THE EMPIRE MUST DIE

ALSO BY MIKHAIL ZYGAR

All the Kremlin's Men: Inside the Court of Vladimir Putin

THE EMPIRE MUST DIE

RUSSIA'S REVOLUTIONARY COLLAPSE, 1900–1917

MIKHAIL ZYGAR

PublicAffairs
New York

Hachette Book Group supports the right to free expression and the value of copyright. The purpose of copyright is to encourage writers and artists to produce the creative works that enrich our culture.

The scanning, uploading, and distribution of this book without permission is a theft of the author's intellectual property. If you would like permission to use material from the book (other than for review purposes), please contact permissions@hbgusa.com. Thank you for your support of the author's rights.

PublicAffairs
Hachette Book Group
1290 Avenue of the Americas, New York, NY 10104
www.publicaffairsbooks.com
@Public_Affairs

Printed in the United States of America
First Edition: November 2017

Published by PublicAffairs, an imprint of Perseus Books, LLC,
a subsidiary of Hachette Book Group, Inc.

The Hachette Speakers Bureau provides a wide range of authors for speaking events. To find out more, go to www.hachettespeakersbureau.com or call (866) 376-6591.

The publisher is not responsible for websites (or their content) that are not owned by the publisher.

Editor of the Russian version: Karen Shainian
Translator: Thomas Hodson
Illustrations: Yuri Buga

Library of Congress Cataloging-in-Publication Data has been applied for.

ISBNs: 978-1-61039-831-2 (hardcover); 978-1-61039-832-9 (ebook)
LSC-C
10 9 8 7 6 5 4 3 2 1

I want to voice support to my friend
Kirill Serebrennikov, an outstanding
Russian filmmaker and theater director,
who was arrested on August 22, 2017 on
made-up charges. I hope he won't share
the fate of any character of this book.

CONTENTS

PREFACE

I am not a historian, but a journalist. As such, this book was written according to the rules of journalism: as if the characters were alive and I had been able to interview them—rather like my previous book, *All the Kremlin's Men.*

Fortunately, most of my protagonists told their own stories, having left behind detailed diaries, letters, memoirs, and public statements. In order to recreate the picture of early twentieth-century Russia, I tried to read as many of the available sources as I could. There is no doubt that although many people lied (especially in their memoirs), most did so sincerely, convinced that they were telling the truth.

My primary objective was to view the world through contemporary eyes. I did not have a ready-made answer to the question of why the Russian revolution happened. I did not have a theory that I wanted to prove to the reader; that would have required some fact-filtering. On the contrary, it took me a great deal of work to clear the picture of prejudices and stereotypes, and to peel away the layers of sediment deposited by dozens of professional historians. Many had their own preconceived concepts and off-the-shelf answers. Many looked upon Russia's revolution as a single, irreversible process.

My protagonists knew—or rather, know—nothing about this. They live their own lives, little suspecting that many years later they will be considered grains of sand in the historical process.

The book starts at the turn of the twentieth century. It is a fascinating time. Many of Russia's young metropolitan intellectuals—the "noughties" generation—are apolitical and totally unlike the older generation of dissidents. They consider politics to be yesterday's game, something old-hat and unfashionable. But politics enters their lives uninvited as the tsarist regime stifles creative freedom, banning and blocking arbitrarily. The result is a gradual swelling of mass protest—the first in Russian history, which is only bolstered by the regime's cack-handed response. During this brief window of opportunity, Russia has a civil society that is active, demanding, and self-aware. Many of the most vibrant figures from this time are forgotten or willfully misunderstood in Russia today.

Russian intellectuals are outraged by the unprovoked shooting of a workers' demonstration on 9 January 1905, Bloody Sunday, after which the protest mood becomes overwhelming. The creative class demands general elections, a parliament, freedom of speech, and equality before the law. What's more, it is sure that it will have its way. But the euphoria lasts barely a year. The authorities seem to reach out at first, but soon backtrack on their promises. Yesterday's optimism gives way to bitter disappointment, and society braces itself for a crackdown. At that point, for many, the time has come to topple the regime.

Curiously, this period—from 1905 to 1914—is regarded by some contemporaries as the most prosperous time in the history of the Russian Empire, a "corpulent" decade, while others see it as a gloomy age of repression, electoral rigging, and nod-and-wink justice. Power and influence fall into the hands of religious radicals and witch-hunters, who demand that cultural figures be biblically "chastised with scorpions" for daring to insult the authorities or the feelings of Orthodox believers. Many intellectuals leave Russia for Europe, where they engage in endless debates about the fate of their homeland. Bizarrely, Europe is also home to many imperial family members and courtiers, who shock the locals with their lavish lifestyle. The intellectual and aristocratic Russian elites are hardly in Russia at this time.

This existence—carefree for some, forlorn for others—comes to an abrupt end with the outbreak of World War I, which no one expects. It is not the war itself that plunges Russia into the abyss, but the fact that the Russian state, with its veritable army of bureaucrats and officials, is unable to cope. The early frontline successes are derailed by corruption and incompetence.

Post factum, the course of history seems logical. Armed with hindsight, we are able to trace the hatching of plans and the exposing of plots; good and evil are clearly labeled. But on stepping into the shoes of history's participants, our preconceived concepts turn to dust. Nothing is preordained. Everyone is fallible and error-prone. No one can foresee the future even a couple of days ahead. No one can map out their own life—let alone that of a dying empire—because the circumstances are in such flux. Even Lenin is convinced of his imminent failure just hours before his ultimate triumph.

In turning the stories of the *dramatis personae* into a narrative, I have not attempted to write a complete history of the Russian state. Russian history, in my view, already concentrates too heavily on the state, or rather on the Sovereign, in whatever guise. Russians are accustomed to viewing their history as a set of biographies of leaders—an elegant array of tsars, general secretaries, and presidents behind which Russian society is obscured. What did the people want? What did they fear? For me, what they did and how they went about doing it are far more important than the dreams and desires of the inhabitants of Tsarskoye Selo or the Kremlin. This book is an attempt to tell the history of Russian society, an attempt to study what it strove for and why, by force of popular pressure, the empire had to die.

I selected as my protagonists the most luminous members of society: the leaders and shapers of public opinion—not only politicians, but also writers, journalists, artists, and preachers.

This book is certainly not an academic work. For the sake of the reader, I have taken the liberty of using modern vocabulary and modern geographical names. At the same time, I do not adhere to the customs often found in historical literature: for example, I call the characters by the names that they called themselves and each other, and not as they are usually known in historical literature. Also, in order to speak to the reader in a clear and modern language I provided all the money sums with their today's equivalents. It should be mentioned that these calculations do not pretend to be absolutely precise, giving only approximate numbers.

This work is the result of the efforts of a huge number of people. First of all, I would like to thank my friends and colleagues from the Future History Lab. We have spent the past two years developing Project1917 (project1917.com)—a unique database of diaries, letters, memoirs, and articles written by people in 1917. All the materials are structured as a series of social media exchanges, creating an online drama that offers a glimpse inside 1917 through the eyes of its inhabitants.

This book would not have been written without the editorial direction of Karen Shainyan, the tenacious editing of Anna Shur, or the help of Pavel Krasovitsky, who performed heroic research in the archives, and organizational efforts of Vera Makarenko. In writing this book, I was greatly assisted by the professional advice of the illustrious historians Kirill Solovyov and Boris Kolonitsky. I also wish to thank Clive Priddle and the whole PublicAffairs team for their patience and professionalism. And I am endlessly grateful to Thomas Hodson for his careful and creative translation of the book into English.

Finally, I would like to dedicate this book to my daughter, Liza. I hope that it will be of interest to her—and her generation. If they can avoid the mistakes that we and the people herein are guilty of, the world will be better for it.

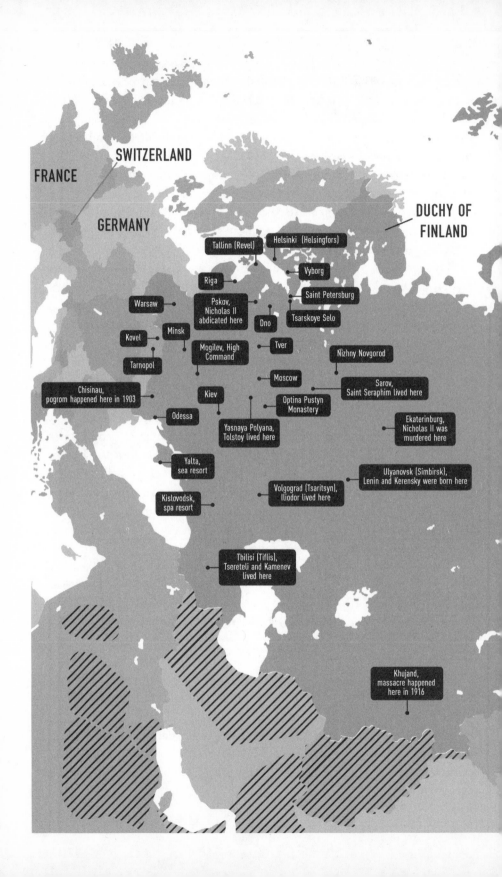

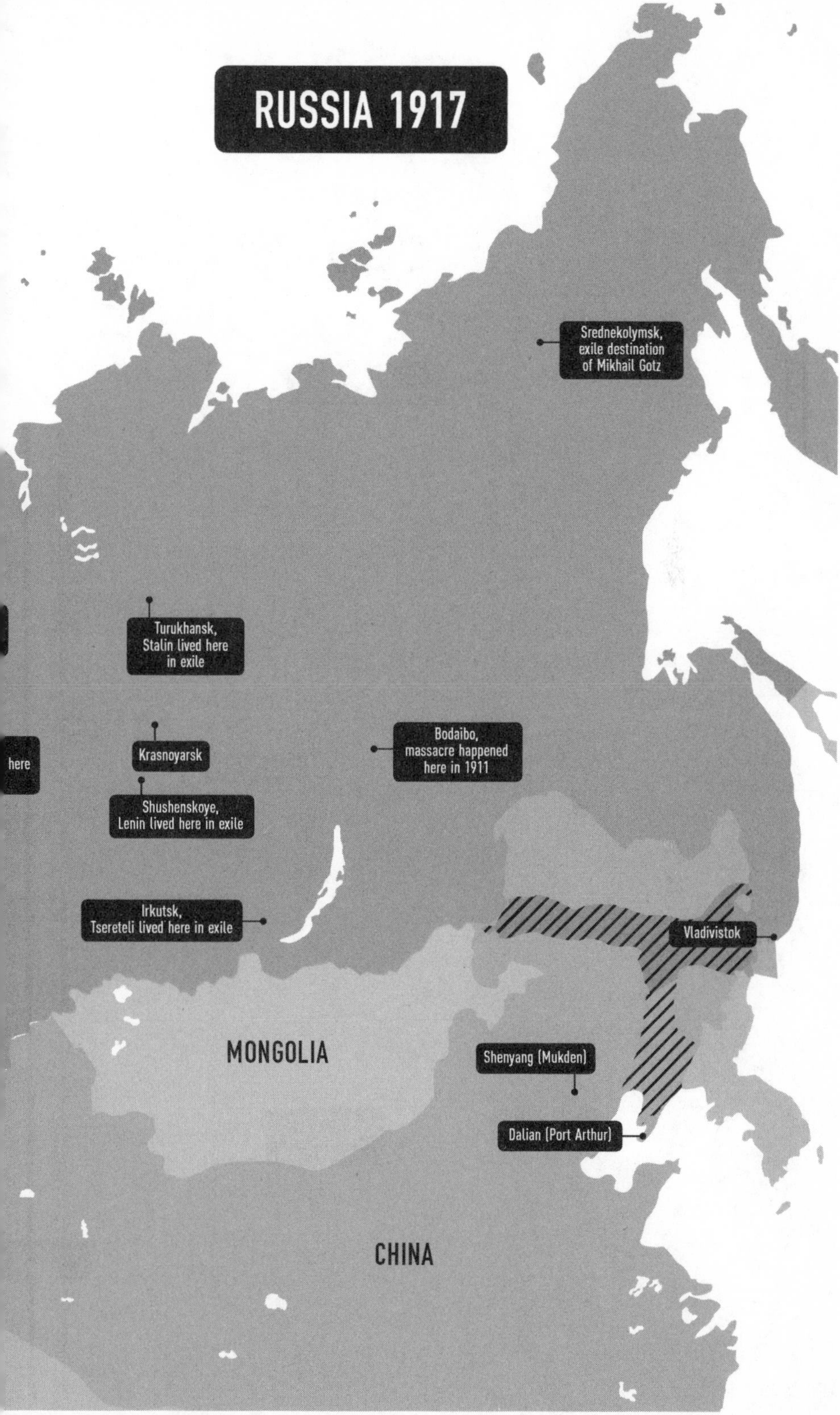

RUSSIA 1917

Srednekolymsk, exile destination of Mikhail Gotz

Turukhansk, Stalin lived here in exile

here

Krasnoyarsk

Bodaibo, massacre happened here in 1911

Shushenskoye, Lenin lived here in exile

Irkutsk, Tsereteli lived here in exile

Vladivistok

MONGOLIA

Shenyang (Mukden)

Dalian (Port Arthur)

CHINA

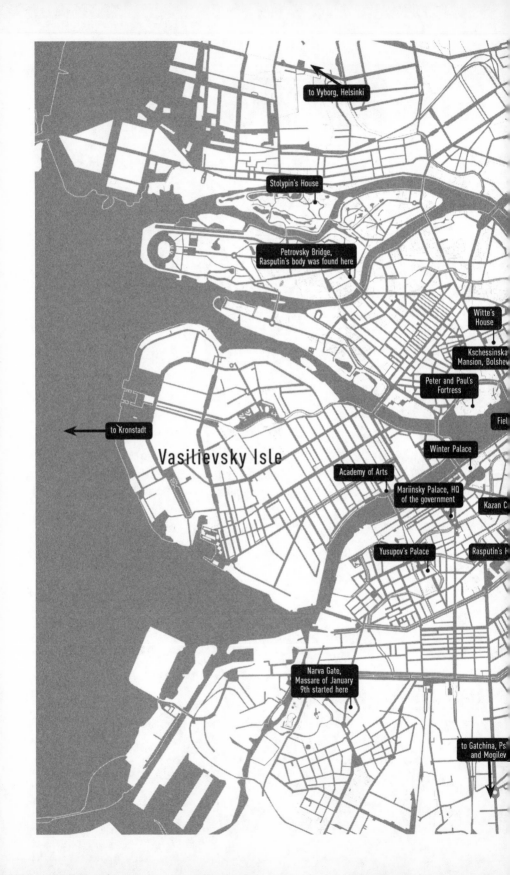

to Vyborg, Helsinki

Stolypin's House

Petrovsky Bridge,
Rasputin's body was found here

Witte's
House

Kschessinska
Mansion, Bolshev

Peter and Paul's
Fortress

Fiel

to Kronstadt

Vasilievsky Isle

Winter Palace

Academy of Arts

Mariinsky Palace, HQ
of the government

Kazan C

Yusupov's Palace

Rasputin's H

Narva Gate,
Massare of January
9th started here

to Gatchina, Ps
and Mogilev

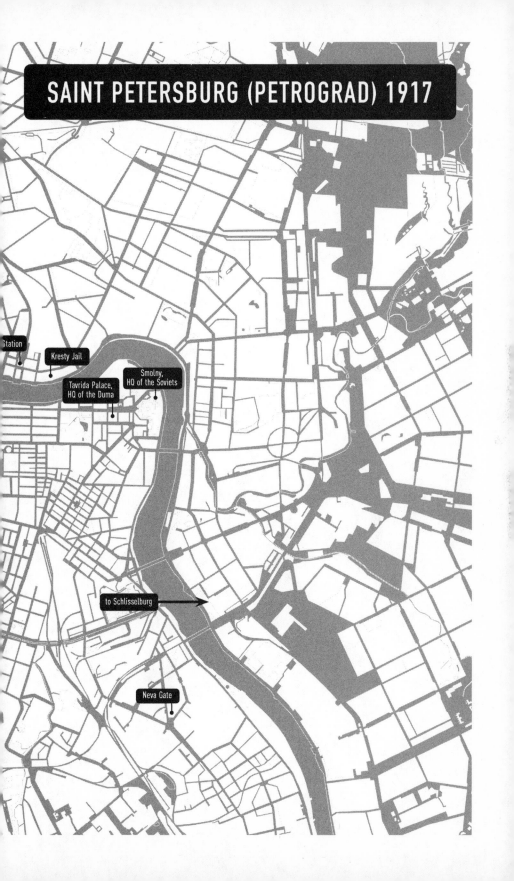

SAINT PETERSBURG (PETROGRAD) 1917

Station

Kresty Jail

Tavrida Palace,
HQ of the Duma

Smolny,
HQ of the Soviets

to Schlisselburg

Neva Gate

|| Chapter 1 ||

LEO TOLSTOY

in which Leo Tolstoy becomes a symbol
of the fight against the regime and the
main ideologist of the opposition

A NEW CENTURY

On 24 February 1901 the *Church Gazette*, the official magazine of the pre-revolutionary Russian Orthodox Church, publishes the text of an edict issued by the Holy Synod on the excommunication of the renowned Russian writer Leo Tolstoy. It is the church's first excommunication in more than one hundred years, the turbulence of the previous century notwithstanding. But Tolstoy is a special case.

Petersburg society, which considers itself the epitome of modernity, is shocked by such archaism. "It must be the first time such news has been conveyed by telegraph," quips Tolstoy's friend, the journalist and writer Vladimir Korolenko. "Excommunication by telegraph is indeed a paradoxical start to the new century."

The next day, 25 February, papers across the Russian Empire reprint the article in the *Church Gazette*, from which Tolstoy learns that he is now officially *persona non grata*. He is in Moscow at the time, on his estate at Khamovniki. According to his wife, Sofia Andreyevna, Count Tolstoy is deeply upset, and the whole family is at a loss: what next?

For many years Tolstoy has lived not so much outside the law as beyond it. His books have been banned, and people imprisoned and exiled for printing and distributing them. Tolstoy's closest friend and loyal follower, the publisher Vladimir Chertkov, has been expelled from Russia. Yet the persecution has not yet extended to Tolstoy personally, perhaps because the writer is now seventy-two years old.

Formally, the Russian Orthodox Church is not separate from the state, which means that a lapse of faith is a crime punishable under secular laws, including exile or imprisonment. For the past two decades, rumors have circulated that the writer could be dispatched to the Suzdal Monastery, effectively a prison for religious offenders, including a number of Old Believers—members of the Russian Orthodox Church who refused to accept the liturgical reforms of Patriarch Nikon in 1653. But so far Tolstoy has remained at liberty. Will the new edict change that?

Tolstoy used to enjoy the patronage of Emperor Alexander III, who loved to read the writer's early works in childhood. But the tsar passed away seven years ago, in 1894, at the tender age of fifty. Still very much alive, however, is the tsar's former tutor and *éminence grise*, Konstantin Petrovich Pobedonostsev, who is Tolstoy's peer (just one year older) and sworn enemy. Pobedonostsev also tutored Nicholas II and retains a grandfatherly influence over the new emperor.

On learning of the Holy Synod's decree, Tolstoy goes into town, where there is public unrest. It has nothing to do with his excommunication: student rioting began in Moscow and Saint Petersburg in 1899 when a university rector ordered that the most politically active students should be conscripted. Battles have been raging in Russia's two capitals ever since, and February 1901 has seen a new surge. Tolstoy arrives at Lubyanka Square in central Moscow* and gets mixed up in a brawl between students and police. News of his excommunication has already spread through the city, and the writer is recognized by the students. In between throwing punches, they give him an ovation.

But not everyone is supportive. "Look, it's the devil in human form," someone shouts at Tolstoy on Lubyanka Square. "The mood of the crowd was split between adoration and loathing. Tolstoy hailed a cab and quickly drove off," is how police officer Alexander Spiridovich later describes the scene. "If there hadn't been so many students, I could have been beaten up," recalls the writer himself.

Waiting for him back at the house are letters from total strangers. On opening them, he realizes that the persecution has begun: "You will die like a dog and rot in hell!", "If the government doesn't get rid of you, we will," and "I'll come and get you, you scum" are some of the more polite sentiments. "Even face-to-face some people expressed similar animosity," writes Tolstoy.

Not all the messages are hostile, but Tolstoy does not note them in his diary.

The Ministry of Interior prohibits all discussion of the Holy Synod's edict, and the ensuing lull generates plenty of rumor and speculation. Vladimir Chertkov, exiled in England, is frantic with worry about stories of Tolstoy's arrest and showers his friend with telegrams. Pobedonostsev watches for the hateful (in his eyes) intelligentsia to react to the Holy Synod's decision, despite the fact that officially all publications on this topic are forbidden by the censor. Even Emperor Nicholas II is perturbed by the hullabaloo surrounding Tolstoy, for he does not like scandals. He summons the ageing Pobedonostsev and asks indignantly why he was not consulted before the decision was taken to excommunicate Tolstoy. Pobedonostsev, whose official title is ober-procurator of the Holy Synod (essentially, "minister of the church") smiles in reply: "What do you mean? I came and showed you the text. You just weren't paying attention."

---

* One of the central squares of Moscow known for housing the headquarters of the KGB.

Pobedonostsev, the personal tutor of two emperors, has a low opinion of Nicholas II. He often recalls how the young tsar would stand there picking his nose while being advised about state business.

AN OLD PROPHET

The now-excommunicated Leo Tolstoy's position in Russia is undoubtedly remarkable. At the age of seventy-two he is one of the most famous people in Russia, yet for the past twenty years he has been at war with the state.

Step back to 1880, and Tolstoy is to be found about to undergo a spiritual revolution. "My father's Orthodox faith ended quite unexpectedly," describes Tolstoy's son, Ilya. "It was Lent. A special meal was prepared for my father and others who were fasting, while the young children, governesses and tutors were served meat. A servant had just put the meat dish on the table when my father turned to me (I always sat next to him) and said, pointing to the meat: 'Ilyushka, pass me a meat chop, there's a good lad. No, I haven't forgotten it's Lent, but I'm not going to fast anymore, so no more Lenten fare for me.' To everyone's dismay, he ate it up and licked his lips. Seeing our father's attitude to Lent, we soon became indifferent to religion."

In terms of global cultural impact, those meat chops can be compared to the Ninety-Five Theses that Martin Luther allegedly nailed to the door of Wittenberg Church in 1517. By renouncing Lent, Tolstoy embarks on his own reformation of Christianity.

Having mastered Ancient Greek, Tolstoy writes his own version of the New Testament in 1880-1881 entitled *The Gospel in Brief*. At heart it is a psychological novel about a young Jesus who is not the son of God, rather his mother Mary knows only that his father is not her husband Joseph. Aware of this fact, Jesus experiences a profound internal drama. His conversations with the devil, for instance, are presented by Tolstoy as an inner dialogue between Jesus and himself. Tolstoy's text makes no mention of miracles, for he does not believe in them, and his *Gospel* ends with Jesus dying on the cross—with no resurrection to speak of. Tolstoy's Christ is an ordinary man, a teacher, and a philosopher, but possessing exemplary moral fiber. For Tolstoy, Christ's gift to mankind lies in his love for humanity, ability to forgive, and rejection of violence, not in ecclesiastical rites.

Tolstoy rejects what the church has become, along with all its rituals, because all they do is divide the Christian world. He sees himself as the creator and founder of a new universal Christianity, free of impurities. Interestingly, in Tolstoy's *Gospel* the word "Pharisees" is replaced with *pravoslavniye*, or "orthodox," meaning those who worship correctly—which is not in fact a literal translation.

Tolstoy knows that *The Gospel in Brief* cannot be published in Russia, so the book is printed in Switzerland. It only appears in Russia in 1906, and even then not in its entirety. Tolstoy's version of the New Testament is followed by the novel *Confession*, the treatise *What I Believe*, and other religious works. His spiritual transformation completely changes his life and upsets his wife. Countess Sofia does not accept her husband's new religion and ceases to be his creative helper and muse. Tolstoy's new "spiritual partner" and chief promoter of his ideas is now Vladimir Chertkov. Sometime in the 1880s, Chertkov and Sofia Tolstoy develop a mutual antipathy for each other, which lasts a lifetime.

Tolstoy's attitude to his work, status, and success also changes. The copyright to all his works printed before 1881 he transfers to his family, and all those printed afterwards he declares to be in the public domain. The pre-1881 period, including *War and Peace* and *Anna Karenina*, he considers less important. Many years later, in response to guests eulogizing about his great novels, he would say: "It's like praising Edison for being able to dance the mazurka." Henceforth, he regards only his religious writings as worthy of attention.

And it is his religious musings that turn Tolstoy into an underground writer, for publishers are no longer allowed to print his works in Russia. Yet his teaching continues to spread. There is a spike in the number of army recruits who refuse to serve, citing that they are followers of Tolstoy and that violence goes against their religious beliefs. The "Tolstoyans," as they are known, continue to multiply, despite the state's persecution of them.

But Tolstoy himself remains untouched, which displeases him. All around, people are under threat, yet he seems to live in a vacuum. He himself would be happy to suffer punishment. In 1890 Tolstoy holds a conversation with the religious philosopher Konstantin Leontiev, a staunch opponent of his: "It's a pity, sir, that there is so little fanaticism inside me," an angry Leontiev says to Tolstoy. "For I would surely send a letter to Saint Petersburg, where I have connections, and ask that you be exiled to Tomsk, and for your wife and daughters not to visit you, and for you to be provided with very little wherewithal. You, sir, are positively harmful!" "My dear, Konstantin!" replies the writer. "For God's sake, please do write that letter. That is my dream. I'm doing everything I can to endanger myself, yet the government turns a blind eye. I implore you to write it."

Tolstoy's protection comes from Emperor Alexander III himself, who values his worth as a writer and reasons that martyrdom would only disseminate his ideas even more. Although Tolstoy's new works are not printed, his popularity grows thanks to his social activity. In 1891, central Russia is hit by a famine. Tolstoy travels to Ryazan and opens up a provincial network of soup kitchens, collecting huge amounts of money to help the starving. On one of his trips he learns that a local priest is telling the starving peasants not to accept help from Tolstoy, because he is the Antichrist. And many take it to heart. Tolstoy's daughter, Tatiana, remembers being told by the starving, as she tried to help them, "Go away, my dear, and take your bread with you. We don't need alms from the Antichrist." Afterwards, the peasants begin to realize that Tolstoy does not mean them any harm and start to wonder why the clergy call him the Antichrist.

Just a few years later several thousand people will describe themselves as Tolstoyans in the Russian Imperial Census of 1897.

Meanwhile, the teaching is denounced as a harmful sect, and the struggle against it is headed by none other than the omnipotent "Minister of the Church" Pobedonostsev. Yet even he is powerless to do anything against Tolstoy himself. Censoring Tolstoy's work brings him into conflict with the tsar. Alexander III overrides Pobedonostsev and personally allows the publication of *The Kreutzer Sonata*, despite the censor having banned it. Yet Pobedonostsev scores a minor victory by stopping a staging of *The Power of Darkness*, despite the fact that Alexander III has seen a rehearsal at the Alexandrinsky Theatre and is reported to have enjoyed it.

SENSELESS DAYDREAMS

But in 1894 Tolstoy's protector dies. His successor, the twenty-six-year-old Nicholas II, is interested in neither politics, nor the elderly Tolstoy, nor the equally elderly Pobedonostsev, who intimidates the young tsar. Nicholas learns from Pobedonostsev one thing: imperial power comes from God and any form of constitution from the devil.

Nicholas II's rule gets off to a bad start. After the coronation the tsar receives delegations from various provinces. During a meeting with a group of subjects from Tver, he reads out a written speech in which he says that all hopes for representative government are nothing but "senseless daydreams."

Petersburg society is prepared to forgive the tsar's poorly worded "mission statement," but Tolstoy is enraged. He writes an article entitled "Senseless Daydreams"—perhaps the most complete exposition of his political views on record—in which he verbally lays into the young emperor.

Having condemned the "insolence of the young lordling," Tolstoy concludes that the monarchy in its present form is a danger to Russia:

> This huge country with a population of over 100 million is managed by one person. And this person is appointed by accident of birth, not according to merit. . . . No one of sound mind would get inside a cab or a train if the driver did not know how to control the vehicle, but the driver's father supposedly did. And no one would board a boat with a captain whose only seafaring pedigree stems from the fact that he is the great-nephew of a man who once commanded the vessel. No sensible person would put his family's life in the hands of such a driver or captain, yet all of us live in a state that is run—and absolutely at that—by the sons and great-nephews of rulers who were themselves no good at managing people.

After giving the monarchy a tongue-lashing, Tolstoy turns his attention to the bureaucracy, concluding that it is Russia's army of civil servants, and not the emperor, that effectively rules Russia.

Tolstoy ends the article by naming the civil servant who irritates him the most: Pobedonostsev. He is a symbol of the regime, a man who "befuddles and corrupts the people." It is a direct challenge to the state, as if Tolstoy were deliberately trying to humiliate the powers-that-be and provoke them into punishing him. But still the authorities do not react.

THE GREAT RESETTLEMENT

In the early years of the reign of Nicholas II, Tolstoy begins his most high-profile social campaign in defense of the Doukhobors, a Christian sect that is very close to him spiritually, since they reject the rituals of the Orthodox Church and any form of violence. In 1895, the Doukhobor community near Tiflis (today's Tbilisi, the capital of Georgia) burns all the weapons it possesses as a protest against forced conscription. The oppression of them intensifies as a result, and they are put in prison, sent to serve in penal battalions, or exiled.

Tolstoy and Chertkov launch a wide-reaching campaign in support of the Doukhobors, whose persecution is soon global news. Tolstoy has the idea of helping the Doukhobors to emigrate to places where they will not be pursued. China, Cyprus, and Hawaii are among the options.

He begins raising money and even considers reversing his decision to forsake royalties. He quickly puts the finishing touches to a new novel *Resurrection* so that all the money from its publication can be given to the Doukhobors.

Tolstoy's human rights activism goes unpunished, but his publisher Chertkov is exiled. In 1897 he moves to England (not the harshest punishment for a journalist fluent in English), where he becomes Tolstoy's mouthpiece in the Western world. While in London, Chertkov seeks new ways to help the Doukhobors. The political émigré approaches another native of Russia, Prince Peter Kropotkin, who has lived in exile for more than twenty years, since 1876. The famous geographer, who uncovered the phenomenon of the Ice Age and wrote what are considered classics of anarchist literature, also supports the Doukhobors. Kropotkin's scientific expeditions have repeatedly taken him to Canada, which, he concludes, is geologically akin to Siberia. He suggests that Canada be the new home of the Doukhobor community.

The great resettlement begins in 1898. At Batumi Port in modern-day Georgia, more than eight thousand people board ships chartered by Tolstoy for Quebec and Halifax. The massive operation to rescue the Doukhobors from state repression comes to an end in 1900, demonstrating that Tolstoy is virtually independent of the Russian authorities.

PRAYING FOR REASON

Nevertheless, the authorities, not to mention the church, are vexed. But still nothing happens. Until, that is, Tolstoy falls seriously ill. In 1899 press reports suggest that the writer's days are numbered. The higher ranks of the Holy Synod are not quite sure what to do if Tolstoy dies. One member of the church hierarchy, the Archbishop of Kharkov, pens the first draft of what will become the edict to excommunicate Tolstoy from the church. In 1900, the oldest member of the Holy Synod, Metropolitan Ioanniky of Kiev, sends a secret letter forbidding all priests in Russia to perform a funeral service for Tolstoy. But the writer recovers, and instead it is the Metropolitan of Kiev who soon departs for the next world.

His successor as elder of the Holy Synod is Metropolitan Anthony of Saint Petersburg, who has a reputation as a liberal, and he decides to get things over and done with. Since the decision to excommunicate Tolstoy has already been made, he decides to publish the secret circular penned by his predecessor and have it approved by the state curator of the church (i.e., Pobedonostsev). But the latter amends the text, making it even more puritanical, and his is the version that ends up in the *Church Gazette**, signed by seven bishops: Anthony and six other metropolitans. Pobedonostsev declines to put his name to the document.

The edict lists the charges against Tolstoy: preaching the overthrow of Orthodox dogma and denying the divinity of Christ, the virgin birth, the resurrection, life after death, the Day of Judgment, and all the sacraments of the church. Tolstoy is accused of having "consciously and deliberately torn himself from all communion with the Church," so that he cannot be considered a member of the flock until he repents. The document ends with a short prayer for Tolstoy, asking God to make him see reason.

Even inside the imperial court, the seventy-two-year-old Pobedonostsev is not held in high esteem. "I've read the Holy Synod's edict regarding Tolstoy. What a load of nonsense. It's a personal vendetta. It's clear that Pobedonostsev is behind it and just wants to attack Tolstoy," writes Vladimir Lebedev, a legal adviser to the government.

Why does Pobedonostsev hate Tolstoy so much when the two men have never even met? Members of the intelligentsia believe they know the answer. Twenty-five years earlier, when *Anna Karenina* was published, readers began searching for prototypes. Konstantin Levin was clearly the author himself. But who was Karenin—the senior official (powerful, but titleless), whose wife's infidelity is public knowledge? Pobedonostsev's wife, Ekaterina, was twenty-one years younger than her husband and rumored to be in a relationship with a military officer. It was even said that after the novel's publication Ekaterina had begun to dress like Anna Karenina.

Although Tolstoy and Pobedonostsev never meet, they do exchange letters on one occasion: five years after the appearance of *Anna Karenina* and twenty years before Tolstoy's excommunication from the church.

In March 1881, on learning of the assassination of Emperor Alexander II, Tolstoy (the celebrated author of *War and Peace*) writes a letter to Pobedonostsev, seeking a pardon for the terrorists. Tolstoy asks for the letter to be delivered to the heir to the throne, the future Alexander III. The letter is a turning point in the history of Russia and in the lives of both Pobedonostsev and Tolstoy.

---

* 100 years later, the Russian Orthodox Church is still not independent. Despite being formally separated from the state it functions, essentially, as a state department under Presidential Administration control.

INESCAPABLE PUNISHMENT

On 1 March 1881 Saint Petersburg witnesses the assassination of Emperor Alexander II by a group of young activists from the terrorist cell known as People's Will. The bomb that kills the tsar is thrown by the twenty-five-year-old Pole Ignacy Hryniewiecki, but the attack is orchestrated by Sofia Perovskaya, the twenty-seven-year-old daughter of the governor of Saint Petersburg. It is she who waves a white handkerchief to signal when to throw the bomb.

The emperor's death shocks the Saint Petersburg elite to the core. Everyone knows that Russia is on the verge of adopting a constitution. Two months earlier, in January 1881, Interior Minister Mikhail Loris-Melikov writes and personally delivers a "most humble report" outlining the reforms. It is in fact a draft constitution, hailed by future historians as the "Constitution of Loris-Melikov." The draft document foresees the phased introduction of a new parliament, and Alexander II approves it. On the morning of 1 March, just an hour before his death, the tsar informs Loris-Melikov that the document will be adopted by the Council of Ministers in just four days. The emperor's son, the future Alexander III, is aware of the plans, since he is involved in all the discussions and also endorses the "Constitution."*

The sudden death of the tsar changes everything. Society is stunned. Only Pobedonostsev, it seems, knows what to do. He targets his former pupil and now the new emperor, Alexander III, who falls under Pobedonostsev's political hypnosis: "The hour is dark and time is short," he writes to the tsar. "Either you save Russia and yourself, or both will perish. Do not be lulled by the sirens of liberalism calling for you to heed the so-called public opinion. For God's sake, Your Majesty, remain vigilant."

At a meeting on 8 March, Pobedonostsev delivers an even more impassioned speech against the liberal reforms. His opponents, fronted by Loris-Melikov, are stunned by the resistance. All of their ideas are rejected out of hand. "Thank God that this criminal step towards a constitution has been rejected by the Council of Ministers, if only by a tiny majority," writes the spellbound Alexander III.

Pobedonostsev suggests placing the capital Saint Petersburg on a war footing and leaving the "wretched place" to take refuge in Moscow. He cannot stand the northern capital, considering it too secular and cosmo-

---

* The unofficial title "Constitution of Loris-Melikov" is given to the document later, after its publication in 1905, although Alexander III himself referred to the document by that name as early as 1881.

politan in comparison to the patriarchal Moscow, the true center of Russia in his view.

Tolstoy is at Yasnaya Polyana, almost a thousand kilometers from Saint Petersburg. News of the attack arrives only two days later, on 3 March, and it comes as a shock. Caring little for court intrigues, his mind is drawn to the death sentence that is sure to be handed down for this act of regicide. For Tolstoy, regardless of the circumstances, capital punishment is a monstrous crime against the very essence of Christianity and in violation of the principle of "turn the other cheek." He writes two letters: one to Alexander III, the other to Pobedonostsev. Yet both are delivered to the latter with instructions to pass the first letter to the tsar. After agonizing over them for more than a week, he finally sends them on 15 March. During this period, he suffers from nightmares, dreaming that he, not Alexander III, is about to execute the terrorists.

"I shall adopt a different tone to the one usually reserved for letters to the Sovereign, and do without flowery obsequiousness and spurious eloquence that only obscure thoughts and feelings. I shall write man to man," begins Tolstoy's first letter. The bluntness is part of a cunning attempt to expound to the emperor an alternative path of political and ideological development: a third way, neither liberal nor conservative.

It starts off simply enough, offering condolences to Alexander III for the "unimaginably terrible situation" in which he finds himself and the "overwhelmingly strong temptation to commit evil" against the perpetrators of the crime: "These enemies of Russia and the people are despicable godless creatures that have violated the tranquility of millions of believers and murdered your father," he writes, implying that they cannot be pitied. However, says Tolstoy, Christ clearly instructs that they should be forgiven: "Do not hate your enemy, be charitable to him. Instead of fighting evil, learn to forgive," Tolstoy paraphrases Christ. But moralism soon gives way to politics. Tolstoy recalls that radical opposition terrorists have been active in Russia for two decades, and so far only two methods have been applied to deal with them: conservative (execution, exile, censorship) and liberal (freedom, softly-softly measures, the offer of a constitution). Both methods have proven ineffective, asserts Tolstoy, because their proponents are divided into those who care about the interests of the state and those who care about the welfare of the masses: "Why not try a third option in the name of God? We should adhere to His law only, without thinking about the state or the masses."

"Punishing three or four criminals only gives rise to thirty or forty more. Evil begets evil." Tolstoy suggests that the tsar should give the assassins money and let them emigrate to America. The letter ends with these words: "As wax before the fire, every revolutionary struggle shall melt before the Tsar who accepts his own mortality and fulfills the law of Christ."

Pobedonostsev, of course, does not show the letter to the tsar, for it employs Pobedonostsev's own trick of using religious arguments, yet arriving, in Tolstoy's case, at the most liberal conclusions. For Pobedonostsev, such an opponent is a real threat. Moreover, Alexander III's former tutor knows something that Tolstoy does not—that the new emperor is very fond of the writer and adores *War and Peace*. For the emperor, Tolstoy's word is law.

Instead, Pobedonostsev writes his own letter to Alexander: "There is an idea floating that appalls me. Some people are so corrupt in mind and thought that they advocate pardoning convicted killers. The Russian people are fearful that Your Majesty could be swayed by these perverted thoughts. Could this happen? No, no, a thousand times, no. It cannot be that You, in the face of all the Russian people, could forgive the murderers of Your father, the Russian Emperor, for whose blood the entire earth (save for those of feeble mind and heart) demands vengeance and groans that it is not swift enough. If this could happen, believe me, Sire, it shall be perceived as a great sin and will shake the hearts of Your subjects. I am Russian, I live among my fellow Russians and I know what the people are feeling and what they are demanding. At this moment they all crave retribution."*

Alexander III tries to calm Pobedonostsev's fears: "Do not worry. No one shall dare approach me with such a proposal. All six will be hanged, for that I can vouch."

However, the emperor is wrong. For Tolstoy has written two versions of his letter. His friend, Fyodor Strakhov, having delivered one to Pobedonostsev, gives the other to the tsar's younger brother, the twenty-three-year-old Grand Duke Sergei, who takes it to Alexander III.

Twenty-four years later, history will repeat itself. Grand Duke Sergei himself is killed by terrorists in exactly the same manner as his father, Alexander II. Sergei's wife, Ella, follows the advice of Tolstoy and visits her husband's murderer in prison, asking for him to be pardoned.

However, back in 1881 Tolstoy and the Grand Duke fail to persuade the tsar. Alexander III replies that if the attack had been against him, he could

---

* This is a very common phenomenon: Russian officials in the twenty-first century are still sure that they know what people really want and that they can speak on their behalf. Opinion polls held in highly questionable ways only give them more confidence.

offer pardon, but he has no right to forgive the killers of his father. On 3 April five of the assassins are hanged. The day after the execution the minister-reformer Loris-Melikov is dismissed.

The sixth defendant, Gesya Gelfman, is granted respite, for she is pregnant. Her case becomes a *cause célèbre*. Alexander III receives letters in her defense from across the globe, including one from Victor Hugo.* Incidentally, she dies soon after giving birth from a lack of medical treatment.

"Pobedonostsev is a dreadful person. God grant that he does not answer me so that I shall not be tempted to express my horror and disgust at him," writes Tolstoy on 3 April 1881, not knowing yet that the execution has taken place. Pobedonostsev has no time for letters just yet. He is busy writing his anti-constitution, the so-called "Manifesto on Unshakable Autocracy," which is published on 30 April.

The essence of the document is simplicity itself: no more liberal reforms, no constitution, no parliament, no representative government.

So begins the Pobedonostsev era, which will last for more than two decades.

> *In those distant, deaf years*
> *Slumber and haziness reigned in the heart*
> *Pobedonostsev's owl wings*
> *Stretched over Russia*
> *There was no day or night*
> *Only the shadow of those vast wings*
> *He drew a spellbinding circle*
> *Around Russia, gazing into her eyes*
> *With the vitreous stare of a sorcerer*

These lines will be written forty years later by the poet Alexander Blok, who in 1881 is just one year old.

Finally, in June 1881, and in spite of Tolstoy's prayers, Pobedonostsev responds to the former's March-dated letter: "Do not hold it against me for not fulfilling your instruction," he writes. "Such an important matter had to be guided by faith. After reading your letter, I saw that your faith and that of the Church are not one. Your Christ is not our Christ. Ours is a man of truth and virtue, a healer of the sick. Yours is weak-minded and

---

* The participation of the international community in the destiny of Russian fighters against the regime will become a long-lasting tradition. Western political and cultural figures will ask to release prisoners and mitigate their sentences both in Soviet and post-Soviet years. The Pussy Riot affair is one of the most recent examples.

in need of healing himself. Thus, my faith did not permit me to fulfill your assignment."

Pobedonostsev wins in the end. He continues to push for Tolstoy to be punished, but is still thwarted by Alexander III.

Tolstoy, incidentally, gets his own back on Pobedonostsev in 1899, just two years before his excommunication. That year sees the publication of his final novel, *Resurrection*. It contains another thinly disguised Pobedonostsev—this time not the hapless Karenin, but the epitome of absolute evil in the form of "Minister of the Church" Toporov.

> Toporov, like all those who are quite destitute of the fundamental religious feeling that recognises the equality and brotherhood of men, was fully convinced that the common people were creatures entirely different from himself, and that the people needed what he could well do without, for in the depths of his soul he believed in nothing, and found such a state very convenient and pleasant. Yet he feared lest the people might also come to such a state, and looked upon it as his sacred duty, as he called it, to save the people from it. . . . His feelings towards the religion he kept were the same as those of the poultry-keeper towards the carrion he fed his fowls on. Carrion was very disgusting, but the fowls liked it; therefore, it was right to feed the fowls on carrion.

This passage from *Resurrection* contains the essence of Tolstoy's hatred of the church in general and of Pobedonostsev in particular. The censors, of course, expunge the offending chapter nine in its entirety before publication, but a privileged few, including Pobedonostsev, see the full version. By that time, however, Pobedonostsev is more than the "minister of the church." He is now the alter ego of the emperor, the chief ideologist of the state.

A GREAT FALSEHOOD

During the life of Alexander II, almost no one in Saint Petersburg harbors any doubt that a constitutional monarchy is on its way and that change is inevitable. But through his iron will, Pobedonostsev single-handedly manages to stem the tide of reform. The most complete expression of his ideology comes in an article entitled "The Great Falsehood of Our Time," written in 1884. The subject is democracy.

Amongst the falsest of political principles is the principle of sovereignty of the people, known as democracy. It is the principle that all power issues from the people and is based upon the national will—a principle which has unhappily become more firmly established since the time of the French Revolution. Thence proceeds the theory of parliamentarianism, which, up to the present day, has deluded much of the so-called 'intelligentsia' and, unhappily, has penetrated certain foolish Russian minds.

It is not that Pobedonostsev believes in Russia's unique destiny and inherent incompatibility with democracy. No, he considers the very idea of "sovereignty of the people" to be insane no matter where in the world it manifests itself. Moreover, he believes that the idea is already showing cracks:

By the theory of parliamentarianism, the rational majority must rule; in practice, the party is dominated by five or six of its leaders who exercise all power. In theory, conviction is affirmed through clear arguments in the course of parliamentary debate; in practice, in no way do they depend on debate, but are determined by the will of the leaders and the promptings of personal interest. In theory, the representatives of the people consider only the public welfare; in practice, their first consideration is their own advancement and the interests of their friends. In theory, they are supposed to be the finest citizens; in practice, they are the most ambitious and impudent. . . . It is sad to think that even on Russian soil there are people who aspire to the establishment of this falsehood among us; that our professors glorify to their young pupils representative government as the ideal of statehood; that our newspapers pursue it in their articles and feuilletons under the name of justice and order, without troubling to examine without prejudice the workings of the parliamentary machine. Yet even where centuries have sanctified its existence, faith in democracy is decaying; the liberal intelligentsia exalts it, but the people groan under its despotism and recognise its falsehood. We may not live to see the day, but our children and grandchildren assuredly will, when this idol*, which contemporary thought in all its vanity continues to worship, is overthrown.

---

*Pobedonostsev's words are surprisingly similar to the Russian TV propaganda in the early twenty-first century. One of its main theses is that democracy does not exist at all, and all Western countries only simulate it: in fact all elections in the world are rigged, all politicians and courts are corrupt, all policemen brutally suppress demonstrations, and there are no democratic values at all. Many cynical Russians and, even more importantly, most Russian officials believe in this sincerely.

The article appears in the magazine *The Citizen*, published on government subsidies by Prince Meshchersky, a friend of Alexander III. Incidentally, for a brief period *The Citizen*'s editor-in-chief is none other than Fyodor Dostoyevsky, a friend of Pobedonostsev.

Emperor Alexander III fully concurs with his former tutor: "It is strange to listen to intelligent people talking earnestly about representative government in Russia," he writes.

The Petersburg nobility pokes fun at Pobedonostsev. The dislike is mutual: Pobedonostsev believes that the main problem in the country is education. And by education he means education itself, not the lack thereof. The most untrustworthy and disloyal segment of the population, in his view, is made of the intelligentsia, students, professors, and civil servants. The knowledge and instruction that they receive do not promote loyalty to the emperor. However, church schools are another matter. Education, according to Pobedonostsev's paradigm, should be limited to literacy and the word of God. Therefore, he devotes a good deal of his life to creating a network of church schools that do not teach history, mathematics, geography, or literature. In his lifetime their number increases tenfold from 4,404 to 42,884 and the number of students twentyfold from 104,781 to 2,006,847. At the same time, church newspapers and magazines double in number, all thanks to Pobedonostsev.

A KILLER AT THE WINDOW

On 8 March 1901, just two weeks after Tolstoy's excommunication, Ober-Procurator of the Holy Synod Pobedonostsev is sitting near the window in his office at his government residence. The window overlooks Liteyny Avenue in central Saint Petersburg. Pobedonostsev is accustomed to working late, and his silhouette is easy to make out from the street. Late that evening Nikolai Lagovsky, a twenty-five-year-old civil servant and statistician from provincial Samara, approaches the window. He pulls out a gun and fires six times at Pobedonostsev.

The first five bullets hit the ceiling, while the sixth shot misfires. Amidst the uproar the terrorist tries to flee, but is seized by staff who have come running out of the building.

The police are at their wits' ends, since this is not the first such incident. The Minister of Education Nikolai Bogolepov is still warm in his coffin, having been shot just one week before. But the "minister of the church" is not even scratched.

Following the unsuccessful attempt on his life, church services are held for Pobedonostsev across the country. Not everywhere do they go smoothly. During prayers in Ryazan, for example, local students shout out, "Hail the inquisitor!" The seventy-four-year-old Pobedonostsev is perhaps the most hated official in the country and the chief enemy of all oppositionists, students, revolutionaries, and the Petersburg intelligentsia. During his interrogation Lagovsky says that he "wanted to eradicate the main obstacle to progress and freedom"; for him, Pobedonostsev's crime is to have "spread superstition and ignorance among the people through church schools."

Lagovsky is sentenced to six years of hard labor and dies in Siberia. Pobedonostsev not only outlives him, but also survives several more assassination attempts. In the wake of the first attempt on Pobedonostsev, Saint Petersburg sees an epidemic of political killings.

THE BATTLE OF KAZAN

On 4 March 1901, three days before the attempt on Pobedonostsev's life, a huge crowd gathers on the square outside Kazan Cathedral in Saint Petersburg that includes not only young people, but also persons of note, among them two young socialist writers. They are the exact opposite of each other. One is Peter Struve, from a "good" family, the son of the governor of Perm; the second, Alexei Peshkov, is a man of working-class origin who goes by the pseudonym Maxim Gorky. Struve is professionally engaged in politics in a country that has no politics (at least as far as ordinary citizens are concerned). The year before in the town of Pskov, he and his friends founded Russia's first socialist newspaper *Spark* [*Iskra*]. Gorky has not yet read *Spark* or made the acquaintance of Struve or the two other founders, Georgy Plekhanov and a certain Vladimir Ulyanov. For his part, Gorky has written several short stories to great acclaim from the upcoming generation, but he has not yet moved to the capital. Struve is thirty-one, and Gorky is thirty-two, the same age as Tsar Nicholas II.

The rally at Kazan Cathedral is quite possibly the first mass public demonstration in Russian history. The crowd has gathered in defense of students' rights and is demanding a repeal of the "provisional rules" that allow any politically active student to be expelled and called up by the army. Although the rally has been approved by the authorities, the murder of the Minister of Education Bogolepov changes everything. In light of the death of his colleague, Interior Minister Dmitry Sipyagin has decided not to allow the gathering to take place.

"We are on the square. The crowd is noisy, bustling and full of nervous excitement. There's not a single policeman in sight," later recalls the mathematics student Razumnik Ivanov, who at that time was twenty-two years old.

> The police, both mounted and unmounted, along with Cossack units, are still hidden away in the surrounding courtyards. We are waiting for the signal. The midday cannon fires and everything kicks off. . . . A red flag is unfurled amid the dense crowd of young people in the middle of the square, when suddenly the gates on the side of Kazan Street and Ekaterina Canal swing open, releasing the Cossack troops. They smash into the crowd, striking people with whips. There are cries of pain and rage, blood spills, the wounded groan; even passers-by on the pavements, despite the shouts of indignation, are attacked by the police.

The battered crowd consists not only of students, but also the metropolitan elite. Gorky says that many commissioned officers refused to obey the head of city police, Kleigels, who was in charge of the dispersal, and many came to blows with the police and the Cossacks.

"I saw one officer break through the chain of gendarmes. He was drenched with blood, his face mutilated by whips," writes Gorky in a letter to his friend Anton Chekhov. "Another was shouting: 'They have no right to beat us, we are the public!' All the while, officers were pulling women from under horses' hooves, rescuing people from the clutches of the police and generally behaving very decently," says Gorky.

A hero of the Kazan Cathedral rally is Prince Leonid Vyazemsky, the former governor of Astrakhan and a member of the State Council. On seeing the carnage, he runs up to Kleigels and yells at him to stop the brutality, accusing him of exceeding his authority. Kleigels does not respond.

The student Ivanov recalls that the protesters are crushed, beaten, and driven back to the steps of Kazan Cathedral. They stumble through the doors of the shrine, dragging the wounded, who are placed on the marble benches around the tomb of General Kutuzov, the conqueror of Napoleon. "The Sunday service at the cathedral was just coming to an end when we came bursting in," says Ivanov.

> The deacon appeared from behind the altar, saying: 'Are you people or beasts? You ungodly creatures storm into a place of worship during a divine service, don't even remove your caps and run amok. . . . Shame on you!'

'Father, it's not us running amok, but the police. Take a look at the blood. We were driven inside the cathedral. We didn't mean to come here.'

He is broken off by a police colonel who has just entered the cathedral and declares that all present have half an hour to disperse and thus prove that they are law-abiding people. "We hadn't come to demonstrate our civil obedience," recollects Ivanov. Half an hour later the injured have been carried away and the rest of the crowd (around five hundred to six hundred men and a few hundred women) are arrested.

Gorky writes to Chekhov that, according to official figures, four people are dead, sixty-two men and thirty-four women have been assaulted, and fifty-four police, gendarmes, and Cossacks are wounded. "I shall never forget that battle! The fight was wild and savage on both sides. Women were grabbed by the hair and lashed with whips. A classmate of mine had her back beaten black and blue, another had her head smashed in, another lost an eye. But even soaked in blood, we weren't defeated," says the writer.

Struve is detained and exiled to Tver. Gorky escapes arrest. Prince Vyazemsky is exiled for resisting the authorities and inciting unrest. Tolstoy, who at this moment is in Moscow, is struck by what has happened. Once again he is ashamed that others, including the aristocrat Prince Vyazemsky, have been punished, yet he remains untouched.

"Dear Prince Leonid Dmitrievich [Vyazemsky]," he writes to the exile. "Your noble, courageous and philanthropic actions on 4 March outside Kazan Cathedral are known throughout Russia. We hope that you, like us, attribute the emperor's punishment of you solely to the brutality and cruelty of those who surround and deceive him. You have done a good deed, and Russian society will be forever grateful to you. You chose to sacrifice yourself in the struggle against brutal violence and to serve humanity, rather than the conventional decorum demanded by your status. Your deed commands all the respect and gratitude that we extend to you in this letter."

A few days later Tolstoy writes a letter "To the Tsar and his aides"—his most important and opinionated text since "Senseless Daydreams," which sets out a political reform plan consisting of three proposals:

"First, grant the peasants the same rights as other citizens" (in particular, "outlaw the nonsensical, humiliating act of corporal punishment"). Second, reform the law enforcement agencies (since police omnipotence encourages denunciations, spying and brutal violence), and "repeal the unlawful death penalty that so corrupts the people, violates the Christian spirit of the Russian folk and represents a terrible crime against God and the human conscience. Third, remove all barriers to education, upbringing and learning," (in particular, allow schools for Jews and other minorities, as well as private schools).

Tolstoy sends the letter to Saint Petersburg. It is not published and no one takes the proposals seriously, save for the metropolitan intelligentsia, who carefully study it. The letter is circulated widely, as indeed are the rest of Tolstoy's prohibited works. They are published abroad by Chertkov and clandestinely distributed.

Alexei Suvorin, a friend of Anton Chekhov and the publisher of Russia's most widely read tabloid, *New Time*, on reading Tolstoy's letter, notes in his diary on 29 May:

> We have two tsars: Nicholas II and Leo Tolstoy. Who is the stronger? Nicholas II cannot touch Tolstoy or shake his throne, while Tolstoy can undoubtedly shake the throne of Nicholas and his dynasty. He is cursed by the Holy Synod, yet Tolstoy's response finds its way into manuscripts and foreign newspapers. Just try to touch Tolstoy. The whole world will cry out and our administration will turn tail. A new age is dawning. It's already evident in the way the government is so hopelessly confused that it doesn't know whether to wake up or go to sleep. How long will this muddle last? Despotism is on its last legs and will surely collapse at the slightest breeze, never mind a gale.

WAR AND ART

On the morning of 15 March 1901, the twenty-eight-year-old Sergei Diaghilev opens a newspaper and learns from the government news section of his dismissal from the Directorate of the Imperial Theatres "without petition or pension under article three"—the most terrible wording imaginable for a Russian official. Translated into modern language, it means expulsion from the civil service, blacklisting, and disgrace.

Diaghilev cannot believe his eyes. He has always believed that he has the Directorate of the Imperial Theatres in the palm of his hand; moreover, he supposedly has the support of the emperor himself and many other influential people. And now everything has been wiped out by a stroke of the pen of his pigheaded superior.

Prior to this morning, Diaghilev has served as the editor-in-chief of two artistic publications. One of them—the aesthetic *World of Art*—he created himself and publishes with the help of billionaire Savva Mamontov and other sponsors. The second is the state-run, semi-official *Annual of the Imperial Theatres*. It goes without saying that Diaghilev's reputation in the capital city comes from the former.

Back in 1898, the twenty-six-year-old law graduate Diaghilev, together with classmate Alexander Benois, finds the money to publish a magazine devoted to modern art. The two young law grads intend to shake up the Russian cultural community. Traditional Russian art, typified by the realism of the Itinerants movement, seems boring and outdated. Diaghilev and Benois have absolutely no interest in the politics or social issues. They are looking for a new kind of voguish and provocative art—like in the West—and the new magazine will serve that purpose. In May 1898 Diaghilev and his sponsor Mamontov jointly announce their mission: "The magazine will revolutionize the art world and shake up the public, which has hitherto fed on trends that Europe has long outgrown," reads the bold statement.

The editorial board of *World of Art* includes the twenty-six-year-old Dima Filosofov, who happens to be a (male) cousin and lover of Diaghilev, and the thirty-five-year-old artist Léon Bakst. At the same time, Diaghilev arranges exhibitions of works by progressive artists, including his friends Benois and Bakst, as well as Mikhail Vrubel, Konstantin Somov, and other young innovators.

Both the exhibitions and the very first issue of the magazine manage to offend the older generation. But not all are insulted by Diaghilev. Russia's preeminent artist of the age, Ilya Repin, has a soft spot for the young and promises to contribute articles to *World of Art*. But the classical landscapist Vasily Polenov is beside himself with rage. The infuriated old guard is backed by Vladimir Stasov, the most influential literary critic in Russia and a close friend of Leo Tolstoy and the now late Fyodor Dostoyevsky. He is indignant that the young generation is so "irresponsible" and "insensate" ("There is no socio-political content in their work at all").

"An orgy of debauchery and madness" and "decadent absurdities and deformities" is how Stasov describes anything and everything that appears in *World of Art*, while Diaghilev is labeled the magazine's "decadent warden."

The resentment of the older generation raises public interest in Diaghilev and his team, but discourages sponsors. Their money runs out, and former backers keep their distance. However, help arrives from unexpected quarters. The artist Valentin Serov, seemingly unattached to the Diaghilev circle, decides to help the young provocateurs. The thirty-five-year-old Serov is the most sought-after portraitist in Russia and the emperor's favorite. In the spring of 1900 he is commissioned to paint the portrait of Nicholas II, during which he tells the tsar about Diaghilev's problems. "I don't understand finance," remarks Serov naively. "Me neither," echoes the emperor, who subsequently makes arrangements for *World of Art* to receive the sum of 15,000 roubles.*

Royal patronage turns Diaghilev from a rowdy maverick into a respected innovator overnight. Sensing that *World of Art* is gaining cultural weight, officials start to curry favor, and by autumn he has been appointed to an important post: Officer for Special Assignments under the Directorate of the Imperial Theatres. One of his duties is to produce the annual journal, and he turns the para-governmental almanac into a sumptuous art brochure.

Diaghilev's career takes off. He conceives bold and innovative projects, one of which is the staging of the ballet *Sylvia* by Léo Delibes. Sergey Volkonsky, the director of the Imperial Theatres, gives the go-ahead, but despite everything still fears a backlash from the "cultural community" if Diaghilev is credited, so the press release says that the new ballet is being staged by the director himself, with no mention of Diaghilev.

The ambitious Diaghilev is not one to give ground. Believing that he enjoys the patronage of the emperor himself, he informs his superiors that, if he is not officially appointed to an artistic role, he will have nothing more to do with the ballet or the *Annual of the Imperial Theatres*. Filosofov, Bakst, and Benois pledge to go with him if he walks. The young artists are sure of their invulnerability, since Diaghilev has the ear of an admiring grand duke who personally intercedes for him with Nicholas II. "Diaghilev has no reason to leave," is the tsar's alleged response. But the cultural functionaries are more tenacious than the fickle emperor, and so Diaghilev learns of his dismissal from the papers.

TWENTIETH-CENTURY HIPSTERS

On 8 October 1901 Pobedonostsev receives a visit from a group of young people; at least to Pobedonostsev they seem young, yet all but one are over thirty and roughly the same age as the tsar. The visitors consider themselves professional journalists, but, in the presence of the grey cardinal of the Russian Empire, they are daunted. The oldest of them is forty-five, but he is shy and does not say a word. He is Vasily Rozanov, the future philosopher and essayist. The youngest, Dima Filosofov, is twenty-nine. It is mostly the thirty-five-year-old Dmitry Merezhkovsky who does the talking.

---

*About $197,750 in 2017.

The purpose of their visit is to obtain permission for a public debate to take place between the metropolitan intellectual elite and the clergy. The goal at first sight is naive. Church censorship is rife in Russia, all discussion of religious issues is banned, and not a single one of Tolstoy's books about religion can be published legally. Yet this group of youngsters is petitioning the country's chief suppressor of freedom to relax one of the most ingrained prohibitions. They ask of the "ideologue of censorship" nothing less than freedom of speech and freedom of assembly. Pobedonostsev, however, does not shoo them away.

Oddly enough, for these young people Pobedonostsev is not the monster he is to the older generation of Russian intellectuals. The "elders," whose youth and maturity came and went with the reforms of Alexander II, back in the 1860s and 1870s, are horribly politicized. The *shestidesyatniki*, or "sixtiers," spend their time endlessly reading, writing, and conversing about politics, government, censorship, and the press. A mark of the older generation is their division into rival camps.

Compared to this set of venerable intellectuals, the generation of the 1890s is extremely apolitical. Many of the young provincials newly arrived in the Russian capital have no intention of recognizing the established circles. Merezhkovsky's young wife Zinaida Gippius writes that they visit liberal journalists, conservative journalists, and even censors. On one occasion, at a social function, Gippius notices a wizened figure in the corner, but fails to recognize him. The figure stares at her through his Scrooge-like eyes, as if studying her. Only when he departs does Gippius ask the host who it was: Pobedonostsev, the all-seeing, all-knowing state ideologue.

Merezhkovsky, who has come to talk to the ober-procurator, knows Pobedonostsev only too well, but is not prejudiced against him in any way. For Merezhkovsky, he is not the medieval inquisitor who six months ago excommunicated Tolstoy from the church. Besides, this younger generation does not hold Tolstoy in any particular reverence.

Pobedonostsev has no great liking for the company assembled before him, but decides not to create problems for them just yet. He sends them to Metropolitan Anthony—let him decide, he thinks. The young men immediately depart for Alexander Nevsky Monastery. With the consent (or at least without the opprobrium) of Pobedonostsev, persuading the liberal metropolitan will be a cinch.

The idea for a public discourse on religion is the brainchild of Gippius, who happens to be a rather hip poet and journalist (officially she is known by her husband's surname Merezhkovsky, but usually publishes under her maiden name). In September 1901, shortly before the visit to Pobedonostsev, she and Dmitry go for a stroll in the woods near their summer dacha at Luga outside Saint Petersburg and discuss returning to the capital in autumn. "What are we going to do this winter? Continue these conversations of ours?" she asks. Merezhkovsky nods.

By "conversations" Gippius means the weekly meeting of Petersburg bohemians at their apartment in Muruzi House at 24 Liteyny Avenue. The Merezhkovskys host receptions for the most celebrated young literati and artists, among them Sergei Diaghilev and friends: Filosofov, Benois, Bakst, Lanceray, and others. And every Wednesday the entire company, including the Merezhkovskys, visits Diaghilev, the editor of *World of Art*, at his spacious flat. The apartments of Diaghilev and the Merezhkovskys attract the Petersburg in-crowd. They host get-togethers for the capital's most "with-it" people, where views are exchanged on everything under the sun from art to literature to religion—everything, that is, except politics. Politics and social problems are for the older generation. The young hipsters despise all of that.

Sergei Diaghilev is interested in art and Dmitry Merezhkovsky in religion and philosophy, but they rebel as a team—not against the government, but against the older generation, against dull social affectation, against old-fashioned journalism. The future belongs to them.

Merezhkovsky at this moment in time is working on his *Christ and Antichrist* trilogy, the first two parts of which have already been published. He and his wife want to create an "open, semi-official society of people of faith and philosophy for the free discussion of Church and cultural issues."

The only one in their bohemian company who is acquainted with the clergy not simply by hearsay is Vasily Rozanov—also a well-known journalist and critic, although somewhat outside their circle. Rozanov likes to play the fool and pranks around in both print and conversation. He obliterates stereotypes and clichés, making fun of everyone, especially himself. He has no qualms about insulting friends or (unusually for the time) writing frank and unflattering things about himself. Rozanov is fond of internal contradictions in his arguments and often defends both points of view. "Morality? Don't even know how to spell the word."

Rozanov's offensive nature is partially explained by his background. He used to be married to Apollinaria Suslova, the former mistress of his idol, Fyodor Dostoyevsky. She is sixteen years his senior. During their seven-year marriage she terrorizes Rozanov, physically beats him and then dumps him, without granting an official divorce, so that he is forced to live in a civil partnership with his new "wife" and the mother of his five children.

Rozanov does not mix with high society and lives in comparative poverty—even as a renowned journalist he still works on the side as a civil servant. In between government tasks he pens endless articles for all kinds of magazines, even ones he would rather not touch ("I write trifles for peanuts," Rozanov says apologetically about his journalistic endeavors).

For the Merezhkovskys, Rozanov is valuable because he is visited not only by bohemians, but also by men of the cloth. Gippius and her husband use these social gatherings to test the waters for their new project.

The first meeting of the Religious-Philosophical Assembly (to which Metropolitan Anthony gave his consent) takes place on 29 November 1901 in the small hall of the Russian Geographical Society. Inside stands a huge statue donated to the Society after a recent expedition, but it is covered with a cloth so as not to distract the participants. From the outline Gippius guesses that the figure belongs to the Buddha—and that is how she refers to it in her memoirs. But she is wrong. The curious Alexander Benois decides to take a peek and discovers that the silent witness is "not the Buddha, but a gigantically fearsome Mongolian *shaitan* [devil], with horns, fangs and shaggy hair."

The chairman of the meeting is the dependable rector of the Theological Academy, Bishop Sergius Stragorodsky. Forty-two years later, during the Great Patriotic War, he will become the Patriarch of Moscow and All Russia appointed by Stalin. But in 1901 the thirty-four-year-old pontiff belongs to the same generation as Merezhkovsky and Gippius, although he effectively speaks on behalf of last century's overlord, Konstantin Pobedonostsev.

Almost all the top hierarchs of the Russian Orthodox Church are present. The assemblies (twenty-two are held in total) spark an intellectual revolution: for the first time the Russian cultural elite has an opportunity to converse with the top echelons of the church (although not the government just yet). Officially the assemblies are not considered public events. If they were, a police presence would be required and the proceedings could be broken up at any moment. In theory only official participants are allowed to attend, but in practice the Merezhkovskys and company hand out membership cards to all comers.

Saint Petersburg's liberal mainstream does not wholly approve of the meetings, recalls Gippius, because everything connected with religion seems backward and reactionary to liberal journalists. That said, the liberal press considers anything outside politics, including the young aesthetes and idealists of *World of Art*, to be backward and reactionary.

A BAD MONK

Merezhkovsky and friends are not the only young supplicants that Pobedonostsev receives in his office. Back in the summer of 1898 he is visited by a forlorn priest from Poltava who is desperate to enter the Saint Petersburg Theological Academy (which will be headed by the future patriarch, Bishop Sergius). The priest presents his graduation certificate from a local seminary, showing poor grades. It allows him to work in a provincial backwater, but is not sufficient to enroll at the capital's premier academy. The petitioner understands that without Pobedonostsev's personal approval the road to further education is barred to him. He sits and waits for the "minister of the church" in the latter's empty office for what seems like an eternity.

"'What can I do for you?' a voice suddenly rang out behind me," recalls the priest.

> I turned round and saw the 'grand inquisitor' creeping towards me through a secret door concealed by the curtains. He was of medium height, skeletal, slightly stooped and dressed in a black coat.
>
> 'Who is your father? Are you married? Do you have children?' The questions rained down on me, and his voice was harsh and dry. I replied that I had two children.
>
> 'I see,' he exclaimed. 'I don't like that. What sort of monk has children? A bad one, that's what. I can't do anything for you,' he said and promptly went away.

The young priest is shocked by Pobedonostsev's abruptness, but calls out after him: "But, Your Excellency, you must listen to me. This is my life. All I want is to study and learn how to help people. I cannot accept rejection."

The applicant's voice sounds so desperate that it stops Pobedonostsev in his tracks. His temper softens, and he begins to question the priest in detail.

"Remind me, what's your name?"

"Georgy Gapon," replies the young man. Pobedonostsev has, of course, already made inquiries before Gapon's arrival. Gapon is an ardent Tolstoyan, which is the root of his problems. Pobedonostsev is aware of that.

Gapon's poor grades from the Poltava seminary are not because he was a bad student. On the contrary, he was the best student, but too feisty. While at ecclesiastical school in Poltava, one of his teachers, Ivan Tregubov, a prominent Tolstoyan and a friend of the count, gives the fifteen-year-old Gapon some of Tolstoy's religious writings. The books have a powerful influence on the young priest: "My eyes were opened to the fact that the essence of religion lies not in external forms, but in spirit—not in ritual, but in love for one's neighbor," remembers Gapon. He becomes so immersed in Tolstoyism that he changes his mind about becoming a priest. Warned that he is about to lose his scholarship, he makes a point of rejecting it himself and starts giving private lessons to finance his studies.

After graduating from the seminary, Gapon intends to get married. His future wife convinces him that the priesthood is not incompatible with his Tolstoyan principles. "A doctor treats the body," she said, "but a priest heals the soul. . . . People need the latter far more than the former." Gapon argues that his beliefs contradict the teachings of the Orthodox Church, but his wife insists that "the main thing is not to be faithful to the Orthodox Church, but to Christ, who taught us how best to serve humanity."

In the end, Gapon combines the two and becomes a Tolstoyan priest. For five years he serves at a rural cemetery church in Poltava province and becomes so popular that people from neighboring parishes join his congregation. But his wife dies in 1898, and Gapon decides to start a new life. He leaves his small children with his parents and travels to Saint Petersburg to ask (or beg) Pobedonostsev to make an exception and allow him to enter the academy.

All contact with the church establishment appalls Gapon. At the Trinity-Sergius Lavra, where he stops by on his way to Saint Petersburg, he encounters the entourage of the Moscow Metropolitan consisting of "obese monks" who banter with each other during the church service he attends. "Their insincerity in the house of the preacher of righteousness Saint Sergius filled me with disgust, and I left without waiting for the end of the vigil and without genuflecting before the holy relics, as I considered it blasphemy to do so in front of these Pharisees," says Gapon.

In Saint Petersburg, Gapon requests an audience with Pobedonostsev from his deputy, V. K. Sabler, who has made a career for himself because "as a student at Saint Petersburg University he regularly attended the same churches as Pobedonostsev and caught the latter's eye by praying fervently."

"We know about your disruptive behavior at the seminary," Pobedonostsev's deputy greets Gapon. "We know what ideas you nurtured back then. But the bishop tells me that you are a reformed man since becoming a priest and have abandoned all your silly notions. All right, we will accept you and we trust that you will become a faithful servant of the Church."

Gapon nods. He decides to conceal his true beliefs from the church officials and enrolls at the academy.

However, just one year later Gapon becomes utterly disillusioned with
his studies. He sees that his dream will never materialize. He attends
church services for workers on the outskirts of Saint Petersburg and hears
sermons all about the Last Judgment and nothing else. He tries to put
forward his own ideas, but the ecclesiastical authorities resist. He becomes
depressed.

"I felt that the work I was doing contradicted my views. I felt unable to
do anything for the very people I was ordained to instruct," he recalls. "In
desperation I abandoned my missionary work and started to dream of a
peaceful life in a monastery where I could pray to my heart's content in
nature's bosom. My mood and health deteriorated. My friends were concerned and decided to send me somewhere I could recover. The Academy
itself contributed to the cost."

His doctors suspect tuberculosis and send Gapon to Crimea, where
he resides not in the "bosom of nature," but at a monastery outside Yalta,
the most sumptuous city in all the empire. Back then, Yalta is the focal
point of the Russian *beau monde*: Livadia Palace is the summer residence
of the tsar; the entire court relocates there during the warm season. "Not
far from the luxury homes oozing wealth and grandeur, the city was
home to thousands of unfortunates—hungry, cold and homeless. Indeed,
the impressionable soul is struck by the contrast between the resplen-
dent palaces in the center and the horrible shacks in the suburbs," writes
Gapon. He is interested in all walks of life and makes the acquaintance
of both the poor and the vacationing bohemia. In particular, he befriends Vasily Vereshchagin, at that time the most famous Russian artist
in the world.

Vereshchagin is at the zenith of his fame and, unlike most of his peers,
very politicized. Had he been born a century later, he would most likely
have been a photojournalist or a war reporter: Vereshchagin's trademark is
to travel to hot spots to capture on canvas the horrors that he sees. Although his antiwar paintings are exhibited all over the world, in his homeland he is accused of sympathy for the enemy and lack of patriotism.

When Vereshchagin, aged thirty-two, held his first exhibition in Saint
Petersburg, the future Emperor Alexander III is said to have remarked:
"His tendentiousness goes against national pride. One might conclude that
Vereshchagin is either a brute or quite mad." In the summer of 1899, the
now fifty-seven-year-old Vereshchagin forms a fatherly relationship with
Gapon.

"I clearly see that you have gone through some kind of inner turmoil. Let me give you my advice. Ditch the cassock!" the artist urges the priest during one of their walks together. "You don't need it! There are better ways to spend your energy in this world." But Gapon does not listen to the celebrity painter. Having rested, he returns to Saint Petersburg in October 1899 and keeps the cassock firmly in place. Vereshchagin, meanwhile, sets off on a world trip: first to the Philippines, then to the United States and Cuba, and four years later to Japan.

PREPARING FOR THE TRANSITION

In August 1901, six months after his excommunication, Tolstoy again falls seriously ill. His family fears that he will not survive the winter and decides to send him to Crimea in the hope that the local climate will help the old man recover.

Countess Panina, a fan of Tolstoy's works, rents a luxury dacha for him at Gaspra, which on one side borders the Crimean estate of the richest family in Russia—the Yusupovs (richer than the Romanovs)—and on the other Ai-Todor, the manor of a childhood friend of the emperor, Grand Duke Alexander Mikhailovich (known as Sandro by his relatives). A stone's throw away is Livadia Palace, the summer residence of the tsar himself. The excommunicated outcast travels with his family to the most upmarket resort in the empire.

The entourage travels by train. On the way, the train stops in Kharkov, where Tolstoy is given an ovation on the station platform. Ovations in Tolstoy's honor have become a tradition this year: when news of his excommunication first breaks, admirers in the Russian capital gather inside an art gallery in front of his portrait by Ilya Repin and rapturously applaud their idol. Immediately afterwards the portrait is removed and the exhibition closed down.

Tolstoy writes a short note to *The Petersburg Gazette* about his relocation to Crimea, whereupon Interior Minister Sipyagin prohibits the sale of this issue of the newspaper. The publisher Suvorin notes in his diary that the minister is upset with Tolstoy for having mentioned him in the "Letter to the Tsar and his aides." Tolstoy did indeed write that the Interior Minister is mistaken if he believes that "were the police to fire into a crowd in good time, it would disperse peacefully."

The young writer Maxim Gorky is not so lucky as Count Tolstoy. Back in April he is sued for an article about the "Battle of Kazan" and exiled to a district town in Nizhny Novgorod province (not far from his home, but away from the action). Gorky writes an appeal asking that he be allowed to serve his exile in Crimea, since he has tuberculosis. Permission is granted with the caveat that he must not reside in Yalta, a large city full of the metropolitan elite. Also in Yalta is Anton Chekhov, and Tolstoy has just relocated to Gaspra, a nearby spa town. Gorky moves into a house close to Alupka, next to Tolstoy and not far from the summer residences of the grand dukes.

In Crimea Tolstoy's health continues to deteriorate. He is diagnosed with malaria, a potentially fatal disease. Tolstoy is seventy-three years old. He is sure that he is about to die and describes his condition as "preparing for the transition." He is suffering from a fever and cannot get out of bed. Those brave enough come to bid the great writer farewell.

On 12 September Tolstoy receives a visit from Anton Chekhov, followed by a neighborly social call from Grand Duke Nicholas Mikhailovich, the great uncle of the tsar, who, like Chekhov, is only forty-two years old. He has a reputation as an enlightened member of the royal family, a historian and writer. Tolstoy is perplexed as to what the tsar's relative wants from him. Later, when Tolstoy recovers, Chekhov brings with him Maxim Gorky.

Tolstoy is thirty-two and forty years older than Chekhov and Gorky, respectively. He considers them the best young writers in Russia and receives them warmly and paternally. "It pleases me that Gorky and Chekhov are much to my liking, especially the former," writes Tolstoy after their visit on 29 November.

As for his "transition," Tolstoy is wrong. His condition abates. The three great Russian writers spend the winter of 1901-1902 together. Gorky at this time is writing *The Lower Depths*, his most successful play, which will bring him worldwide fame. Chekhov has come up with the idea for his final play *The Cherry Orchard* and begins work on it, which will last for three years. Tolstoy slowly puts the finishing touches to *Hadji Murad*, but his thoughts are firmly elsewhere.

Both ill with tuberculosis, Chekhov and Gorky have spent a considerable amount of time over the past few years in Crimea. It is here that Chekhov recovers from his literary failures. The fiasco of *The Seagull*, staged in Saint Petersburg in 1896 to boos and catcalls from the audience, prompted him to head south and forget about the theatre.

However, two years later Chekhov's friend, the director Vladimir Nemirovich-Danchenko, persuades him to stage a new production of the play in Moscow. The writer knows the new theatre founded by Nemirovich-

Danchenko and his partner Konstantin Alexeyev (who uses the stage name Stanislavsky), and agrees. Moreover, Chekhov is besotted by the thirty-three-year-old actress Olga Knipper, who is due to star in the new production. "I'd marry her if I lived in Moscow," says Chekhov only half-jokingly.

The production of *The Seagull* at the Moscow Art Theatre is a triumph, and Olga Knipper becomes a sensation. In 1900, the cast makes a special trip to Crimea to show the play to Chekhov, who has not yet seen it. He likes the production very much and attends all the performances together with Gorky, including plays by other writers. After a staging of *Hedda Gabler* by Henrik Ibsen, Chekhov and Gorky go backstage to meet the leading lady, Maria Andreyeva.

"God damn it, you're great," says the celebrated but overawed Gorky at the sight of the young actress, and shakes her hand rather violently.

"I looked at him with deep emotion, awfully glad that he liked the play. Everything about him seemed strange: his profane language, his suit, high boots and loose-hanging shirt, his long straight hair, coarse facial features and reddish moustache. Not the way I'd imagined he should be," says Andreyeva. "And suddenly those blue eyes lit up under the long eyelashes, his lips curved into a charming childlike smile. His face seemed more beautiful than beauty itself, and my heart skipped a beat. I was wrong. He was exactly the way he was supposed to be, thank God!"

After that first acquaintance, they begin to meet more often. On the next occasion, Gorky visits Andreyeva with the twenty-seven-year-old opera singer Feodor Chaliapin—they are collecting money for the Doukhobors to help Tolstoy send the persecuted sect to Canada.

Chekhov, for his part, is seeing more of Olga Knipper. In 1901, they marry and spend their honeymoon at a tuberculosis sanatorium in Bashkiria. However, they soon part company, at least physically: he spends most of his time in Yalta, while she is in Moscow at the theatre.

Tolstoy is warm yet critical towards the young writers. About *The Seagull*, he has this to say: "It's a bit cluttered, not sure why. Yet Europe cries that it's amazing and that Chekhov is the most talented of them all. But *The Seagull* is in fact very poor." When Gorky reads the first scene of his play *The Lower Depths*, Tolstoy "listens attentively and then asks: 'What are you writing it for?'"

Although Tolstoy is affable, both Chekhov and Gorky tremble before him. Chekhov makes sure to dress properly before visiting Tolstoy, whatever the season or time of day. "Just think," Chekhov says to Gorky, "it was he who wrote: 'Anna felt her eyes glow in the dark.'"

"I once saw him as maybe no one had ever done before," says Gorky.

I was on my way to his house on the coast at Gaspra, just below Yu-supov's estate. On the beach among the rocks I saw this small, angular figure in grey tattered rags and a crumpled hat. He was sat with cheek-bones cupped in both palms, the silvery strands of his beard flowing through his fingers, staring far out to sea, the greenish wavelets rolling obediently at his feet, as if telling the old sage about themselves. Sud-denly, the mad thought possessed me that he would rise up and wave his hand, and the sea would freeze and glass over, and the stones would stir and cry out, and all around nature would come to life, rustling and mur-muring to itself in different voices. I cannot describe in words what I felt at that moment. My soul was full of rapture and horror, but then every-thing merged into a happy thought: 'I am not an orphan in this world as long as this man is in it.'

The atheist Gorky practically deifies Tolstoy: "He looks like a god. Not like Jehovah or Zeus, but a sort of Russian god who sits on a maple throne under a golden lime tree. Although not very majestic, he is more astute than any other god. I, a non-believer, look at him and for some reason think, somewhat timidly, that this man is godlike!"

According to Gorky, not only the waves, but also royal personages step aside to let Tolstoy pass. He recalls one incident when Tolstoy, on the road to Gaspra, discovers that his way is blocked by three grand dukes, all uncles of the tsar: Alexander Mikhailovich (Sandro), Georgy Mikhailovich, and Peter Nikolaevich. Tolstoy "fixed the Romanovs with an inquisitive stare," writes Gorky. The Romanovs looked away at first, but the horse of one of them, withering under Tolstoy's gaze, moved aside to let Tolstoy by. "Even horses understand that Tolstoy must be allowed to pass."

"LYOVOCHKA IS DYING"

In January 1902, after a long walk on a cold, windy day, Tolstoy falls ill with pneumonia. He desperately wants to write, but his health does not permit it.

On 26 January, his wife Sofia notes in her diary: "My Lyovochka [Leo] is dying." The next day the papers write about Tolstoy's "dangerous, hope-less illness." Back in Saint Petersburg, Suvorin writes in his diary that Tolstoy's health is the talk of the town. He sends a telegram to Chekhov to inquire about the count's health. Chekhov replies: "Inflammation of the lungs. It's dangerous, but there's hope." Afterwards a friend explains to Suvorin that he was lucky to get any news from Crimea, since all letters and telegrams mentioning Tolstoy are being intercepted on the Interior Ministry's orders: not only newspapers are being censored, but correspondence too.

Suvorin also mentions that instructions have been issued in the event of Tolstoy's death: obituaries and articles about his work can be printed, but any mention of his excommunication is prohibited. In addition, the Ministry "requires that all news and articles about Count Tolstoy be objective and circumspect."

Tolstoy's relatives are panicking. Manuscripts and letters are put in a suitcase and deposited with Gorky for safekeeping, just in case Tolstoy's death prompts a search of his dwellings. Negotiations begin on the purchase of a plot of land in Crimea to bury Tolstoy without the knowledge of the authorities.

But the dying Tolstoy has his own idea to write a "political will" in the form of a letter to Emperor Nicholas II. He remembers Grand Duke Nicholas Mikhailovich, who once came to visit him, and sends a telegram asking if the duke is prepared to mediate between him and Tsar Nicholas. The duke immediately agrees. Tolstoy strains every fiber to compose the letter to the tsar. It is not a political message, rather a lecture from an elder to a pupil, a word of advice passed from one generation and one century to the next.

"My dear brother," writes the count.

I consider this form of address to be most appropriate because I am writing to you not as the tsar, but as a man and a brother. Moreover, I am writing to you as if from the next world in anticipation of my imminent demise. . . . Most likely, you are under the delusion that the people love autocracy and its representative, the tsar. Everywhere you go, crowds of people greet you with cries of 'hurrah'. Do not take it as an expression of loyalty. The masses are merely curious and would behave likewise if treated to any other spectacle. Often, these same people you take to be expressing adoration for you have simply been handpicked by the police to play the part of loyal subjects. The same as when your grandfather in Kharkov visited a cathedral full of people, yet all were plainclothes policemen. If you were able, as I am, to mingle with the peasants arranged behind the troops all along the railway and listen to what they are saying as they stand there in the cold and slush for days waiting for your train to pass by, you would hear from these genuine representatives of the people, simple peasants, an entirely different speech wholly at variance with love for autocracy and its representative.

However, Tolstoy is unlikely to be heard, even less understood. The emperor, tutored by Pobedonostsev, firmly believes in autocracy.

"Autocracy is an obsolete form of government," writes Tolstoy, "suitable only for people somewhere in central Africa, separated from the world, but not for the people of Russia, who are becoming part of the global enlightenment. Hence, this form of government can only be maintained through violence: heightened security, exile, executions, religious persecution, prohibition of books and newspapers, distorted education and all kinds of cruel and foolish doings."

Next, he turns to the abolition of private ownership of land. For some reason, the deathbed-ridden Tolstoy decides to counsel the emperor on this particular topic:

> Your advisers will tell you that the abolition of private land ownership is a fantasy. . . . I personally think that in our time landed property is a blatant injustice, as serfdom was fifty years ago. I think its destruction would grant the Russian people a high degree of independence, prosperity and contentment. I think also that such a measure would surely eradicate the socialist and revolutionary petulance that is erupting among the workers and poses a grave threat to the people and the government. But perhaps I am mistaken, and maybe this issue can only be resolved by the people themselves if they have an opportunity to speak forth.

On 31 January 1902 Suvorin learns that Interior Minister Sipyagin has banned all portraits of Tolstoy from being exhibited. "Tolstoy will not have to wait [long] for a monument, nor Sipyagin for a stigma on his stupid forehead," writes the outraged pro-government publisher Suvorin in his diary. "Does this gentleman take advice from anyone? Do others simply acquiesce to his stupid orders?"

The ban is followed by guidelines on how to proceed on the occasion of Tolstoy's likely burial: processions and marches are prohibited, and the coffin is to be placed on the back of a wagon, covered with a black cloth, and carried to his estate at Yasnaya Polyana.

But yet again death retreats and Tolstoy recovers. He does not, however, receive a response from the tsar.

|| Chapter 2 ||

SERGEI WITTE

in which Sergei Witte fails to stop Russia
from invading China and seizing Beijing

RUS OR ROUBLE

On a winter's morning in 1895, Finance Minister Sergei Witte receives a batch of newly minted gold coins at his office in Saint Petersburg. He looks at them with a satisfied smile. Witte himself has "coined" a name for Russia's new currency: the *rus* [an old name for Russia].

He believes that the rouble is overvalued. The official exchange rate against the French franc is one to four, and on the black market one rouble is selling for 2.5 francs. It is unprofitable for both industrialists (who buy equipment abroad) and for the state (which pays interest on loans). Therefore, the minister of finance wants to introduce a new gold standard and devalue the currency "to make life cheaper," in his own words. After admiring the new coins, he ponders the backlash that will surely follow his monetary reform. He has no allies in the civil service—all members of the State Council oppose Witte's plan. Also opposed are Russian landowners who sell agricultural produce abroad (to them the exchange rate is beneficial), as well as Russia's most important foreign partner and creditor, France.

Witte makes a special trip to Paris to discuss his plans with French ministers and Alphonse Rothschild, the head of the financial empire. Rothschild is critical of Witte's plans. He believes that the switch to gold is a mistake and advises Witte to go for the bimetallic standard: a currency based on gold and silver. But Witte does not trust silver, believing that it will soon be devalued and cease to be a precious metal. French Prime Minister Jules Meline is also against Witte and even writes a letter to the Russian tsar, asking him to make his finance minister see sense. But Witte stands firm.

"The educated classes of Russia oppose the reform almost unanimously," recalls Witte. "Firstly, due to ignorance; secondly, out of habit, and, thirdly, for personal, albeit imaginary, interests. Thus, I had to swim against the tide that wanted somehow to preserve the status quo."

In view of the scale of the opposition, he decides to sacrifice his new name for the currency. Let it be the rouble as before, then people probably won't even notice. It will just be devalued.

Realizing that it will be easier to go through the tsar, rather than the many-membered State Council, he decides to ask Nicholas II to approve the monetary reform. Nicholas obliges. Witte's authority in economic matters carries weight, since he was the favorite minister of Alexander III. Not only that, he is greatly respected by Maria Feodorovna, the mother of Nicholas. On 15 January 1897, the emperor signs a decree to mint the new gold rouble. "I have only one ally, but the only one that matters—the emperor," says Witte.

Witte enjoys a good deal of influence in the early years under Nicholas II. In the second half of the nineteenth century, Russia becomes increasingly tied to the global financial markets, so the minister in charge of the country's coffers wields clout. One of his colleagues is reported to have said: "Witte holds everyone in contempt because he knows he can buy the lot of us."

Witte's predecessors have borrowed heavily from abroad. The humiliating defeat in the Crimean War has highlighted Russia's economic backwardness compared to Europe and the urgent need to modernize the economy. French bankers have stepped in. The thrifty Alexander III is grateful, describing France as Russia's number one partner. During the visit of a French squadron to Russia, Alexander III listens humbly to the revolutionary anthem *La Marseillase* (at that time it was a crime to perform the tune in Russia, but French loans have changed all that).

It is Alexander III who appoints Witte as Russian finance minister, and he proves to be even more pragmatic than his predecessors. Many, including Nicholas II, subsequently describe Witte as a chameleon. Indeed, Witte's political views do change radically over his thirty-year political career.

Emperor Alexander II's assassination in March 1881 is a turning point in the career of the young provincial Sergei Witte, as indeed it is for Konstantin Pobedonostsev. Witte at the time is only thirty-one years old, nearly half the age of Pobedonostsev.

Witte has not yet entered the civil service and works as a manager for a private corporation in charge of the railway line to the southwest corner of the empire (modern Ukraine). But after the assassination of Alexander II, the young careerist Witte immediately decamps to the capital Saint Petersburg with the idea of setting up a secret society to protect the new monarch from the revolutionaries. He proposes to deal with the nihilists by applying their methods. The plan is to create a secret organization made up of the tsar's most loyal servants to destroy the monarch's opponents. He outlines his idea to Minister of Imperial Properties Count Vorontsov-Dashkov, who approves. The organization is called the "Holy Militia."

Alexander III knows about the organization and showers it with public money. Even though the Holy Militia eventually disbands after two years with limited success, Witte catches the imperial eye. Of all the tsar's "men-at-arms," it is railwayman Witte whose career is assured.

In 1889, he moves to the Ministry of Finance, and in 1893 becomes transport minister. It is Witte who starts building the Trans-Siberian Railway and develops a reputation as a *pochvennik* [nationalist loyalist] and a Slavophile. The conservative entourage of Alexander III lobbies for Witte's appointment as finance minister in the hope that, as a patriot, he will keep the protectionist customs tariffs introduced by his predecessor. However, on finding himself in the finance minister's chair, Witte begins to borrow even more from the West than his predecessors did, and invests the money in a sweeping industrial modernization program. He opens up the country to foreign capital.

The Russian economy starts to develop rapidly. Awash with cash, Witte decides to create a newfangled stabilization fund—for a rainy day or (just as likely) a war.

"I was constantly criticized for holding too much cash in hand," recalls Witte. "Many people, especially the papers, thought the national reserves would be better spent on industry. They said that no other country has a 'cash storage system', including those with well-managed finances, such as France, England and even Germany. I maintained that, for the Russian Empire, the concept of holding reserves worth hundreds of millions of roubles* was not only sound, but necessary."†

Another of the new finance minister's innovative reforms is the introduction of a state monopoly on vodka production. One of Witte's advisers on this issue is the great chemist Dmitry Mendeleev. Witte acts as Mendeleev's patron after the latter is kicked out of Saint Petersburg University for being too quarrelsome. The chemist is appointed to a specially created position where he will cause minimal trouble: head of the Bureau of Weights and Measures.

The Witte-Mendeleev alcohol reform does not go down too well, metaphorically speaking. The vodka lobby tries to resist and even complains to Nicholas II's uncle, Grand Duke Vladimir, that it could lead to public disorder in the capital. But Witte convinces the duke and the tsar that all talk of unrest is exaggerated. "Reforms in Russia should be carried out quickly and urgently, otherwise they will stall," says Witte. And he is right. There is no unrest in Saint Petersburg. Further south in Moscow, however, the introduction of the new state monopoly is delayed. According to the journalist and publisher Alexei Suvorin, Grand Duke Sergei, another of the emperor's uncles, takes a bribe of two million roubles‡ to postpone the introduction of the proposed liquor monopoly. Both Witte and the tsar are aware of this, adds Suvorin suggestively.

---

*About $1,318,333,333 in 2017.
† A similar argument is given by Finance Minister Alexei Kudrin a century later when the decision is taken to create a stabilization fund from oil and gas revenue.
‡ About $26,366,666 in 2017.

Having started his political career in the Holy Militia, Witte becomes more liberal with age, yet he retains an authoritarian streak. Suvorin, who is well versed in governmental affairs, asserts that Witte was one of the masterminds behind the crackdown on students in 1899–1901, and that Minister of Education Bogolepov issued his brutal order to dispatch rowdy students to the army at Witte's behest. According to Suvorin, even the old Pobedonostsev had opposed that measure: "No, Sergei Yulievich [Witte], that is too much."

In his memoirs, Witte paints himself as the main liberating force in the country. He does in fact become a liberal—but only later, in 1905, when forced to draft the first Russian constitution.

THE GILDED YOUTH

Russia's economic growth in the latter half of the nineteenth century produces a burgeoning merchant class, which plays the role of the bourgeoisie. The new Russian middle class is made up of former serfs who have gone into trade and become rich. However, according to the census of 1897, merchants account for just 0.5 percent of the population; even nobles outweigh them with 1.5 percent. Generally speaking, the most powerful merchant dynasties come from Moscow and belong to the Old Believer clans.

The merchant dynasties appeared in Russia only at the beginning of the nineteenth century. The founder of the Morozov dynasty, Savva Morozov Sr., was a serf who redeemed himself (in the original sense) and then made a vast fortune from selling fabrics—assisted by Russia's alliance with Napoleonic France and the continental blockade of England. The disappearance of cheaper English cloth from the Russian market and the need for import substitution enriched domestic producers. Savva Morozov Sr. eventually purchased English looms and his cotton-producing enterprise turned into a textile empire.

The Old Believer merchants are far more conservative in everyday life and in economic policy than the nobles. They are in favor of protectionism and import substitution and against the opening of Russia's economy and the influx of Western capital—not only because they believe in Russia's "special way," but also because foreign bankers are their direct competitors. In the early twentieth century, memories of how the Old Believer merchants defended traditional values are anathema to the reformists.

Put simply, the nineteenth-century mores and moral precepts of the Old Believer merchants are much closer to the peasantry than to the nobility. "Merchants had almost no affinity with their children," says Zinaida Morozova. "I think it's because peasants demand respect for parents. For them, fear before God and fear before parents are paramount."

At the turn of the century, when the new generation of merchants comes of age, the situation changes. The captains of Russian industry, who became fabulously wealthy during the reforms of Alexander II, are replaced by the "gilded youth," who do not resemble the children of "semi-literate peasant traders" at all. They are well educated, travel to the West, and have a very different outlook on their position in the world.

The heir to his family's textile empire, Savva Morozov, studies in Cambridge. Another Savva (a popular name in those days), the third son of the vodka merchant, railway builder, and "king of state procurements" Ivan Mamontov, is so beguiled by the theatre that he goes to Milan to study opera singing and even performs on stage at La Scala. The children of the austere Old Believers discover the Impressionists and make them fashionable all over Europe. Industrialist Ivan Shchukin's son Sergei and the cousins of Savva Morozov, Ivan and Mikhail, are the first in the world to start collecting French Impressionism art. Meanwhile, the heir to the Tretyakov "paper empire," Pavel Tretyakov, and silk manufacturer Kozma Soldatenkov (nicknamed "Kozma Medici") assemble a huge collection of Russian art.

But when it comes to passion for the arts, no one beats the son of the merchant Sergei Alexeyev, a close relative of both the Mamontovs and the Tretyakovs. Konstantin decides not to go into the family business (there's no need, since he has nine brothers) and instead devotes his life to the theatre. Alexeyev becomes an actor and a director, taking the stage name Stanislavsky.

Zinaida Morozova recalls that at the beginning of the twentieth century the merchant class represented the *beau monde* of Moscow: "The nobility had begun to withdraw from the limelight. The merchants were the ones interested in the arts. The Philharmonic Society consisted almost entirely of members of the merchant class. Merchant ladies were beautiful, well dressed and well-traveled, and their children studied foreign languages and attended to balls."

Such a radical change in lifestyle, notes Zinaida Morozova, affected the psyche of the gilded youth, or, in her words, "the third generation" (i.e., the grandchildren of the founders of the merchant dynasties, the generation of Savva Morozov and Zinaida herself). "Most members of the third generation were not touched by culture. Most went through university and came out neurotic; only a tiny percentage came out normal. . . . The culture change was overwhelming. Our grandfathers didn't know how to read and write. They were former serfs and self-made men who set up large facto-ries. They gave their children governesses and tutors. The children had to study, but their brains couldn't cope with the load."

The psychological dissonance between external freedom and the patri-archal setup experienced by the "third generation" can perhaps only be compared with, say, the current crop of princes in today's Saudi Arabia, who have to combine a forced respect for the traditions of their own coun-try with a fascination for Western pop culture. "Some families preserved a peasant wildness, while others rapidly degenerated into nervous angst," says Zinaida Morozova. "The older generation believed in God and had a moral compass, while the young rejected everything and didn't find any-thing to replace it."

The gilded merchant youth, unlike their parents, do not believe that they owe everything to the authorities. They argue with officials, defend their interests, and give Finance Minister Witte a headache. The relation-ship between the "Petersburg liberals" in the government, headed by Witte, and the Moscow "oligarchs"* is becoming increasingly strained.

In 1896 Nizhny Novgorod hosts the Congress of Industrialists, at which excise tariffs are discussed. In attendance is the sixty-eight-year-old Dmi-try Mendeleev (the author of the Customs Tariff Act), who, wishing to put his opponents in their place, states that arguing with him is futile because he has the backing of the emperor. The hall falls silent. But suddenly one of the young participants pipes up: "Scientific findings underpinned by the opinion of the tsar are not persuasive and a discredit to science."

Sitting in the audience is the twenty-eight-year-old Maxim Gorky. He asks the people next to him: Who is this upstart? He is told that he is the heir to Russia's largest textile empire, Savva Morozov. Morozov is thirty-four years old, half the age of Mendeleev.

Just a few days later Morozov becomes embroiled in another scandal. Members of the Nizhny Novgorod Fair, a major annual trade event, learn that Finance Minister Witte has refused the Committee of Industrialists an extension on its state loans. Morozov begins by delivering a rousing speech: "The state must be built on iron girders. . . . Our straw monarchy is not viable. . . . When officials talk about helping factories and workers, you all know it's about helping them to an early grave." Gorky reproduces Morozov's words. Morozov subsequently writes a much more acerbic

---

* The word was not in vogue back then, and in any case the merchants and industrialists of the early twentieth century were not oligarchs in the full sense of the word—if only because they had very little political influence. Incidentally, today's oligarchs also have little political influence.

telegram to Witte, demanding more credit from the state banks. Other business leaders approve it, despite their reservations that the text is provocative. The next day Witte acquiesces to their demand.

OPERA, DRAMA, TRAGEDY

Konstantin Stanislavsky recalls that, when he was very young, Moscow was home to two popular domestic theatres: one owned by his family, the Alexeyevs, the other run by Savva Mamontov, who was also the artistic director. But it is at Mamontov's theatre that the seventeen-year-old Kostya [Konstantin] Alexeyev begins his acting career under the stage name Stanislavsky.

"Mamontov had this amazing ability to work with people and do several things at once," Stanislavsky recalls.

> He was in charge of the whole production, yet found time to write dialogue, dictate telegrams about his railway business, and laugh and joke at the same time. As a result, the two-week job of staging a play was a kind of performance in itself. It was delightful and frustrating at the same time. On the one hand, the wonderful scenery was decorated by the finest artists of the day [for example, Viktor Vasnetsov], and the director's creative vision ushered in a new era in the theatrical arts, forcing Moscow's best venues to take note. On the other hand, it was full of amateurs who didn't rehearse or even learn their lines properly.

According to Stanislavsky, Mamontov lacks patience. He becomes infatuated by an idea, then loses interest before seeing it through to completion. "It is strange that Mamontov, himself a sensitive artist and a painter, adopted such a slapdash approach to his theatrical work. We constantly quarreled with him about it. It created antagonism," writes Stanislavsky.

Fascinated by Italian opera, the "railroader" Mamontov decides to create his own private opera, thereby encroaching on the state monopoly: hitherto all opera in Russia has been funded by the government.

This is Mamontov's finest hour. He invites his fellow artists to design the scenery, including Valentin Serov, Mikhail Vrubel, and Konstantin Korovin. His opera singers are mostly Italian. One exception is Tatyana Lyubatovich (with whom he is having an affair) and the twenty-three-year-old Feodor Chaliapin, whom he met in 1896 and immediately invited on board.

"Fedenka [Feodor], at my theatre you can do whatever you like! If you need costumes, there'll be costumes. If you want to stage a new opera, just say the word," Chaliapin recalls the theatre owner's invitation.

In 1897 Mamontov brings in the twenty-five-year-old Sergei Rachmaninoff as an assistant conductor. "Mamontov was a great man and had a great influence on Russian operatic art," remembers Rachmaninoff. "In a way, Mamontov's influence on opera was similar to Stanislavsky's on drama. Mamontov was a born director. Many times I heard him give advice, even to Chaliapin. His tips were generally very brief: a casual remark, a general comment, a short phrase. Chaliapin immediately grasped what he meant."

But Rachmaninoff also recalls that Mamontov often rushed things: "I remember the first performance of the opera *Sadko*, which Rimsky-Korsakov had just finished. Mamontov's stage decorations, costumes and makeup were magnificent, but the orchestra was bad and the choir even worse," says Rachmaninoff of the choristers who awkwardly hid sheet music up their sleeves. On one occasion, recalls Rachmaninoff, when the character Sadko is about to depart for the kingdom of the Sea Tsar, a wooden plank falls off the ship into the "water" with a terrible crash, and the "fish" swim across the stage facing the wrong way, so the audience doesn't know what they are. Despite all this, Rimsky-Korsakov's new opera is a huge success.

At the same time, other wealthy merchant families are busy setting up their own theatres. In 1898, the thirty-five-year-old Konstantin Alexeyev (Stanislavsky) makes the acquaintance of the thirty-nine-year-old playwright Vladimir Nemirovich-Danchenko, and together they come up with the idea of creating a private drama theatre, free of pomp and affectation and with a topical, contemporary repertoire. The first performance, a staging of *Tsar Fyodor Ivanovich* by Alexei Tolstoy, is attended by the thirty-six-year-old textile mogul Savva Morozov. Morozov enjoys the show so much that he buys out all the other investors in the theatre, leaving himself, Stanislavsky, and Nemirovich-Danchenko as the sole shareholders; he soon starts building a new home for the theatre.

The Moscow Art Public Theatre is the name given by Stanislavsky and Nemirovich-Danchenko to their new venture (the word "public" is later dropped from the title). They use it to stage contemporary drama: Chekhov, Ibsen, Tolstoy (Alexei and Leo). Problems arise with Leo Tolstoy, since his plays are in the clutches of the censor.

At the time when Savva Morozov is in charge of Nizhny Novgorod Fair, a large annual trade event, a fierce cholera epidemic breaks out across the whole province. It requires a superhuman effort from Morozov to keep it in check, and he is left exhausted. According to his wife, on returning to Moscow, he lies on the floor of his office and says: "I'm tired. I can't work any more." It is then that he decides to see a play at the new Moscow Art Theatre, after which Stanislavsky and Nemirovich-Danchenko invite him to join them. His wife opposes his new hobby, writing in her memoirs that she foresaw many of the problems that her husband would face: "Savva, I know the [Moscow Art] theatre is like a holiday for you, but I cannot accept that you will swap it for the factory and the people. The workers love and admire you. You have no right to abandon them. You will become a stranger to them." He replies: "I have to follow my feelings." Zinaida insists that "people have duties as well as feelings," but her husband ends the conversation with the words: "I'm tired."

He does not grow tired of the theatre, however. He helps to build it, takes an interest in the set design and lighting, and even makes sure that the paint is thinned to achieve the right "moonlight effect" on stage. Not only that, Savva Morozov falls in love with one of the company's rising stars, the actress Maria Andreyeva.

Morozov and Mamontov's social and charity work is renowned not only in Moscow, but also in the capital Saint Petersburg. They make the acquaintance of Witte and try to take advantage of it: Morozov seeks permission from the censorship committee to stage prohibited plays, while Mamontov tries to secure railway construction contracts for his firm. He soon wins a tender for the construction of the Donetsk coal railway followed by another to extend the Yaroslavl railway (built by his father) to Arkhangelsk. Witte is very grateful to Mamontov for taking on this project and awards him the Order of Saint Vladimir, Second Class, for services to the Russian Empire.

In 1899 Mamontov and Morozov decide to set up a joint newspaper to challenge Alexei Suvorin, the owner of the country's most popular tabloid, *New Time*. They lure Suvorin's best journalist, Alexander Amfiteatrov, offering him the post of editor. The new paper is called *Russia*.

However, despite Witte's patronage, Mamontov's business ventures do not go too well, perhaps because he spends too much time and money on the theatre instead of on his railway company. The railroad to Arkhangelsk, though important for the development of Russia's far north, is not profitable. Mamontov comes up with a new idea to build a mighty corporation that will include not only railways, but also wagon- and ship-building plants, and a steelworks.

The new enterprise requires money, which he withdraws from the accounts of other companies he owns and channels through various business structures. To keep the enterprise afloat, various shady schemes are employed by Mamontov (and, more likely, his assistants). "Through fictitious transactions, fake accounts and reusing entries in the books, they contrived to transfer money from the railways to the factories and back again, while making it all seem creditworthy on paper," then-Prosecutor of Moscow Aleksander Lopukhin describes the process.

Mamontov's proximity to Witte soon helps him find a better solution. His company, the Society of the Moscow-Yaroslavl Railway, wins a concession to build an important railroad from Petersburg to the Volga region. The results of the tender are approved by the State Council, and Mamontov is sure that the high profitability of the new line will compensate his losses from the Arkangelsk project. But because he does not have the money to build it, he takes out a loan secured against the as-yet-unconstructed railway.

Suddenly, in 1899, the economy nosedives. Several railway companies in the United States go bust, and Europe suffers a stock market crisis. "The banks, the gold standard and Sergei Witte are all coming apart at the seams," writes Suvorin in his diary.

In order to save his position and with it the banking system, Witte goes on the offensive against yesterday's friend Savva Mamontov. He orders the banks to reclaim the loan. If Mamontov cannot pay it back, then his Vyatka concession will be forfeit. What's more, the decision is taken in circumvention of the State Council, simply by obtaining the signature of the emperor.

"Witte launched criminal proceedings against Mamontov and his colleagues for their illegal financial dealings. But not only had the Ministry of Finance been fully aware of them, it had petitioned the State Council to award a concession to the very people it then decided to put in the dock," recalls Prosecutor Lopukhin. "It was not so much that these people were dishonest, they had simply overreached themselves. Their actions were hardly moral, but the Ministry of Finance's decision to throw them to the lions was incomprehensible."[*]

Subsequent events play out like a bad opera. Savva Mamontov cannot repay the loan to the bank, and Witte forces him to sell his shares in the Moscow-Arkhangelsk railway to the state for a symbolic price. Mamontov

---

[*] The case of Mamontov in some ways resembles the first trial of Mikhail Khodorkovsky and the Yukos affair of 2003. In both cases market participants are profoundly surprised by the prosecution, as it contradicts the established rules of the game. Everybody committed fraud, and the colleagues of Mamontov (Khodorkovsky) do not understand why is he the only one who got punished. In both cases a biased trial resulted in business bankruptcy, even though initially it could have been saved.

is bankrupt and charged by the state with embezzlement. He is arrested and paraded on foot all the way through Moscow to Taganka prison.

Mamontov tries to save his business. His friends, led by Savva Morozov, want to pay his bail, but the authorities demand an exorbitant 5 million roubles.*

His fellow artists—Serov, Vrubel, Repin, Surikov, Polenov, Levitan, Vasnetsov—publicly support him. The portraitist Valentin Serov even approaches Nicholas II to let the unwell Mamontov be put under house arrest. The emperor concurs, but nothing happens. Feodor Chaliapin, however, who has walked away from Mamontov's opera, declines to support the disgraced businessman.

Before his trial, Mamontov is finally allowed home. The court session is attended by Gorky. In a letter to Chekhov he describes the scene: "I saw Mamontov—what an unconventional figure! I don't believe he's a crook at heart. He simply got carried away by it all."

Mamontov's fate hangs in the balance. The courtroom awaits the jury's decision with bated breath, no one more so than Stanislavsky. When the jury delivers a not guilty verdict, "the hall broke into applause. People tearfully rushed to hug their beloved [Mamontov]," he recalls. However, it is Mamontov's swan song. He is bankrupt and unable to return either to business, the theatre, or his wife, who has not forgiven his affair with an opera singer.

Witte, too, is washed up. The Russian economy sinks into a recession from which it emerges only in 1907, when Witte himself is no longer in government—thanks to his sworn enemy, Stolypin.

ARTISTS AND SLAVES

Sergei Diaghilev, although dismissed from the Directorate of the Imperial Theatres, continues to receive financing for his magazine. In July 1902, it is officially announced that *World of Art* will continue to be subsidized, albeit to the reduced tune of 10,000 roubles a year†—out of the emperor's own pocket. At the same time, Diaghilev believes that the young artistic community should unite against the moribund authorities in line with global cultural trends: Germany has the Secession, France the Champ de Mars, and England the New Gallery. He urges all young Russian artists to rally round him because he will bring them glory. "I want to nurture

* About $65,916,666 in 2017.
† About $131,833 in 2017.

Russian painting, purify it, and glorify it in the West," he writes to his friend Alexander Benois. But Benois considers it delusional.

Diaghilev's personal relations are complicated, none more so than with the one closest to him—his cousin and lover Dima Filosofov. He is caught up in a "love quadrangle." Dima is becoming very close to the family of Zinaida Gippius and Dmitry Merezhkovsky. Filosofov becomes a permanent guest at their home and goes to all their religious-philosophical get-togethers. Merezhkovsky and Gippius contribute to *World of Art*. Filosofov is in charge of the literature section, for which Gippius writes literary criticism under male pseudonyms.

Intimate friendship with the Merezhkovskys distances him from Diaghilev. They describe their alliance as a "trinity." Gippius is very attracted to Filosofov, even though she knows about his homosexuality. Moreover, their threefold relationship is far more equal than Filosofov's partnership with Diaghilev: "Dima is Sergei's slave," say the Merezhkovskys.

Filosofov is not the only one who wants to break free of "Diaghilev's enslavement." Other artists also think that *World of Art* is run like a dictatorship; they want more say in its editorial and exhibition policy. Diaghilev's authoritarianism irks the Moscow artists most of all, since they are always given less space than Diaghilev's Saint Petersburg chums.

On 16 February 1903, after *World of Art*'s latest exhibition, the finest artists of both Saint Petersburg and Moscow pay a visit to the magazine's office, Diaghilev's apartment. The meeting turns into a revolt against Diaghilev. They talk about his dictatorial ways and demand that decisions be taken by a standing committee. Diaghilev is particularly wounded by the fact that his friends Benois and Filosofov are not on his side. When the former says that a new society is needed, the latter adds, "Amen to that."

Diaghilev realizes that the only way to save his project is to bring in new stars to replace the ones on their way out. Filosofov's departure means that he needs a new literary editor. His eye falls upon Anton Chekhov, and he showers the playwright with letters. But the latter writes a long and very polite refusal to every one of them. The reason is twofold: for health reasons, he cannot move to Saint Petersburg ("and the magazine cannot move to Moscow"), and he cannot work with Merezhkovsky because of the latter's attitude to religion. "How could I get along with Dmitry Merezhkovsky, whose faith is didactic, while I lost mine a long time ago. I am bewildered by intelligent believers."

But Diaghilev does not give up. Though he fails to lure Chekhov, he manages to pull Filosofov away from the Merezhkovskys. In the spring of 1902, after much persuasion and the odd scandal, Filosofov leaves the married couple, writing the following note: "I am withdrawing from our union not because I no longer believe in it, but because I personally cannot partake in it." Diaghilev is pleased. He and Filosofov immediately go on a long trip to Italy together.

CONSTANTINOPLE IS OURS

Nicholas II has inherited from his father the imperial court, the government, the military—and countless problems. As his first major foray into global affairs, he sets his sights on capturing Istanbul (then Constantinople, but known in Russian as "Tsargrad," an Old Church Slavonic rendering of the Greek name).

The "return of Constantinople" (even though it never belonged to Russia) is a highly voguish idea in Russian society in the late nineteenth century. Russian forces already stood at the threshold of the ancient city, during the Russian-Turkish war in 1878, towards the end of Alexander II's reign. The "Slavophile patriots" dream of seizing Constantinople, and the press covers the idea widely. The most ardent supporter was Dostoyevsky: "The Golden Horn and Constantinople will all be ours, but there will be no capture or violence," wrote Dostoevsky in his *Diary of a Writer.* "It will happen by itself, because the time has come or is at least very close. The signs are there. It cannot be otherwise. Nature has spoken."

Witte recalls that, ever since the time of Alexander II, the Russian military has harbored thoughts of seizing control of the Black Sea straits and the Ottoman capital. The plan involves dispatching Russian troops through the Bosporus on rafts. However, Alexander III, later called a peacemaker, refrained from going to war with Turkey (although he liked the idea of taking Constantinople, but could not find the right time). The arrival of Nicholas II rekindles hopes of "hoisting an Orthodox cross over the Hagia Sophia."

Shortly after the coronation of Nicholas II, the Russian government discusses whether to proceed with plans to take Constantinople. The talks are initiated by the Russian ambassador to Turkey, Alexander Nelidov, who predicts an imminent political catastrophe in the Ottoman Empire, which Russia should exploit by capturing the Bosporus.

Almost all those at the meeting are in favor, including the head of the general staff, the military and navy ministers, the foreign minister, and Nicholas II himself. "The only one to object, and very forcefully at that, was me," says Witte. "I pointed out that it would lead to a European war and shake the great political and financial foundations of the Russian Empire bequeathed by Alexander III."

Nicholas II listens to all the arguments—and gives the nod to proceed with the operation. The plan is to dispatch a landing force from Odessa and Sevastopol to Turkey, provoking unrest in Constantinople that could become the pretext for an invasion. Finance Minister Witte insists on a special entry in the minutes of the meeting outlining his position: "According to minister Witte, given the present circumstances, the occupation of the Upper Bosporus without the consent of the Great Powers is very risky and could have disastrous consequences." The tsar ignores Witte.

But Sergei Witte is an experienced bureaucrat. He has been in the government for many years, knows the imperial court, and enjoys good relations with the emperor's mother and older ministers. He takes his grievances to the tsar's uncle, Grand Duke Vladimir, commander of the Imperial Guard and the Saint Petersburg Military District. Vladimir is a veteran of the aforementioned Russian-Turkish war, when Russian troops could have taken Constantinople, but stopped within striking distance. Grand Duke Prince Vladimir is both the country's top military authority and a patron of the arts. A man of culture, he heads the Imperial Academy of Fine Arts.

After talking to the tsar's uncle, Witte goes to see Pobedonostsev. The tsar's mentor, despite his friendship with Dostoevsky, does not share the writer's vision that Russia, as the "leader of Orthodoxy" and the "capital of pan-Slavism," has a duty to seize Constantinople. "God have mercy on us," Pobedonostsev writes to Witte on learning of the tsar's approval of the proposed military operation. Pobedonostsev fears upheaval of any kind.

Witte's efforts bear fruit in the end, and the elder statesmen manage to bring Nicholas II round to their point of view. Having just arrived in Constantinople, Ambassador Nelidov receives instructions to do nothing. The war is called off. The tsar finds himself unable to gainsay his uncle or Pobedonostsev, whom he fears. He calls off the Tsargrad operation—and blames Witte for everything, including his own indecision. He is particularly annoyed by Witte's public criticism and belittlement of his royal ambitions. The emperor wants glory, and Witte is the spoiler-in-chief.

THE NOT-SO-GRAND DUKES

"What will I do?! What will happen to Russia? I'm not ready to be tsar! I can't rule an empire. I don't even know how to talk to my ministers. Help me, Sandro!" Grand Duke Alexander Mikhailovich (Sandro) recalls the words of Tsarevich Nicholas immediately after the death of his father, Alexander III. It is October 1894, and the twenty-six-year-old Nicky (as he's known in the family) is not mindful of state affairs.

His father, Emperor Alexander III, never took his son and heir seriously. An official recalls how one day at dinner, during a discussion of government business, the young Nicky tried to take part, whereupon his father began throwing bread rolls at him.

In 1894 Nicholas is certainly not interested in politics: he is in love. In the spring of that year he travels to Germany to propose to a young German princess called Alix. The engagement is announced on 7 April. Nicholas spends almost the entire summer with his fiancée in London before returning home in September. Alexander III is seriously ill and his doctors advise him to go to Crimea. But he ignores the quacks and instead goes hunting in Poland. There his condition worsens, after which the imperial family does indeed go south to Crimea.

However, there at Livadia Palace, the forty-nine-year-old tsar's condition deteriorates further; the best doctors are called in from all across Russia. His relatives gather round, including Nicky and Alix, who has traveled to Russia specially. Also summoned is Father John of Kronstadt, Saint Petersburg's most respected priest with a reputation as a healer and miracle worker.

On 20 October 1894 John of Kronstadt administers the Eucharist to Alexander III, after which (despite Father John's legendary healing abilities) the tsar dies. The sudden death of the hardy, middle-aged monarch is a shock. And in the words of Grand Duke Sandro, the heir to the throne flies into a panic.

In 1901, five years after his coronation, Nicholas II still feels insecure. Even after his father's death he is not the head of the family. Alexander III had four brothers: Grand Dukes Vladimir, Alexei, Sergei, and Pavel. In addition to them, Nicholas has more than ten uncles once removed—the grandsons of Nicholas I (of which Sandro is one, even though he is only two years older than Nicholas II).

And while in public the uncles behave respectfully, inside the family each grand duke has his own area of authority and expertise: Vladimir is commander of the Imperial Guard and president of the Imperial Academy of Fine Arts; Alexei is commander of the navy; Sergei is governor-general of Moscow. They all consider themselves to be far more competent than their nephew and do not hesitate to say so. The young emperor is afraid to contradict them.

Witte recalls an incident during the early days of the reign of Nicholas II. He is about to approve an order from the tsar to establish a new base for the Russian fleet at what is today the city of Murmansk. Originally it was Alexander III's decision, of which Nicholas is aware. However, his uncle Grand Duke Alexei intervenes, suggesting that the base should be sited at Libava (now Liepaja in Latvia). The young emperor has already assured Witte that he will implement his father's decision, but now signs another order at the behest of his uncle, effectively behind the minister's back. This decision proves to be a fatal mistake: during World War I the Russian fleet is trapped in the Baltic Sea by German vessels, forcing all supplies from Britain and elsewhere to come through Arkhangelsk; a railway to Murmansk is hastily constructed only in November 1916.

"It is regrettable that the grand dukes really do believe that they are *grand*," writes Sergei Witte in his memoirs. "But the role they play is incommensurate with their limited knowledge, talent and education. Their influence on the Sovereign is mostly malign." It should be noted, however, that Witte has no scruples about exploiting that very influence in his own interests.

Sergei Witte considers himself an expert on the Far East and is proud of his ability to establish relations with the Chinese. As transport minister, he initiated the construction of the Trans-Siberian Railway, known originally as the "Great Way." It was in fact the long-dead Alexander III who first entrusted him with the project, and Witte treats the assignment as his life's mission.

In 1895, the First Sino-Japanese War comes to an end. The Chinese army is defeated and, just before her sixtieth birthday, the Empress Dowager Cixi seeks and signs the infamous (in Chinese eyes) Treaty of Shimonoseki, ceding Taiwan and the Liaodong Peninsula to Japan. Taiwan and the city of Dalian on the peninsula are a long way from the Russian heartland, yet Witte believes that his pet project is at risk. Japan's incursion into mainland China threatens the construction of the Trans-Siberian Railway. Moreover, Witte is pondering two options: the railway to Vladivostok can either remain within the borders of the Russian Empire and skirt around the Amur River, or it can cut through the Chinese territories of Mongolia and Manchuria. He prefers the second, more direct alternative.

So Witte issues an ultimatum to Japan: it must not violate the territorial integrity of China and must (despite the recently signed treaty) return the Liaodong Peninsula to the Chinese. Other members of the Russian government are indifferent to the proposal, since, according to Witte, they are only interested in the West and have no concept of Chinese geography.

But Nicholas II supports it. He has a personal grudge against the Japanese dating back to a visit he made there as heir to the throne, when an attempt was made on his life (the so-called Otsu incident). He likes Witte's idea to suppress Japanese expansionism.

France and Germany also back Russia's ultimatum—the European powers are averse to a powerful Japan, since they want to build relations with China themselves. In the end, Japan backs down and withdraws from the peninsula, accepting monetary compensation in return. Witte helps the Chinese government secure a loan from French banks to pay off Japan.

During the course of Witte's highly successful talks with China, it is agreed with the Chinese court diplomat Li Hongzhang that the Trans-Siberian Railway will follow the shortest route through China, yet remain Russian property under the protection of the Russian military. This agreement (which is crucial for Witte) is part of a wider Russian-Chinese security alliance: Russia undertakes to protect China if attacked by Japan.

The negotiations between Witte and Li Hongzhang are overshadowed by a tragic incident. A Chinese delegation, headed by the latter, comes to Russia to attend the coronation of Nicholas II. On 18 May 1896, shortly after the coronation, there is a major stampede at Khodynka Field near Moscow. Witte and Li Hongzhang are practically eyewitnesses.

Witte says that the post-coronation festivities at Khodynka got underway early, before the arrival of the tsar. Food and gifts were being handed out. People rushed forward and stumbled. In the resulting melee two thousand people were crushed. "I was tormented above all by what to do with all the injured and how to deal with all the corpses," writes Witte. "Would there be time to take the dying to hospital and move the dead to a place where they wouldn't be in full view of the Sovereign, his retinue and foreign guests, and the jubilant crowd? The next question was, will the emperor cancel the celebrations and hold a liturgy for the dead instead?"

The Chinese envoy Li Hongzhang arrives at the scene at about the same time as Witte. "Is it really the case that the details of this misfortune will be reported to the emperor?" he asks.

Finance Minister Witte replies that the tsar has already been informed, that very morning.

"Your statesmen are inexperienced. When I was a governor, our province was hit by the plague. Tens of thousands of people in my area perished, but I always wrote to the emperor that everything was in order. When asked about disease, I replied that there was none. Tell me, how could I disappoint the emperor by announcing that the people were dying? If I was a dignitary of your Sovereign, I would conceal everything from him," Witte paraphrases the Chinese envoy. "Well, we're far removed from China in that respect," the finance minister notes to himself with satisfaction.

However, the festivities are not cancelled, and everything proceeds as if nothing has happened. The emperor attends the royal concert as planned, although looking sadder than usual, according to Witte.

In the evening that same day, 18 May, a ball is held at the residence of the French ambassador, Count Montebello. Witte arrives and goes straight to the Moscow governor-general, Grand Duke Sergei, one of the tsar's uncles. The latter says that the emperor has been advised to request that the ambassador cancel the ball and not to attend in any circumstance, should it go ahead. But Nicholas II ignores the advice, saying that the coronation should not be clouded by the Khodynka tragedy. Witte recalls the words of Li Hongzhang and realizes that Russia is not so far removed from China after all. Nicky and Alix arrive at the ball; the tsar dances the first *contredanse* with Countess Montebello, and the tsarina with the count.

Almost concurrently with the China agreement, Russia signs a treaty with Japan on joint actions in Korea. Korea, until recently considered a Chinese protectorate, is now in the zone of privileged interests of both Russia and Japan.

According to Witte, the young tsar is desperate to spread Russian influence in the Far East: "The emperor is fond of this idea because he came of age, so to speak, on a trip to the Far East. But he has no specific program, only an elemental desire to expand into the Far East and take control of the countries there."

Witte indulges such fantasies, painting the Far East as the Russian Empire's answer to British India. According to Witte's memoirs, Nicholas dreams of adding emperor of China, Korea, and perhaps even Japan to his list of titles.

However, a problem soon arises in the shape of Kaiser Wilhelm II. The German emperor pays his first official visit to Saint Petersburg, staying at the Peterhof residence outside the Russian capital. The two monarchs are riding together in a carriage one day when Wilhelm suddenly asks: "Does Russia need the Chinese port of Qingdao?" Wilhelm explains that Russian ships never use the port, but German vessels, on the other hand, need a place to drop anchor. Germany, of course, would never enter the port without the consent of the Russian emperor, says Wilhelm.

Nicholas is taken aback and recounts the episode to his uncle, Grand Duke Alexei, the commander of the Russian fleet, adding that the German emperor has placed him in a very awkward position, since he is a guest and it would be impolite to refuse his request.

A few weeks later Saint Petersburg learns that the German fleet has captured Qingdao. It seems that Wilhelm took Nicholas's diplomatic tip-toeing as consent. The tsar convenes a meeting of the Committee of Ministers at which Foreign Minister Muravyov proposes that Russia follow Germany's example by grabbing one of the Chinese ports on the Liaodong Peninsula: Port Arthur or Dalian. Witte argues that Russia, a "friend of the Chinese," cannot break the freshly signed agreement with China so abruptly. Moreover, it would throw down the gauntlet to Japan, since Russia only recently demanded that the Japanese show "respect for China's territorial integrity." Just because Germany has seized a Chinese port is no reason for Russia to do the same, says the finance minister. The emperor vacillates, but ultimately concurs.

A few days later, when Witte reports to Nicholas, the tsar remarks casually: "Do you know, Sergei Yulievich [Witte], I've decided to take Port Arthur and Dalian and have dispatched a flotilla. I did it because the foreign minister informed me that English ships are cruising in the areas around Port Arthur and Dalian, and that if we do not seize the ports, the British will."

The emperor appoints a new minister of war: the young General Kuropatkin, celebrated in the press as a former chief of staff under the legendary General Skobelev, hero of the Russian-Turkish wars. Kuropatkin is known as an ardent supporter of taking Constantinople. But on becoming Russia's new war minister, he quickly shifts his focus to the Far East. He wants to seize not only Port Arthur, but also all the adjacent territories along the Liaodong Peninsula, otherwise it will not be possible to protect the port. China is sent a demand to transfer the entire Liaodong Peninsula to Russia for a period of twenty-five years rent-free.

Witte says that he desperately resisted these plans, threatening to resign in protest. Yet this contradicts the memoirs of other officials. They claim that Witte was captivated by the idea of assimilating the Far East, and his Ministry of Finance allocated huge sums to build a new port in China. It was also Witte who came up with Dalian (Dalny in Russian, meaning "far") as the name of the port.*

But Witte's version of events is that on receiving the emperor's order to occupy Port Arthur he instructed the Ministry of Finance's envoy in Peking (Beijing) to give Li Hongzhang a bribe of half a million roubles†

---

*Witte wrote his memoirs after the Russian-Japanese War and is therefore sure that he foresaw that everything would end in disaster and asserts that he always persuaded Nicholas II to refrain from expanding into the Far East. This adjusted view of reality was probably designed to demonstrate his prescience in the eyes of the reader.
† About $6,591,666 in 2017.

(according to some officials, all contracts signed between Witte and Chinese officials involved a backhander; Witte himself denies it). As a result, the Chinese government agrees to transfer the peninsula to Russia for twenty-five years rent-free. Russian troops immediately land at Port Arthur and occupy the entire region. Not a single shot is fired, since the Chinese admirals at Port Arthur have also been given a sweetener.

"Capturing the port has severed our traditional relations with China forever," reflects Witte. "The capture itself and the events that followed have led the Chinese Empire to its present state: it will crumble and be replaced by a republic. The fall of the Chinese Empire will shake up the Far East, and the consequences will be felt by Russia and Europe for decades to come."

YELLOW RUSSIA

At the turn of the twentieth century Russia is not overly prosperous, yet many of its neighbors are in far greater trouble, none more so than the ancient Chinese Empire. As in Russia, the ruling dynasty has been in power for three centuries: the Qing are the Chinese Romanovs. For much of the nineteenth century the empire has been engulfed by a struggle between the supporters of reform, modernization, and open relations with the West on one side, and the adherents of isolation, tradition, and China's "special way" on the other. The antagonism runs deep, because free and unrestricted trade with the West has brought China a lot of problems. Great swathes of the population are addicted to opium, shipped in aboard British and Indian ships. The drug epidemic is accompanied by an outflow of hard currency (silver), since almost all the money is being spent on opium imports.

In 1839, Chinese opponents of opium take the extreme measure of closing all the country's ports to foreigners. In response, the British navy prepares to land at Nanjing, the country's southern capital. The Chinese army, equipped with medieval weapons, cannot compete with the British. In 1842, at the end of the First Opium War, China and Britain sign a treaty guaranteeing access to all Chinese ports and ceding Hong Kong as a British colony. Nanjing is the first of several humiliating treaties that China is forced to sign over the coming decades.

To add to its woes, China has leadership problems. The last adult emperor, Daoguang, dies in 1850 (aged sixty-eight), whereafter China is headed for half a century by youngsters. Xianfeng becomes emperor at the age of nineteen and dies at thirty; Tongzhi takes over aged five and dies at nineteen. Guangxu rules from the age of four to twenty-seven (when he is removed from power and placed under house arrest). Lastly, Pu Yi manages to rule from the age of two to the ripe old age of six.

Against the backdrop of successive child emperors, the country is effectively ruled by Empress Dowager Cixi (the former consort of Xianfeng), who skillfully takes over the reins of power. Like Empress Alexandra, she comes to the throne by chance, but believes that she is God's chosen one and that a thirst for power and suspicious nature are prerequisites for a successful leader.

In the 1890s China's rulers are split into two opposing camps: the conservatives (led by Cixi) do not want reform and favor closer ties with Russia; the other (smaller) group wants to modernize and looks instead to Britain and Japan, the latter having opened up to the West in the 1860s-80s under Emperor Meiji. The young Chinese emperor wants change, but is afraid of his adoptive mother, Empress Dowager Cixi.

Germany's occupation of Qingdao is a turning point. Chinese society is outraged, and patriotic sentiment starts to swell. The philosopher Kang Youwei appeals to the Chinese emperor for liberal reform, essentially proposing a constitutional monarchy. Six months later, Emperor Guangxu starts to act. In June 1898, carefully so as not to alarm his adoptive mother Cixi, he begins to issue reform decrees: to set up Peking University, build railways, reshape the Chinese army along European lines, translate foreign books, purchase steam engines and machinery, combat systemic bribery, and publish government budgetary figures, among others. The reforms last for one hundred days and end in September, when Cixi stages a coup. The emperor is arrested and put under house arrest inside the Forbidden City. Almost all the decrees issued during the "Hundred Days' Reform" are scrapped, and a wave of anti-reform repression begins. The emperor's closest advisers are executed without trial.

Russia strongly supports the coup. Foreign Minister Muravyov informs Empress Cixi that she can rely on Russia's help in the fight against the pro-Western reformers.

The reprisals against the pro-reformists degenerate into a state-sponsored pogrom. The empress and her court blame all of China's ills on external enemies, the humiliating treaties, and the painful reforms. This is the start of the Yihequan [Harmony and Justice] Rebellion, which is less a rebellion and more an orchestrated uprising on the part of the authorities, which prompts a wave of attacks against foreigners and "national traitors," in particular Chinese Christians. "Let us all strive to protect our homes and our ancestors' graves from the dirty hands of foreigners. Let us spread the word to every corner of our domain," reads a decree issued by Empress Dowager Cixi. In Europe the uprising goes by a different name: the Boxer Rebellion.

The situation soon flies out of control: diplomats in the capital Beijing are killed and Christian churches across the country are set on fire.

"This is the consequence of our occupation of the [Liaodong Peninsula]," Russian Finance Minister Witte says bitterly to War Minister Kuropatkin on learning of the unrest in the Chinese capital. But Kuropatkin, on the contrary, is pleased that he now has an opportunity to seize Manchuria.

Witte argues in his memoirs that he opposed the annexation of Manchuria, although he acknowledges that economic expansion into Korea appealed to him at the time.

The Boxer Rebellion erupts across China, and the European press describes monstrous pogroms on a daily basis. The European powers set up an international coalition to invade China and suppress the movement. Russia, Britain, France, Germany, Italy, Austria-Hungary, the United States, and Japan all send troops. On 20 June, the "Boxers" lay siege to the Legation Quarter in Beijing, and the next day Empress Cixi declares war on the eight-nation alliance. The night of 23-24 June witnesses what is described as the "Chinese St. Bartholomew's Day Massacre": the brutal extermination of almost all Christians in the Chinese capital.

On the same day as the massacre, Russian Foreign Minister Muravyov, whom Witte blames for the capture of Port Arthur and the war in China, pays the latter a visit. Witte recounts that Muravyov was in a reconciliatory mood. According to Witte, Muravyov arrived drunk and drained another large bottle of champagne during the conversation with Witte and (mostly) his wife. "What a jolly life this Count Muravyov leads. If I'd made such a mistake, come morning I'd be dead. But he just drinks and makes merry. It's all water off a duck's back to him," Witte recalls his thoughts that evening, without knowing that the next morning the foreign minister will indeed be found dead in his office.

War Minister Kuropatkin insists that Russian troops be dispatched to Beijing to punish the instigators of the pogroms. Witte objects, arguing against antagonizing the Chinese even further—let the Japanese handle the reprisal, he reasons. But Nicholas II takes the side of Kuropatkin, and Russian troops enter the Chinese capital and plunder its palaces. The Russians are joined by the Americans and the British. Empress Cixi flees the city, taking with her the arrested "emperor-reformer" Xianfeng. The commander of the Russian force, General Linevich, who received the Order of Saint George for his role in the operation, will return with ten chests full of stolen jewels.

Meanwhile, anti-Russian sentiment in Manchuria is on the rise, and the construction workers laying the railway line to Port Arthur are coming under attack. Witte demands a stronger military presence in Manchuria. Kuropatkin's dream of occupying the region is about to come true. Officially it is announced that the occupation will last only until the Boxer Rebellion is put down, but in reality the Russian military has no plans to leave Manchuria, even when its mission is accomplished.

The first, most successful, and least known war of Nicholas II, the so-called Chinese campaign, comes to an end, leaving Russia in de facto control of northeast China. The tsar is pleased, not least because he has expanded his dominion. Members of his inner circle ponder the idea of creating a "Yellow Russia" by resettling Russians or even setting up a local Cossack corps in the region.

Only Leo Tolstoy is indignant and writes an "Address to the People of China":

> You have been invaded by armed Europeans, who, like wild animals, attacked, ravaged, pillaged, raped and killed you. These people describe themselves as 'enlightened' and (it pains me to say) Christians. Do not believe them. Not only are these people not enlightened (if by 'enlightenment' we mean an understanding of the eternal universal virtues of morality, temperance, humility, diligence and kindness), they are feral, corrupt, idle, selfish and evil, serving only their worldly lusts. Not only are they not Christians, they are the mortal enemies of Christianity. As they rampage among you, committing self-righteous evil deeds, their rulers, parliaments, ministers, kings and emperors sit at home and indulge in debauchery and lust, prescribing all the horrors that are perpetrated against you.

BATTLING DEATH AND THE REGIME

In March 1902, the young writer Maxim Gorky receives a telegram from Saint Petersburg. The Department of Russian Language and Literature of the Imperial Academy of Sciences has elected him an honorary member. Just shy of thirty-three, he is the youngest academician in the country. He immediately reports the good news to his neighbors in Crimea: Anton Chekhov and Leo Tolstoy, both of whom are already academicians.

Tolstoy is feeling better. His fever has abated, yet he still does not leave the house. "The doctors say I'm recovering, but I'm still very weak. I do very little, scribble a few words here and there, and ponder all kinds of ideas that I will never be able to finish. But my soul is at rest, and I am surrounded by peace and tranquility," he writes. His friends and family think about applying for a passport to send him abroad for treatment.

It doesn't happen. Having only just recovered from pneumonia, the count falls ill with typhoid fever. But after ten days the seventy-two-year-old writer's condition improves slightly. For the third time in three months he has cheated death.

Chekhov and Gorky continue to visit the convalescent Tolstoy. One day, at the end of March, Gorky arrives in a puzzled frame of mind. The governor of Crimea has just sent a telegram requesting that he return the notification about his election as an academician. There is something strange going on, which the three vacationing writers do not understand.

Meanwhile, Saint Petersburg is in a state of commotion. On learning of the "dissident" Gorky's election, Interior Minister Sipyagin presents the tsar with a report on the writer's activities. Nicholas II studies the document (he has never read Gorky, of course) and delivers his verdict: "More than peculiar." He proceeds to dictate a letter to his education minister:

> What guided the venerable sages in their decision, we cannot say. Neither Gorky's age nor his brief works constitute grounds for his election to this honorable title. Far more serious is the fact that he is under investigation. How can the Academy of Sciences elect such a person in these troubled times? I am deeply disturbed by this and command that Gorky be deselected forthwith. I hope that this will help to sober up the Academy's thinking.

The education minister (having replaced the murdered Bogolepov) is the seventy-nine-year-old General Pyotr Vannovsky, himself a former war minister. He hurriedly and blushingly informs the president of the Russian Academy of Sciences, Grand Duke Konstantin Konstantinovich, of the tsar's decision.

Grand Duke Konstantin is not only another of the tsar's uncles, but also a refined and distinguished poet, publishing works under the pseudonym KR. However, he does not stand up for his fellow writer or try to convince his nephew of the young Gorky's merits.* On the contrary, he

---

* In Soviet times the head of the Union of Writers also often failed to stand up for its members.

requests that the Crimean governor withdraw the telegram informing Gorky of his election to the academy. Gorky refuses, saying that he will return the notice only if the academy itself asks for it.

The forty-seven-year-old Vladimir Korolenko, also an academician and Gorky's number one admirer, tries to persuade the academy to stick by its decision, but to no avail. He is ignored and Gorky's election is annulled.

Korolenko and Chekhov both resign from the academy in protest against Gorky's expulsion. The apolitical Chekhov asks Tolstoy to support their démarche, but the ageing count says that he would prefer not to partake in bureaucratic squabbles and, in any case, he does not consider himself an academician, despite being an honorary member.

Chekhov, who has always avoided politics, is terribly offended. "Tolstoy is a weak man," he complains to his friend Suvorin, the publisher of Russia's main pro-government newspaper. "I know he considers himself an academician."

A TRENDY PRIEST

The thirty-year-old priest Georgy Gapon returns to Saint Petersburg. Having recovered from his illness, he goes to serve in a church at Galernaya Gavan—a very deprived neighborhood not far from the Baltic shipyards, where workers, beggars, the homeless, and the unemployed all live next to the factories—in short, the protagonists of Gorky's *The Lower Depths*. They adore Gapon's sermons and pack the church full every time he preaches. Gapon, for his part, goes out of his way to communicate with his parishioners and listen to their grievances. After each service, Gapon visits the homeless shelters of Saint Petersburg and tries to come up with ways to help them (including financially), but his ideas are rejected by the church authorities.

Gapon simultaneously works as a teacher and priest at two orphanages, including the Olginsky asylum—a special children's home patronized by Empress Alix and whose board of trustees includes many wealthy ladies. The thirty-year-old priest from the outskirts of Poltava becomes acquainted with the capital's socialites, who fall for his simple charm: he is handsome, charismatic, well-spoken, and, in the words of his female admirers, "Christ-like."

One of the priest's new acquaintances is Senator Anichkov, the main custodian of children's shelters in the capital and effectively Gapon's boss. He often invites the priest to his home for a chat about charity work, plies him with good food and wine—which, he says, is all stolen by his uncle, who is in charge of procurements at the Winter Palace. Gapon is amazed by such an open admission.

Gapon unsettles his secular friends—especially women—with stories about the lives of the poor. He does not do it to shock. He passionately wants to alleviate the plight of the poor by getting them to do community work. Gapon's admirers pass the word to Saint Petersburg Governor Kleigels, who summons the priest and asks him to write a report on the social rehabilitation of the unemployed.

Gapon writes a treatise entitled "On Measures to Combat Abject Poverty and Parasitism." It is, in essence, a detailed program for setting up corrective institutions for homeless people. The report makes Gapon even more famous, and the text does the rounds with enlightened officials—and especially their wives—so that it soon ends up in the hands of the empress, who likes it, too. Alexandra intends to hold a special meeting to discuss Gapon's proposals. The Tolstoyan from Poltava is on the cusp of fulfilling his dream.

However, no serious discussion of Gapon's ideas takes place. A few months later the society ladies' eyes and ears have wandered elsewhere, and Gapon is out of fashion. "I had the opportunity to observe the way high society works and did not envy it," says Gapon. "Their conversations and actions were never sincere. Their lives were dull, boring and pointless. Their interest in charity was fleeting and superficial."

However, those are Gapon's later words. In 1902, he gets along with the *beau monde* and thinks he can utilize it. The church authorities are irritated by Gapon's new existence and come into conflict with him. As a result, he decides to quit the orphanages and takes up a job offered by one of the society ladies, who is the head of the Russian Red Cross.

But again everything falls flat. Senator Anichkov, who has gotten to know some of the details of Gapon's private life during their conversations, reports him to the authorities. No doubt he is offended by Gapon's unflattering remarks in his widely read report about Saint Petersburg's orphanages (for which Anichkov is responsible). He informs the church and the secular powers-that-be about the real life of Georgy Gapon. It turns out that the widower priest is in a relationship with an orphan at the shelter where he worked—the eighteen-year-old Alexandra Uzdaleva. Moreover, they are living together in a civil marriage, which the church forbids.

Anichkov's revelation destroys Gapon's reputation: in July 1902, he is expelled from the Theological Academy and officially defrocked. The thirty-year-old priest, who was so close to his life's aim, has lost everything.

He says goodbye to his parish and on 2 July 1902 delivers an impassioned farewell sermon: "Brothers, I am being forced out, but so be it. I am a martyr, yet for all my suffering the Lord has heard my prayer and provided a dwelling place. It is not far from here. Come and visit."

But having nearly ruined Gapon, Anichkov inadvertently saves him. He writes a second denunciation to the secret police (Okhrana, a forerunner of the KGB). Gapon is paid a visit by a member of the secret police by the name of Mikhailov, who conducts an informal interrogation. The conversation plays a decisive role in Gapon's fate, for Mikhailov offers him a job as a police informant.

As a child, Gapon was greatly moved by the tale of Saint Ioann of Novgorod, who was said to have straddled the devil and flown to Jerusalem (in a story by Nikolai Gogol, born in the same province as Gapon). According to his own memoirs, Gapon the little boy dreamt of the day when he would be able to "straddle the devil." Now a stoolpigeon, that day has arrived.

Mikhailov not only commends Gapon to his superiors, but also writes a letter to Metropolitan Anthony of Saint Petersburg requesting that he be reinstated at the academy. Anthony immediately complies. Henceforth, Gapon begins a new life independent of the church authorities and never looks back.

THE ADMIRAL OF THE PACIFIC

Following the successful Chinese campaign, Nicholas II is brimming with confidence. Yearning for new adventures and victories, he pays ever less attention to warnings and ever more to risky undertakings. The retired officer Alexander Bezobrazov comes up with a plan to take over Korea by "creeping occupation." His idea is for Russia gradually to buy up as much land as possible in and around the country, and then seize control before Japan does.

To begin with, Bezobrazov sets up a private timber company to develop forestland in the Yalu River basin between Korea and China. He buys a logging concession from the renowned Vladivostok merchant Yuliy Brynner (grandfather of the Hollywood actor Yul Brynner).

Witte recalls that Bezobrazov first tries to pitch his plan to Grand Duke Sandro, a childhood friend of the tsar. The latter agrees to press ahead with the idea. Sandro is a former sailor, has toured the world, knows the Far East reasonably well, and, importantly, does not like Japan. Adamant that the Japanese are dangerous and hostile to Russia, he advocates making preparations for war. Bezobrazov's project appeals very much to the grand duke, who dutifully puts it to his nephew, the tsar. Nicholas II is easily swayed by the idea and offers Bezobrazov every kind of assistance. Not content with being the emperor of Great Russia, Little Russia (Ukraine), and White Russia (Belarus), Nicholas aspires to be the emperor of "Yellow Russia," too.

Witte, although in favor of Russia's economic expansion, writes in his memoirs that Bezobrazov's idea is not to his liking and says that he refused to allocate money from the budget.

However, public opinion is sure of the opposite—that Witte supports the idea. It is he who "squandered millions on the city of Dalny (Dalian) and used public money to set up the Russian-Chinese Bank, which funded fraudsters in the Far East, such as Admiral Abaza, the crazy Bezobrazov and their chum Vonlyarlyarsky," thunders Alexei Ignatiev, an army general. "Nothing good will come of this venture. . . . They've taken forest concessions from under the noses of the Japanese, who consider themselves the rightful owners of the Yalu region. Such greed will cost Russia dear."

In the summer of 1902 Nicholas II travels to Tallinn (now the capital of Estonia, then known as Revel) to observe a naval exercise. In June he is joined by German Emperor Wilhelm II, who is a friend and cousin of Empress Alix. Witte says that when Wilhelm's yacht was departing for Germany, it sounded the horn. "Translated into human language, the Admiral of the Atlantic Ocean was giving his regards to the Admiral of the Pacific Ocean," writes Witte. "Wilhelm was saying: I intend to dominate the Atlantic, and I advise you to dominate the Pacific."

According to Witte, Nicholas is a little bemused, but finds the idea of taming the Pacific irresistible. The Korean expansion continues. When the Japanese envoy Marquis Ito pays a visit to Saint Petersburg, Nicholas does not receive him. Ito brings a proposal that Tokyo will accept Russia's occupation of the Liaodong Peninsula and Port Arthur, but in exchange Russian troops are to be withdrawn from Manchuria, especially since officially they were due to leave after the Boxer Rebellion, which is long over. He does not get a response. Even Witte does not seek a meeting with him. Witte considers himself an expert in negotiations with the Chinese, but has no empathy with the Japanese. The envoy leaves insulted.

In the fall of 1902, aware that the Far East is now the most important realm of Russian politics, Witte goes on a tour of the region, stopping over in Vladivostok, Port Arthur, and Dalian. The reality is sobering. It dawns on the pragmatic financier that negotiations with Japan are imperative, or else there will be serious trouble. On his return to European Russia, he immediately heads for Crimea, where the emperor is on vacation. Blindly believing Bezobrazov's affirmations that everything is under control, Nicholas is irked by Witte's intervention. He does not trust his finance minister, considering him to be a schemer. The tsar even refuses to hear Witte's verbal report of his fact-finding trip to the Far East, asking him to send it to him in writing.

But Witte, ever the arch-bureaucrat, goes to see Prince Meshchersky, the publisher of the ultra-conservative newspaper *The Citizen*, and implores him to make the tsar see sense. Meshchersky, one of the most popular journalists even under Alexander III, is on first-name terms with the tsar. He promises to help. The prince writes a letter to the emperor, but receives a mysterious phrase in reply: "On 6 May [everyone] will see what opinion I hold on this matter." Meshchersky and Witte wait for 6 May with bated breath. On the fateful day a royal decree is issued appointing Bezobrazov as Russia's new secretary of state. His view of the Far East is well known: no troop withdrawal from Manchuria, no concessions to Japan, no step back in Korea.

In July 1903 Nicholas goes ahead with another of Bezobrazov's ideas. The Liaodong Peninsula is transformed into a Far East governorship. The only other region in the Russian Empire to be classified as such is the Caucasus, where a "Russification" policy is in full swing. On the rare occasions that the emperor is asked whether he fears that his actions could lead to war with Japan, he replies: "There will be no war, because I do not want one."

|| Chapter 3 ||

GREGORY GERSHUNI

in which Jews go on the war path:
Mikhail Gotz and Gregory Gershuni create
the most powerful opposition party in Russia

NEW YEAR WISHES

On 31 December 1900, the twenty-nine-year-old pharmacist Gregory Ger-shuni from Minsk (today the capital of Belarus) holds a New Year's Eve party. "Comrade Dmitry" (Gershuni's nickname) invites his friends, who happen to be revolutionaries. Gershuni's neighbor, the fifty-six-year-old Yekaterina Breshko-Breshkovskaya, nicknamed Babushka, a legendary dissident of the previous generation, also looks in.

Babushka is a figure of authority for everyone at the party. During an argument about whether revolutionaries should adopt terror tactics like before, Gershuni asks Babushka for her opinion. Her answer surprises many: "We, too, were once tormented by this question and spoke the Biblical words: 'Father, let this cup pass me by.' We stare into the abyss, and the abyss stares back. Once again, terror is the only option." Gershuni is one of the few in agreement. It is time to start killing again.

At the end of the high-spirited party, Babushka takes "Comrade Dmitry" to one side and says: "Keep control of your thoughts. Do you want to end up at the Peter and Paul Fortress or doing hard labour? Change your passport, go underground. Now!"

After this conversation Babushka leaves Minsk forever. She has restless feet. For many years now she has been traveling around the Russian Empire under false documents.

NOT MY CUP OF TEA

A few weeks later, in late January, a young affluent Jew boards a train in Odessa bound for Paris. He is thirty-six years old and one of the most renowned people in the city. He is the heir to a wealthy Russian dynasty of tea producers and the highly efficient manager of the family's Odessa branch. His name is Mikhail Gotz.

Mikhail was born in Moscow, where the rich include not only Old Believers, but also Jews. The tea market is controlled by David Wissotzky and his brother-in-law Raphael Gotz. The business climate for Jews is even tougher than for Old Believers, but Wissotzky and Gotz do very well. At the turn of the twentieth century, their company has a market capitalization of 10 million roubles and an annual turnover of 45 million roubles.* Branches are opened in New York and London a few years later.

---

*About $131,833,333 and $593,250,000 in 2017

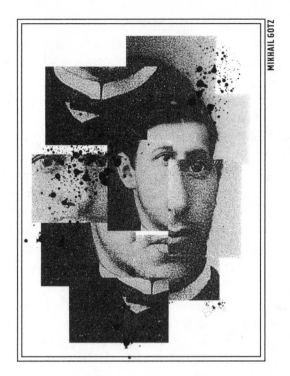

MIKHAIL GOTZ

Wissotzky and Gotz are the most prominent Jewish figures in the Russian Empire. But as in the case of the Old Believers, the "golden youth"—the third generation of Moscow billionaires—has fallen short of its forebears' expectations. Mikhail Gotz, Wissotzky's nephew and Raphael Gotz's son, is not into business or even the theatre (like Morozov and Mamontov). In 1884, at the age of eighteen, he joins the underground revolutionary circle. The group holds its secret meetings at a library run by Gotz's former classmate Sergei Zubatov. In 1886, the library is raided by police, after which Gotz is exiled to Siberia for ten years and barely survives. But that is in the past. Barred from the Russian capital, the "tea heir" is now running the family business in Odessa.

His health weakened by hard labor in Siberia, his family has decided to send him to Paris for treatment. But the patient has other plans. He wants to make the acquaintance of his idol, the legendary revolutionary Pyotr Lavrov, but news arrives from the French capital of his recent demise. Now Gotz can only attend the funeral—and arrives late.

Lavrov's funeral turns into a congress of *Narodniks*—a once mighty movement that in the latter half of the nineteenth century did battle with the Russian Empire. Back then, members of the intelligentsia considered it their sacred duty to "go to the people" and inform the uneducated classes, primarily the peasants, of their rights and foment revolution among them. They told the peasants about the imminent "black repartition"—the cherished day when all the land would be taken from the nobles and distributed to the people. The Narodniks (or populists) set up circles in the capital and provinces. They were the first to use political terror as a weapon. The assassins of Alexander II were bound up in a powerful secret organization called *Narodnaya Volya* (People's Will), and the Narodnik circles were home to the leading lights of the Russian "non-systemic opposition"* of the nineteenth century.

But during the reign of Alexander III, the Narodnik movement begins to decline. All terrorist groups are destroyed, and the peasants remain unmoved by the populist propaganda. The remaining Narodniks cultivate the "theory of small deeds"—the idea that helping out locally as teachers and doctors will improve the lives of ordinary people. The Narodniks curtail their political activity, and the movement's leaders emigrate abroad. The only exception is Babushka. Having spent a third of her life in prison and exile, she is amnestied in honor of the coronation of Nicholas II and now travels in rural areas, campaigning on behalf of the peasantry. Almost nothing is left of the once-formidable People's Will. By the early twentieth century the underground circles are scattered and barely in contact with each other.

Once in Paris, Gotz gets acquainted with the resident Narodniks. Welcomed as an affluent and influential member, he yearns to unite the underground circles of Russian revolutionaries and breathe new life into the withering opposition. Gotz's Paris apartment turns into a rendezvous point for Narodniks of all ages. After almost a year in the French capital, he chucks in the family business, despite limited revolutionary success.

In Minsk, in June 1900, police round-ups are in full swing. The underground printing press and local revolutionary cell are uncovered. Its leader, pharmacist Gregory Gershuni, is arrested and sent to Moscow for questioning by Sergei Zubatov, the head of the Moscow secret police.

Zubatov begins a cat-and-mouse game with the detainee, whose proven links to Babushka are enough to send Gershuni to Siberia. But Zubatov takes a deeper interest in this young revolutionary and decides to reform him.

The thirty-six-year-old Zubatov has his own method of dealing with "politicals." More preacher than detective, he is a romantic in uniform.

As a child, Zubatov is fond of the idea of revolution and even set up his own group at school. But in year seven his father finds out about his passion and removes him from the school. The well-read youngster takes

---

* The term used to describe the real opposition to today's Kremlin.

a job at a library where he discovers a vast number of prohibited books in the vaults. He hands them out to readers, unwittingly turning his library into a center of underground activity. Among the readers are young revolutionaries, including the tea heir Mikhail Gotz. They become friends and, according to Gotz, Zubatov takes a serious interest in Gotz's circle. One day the police arrive for Zubatov. During the first interrogation, he learns that his "friends" have been using his library for clandestine revolutionary meetings of which he was unaware (or so he claims). It does not take long for him to agree to work as a police informant.

With the help of the new secret agent Zubatov, the police arrest, try, and exile many revolutionaries, including Gotz. Wanted by the revolutionaries as an agent provocateur, Zubatov is forced out of the underworld and into a career as a regular police officer. After seven years, he is promoted to chief of the Moscow secret police.

Now an ideological statist, Zubatov loves to deliver long sermons to his subordinates: "Without the tsar there is no Russia.* The prosperity and greatness of Russia come from her sovereigns. It will be ever thus. Opponents of the monarchy are opponents of Russia. The struggle against them is a matter of life and, even more so, death."

After every group arrest, Zubatov spends a long time talking to the detainees who interest him. It is less an interrogation and more a conversation over tea about the ills of revolution and the road to destruction. During these tête-à-têtes, Zubatov invites his interlocutors to assist the government in the fight against the revolution. Some agree. Others, flummoxed by Zubatov's approach, simply renounce their revolutionary activity.

Zubatov offers Gershuni a deal. In exchange for abandoning the revolution, he will be allowed to sign a deposition stating that he is not a member of any secret organization, but simply in despair at the harassment of the Jews. Gershuni pretends to agree. The unwritten revolutionary "code of conduct" prohibits such cowardice, but Gershuni decides to play Zubatov's game. He signs everything that is put in front of him. Zubatov believes that Gershuni is broken and will never return to his revolutionary ways, and although the young pharmacist does not become a collaborator, he is allowed to go home to Minsk.

Zubatov is mistaken. Far from abandoning his revolutionary plans on being released, Gershuni reactivates them. As advised by Babushka, he

---

*In 2014 Kremlin's chief political strategist Vyacheslav Volodin in his speech during high-profile forum in Sochi will announce his view on new Russian ideology: "There is no Russia without Putin and no Putin without Russia."

acquires false papers and goes to Paris, where most of his fellow revolutionaries are based. There he meets Mikhail Gotz.

Gotz and Gershuni have lots to talk about, not least their mutual acquaintance Sergei Zubatov. Zubatov played a decisive role in Gotz's fate when in 1888 he shopped the latter's clandestine circle to the police. The trial lasts for several years. The young metropolitan intellectuals who had gathered in the library to read prohibited works of literature and hold spirited discussions—and nothing more—are all sentenced to ten years' exile in Kolyma.

Sent from Moscow in May 1889, the exiles arrive at Yakutsk (five thousand kilometers from Moscow, but still three thousand kilometers from Kolyma) only in November. There they wait out the winter before the long slog to the settlement of Srednekolymsk in northeast Siberia.

In March, with the ground still covered in snow, the exiles are informed that it is time to move on. The two-month walk in temperatures of minus fifty degrees Celsius is the equivalent of a death sentence, so as a last resort they decide to write to the local governor, begging to postpone their departure.

On 21 March the twenty-five exiled revolutionaries take the letter to the local police department in Yakutsk, where they are given an address at which they are to meet the following day at 11 a.m. to receive a reply. Suspicious, the revolutionaries amass all the weapons they can: ten revolvers and a rifle (security seems to have been rather lax).

Come the appointed hour, the building is surrounded by soldiers and a gunfight breaks out. One officer is injured and six exiles are killed on the spot. Four other revolutionaries are hurt, including Gotz, who has been shot through the lung.

Following a court hearing in Yakutsk, all the insurgents (including the few women among their number) are sentenced to death. The judge subsequently mitigates the punishment for those who did not fire at the police. As a result, three are hanged and the rest are given hard labor.

The badly wounded Mikhail Gotz is expected not to survive, but he eventually recovers and is duly sent to the labor camp.

Despite the remoteness of Yakutsk, the uprising makes the news. Among those who hear about it is the American journalist George Kennan. In 1891, after a trip to Russia, he writes a series of articles about political prisoners in Russia, followed by the book *Siberia and the Exile System*, in which the Yakutsk rebellion features prominently. Western society is shocked by the revelations in the book, and the British parliament even sends an official request to Saint Petersburg for information about the incident.

Other political prisoners in Yakutsk express support for the uprising, but Gotz is unimpressed: "Enough about victims!" he says. "We should have rebelled properly or not at all. By 'properly' I mean kill the person to blame for the massacre, the governor of Yakutsk."

But after the death of Alexander III, the hard labor is annulled in 1894, and the revolutionaries only have to see out their original sentences handed down after Zubatov's denunciation. In 1898 Gotz is set free and heads for the fourth-largest city in the empire, the port capital of Odessa, to take charge of the family company's local operations.

The affluent heir Gotz, who has spent a third of his life in Siberia, and the humble pharmacist Gershuni, who escaped exile thanks to a deal with Zubatov, unexpectedly find a common language. Their meetings in Paris mark the start of a new era in Russian political history. They revive the spirit of People's Will under a new name—the Party of Socialist Revolutionaries. Over the next two decades the socialist revolutionaries (SRs) become the main enemy of the tsarist regime.

THE JEWISH THREAT

In 1900, the authorities do not consider the Narodniks particularly dangerous. The same cannot be said for the Bund—the first underground political party of Russia in the twentieth century. The full title of this influential organization, translated from Yiddish, is the General Jewish Labor Bund of Lithuania, Poland and Russia.

In the late 1890s the Jews are the most politically active people in the world. A turning point in the lives of many European Jews is the case of Alfred Dreyfus—a lawsuit against a French army officer accused of spying for Germany. In December 1894 Captain Dreyfus is found guilty and sentenced to exile for life. But that is only the beginning of the story: over the next five years the entire European intellectual elite hold fierce debates about whether Dreyfus is guilty or not. All the French military (together with all the anti-Semites in Europe) have no doubt, while all the French socialists argue that he is a victim. The most ardent champions of Dreyfus are the leader of the French left Jean Jaurès and the writer Émile Zola, who in January 1898 writes a famous article entitled "J'accuse." In it, he asserts that the real spy is not the Jewish Dreyfus, but Major Charles Esterhazy, a Frenchman of Hungarian origin, who enjoys the protection of the military. Zola is convicted of libel and forced to flee France, but it later transpires that his hunch is correct; in 1899 the case is sent for review and the convicted Dreyfus is pardoned.

Society in Russia is gripped by the Dreyfus affair just as much as in France. Anton Chekhov, on the other hand, is convinced that Dreyfus is innocent and quarrels fiercely with his friend, the publisher Alexei Suvorin, who writes in his magazine *New Time* that the Jewish Dreyfus is obviously guilty. Leo Tolstoy agrees with Suvorin. "I don't know Dreyfus himself, but I know many similar 'Dreifuses', and they all are guilty," Tolstoy tells in an interview.

The Dreyfus affair occupies the minds of many, one of which belongs to the Austrian journalist Theodor Herzl, who works as the Paris correspondent of the liberal Viennese newspaper *Neue Freie Presse*. After Dreyfus's conviction, Herzl, on hearing cries of "Death to the Jews" on the streets of Paris, concludes that his people are not safe in Europe and should seek prosperity abroad. He starts work on a book entitled *The Jewish State*, which is published in Vienna in 1896. That same year the book is translated into English, French, and Russian, and the following year Herzl founds the World Zionist Organization. His goal is to create a separate Jewish state.

Initially, Herzl looks to Africa and ponders the idea of a Jewish state in Kenya, where land has been offered by British politicians sympathetic to the cause. However, most of his adherents consider the area to be uninhabitable, so Herzl switches his focus to Palestine, where he foresees no problems with the Arab population, who presently live under the Ottoman Empire. Herzl believes that the Arabs will welcome Jewish settlers in a neighborly spirit.

At the same time as Herzl is creating his Zionist organization and hatching plans to take the Jews from an increasingly hostile Europe, the Jews of the Russian Empire decide to follow different paths. In 1897, the year of the birth of Zionism, the Bund is set up in Russia. Unlike Herzl and his followers, members of the Bund believe in remaining and fighting for their rights at home. Their slogan is: "Our country is where we live." They are proud to speak a variant of German Yiddish, whereas Herzl's supporters are busy reviving Ancient Hebrew. The Bund activists are completely secular, very left-wing (like most of Europe's politicized youth), and indignant about the unfair accusations against Dreyfus.

The Bund's first congress in 1897 is attended by Gregory Gershuni. Unlike most of the other participants, he does not like the idea of fighting exclusively for Jewish rights and prefers a political struggle for the rights of all the peoples of Russia. He declines to join the Bund and instead sets up his own circle in Minsk, where he meets "Babushka" Breshko-Breshkovskaya.

AN ISLAND OF CALM

Back in 1898 Russia adopts a law limiting the working day to eleven-and-a-half hours per day (ten hours for public holidays and night shifts). The main lobbyist of the law is believed to be Finance Minister Sergei Witte, whose ulterior priority is to protect the major industrialists and not curtail the working day too much. The Ministry of the Interior, meanwhile, is making efforts to slash the number of hours in the working day. It does not care for big business, but about the regular strikes that it has to police. The security services are alarmed at how aggressively the Bund activists and other revolutionaries are stirring up the workers.

The head of the secret police in Moscow, Sergei Zubatov, believes that his service should take charge of the struggle for acceptable working conditions. Paradoxically, if the Interior Ministry is on the side of the workers in the conflict with employers, it will be easier to suppress anti-government propaganda and subdue those disaffected with the regime.

Zubatov begins what is known as the "legalization of the working-class movement" by creating a union under the auspices of the Interior Ministry. It is a challenge not only to employers, but also the Ministry of Finance, which is responsible for employment labor relations. Witte is unhappy about Zubatov's undertaking, but turns a blind eye to begin with, since it is limited to Moscow.

Zubatov sets up workers' circles that host lectures by university professors to educate the people and, in case of conflict with employers, hire Interior Ministry lawyers. Zubatov's movement is very successful: a large-scale demonstration on 22 February 1902 sees forty-five thousand people march in the direction of the Kremlin to lay a wreath at the monument to Emperor Alexander II.[*] A requiem service is being held at the time, attended by the son of Alexander II, Grand Duke Sergei. There are no police; the workers themselves provide security.

The rally has an obvious political purpose. Zubatov has timed it to coincide with the latest student unrest to demonstrate that, unlike the young, the workers are as loyal as ever. He succeeds.

At this moment Moscow is considered the most peaceful city in the empire. The revolution is stifled, the workers obedient. The Moscow authorities are considered the most effective in the country.

During his heart-to-hearts with young detainees, Zubatov comes to the conclusion that most revolutionaries are not fanatics, but have no way to

---

[*] Knocked down by the Bolsheviks in 1918 and restored in 2005 in a flower garden near the Christ the Savior Cathedral in Moscow.

express themselves other than joining the underground movement. "The Bund has already sprung surprisingly deep roots among the Jewish population, and simple folk are using banned publications to teach their children how to read and write," recalls Zubatov.

Based on the success of the trade unions, Zubatov comes up with a similar way of dealing with the Bund. He creates an anti-Bund, or spoiler party,* tasked with attracting all of Russia's politically active Jews, where they can be controlled. Zubatov's brainchild morphs into the Independent Jewish Workers' Party, essentially the first legal political party in Russia—created and funded by the state, but not pro-government (at least superficially). On the contrary, its manifesto is to fight for the rights of Jews.

The Russian Interior Ministry does not only confront the Bund. In 1900, a group of Narodniks in Kuokkala in the Grand Duchy of Finland (part of the Russian Empire) try to publish an underground newspaper called *Revolutionary Russia*. The newspaper is published just once in 1900 and again in 1901, this time in Tomsk. Another issue is in the planning, but in September that year the police raid the printing house and arrest all the employees.

The raid is a deft operation made possible by a new undercover agent who has infiltrated the ranks of the populists. He is the thirty-year-old son of a poor Jewish tailor from Grodno province, an engineer by trade, who once studied in Karlsruhe, Germany. Born Yevno Azef, he has changed his name to sound more melodious to the Russian ear: Yevgeny.

Azef's background is very similar to Gershuni's. Both come from very poor Jewish families and grew up in the Pale of Settlement.

Gershuni and Azef are peers. Having both joined the underground revolutionary movement of Narodniks at a very early age, they have since followed very different trajectories: Gershuni is the life and soul of the party, a natural leader, a good speaker, and everyone's favorite, while the fat, clumsy Azef is disliked and untrusted even by close comrades. Just as Zubatov once took offense at Gotz and company and informed on them to the police, so too Azef, on leaving Rostov for Germany, writes a denun-

---

*One hundred years later, Zubatov's tactics will become the main method of fighting political opposition in Russia. In the early twenty-first century real opposition parties do not have a chance of being registered by the Ministry of Justice, so they function illegally and are called "non-systemic opposition." On the other hand, spoiler parties, created and controlled by the Presidential Administration, get registered. These are called "systemic opposition," though in fact they are not an opposition at all, they only create an illusion of its existence. One example is the party "A Just Russia," created by the government to take votes from the Communists.

ciation against his old comrades to the Moscow secret police (Okhrana), asking for fifty roubles* for the service.

As a student in Karlsruhe, Azef is of scant use, but in Moscow he becomes far more valuable and delivers reports directly to Zubatov, who rates them highly. Zubatov always teaches his subordinates to treat agents "like a woman with whom you're having a secret affair—one wrong move and you'll dishonor her."

Like Zubatov, in due course Azef would probably have been compromised and moved to a regular police job. But in December 1901, during a trip to Berlin, he meets Gershuni.

Azef takes a liking to Gershuni and protects him from the police. Gershuni becomes Azef's best friend.

Gershuni's activity is truly remarkable. By 1902 he has managed the improbable. Years of underground shuttle diplomacy across Russia under a false passport, urging disparate groups of Narodniks to unite, have borne fruit. All the largest Narodnik organizations in Russia and abroad in Paris and Switzerland have agreed to join forces. Azef is not the only one to fall under Gershuni's spell.

THE NEW RUSSIAN ÉMIGRÉ CAPITAL

Following his successful mission in Russia, Gershuni travels to Paris to see Gotz. They discuss the failure of the opposition press in Russia, namely the raid of the printing house in Tomsk. Gotz argues against an underground newspaper at home, especially one that is published only once a year: it is nothing more than "a cry in a vacuum." Using his experience of having managed a large company in Odessa, Gotz decides that the best option is to take over the reins of *Revolutionary Russia* and publish it in Europe. His choice of location falls on Geneva, where the old printing press of the group People's Will still stands. The fact that there are no prominent Narodniks in Geneva is not a problem, believes Gotz. It's more important to get printing.

Gershuni advises Gotz to contact the young, talented journalist Viktor Chernov, who has recently moved from Tambov to Bern, the backwater capital of Switzerland. Chernov is another of Zubatov's "detainees." He spent six months at the police station on Moscow's Prechistenka Street, where Zubatov tried to persuade him to cooperate with the police. But

---

* About $659 in 2017.

Chernov refused and was transferred to the Peter and Paul Fortress for six months, before being exiled to Tambov, south of Moscow.

Gotz goes to visit Chernov in Bern. During their first meeting he explains to this virtual stranger that there is nothing to be done in Bern, and he should move to Geneva, where together they will publish a new newspaper. "I'll be there tomorrow," Chernov readily agrees.

Geneva is not the most popular place for Russian émigrés in the late nineteenth century. Like Bern, it is a relative wilderness where nothing happens. Active politicians and journalists have no one to talk to there. Political refugees usually live in larger cities, with London the first option. That is where Alexander Herzen first published his opposition journal *The Bell* in 1857. London is also the home of Peter Kropotkin, the patriarch of the anarchist movement. Second is Paris, where the late Narodnik leader Pyotr Lavrov resided, and where the left is strong and supportive of their Russian comrades. The third most popular choice is Germany, primarily Munich. The German classics of socialism (Marx, Engels, Bebel) are sacred texts for many Russian revolutionaries.

However, Geneva, chosen by Gotz as the new capital of the Russian émigré opposition, is already home to one fairly well-known and rather odious character: the forty-six-year-old Georgy Plekhanov.

He, too, was once a Narodnik, but in 1880 (a year before the assassination of Alexander II and the annihilation of People's Will) he emigrated to Switzerland. There, having reconsidered his views, he took an interest in Marxism, becoming the first Russian preacher of this doctrine, which later became fashionable. Plekhanov is one of very few revolutionaries not to have suffered for their beliefs.

In 1901, when Gotz decides to take over the publication of *Revolutionary Russia*, three young journalist friends arrive in Geneva. They also want to publish a newspaper—not populist, but Marxist. They go to their idol, Plekhanov, for his blessing. He is a living legend for Russian Marxists, like the late Lavrov for the populist Narodniks.

The three newcomers are often published in the underground press. The youngest of them, and most famous at the time, writes under the pseudonym Martov, but his real name is Yuly Tsederbaum, a twenty-eight-year-old Jew and a convinced social democrat. The second is Alexander Potresov, already a hardened revolutionary at the age of thirty-two. The third is the thirty-one-year-old Vladimir Ulyanov, who publishes under the name Petrov. He has yet to invent for himself the more recognizable sobriquet of Lenin.

However, the meeting with the legendary Plekhanov does not justify their expectations. The three comrades hope that the "patriarch" will use his authority to help them set up a newspaper in Geneva called *Spark* (*Iskra*). But Plekhanov wants control of the paper for himself, and expects his young audience to comply. Horrified, the three depart for Munich and open an editorial office there.

The main role is played by Martov, who writes most of the articles. Plekhanov, too, regularly submits pieces, despite what happened earlier. "Petrov" does much of the donkey work. While his stellar comrades create, this fanatical workaholic edits, proofreads, typesets, and orders new texts. Plekhanov visits the editorial office in Munich and likes what he sees— above all, the future Lenin. "Petrov is a great guy. I didn't doubt it before and even less so now," he writes to a friend. "It's just a pity that his administrative work prevents him from reading and writing."

LITTLE RUSSIA

The year 1902 marks a watershed in Russian politics, although the Russian capital barely notices it, since the major changes are all taking place abroad. And at the end of the nineteenth century Europe is teeming with Russian political émigrés. Hitherto, they have felt like outcasts, unable to influence the situation in their home country. But in 1902 everything changes. The number of Russian political émigrés becomes so great that there is talk of the emergence of an alternative Russian civil society—a huge number of Russia's most educated and active people are concentrated in Europe, because they cannot return home. Henceforth, the most important discussions about the future of Russia take place in Europe, where the shapers of public opinion now live. The Russian diaspora is no longer a branch of Russia; it is no longer clear which is the branch and which the trunk. Europe is becoming a testing ground for ideas that will be implemented in Russia over the next fifteen years.

The Russian-speaking community in Europe is self-sufficient and immersed in internal disputes, conflicts, and debates. It is constantly replenished with new arrivals fleeing Russia. Until 1902 this "Little Russia" (although the thirty-five-thousand-strong community is not so little) had two capitals: Geneva and Munich. It was these cities that hosted the most important émigré Russian-language newspapers *Revolutionary Russia* and *Spark*.

In January 1902 *Revolutionary Russia* triumphantly announces the creation of a unified Socialist Revolutionary Party. Moreover, its new leaders, Gotz and Gershuni, decide that the successor party to People's Will should return to what brought it notoriety in the last century: terror.

Gotz draws up the charter of the SRs and instructs Gershuni to hunt down and destroy Russian officialdom. "The purpose of the militant organization is to fight the existing order by targeting its representatives, who are the most criminal and dangerous enemies of freedom," reads the charter. "By eliminating them, the militant organization not only acts in self-defense, but sows fear and disorganization in the ranks of the ruling classes with the aim of making the government aware that the autocratic system can be maintained no longer."

On 2 April 1902, Interior Minister Dmitry Sipyagin attends a government meeting. An officer approaches him and hands him an envelope, saying that it is a letter from the Moscow governor general, Grand Duke Sergei. Sipyagin holds out his hand, whereupon the officer takes out a gun and shoots the minister point-blank. The other ministers come running.

"If he'd had several revolvers, he would have shot us all," recalls the transport minister. "There was no guard. Just the doorman and Sipyagin's wounded valet."

The killer is the expelled university student Stepan Balmashev, disguised as an officer. His victim dies on the way to the hospital.

Leaflets are distributed in the capital explaining the motives of the murder and signed "The militant Socialist Revolutionary Party." There is a subheading: "You will be rewarded according to your deeds." The mastermind behind the assassination is Gregory Gershuni.

Witte is struck not so much by the death of Sipyagin as society's reaction to it. It turns out that many people despised the minister and are jubilant at his death. Ten days later the publisher Suvorin visits the finance minister and finds him despondent: "Yesterday I was with Witte. I have never seen him so depressed, like a bedraggled hen. He said that if he had a good enough reason, he would retire. It was obvious from what he said that he has few tools with which to govern. He spoke about Sipyagin, calling him a 'wonderful and noble' man, who acted honestly and sincerely and knew no other way."

Witte recalls his last conversation with Sipyagin. They talked long and hard about who should be the new head of the Interior Ministry if the worn-out Sipyagin were to resign. "Anyone except Plehve," said Sipyagin. A few days after the assassination, Vyacheslav von Plehve is duly appointed.

Plehve's appointment to head the Interior Ministry at such a difficult time is logical. He has the most experience dealing with terrorists. In 1881, immediately after the assassination of Alexander II, he took charge of the police department that spearheaded the investigation. It is widely believed that his quick, no-nonsense response is what crushed the terrorist organization People's Will.

The careerist Plehve has dreamt of heading the Interior Ministry, and for the past ten years tsarist circles have considered him the most likely candidate to succeed to the position. When in 1894 Nicholas II was vacillating between Sipyagin and Plehve, Pobedonostsev characterized them as follows: "Plehve is a scoundrel, Sipyagin a fool." He promptly recommended his own man, then Deputy Interior Minister Ivan Goremykin. But Goremykin, insipid like his patron Pobedonostsev, did not inspire Nicholas, who opted instead for the "fool" Sipyagin. Goremykin will later become a government fixture and two-time prime minister, but in 1902, after the murder of Sipyagin, he is overlooked by Nicholas II in favor of the "scoundrel."

Plehve cannot stand Witte and believes that the latter's conniving has prevented his appointment for such a long time. The feeling is mutual, with Witte considering Plehve to be wholly unscrupulous (something that Witte himself is accused of by his detractors).

In fact, Plehve is a professional police officer and has principles. On becoming the new interior minister, he immediately begins to enforce his own system of combating the revolutionary organizations. His plan is to embed a police agent in every terrorist group. To defeat the enemy, you must get close and take control of it, he believes.

Soon after his appointment Plehve meets Zubatov, who delivers a detailed report on the revolutionary movement and the plan to deal with it. "Plehve was gripped by a single idea: there is no revolution. It's all a fantasy made up by the intelligentsia. The broad masses of workers and peasants are deeply monarchist. The agitators and revolutionaries must be caught and straightened out," recalls Alexander Gerasimov, the then-head of the Kharkov police.

Plehve is primarily attracted by Zubatov's ability to recruit provocateurs and his surveillance know-how, and wants to extend these methods throughout Russia. He moves Moscow's police chiefs to Saint Petersburg, making Zubatov the head of a special department and dispatching his assistants across the country to head up the law enforcement agencies in all the major regions of the empire.

Plehve creates a colossal system of surveillance to keep tabs on those suspected of political offenses—a "revolution" in the history of Russian law enforcement. Never before have the secret services been so active, employed agents provocateurs, or invaded society's privacy so deeply. Plehve is one of the first security officers in the world to be tasked with fighting terrorism. His solution resonates to this day: society must sacrifice privacy for the sake of its security.

Plehve effectively establishes a new approach to policing whereby the intelligence agencies have the right to commit crimes in order to prevent them. He could be considered the "spiritual grandfather" of the future Cheka and all its subsequent iterations, up to and including the KGB and today's FSB.

Ever since Gershuni's call to eliminate Russian officialdom, the police have been in disarray. To begin with, they do not know which organization is behind the crimes, if any. Sipyagin's assassination is initially considered to be a lone-wolf attack.

"The police were determined to show that the acts of terrorism were not due to widespread militant sentiment among the masses as a result of government atrocities . . . but because of the ill will and mischief of a few individuals, needless to say the Jews," recalls Gershuni. Plehve "did not understand the broad social nature" of the revolutionary movement, Plehve's subordinate, the gendarme Alexander Spiridovich, agrees. The new minister "saw it as the reincarnation of People's Will and a manifestation of the malevolence of a handful of energetic revolutionaries. He thought it would suffice to remove them and the revolution would stall."

But by 1902 the menace of People's Will seems to be stalking the streets once more. In January, the Russian authorities learn from *Revolutionary Russia* that the Narodniks have joined the Socialist Revolutionary Party, with devastating consequences. The assassination of Interior Minister Sipyagin is the hard-hitting start to the new party's "advertising campaign."

Henceforth, the SRs become a byword for the struggle against the regime. The authorities understand that the main danger is not the Bund after all, but the reincarnated People's Will, revived and ready to resort to tried-and-tested terror.

The next generation of Narodniks is led by Mikhail Gotz, Gregory Gershuni, and Viktor Chernov. Their immediate forebears have departed the scene almost entirely, save for the celebrated Babushka.

NUMBER ONE ENEMY OF THE STATE

Gregory Gershuni's terror continues. He selects a volunteer, a worker named Foma Kachura, to assassinate the governor of Kharkov, Prince Obolensky, who has brutally suppressed a peasant uprising. Kachura shoots twice, but misses.

The police struggle to put a face to the crimes. It takes nearly a year of investigation to conclude that Gershuni and Babushka are behind them. Plehve gives Zubatov a photo of Gershuni, instructing that it should stand on his desk until the leader of the SRs is caught.

For the police, Gershuni is the devil incarnate, able to cloud the minds of recruits and get them to commit crimes against their better judgment. "Slowly but surely Gershuni ensnared his targets until they had no choice but to carry out his orders," describes the gendarme Spiridovich. "There is something satanic about Gershuni's sway over his victims. Always equipped with forged passports, he was highly elusive."

For a long time the police cannot figure out if another mastermind is behind Gershuni. Gershuni reports on the terror operations to his "boss" Mikhail Gotz, and together they develop a special cipher. They exchange postcards, but the text is not important; only the picture matters. If the card depicts a woman (usually a popular Italian opera singer), it means bad news—the operation has failed. A male figure means success. The unwitting harbingers of glad tidings include the writers Maxim Gorky, Leonid Andreyev, and Anton Chekhov.

HARNESSING THE DEVIL

In developing a nationwide network of agents provocateurs, Sergei Zubatov acquires huge influence over Interior Minister Plehve, which he uses to persuade the minister to back another major experiment—a network of trade unions. Outlining the idea, he does not fail to mention that Finance Minister Witte is an ardent opponent, which makes Plehve immediately give the go-ahead to launch the experiment in the major cities of Saint Petersburg, Moscow, Minsk, Odessa, and Kiev.

Zubatov starts searching for people to set up the trade union circles. A promising candidate for the role of trade union leader of Saint Petersburg's workers is the priest Georgy Gapon.

In his memoirs Gapon claims that he never trusted Zubatov. However, after talks lasting until three in the morning, the priest agrees to work for him.

Zubatov does not conceal his hatred of the revolutionaries: "Look at the poison they're spreading among the people," he says to Gapon, holding up a confiscated copy of *Revolutionary Russia*, published abroad and illegally brought into the country. The priest is curious and asks to be allowed to read the article by Peter Kropotkin. His wish is granted. In return,

Gapon promises to go to Moscow over Christmas to see how Zubatov's trade unions are getting on.

In Moscow, Gapon meets with journalists, who explain to him the true purpose of Zubatov's "trade unions." "It's an alliance," says one reporter, "a cunning trap set by the police to separate the working class from the intelligentsia and kill the political movement. It undermines the power of the workers. At first we didn't understand the real motive. We agreed to help educate the workers, but when we realized what was happening we withdrew from the organization."

Afterwards, Gapon attends an Epiphany service and sees all of Moscow's top officials, headed by the chief of the Moscow police, Dmitry Trepov, Zubatov's patron. "Instead of heartfelt prayerfulness, I saw nothing but a parade of uniforms. No one seemed to care about the meaning of this holy day, only about their positions. The police treated the common folk in a most unceremonious manner. I had to intervene on behalf of a poor parishioner who had been hit in the face by a policeman for no reason. These self-appointed defenders of the people, I thought to myself, treat them like cattle."

Gapon comes to the conclusion that all the higher ranks of the Russian Orthodox Church and top officials are secret police agents. The editor of the church journal *Missionary Review*, for instance, as well as Pobedonostsev, regularly report to the security services. "Russian priests are police officers in cassocks. What's worse, the police catch only the bodies of their victims, while the priests capture their souls; they are the real enemies of the working people and the suffering classes," concludes Gapon. However, true to his dream of "harnessing the devil," he decides that he can play along. "By pretending to join Zubatov, I could achieve my own goal of setting up a genuine workers' union."

TWO WORLDS, TWO GERMANS

Like Zubatov, Plehve believes that if society is under tight control it will calm down. However, their notion of control differs. After being appointed the new interior minister, Plehve continues to serve as the secretary of state of the Grand Duchy of Finland, where, together with Governor-General Bobrikov, he starts a policy of Russification. Through Plehve's efforts, Russian becomes the region's official language. That is followed by conscription of Finnish nationals and tighter censorship.

The new head of the Ministry of Interior continues the Russification drive. The Russification of the Caucasus and repressive measures against the local indigenous people are top of the agenda. Most of the Committee of Ministers, including Witte and Pobedonostsev, are against Plehve's campaign. But he has the support of Nicholas II.

National policy is a cause of permanent conflict between Finance Minister Witte and Interior Minister Plehve. They both descend from German nobles who adopted Orthodoxy, but have taken different paths in life. Witte was born in Tbilisi (now capital of Georgia, at that time called Tiflis), studied at grammar school in Chisinau (now the capital of Moldova) and at university in Odessa, and then worked in Odessa and Kiev (in modern Ukraine). In 1871, when Witte had just graduated from Odessa University, the city witnessed a pogrom. Many students were Jews, who tried to defend themselves. But the Jewish students were arrested by the police, while the "pogromists" were given free rein. Witte's sympathies lay with his fellow students.

Plehve's experience was more traumatic. Born in Warsaw (now capital of Poland, then part of the Russian Empire), he attended grammar school until the Polish uprising against Russia in 1863. Warsaw was in uproar, tearing down signs in the Russian language, threatening ethnic Russians, and raiding Orthodox cemeteries, where graves were trampled and flower beds torn up. Plehve felt like a "Russian occupier." In 1863, aged seventeen, he moved to his mother's relatives in the Kaluga province of Russia, where he finished secondary school, before studying law at Moscow University. Having been a Russian in Poland, he was considered a German in Moscow, yet always did his best to look Russian and prove his "Russianness." This is what Witte has to say about his hated "comrade" Plehve: "Like any renegade, he developed a hostility towards anything that was not Orthodox. I don't think he believed in God any more than in the devil, but to curry favor with the higher-ups and the governor general of Moscow, Grand Duke Sergei Alexandrovich, he showed particular devoutness."

Plehve is highly suspicious of all ethnic minorities, but particularly the Jews. He consistently supports the increasing restrictions against them. An even more forceful proponent of the anti-Jewish laws is the tsar's uncle, Grand Duke Sergei. No sooner having taken over as Moscow's governor general, he prohibits Jews from settling in Moscow and evicts all Jewish artisans, about thirty thousand in total. But the grand duke does not stop there, and in 1897 orders the eviction of all Jews studying medicine.

Both Grand Duke Sergei and Interior Minister Plehve support the introduction of nationwide restrictions on the Jews. Witte does not. In his memoirs, he hints that the late Emperor Alexander III once asked him if he sympathized with the Jews. Witte asserts that he replied: "I asked His

Majesty: 'Is it possible to drown all the Jews in the Black Sea?' If not, the only solution to the Jewish question is to let them live normally and phase out the laws created specifically for them, since ultimately there is no other solution to the Jewish question than to afford Jews the same rights as Your Majesty's other subjects."

Even if Witte's memoirs are slightly embellished, he has a personal reason to advocate for the rights of Jews. In 1891, he married his second wife, Matilde Ivanovna (Isaakovna) Lisanevich, a Jewish convert to Orthodoxy. The fact that Matilda is a Jewish divorcee represents a serious obstacle to her being accepted at court. It is no secret to him that not only Grand Duke Sergei and Plehve are prejudiced against the Jews, but Nicholas II as well. In 1895, when a ready-made decision from the State Council to relax the anti-Jewish laws is presented to the tsar, he rejects the document, writing his own resolution: "I will do it when I feel like it."

According to Witte, the numerous anti-Jewish laws exacerbate the problem of corruption: "The administration takes more bribes from them than anyone else. In some places Jews are subject to a special 'bribe tax.' It goes without saying that the poor shoulder the burden of the anti-Jewish measures, for the rich can easily afford to pay. Far from being oppressed, rich Jews sometimes benefit from the discrimination, for it gives them influence over the local administration."

As a result, writes Witte, the harassment of the Jews has "sown the seeds of revolution among the Jewish masses, especially the young. Thirty years ago, they were considered cowards, but now they are willing to sacrifice themselves for the revolution as bandits and killers. Not all Jews are revolutionaries, of course, but there is no doubt that they make up a larger percentage of the movement than any other ethnic group in Russia."

For a long time, Jews have had a particular status in the Russian Empire. Their numbers increased sharply in the eighteenth century when Empress Catherine II added parts of Poland to her dominion. However, the extensive curtailment of their rights only began in the nineteenth century.

Emperors Alexander I and Nicholas I were both ill disposed towards the Jewish people, believing, as they did, in "blood libel"—the widespread notion in Western Europe, dating back to the Middle Ages, that Jews commit ritual sacrifice of Christian children (from the seventeenth century onwards, another myth circulates in Western Europe that the recipe for *matzo* bread includes the sacrificial blood of Christian infants). On one occasion, Alexander I orders a review of a case involving the alleged murder of a three-year-old child in the town of Velizh, near Smolensk. Dozens of Jews have already been acquitted of any wrongdoing, but the conqueror of Napoleon is not convinced. They are again acquitted (by this time Nicholas I is on the throne), but he, too, on signing the State Council resolution, adds his "personal opinion" that the Jews are not to be trusted.

It is Nicholas I who initiates the anti-Jewish laws in the Russian Empire and introduces the Pale of Settlement, allowing Jews to live only in the western and southwestern provinces of the empire (today's Belarus, Moldova, Lithuania, Poland, and a part of Ukraine) and forbidding them from certain cities and rural areas, confining them largely to the *shtetls*. The Jews are expelled from Saint Petersburg in 1826 and from Kiev the following year (despite the fact that Kiev is part of the Pale of Settlement), and later they are also banned from residing in Yalta, Sevastopol, and Nikolaev. The year 1835 sees the adoption of "the Statute on the Jews," which entrenches their status as an oppressed people.

Under Alexander II, the architect of Russia's most important reforms of the nineteenth century, there have been some concessions. Jews with higher education now have the right to settle outside the Pale, as do goldsmiths, dental technicians, and other artisans in sought-after professions, plus "first-guild merchants." The fee to become a first-guild merchant is 575 roubles* annually for ten years (which have to be spent inside the Pale of Settlement). In the eleventh year (i.e., after paying almost 6,000 roubles†) a Jewish merchant can move. Having met these requirements, Wissotzky and Gotz are allowed to live in Moscow and enjoy benefits denied to other Jews.

The nineteenth century sees numerous anti-Jewish pogroms in Russia. The first takes place in Odessa and is started by local traders of Greek origin who resent the competition. A powerful wave of pogroms surges across the country after the assassination of Tsar Alexander II, even though the Jews have little to do with it. The killer himself is Ignatius Grinevitsky, a Pole, while most members of his group are ethnic Russians. Only one of the conspirators, Gesya Gelfand, has Jewish origins and is also one of the few women involved.

After the murder of his father, Alexander III initiates a series of anti-Jewish laws. The year 1882 sees the publication of the "Interim Rules," forbidding Jews to acquire real estate outside the Pale of Settlement or to trade on Sundays and Christian holidays. The pogroms and anti-Jewish laws draw a sizeable response from European liberals; for example, the writer Victor Hugo becomes an active member of the French Committee

---

*About $7,580 in 2017.
†About $79,100 in 2017.

for Assisting Russian Jews. Among Russian conservatives, such organizations are perceived as part of Europe's ingrained prejudice against Russia.

KING SOLOMON'S PLOT

In April 1902, the renowned Russian journalist Mikhail Menshikov publishes an article in Suvorin's newspaper *New Time* under the title "Conspiracies Against Humanity." In it, he mentions a letter from a female reader. Citing a terminal illness, she wants to see him to hand over some "invaluable documents." Menshikov agrees, meets the old lady, and then makes fun of her in his article. The "matter of worldly importance imparted from above" that she alludes to seems to him like a case of senile delirium. This curious incident results in the first ever mention of the "Protocols of the Elders of Zion."

The sixty-six-year-old woman's name is Yustinia Glinka, the daughter of a Russian former ambassador to Brazil, who has lived abroad for many years. She recounts that during a sojourn in Nice ("long chosen as the secret capital of Jewry") she discovered documents about a Jewish plot dating back to the year 929 BC in Jerusalem. Although Menshikov has a reputation as a conservative and even a nationalist (which is why Glinka turned to him), he declines to publish the documents.

He does not believe in their authenticity and paraphrases them in an ironic tone: "Startled by their contents, I asked her to give me a brief summary," he writes.

I heard terrible things. The leaders of the Jewish people, it seems, as far back as the time of King Solomon, decided to subordinate all of humanity to their will and assert the primacy of the kingdom of David for all eternity. A secret alliance was concluded to take over the trade and industry of all nations. Scattered across the Earth, the Jews sought to undermine the material and moral well-being of others and to seize control of the world's capital cities to suck dry and enslave the masses. With Jesuit, nay, devilish cunning, the Jews adopted the propaganda of liberalism, cosmopolitanism and anarchy to undermine the foundations of order and Christianity with the aim of ensnaring the whole of humanity in brutal despotism. It took one-and-a-half thousand years to destroy the ancient pagan kingdoms, and now Christianity stands on the verge of collapse. The Jews (according to Glinka) represent the serpent of the Apocalypse, crawling from country to country. It already has its coils wrapped around

France, Germany and England. Now the serpent is raising its head above Saint Petersburg. All the events of recent years—the assassinations, the public disorder, the gold standard, the unrest in China—are the work of this abominable creature. Having swallowed Saint Petersburg, the serpent will proceed to Moscow, Kiev, Odessa and Constantinople. When it once more reaches Jerusalem, humanity will be forever enslaved. The Jews will consolidate their eternal kingdom. Mankind will not guess who its masters are, but will bear the yoke submissively, like domesticated animals.

Menshikov does not try to establish the identity of the real author of the text, since he considers it to be a delirious hoax. However, he notes that copies of the "Protocols" may be in the possession of other journalists. A few years later these journalists will make themselves known, but for now, having been roundly derided by Menshikov, the "Protocols" remain on the shelf.*

JEWISH SELF-DEFENSE

Rumors of the imminent pogroms spread throughout the Pale, including one of the most Jewish cities of the Russian Empire, Odessa. The journalist Vladimir Zhabotinsky (later Ze'ev Jabotinsky) of *Odessa News* recalls that some dismissed the rumors as idle chitchat, believing that the police would not allow it to happen; others are whispering that the police themselves will instigate the violence. Everyone is very alarmed. For the past twenty years Odessa has been relatively calm.

Zhabotinsky decides that self-defense units are needed and writes to Odessa's most influential Jews, urging them to buy weapons to protect themselves from the pogroms. The letters remain unanswered. A few weeks later Zhabotinsky is paid a visit by a childhood friend. First, he says that the letters were a waste of time: the rich Jews are too frightened to budge. Second, self-defense units are being set up anyway, and Zhabotinsky can help if he wants. To his surprise, the self-defense units in Odessa are run by Zubatov's local cell, the Independent Jewish Workers' Party.

Zhabotinsky comes on board. In a few days he and his new comrades manage to raise more than 500 roubles† (a large sum), plus an arsenal of guns,

---

*One hundred years later conspiracy theories are not mocked or refuted by officious journalists anymore. In the early twenty-first century conspirology almost becomes state ideology in Russia—belief in a conspiracy against Russian people unites the officials, loyal journalists and most of the public consuming the conspiracy propaganda.

† About $6,592 in 2017.

crowbars, and knives. Leaflets are printed in Russian and Yiddish: "The content was very simple: two articles of the Criminal Code clearly stating that killing in self-defense is exempt from punishment, and a few words exhorting young Jews not to let their people be slaughtered like cattle."

At first, Zhabotinsky wonders why the police are so relaxed about the Jews amassing arms. That is before he realizes that the self-defense units are being set up under the direction of Genrik Shayevich, the head of Zubatov's cell in Odessa.

In the end, there is no pogrom in Odessa. It happens instead in Chisinau. Zhabotinsky visits the scene and recalls that reports of the first pogrom made little impression, apart from a few donations from European Jews sent to his newspaper in support of the victims.

A few months later he is elected as Odessa's delegate to the World Zionist Congress, launching his international career. History will remember Zhabotinsky as the organizer of the first Jewish self-defense units in Russia. In 1918, he will travel to Palestine and become one of the forerunners of the future Jewish state.

HOUSE NO. 13

One of the owners of the still unpublished "Protocols of the Elders of Zion" is Pavel Krushevan, a Moldovan-born publisher of two newspapers: *Znamya* [Standard] in Saint Petersburg and *Bessarabian* at home in Chisinau. *Bessarabian* is the only daily newspaper in the provincial Chisinau, where Jews make up nearly forty percent of the population. The "Jewish threat" is a constant topic in the paper.

In March 1903 *Bessarabian* reports that Jewish residents of the village of Dubossary have allegedly carried out the ritual murder of a fourteen-year-old Ukrainian.*

The investigation quickly unmasks the real killer, who turns out to be a cousin of the murdered boy. However, the local authorities ban all coverage of the case, and the article in *Bessarabian* goes uncontested. On 6 April, Easter Sunday, a pogrom breaks out. News of the attack spreads around the town, but the police do not intervene—the governor is awaiting orders from higher up.

This is how Russia's top reporter at the time, Vladimir Korolenko, describes that day in his essay "House No. 13":

---

*In 2014 Russian state owned "First Channel" will make a fake report that Ukrainian "neo-Nazis" had crucified a boy in eastern Ukraine. That story will cause a huge scandal in Russia, but many people will believe it.

At about 10 a.m. a well-meaning policeman advised the Jews to stay indoors and then sat down on the roadside, seemingly able to do nothing more. There he remained, as if posing for a sculptor. Just a few steps away the tragedy of the Jewish shanties unfolded in all its spontaneous horror. The crowd appeared at around 11 a.m., accompanied by two patrols, which, unfortunately, had received no orders. The 50-60 strong crowd was made up of 'neighborly' Moldovans. They went up to a wine store and said to the owner: 'Give us thirty roubles* or we'll kill you.' He paid up, took cover and saved his skin. Then the pogrom began. A few minutes later the square was strewn with glass and bits of furniture.

The most notorious episode of Korolenko's report tells how three Jews—two men and a girl—climb into an attic. Hearing their pursuers, they begin to break through the roof to get out: "They were desperate to smash a hole in the roof with their bare hands. They had to get out of the attic. Up above was sunshine, down below was the crowd," writes Korolenko.

The three scramble onto the roof, and the crowd starts jeering. Someone throws a tub. ("The tub clatters against the roof, and the crowd laughs...") All three are eventually forced to jump down. The girl lands in a pile of debris and survives. The men are killed by the baying crowd.

"The two men [Maklin and Berlatsky] were injured in the fall and then finished off with sticks by the vile mob. Laughing, the bloodthirsty executioners left them for dead in a dirty puddle of spilled wine and debris."

At 5 p.m., having received his long-awaited orders (and seemingly unable to act in the meantime), the governor steps in to restore relative calm. According to official figures, forty-three people have been killed, thirty-eight of them Jewish.

After the Chisinau massacre, self-defense units are established throughout the Pale of Settlement. A month later an attempted pogrom in Homel, Belarus, turns into a full-scale battle when the Jews fight back: five Jews and four Christians are killed. "The Jewish streets changed after Chisinau," remarks Zhabotinsky. "The Jews were grief-stricken, but also ashamed. The shame of Chisinau was not repeated in Homel. The grief cut just as deep, but there was no more shame."

The Chisinau pogrom makes the headlines across Russia and the world. European human rights organizations start collecting donations for the victims. The initial reaction in Russia is unequivocally condemnatory. Leo

---

*About $396 in 2017.

Tolstoy denounces it, as does John of Kronstadt, the most popular priest in the country: "The people of Russia are capable of such stupidity!" he writes in an appeal to Chisinau's Christian population. "What heathenism! What waywardness! A Christian feast is transformed into hell on Earth, a satanic orgy of bloodletting. Russian people, my brothers! What are you doing? Why do you treat your compatriots with such barbarism and savagery?"

Soon, however, the tone changes. Vladimir Korolenko arrives at the scene and writes his essay "House No. 13," only to see it banned by the censor. Yet the Saint Petersburg newspaper *Znamya*, published by the nationalist Pavel Krushevan, is allowed to print its version of events: the Jews allegedly attacked first and provoked the pogrom themselves. The nationalists are outraged by what the Western press is writing, by the collection of donations, and by the fact that so far only Christians have faced trial.

No one about-turns more comprehensively than John of Kronstadt. *Znamya* now publishes a letter of apology from him: "From the various reports I have become convinced that the Jews themselves were the cause of the carnage that marked the 6th and 7th of April. I am assured that the Christians have suffered, while the Jews have been amply recompensed by their own and other brethren for losses and injuries incurred. . . . I appeal to the Christians of Chisinau: forgive me for my reproach of you. Eye-witness accounts have convinced me that a handful of Christians were provoked into action and that the Jews largely brought the pogrom upon themselves."

The British newspaper *The Times* publishes a letter allegedly sent by Interior Minister Plehve to the governor of Bessarabia with a request not to use force against the "pogromists." The letter is a fake (Plehve actually dismissed the Chisinau governor for failing to stop the pogrom), but the global community believes it. A shocking, and in many respects exaggerated, report on the incident appears in *The New York Times*.* The Chisinau pogrom kick-starts a wave of Jewish emigration from Russia, primarily to the United States.

In his memoirs Witte, too, blames Plehve: "I hesitate to suggest that Plehve directly organized the massacre, but he did not oppose this 'anti-revolutionary countermeasure' (as he sees it)," writes the finance minister. According to Witte's memoirs, after the pogrom in Chisinau, Plehve negotiates with "Jewish leaders in Paris" and demands that they persuade young Jews to "stop the revolution," allegedly saying that he will put an end

---

* Bias and stereotypes are still widespread in the world media in the early twenty-first century: in their coverage of the events in Russia they create a much more black-and-white, primitive, and conspirological picture than the real one.

to the pogroms and the anti-Jewish laws in return. But, according to Witte, Plehve receives the following response from the Jewish leaders: "We are powerless to do so, for most young people are wild with hunger and we do not hold them in our hands. But we strongly believe that if you start relaxing the anti-Jewish measures they will settle down."

Meanwhile, the unrest continues to grow. On Saint Petersburg's main street, Nevsky Prospekt, a young Jewish man by the name of Dashevsky, a former student from Kiev, attacks the *Znamya* publisher, Pavel Krushevan, with a knife. Only slightly wounded in the neck, Krushevan seizes the attacker himself. According to the reporter Korolenko, a Jewish doctor on the scene wants to administer first aid, but Krushevan refuses, fearing that it is part of the plot. He demands the death penalty for Dashevsky "on the grounds that he, Mr. Krushevan, is no ordinary man, but a representative of the state idea." During his interrogation Dashevsky says that the attack on Krushevan was revenge for the Chisinau pogrom. Unlike Menshikov, Krushevan takes the "Protocols of the Elders of Zion" at face value and, on a wave of mass hysteria, publishes the text in *Znamya* under the heading "The Jewish Program to Conquer the World." The text spreads around Saint Petersburg, and then the world.

THE PRISONER OF NAPLES

Mikhail Gotz is not only the leader of the Socialist Revolutionary Party and the editor-in-chief of *Revolutionary Russia*. More importantly, he is the main sponsor of the SRs, describing himself, according to Viktor Chernov, as the "steward of the revolution and the overseer of the operation to extract maximum funding for the cause." In other words, the "tea heir" regularly receives money from his billionaire father and uncle in Russia, but takes only a small part, giving the rest to the party.

However, sometimes he has to earn his keep. Chernov recalls how Gotz would "gasp, groan and complain that he had to abandon his favorite pastime [revolution] for a couple of weeks" because of another visit from a rich relative, forcing him to pack a suitcase of suits, tuxedos, luxurious jackets, and ties that his party comrades never saw. Members of the tea dynasty and allied financial magnates would regularly come to Europe to gamble in Monte Carlo or stroll along the Cote d'Azur. It was Gotz's job to "take them for a walk."

Gotz uses the encounters to good effect, persuading the visitors that their donations towards "the liberation movement" will bring them luck at the gambling table. Gotz's work as a tour guide for his relatives and their friends effectively funds the SR party, including its military wing. The tea oligarchs are unaware that their travels are financing the preparations for political assassinations.

In March 1903 Mikhail Gotz and his wife head for Naples, where he is to meet his father, Raphael Gotz, and his sister. In Naples the family intends to travel by boat to the French Riviera, but the trip is unexpectedly called off. On 3 March, Italian police break into Gotz's hotel room in Naples and seize all his documents. He himself is put in jail.

The arrest has been carried out at the request of the Russian police: Gotz is accused of ordering the assassination of Interior Minister Sipyagin. It marks a breakthrough for the investigation, and Gotz is due to be extradited to Russia for trial. But the Russian authorities underestimate the power of European public opinion. Plehve and his subordinates are not accustomed to paying attention to the Russian public and cannot imagine that the European press might thwart their plans.

The Russian vice-consul in Naples gives interviews to local newspapers, which report the details of the operation to capture the leader of the terrorist organization. It turns out that a Russian police agent tracked Gotz from Switzerland and that the vice-consul himself was present during the search of the hotel room. These revelations spark a scandal: why are representatives of a foreign state telling Italian law enforcers what to do, asks the press.

Leftist politicians across Europe start collecting signatures in support of Gotz. The first to sign the petition is the leader of the French socialists, Jean Jaurès, and the future prime minister of France, George Clemenceau. The arrest of Gotz is discussed in the Italian parliament. Left-wing MPs assert that Italian law prohibits the extradition of a foreign national if the charges are politically motivated. Gotz fits this description, and the parliamentarians are close to demanding the resignation of the government, which has knowingly violated Italian law in collusion with the Russians.

The trial begins. All the Italian media, including the pro-government press, are on the side of the accused. According to Chernov, the evidence for Gotz's involvement in the murder was collected by the Italian police in a "sloppy and clumsy manner," making it impossible to link Gotz to the assassination. So the Russian side decides to play its political cards. First, the court hears the Russian ambassador, and then a rumor spreads that Nicholas II is planning to pay an official visit to Italy. If so, it would be very impolite of the king of Italy not to extend the Russian emperor a reciprocal courtesy. When this information is confirmed in parliament, the Italian left warns that if the tsar comes to Italy he will be booed and whistled wherever he goes. In a matter of hours all the whistles in the country are sold. In Florence a special newspaper is published under the title *Whistle* to mobilize young people against Nicholas II. As a result, the emperor is advised by his Foreign Ministry not to travel. The trial comes to an end, and Russia's extradition request is turned down. The defendant is only expelled from the country. On 6 May, after spending two months in a Naples prison, Gotz goes free and heads for the French Riviera, as planned.*

While Gotz is temporarily behind bars in Naples, the police in Russia have one objective: to catch the evil genius of terror, Gregory Gershuni.

In May 1903 he is finally arrested following a tip-off from a member of the SRs' Kiev cell. Gershuni is taken from Kiev to Saint Petersburg. Along the way he recalls that he imagined Gotz appearing at the police station, disguised as a gendarme, to arrange his escape. But Gotz has only just gotten out of prison himself. Now back in Geneva, he is, according to Viktor Chernov, plagued by visions of his own. He has nightmares of Gershuni in shackles.

Gershuni is taken to the Peter and Paul Fortress in Saint Petersburg, the main detention center for political prisoners. The worker Foma Kachura, who shot at the governor of Kharkov, has also been arrested. The gendarme Spiridovich claims that Kachura is terrified of the demonic Gershuni and agrees to testify only after he has seen a photograph of the militant leader in shackles.

Gershuni does not believe at first that his faithful accomplice has told the investigators everything, but changes his mind when they recount details that only Kachura could have known. "My soul descended into hell," recalls Gershuni. "Do you know what mortal terror is? It is horror at the complexity and mystery of what is called the human soul. Kachura is a traitor! Trapped in the jaws of Russian justice, such a psychological blow is crushing indeed."

Three months later the investigators offer him a deal: in return for confessing that he belongs to a militant organization, the death sentence will be commuted to life imprisonment. The prisoner defiantly refuses: "I am a Jew. You and other fools think that Jews are cowards and will do anything to avoid the gallows. Well, I'll show you an example of 'Jewish cowardice'! You say that Jews only know how to rebel? You'll see that we know how to die. Tell your Plehve that we have nothing to bargain over. Let him do his job, I will do mine."

---

*In the beginning of twenty-first century Vladimir Putin will demand the extradition of the exiled oligarchs (and his personal foes) from different European countries. But all those appeals will be rejected by European courts: Spanish and Greek judges will prevent Vladimir Gusinsky from being extradited to Russia, and British court will grant refugee status to Boris Berezovsky.

The "Jewish cowardice" slur haunts not only Gershuni, but also the entire Pale of Settlement. The Jewish community is stunned by the Chisinau pogrom. Many considered such a thing impossible in the twentieth century. Obviously not. Maybe something more radical is needed.

In June the leaders of the Jewish Independent Workers' Party hold a meeting in Minsk. The Chisinau pogrom is still raw, and the fact that Genrik Shayevich, the leader of the Odessa cell, played a key role in establishing the Jewish self-defense units in Odessa has done nothing to improve the party's prestige. On the contrary. There are rumors among Russia's Jewish population that the authorities arranged the pogroms, as if Plehve personally gave out instructions. This makes cooperation with the Independent Jewish Workers' Party shameful, and many former supporters turn their backs on it. Even the "independents" themselves do not want to be part of a puppet party or be regarded as agents provocateurs in the pay of the police. The party decides to disband.

Surprisingly, in Saint Petersburg the "independents" are not regarded as loyal puppets. Quite the opposite, Plehve believes that Zubatov's experiment has gone too far and orders him to curtail the party's activities with immediate effect. Zubatov demurs, insisting that the state needs a loyal social movement, but Plehve is adamant that the most important thing is to disarm the "anti-government criminals," for which purpose the Jewish party is not required, since the leaders of the Bund have already been caught and the "independents" are spinning out of control. Zubatov threatens to resign, but Plehve restrains him from doing so.

Zubatov becomes increasingly irritated by the policing methods of his boss. He believes that "the whole of Russia is seething and the revolution cannot be suppressed through police measures." Plehve's policy is to "drive the malaise inwards, which can only end badly." He decides to take his grievances to Plehve's bitter rival, Sergei Witte. It is not the first time that the reformer of the Ministry of Interior has tried to find a common language with the reformer of the Finance Ministry. The key players' memoirs recount conflicting versions of events.

According to Alexei Lopukhin, the director of the Imperial Russian police, Witte agrees to help Zubatov have the interior minister removed. Their accomplice is Witte's longtime friend Prince Meshchersky, the publisher of the newspaper *The Citizen*, who once recommended Plehve as a minister. The plan is as follows: Zubatov's subordinates are to write letters to Meshchersky made to look as if they had come from various influential figures. Each letter is to describe how disastrous Plehve's policies are for Russia and that only Witte is able to save the situation. Meshchersky, in turn, shall go to the emperor with the letters in hand to prove that Witte should replace Plehve.

But Witte insists that there was no conspiracy, that Zubatov came to complain to him about his boss, but that he, Witte, threatened to tell Plehve about their conversation, whereupon they parted company. Witte's memoirs are often embellished and not entirely reliable, it should be said.

ODESSA ON EDGE

In June a strike begins in Odessa following the unfair dismissal of an iron foundry worker. The city is home to a formidable cell of "independents" (or former "independents," i.e. members of the Independent Jewish Workers' Party). Genrik Shayevich is eager to prove that he is not a provocateur or an agent of Plehve. He makes every effort to stand up for the workers.

By July it has turned into a general strike—forty thousand people stop working. Odessa is now without bread, water, and light. The local authorities are at a loss, including Shayevich.

The official response is chaotic, for the authorities have no clue how to deal with the workers. The matter is complicated by the constant interference of Grand Duke Sandro, a childhood friend of the emperor and the new minister of merchant shipping and ports. Odessa, the largest trade port in the empire, falls under his mandate, and the grand duke demands to know who is to blame for the general strike.

The grand duke's main enemy is in fact Sergei Witte, for the new ministry headed by Sandro has been hived off from the Ministry of Finance. Witte does not conceal his opposition to the move ("It was like having a finger cut off," he says) and is keen to hinder the grand duke. Sandro in response plots against Witte and even tries to inculpate him for the Odessa strike, but the finance minister shifts the blame to Plehve and his subordinate, Zubatov. Plehve denies it, saying that he knew nothing about Zubatov's actions in Odessa. In the end the buck stops at the leader of the Odessa "independents," Genrik Shayevich, who is arrested and put on trial.

From this moment on, Zubatov has serious problems. First, his superiors, fearful of taking responsibility, make him a scapegoat for the Odessa strike. Second, rumors of the alleged plot between Zubatov and Witte reach Plehve. According to the police department head Lopukhin, Zubatov has been betrayed by one of his colleagues. But Witte's version of events states that the "conspirator" Prince Meshchersky informs on the interior minister (again Witte denies any conspiracy and claims that the matter went no further than speculative talk).

"All Zubatov's enemies seemed to unite against him and use the moment to bring about his downfall," says Zubatov's underling Alexander Spiridovich. "It was loudly declaimed that Zubatov had orchestrated the strike and was himself a revolutionary."

On 19 August, Plehve summons Zubatov and openly, in front of a witness, puts the accusations to him, the most serious being the disclosure of classified information. Among the papers seized from Shayevich is a letter written by Zubatov, seeking to recruit the former as an agent with the following words: "Dear Genrik Isaevich [Shayevich], I have unexpectedly found a kindred spirit in the shape of the 'pro-Semitic' tsar. According to the Eagle [Plehve], the sovereign said, 'Do not break up the rich Jews, and let the poor ones live.'" Plevhe is indignant that "Zubatov has taken the liberty of relaying the tsar's words to his agent, the 'yid' Shayevich" and threatens to prosecute him. "The Eagle was livid," recalls a subordinate.

Never having been a civil servant, Zubatov does not mince words and challenges Plehve head on, reminding him that it was he who "legalized" the labor movement in Odessa in the first place. On leaving the room he slams the minister's door so hard the glass nearly shatters, say witnesses. "I was seething with such burning resentment, the door barely survived," recalls Zubatov.

He writes a resignation letter, and the next day goes to Moscow. One of the few to see him off at the station is Georgy Gapon. In just a few years he will replay the fate of Genrik Shayevich, but on a far grander scale.

Shayevich is put on trial and sent to Siberia, while the head of the Interior Ministry exiles Zubatov to Vladimir. "To withstand fifteen years of service under the watchful eye of the authorities and be cursed on all sides by one's enemies, not without risk to life and limb, only to fall under police surveillance oneself is an unprecedented and outrageous injustice," writes Zubatov in his report to the Interior Ministry. "They say that prayers to God and service to the Tsar shall not go unheeded. My service was indeed to the Tsar, but it ended in foul, unheard-of wrongfulness."

|| Chapter 4 ||

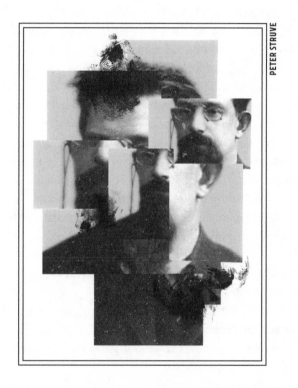

PETER STRUVE

in which liberals come into fashion:
Peter Struve and Pavel Milyukov become the
most popular politicians in the country

THE MOST POPULAR MARXIST

In a Saint Petersburg drawing room a group of young intellectuals is debating a new book, the author of which asserts that humanity is threatened by degeneracy. All agree that the hypothesis is overstated. There is no degeneracy; everything is cyclical. All ages spawn good and bad people alike. Suddenly up jumps a redheaded young man, who tugs on his jug ears and shouts: "What do you mean there's no degeneracy? Take a look at me! At my ears!" "Peter, stop this nonsense," says his embarrassed wife. But "Peter" continues to expound upon humanity's degeneracy with himself as a case study." The incident is described in the memoirs of Ariadna Tyrkova, a young metropolitan journalist and a former classmate of Peter's unfortunate wife.

The performance is not meant to be ironic or provocative. Everyone knows that the thirty-year-old Peter (Pyotr) Struve is a very serious young man with no sense of humor whatsoever. But that does not prevent him from being a popular figure in Saint Petersburg, whose young people are gripped by Marxism. Struve is the most fanatical adherent of this fashionable new philosophy emanating from Germany. The son of a former governor of Perm and a shining member of the "golden youth," Struve is well acquainted with all the latest books on the topic, some of which are not even known to many of his peers.

He set up Russia's first Marxist circle long before this incident, as a twenty-year-old student back in 1890—a time when the future founders of the newspaper *Spark* (*Iskra*), the revolutionaries Martov, Lenin, and Potresov, are still far from Marxism.

Struve is lucky. In 1886, another twenty-year-old member of the "golden youth," Michael Gotz, was arrested and banished to Kolyma for ten years, despite the efforts of his wealthy relatives. But the times are more lenient when Struve catches the Marxist bug.

In 1894 Struve graduates from university and enters the Ministry of Finance. Only then does he end up in trouble. He is arrested by mistake, erroneously identified as a member of the underground movement People's Will. The error quickly comes to light, and the police release the former governor's son and even pen a letter to the Ministry of Finance clearing the young man of all charges. But Finance Minister Witte is not convinced and decides in any case to dismiss the young Struve, which

---

* For several decades Peter Struve is the "face" of the Russian liberals and the main target of attack for their opponents—not unlike the symbol of Russian liberalism a century later, the equally redheaded Anatoly Chubais.

ultimately does him good—instead of becoming a civil servant, he becomes a popular journalist.

At the age of twenty-four, Struve writes a book entitled *Critical Observations on the Problem of Russia's Economic Development*—the first Russian book about Marxism to become a hit among Saint Petersburg's youth. The book's final phrase ("We recognize our lack of culture and shall learn from capitalism") becomes a mantra.

In January 1895, shortly after the death of Alexander III, the twenty-five-year-old Struve distributes an anonymous open letter that ends with the following warning for the new tsar, the twenty-seven-year-old Nicholas II: "You have begun the struggle, and the struggle will not be long in coming." Struve reads the letter to some friends before making multiple copies. However, the public attributes authorship not to Struve, but to Fyodor Rodichev, whose recent "Tver Address" prompted the tsar's "senseless daydreams" speech* and for which he was removed from the Tver district council, or *zemstvo*.

Four years later, now twenty-nine years old, Struve publishes the first Russian edition of Marx's *Das Kapital* and adds his own preface. His economic lectures are attended by legions of fans; he is a political rock star.

Struve makes the acquaintance of Vladimir Ulyanov (the future Lenin) in 1894 while visiting friends. Struve takes an immediate dislike to the provincial Marxist: "He was too abrupt," he recalls. "It was something more than mere abruptness, more like mockery, partly deliberate and partly irrepressibly spontaneous, rising from the depths of his being. He immediately sensed that I was an opponent, whereupon he was guided not by reason, but by intuition—what hunters call instinct."

Struve is repelled by Ulyanov's behavior: "The terrible thing in Lenin was that combination of actual self-castigation, which is the essence of all real asceticism, with the castigation of other people as expressed in abstract social hatred and cold political cruelty."

The young Saint Petersburg journalist Ariadna Tyrkova suddenly finds herself surrounded by young Marxist fanatics. And all because of her friends. At school, Ariadna had three best friends: Nina, Lida, and Nadia. All three found politically active husbands. Nina became the wife of Peter Struve, Lida married a member of his circle, the Marxist Mikhail Tugan-Baranovsky (one of the founders of the independent Ukrainian state in 1917 and the first Minister of Finance of Ukraine), while Nadia—Nadezhda Krupskaya—falls for the provincial Vladimir Ulyanov. Deeply in love,

---

* See chapter one.

according to Ariadna, Nadia becomes his common-law wife. The young atheists do not recognize the institution of church marriage.

Through her friends, Ariadna spends a great deal of time in the company of young Marxists and is amazed by their fanaticism: "They reiterated Marxist axioms with the stubborn obedience of a Muslim preaching the Quran." Struve and his companions are "unshakable in the belief that their quotes from *Das Kapital* and Marx and Engels' personal correspondence will resolve all doubts and disputes. Citing the edition and page number of every work, they assume that only an idiot can object. For these doctrinaires of Marxism, every punctuation mark in the writings of Marx and Engels is sacred. Listening to them, I understand how the Muslim conquerors were able to burn down the Library of Alexandria," writes Tyrkova.

"DAMN YOUR OPINION"

In 1898, a year after the establishment of the Jewish Bund, the young Marxists decide to unite the country's numerous circles into a real underground political party, headed by none other than Struve. However, since neither he nor any of his comrades have much organizational experience, the idea barely gets off the ground. Struve does at least come up with a name—the Russian Social Democratic Labour Party (RSDLP)—and writes the party manifesto. The first congress in Minsk is attended by just nine representatives of Marxist circles from different cities (even Struve himself is not there). All are arrested immediately. Struve's virtual RSDLP is in fact the "grandmother" of the future Communist Party of the Soviet Union (in later Soviet textbooks Lenin is named as the founder of everything; Struve does not even get a mention).

Until now, the only opposition in Russia has been the populists or Narodniks. But for the Marxists, the Narodniks are barbarians who believe in the revolutionary spirit of the Russian folk (i.e., the peasantry), whereas for Marx himself the driving force of the revolution is the proletariat. The Marxists despise the Narodniks as ignorant heathens.

The leading lights of Russian Marxism continue to convene, but the underground groups are constantly targeted by the police, and members are arrested and exiled. This happens to the young Vladimir Ulyanov and Julius Tsederbaum (Martov) in 1895.

By 1895 Ulyanov has managed to pass his exams at Saint Petersburg University as an external student, gaining a law degree and moving to the capital to work as a paralegal. It does not go well: all four court cases assigned to him are unsuccessful. On the other hand, he gets to know Tsederbaum and Potresov, who will become his closest comrades.

The new acquaintances set up a clandestine circle and print seventy leaflets that they intend to distribute to the working classes. That is their undoing. Ulyanov and Tsederbaum are arrested and sent to Siberia. Ulyanov is followed by his devoted Nadia, together with her mother. In 1898 Vladimir and Nadia get married in the village of Shushenskoye in Siberia, this time in a church. ("We had to go through the whole farce," recalls Krupskaya. Although the newlyweds despise religious ceremonies, the authorities will not allow Nadia to accompany Vladimir into exile without a church marriage certificate.)

Some details of the future Lenin's exile come from Ariadna Tyrkova via her brother, who is exiled with him. Ulyanov does not hide his contempt for the Narodniks:

"[Ulyanov] did not behave like a comrade. He rudely stated that People's Will was the past and that the Social Democrats were the future," Tyrkova retells her brother's words. "His disdain for the old exiles and their traditions was particularly apparent when an exile escaped, as happened on occasion. Typically, the entire colony helped fugitives and also hid the identities of those who actually supplied money or boots. Ulyanov ignored this unwritten rule and grassed on someone for facilitating an escape, which wasn't even successful. The 'accomplice' was put in a cell for two months. Ulyanov was summoned to a 'court of comrades' [a form of collective justice] at which he stated that he didn't recognize its authority and didn't give a damn about its opinion."

While Ulyanov is in exile, Struve is busy lecturing in Saint Petersburg. A theorist, he declines to join the underground organizations, print leaflets, or agitate among the workers, unlike many of his allies.

In February 1900, after his Siberian exile, Vladimir Ulyanov is allowed to return to European Russia, but not the capital. Instead, he takes up residence in Pskov, where he is visited by all the prominent Russian Marxists of the day: Martov, Potresov, Struve, and Tugan-Baranovsky. Ulyanov and Martov want to publish a newspaper, and Potresov is ready to join them. To do so, they need to enlist the support of the Saint Petersburg Marxist elite.

Struve endorses the idea. Understanding that they need material as well as moral support, Struve finds a sponsor in the shape of a rich friend of his—the young, progressive landowner and Marxist aficionado Dmitry Zhukovsky. He finances the three Marxists to begin publishing a newspaper, whereupon they travel to Europe to curry the favor of their idol Georgy Plekhanov.*

CAPITAL OF RUSSIAN OPPOSITION

A turning point in Struve's life is the rally at Kazan Cathedral on 4 March 1901, when he first encounters state-sponsored violence and feels the blows of Cossack whips for himself, a truly memorable experience. "How dare they whip me! Me!" he cries. His worldly air of invincibility is shaken to the core.

It is now Struve's turn to be exiled. Because he is a first-time offender, the penalty is not severe. He is simply prohibited from living in either of Russia's capitals. Moreover, he is able to choose his place of residence. His eye falls upon Tver.

The choice is not random. Of all the local self-governing authorities in the Russian Empire, the most politically active are Moscow and Tver. Moscow is the cultural and business capital of the empire, home to the richest merchants. Dissidents expelled from Saint Petersburg and Moscow often relocate to Tver—the only major city located between the two capitals. Thus, the turn of the century sees the emergence of a third Russian capital—a city of oppositionists and freedom-lovers.

In 1895 it is the Tver zemstvo that sends the infamous address to Nicholas II, requesting a greater role for society in government, which the young emperor dismisses as "senseless daydreams."

Struve's new social circle is the Tver intelligentsia, which leads to a radical change of outlook. Once faithful to the letter and spirit of the law of Marx, his contact with real life outside the capital alters his credo. He departs from Marxism and becomes a moderate liberal.

The system of zemstvos was introduced in Russia back in the 1860s as part of the reforms of Alexander II. Alongside the liberation of the serfs and the introduction of trial by jury, it was a beacon of progress. Over the course of the next three decades, a full-fledged civil society takes root in Russia in the shape of the provincial intelligentsia, which assumes the authority to decide on all economic and humanitarian issues relating to its region.

Unsurprisingly, universal and equal suffrage is not a feature of nineteenth-century Russia. The right to vote depends on one's social estate.

---

* See chapter three.

The nobles (1.5 percent of the population), the peasants (77 percent of the population), and the propertied classes outside the nobility each elect their own representatives to the zemstvo assemblies. Voting rights are denied to Jews and persons convicted or under police surveillance. All in all, representatives of the nobility control around 57 percent of the seats in the zemstvo assemblies, with the peasantry and non-noble property owners having roughly 30 percent and 13 percent, respectively.

With equality somewhat lacking, the tone inside the zemstvos is set by the provincial nobles and intelligentsia, who profess, nevertheless, to be the most educated and liberal-minded section of the populace.

Struve spends more than six months in Tver, during which period he is visited by his old friend Dmitry Zhukovsky, the landowning sponsor of *Spark*, who offers Struve 30,000 roubles* worth of gold to publish another new magazine on one condition: Ulyanov and his ilk are to be excluded. Zhukovsky is displeased by the Munich-based socialists and their radicalism.

Struve agrees. Denied permission to leave Russia (only his pregnant wife is given a passport), he sneaks across the border illegally. Before decamping abroad, he tours half of Russia in search of potential authors for the future magazine. In winter 1901 he arrives in Crimea, where Russia's three greatest writers are in residence. Struve does not disturb the gravely ill Tolstoy, but approaches Gorky and Chekhov. The latter promises to contribute to the new magazine.

In early 1902 Struve goes to Munich to explain matters to Ulyanov, who, already au fait with the situation and offended, refuses to meet him. Struve takes up residence near Stuttgart and uses Zhukovsky's money to set up a magazine entitled *Liberation*. In just a few months it becomes the most popular and influential Russian-language magazine, both in Europe and Russia. Its circulation reaches seven thousand copies, most of which are smuggled into Russia. The magazine is read by everyone, including the ministers Plehve and Witte and the literary doyens Tolstoy and Chekhov, as well as rank-and-file officials, nobles, merchants, priests, and village intellectuals.

The trick is the editorial board's ability to import the magazine into Russia, something that Struve and friends are far more adept at than the publishers of *Spark* and *Revolutionary Russia*. *Liberation* succeeds for two reasons: the quality of the content and the unique distribution system. First, it is not a party publication intended for a narrow circle of devotees; it is wide-ranging with something for the entire Russian intelligentsia. Second, although the magazine is banned in Russia, the publishers do deals

---

*About $395,500 in 2017.

with purveyors of contraband goods and Finnish nationalists who move freely across the porous Finnish border. Lastly, the magazine is distributed to recipients directly by post. Copies are printed on very thin paper without a dust-cover, and the first page bears the words: "We found your address from open sources and took the liberty of sending a copy of our publication," which relieves the recipient of wrongdoing in the event of the package being opened by the police.

Struve is not the first journalist to receive the patronage of the liberal investor Zhukovsky. The latter makes a similar offer to Pavel Milyukov, a renowned historian and former professor of Moscow University.

Milyukov's reputation as a dissident precedes him since his suspension in 1895 from teaching in Moscow for allegedly criticizing autocracy during a lecture. Having spent several years in Bulgaria, he returns to Russia only to land in trouble once more by speaking at a student gathering in memory of the deceased leader of the Narodniks, Pyotr Lavrov. The speech results in his arrest. A search of Milyukov's apartment reveals a draft document entitled "The Constitution of the Russian State"—a liberal fantasy of what Russia might one day become.

Milyukov spends six months at a detention center before being released, pending trial. Barred from the capital, he moves to Finland.

There, he is visited by an old acquaintance once more in the shape of Dmitry Zhukovsky, who proposes that Milyukov move abroad to become the editor of a new magazine. But he refuses. "I didn't relish the prospect," recalls the professor. "Having just returned to Russia, I did not want to risk becoming a permanent émigré detached from my homeland."

The investigation of Milyukov continues, with all the accompanying legal red tape. The verdict is handed down only in spring 1902, whereupon Milyukov requests a deferral of his prison term, because he wants to spend the summer in England to learn English. Rather bizarrely, the authorities accede to his request, presumably not too bothered if he fails to return.

But in autumn he is back in Saint Petersburg. Having collected his things, he goes to the Kresty jail to serve his sentence. More bizarrely still, it is a Sunday and the prison gates are firmly shut. He has to return the following day.

A few months later, having served more than half his sentence, Milyukov is suddenly shown the door with his coat and other possessions in hand. He is driven to the building of the Ministry of Internal Affairs on the banks of the Fontanka River in Saint Petersburg, where he is led though "some mysterious, empty, dimly lit corridors." "I even got a little scared," recalls Milyukov.

Awaiting his arrival is Interior Minister Vyacheslav von Plehve. The minister sits the convict down at a small tea table and starts to talk about Milyukov's most famous academic work, *Sketches in the History of Russian Culture*. "His Majesty instructed me to make your acquaintance and to decide whether to release you based on my impression of you as a person," says Plehve. They discuss Milyukov's background and his expulsion from Moscow University for "political disloyalty." Suddenly Plehve poses the question: "What if I were to offer you the post of education minister?" Milyukov replies that he would refuse. "Why?" asks Plehve, surprised. "Because the education minister is powerless. Now, if Your Excellency were to offer me your own position, that would give me pause for thought," says Milyukov. With that, Plehve ends the meeting, promising to summon the historian again in a few days' time.

A week later Milyukov is again brought to the Ministry of Internal Affairs, but not to the minister's office. He is made to sit in the waiting room. Suddenly Plehve appears, recalls Milyukov, this time "with a quite different demeanor, carefully intoning his words as if addressing a suppliant: 'I have reached a conclusion. I see that you are irreconcilable. But do not wage war with us, or we shall sweep you away.'" Milyukov is released, prohibited only from living in Saint Petersburg. Plehve walks off, without shaking the professor's hand.

"I felt sorry for him," says Milyukov. "He seemed like a Don Quixote chained to an obsolete idea, far more intelligent than the Sisyphus-type task of propping up autocracy that he was duty-bound to perform."

LEADER OF THE OPPOSITION

On 23 May 1902, fifty-two members of zemstvo councils from across the country convene in Moscow. It is unprecedented: the first people's congress in history, and without the prior approval of the Ministry of Internal Affairs at that.

They meet at the home of the head of the Moscow zemstvo, Dmitry Shipov. The hard-nosed representatives' defiance is driven by the fear that the new interior minister, Vyacheslav von Plehve, intends to dismantle the local government system introduced by Alexander II. Everyone remembers the recent report of Finance Minister Witte asserting that the existence of zemstvos makes the state ungovernable. "To be or not to be, that is the question facing the zemstvos," writes Shipov.

Shipov is an unlikely choice for the first ever opposition leader in Russian history. A suburban Moscow landowner, the son of a district marshal of the nobility and a law graduate of Saint Petersburg University, he has been an avid Tolstoyan since youth: both an opponent of violence and a deeply religious man. There is no trace of rebellion in his character.

The participants in the "zemstvo congress" not only discuss procedural issues, but also draft their own agrarian program: peasants are to be afforded the same rights as the other estates, including equal voting rights in the election of the zemstvos; and corporal punishment of the peasantry is to be abolished.

The "zemstvo congress" (as it is designated at the first meeting at Shipov's apartment) is essentially the first opposition convention. Hitherto, all opposition gatherings have been top-secret affairs. But it never even occurs to the zemstvo representatives that they might be anti-government; on the contrary, they plan to discuss the future work in the government committee.

Not all of zemstvo representatives consider themselves oppositionists. Most are guided by the logic that Alexander II's reforms were not seen through to the end: the liberated serfs did not receive land allotments; society gained no influence over the bureaucracy; and freedom of expression was not guaranteed. All these rights, they assert, are the logical continuation of the "great reforms." Their only motivation is to encourage Nicholas II to follow the example of his grandfather and not to listen to officials and reactionaries like Pobedonostsev and Plehve. But the government sees it as a challenge to its authority. In its eyes, political matters are beyond the remit of local self-government.

The zemstvo congress lasts three days. The representatives depart and rumors immediately begin to spread. In late June, Plehve summons Shipov to the Ministry of Internal Affairs to inform him that the emperor is deeply angered by the attempt "to set up an illegal public organization" and that all members of the zemstvo congress are to be "severely reprimanded." At the same time, the minister is unusually courteous. Shipov is quick to assure him that none of the zemstvo representatives has any intention of doing anything illegal. Plehve believes that Shipov is loyal to the idea of autocracy and that the zemstvos are not revolutionary. He advises Shipov: "The zemstvo representatives must show by their deeds that they have no political desire," in which case he, Plehve, will help them achieve what they want and even involve them in the relevant commissions.

Shipov returns to Moscow satisfied and tells his comrades that the government is ready to listen to them. But nothing changes. There is no dialogue between the local zemstvos and the metropolitan authorities, and Shipov soon notices that his letters and those of his closest colleagues arrive unsealed (i.e., the Ministry of Internal Affairs is now brazenly reading their correspondence). The next meeting between Shipov and Plehve takes place six months later, at which time the interior minister does not hide his hostility: "You continue to lead a public organization with the objective of opposing the government. It is clear that we do not see eye to eye."

BATTLING THE CENSOR

In the summer of 1902 a troupe from the Moscow Art Theatre arrives in Saint Petersburg. It is not a tour. The theatre directors are in fact slightly edgy. The small but highly popular Moscow theatre is seeking permission to stage a play by Maxim Gorky. The writer himself is in exile in Arzamas in the province of Nizhny Novgorod, so the director Konstantin Stanislavsky, the administrator Vladimir Nemirovich-Danchenko, and the theatre sponsor Savva Morozov are there without him. Morozov manages to get in touch with Finance Minister Witte, and although the latter once bankrupted Morozov's friend and partner Savva Mamontov, he does not refuse to help.

Morozov has just finished the construction of a building to house his new theatre on Moscow's Kamergersky Lane, and Nemirovich-Danchenko is desperate to open its doors with a staging of Gorky's scandalous new play *The Lower Depths*, passages from which he read in Crimea, about the inhabitants of a shelter for the destitute. Never before has the Russian stage seen a play about the dregs of society, and the theatre directors know the public reaction will be immense. Everyone is deeply disappointed when, instead, Gorky sends them the text of another drama, far less shocking, entitled *The Philistines*.

On the eve of the final run-through, the city authorities post police officers at the theatre entrance to keep out ticketless youngsters. Nemirovich-Danchenko asks the officers to leave, explaining that their uniforms are scaring the audience. The next day the governor makes a compromise: he dispatches police dressed in tuxedos. "The final dress rehearsal was attended by all the 'rulers' of Saint Petersburg—grand dukes and ministers, all kinds of officials, the entire censorship committee, police chiefs and other heads with their wives and families," Stanislavsky recalls. "The theatre was encircled by police; the square in front of the building was patrolled by mounted gendarmes. You'd have thought they were gearing up for battle, not a dress rehearsal."

In the end, the Saint Petersburg censors allow the play to be staged, albeit with some alterations. For example, the words "the merchant Romanov's wife" are replaced with "the merchant Ivanov's wife," according to Stanislavsky, since the surname Romanov openly hinted at the ruling family.

Censorship and suspicion go hand in hand. Savva Morozov's newspaper *Russia*, for instance, was closed down by the Ministry of Internal Affairs for an inoffensive satirical piece by Alexander Amfiteatrov entitled "The Obmanov Family," in which Nicholas II is portrayed as a weak-minded little boy ("Obmanov" is suggestive of "Romanov" and in Russian sounds like "swindler"). Amfiteatrov was exiled and the newspaper banned.

But Savva Morozov is not afraid of the censor and makes every effort to stage Gorky's plays. In the words of his wife, "He is obsessed with Gorky."

Shortly after the premiere of *The Philistines*, Gorky finally puts the finishing touches to the play he sketched out during the Crimean winter, and which failed to impress Tolstoy. He wants to call it "Sunless" or "The Lower Depths of Life," but director Nemirovich-Danchenko suggests shortening it to "The Lower Depths" (in Russian: "Na Dnye"—literally, "At the Bottom").

Having just been allowed to return from Arzamas, the writer arrives in Moscow and reads the new work in the presence of the entire Moscow Art Theatre, including Stanislavsky, Nemirovich-Danchenko, Morozov, and the opera singer Chaliapin, a close friend of Gorky. On reaching the culmination—the death of the main heroine—Gorky, overcome with emotion, starts to cry. Lowering the manuscript, the writer looks his audience in the eye: "By God, it's well written. Even if I say so myself, it's good, isn't it?" Everyone looks at him adoringly. According to the actress Maria Andreyeva, the whole theatre loves him, no one more so than Stanislavsky. "No worries," Chaliapin reassures him. "Keep reading, there's a good chap."

Staging a play about homeless people is not easy, since no one in the theatre knows how the characters should speak or behave. So Stanislavsky hires the reporter Vladimir Gilyarovsky, known for his portrayal of beggars and vagrants in the seminal work *Moscow and Muscovites*, to give them a guided tour of the most depraved area of Moscow—Khitrovsky Market.

The excursion comes to a dramatic conclusion. The actors treat the vagabonds to vodka and sausage, but the feast unexpectedly descends into ugliness: "They turned purple with rage, lost control and ran wild. They started shouting and swearing. Someone grabbed a bottle, another a stool, and they started swinging at each other," Stanislavsky recalls. "At that moment, in a thundering voice, Gilyarovsky hurled a torrent of invective of such syntactical complexity that it stunned not only us, but the tramps, too. Dumbfounded and delighted, they were in a state of aesthetic rapture. The mood soon changed. Mad laughter and applause broke out for such a brilliant piece of swearing, which saved us from harm or even death."

On 18 December 1902, the new building of the Moscow Art Theatre stages the long-awaited premiere. The cast includes some major stars: Stanislavsky himself, Chekhov's wife (Olga Knipper), and the young actress Maria Andreyeva. Public interest is also piqued by the fact that Gorky is officially banned at all imperial (i.e., state) theatres.

Andreyeva, the *femme fatale* of the Moscow Art Theatre, is having an affair with the co-owner of the theatre Savva Morozov, yet she is also passionately jealous of Olga Knipper, the theatre's prima donna and the wife of Anton Chekhov. The status of sponsor's mistress is much lower than wife of living legend. "As an actress, Andreyeva is useful, but Knipper is indispensable," Stanislavsky characterizes his two stars. Andreyeva cannot accept being second best.

Like many high-society ladies, Andreyeva has a curious streak and keeps up with the latest fads, in particular the new-fangled Marxism. She is even acquainted with Vladimir Ulyanov, the editor of the Munich-based *Spark.*

The unprecedented success of *The Lower Depths* turns Gorky into a major celebrity in Moscow. Street sellers tout calendars bearing his picture. Stanislavsky remembers the endless applause when the author was invited on stage after the performance, unprepared for such an ovation: "It was very funny to watch him appear on stage for the first time, with a cigarette hanging between his lips. He just stood there, smiling with embarrassment, unaware that he was supposed to remove his cigarette and bow to the audience."

The author is congratulated by Andreyeva, known as "Marusya" to her friends. She kisses him on stage, which leaves him totally at a loss.

Wherever he goes, Gorky is met by crowds of admirers. The writer, according to Stanislavsky, is publicity-shy, all the while picking at his moustache and straightening his hair. "Brothers!" he addresses his fans, smiling sheepishly. "You know, it's all a bit awkward, to be honest. . . . Why are you staring at me?! I'm not an opera singer or a ballerina." The situation is particularly tricky when Gorky appears in public with Chekhov, whom nobody recognizes in the flesh. Gorky resorts to shouting: "Look, I'm not a corpse fished out of a river. Stop rubbernecking me!"

The once-penniless Gorky is not only Russia's most successful writer, but also its richest. Together with his friend Pyatnitsky, he invents a new literary business model. They create a partnership called Znaniye ("Knowledge"), through which writers receive practically all the proceeds from their works, instead of a small percentage.

It is a revolutionary way of paying writers. For his first book, the young Leonid Andreyev receives 5,642 roubles 71 kopecks[*] from Znaniye, instead of the 300 roubles[†] offered by the publisher Sytin. The enormous sum instantly turns the poor journalist into a wealthy man of letters.

As a popular author himself, and the founder of Znaniye, Gorky earns more than anyone else. However, he elects to give most of his fortune to his revolutionary pals.

Relations inside the Moscow Art Theatre, however, are less than ideal. Savva Morozov, one of the theatre's shareholders, devotes all his time to it, risking altercations with his wife in the process, yet the company still treats him as a rich patron who dabbles in art without understanding it. Olga Knipper, the leading lady, writes to her husband: "Savva Morozov is in the habit of going to all the rehearsals. He sits up at night, fretting. We joke

---

[*] About $74,390 in 2017.
[†] About $3,950 in 2017.

about it. I think soon he'll be making his stage debut with us, only no one knows in what role." Morozov doesn't notice, but his wife picks up on it. Zinaida is offended by the troupe for treating both her husband and her as a source of money, without any respect. The actor Vishnevsky, for instance, publicly accuses her of spending too much money on outfits, instead of giving it to the theatre.

The worst thing for Zinaida is that her husband does little to conceal his affair with Maria Andreyeva. But Zinaida is mistaken in believing that Andreyeva seduced her husband at the behest of the theatre. It was her own idea, and Stanislavsky for one is deeply annoyed by it. "Your relationship with Savva Timofeevich [Morozov]," the director writes to Andreyeva, "is the kind that ruins lives and forces people to sacrifice themselves. Do you know what sacrilege you are committing? You publicly boast in front of strangers that the painfully jealous Zinaida Grigorievna [Morozova] wants you to control her husband and that he is investing his money at your insistence. . . . If you could look at yourself, you would agree with me."

But prudence is not one of Marusya's virtues. She values Morozov— quite literally, using his money to finance both the theatre and the Social Democratic Party. But once she falls in love with another, she dumps her rich suitor without a second thought. Moreover, her new lover is Morozov's "obsession," Maxim Gorky.

In autumn 1903, after the premiere of *The Lower Depths*, Gorky reaches the peak of his fame. It is also the moment when he offers his long-estranged wife Ekaterina Peshkova a divorce. But it does not happen, and officially they remain man and wife. Gorky's letters to Ekaterina are the simplest and sincerest texts of his literary heritage, describing his innermost cares and secrets.

At a New Year's party at the Moscow Art Theatre in December 1903, he and Andreyeva announce that they intend to live together, despite Andreyeva also being married and the mother of a son.

Gorky's "engagement" gift for his new live-in wife is the text of his latest poem, "The Man." Andreyeva hands the manuscript to Gorky's assistant Alexander Tikhonov: "My dear, hide this somewhere safe. I've nowhere to put it." But the text ends up in the hands of Savva Morozov, who reads the inscription: "The author of this poem has such a strong heart that an actress could make the heels of her shoes from it."

"A New Year's gift! In love, are you?" says Morozov, glancing at the happy face of his beloved Andreyeva, recalls Tikhonov in his memoirs. Morozov takes out his gold cigarette case and starts to light a cigarette—at the wrong end.

Even when Marusya leaves Morozov for Gorky, she does not lose influence over the tycoon. Morozov continues to take care of her, and still finances the Social Democrats. Nor does he lose his admiration for Gorky. Remarkably, Morozov is perhaps the only one who remains by Gorky and Andreyeva's side.

Back at the theatre Andreyeva is unhappy. She is furious that all the best roles go to Knipper instead of her. She first threatens to leave and then announces that she is taking a long vacation. "You are renouncing your privileged position, to which the finest provincial actresses aspire, and are voluntarily joining their ranks," Stanislavsky writes to her in February 1904.

Andreyeva ignores the director's admonitions. She and Gorky have plans to set up their own theatre, using the money of the eternally loyal Morozov. She even begins to lure actors from Stanislavsky's troupe, but to no avail. The Moscow Art Theatre's top-drawer performers stay put.

"HIS NARROW-MINDED VIEWS INFURIATE ME"

Having set up a newspaper in Munich, the Marxists return to the idea of creating a political party, piqued by the fact that their competitors—the Narodniks, rebranded the Socialist-Revolutionaries—have long had one. But whereas the SRs have managed to unite their disparate circles, the Marxists' wild ambitions cause incessant infighting. Both Plekhanov and the editorial board of *Spark* direct all their oratory at crushing their archrival Peter Struve, who has recently penned the RSDLP's manifesto. The dogmatists reproach him for abandoning pure Marxism in favor of wishy-washy liberalism. Most zealous of all in his criticism of Struve is his long-time friend and the editor of *Spark*, Vladimir Ulyanov. Arriving in Munich, he adopts yet another pseudonym, changing his *nom de plume* from "Petrov" to "Frey."

The exiled Marxists begin to write their own party program, adding fuel to the fire. Plekhanov rejects Frey's draft manifesto, declaring it to be unsatisfactory and telling the editorial board of *Spark* to make sweeping changes. The ambitious Plekhanov and the equally ambitious Ulyanov take a personal dislike to each other. "I don't write to Frey. His narrow-minded views infuriate me," Plekhanov informs his followers.

Frey ignores the advice of his comrades on the *Spark* editorial board, just as he once ignored the criticism of the Narodniks. He insists that his texts are to be published without amendment. This enrages not only Plekhanov, who is far away in Geneva, but also Martov. The other members of the editorial board even hatch a plan to expel their obstinate colleague, because he is impossible to work with. But he gets wind of their intentions, and prepares a counterattack.

That is the frame of mind in which the Russian Marxists gather for their first meeting, which they call the "second congress of the RSDLP," a nod to the "first congress" six years earlier in Minsk, at which all nine participants were arrested.

The Marxist congress in Brussels is attended by forty-three people. The chairman is, of course, Plekhanov. One of his deputies is the editor of *Spark*, real name Ulyanov, pen name Frey, but now going by his latest (and last) pseudonym, Lenin. The meeting immediately turns into a squabble, causing the Belgian authorities to politely ask the Russian revolutionaries to leave the country. They promptly set sail for England, and a week later their slanging match continues in London.

One question lies at the heart of the dispute: Who will be in charge of the party newspaper *Spark*? Lenin proposes to reduce the editorial board to three members, and receives the unexpected support of Plekhanov, who sees it as an opportunity to weaken Martov by excluding his supporters from the board. If the editorial board consists solely of Martov, Lenin, and Plekhanov, the latter will establish editorial control as the exclusive arbiter in the unending quarrels between Martov and Lenin.

Since Plekhanov is the party leader and enjoys real authority, most of the congress participants support him. The decision is made. Martov is outraged and incites all the now ex-members of the editorial board to walk out of the congress in protest at the lack of trust in him.

This petty altercation will change the course of world history. No one knows it at the time, but it marks a split no less momentous than that between Sunni and Shia, or Catholic and Orthodox.

The Marxists elect their first-ever central committee, the majority of which is made up of supporters of Plekhanov and Lenin. As a result, they adopt the name "Bolsheviks," from the Russian word for "majority," leaving the disgruntled Martov and friends with the pejorative label "Mensheviks," from the word for "minority." Both terms will soon become known all over the world.

The schism in the party is not due to ideological differences, but personal animosity and three uncompromising egos: the authoritarian Plekhanov, the touchy Martov, and the irascible Lenin. Plekhanov's support for Lenin is only to dampen Martov's influence over *Spark*. Martov's resentfulness and Lenin's venom stymie any chance of compromise.

Despite everything, at first no one believes the split is permanent. The words "Bolshevik" and "Menshevik" are not yet in vogue. Lenin calls his opponents "Martovites" or simply the "minority," while Martov terms Lenin's supporters "Leninists."

Many do not take the quarrel seriously. Plekhanov, used to the antics of the hysterical Martov and the insufferable Lenin, is sure that he can reconcile them.

A POLITICAL SOJOURN

In the summer of 1903, at the precise moment when the Marxists are gathering in Brussels, their former comrade Peter Struve is paid a visit by some new friends from Russia. Struve and his sponsor Dmitry Zhukovsky have invited twenty people: ten members of the zemstvo assemblies and ten representatives of the "creative" intelligentsia.

The trip to Europe is no vacation, far from it. They plan to set up Russia's first liberal opposition party. Zhukovsky outlines the route they are to take: on 2 August, they meet in the Swiss city of Schaffhausen, near the Rhine Falls, a popular tourist trap. Having viewed the waterfall, the liberal travelers head for the resort town of Singen in Germany. The next day they move to Radolfzell, where an entire restaurant is reserved for them. The whole day is spent in lively conversation. On the third day, they move to a third resort: Konstanz on the Bodensee (a.k.a. Lake Constance).

The group is being as surreptitious as possible, with good reason. Unlike the revolutionary Marxists, they have everything to lose. They are not émigrés. They live and work in Russia and do not want to lose their positions in society. Nor are they revolutionaries: "We should be seen as custodians of law and order," says Prince Dolgorukov, a member of the Moscow zemstvo assembly.

The liberals in Russia have always been moderate opponents of the authorities, yet never before have they consolidated as a political party. Three dinners at three resorts in the area of Lake Constance in Germany in the summer of 1903 change all that. The trip is effectively the first congress of Russian liberals, who, still averse to establishing a party, agree to set up an alliance of independent circles known as the "Union of Liberation."

The most debated issue is the question of how to treat the other oppositionists, namely the Marxists and the Socialist-Revolutionaries. "We have no enemies on the left," insists the group's self-appointed leader, the fifty-nine-year-old Ivan Petrunkevich.

Most of them want to unite all opponents of the regime, which is why they favor the term "union"—to allow other dissidents to join them without leaving their own parties. Struve does not concur. A former "comrade" and a target of the Marxist press, he believes that negotiations with them are futile: "It's very easy to start a debate, and very tempting, too. But once started, it cannot be stopped. You will be accused of getting cold feet, of losing the argument. Moreover, we are unable to deliver as much verbal abuse as our opponents, especially the Social Democrats."

The congress draws to a close with the feeling that history is on its side. "Ideologically and organizationally, the 'Union of Liberation' is set to unite the broad strata of the Russian population aspiring to freedom and independence," writes Struve after the meeting. "Ours is not a revolutionary circle, but an organization that resides ineradicably in the minds of all proponents of liberation and manifests itself in their efforts to accomplish, by word and deed, the great national task of the age."

WAR AND GERMANY

It is striking that the summer of 1903 sees so many gatherings of distinguished Russians in Germany. The members of the newly created Union of Liberation, sojourning on the shores of Lake Constance, and the editors of *Spark*, a stone's throw away in Munich, are not the only ones there. Three hundred kilometers to the north, Emperor Nicholas II and his young wife are spending September in the city of Darmstadt at the home of Alexandra's brother, Ernst Ludwig, Grand Duke of Hesse.

In Saint Petersburg, meanwhile, the talk is of war with Germany. The decision has already been made that, in the event of hostilities between the two empires, Grand Duke Nicholas, the great-uncle of the tsar, will command the German front, while the war minister, General Kuropatkin, will take charge of the Austro-Hungarian front. The two commanders have even managed to fall out with each other during the preparations for this hypothetical war: the grand duke is demanding a new railway to western Russia to supply troops with food; War Minister Kuropatkin is foot-dragging.

This does not prevent the imperial family from going on vacation. In late July, Nicholas II learns that his second cousin, Kaiser Wilhelm, is offended that the Russian tsar has been in Germany for so long without arranging a meeting. Finally, Wilhelm arrives to Darmstadt himself to visit Nicholas.

As usual, Wilhelm urges his second cousin Nicky to be more proactive in the Far East and live up to his provisional title of "Admiral of the Pacific Ocean." The Russian tsar likes the idea. Success in China has emboldened him. He craves glory, if not the hassle of actual expansion in the Far East, and, according to Finance Minister Sergei Witte, begins to ponder the idea of conquering India or Turkey.

Economic expansion around the Far East governorship is already underway, in which regard the main advocate of "Yellow Russia," Alexander Bezobrazov, enjoys the total trust of the emperor. Negotiations with Japan, which is still smarting from Russia's occupation of the Liaodong Peninsula in China, are limping on. No one takes the Japanese seriously. The country is viewed disdainfully as small and backward, unable to vie with Russia, even theoretically. Saint Petersburg acts in accordance with this prejudice, taking months to respond to Tokyo's communiqués.

Russia's insouciance is matched by Japan's anger. Aware of the talks, Japanese society is offended by the fact that the Japanese authorities have to negotiate with a minor official by the name of Alekseyev, who is the tsar's governor-general in the Far East.

Witte recalls how the naval officer Alekseyev was said to have attained such a high post. As a young man, he allegedly accompanied Grand Duke Alexis (son of Alexander II, uncle of Nicholas II) on a trip around the world. It is said that on one occasion the grand duke sparked a drunken brawl in a Marseilles bordello and was ordered to appear before the authorities. His place was taken by Admiral Alekseyev, who claimed that the fault was his and that the grand duke had been mistakenly summoned due to confusion between the names "Alexis" and "Alekseyev." The officer was fined, but gained the eternal gratitude of the grand duke, who took command of the Russian Imperial Navy in 1881. With the patronage of the emperor's uncle, Alekseyev's career is assured. His first post of governor of the Far East is followed by the position of commander-in-chief, despite being unable to ride and afraid of horses, quips Witte in his memoirs.

"PHEW"

At the end of August 1904 Nicholas II unexpectedly summons Finance Minister Witte to Peterhof, after a long period of disfavor. The emperor informs Witte of his decision to "promote" him to the position of chairman of the Committee of Ministers. Witte thanks the tsar, but says that he will be of greater service in his current job. Everyone knows that the chairman of the Committee of Ministers is a ceremonial figure, with no influence in government matters. The Committee of Ministers rarely convenes as a body, each member reporting to the emperor individually. A transfer from the important role of finance minister to the chair of the Committee of Ministers is tantamount to retirement. This is clearly what Nicholas has in mind.

After his conversation with Nicholas, the out-of-favor minister goes to the tsar's mother to ask her to intercede on his behalf. The Dowager Empress Maria Feodorovna consoles Witte, saying that her husband Alexander III had been very fond of him, but that she can do nothing for him.

Next, Witte endeavors to find out what the emperor actually said to members of his entourage when discussing Witte's departure. He is told that Nicholas heaved a sigh of relief and emitted one syllable: "Phew."

Witte turns to his memoirs to express his side of the story, writing that he was removed purely for his views on the Far East, namely his supposed opposition to war and insistence on talks with the Japanese.

Deeply insulted by his transfer to a ceremonial role, Witte is stung even more by the fact that not a single colleague stood up for him. But his greatest antipathy he reserves for the emperor himself. "Deceitfulness, tight-lipped mendacity, the inability to say yes or no, optimism grounded in fear—these are all undesirable qualities in a sovereign," he writes about Nicholas. "A tsar who lacks a royal character cannot give happiness to his country."

Enmity between the thirty-five-year-old Nicholas II and the fifty-four-year-old Witte is inevitable. The minister lacks all respect for the tsar. Well aware of this, Nicholas does not trust the ambitious minister. Their fractious relationship will play a crucial role in the history of Russia.

No less important to the country's future is the animosity between two other men. The age gap is similar, hence a comparable lack of trust and respect. They are the forty-six-year-old Georgy Plekhanov and the thirty-two-year-old Vladimir Ulyanov (Lenin). The "elder" of the Russian émigré community looks askance at the ambitious upstart, who shows a disturbing lack of reverence.

In August 1903 Plekhanov takes the side of Ulyanov-Lenin in his wrangle with Martov. When a few months later he tries to reconcile the implacable enemies, it turns out that Martov is not the only one capable of tantrums. Plekhanov tries to restore the editorial board of *Spark* to its former composition, but this time it is Lenin who slams the door in his face. "Plekhanov has betrayed us. The feeling in our camp is bitter. Everyone is outraged," he writes to a comrade. "I have left the editorial board. It might be the end of *Spark*. The crisis is full-on and ominous. The struggle for the editorial board has been irretrievably lost due to Plekhanov's treachery."

Such rhetoric is characteristic of revolutionaries: any opponent is immediately branded a traitor. Like the reformed liberal Struve before him,

Plekhanov feels Lenin's wrath for having reached out to Martov. Lenin abandons *Spark* once and for all, and as of November 1903 the newspaper is edited by Martov and his team. Lenin, it seems, has lost. His former comrades mock his ambitions, calling him "Little Bonaparte." Stung by it all, he plots his revenge.

THE LAST BALL

In January 1904 Nicholas II arrives in Saint Petersburg, and the ball season kicks off "as if nothing had happened," writes Witte. At one of them, the new chairman of the Committee of Ministers is approached (not for the first time) by the Japanese envoy to Russia, who requests that Witte exert pressure on the Russian Foreign Ministry, which is taking an indecently long time to respond to Tokyo's latest missive, especially given the gravity of the situation. Witte goes to the foreign minister, Count Vladimir Lamsdorf, but the latter simply shrugs: "I can't help with the negotiations. I'm not the one in charge."*

On the evening of 26 January, the Winter Palace hosts a grand ball. It opens with a polonaise from Tchaikovsky's opera *Eugene Onegin*, based on the poem by Alexander Pushkin. The ball is attended by War Minister Kuropatkin, who is popular with the press, but not with the *beau monde*. Kuropatkin does not have an aristocratic title, for which reason no one at the ball deigns to talk to him.

Nevertheless, attired in his general's tunic, Kuropatkin cuts a fine figure, while the tsar, dressed in the red uniform of a colonel, barely stands out from the crowd. "Nicholas II does not feel like the lord of the realm, more like a guest performing some kind of duty," recalls Captain Alexei Ignatiev, a young officer, who is "conducting the ball" (i.e., giving instructions to gentlemen on the dance floor not to fall out of step).

The hall is decorated with palm trees in tubs, around which tables are laid for dinner. Wrapped in felt and straw for the journey, the palm trees have been brought specially to the Winter Palace from Saint Petersburg's Botanical and Tauride Gardens. "Petersburg's high society is satiated with luxury," says Ignatiev. "If there aren't baskets of roses, carnations and lilacs all the way from Nice, it doesn't count as a ball."

---

*In the early twenty-first century the Ministry of Foreign Affairs also performs a secondary role in everything connected with foreign policy negotiations: all the crucial decisions are made by the Presidential Administration and Security Council. Russian diplomats can only implement the decisions, but not influence the situation themselves.

Yet this will be the last ball of Imperial Russia. The next day, news breaks that Japan has attacked Port Arthur without warning. All soirees are called off during wartime. A few months later the royal family will move from the Winter Palace to Tsarskoye Selo, thirty-five kilometers from the capital, where they lead a reclusive existence. Imperial balls are consigned to history.

The news of the attack on Port Arthur shocks the recently waltzing officers: "Can a foreign navy really attack us without a declaration of war?" Ignatiev recalls the rhetorical question on everyone's lips. "It seemed so unbelievably monstrous that some were inclined to downplay it as just a serious incident, not the outbreak of war."

The next morning the capital's officer corps convenes once more at the Winter Palace. After a prayer service, the emperor appears wearing a modest infantry uniform and, according to Ignatiev's memoirs, "bearing his usual indifferent look . . . only paler and more agitated than usual." Wearing one white glove, he runs the other through his fingers. "We declare war on Japan," he intones dispassionately. A loud "hurrah" rings out among the officers. Yet Ignatiev notes that the cry is somewhat restrained. It transpires that enthusiasm for the war is low. Very few people volunteer to serve, and those that do see it as a "tour of duty, almost an errand." The lack of volunteers is such that a month after the outbreak of war Plehve issues a decree promising to pardon prisoners if they join the army.

There are court rumors that, for Nicholas II, war with Japan is a personal vendetta. In 1891, on a trip to Asia, the then-heir to the Russian throne visited Japan. In Otsu, a local nationalist fanatic attacked him with a sabre. The head wound was not serious, but the future emperor required stitches and returned home immediately.

Government ministers use the war to try to win the tsar's favor. Interior Minister Plehve organizes patriotic rallies across the country, while War Minister Kuropatkin goes for broke, requesting a transfer to the front line. "You know what, that's probably a good idea," says Nicholas II, who is normally disinclined to take advice from public officials, including his ministers, whom he views as competitors.

Witte writes that Plehve's patriotic rallies are not popular. Yet Plehve remains the most powerful official in the country. "Alexei Nikolaevich, you do not understand Russia's internal situation. To contain the revolution, we need a short victorious war," Plehve says to Kuropatkin, according to Witte (other sources say that Plehve even used the word *voinishka*, the diminutive of "war," basically meaning a "game of toy soldiers"). According to the memoirs of one of his subordinates, during a meeting of the Ministry of

Internal Affairs, Plehve once lashed out at his deputy Lopukhin for questioning the chances of success: "Don't you understand the arithmetic? Which population is greater, 50 million or 150 million?"

It is not known for sure whether Plehve actually uttered the words "short victorious war," but the phrase became a meme in Russian politics. It is possible that Witte came up with it, since it first appeared in print only after Plehve's death. Whatever the case, despite the fiasco of the "short victorious war" against Japan, the concept is still alive and well a century later.*

The Russian-Japanese War is one of the first examples in world history of full-scale information warfare. The entire international press of the day publishes cartoons of Nicholas II and the Russian bear mauling the hapless Japan. Especially zealous is the reaction across the Atlantic. Never before has the American press reacted so sharply to a war in which the United States was not a participant. In this instance, the American audience is invited to sympathize exclusively with the Japanese.

The Western press is full of cartoons, the nature of which changes over the course of the military operation: first the images are of a huge Russian bear (or, oddly, an octopus) attacking little Japan, but later in the campaign, Nicholas II is dressed as a sumo wrestler, hopelessly trying to withstand his far-heavier Japanese opponent.

The Russian press, meanwhile, call the Japanese "monkeys" (the actual word used is "macaques"), and Witte asserts that it was the tsar himself who first used the derogatory term in his handwritten resolutions, saying that they should be "crushed." The word is picked up by the newspapers, especially state-funded ones.

Patriotism infects even Russian political exiles in Europe. Pavel Milyukov recalls that on 10 February 1904, the day when the first telegrams about the Japanese attack on Port Arthur arrive in England, he goes to Brighton to visit the "patriarch" of the Russian émigré community, the anarchist's anarchist Peter Kropotkin. The sixty-one-year-old Kropotkin is incensed by the perfidy of the Japanese. "I was taken aback," says Milyukov. "How could the enemy of Russian politics and state-sponsored war in general be such a flag-waver?"

The jingoistic backdrop is so strong that Nicholas II, as mentioned, decides to send the media-friendly Kuropatkin to the front line, appointing him commander of the army. Yet the emperor employs his usual system of checks and balances by keeping the Far East governor Alekseyev in

---

*The phrase "short victorious war" has been used to describe Russia's twenty-first-century conflicts in Georgia, Ukraine, and Syria.

position as commander-in-chief. In other words, there are two commanders, whose powers are not clearly delineated.

Captain Ignatiev, whose most important duty used to be conducting balls at the Winter Palace, goes to the Far East as a volunteer. According to his memoirs, the army is totally unprepared: "All peacetime items of military clothing and equipment turned out to be useless in conditions of war." The uniforms and tunics are too narrow for soldiers in the field. There are no pockets. Everything is white, unlike the khaki worn by the Japanese (or, incidentally, the British). Russian officers on the battlefield are easy targets. The overcoats are not warm, and the boots are thin-soled, tear easily, and have no grip. The quality of the military uniforms is such, writes Ignatiev, that after six months of war the entire Russian army resembles a "bunch of ragamuffins."

Food is also a problem. The Russian food industry does not produce tinned products. Rich officers can afford to buy British goods, but not the rank-and-filers.

The quality of training is not much better, either. Captain Ignatiev says that even he, a military academy graduate, heard the sound of a bursting grenade for the first time there in Manchuria. Officer training is strictly old school. Russia's military minds still look to the Napoleonic Wars and long to relive them. According to the field manual, for instance, rifle fire should be used only when approaching the enemy in advance of a bayonet charge; at long range, cartridges are to be used sparingly.

Most of the soldiers sent to fight against Japan are illiterate peasants; the rest are largely from the empire's Far Eastern populations of Buryats and Yakuts, who do not speak Russian. Military operations are carried out on Chinese soil, and the locals are often less than pleased about being occupied by the Russian army.

"The more I gazed at this town [Mukden], the less I understood: what are we doing here in Manchuria?" reflects Ignatiev in his memoirs. "What did we want to trade? Who were we trying to civilize? Any Chinese *fanza* is more spacious and cleaner than a Russian *izba* [both are types of hut]. The cleanliness of the local streets and courtyards would be the envy of our towns and cities. And what bridges they have! Made of stone and decorated with ancient sculptures of gray granite! They speak of a civilization that dates back not centuries, but millennia."

Army HQ is in disarray. The two commanders, Alekseyev and Kuropatkin, cannot stand each other and spend their time mud-slinging and telegraphing Saint Petersburg with their grievances. Alekseyev does not like Kuropatkin's retreat tactics, and the emperor agrees. He, too, believes that Russian soldiers should only advance victoriously, and says so in his dispatches to the front line.

Nicholas II spends almost the whole of 1904 traveling around the country exhorting his troops before their departure to the front, handing out religious icons left, right, and center. Witte recalls a "joke" doing the rounds at the time: "We will attack the Japanese with images of our saints, they will slaughter us with bullets and bombs."

On 31 March, two months after the outbreak of war, the *Petropavlovsk* battleship is blown up by a mine, killing around six hundred and fifty sailors. Only eighty survive, including the wounded Grand Duke Kirill, another cousin of Nicholas II. Twenty years after the revolution and the death of the tsar, he will proclaim himself the Russian emperor in exile.

Russian society reacts badly to the military debacle. No one expected the war to be such a complicated affair. The lack of supplies and decent medical care for the wounded is no secret in the capital cities.

In February 1904, the zemstvos decide to help the troops by collecting funds to provide assistance for the wounded and the families of those killed. The charity initiative is led by the head of the Tula zemstvo Prince Georgy Lvov, a neighbor and family friend of Leo Tolstoy and a die-hard Tolstoyan. He follows his mentor's example: twenty years earlier, when central Russia was gripped by famine, Tolstoy collected donations, traveled to the afflicted regions, and set up soup kitchens. Lvov does likewise. Tolstoy himself (still alive) condemns the war and supports the actions of Lvov and other zemstvos.

The zemstvo fundraising organization marks the start of Prince Lvov's political career, which burns brighter than that of most of his colleagues. In 1917 he will head the provisional government of the fledgling Russian state. In 1904, however, he is unknown and very moderate in his views.

Plehve is extremely wary, believing that Lvov and the other zemstvo leaders are above their station. By law, they are obliged to see to their districts, while the war with Japan is a political issue. Hence, the zemstvos are encroaching on the power of the state. Plehve issues a government order prohibiting assistance to the wounded without the prior approval of the Ministry of Internal Affairs. It even prohibits any discussion of the matter without permission. Prince Lvov, who has only just met with Nicholas II, in April 1904, and received the emperor's gratitude for his charity work, is outraged by Plehve's order. He calls upon the zemstvos to disobey it.

The interior minister's war is not actually with Japan, but with the zemstvos; he believes them to be the source of the revolutionary contagion affecting Russian society. Prince Lvov's act of defiance is a Rubicon moment. The general leader of all the Russian zemstvos, Dmitry Shipov, is targeted. In April

1904, he is once more elected as the head of the Moscow provincial zemstvo. But according to the law, the result of the election must be approved by the Ministry of Internal Affairs. Plehve promptly vetoes Shipov's candidacy.

There is uproar. From all across the provinces, letters of support for Shipov pour in. The wave of protest spreads around the country; even the remotest district councils communicate their support for Shipov and Lvov boldly in black and white. It is not the reaction of a "small group of troublemakers," as Plehve believes, but something rather more significant.

In pursuit of the dissidents, the interior minister wants to exile the leader of the Yaroslavl zemstvo, Prince Dmitry Shakhovskoy, a known liberal and publisher of an influential local newspaper. The decision to expel him is not approved by the tsar "out of respect for [Shakhovskoy's] ancestors." Instead, Plehve summons the prince to Saint Petersburg and gives him an official rebuke, warning that exile awaits if he continues his activities.

The journalist Ariadna Tyrkova, a childhood friend of Nadezhda Krupskaya and Nina Struve, is employed by Shakhovskoy's magazine. She recalls that the publisher returns after a conversation with the minister in a rage: "Plehve should be killed," he says.

PRAYERS, TEA, AND DANCING

After Zubatov's exile to Vladimir, Georgy Gapon loses his protector, forcing him to act independently. Using money from his former patron, he rents an apartment in the suburb of Saint Petersburg and sets up a workers' club. Tea and mineral water are served from seven o'clock in the evening until midnight; spirits are prohibited. On Wednesdays and Saturdays workers gather to discuss books and articles, sometimes Gapon lectures on politics and economics (as he sees them), and every meeting begins and ends with a prayer. His club is called the Assembly of Russian Factory Workers of Saint Petersburg. Naturally, he is elected its chairman.

Gapon decides once more to gamble with the authorities, fearing that his unsanctioned tearoom will be closed. He goes to the capital's governor to register his venture and gain support. Oddly enough, he gets it and even receives sixty roubles* a month for books and newspapers, provided that the workers only read conservative publications.

Still working as a prison priest, Gapon devotes all his free time to the club. He is very pleased with it: discussions are held before dawn, and some

---

*About $791 in 2017.

workers go straight from the tearoom to work. "I felt that my life was no longer aimless. I had no time to think about myself. For my prison work I received a salary of around 2,000 roubles* [per year] and gave it to the cause. My clothes were in rags, but I did not care. Opening the assembly, I told the workers that the foundation of our union would be an epoch in the history of the labor movement in Russia, and that through their efforts and exertions they would become an instrument of salvation for themselves and their comrades," he recalls.

Gapon soon quarrels with Metropolitan Anthony of Saint Petersburg, his patron, who first restored him to the academy and then, after Zubatov's exile, found him a new job as a priest in a prison church. Anthony does not approve of Gapon's organization and wants to remove him as chairman.

"I know," says Anthony, "that they want to arrange musical evenings with dancing. How can you, a priest and a member of the church, have anything to do with such frivolity?"

"I think that's exactly what church members should be doing," retorts Gapon. "You can't deny that life for our workers is terrible. They have no joy, only drunkenness. They need healthy entertainment if we want them to be sober and morally minded. Almost the entire intelligentsia with influence over the people has left the church. If we don't start helping the masses, they will leave us too."

Metropolitan Anthony is unpersuaded. No one from the clergy comes to the workers' meetings. Gapon seems to get on much better with the police and city authorities than he does with the priesthood. As proof, the new mayor of Saint Petersburg, Ivan Fullon, pays a visit to the tearoom and even poses for a photograph with Gapon and the workers. The police have no doubt about Gapon's loyalty, for which reason he is offered a large sum to run the organization and open up branches throughout the capital. "I accepted the money to avert suspicion. It was invested anonymously in books for the organization. The money had been taken from the pocket of the people and had to be returned somehow to its rightful owners," writes Gapon.

A DEATH WARRANT

Meanwhile, Gregory Gershuni is awaiting trial at Shlisselburg Fortress outside Saint Petersburg, the central prison for dangerous political criminals. For several months, he has been agonizing over how to behave at his trial

---

*About $26,367 in 2017.

when faced with his betrayers. In February 1904, after nine months of solitary confinement, he is finally allowed to see his lawyer Karabchevsky:

"Is Plehve still in power? Still alive?"

"Yes. But there's more important news. Do you know that Russia is at war?"

"War?! With whom?"

"Japan. Our cruisers have been destroyed. We're facing defeat."

"Like in Crimea? Port Arthur is another Sevastopol?"*

"Looks like it."

"Is the country gripped by patriotism and rallying around the 'almighty leader'?"

"Kind of. But it's largely inflated. The war is unpopular. No one expected it and no one wants it."

The trial begins on 18 February. Gershuni is in a tormented state: "My soul was seething . . . with desire to poison the audience with words of popular hatred. . . . But scrutinizing the room, I saw not a single intelligent, thoughtful face. Are they really enemies? . . . Nothing but cold indifference. . . . The so-called 'judges' were bored and doodling pictures of horses." †

The trial lasts for eight days. Grigoriev and Kachura testify against Gershuni, who remains silent.

There in the courtroom is an unlikely onlooker, Grand Duke Andrei, another of the tsar's long line of cousins. He is the only member of the royal family to attend, simply out of curiosity and to unearth the terrorist movement's motivation. Gershuni is annoyed by the grand duke, who "sat there the whole week constantly sucking sweets of some sort," recalls the defendant. But Grand Duke Andrei is profoundly interested in the hearing and afterwards holds a lengthy discussion with the lawyer Karabchevsky. "I realized that they are not villains and believe sincerely in their actions," says the grand duke.

On the eighth day, the court delivers its verdict: death. Three weeks later the sentence is commuted to life imprisonment. Yet Gershuni is horrified: "The whole of my being, my thoughts and feelings, after such dreadful suffering, were trained in one direction and then suddenly swung

---

*Russian Empire lost the Crimean War (October 1853 to February 1856) to the alliance of Great Britain, France, Ottoman Empire, and Sardinia. The crucial defeat of Russia was the battle of Sevastopol, the major Russian port in Crimea. Russian society was greatly impressed by that humiliation; the Emperor Nicholas I supposedly committed suicide after the defeat became inevitable; after that his successor, Alexander II, decided that Russia needs reforms.

† Russian judges in the twenty-first century demonstrate a similar level of interest in trials. Alexei Navalny in his last plea at the trial on the "Yves Rocher" case in 2014 described the judge and prosecutors as "looking down at the table."

.

around. . . . To go from death to life is perhaps even more difficult than to go from life to death."

The trial of Gershuni is monitored closely by his party comrades in Geneva. His arrest has posed the SRs a question: Who will now lead the militant organization? Gotz wants to take up the cause and delegate the running of the newspaper *Revolutionary Russia* and other organizational issues to Chernov, his assistant. But the remaining members are against, for Gotz's health has deteriorated after two months in a damp Neapolitan prison.

Gotz longs to return to Russia: "I cannot stand this life," he says. "You are depriving me of the joy of martyrdom on the scaffold. Dying here peacefully in a comfortable bed is a wretched fate that I do not deserve."

Back when he was in charge, Gershuni also believed that Gotz belonged in Nice, where he would be of more use to the cause. Gershuni's departing words were: "If worst comes to worst and I am arrested, the militant organization should be headed by my assistant Yevgeny Azef."

Worst has come to worst. Viktor Chernov recalls that Gotz was extremely anxious about the fate of the party and the militant organization. For him, Azef's leadership is a "leap in the dark." He urges his closest comrades to proceed on the assumption that there is a traitor in the party and that everyone must be verified without prejudice: "All for one, and one for all," he is fond of saying. Gotz senses the presence of a traitor, but does not suspect anyone in particular. Moreover, he cannot suspect Azef, for he was appointed "interim leader" by his beloved friend Gershuni.

In July 1903, while Gershuni is inside Shlisselburg Fortress, the twenty-four-year-old exile Boris Savinkov flees Vologda and slips across the border. He is an educated young man and the son-in-law of the popular writer Gleb Uspensky. Back in 1902 he was convicted for being a member of the Union of Struggle for the Liberation of the Working Class, an underground organization in Saint Petersburg, and exiled to Vologda, where his revolutionary career takes off. He meets with Babushka and joins the Socialist-Revolutionary Party. His new party comrades help him get to Arkhangelsk, from where he takes a boat to Norway. Via Oslo and Antwerp he eventually reaches Geneva and calls on Gotz.

He tells Gotz that he wants to engage in terror, because he considers it the most important aspect of the revolutionary struggle. Gotz invites Savinkov to remain in Geneva and wait until the time is right. Ever since Gershuni's arrest, the SRs have had to postpone all terrorist activity.

Savinkov rents an apartment in Geneva and waits patiently for a few months. He is paid the occasional visit by Babushka, who has also moved abroad. Finally, in August 1903, a visitor "around thirty-three years old, rotund, with a broad indifferent face, as if set in stone, and big brown eyes" comes to see him. It is Yevgeny Filippovich Azef.

"He offered me his hand, sat down and said in a lazy manner: 'I hear that you want to engage in terror. Might I ask why?'" recalls Savinkov.

Savinkov tells Azef that he considers the assassination of Interior Minister Plehve to be a top priority. Thereafter, Azef regularly visits Savinkov, asking numerous questions but saying nothing about himself. A few months later he sends Savinkov back to Russia on a special mission.

The plan to assassinate Plehve belongs to Azef, whose operational approach differs greatly from Gershuni's. On past assignments Gershuni's militants generally attempted to shoot their victims—and often missed. Azef decides to play it safe, so to speak, and use only explosives. Moreover, Gershuni's lone assassins are replaced by operational groups tasked with carefully tracking the victim's movements. Azef essentially adopts the police tactics applied by Plehve himself and formerly Zubatov, with secret agents and field surveillance.

The plan is as follows. It is known that Plehve lives at the police department building at number 16 on Saint Petersburg's Fontanka Street and travels weekly to report to the tsar, either at the Winter Palace, Tsarskoye Selo, or Peterhof, depending on the time of year. Since the target is more vulnerable outside than at home, his travel routes and movements are carefully monitored to ascertain the optimum moment at which to throw a bomb under his carriage. The surveillance is meticulous and involves several people: one buys a horse and cab and pretends to be a regular driver, while another obtains a license to sell tobacco in the street. The operation is directed by Savinkov.

Despite the planning, the first attempt to kill Plehve, on 18 March 1904, is unsuccessful. Three terrorists are lying in wait for the minister's carriage, but it speeds by, leaving no time to throw a bomb.

The militants disperse and later regroup to organize a second attempt. They leave Saint Petersburg and travel around various towns and cities to throw the authorities off the scent in case they are being tracked. Savinkov journeys to Kiev, where he learns that a member of the militant organization, Alexei Pokotilov, has been killed by an explosion inside his hotel room. Manufacturing a bomb in the small hours, he accidentally breaks the flask containing the incendiary mixture. Three-quarters of the group's stockpile of explosives is lost as a result, leaving enough for just one bomb.

The militants regather in Moscow. Azef draws up a plan for the next attempt. The task of bombing the minister's carriage falls to two members: Ivan Kalyaev and Yegor Sazonov. Kalyaev listens to Azef's instructions and then joins in the discussion:

"There's a way to guarantee it works."

"What's that?"

"Throw a bomb under the horses' hooves."

"How will you manage that?" asks Azef.

"The carriage rides past. I jump under the horses with a bomb. Even if it doesn't explode, the horses will be frightened and rear up."

All are silent. After a long pause, Azef says:

"Yours will probably explode."

"Of course."

Kalyaev's plan seems to guarantee success, but Azef is opposed: "It's a good plan, but unnecessary. If you have time to get to the horses, you'll have time to get to the carriage. So you can just throw the bomb under it or through an open window. One guy might be enough."

Later, Savinkov and Sazonov go for a walk in Moscow. After a long stroll they sit down on a park bench near the Christ the Savior Cathedral. "You know you probably won't return," begins Savinkov. "Tell me, what do you think we'll feel after . . . after the assassination?"

"Pride and joy," replies Sozonov.

"Nothing else?"

"Absolutely not."

The "first" second attempt, scheduled for 9 July 1904, fails before it starts: Sazonov is late. The next try is scheduled for 15 July. Four terrorists line the route to be taken by Plehve. Sazonov throws his bomb into the carriage. An explosion rings out. Savinkov runs to the scene of the crime and sees Sazonov lying in a pool of blood. His comrade is dead, yet Plehve is alive—or so it seems.

Emperor Nicholas II spends the day at Peterhof. In his diary he writes that early in the morning he "received the grave news of Plehve's assassination." Usually sparing with emotions, on this occasion the tsar lowers the mask a fraction: "Death was instantaneous. The cab driver was also killed and seven wounded, including the commanding officer of my company, the Semenov Regiment. It's distressing. In Plehve I have lost a friend and an indispensable interior minister. The Lord has vented His wrath upon us. To lose two such dedicated and valuable servants in such a short space of time! It is His holy will!"

He then reverts to his usual style: "Aunt Marusya had breakfast. I received Muravyov with the details of this vile event. We walked with Mamá. I went for a sail with Misha. We dined on the balcony. It was a lovely evening."

|| Chapter 5 ||

in which Empress Alexandra and Dowager Empress Maria argue over who will be mistress of the palace and of Russia

A NEW LOUSE

On 30 July 1904, the thirty-two-year-old Empress Alexandra (Alix) gives birth to a boy at the Peterhof estate outside Saint Petersburg. He is christened Alexei. The birth of a male heir is cause for celebration and the end of a distressing time for Alix, who has been driven to the brink of insanity.

The news even distracts her husband, Emperor Nicholas II, momentarily from his misadventure in the Far East. In order to raise army morale, all soldiers fighting in Manchuria are made nominal godfathers of the young *tsarevich* [son of the tsar]. For several weeks Nicholas does not leave his wife and child's side, ignores his ministers, and spends a lot of time walking with his mother and picking mushrooms.

The birth comes two weeks after the assassination of Interior Minister Plehve in Saint Petersburg, but the emperor is in no hurry to appoint a successor; only one month later is a new name announced (a certain Prince Mirsky). Sergei Witte, the chairman of the Committee of Ministers, returns from a European tour and brings a letter from the Japanese ambassador in London. Witte advocates peace talks, noting that the sooner they start, the less severe the terms will be for Russia. His view is seconded by the commander of the garrison at Port Arthur, General Kondratenko, who writes to the emperor that peace talks could avoid some major unpleasantness. Emperor Nicholas leaves both letters unanswered.

Most of society rejoices at the news of the birth of an heir, but not all. The publisher Alexei Suvorin recalls the words of a furniture maker he spoke to shortly after the birth: "I was traveling by train from my dacha. Everyone was happily talking about the birth. Suddenly a gentleman spoke up loudly: 'Russians are strange people. They discover a new louse on their head, yet they only rejoice at the prospect of being bitten by it.' Everyone fell silent. It was incredible that anyone could speak so loosely and freely." That same day Emperor Nicholas II writes a letter to his wife's best friend, Princess Milica of Montenegro: "My dear Milica! Words are insufficient to thank God for His great mercy. Please convey our joy and gratitude . . . to Him. Everything has happened so quickly that I still do not understand it. The child is huge, with black hair and blue eyes. He is called Alexei. The Lord be with you all. Nicky."

Despite the capital letter, "Him" refers not to God, but a French psychic and miracle-worker Nizier Philippe, who enjoyed a brief period of influence over the imperial couple.

The decade of married life preceding the birth of her son has been torment for the young empress. Only after giving birth to a male heir does she begin to feel more confident. Hitherto she has suffered in silence at the hands of the spiteful imperial court, but now she starts to retaliate for the sake of her son, whom she naturally assumes will one day ascend to the throne. Prior to 30 July 1904 Empress Alexandra has participated very little in Russian political life, but that now changes. She enters the political scene to defend the interests of her son, as she envisions them to be.

To understand the position of Empress Alexandra—the favorite grand-daughter, future queen, wife of Jack the Ripper—one has to go back a quarter of a century. On 5 November 1878, the eldest daughter of Princess Alice of the United Kingdom (a.k.a. Princess Louis of Hesse), herself the daughter of Queen Victoria, complains of a stiff neck. The other children think that she has mumps and joke that it "will be funny if she infects everyone." That evening the eldest daughter, fifteen-year-old Victoria, named after her grandmother, reads her younger brothers and sisters a bedtime story (ironically, *Alice in Wonderland*). In the morning Victoria is diagnosed with diphtheria. One by one the other children all succumb to the illness. They are six-year-old Alix, four-year-old Marie, and ten-year-old Ernst. Later their father, Duke Ludwig of Hesse, also falls sick.

On 16 November the youngest sibling dies. For two weeks Princess Alice conceals Marie's death from the other children. On 7 December she herself falls ill and dies a week later.

The only member of the family not to fall ill is Alice and Ludwig's second daughter, Elizabeth (known as Ella). At the time when the family is struck by the epidemic, she is visiting her grandmother Queen Victoria in London. After Alice's death, Victoria takes in all her grandchildren. The now youngest, Alix, is her favorite. In London she acquires the nickname "Sunny."

The beauty of the family, Ella goes on to capture the heart of almost every visiting prince. Even as a twelve-year-old, just before her mother's death, Ella receives a proposal from the heir to the German throne, the future Kaiser Wilhelm II. But she refuses. In 1884, the now nineteen-year-old Ella marries the Russian Grand Duke Sergei, the younger brother of Emperor Alexander III. The wedding is held at the Winter Palace. It is then that Ella's younger sister, Alix, first comes to Russia and meets the sixteen-year-old Nicky, the heir to the Russian throne. She is his second cousin on her father's side.

Alix and Nicky like each other, but they are still children, and no one takes their feelings seriously, particularly as "Granny" Victoria is hatching her own grandiose plans. When her granddaughter turns sixteen, Queen Victoria, now very much attached to Alix, decides that she will succeed her as ruler of the British Empire.

Victoria's heir at the time is her forty-eight-year-old son Edward, Prince of Wales, the future King Edward VII. Since he is no longer in the flush of youth, the seventy-year-old Victoria is looking further down the line. Edward's one-day successor is set to be his eldest son, Albert Victor (named in honor of both his grandparents, Victoria and Prince Albert), but the queen is dissatisfied with him. The prince has learning difficulties (including reading and writing), is bad-tempered, and leads a "dissolute lifestyle," as his disapproving grandmother writes in a letter to her daughter. To make the potential heir more respectable, Victoria decides to find him a wife with a strong character, able to keep a tight rein on him. The role is ideally suited to her favorite granddaughter, Alix.

In 1889 Albert Victor, at Queen Victoria's insistence, proposes to Alix. But soon afterwards the plan is derailed by scandal, and not just any scandal, but one that engulfs the British royal family. London police uncover a male brothel in Fitzrovia on Cleveland Street. At the time homosexuality is a criminal offence in Britain and its empire. An indirect victim is the writer Oscar Wilde, who alludes to the scandal in his 1890 novel *The Picture of Dorian Gray*. He will be imprisoned for "gross indecency" six years later.

Soon after the raid on Cleveland Street it turns out that this is no ordinary brothel. One of its clients is Lord Arthur Somerset, the head stableman of Prince Edward. The investigation is slow and sluggish, but details are leaked to the press bit by bit. No British newspaper dare mention the name of the highest-ranking suspect, but the leftpondian *New York Times* has no qualms, openly writing that Prince Albert Victor is implicated. The paper calls him a "stupid perverse boy" unfit for the British throne.

To this day British historians argue about whether Albert Victor used the services of rent boys or whether it was just slander (Oscar Wilde, for his part, believed the former). Either way, the scandal erupts right after Albert Victor's proposal to Alix. She refuses. The prince immediately sets off on a long journey to India, while Alix departs for Russia to visit her elder sister Ella.

Ella's marriage, incidentally, is not a happy one. A few years later, when her husband Grand Duke Sergei becomes governor-general of Moscow, the whole city starts gossiping about his alleged homosexuality (illegal in the Russian Empire, too). Ella's fate unfurls in tragic fashion. After the murder of her husband she abandons high society and founds the Marfo-Mariinsky Convent in Moscow. Soon after the revolution Ella herself is brutally killed (and canonized almost a century later).

During a trip in the summer of 1889, the seventeen-year-old Alix again meets Nicky, the heir to the Russian throne. They strike up a platonic

romance. Nicky's parents, Emperor Alexander III and Empress Maria Feodorovna, dislike her so much that they bar her from the royal court and
try to prevent her from seeing their son.

But Alix is nothing if not persistent. Back home in London, the German princess starts studying the Russian language and Russian literature,
and even takes lessons in Orthodoxy from a priest at the church of the
Russian Embassy in London.

Queen Victoria is less than overjoyed about her beloved Alix's new
hobby: she does not like Russia at all, in particular Alexander III. Nevertheless, she intercedes on behalf of her granddaughter, and at her request Ella
goes to see her brother-in-law, Alexander III, and his wife, to clarify their
attitude to the young Alix and her potential betrothal to Nicky. They reply
that the twenty-two-year-old heir is too young for marriage, since he has yet
to make a trip around the world to expand his horizons or perform military
service. In any case, they assert, even if Alix and Nicky are fond of each other,
such feelings between young cousins are commonplace and will soon pass.

The heir to the Russian throne soon sets sail on a global trip, and Alix
is confirmed in the Church of England, although Queen Victoria initially delays the ceremony so as not to hinder her possible conversion to
Orthodoxy.

It is only in 1893, when Alexander III's health begins to fail, that his relatives raise the issue of the heir's marriage. They ask Nicky's opinion: he says that he dreams of marrying Alix.

THE BRIDE IN BLACK

In the spring of 1894 Nicholas attends the wedding of Albert, the elder brother of Alix, at the Veste Coburg in Bavaria, the ancestral home of the late husband of Queen Victoria. The wedding is organized by the queen herself, who is the groom's grandmother and the doyenne of the family. Also present is Germany's Wilhelm II. The heir to the Russian throne is accompanied by his uncles Sergei (with his wife Ella), Vladimir, and Pavel.

On the very first day, Nicky proposes to Alix, yet she refuses, saying that she no longer wants to convert from the Anglican Church to Orthodoxy. But Ella reassures her sister and persuades her to go ahead. The engagement is announced on 7 April, and Nicholas spends almost the whole summer in London with his bride, returning home in September. He only just manages to see his father, Alexander III, one last time before the latter's untimely demise.

Alix is also summoned to Alexander's deathbed in Crimea. She and Ella have to make the trip to Livadia Palace aboard an ordinary passenger train. Alexander III gives his blessing to the marriage, before passing away on 1 November 1894. The next day Alix converts to Orthodoxy. She wants to take the name of Catherine—in honor of another modest German princess who ascended to the Russian throne in the eighteenth century, to become Catherine the Great. But Nicky prefers the name Alexandra,* after the wife of Emperor Nicholas I, Alexandra Feodorovna. Alix does not demur.

The entire family travels with the deceased emperor's hearse to Moscow and onwards to Saint Petersburg, where he is buried on 19 November. Just a week later, on 26 November, Nicholas and Alexandra are hastily crowned at the church of the Winter Palace.

"Our wedding seemed a continuation of the funeral liturgy for the late tsar, with just one difference: my dress was white, not black," Alexandra writes to her sister.

Alexandra's relationship with her mother-in-law is awkward. Maria Feodorovna is still quite young and active. Christened Princess Dagmar of

---

*Despite the similarity, Alix is not short for Alexandra, but is a Germanic and Old French form of Alice.

Denmark, she is widowed at the age of forty-seven and has no plans to retire to the background. For her, Alix (now officially Alexandra Feodorovna) is a symbol of unwanted upheaval in her life. Along with the death of her husband, Alexander III, she has to cope with the arrival of this cold, unfamiliar woman who immediately takes her place as empress. "She arrived here with the coffin [of the tsar]. She spells misfortune," residents in the capital say about Alix, calling her the "bride in black." The now empress dowager, Maria Feodorovna, concurs.

Maria Feodorovna has no intention of ceding her role as lady of the court. During the early years of the reign of the now Tsar Nicholas II, the empress dowager takes pride of place. She is always on view at the head of any royal procession, arm-in-arm with her son, while Alexandra walks behind on the arm of one of the grand dukes. The influential society lady and general's wife Alexandra Bogdanovich writes in her diary: "The young tsarina, who draws well, once sketched a picture of a boy on the throne (her husband) frolicking about. At his side was the queen mother, telling him not to mess about. The tsar was said to have been greatly offended by the drawing."

Nor does Petersburg high society warm to Alexandra, continuing as it does to revolve around Maria Feodorovna. At receptions, she and even her husband Nicholas II are left in a corner talking to members of their entourage. The empress dowager is considered arrogant, although her haughtiness masks a certain shyness.

The only friends of the new empress are two Montenegrin princesses, Stana and Milica, the daughters of Prince Nikola of Montenegro, who were married off by the then Tsar Alexander III to "minor grand dukes" (according to Witte, who writes: "Back then, our grand dukes were breeding an entire herd"). Metropolitan society looks down its nose at the Montenegrins, for which reason Alexandra seeks their company.

"The Montenegrins didn't just kowtow to the Empress. They displayed endless love and devotion to her. When the Empress fell ill with a gastrointestinal disease, the Montenegrins did not leave her side, even taking over some unpleasant duties from the housemaids. That way, they insinuated themselves into her favor and became her closest friends," writes the somewhat-skeptical Witte.

On 3 November 1895, a year after the wedding, the empress gives birth to her first child—a girl, Olga. "Nicky and Alix are overjoyed at the birth of a daughter, but it's a pity it's not a son," reads the diary of the tsar's sister Xenia, who is very close to the imperial couple. "The joy is immense, while the disappointment of giving birth to a girl is fading from the realization that all is well," writes Ella.

The birth itself has not been without complications. "You are aware of the terrible rumors that Alix is dangerously ill, cannot bear any more children and needs an operation," Ella writes to her grandmother, Queen Victoria, shortly afterwards.

Yet a year later she is pregnant once more and gives birth to her second child on 29 May 1897. "This morning God gifted Their Majesties . . . a daughter. The news spread quickly. Everyone is disappointed. The hope was for a son," writes Grand Duke Konstantin in his diary. The daughter is christened Tatiana.

On 14 June 1899, at Peterhof, a third daughter is born—Maria. Two weeks later news arrives from the Caucasus that the tsar's younger brother, the twenty-eight-year-old Crown Prince Georgy, has died of tuberculosis. The new heir to the throne is the next brother in line, Mikhail. But officially the title of crown prince is not conferred upon him, for it is rumored at court that the superstitious Alix fears that it will jinx her chances of bearing a son.

A year later, in 1900, the life of the emperor himself hangs by a thread. Vacationing in Crimea, the thirty-year-old Nicholas II suffers flu complications. His doctor, who arrives late having traveled from Saint Petersburg, diagnoses Nicholas with typhoid and declares that he has not been treated adequately by local medics. His condition is so severe that an emergency meeting is held on the succession in case he dies. The meeting, held in Yalta, is attended by State Council Chairman Grand Duke Mikhail Nikolaevich (the tsar's great uncle and the son of Nicholas I), Court Minister Baron Fredericks, Interior Minister Sipyagin, Foreign Minister Lamsdorf, and Finance Minister Witte. The latter recalls that there was nothing to discuss in his opinion—the emperor has no son, therefore by law the throne must pass to his younger brother, Grand Duke Mikhail.

"What if the empress is pregnant?" asks Baron Fredericks, who is very close to the imperial couple. Witte says that it would make no difference. An autocratic country cannot survive without an autocrat, so there must be no pause between the emperor's death and the appearance of his successor. "What if the empress's next child is a boy?" continues Fredericks, unappeased. Witte says that Grand Duke Mikhail Alexandrovich, the younger brother of Nicholas, is a very honorable man and would be able to decide for himself whether to remain on the throne or abdicate in favor of his nephew. All those present agree. An ulterior motive comes from Witte's close ties to Mikhail—he teaches economics to the young grand duke. Everyone in the room knows full well that the finance minister is lobbying for his "own" candidate.

A few days later War Minister Kuropatkin comes to see Witte. Striking his chest with his fist (according to the latter's memoirs), the minister states that he will stand up for the empress. Witte notes sardonically that such is the duty of every citizen, including himself. Later he learns that the empress has been informed of the details of the meeting in Yalta. She will never forgive the finance minister.

Nicholas gradually recovers. Moreover, Alexandra really is pregnant and on 5 June 1901 at Peterhof gives birth to her fourth daughter, Anastasia.

It is a tragedy for the whole family. "Good Lord, what a disappointment! A fourth girl!" writes Grand Duchess Xenia. "Forgive me, Lord! Instead of joy, there was nothing but disappointment. Everyone was hoping for an heir, but now there is a fourth daughter," sighs Grand Duke Konstantin. Alexandra herself is in despair.

The agitated emperor inquires of the grey cardinal Pobedonostsev as to whether it would be possible to appoint his eldest daughter, Olga, as his successor. Pobedonostsev replies in the negative: under current law it is not permitted. Emperor Paul I, who hated his mother Catherine the Great, passed a law according to which the title of sovereign can only be handed down through the male line. As a favor to the imperial couple, Witte investigates having the law amended.

After the birth of a fourth daughter, Empress Dowager Maria Feodorovna begins to talk openly about divorce, for if Alexandra cannot give birth to an heir, her son must choose another wife. The tsar genuinely loves his wife and does not even consider it, but the court gossip is too much for Alexandra to bear.

Maria Feodorovna might have gotten her way, had she not been distracted by an unexpected turn in her own personal life. The fifty-year-old widow of Alexander III falls in love with the Abkhazian Prince Georgy Shervashidze, the royal chamberlain. In 1902 they conclude a morganatic marriage, that is, a semi-official union in which Prince Shervashidze does not become a member of the imperial family (which, incidentally, does not prevent him from becoming one of the most powerful courtiers). The emperor's new stepfather is privy to many issues that government ministers are not.

THE CHRIST OF LYON

Empress Alexandra seeks solace in religion and mysticism. She enjoys reading hagiographies about the lives of Orthodox saints, diligently places candles in front of icons, and performs esoteric church rituals more common of tsarinas in the days before Peter the Great. She is imbued with a belief in "God's people"—recluses, hermits, and holy fools, who now form an endless stream into the royal residence, sometimes into her own chambers, where she converses with them for hours on end.

In 1900 Grand Duke Vladimir, the tsar's uncle and the president of the Imperial Academy of Arts, makes the acquaintance of the preacher Nizier Philippe in France. Dr. Philippe, as his followers call him, heads a sect that considers him to be the reincarnation of Christ on Earth. Mysticism is in vogue at the Russian court, with many imperial family members drawn to spiritualism. The impressionable grand duke invites the "doctor" to Saint Petersburg.

In the Russian capital, Philippe acquires some fanatical acolytes, among them another of the tsar's uncles, Grand Duke Nikolai Nikolaevich. A military man, and one of the most experienced in the country at that, Nikolai is, nevertheless, something of a "mystical oddball." According to Witte's memoirs, he once told the finance minister that the sovereign is not human: "He is neither man nor God, but somewhere in between."

Nikolai introduces Philippe to Alexandra's Montenegrin princess friends, Stana and Milica, who in turn acquaint him with the tsar and tsarina. The French quack makes a great impression on Alexandra. Her only thought is to give birth to a son, and Dr. Philippe says that he will make it happen.

Witte recalls that there developed around Philippe a kind of "secret society of illuminati" consisting of the Montenegrin princesses, Grand Duke Nikolai Nikolaevich, Peter Nikolaevich (Milica's husband), and the imperial couple. This inner circle of admirers tries to conceal the activities of the French miracle-worker. Even inside the imperial family, many members do now know who or what he is.

Under the spell of the French preacher, Nicholas II asks his foreign minister to request the French government to confer a proper doctoral degree on Philippe, so that he can officially invite him to the imperial court. The French government declines the request, so the tsar awards the title of doctor himself.

War Minister Kuropatkin arranges for Philippe to sit an exam at the Saint Petersburg Military Medical Academy, whereupon in November 1901 the Frenchman receives the rank of state councilor by "secret order" (i.e., the award is not made public knowledge). "Philippe promptly ordered a military medical uniform from the official state tailor," writes Witte.

The French guest holds not only spiritual, but also political conversations with the tsar and tsarina. He advises them not to introduce a constitution, since that would be the downfall of Russia. Grand Duke Sandro, who is more grounded than his relatives, recalls that Philippe "claimed that through the power of suggestion he was able to influence the sex of a child developing in its mother's womb. He did not prescribe any medication that could be verified by the court physicians. The secret of his art lay in hypnosis. After two months of treatment, he announced that the Empress was with child."

Following the conception in November 1901, the imperial couple decides to conceal Alexandra's fifth pregnancy even from their closest relatives. Only in the spring, when the empress is visibly much stouter and no longer wearing a corset, is the pregnancy announced officially. However, on Philippe's advice, the empress does not allow physicians to examine her until mid-August (i.e., until the end of the pregnancy).

Even the entreaties of the court obstetrician, Professor Ott, are ignored. "Rest assured, the child is fine," she says. Ott recalls his amazement at Alexandra's routine: almost every day at eleven o'clock in the evening she travels to Znamenka, the estate of Grand Duke Peter Nikolaevich, returning only at three in the morning. But the obstetrician dare not criticize her.

Dr. Philippe lives at the palace of Peter Nikolaevich, the brother of Grand Duke Nikolai Nikolaevich and the husband of Milica, where he "watches over" the empress and assures her that everything is in order. Philippe enjoys colossal influence over the imperial couple. In July 1902 Nicholas II writes in his diary: "Mr. Philippe spoke to us and counseled us. How wonderful!!!" A few days later the empress writes to her husband, who is about to embark on a short trip to Germany for talks with Kaiser Wilhelm II: "Our dear friend will be by your side. He will help you to answer all Wilhelm's questions." Clearly, the doctor has become a political as well as medical adviser.

The birth is expected on or around 8 August, but the contractions do not begin. Only on 16 August does the empress summon Professor Ott when she starts bleeding. "She's sitting upright but agitated, with drops of blood on her chemise. The Emperor is pacing around the room. He is very anxious and wants me to examine her," recalls the doctor.

After the examination, the professor informs Alexandra that she is not pregnant. Only three days later is the diagnosis made: false pregnancy. It is a terrible blow to Alexandra's psyche. Grand Duke Sandro recollects that she suffered a nervous breakdown. "We've all been utterly dejected since yesterday. . . Poor A.F. [Alexandra] was not pregnant," Sandro writes to his wife, Grand Duchess Xenia.

The city is rife with rumors. It is said that the tsarina has "given birth to a monster with horns." The censors hurry to remove a line from

Rimsky-Korsakov's brand new opera *The Tale of Tsar Saltan*, based on Alexander Pushkin's poem, written in 1831:

> *Late last night inside the house,*
> *Not to a son or daughter, frog or mouse*
> *Did the tsarina give birth*
> *But to a creature not of this Earth.*

THE SAINT FROM SAROV

Yet the false pregnancy does not ruin Alexandra's faith in the "Christ of Lyon." Nicholas II, however, is presented with a report on the activities of Dr. Philippe, prepared by the French Interior Ministry, exposing him as a charlatan. But he says nothing about it to his wife. To the end of her life, the empress remembers him fondly and keeps his gifts: an icon with a bell and dried flowers. Nevertheless, Philippe leaves Russia.

Before leaving, he tells the empress of someone who can help her give birth to a son: Seraphim of Sarov, a renowned hermit monk from Nizhny Novgorod province, who (unfortunately) has been dead for seventy years. Soon after the death of Father Seraphim, a contemporary of Pushkin, the first stories appeared of his miracle-working: he fed on grass, could stand for weeks on a rock without moving, and was able to converse with animals. By the early twentieth century, Seraphim of Sarov is a legend and very popular among the people.

In autumn 1902 the imperial family invites Pobedonostsev for breakfast. The "minister of the church" is taken aback, since he has not met with the emperor in a domestic setting for a long time. Even more of a surprise is Nicholas's request to canonize Seraphim of Sarov, and to do so by 2 January, the date of the future saint's death. The legal scholar Pobedonostsev says that it is against the law, since such a decision can only be taken by the Holy Synod. "The sovereign can do anything!" objects Alexandra.

Witte says that she uttered these words on more than one occasion. And General Vasily Gurko, chief of staff of the Russian Imperial Army, writes in his memoirs that Empress Alexandra was not aware that the Russian tsar was bound by any laws. In her mind's eye, the emperor's will is law, both supreme and divine.

Nicholas does not gainsay his teacher Pobedonostsev, but later that evening sends him a letter (evidently dictated by his wife) stating that Seraphim of Sarov is to be canonized as soon as possible.

The Holy Synod dispatches a special commission to Nizhny Novgorod province to open the grave of Seraphim and inspect his remains. Orthodox canon states that a prerequisite for sainthood is the presence of imperishable relics. Unsurprisingly, the opening of the grave reveals nothing but Seraphim's bones, causing a dilemma. All members of the Holy Synod are against the canonization, but everyone knows that the emperor's order must be executed.

In the end, the Holy Synod announces the canonization date: 20 July 1903, Seraphim's birthday. Better late than never. On receiving the Synod's report, Emperor Nicholas II makes a note of his reaction: "I read [the report] with sincere joy and profound emotion."

Meanwhile, in Saint Petersburg, anonymous leaflets are being distributed, signed by the unknown "Union Against Orthodoxy." The leaflets state that the relics of Seraphim of Sarov are fake and threaten that "Union" activists are ready to open the grave once more to expose the deception. To counter this, on 22 June Metropolitan Anthony of Saint Petersburg writes an article in Suvorin's newspaper *New Time*, asserting that the preservation of the skeleton is sufficient and the presence of imperishable relics is not a barrier to apotheosis. This scandalizes public opinion even further.

The ceremony on 20 July in Sarov, at which the relics are again inspected and this time venerated, is attended by sixteen members of the imperial family. Public interest is so great that Cossacks have to disperse the crowd with whips. The empress is in a state of bliss. At night she bathes in the healing spring of Saint Seraphim in Sarov forest and prays for an heir. Everyone says that the new saint is sure to give the emperor a son. The court press writes that the canonization of the "people's saint" is a symbol of unity between society and the tsar.

Exactly one year after the canonization of Saint Seraphim, Alexandra's wish is fulfilled and she at last gives birth to a boy. Nicholas II hangs a large portrait of the Sarov elder in his office and says to his inner circle: "Nothing will ever shake my belief in the sanctity and miracles of St. Seraphim. I have conclusive proof."

The tsar and tsarina continue to correspond with Nizier Philippe, for Alexandra believes that it was his advice that helped her to give birth to an heir. In letters to her husband she still refers to him as "Our Friend." Philippe dies in August 1905, a year after the birth of the heir. In his final letter he foretells that after his death Alexandra and Nicholas will find a new "Friend," who will preach the Bible full of ecstasy and fire.

THE WANDERER FROM SIBERIA

In 1903 a peasant from the village of Pokrovskoe in Tobolsk province arrives in Saint Petersburg. He is thirty-five years old and has spent almost his whole life traveling from monastery to monastery. The monastery of John of Kronstadt makes a great impression on the stranger. He later recalls that, on crossing the threshold, he felt as if the monastery gates had severed all the defilements of his past life.

The wanderer's name is Grigory Rasputin—just one of thousands of "God's people" who make the journey each year to Saint Petersburg in the knowledge that society ladies are addicted to mysticism. Rasputin is the same age as Georgy Gapon and tries to wheedle his way into the same company. But whereas Gapon idolizes Tolstoy and dreams of social transformation, Rasputin's role model is John of Kronstadt, a very popular but slightly less liberal man of the cloth.

Every morning John serves at Saint Andrew's Cathedral in Kronstadt, twenty miles west of Saint Petersburg, before heading for the capital, where he visits the homes of the wealthy and prays for their health. John is accompanied by a huge entourage tasked with collecting donations and arranging the itinerary of the "celebrity father." He visits dozens of homes each day. Each visit costs—and brings in—a lot of money. His large retinue deals with the bean-counting.

John of Kronstadt is a pop star of his own megachurch. To maximize his flock, he comes up with the idea of collective confession: thousands of people at once gather in his cathedral to confess, shouting out their sins.

One such collective confession is attended by Rasputin, and it makes a deep impression on him. Father John notices the stranger from Siberia. They meet, after which John invites his new acquaintance to live in the monastery.

Rasputin soon surpasses his host in terms of popularity and wealth. It is John who acquaints Rasputin with Bishop Theophan, spiritual councilor to the imperial family, who in 1904 takes him to the house of the Montenegrin princess Milica. Grigory Rasputin soon becomes another fashionable frequenter of the salons of rich ladies in search of mysticism.

CHAMPAGNE AND OYSTERS

In the summer of 1904 Anton Chekhov's health is deteriorating. Tuberculosis has kept him in hospital in Moscow and in Crimea for much of the past few years. In June 1904 his wife, the Moscow Art Theatre actress Olga Knipper, takes him to Germany for treatment.

Since the start of the war with Japan, the once-apolitical Chekhov has been avidly following the news. A Russian victory, he tells his brother-in-law Viktor Knipper, is highly undesirable, since it would consolidate autocracy and set back the revolution. He voices the same opinion to Stanislavsky: "It's terrible, but necessary. Let the Japanese give us a push in the right direction."

Winter 1904 sees the premiere of *The Cherry Orchard* at the Moscow Art Theatre, after which Chekhov's pen falls silent. On the night of 1–2 July 1904, at the resort of Badenweiler with his wife, he wakes up suddenly and calls for a doctor—and champagne. When the doctor arrives, he says in German "Ich sterbe," and then the same to his wife in Russian, "*Ya umirayu*" ("I'm dying"). He takes a sip of champagne with the words, "I haven't tasted that for a while," before rolling over on his side and closing his eyes.

His body is taken to Moscow in a train carriage equipped with a refrigeration unit inscribed with the words "For the transportation of fresh oysters." The writer Maxim Gorky is outraged: "This wonderful person, this magnificent artist, who spent his entire life battling vulgarity, finding it everywhere and shining a gently reproachful light on its rottenness, like that of the moon, Anton Pavlovich [Chekhov], who shuddered at all things trite and vulgar, was transported in a fridge for oysters. My heart is wrung and ready to howl with anger. He personally would not care if his body were transported in a basket for dirty linen, but I cannot forgive us, Russian society. It is this vulgarity of Russian life, its lack of culture, which so perturbed the deceased writer."

Gorky goes to Chekhov's funeral, along with Savva Morozov. During the procession, they decide to head off to Morozov's place on Moscow's Spiridonovka Street for a coffee and only then on to the cemetery. There, they walk around among the tombstones. "All in all, it's a bit of a downer that life ends in putrefaction," philosophizes the tycoon Morozov. "It's untidy. There's always cremation, yet they say combustion and decomposition are essentially the same thing. As for me, I'd prefer to explode like a stick of dynamite. I'm not afraid of death, only squeamish about it. I imagine death to be like falling into a compost pit."

CROOKS AND THIEVES

The joy of the birth of Tsarevich Alexei is short-lived compared to the terrible news from the Far East, which continues unabated. The publisher

144 | MIKHAIL ZYGAR

Alexei Suvorin, a friend of the late Chekhov, notes in his diary entry for 6 August that the editors-in-chief of Russia's leading newspapers were summoned to the Interior Ministry and asked to prepare public opinion for the imminent fall of Port Arthur.* "It's a frightful time," writes Suvorin.

On 21 August 1904 it is reported that General Kuropatkin has surrendered Liaoyang fortress in southern Manchuria. The reasons for Russia's military setbacks are manifold: abysmal preparation, a monstrous lack of coordination between the generals, and scant information on the number of enemy troops, to name a few. Captain Ignatiev says that the Russian officer corps considered prewar intelligence gathering to be something dirty and dishonorable, so army reconnaissance skills were minimal. Chinese scouts were hired instead, but many of them turned out to be Japanese spies, as did the interpreters.

Without delving too much into the detail, metropolitan society blames the defeats on specific individuals, primarily Kuropatkin. The public is incensed by news of Russia's military failures in the Far East. Particular opprobrium is reserved for members of the imperial family: the defeat inflames talk of appalling levels of corruption on the part of the tsar's relatives.

Even before the war started, the public was outraged by the staggeringly high cost of sending telegraphs to the Far East. Suvorin notes that one word cost eight roubles†, the reason being that Empress Dowager Maria Feodorovna insisted on a special tax for the benefit of the Great Northern Telegraph Company, which, like her, was of Danish origin.

Another target of gossip is Grand Duke Sandro, the minister of the merchant fleet and one of the architects of the Korean adventurism that led to the war. Even in the prewar period he held the reputation of being perhaps "the most venal of all the grand dukes" (according to Suvorin), an impressive achievement given the competition.

Whereas in peacetime many a blind eye has been turned to corruption, during the war attitudes harden and unbridled disgust is openly voiced. When the Russian Pacific Fleet is routed in the first months of fighting, the question arises as to where to get new ships. Sandro wants to buy Argentina's fleet, but the deal falls through because the Argentines refuse to pay the grand duke a kickback worth 500 thousand roubles.‡

---

*One hundred years later this practice will become even more widespread. In the early twenty-first century Kremlin administrators organize weekly meetings with editors-in-chief of major media outlets—usually on Fridays. At these meetings editors-in-chief receive detailed instructions on how to cover different events, even the minor ones.
† About $105.50 in 2017.
‡ About $6,591,666 in 2017.

Yet the main object of universal hatred and the official culprit in the shameful defeat is Grand Duke Alexei, the commander-in-chief of the Russian Navy. His public appearances are explosive affairs. In October 1904, when his carriage is riding along Bolshaya Morskaya Street in Saint Petersburg, a crowd gathers along the roadside, shouting: "State thief!" and "Where's our navy? Give us our fleet back!" The grand duke takes cover in a restaurant. Duly summoned, the city governor helps the tsar's uncle get back home via the backstreets.*

All year the naval command ponders how to replace the Pacific Fleet. After the failure to purchase ships from Argentina, all eyes fall on its Baltic and Black Sea sisters. The Baltic Fleet, under the command of Admiral Zinovy Rozhestvensky, is the preferred option, but still the debate about whether to send it drags on for several months. It is a risky expedition, but finally Nicholas II announces, according to Witte, "with his characteristic optimism that Rozhestvensky will turn the war around, because Seraphim of Sarov has predicted that a peace agreement will be signed in Tokyo and only the yids and intelligentsia can think otherwise."

The decision to dispatch the Baltic Fleet under Rozhestvensky is taken. As for the admiral himself, his opinion is thus: "The expedition is an arduous one, but if it be His Majestry's order, I shall lead the fleet into battle against Japan." Before Rozhestvensky sets sail, the emperor introduces him to the newborn heir to the throne, Tsarevich Alexei, and presents the admiral with a small icon of the now-holy Seraphim of Sarov.

"If I'd had a bit of civic courage," writes the admiral a few years later, "I'd have shouted from the rooftops: safeguard the last vestiges of the Navy! Do not send it to its destruction! But I lacked the necessary spark."

The fleet departs in October. After an accidental skirmish with British trawler boats (the Dogger Bank incident), Britain forbids the Russian ships from sailing through the Suez Canal, forcing them to skirt the southern tip of Africa. Only in spring the following year does the fleet reach Japan.

The European and American media are fully on the side of the Japanese. Russia and Russians are remorselessly caricatured, in particular sailors for alleged cowardice. Suvorin recalls that *Punch* magazine published a cartoon in the form of a job seeker's notice: "Young man, ashamed to be

---

* In the early twenty-first century corruption in the higher spheres still provokes the strongest protests. However, this does not concern military operations held by Russia. Sergey Fridinsky, Chief Military Prosecutor, prepared a report in 2017 about the inspection of the Ministry of Defense's actions during the military operations in Syria. However, the results of this inspection were never published and didn't even attract any public interest, whereas Prosecutor Fridinsky resigned immediately instead of reporting to the Federation Council.

Russian, seeks employment" with an editor's note: "The word 'young' rules out Rozhestvensky. It's probably the Tsarevich looking for a job."

Never before has Alexei Suvorin, the publisher of *New Time*, the most pro-government newspaper in Russia, been so outspoken as in autumn 1904: "Does the government have friends? No. How can fools and block-heads, robbers and thieves have friends?"

PARIS CONGRESS

In late summer Peter Struve, the publisher of the magazine *Liberation*, encounters major problems: the German police begin an investigation at the request of their Russian counterparts. The entire editorial office has to up sticks immediately and relocate to Paris.

It is there that a general congress of Russian oppositionists soon takes place, involving everyone from moderate liberals to Marxist desperados. The diverse gathering includes Struve (from the Union of Liberation), the historian Pavel Milyukov (acting alone for now), and the Geneva Social-ist-Revolutionaries (SRs) Yevgeny Azef and Boris Savinkov. The congress is organized and sponsored by the Finnish nationalist Konni Zilliacus. No one at the time knows how he is able to afford it, but it later transpires that Zilliacus is in receipt of direct funding from the Japanese General Staff for the purpose of promoting the revolutionary movement in Russia.

All participants agree that terror is what is needed. The assassination of Plehve is praised and Azef branded a hero. But it does not take long for the infighting to begin; the Finns and Poles demand autonomy and even independence from the Russian Empire, while the Russian revolutionaries are split: Struve supports their agenda, but not Milyukov. Nothing is re-solved after nearly two hours of bitter wrangling, and the congress partic-ipants depart, leaving a raft of contradictory resolutions in their wake.

During the congress Ariadna Tyrkova, together with Struve and other members of the Union of Liberation in Paris, meets up with Azef. He is there on behalf of Gotz. "Why did you send this abominable specimen? You can smell he's a spy a mile off," writes the inexperienced young jour-nalist to Gotz after the meeting. The leader of the SRs replies resentfully: "I encountered the rogue Zubatov in my youth, so I know a crafty spy when I see one. My recommendations are based on personal experience." "Well," replies Tyrkova sardonically, "I'm sure you are well versed in dealing with spies, but I do not relish the prospect." Five years later the SRs will remember that the young Ariadna was the only person who exposed Azef at first glance—something that the party's professional conspirators were unable to do.

But for now, the SRs still trust Azef, who is plotting more assassinations. The decision is taken to dispatch three groups to Saint Petersburg, Kiev, and Moscow. The target in Moscow is the city's governor-general, Grand Duke Sergei. His assassination is assigned to Boris Savinkov.

After the assassination of Interior Minister Plehve, the question arises as to who will replace him in the firing line, quite literally. Witte feels that his hour has come to regain real power.

But one of the late Plehve's accomplishments was to persuade Nicholas II not to trust Witte. Plehve has regularly supplied the emperor with reports denouncing Witte as a conspirator, a revolutionary, and a freemason. The latter himself asserts that Plehve's briefcase (which survived its owner's assassination) contained a report for the tsar alleging that Witte was involved in a plot to kill Nicholas II. The emperor did not fully believe Plehve's claims, but became suspicious all the same.

The front-runner for the vacant post of interior minister is Boris Stürmer, a former member of the "Holy Militia,"* a metropolitan conservative, and Plehve's ex-chief-of-staff. The emperor meets him and even signs a decree on his appointment as the new minister. But the tsar's next visitor is his mother, Empress Dowager Maria Feodorovna, who persuades her son not to give the job to Plehve's man.

She never liked the deceased minister and now convinces her son that his repressive policies only served to worsen the situation in Russia. Plehve tackled terrorism with prison and exile, and was blown up as a result. What Russia needs, says the empress dowager, is a skilled civil servant able to pacify society and avert a revolution. Maria Feodorovna recommends Prince Mirsky, a former chief of police and deputy of Sipyagin (Plehve's predecessor). Having resigned after Plehve's appointment, Mirsky moved to the western provinces, where his liberal reforms have so far produced excellent results. He should be the next minister for the sake of Tsarevich Alexei, says Maria Feodorovna.

Nicholas II never argues with his mother. In late August he summons Mirsky and offers him the post. The latter states quite bluntly that there needs to be a radical shift in government policy: "The situation has deteriorated so much that the government is effectively at war with Russia. The two must be reconciled, or else Russian society will split into the watchers and the watched, and then what?" he asks the tsar rhetorically. The prince

---

* See chapter two.

says that as interior minister he would seek to relax censorship, adopt a law on religious tolerance, and soften the punishment for political crimes. The emperor agrees with everything.

In addition, Mirsky proposes not to punish workers for strikes and demonstrations, and calls for an expansion of self-government and more elected representatives. Once more, the emperor does not demur.

Lastly, Mirsky complains of poor health and his lack of public-speaking skills, fearing that it will hinder his work with other officials: "I can't speak either," replies Nicholas. The tsar promises to give the new minister a few months' holiday every year to freshen up. However, the prince knows that such perks might be irrelevant: the previous two interior ministers, Sipyagin and Plehve, were assassinated twenty-five and twenty-seven months into the job, respectively.

A predecessor who did survive, the former Interior Minister Ivan Goremykin, tries to dissuade Mirsky: "You can't trust him [the tsar]. He's the most insincere man in the world." But Mirsky accepts the job.

After taking office, the prince gives an interview to foreign correspondents in which he announces that the Russian government should be based on public trust. He then speaks to ministry staff, calling on them to form a "trusting relationship with public institutions and the population in general." Mirsky is going to have problems after reading the interview. Indeed, Nicholas is very unhappy, and when the minister reports to him for the first time, on 22 September, the tsar demands that he give no more interviews.

The establishment soon starts to loathe Mirsky. No one more so than the governor-general of Moscow, Grand Duke Sergei, who is battling on all fronts with the Moscow zemstvo and will not hear of granting it greater rights. He is echoed by Pobedonostsev. When Mirsky lobbies for a new religious tolerance law, the old "minister of the church" reiterates that Mirsky's ideas "will result in a massacre on the streets of Saint Petersburg and the provinces." Mirsky seeks support from Witte, who seems to back his initiatives, but replies evasively that he (Witte) is now so out of favor with the tsar that his support will likely wreck Mirsky's plans. In reality, Witte plots against the new minister and tries to derail all his proposals.

Saint Petersburg's conservative elements are angered by the liberal minister. In autumn 1904 Russia's twin capitals are simmering. In Saint Petersburg the aforementioned socialite and general's wife Alexandra Bogdanovich writes in her diary that Mirsky's liberal reforms will spark revolution.

Mirsky is accused of "tactlessness" for having received a deputation of Jews and promising equality for all nationalities of Russia. General

Bogdanovich recalls that he saw a demonstration in Moscow with two red flags, one bearing the words "Down with the tsar," the other "Down with the war." His wife bewails that the history professor Yevgeny Tarle is giving lectures on the French Revolution, after which his students are "so roused that every Monday you can expect trouble." A friend of the general and his wife, the might-have-been interior minister Boris Stürmer, is deeply "gloomy and upset about everything and says that we are heading for revolution. Even if we come to our senses and get rid of Mirsky, the old order is ruined." (The real revolution, incidentally, is still thirteen years away and happens, ironically, after Stürmer's premiership.)

In the end, Prince Mirsky's fragile health fails and he suffers a nervous breakdown. While he is convalescing, the tsar issues an order to the minister stating explicitly that there shall be no change of policy. In Saint Petersburg it is said that Mirsky is on the verge of retirement, but once more the tsar's mother, the empress dowager, steps in: "If Mirsky is pushed, I shall return to Copenhagen," threatens the former Danish princess.

Prince Mirsky's interview and the beginning of his reforms make an impression not only on Russia's conservatives, but its liberals, too—wherever they may be, in exile or emigration. Peter Struve's newspaper *Liberation* writes that Plehve's successor will find it difficult to achieve reform, but Russian society is prepared to wait, because it understands that real change takes time.[*]

Just a week before Mirsky's appointment, several zemstvo activists, led by Princes Shakhovsky and Dolgorukov, convene a large zemstvo congress in Moscow, such as the one that took place in 1902 at the apartment of Dmitry Shipov, the head of the Moscow zemstvo. They had wanted to convene it earlier, but all meetings were banned by Plehve.

The zemstvo representatives are impressed by Prince Mirsky's performance. "The speech wafted across the country like a breath of fresh air," recalls Shipov. District councils from across the country respond to Mirsky's words with approving telegrams. Mirsky, for his part, asks the tsar's permission to hold a zemstvo congress in Saint Petersburg. He explains that it will be a quite innocent gathering simply for participants to pool their experience and discuss everyday matters. Nicholas does not object.

The apparatchik Witte claims that he warned Mirsky right from the start that the congress would be a mistake. "The so-called intelligent

---

* The reaction to the appointment of Mirsky and to his policy of trust in Russian society somewhat resembles the reaction to the presidency of Dmitry Medvedev who proclaimed, "Freedom is better than non-freedom." Conservative officials considered his rhetoric strange and harmful, whereas the progressive part of the society saw it as too weak and inconsistent.

people," Witte allegedly told his younger colleague Mirsky, "only pretend to fight bureaucracy. But if you ask them what they mean by bureaucracy, they will answer 'unlimited sovereign power.' This congress is sure to end in misunderstanding. It is bound to adopt a resolution demanding a constitution, and instead of reconciliation between government and society, there will only be further aggravation."

On learning that the tsar has consented to the congress, the zemstvo bureau decides to change the agenda completely and discuss political and economic issues. All members of the bureau, apart from Shipov, are members of the Union of Liberation and vote in favor of discussing the state system, the creation of a parliament, and the introduction of a constitution.

A month later Shipov receives a call from the Interior Ministry in Saint Petersburg to say that Prince Mirsky wants to discuss the forthcoming congress with him. Shipov replies that he is ready to come, but then the minister falls ill. The congress is scheduled for 6 November. Only on 25 October does Mirsky's health allow him to receive the delegate from Moscow.

The interior minister gives Shipov a cordial welcome and proposes that they discuss the "upcoming conference of the chairmen of the provincial councils, the importance of which is greatly inflated, as if it were some kind of constituent assembly." Shipov replies that Prince Mirsky is probably not aware of the new agenda and promptly shows it to him.

Mirsky is shocked. "I informed His Majesty that these meetings would not touch upon political issues or constitutional changes to our system," says the bemused minister. "I agree with all the items and am ready to put my signature to them, but the raising of such an agenda is tantamount to my dismissal. If the congress goes ahead with this program, I have no doubt that I shall be discharged the next day," Shipov recalls Mirsky's words. "Personally I care little for the position I hold, but my departure could have undesirable consequences. My policies have made many enemies, who will take full advantage of my exit."

Shipov advises Mirsky to show the congress agenda to the tsar as quickly as possible, so that the latter does not believe he has been deceived. Later that evening Mirsky tells his wife that he is fearful: "Today there was unpleasantness. The program is militant and demands a constitution." The next day the minister is visited by Grand Duke Nicholas Mikhailovich, who warns that Mirsky's enemies are becoming emboldened. The governor-general of Moscow, Grand Duke Sergei, is said to be "chomping at the bit."

Shipov returns to Moscow and urgently convenes a meeting of bureau members from other cities. All those assembled say that the hullabaloo surrounding the congress is such that it cannot be put off—all the newspapers are writing about 6 November, the appointed date. However, because permission for the congress is likely to be withdrawn in light of the new agenda, the participants decide to hold it semi-officially—not in the building of the Saint Petersburg zemstvo, but in a private apartment.

On 31 October Shipov again travels to Saint Petersburg to see the minister and states that the zemstvo members have decided not to change anything. The next day Mirsky goes to see Nicholas II and tries to persuade him to involve the people's elected representatives in the legal system, because the political situation is "very critical." "Yes, that will allow them to sort out the veterinary issue," replies Nicholas II, rather off topic. "Your Majesty, I am speaking not about that, but about their right to permanent participation in the lawmaking process. I would not be so persistent if the throne were secure, but given the terrorist movement, what situation might Russia find itself in?" continues Mirsky. But the tsar is unfazed. As a last resort, the minister recommends banning the zemstvo congress, with which the tsar immediately agrees.

In the evening Mirsky receives Shipov once more and informs him that the government cannot entrust the discussion of such important state matters to a "group of private individuals," but also that private conversations in private homes cannot be banned and that the police will provide them with assistance.

Petersburg society is agitated. The general's wife, Bogdanovich, writes in her diary that the forthcoming "zemstvo congress" is reminiscent of the Estates-General, which sprouted the French Revolution. As if to prove the point, the Saratov delegation bound for Saint Petersburg is seen off at the station to the accompaniment of the revolutionary *La Marseillaise*.

In the meantime, on 4 November, without waiting for the congress, Interior Minister Mirsky starts drafting his own program for the "internal transformation of the imperial order," which he intends to present to the tsar.

At long last, the zemstvo representatives gather in Saint Petersburg on 6 November. The decisive third day is held inside the apartment of the law professor Vladimir Nabokov, the father of the future author of *Lolita*. They argue long and passionately about how the Russian state should be structured: whether a constituent assembly is required, or whether all changes can be made from the top down.

The congress adopts a program consisting of eleven points. The demands include: integrity of the individual and the home; freedom of conscience and religion; freedom of speech and the press; freedom of assembly and association; equal rights (civil and political) for all citizens of the Russian Empire, regardless of social estate or class; and local government in all parts of the Russian Empire.

"It's terrible. They are giving advice when no one is asking for it," Empress Dowager Maria Feodorovna says to Prince Mirsky about the congress.

On 11 November Mirsky receives Shipov and says that he personally will hand the congress resolution to the tsar. The zemstvo representatives depart Saint Petersburg, satisfied. The emperor meets the minister in good cheer after a successful hunt (he personally shot 144 of the 522 pheasants killed that day). The prince tries to resign, taking the blame for the congress, but the emperor does not let him.

Mirsky's nerve is starting to fail. Grand Duke Nicholas Mikhailovich, the tsar's uncle and a supporter of the reforms, warns him that storm clouds are gathering. Meanwhile, the less liberal governor-general of Moscow, Grand Duke Sergei, travels from the old capital to attend the birthday of the empress dowager with the intention of offering an ultimatum: either him or Mirsky. He is convinced that the minister is a revolutionary.

Suvorin is sure that the convalescent Prince Mirsky will achieve nothing: "He lacks not only the character, but the mind." Saint Petersburg is whispering that a successor for Mirsky has already been found, but, as the diarist and general's wife Bogdanovich is informed by Stürmer, the tsar has asked the prince to remain temporarily. General Bogdanovich himself goes to see the interior minister and tells him to his face that the zemstvo congress is nothing but a bunch of revolutionaries. Mirsky replies that they are good people, and that the real enemies of the state are "shitheads like Stürmer."

THE "THIRD ELEMENT"

The successful "private meeting" in Saint Petersburg spurs the intelligentsia. At the time its members are known as the "third element"—after the fashion of drawing parallels with the French Revolution. In France, the driving force of the revolution was the Third Estate, that is, the bourgeoisie (the other two being the nobility and the clergy). In Russia, there is no bourgeoisie *per se* (in the sense of a fully formed class of small business owners), but there is a class of educated people who consider themselves to be the equivalent.

In some respects, the gathering in Saint Petersburg has achieved nothing, yet the fact that it has been widely proclaimed and not been punished is cause for celebration. (The exception is the law professor Vladimir Nabokov, whose home was used to draft the resolution; a week after the congress he is removed from his post at the Imperial College of Law.) Moreover, the congress's resolution is printed all across the country, and most of its members become celebrities.

Similar "private meetings" are held all over the place, adjusted for scale. Urban intellectuals gather for drinks and snacks to toast the success of the zemstvo congress and adopt their own resolution. The "liberal banquet" campaign spreads across Russia: "It was like a dam bursting. In the space of just 2-3 months Russia was gripped by a newfound thirst for change. People are speaking loudly," Grand Duke Konstantin Konstantinovich, the president of the Imperial Academy of Sciences, writes in his diary. "Revolution seems to be knocking at the door. The talk of a constitution is becoming more open. It's shameful and frightening."

Even provincial marshals of the nobility* petition the tsar to demand government reforms. "They, too, have fallen under the influence of the zemstvo congress," Nicholas dismisses them in conversation with Mirsky. "If you do not even trust the marshals of the nobility, whom are you going to rely upon? After all, they certainly cannot be accused of lacking conservatism," replies the minister, somewhat reproachfully.

The workers are also fairly conservative at first. Gapon's trade union organization is growing steadily, and he sets up a branch of his "tea-drinking" workers' club near the Putilov factory in Saint Petersburg, which immediately attracts seven hundred members. The next few months see eight more branches opened, but their members are far removed from revolutionary ideas. During the blessing of one of the new affiliates (Gapon is a priest, after all), he notices that some workers kiss first the cross and then the hand of Saint Petersburg Governor Ivan Fullon. Gapon is outraged. When Fullon departs, he delivers a full-on lecture to the workers that the world is divided between the poor and the rich, and relations between them can never be good so long as this divide exists. Fullon is on the side of the rich and does not care about the poor. Gapon ends by saying that self-esteem and self-respect must be maintained at all times.

Gapon does well to avoid problems with the police. By October he has nine branches with five thousand members, rising by November to eleven and seven thousand, respectively. In November Gapon rejects the restrictions on nationalities prescribed in the state regulations, and openly invites Finns, Poles, and Jews to his "assemblies of Russian workers."

---

* Elected local representatives in pre-revolutionary Russia.

The discussions at the assemblies rapidly turn political. Gapon invites new speakers and meets with members of the "Union of Liberation," who recommend drafting a workers' petition to the tsar. Many of Gapon's comrades like the idea. After all, the marshals of the nobility have already done it, so why wait?

Gapon struggles to restrain the enthusiasm of his comrades. He is afraid that his brainchild will be banned by the authorities, and fears that a workers' petition will simply drown in the general stream. He prefers to wait for a specific pretext to arise, believing that "the petition should be lodged at a critical moment, such as the fall of Port Arthur and or the rout of Rozhestvensky's fleet, which seems inevitable." Moreover, it will have more success if accompanied by a mass workers' strike.

The political debate in Russia is moving so quickly and stormily that the revolutionaries in exile are out of touch. Ariadna Tyrkova recalls that the Paris-based Struve cannot sit still. Several times a day he runs to a newsstand to buy up all the latest papers to monitor the developments back home.

The monthly newspaper *Revolutionary Russia* is redundant. "Things are changing too fast," Chernov says to his fellow revolutionary Gotz. "We can't keep up here. We have to go back to Russia and immerse ourselves in the public mood." Chernov believes that they should try to publish in the legal press: "Only that will work. Abroad, we are simply beating the air."

"They'll just arrest you one by one," Gotz tries to dissuade his comrade. Chernov stands his ground and tables the matter with the central committee of the Socialist-Revolutionary Party, but his senior comrades order him to remain put. Mikhail Gotz's illness is progressing. The doctors have diagnosed a tumor in his spinal cord. He can no longer walk, moves only in a wheelchair, and cannot sleep without morphine.

Strikes break out in the autumn of 1904 not only in Saint Petersburg, but also in Moscow, where the skies had seemed relatively cloudless. That summer the governor-general of Moscow, Grand Duke Sergei, and the police chief Trepov write to Saint Petersburg to request that action be taken against Gapon. But all minds in the capital are focused on Plehve's assassination and the advice goes unheeded. The grand duke becomes increasingly irate and accuses Mirsky of "criminal weakness," blaming him for the disorder.

Of all the tsar's relatives, Grand Duke Sergei and his wife Ella are the closest and most influential. Ella (whose Orthodox name is Elizabeth Feodorovna) is the elder sister of Empress Alexandra and the only member of the imperial family still trusted by the tsarina (Alix steers clear of her mother-in-law, the empress dowager, and simply hates her Aunt Miechen, for instance).

Grand Duke Sergei is only nine years older than Nicholas II and on very good terms with the emperor. This is the same man who in 1881 ventured to convey to his elder brother, Alexander III, a letter from Leo Tolstoy asking for their father's regicides to be pardoned. He has changed a great deal since then. Besides favoring repression and opposing reform and the introduction of a constitution, he has also become deeply religious.

But that does not prevent Moscow society from gossiping about his homosexuality, alleging that all his adjutants are in fact male lovers. There is not a word about it in his diaries, while his wife Ella is one of the most beautiful women in Europe (so says the imperial court, partly to belittle her sister, Empress Alexandra). Moreover, unlike Alix, Grand Duchess Elizabeth Feodorovna speaks excellent Russian and is very popular with society.

Still, the severest blow to Sergei's reputation is the Khodynka tragedy.* As governor-general of Moscow, he was responsible for the new tsar's coronation in 1896. In Moscow he is even nicknamed "Prince Khodynka." The two government commissions set up to investigate the tragedy reached opposite conclusions, as a result of which no one was ever punished. Only later do two officials, the head of the Moscow police and the minister of the court, tender their resignations.

Sergei and Ella have no children of their own, but they have custody of their nephew and niece. In 1902 Sergei's younger brother, Grand Duke Pavel, without the permission of the emperor (his nephew), marries for a second time—to a divorcee. Knowing that Nicholas II will never give his consent to such a misalliance, Grand Duke Pavel marries in secret in Italy. Nicholas II subsequently punishes his uncle to exile abroad, and places the latter's children, twelve-year-old Maria and eleven-year-old Dmitry, in the care of Uncle Sergei and Aunt Ella. The childless Moscow governor-general is overjoyed. He is very fond of his brother's children, who even before the forced separation with their father have long been living with their aunt and uncle. Maria later recalls: "Despite the deep regret that my uncle had over his brother's misalliance, he could not hide his joy at what were now his children. He said over and over again: 'Now I am your father and you are my children.' Dmitry and I sat side by side, staring blankly at him in silence."

These effectively orphaned children (their mother, Princess Alexandra of Greece, died giving birth to Dmitry) will play a major role in the life of

---

* See chapter two.

Nicholas II. The young Dmitry is set to become one of the assassins of Rasputin. But that is fourteen years down the line.

For now, they are getting used to permanent life in Moscow with Grand Duke Sergei. Grand Duchess Maria ("little Marie") recalls that in 1903 the emperor arrived in Moscow for his Easter vacation. He was greeted by such an enthusiastic crowd that it was a miracle that the children, who were out for a walk with the tsar, were not trampled.

Just one year later the war with Japan has caused a violent shift in the public mood. In 1904, a crowd gathers under the windows of Grand Duke Sergei's residence, not with the intention of expressing loyalty: "They started throwing bottles and stones at our windows. We had to call the police and put sentries along the pavement to protect the entrance to our palace," recalls little Marie.

Arriving in Saint Petersburg in November 1904, Grand Duke Sergei, the man who nurtured the police chiefs Trepov and Zubatov, is angered by the new liberal practices and delivers his aforementioned ultimatum to the tsar: him or Mirsky. Nicholas II is known to hate being cornered and to punish anyone who demands resoluteness from him. As a result, Uncle Sergei is pensioned off and left only with the symbolic post of commander of the Moscow Military District. At the same time, Trepov tenders his resignation and asks to be sent to the front line in the Far East.

Yet the now-retired grand duke's influence only increases, since the tsar always has more faith in persons with no public office. Throughout December Sergei is ever present in the emperor's company.

On 24 November 1904, Interior Minister Mirsky presents the tsar with his own set of draft reforms. It is difficult to say who is the more agitated of the two: Prince Mirsky, who is being hounded by the metropolitan elite, or Emperor Nicholas II, who is being harassed by his own family. In addition to his mother and Uncle Sergei, all the senior Romanovs are weighing into the debate over governance and reform, including Alexander III's brothers Vladimir (president of the Imperial Academy of Fine Arts and commander of the Saint Petersburg Military District) and Alexei (commander of the Imperial Navy), as well as the late tsar's cousins Alexander (Sandro) and Nicholas Mikhailovich. Lastly, there is Empress Alexandra, who in late November asks her husband to introduce her to Prince Mirsky.

"If we do not press ahead with liberal reform, change will come in the shape of revolution," the interior minister urges the empress, saying that most members of the nobility and the educated classes want the reforms to happen, but "without touching the autocracy." Mirsky hopes to persuade the tsar and tsarina to meet society halfway, without the need to introduce a constitution. Alexandra replies that the proposed changes are "frightful" and need to be implemented very gradually: "The intelligentsia opposes Tsar Nicholas and his government, but the nation as a whole has always supported him and always will do," she says, in response to which Mirsky notes that the opinion of the intelligentsia has greater value, since the people are very changeable—today they "can kill intellectuals for sake of the tsar, but tomorrow burn down royal palaces. They are a force of nature."

But Nicholas II hates the intelligentsia. Mirsky recalls that during his spell as governor in Vilnius, he once mentioned the word "intelligentsia" in the presence of Nicholas II, who snapped that the word was detestable and should be expunged from the dictionary. According to Witte, the tsar deliberately took no interest in public opinion, because he believed that public opinion had been hijacked by the so-called intellectuals.

In his memoirs, General Mosolov, head of the imperial chancery, tells in detail about the "partition wall" theory, which was very popular with courtiers and the imperial couple at the time. According to this theory, for Russia to live in peace and harmony there must be a direct link between the sovereign and his subjects. The tsar stands above all social strata and possesses unlimited resources. He does not make mistakes and does not seek personal gain. His subjects live in the knowledge that the emperor does everything in his power to ensure that they receive their fair share of the country's wealth. If something is wrong in society, it simply means that the emperor does not know about it.

The trouble is that there exist two forces that benefit from keeping the tsar uninformed. One part of the "wall" around the tsar is formed of the bureaucracy (including ministers); the second—the instigator of all unrest—is the intelligentsia. The intelligentsia's dream is to become the bureaucracy under a new regime brought about by revolution. The task of the intelligentsia, the self-styled "third element," is to use newspapers, pamphlets, lectures, and dubious foreign connections and money to distort the relationship between the benefactor and his people. The tsar rightly hates intellectuals, propagandists, agitators, and revolutionaries. The competing bureaucrats and intellectuals construct a wall of lies around "the good tsar," immuring him inside his palace and preventing him from telling his subjects how much he loves them.

The empress adheres passionately to this point of view. For her, one of the primary motives for canonizing Seraphim of Sarov was to strengthen the bond between the tsar and the people. Yet the court is unaware of Alexandra's growing political awareness. The conversation with Prince Mirsky marks her debut in the arena of politics.

Having examined Mirsky's draft reforms, Nicholas is minded to endorse them. The document is moderate, especially compared to the resolution put forward by the zemstvo congress. It proposes that the State Council be partially elected (i.e., turned into a proto-parliament) and that the Old Believers be granted freedom of worship. At the same time, crucially, it seeks to preserve the autocratic system. But Nicholas does not immediately put pen to paper (perhaps he only pretended to endorse Mirsky's plan). Instead, he decides to convene a plenary session of the Committee of Ministers. Nicholas II and Mirsky discuss who should be summoned. The emperor does not want the "freemason" Witte to be present, while Mirsky is disinclined to see Pobedonostsev, whom he despises for his know-all attitude. The tsar eventually agrees to invite Witte, but when Mirsky departs he sends Pobedonostsev a note: "Everything's a mess. Come and help sort out the chaos."

"I CONGRATULATE YOU, GENTLEMEN!"

November 28, 1904, sees another demonstration outside Saint Petersburg's Kazan Cathedral, which is dispersed by police like the one three-and-a-half years before. All officials set to attend the session with the tsar on 2 December are unsettled by the new wave of unrest.

The first person whom Mirsky bumps into on the way to the meeting that will decide the fate of the reform program is Pobedonostsev. During the session, the latter delivers a coruscating speech against the reforms, accusing Mirsky of wanting to curb the monarchy's powers—something that even the tsar himself has no right to do, for it would violate the oath he gave during his coronation. The emperor is not entitled to limit the authority bestowed upon him from above.

Interior Minister Mirsky remains mostly silent. After the first sitting, Nicholas instructs Witte to draft a new decree in place of Mirsky's proposals.

"The bureaucracy has triumphed. The case against it has collapsed, and there is nothing left to do except build more prisons and tighten the screws," Mirsky says to Interior Ministry staff after the meeting. He complains of being "marginalized" by Witte. However, the new draft is not much different from his own, which gives him hope.

Ahead of the final sitting scheduled for 8 December, the tension is rising palpably. On 5-6 December student riots break out in Moscow right in front of the house of Grand Duke Sergei.

Unexpectedly, the final sitting on 8 December is attended by the tsar's uncles, Grand Dukes Sergei, Vladimir, and Alexei. The idea of reform seems to be dead and buried, but Count Dmitry Solsky, a member of the State Council, tables an amendment to create something like a lower house of parliament (he calls it the "first instance" of parliament), whose task would be to review laws before submission to the State Council. Solsky is backed first by Grand Duke Vladimir and then by the tsar, whereupon everyone agrees unanimously, including Grand Duke Sergei and Prince Mirsky, who diametrically oppose each other. According to Witte's memoirs, the grandeur of the historical moment caused some ministers to shed a tear.

But the family drama does not end there. The next day the emperor is paid a visit by two of his most influential political advisers: Uncle Sergei and his mother. They hold a long discussion.

On 11 December Empress Dowager Maria Feodorovna informs Mirsky that she generally approves of the decree, expect for the paragraph about elections, which disturbs her greatly. That same evening Witte goes to see the tsar with his freshly drafted decree in hand. Grand Duke Sergei is there in the tsar's office. Nicholas expresses concern and asks that the paragraph about elections be amended. Witte says that it is a precursor to a new constitution, but if the emperor does not wish to go down that path, the offending paragraph can simply be crossed out. Exchanging glances with Grand Duke Sergei, the tsar replies: "I will never agree to any representative form of government, for I consider it harmful to the people entrusted to me by God. Therefore, I shall follow your advice and cross out this paragraph."

The emperor later pours out his soul to Pyotr Trubetskoy, the marshal of the nobility for Moscow. "Only autocracy can save Russia," the tsar is alleged to have exclaimed. "The common man would not understand the idea of a constitution. He would think only that the tsar's hands have been tied, and in this case, I congratulate you, gentlemen!"

Nicholas II agrees that Prince Mirsky should resign, but only a month later, in mid-January 1905. The prince is dispatched as governor-general of the Caucasus.

On 14 December the new decree, written by Witte, appears in print. It makes no mention of elections. Moreover, it is accompanied by a statement that the very idea of elected representatives having a role in government is "alien to the Russian people, who are loyal to the age-old foundations of the political system as it exists." The decree also prohibits "liberal banquets" and other private meetings at which reforms might be discussed.

DEFEAT

On 21 December, the tsar and his brother Mikhail travel by train to Minsk to inspect military units bound for the Far East. On the train he receives the news that Port Arthur has fallen. The news does not come as a surprise: "Although it was foreseen, one had hoped that the army would prevail. Yet the defenders are heroes and did more than what might have been expected. It is God's will!" reads the tsar's diary.

His reaction stuns even his inner circle. "The news that dispirited all those who love their country was received by the tsar with indifference. He showed not the slightest trace of gloom," the general's wife Bogdanovich conveys the tsar's attitude. "Sakharov [the war minister] started telling anecdotes, and there was no end to the chortling. Sakharov knows how to make the tsar laugh. How deplorable! God forbid that such behavior should become known to the people or [the tsar's] enemies."

A couple of days later Saint Petersburg learns of the fall of Port Arthur. "Its defenders ran out of shells, the soldiers are sick with scurvy and typhus, the wounded are multitudinous, Japanese bombs hit hospitals and injured them even more. We blew up our own forts and ships at port. It is a repeat of Sevastopol precisely 50 years on," Grand Duke Konstantin describes the situation.

In December 1904, everyone is comparing Port Arthur to Sevastopol and the war with Japan to the Crimean War. For the past half-century the Crimean War has been a symbol of shame and humiliation. Emperor Nicholas I did not live to see the end of the war, dying after Russia's failed assault on the city of Yevpatoria (he is rumored to have committed suicide). Sevastopol fell just six months after the tsar's death. The excessive sangfroid of Nicholas II stands in sharp contrast to the anxiety and shock felt by his great-grandfather.

Alexei Suvorin writes that "never before have I thought that a revolution might happen in Russia, but now we have to consider the possibility." Witte is dreading the arrival of spring: the Petersburg *beau monde* is sure that the fall of Port Arthur spells revolution.

|| Chapter 6 ||

GEORGY GAPON

in which Russia gets a new leader of popular
protest: his name is Georgy Gapon

A NIGHTMARE AFTER CHRISTMAS

On Christmas Day, 25 December 1904,* Georgy Gapon's trade union arranges fairs throughout the capital. Workers bring their families along to the festivities, but among them the talk is serious. They intend to help a group of colleagues who have been dismissed from the Putilov factory (unlawfully in their eyes). However, they are concerned less by the plight of their comrades than by the public condemnation they will face if they do not make a stand. Gapon's organization has a dubious reputation in revolutionary circles, where it is accused of working for the regime. Gapon's trade unionists do not wish to be branded as cowards and stool pigeons. They are shamed into becoming ever-more radicalized.

On 27 December, the "Gaponites" hold a general meeting at which they propose to write a petition and call a strike in support of the dismissed workers. Gapon is against the idea. He knows full well that a general strike will put an end to his career, if not to the movement, for his benefactors will not forgive him for an outburst of real protest. However, the moment gets the better of the ambitious priest. As the head of the organization, he must be seen to take the lead: "You want to up the stakes? Go on then!" he says with his heart, not his head.[†]

The strike begins at the Putilov factory on 3 January 1905, when thirteen thousand people put down their tools. The plant director comes out to see the workers and suggests that they all sit down for a friendly chat to sort things out. The workers reply that they want to be represented by Father Gapon. The director, whose name is Smirnov, refuses, saying that Gapon is "the enemy of the workers and is leading them to ruin." In response, one of the activists rushes at him with a knife. The director only just manages to escape harm.

A rally starts outside the factory building, and Gapon, standing on a cart, reads out a list of demands, which includes restoring the laid-off workers, establishing an eight-hour working day, scrapping overtime, improving ventilation on the factory floor, increasing wages, and legalizing the trade union movement.

---

* Pre-revolutionary Russia used the Julian calendar.
† This is a very typical scene—one hundred years later organizers of almost all protest actions will split into radicals (those in favor of more decisive and offensive actions) and moderates (those in favor of waiting and negotiating with authorities). Leaders who are ready to aggravate the situation will be compared to Georgy Gapon—even though initially Gapon stuck to a different tactic. For example, Alexei Navalny in the early twenty-first century is often called "the new Gapon."

In the evening Gapon receives a call from Saint Petersburg Governor Fullon, who says that Witte has promised that the dismissed workers will be reinstated. Still, Gapon persuades the governor to let the negotiations continue and secures an assurance that no one will be arrested.

But Smirnov refuses to accept the workers' demands and the talks break up. He does not have much choice, since he himself is a hired manager and under pressure from the factory shareholders. The factory is a major supplier of the Russian military, and its owners are demanding that all arms contracts are fulfilled on schedule. For their part, the shareholders are under pressure from the government. The result is more strikes. On 5 January other factories join in, swelling the total to twenty-five thousand people.

A SHOT ON THE NEVA

The year 1905 begins with a symbolic event. On 2 January Grand Duke Sergei, who has just left his post as Moscow's governor-general, leaves the old capital for the imperial residence Tsarskoye Selo outside Saint Petersburg. It is customary for all city officials to see him off at the station. The train has not yet departed when a young man approaches the Moscow police chief Dmitry Trepov and shoots at him three times. Alarmed, the grand duke rushes out of his carriage, but Trepov is unharmed. Three shots, three misses. No one can imagine that in just two weeks' time the bullet-dodging Trepov will become the most influential person in Russia, or that the real threat is in fact hanging over the grand duke.

On 6 January, the Epiphany, Emperor Nicholas II, together with senior members of the clergy, is standing inside a pavilion on the frozen Neva River, watching the ceremonial blessing of the water. After the ritual, cannons begin to fire from the direction of the Peter and Paul Fortress, opposite the Winter Palace. One of them, it turns out, is loaded with live ammunition. Several windows in the Winter Palace are shattered. The tsar and his retinue are safe; the only injured man is a policeman, whose surname, ironically, is Romanov.

Everyone, including Nicholas himself, is sure that this was an assassination attempt, and within a few hours rumors have spread throughout the city that revolutionaries have tried to kill the tsar. An investigation begins, headed by Grand Duke Sergei. The general's wife Alexandra Bogdanovich notes in detail all the gossip about when the next attempt on the tsar's life is apparently set to take place. The word on the street is that anarchists have arrived from Switzerland. Some say they plan to assassinate the imperial couple and Pobedonostsev. Others think the targets are Dowager Empress Maria Feodorovna, Grand Duke Sergei, and Grand Duke Alexei.

The startled tsar leaves Saint Petersburg for Tsarskoye Selo the same day. Were it not for these rumors, Nicholas would have stayed in the city and subsequent events would have unfolded differently. But he decides to take cover, and in doing so he effectively vacates the Winter Palace for good. The main residence of the Russian emperors, commissioned by Empress Elizabeth, the daughter of Peter the Great, is no longer the seat of the royal house. The next head of state to reside at the Winter Palace will be Alexander Kerensky, the leader of the Provisional Government in 1917.

The gossip in Bogdanovich's diary is not far from the truth. As Boris Savinkov recalls, three groups from the Socialist-Revolutionary (SR) militant organization have indeed arrived from Switzerland, one in Saint Petersburg. Moreover, one of the female militants has successfully infiltrated high society and is due to present the tsar with flowers at an imperial ball. Without waiting for confirmation from the SR central committee, the Saint Petersburg group decides to act. Only at the last moment is the ball cancelled, forcing the militants to select new targets: Justice Minister Muravyov and Grand Duke Vladimir. By January, the tsar is effectively safe. The immediate threat to his life has passed.

Everyone is so caught up by it all that little attention is paid to the workers' strike. The authorities ignore Gapon's demands, with Finance Minister Kokovtsov describing them as "illegal and generally infeasible." The director of the Putilov factory, Smirnov, says that he cannot fulfill any of them, because it would ruin the shareholders. Given the disastrous state of affairs in the Far East, his bosses are jittery enough as it is.

Twenty-four hours after it began, the strike numbers a hundred and fifty thousand members. Gapon already feels like a hero, and is accompanied everywhere by fans and up to twenty volunteer guards and correspondents, including some from abroad. He delivers speech after speech to various gatherings. On 6 January, he recalls that he spoke the same fiery rhetoric twenty to thirty times.

The underground revolutionary newspapers abroad have no sense of the febrile atmosphere, and continue to write disparagingly of Gapon. But in Saint Petersburg it is clear to everyone that he is in charge. He is the focus for all the capital's oppositionists and politically active members of the public: the SRs and liberals from the Union of Liberation coalesce around him. In a matter of weeks Gapon is the head of the largest organization in Saint Petersburg. Among his new associates is Pinhas Rutenberg, a twenty-seven-year-old Socialist-Revolutionary and former workshop manager at the Putilov factory. He accompanies Gapon everywhere and assists with writing and editing his speeches.

With the factory refusing to fulfill the workers' demands, Gapon adds some that are overtly political: the convocation of a constituent assembly of representatives of the entire Russian people to be elected by universal, equal, direct, and secret ballot; equality for all estates and creeds; civil liberties; and the release of political prisoners. The proposals do not come from Gapon himself, but rather the political activists who are now thronging around him.

On the same day of Epiphany, 6 January, Gapon decides to write a petition to the tsar and present it to the Winter Palace as part of a mass demonstration. It is a bold move. Although petitions are commonplace, no one before has ever tried to gather thousands of protesters in the capital.* Gapon writes a draft to the tsar, and Rutenberg edits it.

This remarkable document is fully consistent with the belief of Nicholas II and his entourage in the people's love for the tsar, which is obstructed by a "wall" of bureaucrats and intellectuals. "We have been enslaved by Your officials ... a bureaucratic government made up of embezzlers and thieves," begins Gapon.† He continues: "Do not refuse assistance to Your people, but lead them out of the grave of deprivation, poverty and ignorance. Knock down the wall between You and Your people, and let them rule the country with You. Your will is to make the people happy, but happiness is denied by the bureaucracy."

The loyalist mantra states a revolutionary demand, something that even the recent zemstvo congress baulked at: the creation of a constituent assembly: "The people must be represented and self-governing. Let there be free and equal electoral rights for all."

For safety reasons, Gapon decides not to spend the night of 6-7 January at home. "For one final time I gazed upon the painting *Christ in the Desert* [by Ivan Kramskoy] and upon the furniture made for me by pupils at the orphanage," he describes this sentimental moment. "Trampled by grief, yet full of resolution and determination, I left my dwelling never to cast eyes over it again." Consciously or not, Gapon is comparing himself with the protagonist of the painting on his wall. Having heard from female admirers that he "looks like Jesus," Gapon is beginning to feel like a messiah.

---

*Some describe Gapon as the world's first human rights activist. Mahatma Gandhi (influenced by Tolstoy) preached non-violent resistance and peaceful demonstrations in the 1920s, and Martin Luther King, Jr. made them mainstream in the 1960s. But the pioneer was Gapon, even though his peace march was not altogether peaceful.

† This is an almost exact match to Alexei Navalny's phrasing "party of crooks and thieves," which united the Russian protesting public in 2011.

On 7 January the now one hundred and eighty thousand striking workers seize Saint Petersburg's Warsaw and Baltic railway stations, paralyzing the capital. Gapon's petition is read out at all branches of his organization, and workers put their signatures to it (more than one hundred thousand, according to Gapon himself). Everyone awaits Sunday 9 January as if it were the second coming or the end of the world. The authorities take a long time to react. Both the police and the governor consider Gapon as one of their own and not a troublemaker, so they do not attach much significance to the strike until the very last moment.

Only in the morning of 7 January is Gapon summoned to the Ministry of Justice. He arrives accompanied by assistants.

"Tell me frankly, what is all this about?" asks Justice Minister Nikolai Muravyov, a former prosecutor at the trial of the assassins of Alexander II. Before replying, Gapon asks for a promise that he will not be arrested, which is granted.

"The country," Gapon later recalls his own words, "is experiencing a deep political and economic crisis. The workers can suffer no more. I ask that you write a letter to His Majesty and request that he appear before the people. We guarantee his safety. Fall to his feet if need be, and beg him for his own sake to receive our delegation. Russia will be eternally grateful to you for doing so."

Muravyov's mien changes. He rises from the table and, indicating that the meeting is over, utters the words: "I shall perform my duty." Gapon takes this to mean just one thing: he will go to the tsar and advise him to open fire on the demonstrators.

Gapon is sure that public disorder is unavoidable. That evening he visits all eleven branches of the union, where, in an unwise attempt to avert bloodshed, he tells the workers that they must march on to the Winter Palace in the company of their wives and children, adding that if the tsar does not want to listen to them or greets them with bullets, then he is no longer their sovereign.

It is difficult to say whether the organizers of the procession were in fact expecting bloodshed, but the petition certainly suggests that they were. It begins thus: "Sire, we are exhausted! Our patience has reached its limit. The terrible moment has come when death is better than to continue our insufferable torture." And it ends in a similar vein: "If You do not respond to our plea, we shall die here in this square, in front of Your palace. We have nowhere else to go."

On the night of 7–8 January, high on adrenalin, Gapon meets with professional revolutionaries, Socialist-Revolutionaries, and Social

Democrats, and draws up another plan. Unlike the tens of thousands of workers, he knows that Nicholas II is not in the capital. He wants to wait for the tsar to arrive from Tsarskoye Selo and meet with him on Palace Square (outside the Winter Palace). Together with a group of negotiators, the plan is to issue two demands: an amnesty for political prisoners and the convocation of an all-land assembly. If Nicholas II agrees to the demands, Gapon will approach the crowd holding aloft a white handkerchief and "a great public holiday will commence." If not, says Gapon, he will throw up a red handkerchief to let the people know that they have no tsar, and the people's revolt will begin. Until that happens, the socialists are not to lay a finger on Nicholas or provoke the crowd.

On the last day before the demonstration, Gapon rushes around the city non-stop, giving dozens of speeches, urging everyone to go out into the street. He even states in an interview with a British journalist that, if the demands are not met, the telegraph office will be seized. He asks for these words not to be printed.

TROOPS IN THE CITY

On 8 January Interior Minister Mirsky gathers his deputies, together with the police chief Lopukhin, Finance Minister Kokovtsov, Justice Minister Muravyov, and Saint Petersburg Governor Fullon, at the Mariinsky Palace. Muravyov proposes to arrest Gapon, but Mirsky and Fullon are opposed, saying that it will only make matters worse. Mirsky suggests that a small group of workers' representatives be allowed onto Palace Square, and asks if it would be better to evacuate the tsar from Tsarskoye Selo to Gatchina Palace, further south. With nothing decided, the meeting breaks up, whereupon Mirsky and Lopukhin go to see the emperor.

They find Nicholas in a calm state of mind. The hope is that everything will soon blow over. After the trip to Tsarskoye Selo, the worn-out Mirsky holds another meeting on the deployment of troops in the capital. In attendance is Grand Duke Vladimir, art connoisseur, president of the Imperial Academy of Arts, and part-time commander of the Saint Petersburg Military District. He says that additional troops have been dispatched to the capital from Peterhof, Pskov, and Revel (today's Tallinn).

The question of how to pacify the protesters is not discussed. There is unanimity on this front. The ministers are sure that if the workers do indeed take to the streets, they will disperse of their own accord on seeing the police cordons. No special orders are given, since everything will be done according to the military regulations: the troops will be armed with live ammunition, sabers, and whips in order to restore order, should the need arise. How else to pacify the demonstrators? Rubber bullets and water cannons have not yet been invented.

Writer Maxim Gorky meets his friend Savva Morozov to ask what the business community thinks. Morozov is pessimistic and repeats rumors that he has heard from his Saint Petersburg colleagues: "It is possible that tomorrow Grand Duke Vladimir will be in charge of the city and newspaper editorial offices will be violently raided. Members of the intelligentsia will probably be arrested." Just in case, Morozov gives Gorky his Browning pistol.

A few hours later Morozov receives new information that the authorities have decided not to let the workers near the palace to stop them from "organizing carnage," for which purpose the army has been brought in from the provinces. Gorky hurries to the editorial office of the literary magazine *Son of the Fatherland* and urgently demands that a "delegation of intellectuals" go to Prince Mirsky with a request not to use force.

Gorky goes himself in the company of seven professors and lawyers. The interior minister does not receive them. Instead, a member of staff inquires in whose name the venerable delegation has been sent. "I could explain 'in whose name' we are here, but I fear that you would not understand. The name is completely unknown here. It is the name of the Russian people," replies Gorky. They eventually see the head of the gendarmes, Deputy Interior Ministry Rydzevsky (with whom all talks fail) and finally Sergei Witte. But Witte washes his hands of all involvement: "I am powerless to assist in your endeavor."

In the end, Prince Mirsky decides to arrest Gapon and to post notices around the city banning gatherings and processions. The printing presses are on strike, so the notices are thinly spread. What's more, the posters urging workers to march on the Winter Palace are not removed, making some feel that the authorities are not actually opposed to the procession.

Gapon avoids arrest for the time being. A high-ranking police officer named Rydzevsky explains to the head of the tsar's chief of staff that Gapon has moved to a workers' district and it would be dangerous to send the police there at night. "Do you want me to have the lives of ten people on my conscience for the sake of one wretched priest?" he says. The arrest is rescheduled for the morning.

In the evening of 8 January Prince Shervashidze, the husband of Dowager Empress Maria Feodorovna and the stepfather of Nicholas II, is on his way to the theatre. He is approached by a journalist acquaintance called

Filippov, who has just spoken to Gapon and conveys a request from the latter to the influential prince: the people must not be met with violence and they must be given an opportunity to see the emperor. Shervashidze chuckles in response. He is sure that there will be no procession. The workers will not go anywhere in such weather—the temperature in Saint Petersburg is minus fifteen degrees Celsius.

The night before what will become known as Bloody Sunday, Gapon and his closest associates appoint successors in case worst comes to worst, and take memento photographs of themselves. In his memoirs Gapon writes that there was no plan in the event of a clash with the imperial troops. In the morning, he asks the workers to take icons and processional banners from churches. The local priests do not want to hand them over, so the workers take them by force. Gapon, the new Christ in their eyes, needs them more. The procession starts at 10 a.m., and half an hour later the workers reach the soldiers' barricades.

According to Gapon's memoirs, a detachment of Cossacks cuts into the crowd brandishing sabers, after which the troops open fire without warning. Gapon survives by falling to the ground during each salvo. Others are dying or fleeing. According to legend, he cries out: "God is no more, the tsar is no more!" (Gapon himself does not mention using such a theatrical phrase). He writes that "someone took me by the hand and led me into a side street a few paces away from the carnage." It is Rutenberg. He pulls out a pair of scissors and cuts Gapon's hair to disguise him (the workers later share the hair among themselves). Gapon is given a "ragged coat and hat" to complete his transformation.

The whole city is a battlefield. In total six columns are converging on Palace Square, three from the north and three from the south. At 11:30 a.m. the southwest column led by Gapon comes under fire at the Narva Triumphal Gate, five hundred meters south of the Winter Palace. At about midday the three northern columns—from the direction of Vasilievsky Island and two districts known as Vyborg Side and Petersburg Side—are attacked. The "Petersburg" column reaches Trinity Bridge (i.e., the heart of the city). To the right is the Peter and Paul Fortress, where all the Russian emperors* are buried, and to the left stands a mansion built for the former mistress of Nicholas II, the ballerina Matilda Kschessinskaya.† This is where the shooting described by Gorky takes place.

---

* Peter the Great founded the Russian Empire in 1721 and introduced the European title of emperor; previous Russian tsars (who were not emperors) are buried in Moscow.
† A biopic of her life in 2017 caused scandal in Russian religious circles, for by that time Nicholas II was a saint.

Half an hour later the "Vyborg" column advances from Finland Station past Kschessinskaya's mansion, before being dispersed with whips, not bullets. Twelve years later the same topography will be exploited by Vladimir Lenin, who, on arriving at Finland Station, proceeds along the same route to Kschessinskaya's mansion, now abandoned by its owner. Lenin will occupy that very building, which, on 9 January 1905, has just witnessed the shooting of the first victims of the Russian revolution.

The worst of the slaughter, however, happens around the Imperial Academy of Arts on University Embankment almost opposite the Winter Palace, where the column from Vasilievsky Island is advancing. Here the soldiers meet resistance from university students and revolutionary activists. The column is not dispersed, and instead manages to seize an arms depot and build a barricade. Symbolically, the fiercest fighting takes place right by the walls of the academy, which is headed by Grand Duke Vladimir, who also doubles up as commander of the Saint Petersburg Military District. It was he who ordered troops to the capital in the first place.

"I will never forget the restrained, majestic, unarmed crowd heading towards the cavalry and rifle attack. What a terrible sight," writes Valentin Serov, who observed the scene in horror from a window of the academy. The forty-year-old court painter has produced dozens of portraits of the imperial family and is well versed in politics. He understands what is unfolding outside his window. A few days later he announces his resignation from the Imperial Academy of Arts because he no longer wants to be part of the same institution as Grand Duke Vladimir. He does not paint any more portraits of the Romanovs from that moment on.

The battle on Vasilievsky Island continues for two days. Only in the evening of 10 January do the authorities finally crush the resistance of the armed students.

The columns advancing from the southeast down Shlisselburg Tract have more luck. The officers dare not open fire on the unarmed marchers because they have not received instructions to do so. Meanwhile, the commander at the Neva Gate has complied with the order not to let people pass overland, but for some reason he is not responsible for guarding the river. Realizing that they are safe on the ice, the crowd walks over the frozen waterway to Nevsky Prospect and Palace Square. Back on land the troops again open fire, shooting at people near Kazan Cathedral and on the bridge across the Moika River, as well as around Palace Square itself and the Admiralty.

There is no precise data on the number of casualties. According to official figures, one hundred and thirty people lie dead and about three hundred are wounded. Gapon writes that the number of dead is between six hundred and nine hundred. Abroad, Peter Struve's newspaper *Liberation* reports some twelve hundred victims.

Rumors soon spread that the government has hidden most of the corpses and ordered them not to be handed over to relatives. Public funerals are prohibited; the massacred are buried at night, in secret, in mass graves.

Rutenberg takes the shell-shocked Gapon to the home of Savva Morozov, where Gapon now shaves off his beard. Dressed as a university student, Gapon heads for Gorky's apartment.*

Gorky is distraught at the sight of massacred, abandoned corpses. But instead of being cowed, the writer is stirred by the horror. Having put the exhausted priest to bed in a room in his apartment, he pens a letter to his ex-wife Ekaterina Peshkova in Nizhny Novgorod: "So, my dear, the Russian revolution has started. I offer you my hearty congratulations. We are not daunted by the dead. History will be repainted in the color of blood. Tomorrow will see even more drama and heroism, though, of course, not much can be done with one's bare hands."

That night sees a meeting of the Free Economic Society, effectively a continuation of the intelligentsia's "liberal banquets," only this time several thousand people are packed into the hall. All the capital's leading intellectuals are there, including Zinaida Gippius, her husband Dmitry Merezhkovsky, the religious thinker Dmitry Filosofov, and a guest from Moscow, the young poet Boris Bugaev (pen name Andrei Bely). "You can imagine the commotion that ensued. All were outraged. How could they open fire on an unarmed crowd? Purely out of blind fear of any peaceful gathering, without understanding the nub of the matter," writes Gippius in her diary.

Having caught a few hours' sleep, Gapon arrives with Gorky and Rutenberg. The writer stands on the podium, reads out Gapon's petition, and gives the floor to "his representative," without introducing him by name. The clean-shaven and newly attired Gapon says that this is "not a time for speeches, but for action. The workers have shown that they are prepared to die, but unarmed they have no chance against bayonets and revolvers. Now it is your turn to help them," he says to the hall. Even if the audience recognizes him, they do not show it. Gapon, Rutenberg, and several others next discuss how to get hold of weapons and organize a popular uprising, while Gorky keeps a watchful eye over the entrance to the

---

*This address, 20 Vosstaniya (Uprising) Street (then called Znamenskaya [Apparition] Street), is right next door to Vladimir Putin's childhood home on Baskov Lane, where he grew up half a century after the events described.

building. The participants at the meeting write an appeal to the officers of the Imperial Guard, which is signed by 459 people. A few days later, when the roundups begin, the incriminating list of signatures is burnt.

Later that same evening Gapon writes another appeal, this time to both the soldiers and the officers, condemning those responsible for killing his "innocent brothers" and blessing members of the military willing to help the people achieve freedom.

The liberal finance minister and future prime minister Vladimir Kokovtsov remembers the day largely as one of delays. In his memoirs he describes in detail how two visiting ladies overstay their welcome in his office because "people are being shot in the streets." In the evening he is late for a dinner appointment because his coach is held up at every turn. In any case, he has to wait a dreadfully long time for supper because his dining partner—the head of the prison service—has been delayed by protesters pelting stones at his carriage.

"What a difficult day! There were serious disturbances in Saint Petersburg due to the workers' desire to march on the Winter Palace. The troops had to open fire in various parts of the city. There are many dead and wounded. Lord, how painful and dispiriting! Mamá came to us from the city for morning mass. We had breakfast," writes Nicholas II in his diary in the evening of 9 January. The characteristic telegraphic style suggests insensitivity, but more likely he is bewildered. During the day, he has not received anyone or taken any decisions.

Nor are they taken by anyone else in authority. Only on Tuesday 11 January does the minister of the court, Count Fredericks, visit the emperor with a weekly report and request that the chief of staff, General Mosolov, ascertain whether the security forces are coping with the disorder. Mosolov goes on foot to Governor Fullon, who says that the police are overwhelmed because new hotbeds of unrest are popping up everywhere. Moreover, the army is not helping in any constructive sense, and there is reason to fear that "some of the instigators will now head for Tsarskoye Selo."

The commander of the army, for his part, radiates calm. Relieving himself of any blame, he reports to Mosolov that he gave no instructions to his officers, who acted purely according to the military regulations, adding that there is no reason to doubt their loyalty.

Speaking over the phone to Fredericks, who is waiting to be received by Nicholas at Tsarskoye Selo, Mosolov informs him that the situation is febrile and that even at Tsarskoye Selo the tsar is not safe. Fredericks says that he must advise the tsar to take precautions, whereupon Mosolov suddenly recalls a domestic conversation he had that morning with a relative.

Earlier that day, 11 January, Mosolov was paid a visit by his brother-in-law from Moscow. Aware of the situation in Saint Petersburg, his brother-in-law is harshly critical of the police. There is no need, he opines, to use violence against the crowd—that only increases the anger and desire to resist. A far more effective tactic would be to split the crowd up and drive each part into a cul-de-sac. There, they can be processed: the hardcore arrested, the periphery released. That's how it's done in Moscow, he says, with never a drop of blood spilt.

The brother-in-law, a certain Dmitry Trepov, knows what he is talking about. He has just resigned from his post as chief of the Moscow police with the intention of heading to the capital.

Mosolov shouts down the phone line that Nicholas should appoint Trepov as the capital's new governor-general, for he will suppress the uprising in no time. Half an hour later Fredericks summons Trepov to Tsarskoye Selo and, by evening that same day, the now Governor General Trepov moves into his new residence at the Winter Palace. He will soon be known by the epithet "dictator," a common term at the time to describe someone who dictates his will to the emperor.

Prince Mirsky finally retires and his powers are transferred to the team of Grand Duke Sergei, Mirsky's main adversary, who demands tougher action from Nicholas II. The new head of the Interior Ministry is Grand Duke Sergei's assistant, Alexander Bulygin, although he is overshadowed in the policing stakes by the tsar's new right-hand man, Trepov. The latter is given *carte blanche* to implement drastic measures.

On 14 January, the emperor writes to his mother: "For me, Trepov is irreplaceable, a kind of secretary. He is experienced, clever and circumspect in his advice. I give him Witte's dense reports and he filters everything quickly and concisely. It's a secret [that Trepov reads them], of course!"

Most official accounts of the early days after 9 January are written many years after the event, but even so the paranoia gripping the ministerial corridors is palpable. Officials do not believe that the multitudinous procession was a grassroots phenomenon and led by one man, Father Gapon. Everyone is sure that it was a vast, well-planned conspiracy involving members of the government.* The title of schemer-in-chief belongs to Witte, and many ministers suspect that he knew about everything in

---

*A typical situation for the early twenty-first century. For example, in winter 2011-2012 after the rally for fair elections at Bolotnaya Square many senior officials will not be able to believe that protests were spontaneous—among themselves they will be earnestly discussing that there was a carefully planned operation involving some Presidential Administration officials (for instance, Vladislav Surkov).

advance. Finance Minister Kokovtsov, for instance, writes that there is no way that Witte could not have known: first, he had his own agents; second, Mirsky consulted him on all matters; and third, the "interim government" had been to see him and urged him to take measures (by "interim government" Kokovtsov means the delegation of intellectuals led by Gorky).

Despite his criticism of the police, Trepov is also more inclined to believe in conspiracy theories than in across-the-board sloppiness: one of the first orders he issues is the immediate arrest of all "conspirators" and all members of the "interim government"—the same people who tried to prevent bloodshed the day before it happened.

When Grand Duke Sergei returns to Moscow after the New Year holidays, the city's *siloviki* persuade him and his family to move from Alexandra Palace in Neskuchny Garden to the Kremlin. Moscow workers are on strike in the vicinity of the palace, so at 11 p.m. the Grand Duke pulls the children out of bed and goes to the Kremlin.

The palace they move to has not been heated or ventilated for a long time. "A humid, icy chill hung in the air," writes the grand duke's niece Maria. Even the stoic grand duke complains in his diary about the "biting cold." The next day, on learning about the appointment of his trusted assistant Trepov as Saint Petersburg's new governor-general, Sergei adds to his diary: "I fear for him."

In the meantime, the revolutionaries Boris Savinkov and Ivan Kalyaev have been preparing an assassination attempt on Grand Duke Sergei for a month. They initially planned to kill him on Tverskaya Street as his carriage pulled out of the drive of his residence; then they switched to Neskuchny Garden, before finally focusing on the Kremlin itself. They believe that they can identify Sergei's carriage by its lanterns, but later discover that his wife travels with exactly the same lanterns. So as not to get the wrong victim, they have to remember the faces of the coachmen, which means the hit must take place in daylight.

Savinkov is putting the finishing touches to the plans when he receives an unexpected visit from Pinhas Rutenberg, a former course mate at university. He talks about his role in the events of 9 January. He wants to take Gapon abroad and needs fake passports, which Savinkov helps to secure.

A FINANCIAL ILLITERATE

On 11 January, despite the ongoing unrest in the Saint Petersburg, Gorky boards a train for Riga, where his beloved actress, Maria Andreyeva, is dying.

His letter on Bloody Sunday to his first wife also contained the words: "The day after tomorrow I will go to Riga—my friend is dangerously ill. M.F. [Maria Feodorovna Andreyeva] has peritonitis. Savva and the doctor say it could be fatal. Yet all personal sorrows and failures are meaningless at this time of Russia's awakening." Savva Morozov, Andreyeva's previous lover, whom she rejected for Gorky, keeps vigil at her hospital bed, which is why he is not in Saint Petersburg during the disturbances, and his house is empty (and Gorky's got a key) when Gapon goes there for a change of clothes.

Andreyeva had left the Moscow Art Theatre the year before. She moved first to Staraya Russa near Novgorod, and then to Riga. It is on stage in Riga around the time of Bloody Sunday that the pregnant Andreyeva has an accident. During a rehearsal, she falls through a trap door. She loses her child and contracts peritonitis. "My dearest, my darling, I'll be there tomorrow. Hold on. There is no earlier train. Be strong. Wait for me. I love you with all my heart. Alexei," Gorky telegraphs her on 10 January.

However, when he arrives in Riga, Gorky is immediately arrested as a conspirator and member of the "interim government," and promptly taken back to Saint Petersburg. "Idiots! They should have arrested all the people," Gorky's friend, the writer Leonid Andreyev, writes to Andreyeva. "It's terrible it's happened during your illness. Alexei has gone to prison with a heavy heart. But do not worry. His punishment should not be too severe. The times of Chernyshevsky* are over." But soon Leonid Andreyev himself is arrested for holding a meeting of the Russian Social Democratic Labor Party in his apartment.

Inside the Peter and Paul Fortress, Gorky is mad with anxiety about the health of "Marusia" [Maria]. Meanwhile, an important yet apocryphal conversation takes place between her and Savva Morozov. Allegedly, the thirty-six-year-old Maria says that she can feel the approach of death, at which the forty-two-year-old Savva replies that he has no doubt that she will outlive him. The actress says that she does not want to, because without Morozov there will be no one to take care of her. Morozov says that he will take care of her even after his death by giving her a life insurance policy.

"Morozov considered me financially illiterate and feared that I would die under a fence somewhere," recalls Andreyeva. "He thought my relatives would try to fleece me, so he made sure that his life insurance policy, worth 100,000 roubles,† would go straight to me. Mental illness runs in the Morozov family, and he is sure that he will succumb to it."

---

* The philosopher Nikolai Chernyshevsky was exiled to Siberia for political activism for twenty years (1864–1883).
† About $1,318,333 in 2017.

Despite all the concern, Andreyeva slowly recovers. Morozov takes her to Saint Petersburg and departs himself for Moscow, since his factory is affected by the unrest. But first he makes Maria promise to "call him if he can be of any assistance" and he will immediately return.

In his damp cell Gorky suffers a violent coughing fit. The medical diagnosis is hemoptysis. His official wife, Ekaterina Peshkova, takes care of the writer. When the authorities agree to release him on bail, it turns out that the wealthy Gorky cannot afford it. So Peshkova goes to Morozov for money. Gorky is released a month after his arrest, on 14 February, whereupon he and Andreyeva leave for Majorenhof (today's Jurmala in Latvia).

GAPON FLEES

On 12 January, the smooth-shaven Gapon attired in an old-fashioned suit, a "magnificent coat," and wearing pince-nez arrives at Tsarskoye Selo Station. The route to his destination, a suburban estate, is deliberately circuitous to throw off any potential trail. Rutenberg is due to meet him there with a forged passport. To calm his nerves during the wait, Gapon does a bit of cross-country skiing, but it does not help. A week later Rutenberg still hasn't appeared, so Gapon decides to make a dash across the border without papers.

It is probably the right option, for the police have his description. They are looking for a man of "middle height, a gypsy type, swarthy, cropped hair, recently shaved beard, crooked nose, darting eyes, Malorussian [Ukrainian] accent."

Gapon joins a group of smugglers. "Russia's entire western border was crisscrossed by professional smugglers and fugitives making deals with the border guards," he writes in his memoirs, addressed primarily to foreign audiences. "Jews, Poles, Lithuanians and others were driven by despair and turmoil to leave Russia mainly for America."

On the way, Gapon almost dies of suffocation while spending a night in a house heated with a chimneyless stove. At the border he has another lucky escape: a border guard spots him and gives chase, but falls over in the snow. The former priest manages to crawl under a barbed-wire fence into German territory. From there, he makes his way to Switzerland, where he describes himself for the first time as a "free man in a free country."

Anti-Gapon Trepov comes up with the idea that the "Gaponite" workers should be countered with laborers of their own. He arranges a meeting between Nicholas II and a group of "correct workers."* The text of the tsar's words at the meeting is printed in official newspapers the next day. It ends with the words: "I have faith in the honest feelings of the working people and in their unshakable devotion to Me.† Therefore, I forgive them their guilt." The words anger many supposedly devoted workers: first the tsar opens fire on them, and then forgives them for having been shot at. Another paragraph from the royal speech is edited out. It reads: "What will you do with your free time if you work no more than eight hours a day? I, the Tsar, work nine hours a day. My work is more stressful. You work only for yourselves, but I work for all the people. If you have free time, you will engage in politics. That I will not allow. Your only purpose is work."

Although the investigation finds no signs of pre-planned slaughter in Saint Petersburg, some fingers point at foreign masterminds.‡ The Russian Orthodox Church is the first to voice its opinion: "The Russian people, Orthodox since time immemorial, stand for Faith, the Tsar and the Fatherland. They are being incited by malicious enemies of the Fatherland, domestic and foreign." The Holy Synod officially defrocks Gapon.

The next day several newspapers, including Suvorin's *New Time*, print a sensational scoop that the Japanese government has allegedly financed the unrest in Russia to the tune of 18 million roubles.§ The information is not, in today's terminology, fake news. The Japanese really have allocated funds to destabilize Russia (by financing, for instance, the recent opposition conference in Paris). But they have no links to Gapon and Bloody Sunday. Even the Japanese could not conceive of such an audacious operation.

---

*In the early twenty-first century, pseudo-public organizations are created to simulate civil engagement, although their real purpose is to approve the actions of authorities. It is a very important feature of Russian political system. One such institution is the Civic Chamber, created in 2005. It is supposed to simulate the discussion about key issues, but it acts under close supervision of the Presidential Administration. Such fictitious public organizations became especially popular during the time when Vyacheslav Volodin was in charge of domestic policy. After he left for the Duma (Russian parliament) this method remained popular. Thus, on 12 June 2017, at the time of an anti-corruption demonstration, in the center of Moscow with numerous teenage participants, Vladimir Putin received the "proper" school pupils, gave them passports, and was photographed with them in his office.

† Nicholas refers to himself with a capital letter.

‡ Any protest activity in Russia in the early twenty-first century gets accused of having "foreign sponsors" and of being funded by the State Department of the USA. Quite often such accusations are made by Russian Orthodox Church members. For instance, patriarch Kirill and Tikhon Shevkunov, father superior of the Sretensky Monastery, are among the most vocal advocates of the theory that Russian opposition is commissioned by the West.

§ About $237,300,000 in 2017.

DEATH IN THE KREMLIN

On 2 February Grand Duke Sergei, the former Moscow governor-general, is taking his wife Ella and their adopted children, fourteen-year-old Maria and thirteen-year-old Dmitry, to the Bolshoi Theatre. Chaliapin is singing, Rachmaninoff conducting.

Savinkov knows in advance that Sergei will be at the theatre for a charity event in support of the Red Cross, which is patronized by Ella, the grand duchess. Before the performance, the terrorists occupy positions around the theatre: one bomber stands on Voskresenskaya [Resurrection] Square (today's Revolution Square), and the other on Manezhnaya Square. They know that Sergei will go to the theatre via the Kremlin's Nikolsky Gate, so he is sure to pass one of them. Savinkov sits down on a bench in Alexander Garden in front of the Kremlin and waits for the sound of an explosion.

The coach turns onto Voskresenskaya Square, right towards Kaliayev, the first bomber. He recognizes the coachman and rushes to intercept the carriage. The terrorist's arm is already raised when suddenly he spots Grand Duchess Elizabeth and her little niece and nephew. He cannot go through with it. The carriage wends its way to the Bolshoi Theatre.

Kaliayev goes to Savinkov in Alexander Garden: "I think I did the right thing. How can we kill children?" Savinkov recalls his words. Savinkov replies that far from condemning his actions, he applauds them. But Kaliayev's resolve soon returns. He says that if the organization sanctions the killing of the grand duke together with his family, he will do it that very night after the performance at the Bolshoi. Savinkov says it will not be necessary.

"The performance that evening was magnificent. Chaliapin was at the peak of his powers," recalls Maria. "The hall sparkled with jewels and uniforms. There were no thoughts of misfortune." Incidentally, it is the first and last time that Chaliapin will play the role of Eugene Onegin in Tchaikovsky's opera based on Pushkin's poem.

Two days later Grand Duke Sergei, after lunch at the usual time, leaves the Kremlin in an open carriage. He kisses his niece Maria, who asks him to buy her a mandolin. He ponders the request and tells her to wait until evening. The girl goes to see her mathematics tutor; the grand duke heads out.

At that same moment, Savinkov and Kaliayev are on Red Square. The latter wants to make up for the failed attempt near the Bolshoi Theatre and assures his friend that he can cope with the task all by himself: "I cannot fail. If the grand duke comes, I will kill him. Rest assured."

They embrace and say their goodbyes. Kaliayev goes to Nikolsky Gate; Savinkov enters the Kremlin through Spassky Gate and heads up the hill to the Alexander II monument, offering a fine view of the grand duke's home. Without waiting for the grand duke to come out, he goes to meet his accomplice, the superbly named twenty-four-year-old Dora Brilliant.* She has assembled the bomb that Kaliayev is about to throw.

The fourteen-year-old Grand Duchess Maria is with her mathematics tutor in a classroom overlooking the Kremlin's Cathedral Square and Ivan the Great Bell Tower.

"Suddenly a terrible explosion shook the air and rattled the window frames," Maria recalls. "Thoughts raced through my mind. Has one of the Kremlin's old towers collapsed? Has an avalanche of snow fallen off the roof? And where's my uncle? Dmitry came running from his classroom. We looked at each other, not daring to express our thoughts aloud. A flock of crows was swirling frantically over the tower, and then disappeared. The square began to come to life."

Throwing a cloak over her shoulders, Grand Duchess Ella runs out of the house to the site of the explosion. "The minutes were indescribably excruciating," Maria writes. "The area was swarming with people, but still no one reported to us the dreadful news that we did not doubt would come."

Her Aunt Ella arrives at the scene. Pieces of her deceased husband are strewn everywhere. She picks them up one by one and puts them on an army stretcher that has been brought from nearby. Soldiers from the barracks opposite cover the remains with their greatcoats. They hoist the stretcher onto their shoulders and take the body to Chudov Monastery, which adjoins the palace of the late Grand Duke Sergei.

Ivan Kaliayev, who threw the bomb, is slightly wounded by the explosion. Dazed and deafened, he picks up his hat and is about to walk off when he is grabbed. "What are you doing?" he cries. "I'm not going to run. I've done my job. Down with the wretched tsar, down with the wretched government, long live freedom!"

The children are taken to a church. "My aunt was kneeling by the stretcher. Her bright dress looked ridiculous among the modestly clothed people around her.... The service finished. People got up from their knees. I saw my aunt coming towards us. Her face was white—a terrible frozen mask of pain."

Grand Duchess Elizabeth does not cry. But for some reason Dora Brilliant is sobbing on the shoulder of Savinkov: "We killed him. . . . I killed

---

* *Brilliant* in Russian means "diamond."

him.... I ..." "Who?" Savinkov asks, thinking that she is talking about the soon-to-be-hanged Kaliayev. "The grand duke," she replies.

That evening Ella goes to visit the wounded coachman. So as not to upset him, she does not change into black, but remains in the same bright blue dress. With sleeves and fingernails stained with blood, she assures the injured coachman that everything is all right and that the grand duke survived. The coachman dies later that night.

AT ANY COST

"Terrible, terrible," repeats General Trepov at his royal chambers inside the Winter Palace when he is informed of the death of Grand Duke Sergei. It is also his first meeting with the new head of the secret police, Alexander Gerasimov.

"I have learned that a new terrorist group is operating in Saint Petersburg," he says to the newcomer, who has come from Kharkov. "It recently arrived from abroad. Preparations are being made for an assassination attempt on Grand Duke Vladimir, on me and on who knows who else. Listen: your first task is to eliminate this group. You must get these people at any cost. Do you understand? At any cost!"

Arriving for work, Gerasimov realizes that Saint Petersburg's legendary security department—the powerful secret police—which the entire country fears, is in chaos. There is no information at all about who is preparing the rumored assassinations. Gerasimov takes a bold decision: he informs all potential targets that they must not leave their homes until he is on top of the terrorists. Trepov, Grand Duke Vladimir, president of the Imperial Academy of Arts and commander of the Saint Petersburg Military District, and even the emperor himself obey. They place themselves under voluntary house arrest—for a few months.

Three days later Ella goes to visit her husband's assassin, Ivan Kaliayev. They meet at the police station, in the presence of the governor and a police officer. Kaliayev has been brought specially from the detention facility where he is being kept.

"Who are you?" asks Kaliayev.

"The wife of the one you killed," answers the grand duchess. "Tell me, why did you kill him?"

"The ones who instructed me to do it know the reasons. It is the result of the current regime," replies the terrorist.

"Knowing the kind heart of the deceased, I forgive you," she says, and asks the governor and officer to leave. She spends about twenty minutes alone with the arrested killer.

"We looked at each other," says Kaliayev himself after the meeting, "with a certain mystical feeling. Mortals both of us, I survived by chance, while she still lived because I consciously avoided bloodshed. Looking at her face, I could not help but notice signs of gratitude, if not to me, then to fate, for having spared her life."

"She asked me to take her icon and said she would pray for me. For me, it was a symbol of her gratitude and repentance for the crimes of the grand duke. I said that my conscience was clear. I told her I was sorry for her grief, but had acted knowingly, and if I had a thousand lives, I would sacrifice all of them for the cause. The grand duchess got up to leave. I also stood up. I repeated I was sorry, but that I had done my duty and would bear the consequences. I said farewell, for we would not see each other again."

What Kaliayev and the grand duchess actually talked about is unknown. She did not tell even her children about it. The newspapers write that Kaliayev allegedly wept on his knees and asked for forgiveness. On hearing this, he writes a long indignant letter to the grand duchess: "I am fully aware of my mistake. I should not have been so kind as to engage in conversation with you. You have turned out to be unworthy of my generosity."

Kaliayev returns the icon together with the letter. However, his correspondence is not conveyed to Ella. A week later Kaliayev asks for a second meeting, but she refuses.

The trial of Kaliayev begins on 5 April. The bomber delivers a speech that makes his party comrades proud: "I am not a defendant. I am your captive. We are two warring parties. You represent the imperial government, the hired servants of capital and violence. I am one of the people's avengers, a socialist and a revolutionary. We are separated by piles of corpses, countless broken human beings and a sea of blood and tears. You have declared war on the people, we accept the challenge."

He then utters a speech addressed to the murdered grand duke, blaming him for the Khodynka tragedy and explaining that "since the grand duke was not accountable to the law, the militant organization's duty was to make him accountable to the people." Kaliayev is sentenced to death. His appeal is rejected. Nicholas II asks the Ministry of Justice to extract a plea for mercy from the convicted man, who refuses. On 10 May, Kaliayev is hanged at Schlisselburg Fortress outside Saint Petersburg.

ON TOUR IN EUROPE

Gapon makes his way to Geneva in early February. He stumbles upon a Russian émigré library, where he asks for the address of Plekhanov. All Russian revolutionaries know it by heart: 6, Rue de Candolle. They also know that the celebrity Marxist spends most evenings drinking beer in a nearby tavern. On presenting himself, at first Gapon is not allowed in. Only when he discloses his name does Plekhanov agree to meet.

Soon he is the center of care and attention. He is given a place to stay with the revolutionary Leo Deutsch and supplied with books on socialism to prepare the defrocked priest for life as a Marxist. Gapon acknowledges himself that he feels like a Social Democrat. But then, suddenly, the long-lost Rutenberg shows up, also on the run from Russia. The Socialist-Revolutionary (SR) Rutenberg extracts his ally from the clutches of the Mensheviks. Plekhanov is offended and breaks off contact with Gapon.

Rutenberg introduces Gapon to his friends "Babushka" Breshkovskaya, Viktor Chernov, and Yevgeny Azef. They all want to get close to the celebrated priest. Gapon himself fancies the idea of uniting all the Russian revolutionary parties under his leadership, as he had done with the Saint Petersburg workers' union. He already knows that Plekhanov despises Lenin and is extremely distrustful of the SRs. Gapon senses that only he can lead the Russian émigrés to revolution.

In Gapon's own words, Russian Geneva is bewitched by him—all except Azef. The antipathy is mutual. Gapon does not like the rude and authoritarian Azef, who places his own leadership qualities above Gapon's. "He bosses everyone around and they meekly comply," recalls Gapon. "He is deaf to criticism. We do indeed dislike each other."

Azef is particularly appalled by Gapon's idea to create a new militant organization, which, in his capacity as "Agent Raskin," he immediately reports to Saint Petersburg.

Gapon enjoys learning how to fire a gun (unusually so for an ex-priest) and ride a horse, but is not too interested in reading the classics of Marxism. True to his idea of uniting all Russian oppositionists, he seeks an appointment with the leader of the Bolshevik faction, a certain Vladimir Lenin. On the eve of the meeting, according to the memoirs of Nadezhda Krupskaya, Lenin's wife, her husband spends the whole evening pacing around the living room in eager anticipation. Gapon's reputation precedes him, and he impresses Lenin with his fiery talk. Lenin advises his new friend: "Father, don't listen to flattery. Read more and learn. Otherwise you'll end up you know where," he says, pointing to the ground.

Rutenberg takes Gapon to Paris, where the "organizer of 9 January" is awaited by leading French politicians, including Jean Jaurès, the head of the United Socialist Party, and the future Prime Minister George Clemenceau. The attention of Western luminaries turns Gapon's head. He sees his picture on the front pages of newspapers and is offered a huge fee for his memoirs. This is only the beginning, he thinks.

PANIC IN CHINA

In the Far East, meanwhile, the fighting continues around Mukden (present-day Shenyang), the capital of Manchuria and the largest city in northeastern China. It is the birthplace of China's ruling Qing dynasty and presently a Russian outpost in the Far East. Governor-General Alekseyev likes to stroll among the mausoleums of the Chinese emperors. Commander-in-Chief Kuropatkin, for his part, is more concerned about military matters.

The battle of attrition around Shenyang lasts for a month. After a heroic effort, Kuropatkin orders his troops to retreat from the advancing Japanese. In doing so, three army corps are cut off from the main force, and panic sets in. Both armies are depleted. Japanese losses are at least twice as high as Russia's, yet on 10 March 1905 it is the Russian army that withdraws from the city.

"It was our last, but greatest defeat," writes Witte. "I do not recall such a colossal defeat on land as that suffered by the Russian army at Mukden."

Captain Denikin is highly critical, believing that "the whole operation would have been different if just a few people on the command ladder had been replaced in good time." General Kuropatkin, the darling of the press for the past two years, is now in disgrace. Nicholas II dismisses him as commander-in-chief.

The Mukden defeat poleaxes the whole of Russian society. The regime seems to be coming apart at the seams. It faces a stark choice: reform or die.

Meanwhile, the Japanese army is also at the breaking point. It has been victorious in every battle thus far, but the casualties have been debilitating. At Mukden, the Japanese have lost more than seventy thousand men. It is very much in Tokyo's interests to end the war as soon as possible. Russia's weakness lies in the fact that its main forces are far from the front line. If Russia were to hang in and deploy fresh units from Europe, Japan would eventually succumb.

The question occupying the Japanese General Staff is how to get the Russian authorities to surrender. It is then that Japanese intelligence suggests sponsoring the revolution, for the Russian regime is still shell-shocked by Bloody Sunday. Japan's former military attaché Akashi Motojiro tries to make contact with the revolutionaries, and does so through the Finnish separatist Konni Zilliacus. The next goal is to find and finance someone to catalyze the people's revolution. There is only one option: Georgy Gapon.

The events of 9 January have deeply affected Savva Morozov, even though he was in Riga at the time. The tycoon begins to develop his own reform plan and writes a report entitled "On the causes of the strike movement. Demands for the introduction of democratic freedoms," which he plans to submit to the government on behalf of big business.

In the report, Morozov argues that the strikes are not just economic, but political. The backwardness of the Russian state is hindering the country's industrial development. Consequently, systemic reform is not the whim of a group of rabble-rousers, but the driving force of national prosperity.

To increase Russia's global competitiveness, Morozov proposes making all citizens equal before the law, guaranteeing the inviolability of the individual and the home, introducing freedom of speech and of the press, providing universal compulsory schooling, and drafting laws with the participation of representatives elected by all classes of the population.

Morozov meets with Witte, who snootily advises him not to meddle in politics: "See to your business interests, and do not get mixed up in the revolution. Take my advice and pass it on to your colleagues." Morozov departs in silence.

A couple of days later the tycoon hurries to Moscow: strikes have broken out at his own production facilities. Savva, who has not had a hands-on role in the business for many years, is out of touch with the workers. Arriving at the factory, he goes to meet the strikers. The large hall where they gather is packed to the rafters: people are sitting on the windowsills and stairs. Morozov listens carefully to the workers' demands and tells them that he will convey them to the governing board (which is headed by his mother). "What board?!" shouts the outraged crowd. "We don't care about that. You're the boss. You sort it out!" Morozov is taken aback and, according to his wife's memoirs, leaves early and drives off in his carriage.

Morozov is unable to persuade the governing board to satisfy the workers' demands. His mother, the de jure head of the family company, is categorically opposed to any politically motivated change. She forbids her son to offer concessions to the workers and threatens to remove him from the business altogether. On 17 March the board re-elects his mother, Maria Feodorovna Morozova, as managing director and Savva as her deputy. The decision is also taken to send troops to the factory to suppress the unrest. Morozov's mother places the blame squarely on his shoulders: "Look at the mess you've made. This isn't England, you know. Workers in Russia need to be afraid. That's what they're used to."

On 25 February, the so-far peaceful strikes turn violent. The workers attack the recently stationed troops, who open fire. As a result, four people are taken to hospital in a serious condition. The newspaper *Spark* publishes an article on the "monstrous exploitation and abuse of workers by Savva Morozov." Morozov, who financed *Spark* for several years, plunges into depression.

The forty-year-old Savva Morozov finds himself isolated. He has a poor relationship with his family, who considers him a mad socialist, while the Bolsheviks are only interested in his money, as indeed are Stanislavsky and Nemirovich. He does not even have the Moscow Art Theatre to fall back upon, since he left it in 1904 after Andreyeva's departure.

His closest friends, Gorky and Andreyeva, have moved away, first to Jurmala and then to Crimea to treat Gorky's tuberculosis. Gorky has been released from prison on bail pending trial. He plans to use the courtroom as a platform from which to rant about the injustices of the world.

On 15 April, at the insistence of his mother and his wife, Savva seeks medical treatment. He is diagnosed with a nervous disorder, exacerbated by overexcitement, anxiety, insomnia, and depression.

"Savva's mother and wife have declared him insane and want him confined to hospital. I thought about visiting, but was sure they wouldn't let me see him. Such a strong person, but not invincible," writes Maria Andreyeva.

However, Savva is not confined to hospital, but sent for treatment to Europe. On 17 April, he and his wife Zinaida, accompanied by a doctor, depart for Berlin.

"TO THE RUINED WALLS OF BEAUTIFUL PALACES!"

On 5 March the tsar, his family, and the *beau monde* gather at Tauride Palace in Saint Petersburg. The palace, which a year later will host the first assembly of the State Duma, is hosting an exhibition of Russian portraits painted from 1805 to 1905. Despite the recent January massacre and the defeat at Mukden, high society is seemingly oblivious to it all.

The exhibits have been assembled by the thirty-two-year-old Sergei Diaghilev, who has spent the past year traversing the old estates around Moscow and Saint Petersburg and selecting more than four thousand paintings from their private collections. "The collection should remain permanently at Tauride Palace. It is the finest example of portraiture in Europe," the painter Borisov-Musatov writes to fellow artist Valentin Serov. "It would make Diaghilev's already historic name immortal."

The exhibition is so successful that even his enemies grudgingly praise Diaghilev. His Moscow friends and acquaintances, including those who disapprove of his dictatorial ways, hold a feast in his honor at the Metropol Hotel. It is attended by Moscow's leading lights, among them Valentin Serov, Savva Mamontov (now bankrupt), the merchant dynasty heir and collector of impressionist works Sergei Shchukin, the young poet and publisher Valery Bryusov, and the architect Fyodor Shekhtel.

They discuss art and politics. All of a sudden, Diaghilev rises to his feet and proposes a toast that might be described as a stump speech had it come from someone less apolitical. But even having spent the past year rummaging through eighteenth-century paintings, Diaghilev cannot be oblivious to what is happening in the country or fail to have an opinion.

The Tauride Palace exhibition, he says, marks the end of a dazzling era. Traveling around Russia's boarded-up estates and dilapidated yet "fearsomely splendid" palaces in search of exhibits, Diaghilev understood that he is witnessing a great turning point in history: "We are condemned to die so that a new culture may live, which will take what remains of our old wisdom."

The speech, which echoes the world-weariness of *The Cherry Orchard*, is published by Bryusov a few days later in his magazine *Vesy*. Yet Diaghilev is more optimistic than Chekhov. For Chekhov, *The Cherry Orchard* marked the end of his life, while for Diaghilev the Tauride Palace exhibition is merely his last project in Russia, although that evening at the Metropol he does not know it.

"We are witness to a seminal historical moment—the birth of an unknown culture that will ultimately sweep us aside. Without fear or disbelief, I raise a glass to the ruined walls of beautiful palaces and the laws of the new aesthetic." The Moscow intelligentsia applauds.

Back in March, Azef reports to the police that Georgy Gapon allegedly received 50,000 roubles* to organize a conference for all Russian revolutionary parties abroad. The source of the funding is unknown, but Gapon

---

*About $659,167 in 2017.

gladly takes on the assignment and sends out invitations to potential participants. The example of the French socialists is very much on everyone's mind: in 1899 all the French socialist parties merged into one under the leadership of Jean Jaurès. Moreover, in 1904 the Socialist International (a.k.a., the Second International) called for the unification of all socialist parties of Europe. Thus, Gapon, now Russia's leading oppositionist, is following not only his dream, but also the global trend.

However, Russia's socialists are not so straightforward. The SRs generally support the idea of unification, but the party leader Mikhail Gotz does not. He believes that all other revolutionaries should simply join his party, since the assassinations of Plehve and Grand Duke Sergei have turned the SRs into the most influential revolutionary organization. Georgy Plekhanov does not want to unite under Gapon's leadership. He has been disillusioned with the former priest even since the latter switched camps to the SRs.

The only party leader in favor from day one is Vladimir Lenin. On the eve of the unification conference, the leader of the Bolsheviks publicly expresses support for Gapon and the hope that the former priest will join his party in the foreseeable future.

The congress begins on 2 April, attended by representatives of eleven of the eighteen parties invited. The leading figures are the presiding Gapon, Viktor Chernov, and "Babushka" Yekaterina Breshko-Breshkovkaya of the SRs, and Vladimir Lenin of the Bolsheviks. Other participants include opposition parties representing various minorities of the Russian Empire: Poles, Finns, Jews, Georgians, Armenians, Latvians, and Belarusians. On the very first day of the congress, Lenin opposes the uneven makeup of the participants: too few Social Democrats, too many potential allies of the SRs, in his opinion. He theatrically walks out of the hall.*

Gapon is upset by the gesture. Yet his disillusionment with the Social Democrats does not extend to Lenin himself. In a letter to his comrades in Saint Petersburg, he describes them as follows: the Social Democrats have no unified spirit, and their generals (except for Comrade Lenin) are mostly "Talmudists, Pharisees [hypocrites] and liars who masturbate words and phrases full of self-importance."

The congress continues without the Social Democrats: only the Socialist-Revolutionaries and ethnic minority parties remain. The main topic is now the ethnic question. The delegates discuss the transformation of

---

*Russian non-systemic opposition parties tried to unite their efforts in the early twenty-first century as well, but failed due to personal ambitions of their leaders. Later, almost all of them left politics. They lost all their popularity after having become marginalised political groups.

Russia into a federation, which annoys Gapon: "Everyone is talking about the rights of outlying regions but not of Russia herself. It will end in Russia being torn apart," he interjects. Gapon intervenes once again by offering to give the Jews their own territory inside the Russian Empire. It is 1905, and Gapon is still unfamiliar with the ideas of the leader of the Zionist movement. The idea of creating a Jewish autonomous region in Russia will return twenty-nine years later.

In May Gapon briefly joins the Socialist-Revolutionary Party, but then withdraws. He departs for a tour of Europe, traveling first to Geneva and on to London, where he receives an offer to publish his memoirs. He is joined by his common-law wife and former pupil Sasha Uzdaleva. For the book, he is promised a fee of 10,000 roubles*—a huge sum that will free him from political allegiance and allow him to become a properly independent activist. The writing, of course, will not be done by Gapon himself. He hires a journalist to take extensive interviews and rework them into a narrative.

PORTRAIT OVER THE ENTRANCE TO THE BUFFET

Also in Europe, following his doctor's instructions, are Savva Morozov and his wife Zinaida, who go first Berlin, then Vichy, then Cannes.

On 11 May, in Vichy, Morozov receives an unexpected visit from the head of the Bolsheviks' militant organization, Leonid Krasin, who finds the tycoon depressed. Morozov keeps the meeting a secret from everyone, including his wife, and uses the encounter to make another timely contribution to the party coffers.[†]

Formally, Leonid Krasin holds the same position in the Social Democratic Party as Azef in the Socialist-Revolutionary Party (i.e., head of combat operations). A well-educated engineer who does not hide in underground circles, Krasin is at once Azef's double and antithesis. He is charming, sociable, and friends with people like Gorky and Andreyeva—the opposite of the sullen Azef. Another difference is that Azef plots political assassinations, while the militant wing of the RSDLP does not engage in murder, but "fundraising," which often means looting.

The next day, 12 May, Morozov and his wife move to Cannes, where Savva's mood seems to be improving. But the appearance is deceptive, for it is there in Cannes, on 13 May 1905, in a room at the Royal Hotel, that

---

*About $659,167 in 2017.

† This meeting is mentioned in the memoirs of both Gorky and Krasin himself. Since Zinaida writes that Morozov did not receive Krasin, the meeting was most likely a secret.

Savva Morozov's body is found. He died from a gunshot to the heart and left lung, says the medical report.

Although the memoirs of Savva's contemporaries make no such suggestion, a century later Morozov's great-grandchildren will allege that the businessman was murdered by Leonid Krasin. In the twenty-first century, the theory is quite widespread.

The body is taken to Moscow and buried only two weeks later on 29 May at Rogozhskoe Cemetery—the main resting place for Old Believers in Moscow. This is significant, for it means that the family was able to convince the Old Believer community that it was not suicide; otherwise he could not have been buried there. Yet still no one speaks of murder—neither his family, nor the authorities. No further investigation is carried out following the initial probe by the French police.

Forty years later Zinaida Morozova writes in her memoirs that suicide was common among the third generation of merchants—the grandsons of the first free peasant entrepreneurs. The heirs of the Zhuravlev, Tarasov, and Gribov merchant dynasties "all shot themselves on the same day, perhaps the same hour, out of boredom," she writes.

Andreyeva arrives from Finland, where she is now living with Gorky at a country dacha, but she catches cold and cannot attend the funeral ceremony. A month later she claims the insurance policy left to her by Morozov. His widow Zinaida sues to have the sum returned, but Andreyeva (or, more accurately, Krasin, her legal representative) wins in court. Most of the money, 60,000 roubles,* ends up going to the Social Democratic Party.

"RUSSIA HAS GONE MAD"

Despite the fact that the "dictator" Trepov has been given *carte blanche* by Nicholas II, the Saint Petersburg authorities are still torn apart by controversy. Finance Minister Kokovtsov recalls that Bloody Sunday very nearly derailed talks with the French government for a loan that Russia desperately needed to continue the war with Japan. Kokovtsov and Witte arrange a personal meeting between the tsar and a French banker. Nicholas handles the task admirably. He calms the banker's nerves by promising to carry out political reform and assuring that Admiral Rozhestvensky's Baltic Fleet will swing the war in Russia's favor. The money is practically in his pocket, he thinks.

---

* About $791,000 in 2017.

That evening, Empress Alexandra brings her husband a decree drafted by a member of her entourage. It says that the strike movement will be harshly suppressed, making no mention of any reform. The only minister who knows about it in advance is Pobedonostsev. He says that the text is so good that not a single word should be changed. The tsar signs the decree without looking at it. Finance Minister Kokovtsov is shocked, for it means the French could withdraw the loan. As a counterweight, in typical fashion, Nicholas signs a second decree on the very next day that completely contradicts the first, promising to set up a new legislative body.

On 14 May, the long-awaited news arrives that the Baltic Fleet is approaching Japanese waters. In his memoirs, Witte repeatedly cites the tsar's phrase: "Seraphim of Sarov has predicted that a peace agreement will be signed in Tokyo and only the yids and intelligentsia can think otherwise." It is hard to say if Nicholas II was alone in his miscalculation. In hindsight, of course, all officials claim that they foresaw the annihilation. Captain Denikin, who fought in the war, writes that the military bowed to public and media pressure. The decision to send the fleet "12,000 miles around the world to a place with no military base" Denikin describes as "reckless."

During the six months that Rozhestvensky's vessels have been at sea, Port Arthur has fallen. In other words, the whole purpose of the campaign—to break through the blockade of the port—is now irrelevant. When Nicholas II sets the new goal "to seize control of the Sea of Japan," Rozhestvensky decides to break through to Vladivostok. There are three points of entry to the sea. The admiral chooses the Tsushima Strait. It is there that the Japanese fleet is lying in wait, presumably tipped off by intelligence reports.

The battle (or rather, massacre) of the Tsushima Strait lasts for two days. Of Russia's thirty-eight ships, only three break through to Vladivostok and one "runs away" to Madagascar; the remaining thirty-four are sunk or interned. Japan loses only two small torpedo boats.

After the Tsushima debacle, the tsar's uncle and commander of the fleet, Grand Duke Alexei, resigns. He has already been hissed and jeered at in the streets for months, and the windows of his palace are regularly smashed with stones. However, at a meeting with the tsar, many military leaders say that the war must continue, arguing that Japan is still weaker than Russia.

With the domestic situation becoming ever-more explosive, Nicholas appoints Dmitry Trepov as deputy head of the Interior Ministry, in addition to his position as governor-general of Saint Petersburg.

The military defeat makes a huge impression on society, which is accustomed to viewing the Russian state as an implacable, all-powerful machine that grinds up everything in its path. Yet it turns out that it cannot even beat a "bunch of monkeys," as the enemy was called by semi-official propaganda a year previously.

Witte, a firm believer in Russia's military might, writes that his country "has gone mad." With Russia now seen as all bark and no bite, "the whole picture changed. Russia's enemies, both internal and external, suddenly came out of hiding."

Interestingly, even the "reformer" Witte uses the phrase "internal enemies"—Saint Petersburg now seems like a besieged fortress, not unlike Mukden on the other side of the world.*

GO BACK AND CRY

April 17th sees the publication of a new law on religious tolerance, abolishing the degrading restrictions on Muslims, Buddhists, Catholics, and Old Believers. It is also no longer a criminal offence to leave the Orthodox Church. Moscow's merchant class rejoices. Their religion (officially known as Old Belief) is, at long last, lawful, meaning they are no longer second-class citizens.

Conservatives, on the other hand, see the law as another in a list of defeats, the latest after Tsushima. Another potential blow is the bill to set up a new legislative body, currently being drafted. Three names are under consideration: the Zemsky Sobor, the Sovereign Council, and the State Duma. The tsar chooses the latter. Post-Tsushima, recalls Moscow Governor Vladimir Dzhunkovsky, the convocation of a new nationwide representative assembly is the most pressing issue of the day.

There is intense debate among ministers over the issue of whether illiterates should be allowed into the Duma. Most are in favor, because illiterate former peasants are devoted to the tsar: there should be as many of them as possible to shore up support for the regime, it is argued. Finance Minister Kokovtsov is against, saying that "enthusiasm for the regime is no

---

*Seeing Russia as a besieged fortress is still popular in the early twenty-first century. This idea captured the minds of the political elite at least twice: 100 and 110 years after the Tsushima tragedy. In 2004 and 2014, after two Ukrainian revolutions, many Russian officials have gotten carried away by the theory that Russia is surrounded by enemies who are planning a revolution with the help of planted influence agents (opposition activists). Such times of acute government paranoia haven't lasted for long: their concerns that there is a global anti-Russian conspiracy haven't come true. However, prejudice against opposition remains.

use if they cannot read what they are being asked to consider." Ultimately, Nicholas II takes the side of the illiterate. There is one more proposal: to ban Jews from the elections. Witte is vigorously against the motion; finally, Jews are allowed to vote.

BORSCH AND VODKA

The disturbances spread across the country, but for some reason the censors do not ban the press from reporting them. Suvorin's *New Time* features a special section under the heading "Unrest."

Maria Andreyeva, in a letter to her sister, expresses concern that the latter is in Saint Petersburg with her children. Yet no city in Russia is safe at the present time. Curiously, the "revolutionary" Andreyeva describes the situation in the same terms as the monarchist Alexandra Bogdanovich: "It's dreadful what's happening in Odessa! It breaks the heart to see so many lives ruined. It's not so much a political tragedy as a human one."

The general strike in Odessa has been ongoing for about a month. Cossack regiments are eventually sent in, but still the unrest carries on until June and beyond. Earlier in the month a Black Sea Fleet vessel performing maneuvers off the coast of Odessa sends a boat to the shore to stock up on food. Everyone in the city is on strike, so fresh goods are not easy to come by. The ship's cook buys stale meat crawling with maggots. He takes it back to his vessel, the *Prince Potemkin-Tavrichesky*, and promptly uses the meat to make borsch. The revolutionaries, incidentally, have been agitating among sailors in the region, yet the one ship they do not count on is the *Prince Potemkin-Tavrichesky*—its crew is weak and apolitical.

On 14 June, the sailors aboard the ship receive their daily ration of vodka, dried bread, and borsch. On seeing maggots wriggling around in the soup, they go on strike. Only one young sailor, obviously hungry, slops it down.

On learning about the mutiny, the captain consults with the ship's doctor, who inspects the soup and declares it fit for consumption. The captain lines up the sailors—with those willing to eat the soup standing on the right and those who are not on the left. Giving them one last chance, he summons the ship's security service to make a note of the names of the mutineers. At this point, many try to move from the left to the right, but the captain orders them to be arrested and shot for insubordination. A tarpaulin is brought out, indicating that the cleanliness of the deck is more important than human life.

So begins the most famous uprising of the 1905 revolution, glorified twenty years later by Sergei Eisenstein in his classic silent film *The Battleship Potemkin* (using the shortened version of the ship's name). Within minutes the sailors kill the captain and all the officers, and then go after anyone who has taken cover on board the vessel. The ship's cook and doctor are murdered, as are some young sailors who have jumped overboard to escape, including the one who ate the offending soup.

During the period 16–25 June, the battleship roams around the Black Sea, periodically opening fire on Odessa. Vessels sent to intercept it fail to do so. Finally, on 25 June, the ship runs out of fresh water and food, causing arguments on board. The sailors decide to head for Constanta on the coast of Romania to claim asylum. Back on *terra firma* and having avoided arrest, the crew disperses across Europe. One of the ringleaders of the mutiny, the "chairman of the ship's committee" Afanasy Matyushenko, travels to Geneva, where he dreams of joining up with the "damned priest" (as Gapon is known in various circles). The battleship itself is towed back to Sevastopol on 29 June.

"Europe, England and America are eager to hear my words and my opinion," boasts Gapon to his old friend, Pinhas Rutenberg, when the latter comes to visit him in London. The former priest even says that local workers are planning to put up a monument to him in his lifetime. Gapon feels like an ancient prophet in the days before organized religion: "Nicholas II faces the same fate as [Charles I or Louis XVI]. Those of his dynasty who manage to escape the horrors of the impending revolution will soon seek refuge in the West." So ends his book of memoirs published in London in summer 1905.

Even the patriarch of "Russian London," the anarchist philosopher Peter Kropotkin, falls under Gapon's spell, writing an article about the Russian Workers' Union, which Gapon wants to revive. Peter Struve, the editor of *Liberation*, also seeks a meeting with him.

It is in London that Gapon draws up a plan to return to Saint Petersburg and start a revolution. The idea is to collect donations from wealthy Europeans and Americans, buy weapons, put them on board a boat, sail down the Gulf of Finland, equip members of the Russian Workers' Union, and stage a rerun of 9 January, only this time the now-armed workers will march on the Winter Palace and seize power. "In what way is the Romanov dynasty superior to the would-be Gapon dynasty?" a friend paraphrases the fiery former priest. "Russia is ready for a manly peasant tsar. I am just a pure-blooded peasant."

Gapon writes to his comrades in Saint Petersburg who survived 9 January, asking them to put the trade union back together. The organization has since been reduced to a few dozen people. The operation to return to Saint Petersburg is planned in London at the apartment of the fifty-five-year-old Nikolai Tchaikovsky, an SR émigré with three decades of revolutionary experience. Responsibility for collecting "foreign donations" is assigned to the Finnish separatist Konni Zilliacus and for purchasing weapons to Yevgeny Azef. Neither the underground veteran Tchaikovsky, nor the younger Gapon (nor anyone else for that matter) suspects that they are dealing with two agents: one working for Japanese intelligence, the other for the Russian secret police.

Zilliacus does indeed raise funds. He tells Gapon that the money was donated by an American billionaire, yet there is no real need to be evasive, since Gapon and his fellow revolutionaries do not care about its provenance. They would just shrug if they knew that the revolution was being funded by the Japanese General Staff.

Lenin catches wind of the impending revolution and tries to join Gapon's project. In early July, when Gapon visits Geneva, the Bolshevik leader takes him to a pub and asks for the Bolsheviks to be part of the conspiracy. Gapon agrees to admit Nikolai Burenin to his circle as Lenin's representative. Lenin, once opposed to any kind of unification, is now desperate not to be left out. The Bolsheviks even urge Maxim Gorky to persuade Gapon to cooperate with them. In mid-August Gorky duly writes his very first letter to Lenin. True, Lenin is not the addressee, but an intermediary postman—he is to hand the letter to Gapon. Gorky is very excited about Gapon's plan to smuggle arms into Saint Petersburg and provoke another uprising.

"Strength in unity, comrade!" Gorky writes to Gapon. "We don't need a party that is detached like the intelligentsia. We need a party overflowing with workers." Gorky ends the letter by suggesting that the Social Democrats play a major role in the seizure of Saint Petersburg, since Gapon's union is not strong enough.

ON TOUR IN AMERICA

In late June 1905, a month after Tsushima, US President Theodore Roosevelt proposes peace talks between Russia and Japan. Nicholas II sends Sergei Witte to the negotiations with the parting words that he desires peace, but will not cede a single square inch of land or pay a single kopeck of war reparations. But (adds Navy Minister Alexei Birilev) "it might be possible to give up some of what we ourselves stole when times were more favorable."

According to the most experienced commander in the imperial family, Grand Duke Nikolai Nikolaevich, Russia can win back the Liaodong Peninsula and the peninsula of Korea, but it will take another year and cost a billion roubles.* It also has to be a ground operation, since the sea option is closed off. What's more, it will have to be funded by printing money. The state coffers are empty (according to Witte), and no one is prepared to grant the Russian government a loan.

In late July Witte travels to the United States via Paris in his role as peacemaker: "For some reason, the European powers had a high opinion of me back then. They all thought I was the man to make peace."

On the way, he formulates his negotiating tactics: "Given the huge role of the press in America, it's important to communicate with its representatives." In other words, the plan is to play to the crowd. On board the transatlantic steamer he gives an interview to *The Times*, and then, having disembarked, holds a large press conference. He is photographed with everyone and willingly signs autographs. Every time he steps off a train, he makes sure to shake hands with the driver. He wears his democratism on his sleeve, and it pays off. The newspapers write that the Russian tsar's representative is "more straightforward and more accessible than President Roosevelt." Lastly, Witte demands that the talks be open to journalists. It is a bluff, of course. He knows full well that the Japanese will object, but for him it is another victory in the information war.

BEFORE: THE RISE OF JOHN GRAFTON

In late August, while Witte is glad-handing in America, Gapon is busy uniting all the forces of the underground opposition and plotting his assault on Saint Petersburg. The plan involves the Socialist-Revolutionary militant organization led by Azef, the Bolshevik militant organization led by Krasin, Gapon's own Russian Workers' Union, and even Peter Struve's liberal Union of Liberation.

Gapon goes to Stockholm, from where he plans to enter Finland and rendezvous with a boat that Azef and Tchaikovsky will load with arms. Azef has reported the purchase of the weapons to his handlers in Saint Petersburg, but in small doses. The Russian police do not know that "Agent Raskin" is the actual head of the SR militant organization, believing him

---

*About $13,183,333,333 in 2017.

to be a revolutionary pawn. So as not to upset the apple cart, Azef greatly understates the extent of his knowledge.

In London, the conspirators purchase the 315-ton steamship *John Grafton*, which they resell to a fictitious business. Reaching the coast of Finland, the *John Grafton* heads for a fjord near Helsinki, where the weapons are unloaded, after which Gapon's now twelve-thousand-strong army of workers is to advance on Saint Petersburg.

Having unloaded the *John Grafton*, Azef is supposed to head for the capital to lead the armed uprising, but at the crucial moment he disappears. The other conspirators think that he has been arrested, or, sensing a tail, has decided to lie low. Savinkov recalls that Azef was in the habit of going AWOL, always explaining afterwards that he had been forced to take cover from the police.

On 3 August, a second misfire occurs when Pinhas Rutenberg, Gapon's trusty right-hand man, is arrested. Yet the operation continues. Due to the depleted ranks of the Socialist-Revolutionaries, the Bolsheviks take the lead: they dig pits to store the weapons, including a secret cache under a slab at Saint Petersburg's Volkov Cemetery.*

But not all the arms get through. The *John Grafton* docks once again, this time not far from Vyborg, but for some reason no one comes at the appointed hour to collect the weapons. After waiting a few days, the vessel returns to Copenhagen.

Gapon himself is not involved in the arms smuggling phase of the operation. He is too important a figure for such a mundane role. His task is to raise morale. In mid-August Konni Zilliacus hires a yacht on which Gapon sets sail for Finland: "St. Petersburg needs a spark. Don't be afraid of victims. It's no loss if 500 workers are sacrificed. They will have achieved freedom for all," says the Finnish separatist Zilliacus.

But Gapon "can see through these Swedes and Finns" (or so he thinks) and realizes that they are exploiting him for their own separatist ambitions. "I will not sacrifice a single Russian worker for the sake of their bourgeois schemes," he says.

AFTER: THE AMERICANS CRY

Sailing only a few dozen kilometers from Gapon's yacht is another, rather more luxurious vessel. On holiday aboard the imperial *Standard*, Nicholas II and family are awaiting the outcome of the peace talks in America.

---

* By a quirk of fate, all of Lenin's relatives will end up buried here, and in the post-communist 1990s the question of moving Lenin's body to this cemetery is a political hot potato.

The talks between the Russian and Japanese delegations are held in the small coastal town of Portsmouth, New Hampshire, where Witte feels like an actor on stage—even his hotel room looks out over the street, so that journalists and passers-by can take pictures of the "Russian prime minister" on his balcony. The all-smiling Witte does not object.

Witte immodestly recalls that it was his openness that swung US public opinion from sympathy for Japan to empathy for Russia. The same change occurs in President Roosevelt. Witte's memories of his trip to Roosevelt's country house are insightful. He is amazed by the president's Spartan breakfast—no tablecloth, no wine ("just icy water"). Even more surprising is Roosevelt's admission that he does not want to be re-elected to the presidency, but would rather become dean of Harvard University. Witte even goes to Harvard out of curiosity.

Another strong impression upon Witte is made by Russia's émigré Jews. At the train station in Boston, a crowd gathers to talk to the Russian minister. They tell Witte that even though they detest the tsarist regime, they miss Mother Russia and will pray for its success in the negotiations.

The most contentious issue is Sakhalin Island. Half of it is already de facto occupied by the Japanese, so Nicholas II telegrams Witte, agreeing to cede the territory. At the same time, there is a flurry of correspondence between the Japanese representative, Foreign Minister Komura Jutaro, and his superiors in Tokyo. The foreign minister does not want to accept Witte's offer, but to claim more substantial war reparations. But he is pressured by Roosevelt—not out of love for Russia, but simply because the latter wants the negotiations to succeed. As a result, the Japanese emperor orders his minister to sign the treaty.

Witte enjoys his time in America and wants to travel around the country, as suggested by Russia's ambassador to Washington. However, according to Witte, Nicholas II pours cold water on the idea, fearing that his representative is becoming too popular.

Witte also writes that during the talks he felt unwell (allegedly from the low-quality American food) and kept himself in working order through "very strict dieting and intense massages with cocaine paste." Back home, on 17 September Witte travels to the Gulf of Finland, where Nicholas and family are resting aboard the *Standard*. Pleased with the outcome of the negotiations, he bestows upon Witte the title of count. The now Count Witte is touched, saying that he is glad that the tsar has not been influenced by all the anti-Witte gossip. "I never believed such slander," replies Nicholas II.

BEFORE: THE END OF JOHN GRAFTON

Meanwhile, the *John Grafton* returns to Finland from Copenhagen and this time delivers its cargo. On this occasion, the unloading is performed by the more reliable Finns, although the weapons do not make it to the cemetery just yet. But that is now a secondary matter. On 7 September, during its third voyage, the *John Grafton* runs aground in the Gulf of Bothnia, the northernmost arm of the Baltic Sea.

The boat, loaded with even more weapons, is immobile on the rocks, and the crew can do nothing except wait for backup from Copenhagen. Spotting the disaster, coastguards come to the rescue. They offer assistance, which is turned down. But the crew senses danger.

The crew eventually abandons the *John Grafton*, blows it up with dynamite, and sails to Sweden in the ship's lifeboats. The following day the police inspect the scene. The vessel is not totally destroyed and not even entirely sunk. The weapons are duly found.

"It's a nasty business," says Nicholas II on learning that his yacht was in the vicinity of the floating arsenal. The emperor is lucky on this occasion. Were it not for the *John Grafton's* inexperienced crew, the armed uprising scheduled for autumn 1905 could have been nastier still.

History books will say that the arms smuggling operation was a gamble, doomed to failure from the start. Yet the preparations involved all the Russian revolutionary parties (which quickly distanced themselves in the aftermath). No one thought of the operation as a gamble until the *John Grafton* ran aground. And if the weapons had reached their destination, the Russian monarchy would certainly not have survived the upheaval of 1905.

|| Chapter 7 ||

in which Black-Hundreder Alexander
Dubrovin creates the first Russian party of
the state, and oppositioner Maxim Gorky
asks the West to stop funding Russia

THE GOOD DOCTOR

Alexander Dubrovin is angry. A popular Saint Petersburg pediatrician who closely follows politics, he cannot stand the chairman of the Committee of Ministers, Sergei Witte. The news of the conclusion of the Treaty of Portsmouth seems terrible to him. He considers Witte a traitor, working in the interests of "world Jewry." Dubrovin is outraged by the peace with Japan: he is sure that Russian troops were halted on the cusp of victory. He is even more indignant about the accolades heaped upon Witte, who has handed half of Sakhalin Island to the enemy. "Count Semi-Sakhalin" he now calls the hated prime minister.

Dr. Dubrovin is not alone in his convictions. Russia is now home to dozens of monarchist organizations, but so far none enjoys nationwide coverage. These organizations are united not only by their love of the autocratic system, but also their hatred of Jews and other "aliens." Their members go by the name of the "Black Hundreds."

The dream of the Black Hundreds—to create a mass patriotic movement—becomes possible only when the state joins the cause. A new organization is sanctioned by the Interior Ministry, and its first meetings are held at Dubrovin's apartment. One of the organizers of the event, Boris Nikolsky, will later describe the doctor in less than glowing terms: "A crude, repulsive animal shunned by all, yet at the same time a wealthy intellectual. Desperate to play a role, he curried favor with everyone and was elected chairman."

In summer 1905, the head of the Saint Petersburg secret police, Gerasimov, asks his colleague, Deputy Police Chief Rachkovsky, why the authorities are not trying to create an organization to "counter the detrimental influence of the revolutionaries on the masses." The surprised Rachkovsky promises to introduce him to Dr. Dubrovin, "who is indeed setting up a monarchist organization." Through the efforts of Dubrovin and the Interior Ministry, the amorphous Black Hundreds gradually turn into a state institution.

TREPOV TAKES CONTROL

The most influential person in the country is still General Trepov, the only police officer able to disperse the crowd after the 9 January tragedy. His people skills have gotten him close to the tsar. In fact, Nicholas II has made Trepov a mediator between himself and outside world, giving him access to intimate family affairs. The tsar's diary in 1905 is all about his children and hunting; state business, it seems, has been outsourced to the trusty Trepov.

However, the skills of a professional police officer are not sufficient to govern the state, which Trepov understands. It is not just that he has no political program; he does not know how to cope with the machinery of the state that has ended up in his hands.

In need of reliable advisers, Trepov turns to the circle he knows best—the *siloviki*. More than anyone else he trusts Pyotr Rachkovsky, an experienced secret police agent who once led Russia's foreign intelligence service. Rachkovsky is Witte's long-time favorite, and the two enjoy good relations. Through Rachkovsky, Trepov gets closer to Witte and soon begins saying, even to the tsar, that Witte is the only person able to bridge the divide between the regime and society, something that is necessary to prevent new unrest, believes Trepov.

At the end of the summer of 1905, Trepov still considers it his task to lure the intelligentsia over to the side of the authorities. To do so, he decides to fulfill one of the main demands of the liberals: autonomous universities, which enjoy freedom of speech and freedom of assembly (but only for people with higher education). Trepov is sure that now the intellectual elites will calm down.

Under the new "temporary rules" adopted on 27 August 1905, higher educational institutions can choose their own rectors, and the police no longer have the right to enter university grounds without permission. The newly elected rector of Moscow University is Sergei Trubetskoy, one of the leaders of the Liberation Union.

But there is no calming the intelligentsia. In a country where all rallies are banned, the introduction of autonomous universities has the opposite effect: educational institutions become a place of free assembly for all layers of society.

"It's all a complete mess," recalls the head of the secret police, Gerasimov. Mass political rallies are held in assembly halls. Some lecture theatres host meetings of workers from specific professions. There are posters everywhere: "Assembly of cooks," "Assembly of shoemakers," "Assembly of tailors," etc. The police meeting is advertised as follows: "Comrade policemen, be ready to talk about your needs."

Trepov and his advisers are astonished by the ingratitude of the intelligentsia. They expected that students and professors would talk only about academic matters, not politics.

THE BIRTH OF THE SOVIETS

While Gapon is abroad, the workers find themselves new idols. One of them is Gapon's namesake, Georgy Nosar, a lawyer specializing in labor disputes. In the summer, he meets members of the Liberation Union and the "Union of Unions" (a wide alliance of trade unions) and tries to create a new working group (based on Gapon's model). As a result, he is arrested for two months. This only increases his popularity. Nosar is younger than Gapon, only twenty-eight.

Another rising star is the twenty-five-year-old Leon Bronstein, nicknamed "Pen" ("Pero" in Russian). Before 9 January 1905 he lived in Geneva, writing for *Spark*. But after Bloody Sunday he breaks loose and returns to Russia. Like Lenin, he has numerous names: according to his passport he is Pyotr Petrovich Vikentiev; his party comrades know him by the surname Yanovsky, but he writes articles under the pseudonym Trotsky. Although he maintains friendly relations with Lenin, he considers himself a Menshevik—like almost all Marxists in Russia.

Trotsky joins the newly formed Petersburg Soviet of Workers' Deputies—the organization leading the workers' strikes in the capital. A year ago Gapon would surely have been elected chairman. If Trotsky had come a day earlier, perhaps he would have become chairman. But he is late, and on the eve of his arrival the Soviet votes for the modest worker Pyotr Khrustalev. This pseudonym conceals the identity of the lawyer Nosar. An intense rivalry arises between Bronstein-Trotsky and Nosar-Khrustalev, which no one except them seems to notice. Trotsky takes the upper hand.

Years later, Nosar will argue that he created an organization called the "Soviet of Workers' Deputies" back in January 1905—an attempt to exaggerate his role. Nevertheless, Nosar's main contribution to history is the name he coins. All the subsequent Soviets, as well as the name "Soviet Union," originate from this Petersburg Soviet.

STRIKES AND STROKES

On 20 September 1905 two Moscow printing houses go on strike, and three days later a further eighty-nine have laid down their fonts. Newspapers are no longer published. The strike is joined by tram staff and confectioners. They all gather for rallies on the grounds of Moscow University.

On 23 September the authorities close the university, so, instead of classes, the students go out into the street. A demonstration of thousands begins from the university building on Manezhnaya Square and advances up Tverskaya Street to the governor-general's house. The crowd chants political slogans: "Down with autocracy!" "Long live the revolution!" "Long live the republic!" Cossack regiments try to disperse the rally, but they are greeted with a hail of stones. The unrest spreads, and soon almost the whole city is on strike.

On 29 September the democratically elected university rector Sergei Trubetskoy travels to Saint Petersburg. During a seven-hour meeting with the education minister, the forty-three-year-old Trubetskoy suffers a stroke and dies. On 3 October the rector's funeral turns into a powerful protest. More than a hundred enterprises in Moscow are already on strike, and the railway workers are joining in. As a sign of solidarity with Moscow, printing houses in Saint Petersburg also stop publishing.

On 10 October trains from Moscow stop running completely. That is followed on 12 October by a strike at the telegraph—Moscow is cut off from the entire world. On the same day, Saint Petersburg's trains also come to a halt. Fuel supplies dry up, bringing plants and factories to a virtual standstill. On 13 October, the Moscow Duma announces a general strike.

In Saint Petersburg, too, everyone is now on strike: the municipal and zemstvo councils, banks, shops, post offices, and the telegraph, even government officials. By the evening of 13 October, both capitals are severed from the world and from each other.

On 9 October, Sergei Witte, now a count and still buoyed by his American triumph, visits Nicholas II. Despite being back in favor, he still has no real authority (other than his formal position). The tsar still sees him as an outsider—after all, Witte has been absent for so long that he did not take part in drafting the new manifesto on setting up a legislative council.

Analyzing the growing unrest, Witte tells the tsar that he has two choices: appoint a "military dictator" who will suppress all demonstrations, or make major political concessions. Witte himself favors the second option. Moreover, he gives the emperor a "note"—or rather a lengthy political treatise on the inevitability of reform.

Witte's "note" is a historical, even revolutionary, document. Never before has the head of government in Russia delivered anything like it to the head of state. He starts by reasoning about why the state exists at all—a question that Nicholas II is unlikely ever to have pondered. "The state cannot live and develop merely because it exists. . . . There must be a goal; the state must live for the sake of *something*," Witte begins. He proceeds to explain that the sole objective of any state is to ensure the moral and material welfare of its people.

The principal "moral" benefit, says Witte, is freedom. "Man always strives for freedom," since freedom is the most ancient and natural human condition. Autocracy, argues Witte, like all other forms of statehood, is something new, a relatively recent invention. The struggle for freedom, however, dates back to the dawn of humankind.

This thought is in itself revolutionary, so to speak. In the worldview of Nicholas II, instilled by Pobedonostsev, autocracy is God's design. It was God who made him tsar. Witte's concept differs from Pobedonostsev's as much as Darwin's theory of evolution from the Book of Genesis.

Witte reinforces his theory with examples: "The liberation movement was not born a year ago. Its roots lie in the depths of time—in Novgorod and Pskov,* in the protests against Peter's reforms,† in the Decembrist revolt,‡ in the Petrashevsky case,§ in the great act of 19 February 1861,¶ and in the nature of every person."

Witte then moves to the present, arguing that man's striving for freedom cannot be suppressed: "Executions and bloodbaths only accelerate the eruption. They provoke the wild revelry of base human instincts." The only solution, in Witte's view, is for the slogan "freedom" to turn into government activity.** Witte seems to have picked up these ideas during his trip to America, although he does not refer to it anywhere in the "note"—so that the tsar does not think that he dreams of being the first president of the "United States of Russia."

Witte believes that the authorities should lead the reforms, rather than trail behind the demands of society: first, no more arbitrary rule on the part of the law enforcement agencies; second, civil rights for all; third, reforms of the system of state administration; and lastly, the worker, agrarian, and regional issues need to be addressed once and for all.

"Historical progress is irrepressible. The idea of civil liberty will triumph if not by way of reform, then by way of revolution. But in the latter

---

* East Slavic republics which existed in the thirteenth–fifteenth centuries.
† Government reforms of Peter the Great of the early eighteenth century aimed to modernize Russia based on European model.
‡ Uprising of army officers and soldiers in the center of Saint Petersburg in 1825.
§ The Petrashevsky circle was a radical literary discussion group; its members were arrested and exiled to Siberia in 1849, among them Dostoevsky.
¶ The Emancipation reform of 1861 which abolished serfdom.
** Russian authorities in the early twenty-first century tried to lead the reforms. During Vladimir Putin's first presidential term the government announced economic reforms as their main goal, but they were halted as soon as oil prices started to go up. Next time it was Dmitry Medvedev who announced economic and political reforms aimed at liberalization of the public life. Some of these reforms have never begun, and some were canceled or even reverted as soon as Medvedev's presidential term ended.

case, it will be reborn from the ashes of overthrowing a thousand years of history. The Russian uprising, senseless and merciless, will sweep everything away and all shall turn to dust," Witte predicts. He will never know just how accurate his forecast is.

The emperor listens attentively to Witte's prognosis, and duly consults his wife. They discuss his report together. Nicholas II promises to think about it.

On the day of Witte's report, 9 October, the situation does not seem alarming from the tsar's perspective at his Peterhof residence outside the capital. But by 12 October everything has changed. He discovers that he is effectively a prisoner. Ministers from Saint Petersburg cannot reach him at Peterhof, since the roads are blocked. They have to commandeer two warships, the *Dozorny* and the *Razvedchik*, to get to him. The railway network across the length and breadth of Russia has stopped working. The telegraph is also silent.

"What lovely times!!" Nicholas II notes ironically in his diary. The emperor is incredibly isolated. He has effectively lost control of the country and only learns about what is happening in the capital in snippets.

In the Gulf of Finland, near Peterhof, there appear two German cruisers. It is not a threat—they have come to rescue Nicholas II. Kaiser Wilhelm II, Empress Alexandra's cousin, who never fails to send the tsar detailed written recommendations on Russian domestic policy, believes that the situation in Saint Petersburg is out of control. The German emperor advises his Russian counterpart to go abroad, and offers asylum in Germany. Moreover, he is ready to assist in suppressing the unrest: German troops can be dispatched to Saint Petersburg, or any Russian region, to put things in order immediately. In the capital, rumors spread that German troops are already on the move to Russia.

Wilhelm's letter becomes the talk of high society—many welcome the proposal. Revolutionaries are everywhere, and they no longer trust their own military, which could join the other side at any moment. German soldiers are far more reliable. Many advise the tsar to leave and let the Germans in. Witte believes that if he does, he will not be able to return. Trepov vacillates.

It is difficult to understand the tsar's emotional state at this time. All his attendants describe him as a man of incredible restraint, able to hide his emotions. Yet at the same time, he is often described as suspicious and distrustful. The brutal assassination of King Alexander I of Serbia and his wife, Queen Draga, by members of their inner circle in 1903 has had a profound effect on Nicholas. He knew Alexander personally and was deeply

MAXIM GORKY

shocked by his murder. Two years later, he still remembers the unfortunate fate of the Serbian monarch and fears a conspiracy.

THEATRICAL MUTINY

With Russia's two capitals roiling in political activism, Maria Andreyeva cannot sit still in the provincial Finnish backwater of Kuokkala (now Repino). Despite all the previous scandals, she returns to the Moscow Art Theatre to rehearse a new play, *Children of the Sun*, by her civil-law husband. Gorky himself still resides in Finland. But it is not really the theatre that draws Andreyeva back to Moscow.

She is a member of the underground revolutionary movement and revels in the role. Back in Kuokkala, she and Gorky gave underground performances to raise money for the revolutionaries. She, her husband, and the writer Leonid Andreyev read poetry and prose, and passed a reticule around the audience marked with the words: "Please donate to the militant organization." The money Andreyeva sent to the leader of the organization, Leonid Krasin.

Now in Moscow, Andreyeva takes an even greater liking to revolutionary activity. She again collects money on behalf of Krasin to help fund the Social Democrats' underground press and help prisoners escape from jail, among other things. Andreyeva copes admirably with the task. Meanwhile, the play is at risk.

On 14 October, the Moscow Art Theatre holds a dress rehearsal of *Children of the Sun*. Suddenly, in the middle of the play, the lights go out. Moscow's power stations have joined the strike.

Andreyeva demands that the theatre should also strike. Three meetings are held to discuss whether or not to take part in the political struggle. Andreyeva delivers a passionate speech. But Stanislavsky and Nemirovich-Danchenko announce that the theatre shall "express sympathy with the strikers by giving a performance for the benefit of their families."

For the most part, protesting is very fashionable. The strikes are supported by university professors, who donate three days' wages to the striking workers, as well as by previously apolitical intellectuals and artists. The Imperial Theater elects a "strike committee," which includes Anna Pavlova, Tamara Karsavina, and Mikhail Fokine, all future stars of Diaghilev's ballets.

The Directorate of the Imperial Theatres plans to fire the instigators and demands that all employees sign a declaration of loyalty (similar to when the captain of the battleship *Potemkin* divided the crew into willing and non-willing soup eaters). Few agree, but some, such as Diaghilev's friend, the choreographer Sergei Legat, go ahead and sign it.*

Diaghilev is in a state of nervous excitement: "It's impossible to describe what's going on: everything's locked—newspaper stands, telephone booths, telegraphs—all in anticipation of machine guns. Last night I walked along Nevsky Proskpekt. It was ghost-like and pitch-black, save for a shaft of light from the Admiralty's vast searchlight. The effect was amazing. The pavements are black, the people are like shadows, the houses are like cardboard cut-outs," he writes to his friend Benois in France.

Diaghilev's cousin and former male lover, Dima Filosofov, has also become interested in politics. He has long since distanced himself from Sergei, and now lives together with Zinaida Gippius and Dmitry Merezhkovsky—the so-called *Troyebratstvo* or "brotherhood of three." Only five years ago the Merezhkovskys despised the politicized older generation and

---

*In the early twenty-first century loyalty of cultural workers is still very important to the authorities: those who receive state funding are usually supposed to publicly support government policy, sign open letters in condemnation of the opposition, and show their loyalty in other humiliating ways.

were focused on spiritual, mystical, and religious matters. But in summer 1905 Merezhkovsky tells his wife: "Autocracy comes from the Antichrist." She writes the phrase on a box of chocolates so as not to forget it.

In October 1905 Zinaida Gippius experiences a mystical presentiment of the revolution, like a doom-monger predicting the end of the world. On 17 October, she writes a letter to Filosofov, which will be published years later as proof of her prophetic ability. In it, she says that, if the regime does not avert disaster by implementing reform, there will be a revolution in March (the year is unspecified) led by the Social Democrats.

The authorities believe that the strike movement is part of a diabolical plan hatched by the opposition. Trepov and even more so Gerasimov are convinced that the strike has been organized by the Union of Unions, which created the Saint Petersburg Soviet of Workers' Deputies. Nicholas II is also convinced of this, writing to his mother about the "infamous Union of Unions, which has caused all the unrest." This, of course, is a slight exaggeration. Following the arrest of Milyukov and company, the central bureau of the Union of Unions ceases to exist. Their places are gradually taken by other less familiar faces. In October, after the strike in Moscow, the new central bureau of the Union of Unions sends delegates to the Saint Petersburg Soviet. It sounds like a coordinated plan, but is in fact spontaneous and haphazard.

What has the former head of the powerful Union of Unions Pavel Milyukov been up to since his release from the Kresty prison? No longer linked to the organization, on 12 October he holds the founding congress of the new Liberal Party—the first legal opposition party in Russia, based on the Liberation Union. Funding for it comes from his former lover Margarita Morozova, a widow of a rich merchant and an ardent fan of Milyukov. However, there is a problem: the railways go on strike and three-quarters of the delegates are unable to get to Moscow for the congress, including almost all the ones from Saint Petersburg. But Milyukov believes that it cannot be postponed. So, a few months after returning from delivering a series of lectures at Chicago University, he ejects all the veterans of the Russian liberal movement and becomes the sole leader of the party, which becomes known as the "party of people's freedom" and, more officially, the Constitutional Democratic Party. Its members are called Kadets.*

Milyukov's personal life and circumstances have a strong influence on the work of the congress. Despite the congress being sponsored by his

---

* Abbreviated from the Russian name of the party: *Konstitutsionno-Demokraticheskaya Partiya*.

former mistress, Milyukov's wife Anna is actively involved. It is she who raises the question of whether universal suffrage should be extended to women (in the liberal constitution drafted by members of the Liberation Union in spring 1905, there was no mention of it). Milyukov is opposed, believing that it is not necessary to burden the party program with unnecessary minutiae. But his offended wife is supported by most of the congress participants. As such, Russia's first liberal party starts to champion women's right to vote.

As the Kadets are discussing women's rights, strikes are breaking out all over Russia.

CONSTITUTION OR DEATH

On 13 October Witte receives a telegram informing him of his appointment as the new chairman of the Council of Ministers. There is no mention of the proposed reforms. Witte requests an audience with the tsar, saying that he cannot accept the position if his political agenda is not adopted.

But Nicholas II cannot adopt the proposals of Witte and Wilhelm II at the same time, both of which seem to violate the oath that he gave on accession to the throne, namely that he would pass it on to his son, just like he had received it from his father. He hears this repeatedly from Alexandra, who is obsessed with the notion that Tsarevich Alexei must receive what is rightfully his. The solution is simple. The rebellion must be crushed.

To this end, the tsar summons Grand Duke Nikolai Nikolaevich (known in the family as Uncle Nikolasha), with whom he has a special relationship. He is forty-nine years old, twelve years older than Nicholas, and one of the tsar's most trusted men. The feeling is mutual.

The grand duke is known for his mysticism, like his brother Peter and the "black princesses"—the best friends of Empress Alexandra, the Montenegrins Stana and Milica. They were all under the spell of Dr. Philippe. Now, in the autumn of 1905, they are passionate about a new preacher in town, Grigory Rasputin.

Yet Nikolai Nikolaevich is not only a mystic, but also a professional soldier. The tsar believes that he is the one to suppress the rebellion.

In the midst of the strikes the task will not be easy. Nevertheless, Uncle Nicky makes the journey to Peterhof on 15 October to talk to his nephew. However, he is in an uncertain frame of mind, not dictatorial at all. Before setting off, he takes out a gun and says to the minister of the court, Count

Fredericks: "I am going to go to see the Emperor to entreat him to sign the manifesto and the proposals of Count Witte. Either he signs, or I shoot myself in the forehead with this revolver in front of his very eyes."

Nicholas II acquiesces, says Witte, and orders that a draft manifesto be drawn up. The tsar spends a few days (15–17 October) in talks with Witte and other officials about the wording of the manifesto. He consults with everyone he can. Uncle Nicky, Count Fredericks, and Witte are in favor. His wife is against. His aide Orlov (nicknamed "Vladi") also tries to dissuade the tsar: "Do not be pressured into granting a constitution; it would better to wait at least half a year," he says.

Nicholas asks Trepov how many days it would take to restore order in Saint Petersburg without bloodshed, if at all possible: "I can give no guarantees. The sedition has spread so far and deep that it now depends on the mercy of God," responds Trepov. "Trepov is a coward," says Vladi Orlov. The emperor disagrees.

At 5 p.m. on 17 October Witte brings a revised version of the text. The tsar puts pen to paper. The manifesto guarantees "civil liberties on the basis of personal integrity, freedom of conscience, speech, assembly and association," and gives the vote to all "classes of the population presently deprived of electoral rights." Lastly, it states that a parliament, or State Duma, is to be set up without the consent of which no law can be passed. It is essentially the first constitution in the history of Russia.

Having signed the document, Nicholas summons Orlov. "Don't leave me today. It's too much to bear," says Nicholas II, holding his head and crying. "I feel like I've lost the crown. It's over." Orlov consoles him by saying that he can still "unite the forces of reason and rescue the situation." Orlov telephones Rachkovsky and urges him to do just that.*

"After such a day, my head is heavy and my thoughts are confused. Lord, help us. Save and reconcile Russia," the tsar writes in his diary.

At the same time, a decree is published to officially set up the new Council of Ministers and appoint Witte as its chairman, based on the model of European prime ministers. Also published is the "Report of Count Witte"—the new government's effective agenda, perhaps the most liberal ever in the history of Russia. The text says that Russia "has

---

*In the twenty-first century the Presidential Administration is responsible for the matters that used to be handled by the Interior Ministry in the early twentieth century. The matters remain the same: creating artificial public organizations and movements that serve as a power base for the regime. Such formations range from the party of the state to niche pro-government organizations. Their number has increased a hundred times over, the scale of their funding, perhaps, a thousand times over.

outgrown the existing system and is committed to building a legal order on the basis of civil liberties." The government undertakes not to interfere with the elections to the State Duma and to "repeal repressive measures against actions that do not threaten the state."

In addition, Witte ponders the needs of Russian society: "It cannot be that Russian society wants anarchy and the dismemberment of the state." However, the new prime minister is only briefly distracted by such thoughts—he has a new government to appoint.

Trepov learns the news from Witte over the phone. "Thank God, the manifesto is signed. We'll have civil liberties and popular representation," says the relieved general to his adviser Rachkovsky. "Tomorrow they'll be triple-kissing* in the streets of Saint Petersburg," echoes Rachkovsky and, turning to Gerasimov, continues: "That means no more work for you." "If that's the case, I'll be happy to resign," responds Gerasimov.

That evening Prime Minister Witte gathers his ministers to discuss the manifesto and some extra details not yet prescribed in law: in particular, the forthcoming amnesty. Witte wants the release of all political prisoners, the return of all exiles, and the emptying of the Shlisselburg prison in order to show that "the old Russia is gone." He is opposed by Finance Minister Kokovtsov, who is against a general amnesty for the "terrorists" inside Shlisselburg Fortress. Witte's nerves get the better of him, and he screams at Kokovtsov in front of all those present: "The finance minister's ideas would be better suited to governing the Zulus."

October 18th becomes a nationwide celebration that is still marked ten years later. Saint Petersburg's intellectuals rejoice. Sergei Diaghilev buys a bottle of champagne and celebrates the constitution with his family. "We're delirious! Yesterday we even drank champagne courtesy of Sergei. It's miraculous!" writes his Aunt Nona, the mother of Dima Filosofov.

The strike comes to an end, and the water supply system, trains, and everything else start working again. There are demonstrations in both capitals: half with portraits of Nicholas II, the other half with red flags. Some sing the national anthem, others revolutionary songs. "Both sides are out of control. Passers-by who don't doff their caps to them risk getting attacked," recalls the Moscow governor Dzhunkovsky. The police do not intervene.

In Moscow the sister of Margarita Morozova arranges a magnificent banquet to mark the end of the congress, not expecting there to be a second, far more momentous occasion. The hall is full and in an enthusiastic

---

* Three times on the cheek as a greeting, especially on Easter Sunday.

mood. "We are gathered here to commemorate the congress and the manifesto together," says Milyukov. As the hero of the day, he is raised aloft and placed on the table to make a speech. But Milyukov acts with restraint, saying that it is only the beginning: "We cannot become complacent or abandon our battle stations." He finishes his speech on a gloomy note: "Nothing has changed yet, the war goes on."

At roughly the same time, the antithesis of the forty-six-year-old Milyukov, the twenty-five-year-old Leon Trotsky, is shouting from a university balcony at the rejoicing crowd below: the "semi-victory" is insufficient; the enemy is implacable; traps lie ahead. He tears the imperial manifesto into pieces and scatters them to the wind.

There is even less clarity in the provinces. No one there has even heard of this seminal document until the morning of 18 October, when it is published in the local newspapers. Even then, no one understands what it means.

Vasily Shulgin, a monarchist and future State Duma member, who at the time is a warrant officer and resident of Kiev, describes how the advent of political freedom is celebrated on Dumskaya Square, which will be known as Maidan (Independence Square) one hundred years later and will become a venue for all subsequent Ukrainian revolutions. The square is packed from end to end, with people hanging from the balconies on either side. In the midst of the "sea of heads" are "huge boxes dripping with people." "I didn't realize at first that they were trams. From the roofs of these trams, people were making speeches, waving their arms, but the roar of the crowd drowned them out. They opened their mouths like fish thrown on the sand," writes Shulgin. The mood is joyous: some celebrate quietly; others are drunk on adrenaline. The City Duma holds an emergency meeting. Its members demand the release of all political prisoners and sing the Eternal Memory to the "champion freedom fighter"—the deceased rector of Moscow University, Prince Trubetskoy. Then the Duma members go out onto the balcony of the building, which is decorated with the tsarist monogram and crown. They dismantle and replace them with a red flag.

The monarchist Shulgin describes it histrionically: "The tsarist crown broke off and crashed onto the dirty pavement in front of the 10,000-strong crowd. The metal cried out on impact with the stone. . . . The crowd gasped. A sinister whisper spread: 'The yids have smashed the crown.'" Shulgin does not even suspect that in twelve years' time he will be the one who really does dismantle the crown—he will take the act of abdication from the hands of Nicholas II himself.

But for now Shulgin is horrified by what is happening in Kiev: students are ransacking the City Duma building, tearing down the royal portraits, piercing the eyes. One student sticks his head through a portrait of the tsar and runs around with the torn canvas around his neck, shouting: "Look at me, I'm the tsar!"

Kiev differs from Saint Petersburg and Moscow in that it is inside the Pale of Settlement. Anti-Semitic sentiments are very strong. *The Kievite*, one of the most conservative, monarchist, and anti-Semitic newspapers in Ukraine (known as "Little Russia" back then), is edited by Shulgin's step-father, Dmitry Pikhno.

In the evening of 18 October, a crowd of students and workers goes to the editorial office of *The Kievite*, planning to loot it. The police threaten to open fire. Meanwhile, Pikhno is trying to get the typesetters to print the latest issue. They are afraid, saying that the revolutionaries have threatened to slaughter their families if they carry on working for a paper that supports the Black Hundreds. The editor delivers an impassioned speech: "I ask you to do it not for yourselves, but for Russia. . . . If we give in now, they will destroy everything and you will not have a single crust of bread to eat, nor will Russia." Two senior typesetters agree. They tearfully ask Shulgin for "a rouble to buy some vodka" and then risk their lives by typesetting the new issue of *The Kievite*, which is only two pages long. It is the only newspaper that comes out the next day, 19 October.

The protests around the City Duma do not last long. Cossack troops arrive and disperse the crowd. A terrible stampede ensues that claims some lives: "Five minutes ago there was a crowd of many thousands. Now there are corpses, crumpled hats, galoshes, umbrellas and a few ladies' garments," *The Kievite* describes the events of that day. "Battles took place on the square and in the side streets between the Black Hundreds on one side, and the intelligentsia and the Jews on the other. By evening, and over the next two days, it turned into a pogrom."

According to Shulgin, the pogrom was provoked by the rumor that "the yids have smashed the crown," which the angry urban poor use as a pretext to raid Jewish shops. Officer Shulgin, the stepson of a pro-Black Hundreds publisher, goes around the city with a detachment of troops, trying to prevent the killing of Jews. The mobs cannot understand why the military is not on their side: "Officer, why are you going after us?! We support you." Shulgin struggles to persuade them not to attack Jewish homes: "No sooner had I dispersed one group, another formed at the edge of the wasteland. It turned into a game of cat and mouse."

THE UNION OF RUSSIANS

Dr. Dubrovin is extremely worked up by the manifesto. His followers gather at his huge apartment the next day. They believe that Witte has "extorted" the manifesto from the tsar with threats, and hence it has no legal force. Dubrovin comes up with a name for the nationwide organization that the monarchists have long dreamed of creating—the Union of the Russian People.

The "unionists" (as members of the organization call themselves) intend to fight the manifesto of 17 October and restore the unlimited power of the sovereign. They also describe themselves as "true Russians"—the very "forces of reason" that the imperial aide Vladi Orlov had in mind.

Dubrovin's apartment becomes the epicenter of monarchist Petersburg. The police supply volunteers. After all, Rachkovsky has long mentored the trusty Dubrovin. Funding comes directly from the Interior Ministry.

REFORM OR TRAP

A couple of days after the signing of the manifesto, the news reaches Geneva, the capital of the Russian opposition. The leaders of the most powerful opposition party—Mikhail Gotz, Yevgeny Azef, and Viktor Chernov—study the latest issue of *Journal de Geneve*, which has published the text of the tsar's manifesto. Chernov does not believe it is for real. "It's a concession. The general strike is clearly having an effect," he says. "But we have to stay on our toes."

Chernov is not alone. Almost all the SRs are unanimous that it is "another trick, a cold-blooded trap" to lure the "underground émigrés back to Russia" and then "sweep Russia clean of sedition."* Only Gotz and Azef disagree. "Do you really think they would turn the entire state system upside down and embolden the whole opposition for the sake of a police operation?" asks Azef.

Gotz agrees: "The old regime is finished. It is the end of absolutism and the start of a new era." Moreover, in his opinion, "terrorism has also run its course." It is time to do away with the militant organization.

---

* Chernov talks in line with many political scientists of the early twenty-first century (both in Russia and abroad): he believes that all actions of the authorities are parts of a very clever and even cunning master plan that is calculated for many steps ahead in order to trap and destroy all enemies of the regime.

The dismantling of the militant organization is opposed by Savinkov. But he is still subordinate to the central committee. But his younger comrade Mikhail Sokolov, who has not yet taken part in any terror operations, but dreams of doing so, does not feel beholden to the central committee. He and others decide to launch their own terror.

Gotz dispatches Chernov to Russia to start printing an SR Party newspaper in Saint Petersburg, which it can now do legally for the first time. Chernov comes to say goodbye to the party's ideologist, who intends to remain in Europe. Gotz is now paralyzed from the waist down, and his hands are becoming numb as well. Gotz's wife plays a gramophone record, and Chernov sings along in a "happy, silly mood." The cause of Gotz's illness is a tumor in the spinal cord, and his doctors have recommended a highly complex operation. But he and Chernov do not discuss health issues. They only talk about the future of Russian politics. "I selfishly did not want to spoil my own joy with pessimism," recalls Chernov.

THE PIG, THE TOAD, AND OTHER MINISTERS

Under the new system, the Russian capital becomes a completely different city. Whereas before it was "ghost-like," now it is one big carnival.

On 21 October, the Petersburg Soviet issues a (somewhat ironic) decree: "Only newspapers whose editors do not send issues to the censors can be published"; the next day every newspaper in the capital is published uncensored. The trade union of typographical workers refuses to typeset the censored newspapers.

The dissidents feel proud that their erstwhile guardians are now lying low. The striking dancers at the Mariinsky Theatre claim victory, but those who signed the declaration of loyalty are disgraced. The choreographer Sergei Legat, who gave in to the authorities, commits suicide. The entire theatre is shocked. Sergei Diaghilev writes an article entitled "The Dance of Death," in which he accuses culture officials of driving him to take his own life.

It is at this time that Diaghilev becomes acquainted with Maxim Gorky, and together they discuss the idea of publishing an art magazine. It is a remarkable alliance: the aesthete Diaghilev's projects are all state-funded, while Gorky, a living symbol of the protests, spent a month in jail last winter and is still awaiting trial. However, no one believes that the trial will now go ahead.

Gorky's civil-law wife, Maria Andreyeva, becomes the publisher of the new magazine, which is called *New Life*. The popular actress is, of course, purely a figurehead—the brains behind the publication are Andreyeva's Bolshevik friends. For them, it is their first lawful outlet of expression.

Autumn 1905 sees the return of political exiles and the release of political prisoners. Crowds gather to welcome home the Swiss exiles Viktor Chernov, Julius Martov, Vladimir Ulyanov, and Peter Struve.

For Struve, who is still in Paris, 17 October is a special day, for his wife gives birth. The contractions have already started when her husband bursts into the ward, shouting, "Nina, there's a constitution!" After a couple of days he leaves his wife and newborn baby, closes the now defunct émigré magazine *Liberation*, and goes to Saint Petersburg to start a new magazine, this time on home soil.

The magazine takes a while to get off the ground. Struve is busy touring around, making speeches, and warning everyone of the danger of dictatorship hanging over Russia. He fears both the "dictatorship of the so-called 'Black Hundreds' and of the so-called 'revolutionary proletariat.'" Struve believes that "Russia does not need any sort of dictatorship, only human rights, freedoms and economic revival."

Lenin at this time prudently takes Andreyeva's *New Life* under his wing, and dismisses the entire staff that she has recruited. Martov, for his part, begins to edit another newspaper, called *Beginning*. The Menshevik paper is far more popular and features articles by the "protester-in-chief" Leon Trotsky. Day after day Trotsky calls for a popular uprising. The main targets of his publications are Sergei Witte and Peter Struve. "Witte is an agent of the stock exchange, and Struve is an agent of Witte," says one of his articles. He is full of bad blood for his enemies. He condemns the liberals even more violently than the government.

Freedom of speech knows no bounds. Right there on Nevsky Prospekt, outside Saint Catherine's Catholic Church, stands a stall selling newspapers from Geneva, Paris, and London, which the day before were illegal, including back issues of *Spark*, *Revolutionary Russia*, *Liberation*, and others. The head of the secret police, Gerasimov, is shocked. Loitering by the counter, he rummages through the piles and buys something out of interest for his personal collection.

The metropolitan press, free from censorship, is forced to fight for readership with the revolutionary publications. A whole galaxy of satirical magazines ridicules the authorities.

Gerasimov's new hobby is to deliver a selection of the latest cartoons to Interior Minister Durnovo: "This is Count Witte as a pig. And here, in the form of a toad, is you, Your Excellency." However, only when the cartoonists mock the tsar does the minister take offence. He orders the immediate confiscation of any such magazines, which only spurs demand for them: instead of the usual five kopecks,* "banned" issues sell for one,† two,‡ or even five roubles.§

Saint Petersburg's "constitutional" civil society tries to assume ever-greater authority, even in areas that the state did not intend. The Petersburg Soviet of Workers' Deputies passes a resolution for a new eight-hour working day (although it fails to implement it). Meanwhile, the Soviet's official newspaper *Izvestia* discusses the regulation of food prices and lower rents for the poor.

The Soviet also forms its own "militia" in order to police the police. Its "officers" are granted entrance to inspect the prisons to verify that the amnesty is being honored. Gerasimov is outraged and dismisses the police officers who let them in.

He is even more indigent about something that randomly catches his own eye: on Liteyny Avenue a man with a bandaged hand approaches a guard and says something to him. Gerasimov goes up to the man and asks him what the problem is. "The sanitary conditions in this yard are unacceptable. There is a cesspit that has not been cleared for a long time and stinks terribly. I suggested to the guard that action should be taken," says the man with the bandage.

Despite the stinking cesspit, Gerasimov is furious. He cannot understand on what basis society has claimed such authority: "Excuse me, but who are you?" he shouts. "I am a representative of the militia under the Soviet of Workers' Deputies," states the bandaged man assuredly. Gerasimov orders the guard to arrest the "representative of the militia," but Gerasimov is not in uniform and the guard does not know who he is. The latter taps his temple, showing that he thinks Gerasimov is a head case, and follows the bandaged man into the yard to draw up a report on the unsanitary conditions.

Witte, who wants to start everything anew, fails to take into account the reaction of the bureaucracy. No one bothered to explain what the new rules of the game would be. And thousands of people sincerely believe that the old order was better and do not want change.

From day one, Gerasimov advises the new interior minister Durnovo to arrest all leaders of social organizations. "Well, if we could arrest half of Petersburg, that would be great," jokes Durnovo, who himself is itching to

---

*About $0.7 in 2017.
†About $13.2 in 2017.
‡About $26.4 in 2017.
§About $65.9 in 2017.

do something. But he restrains himself: "We are a constitutional government. There is no going back and you must behave accordingly." But many,
Gerasimov included, do not want to. They do not believe in the new policy
and demand arrests.

THE WITTE GOVERNMENT

It would seem that Sergei Witte has achieved his life's aim. He is the new
shogun, the grand vizier, as his enemies in Petersburg high society acidly
describe him. He is now the most powerful government official in the
history of Russia, and is suitably placed to carry out his own program of
reforms. Moreover, he is the first head of government able to choose his
own ministers, regardless of the tsar.

Witte begins to look for personnel, but it turns out that most public
figures want nothing to do with him. The first people he summons are
Dmitry Shipov, the former head of the Moscow zemstvo and the first
leader of the opposition, and Alexander Guchkov, an extremely active
member of the Moscow Duma. They are both unhappy with Witte's choice
for the post of interior minister, Pyotr Durnovo, who worked as both Sipyagin's and Plehve's deputy. Next Witte meets with representatives of the
Zemstvo Congress (including Prince Georgy Lvov, who twelve years later
will head the Provisional Government). They all say that the manifesto of
17 October is not a constitution, merely a declaration of intent on the part
of the government. First and foremost, the authorities must convene a
constituent assembly. Witte even seeks out Milyukov, who advises him not
to form a government of national trust, but to select a technocratic "busi-
ness-minded" cabinet.

Witte consults with media owners. The publisher of the popular *Stock
Exchange Gazette* tells him face to face that no one wants to work with him
because no one trusts him.

In the new atmosphere of free speech, the old-timer Witte is an unap-
pealing figure. All prospective ministers shy away, because even talking to
him is a blow to their reputation. The Petersburg Soviet, Trotsky, and the
leftist newspapers *Beginning* and *New Life* are riding high, and the public
is far more radical than a year ago. Leftist ideas are in vogue, and no one
wants to tarnish themselves by shaking hands with Witte. Supporting
Witte, says Milyukov, would mean "losing face."

In his memoirs, Witte complains about the liberal intelligentsia. If it
had not rejected his proposals, everything would have been different, he

opines. Later, even the liberals themselves will remember the moment as a unique opportunity lost.

As a result, Witte's cabinet is formed not of public figures, but of time-worn tsarist officials. Yet the structure of power changes. The tsar's recent favorite, Trepov, is appointed court commander. He is no longer the sole intermediary between the nation and the tsar, but simply the most important confidant, responsible for the sovereign's personal safety.

But perhaps an even more epoch-defining resignation is that of the highly influential Grand Duke Vladimir, who commanded the army on the fateful 9 January 1905 and authorized the Bloody Sunday massacre. But his departure has nothing to do with the killings; it is simply that Nicholas II disapproves of the marriage of his son, Grand Duke Kirill, a first cousin of the tsar himself. Kirill has provoked a scandal by marrying the recently divorced wife of Alexandra's elder brother, Duke Ernst Ludwig of Hesse. The tsar (under the influence of his wife) banishes Kirill from Russia. Enraged by this act, Uncle Vladimir hands in his notice. So begins the most protracted and internecine feud ever to occur inside the imperial family, with Nicky and Alix on one side, and Uncle Vladimir, his wife Miechen, and their children on the other. The feud lasts all the way until 1917.

A SAINT AND A REBELLION

The adoption of the manifesto is not the end of the crisis. On 23 October tempers flare at Kronstadt, Russia's largest military port, just thirty kilometers from Saint Petersburg. In the evening the Kronstadt sailors learn that a commandant has arrested forty soldiers for having demanded better conditions. The sailors stop the train with the arrested soldiers. In response, the convoy opens fire, killing one sailor. It signals the start of an uprising of twelve naval barracks.

The uprising descends into attacks on local shops. Residents start fleeing in panic. On the morning of the 27th, even the most famous local, Father John of Kronstadt, leaves town.

Nicholas II writes in his diary on 27 October: "Disorder and riots broke out in Kronstadt yesterday. News of it was hard to come by, since the phones are not working. What times we live in!!!"

The next day of the uprising turns into a drunken brawl. The sailors smash up shops without making any demands.

The task of suppressing the unrest falls to two generals: Nikolai Ivanov and Mikhail Alekseyev, who will go on to lead the Russian army a decade later and become the tsar's two closest generals in 1917. But in 1905 they are still unknown to the general public, having both just returned from the Manchurian front. They make short shrift of the drunken sailors. General Ivanov uses his stentorian voice, shouting with all his might at the mutineers: "On your knees!" The dumbfounded sailors obey. The rebellion is fully quashed with the help of a machine-gun crew and an infantry regiment. There are fifty dead and two hundred wounded.

The very next day Nicholas II writes: "Things have calmed down after the sailors' drunken unrest." But the story does not end there. After the suppression of the rebellion, the Petersburg Soviet announces a protest strike, which involves around a hundred and fifty thousand people. Strikes in support of the Kronstadt sailors are held in Moscow, Vilnius, Kharkov, and Kiev.

The seventy-six-year-old priest John of Kronstadt stays in the capital for three days until everything in the island town calms down. For a long time afterwards, the liberal press mocks the "people's priest" who fled the uprising: a newspaper prints a cartoon in which he is depicted on a donkey wading through the Gulf of Finland to the mainland.

It is a difficult time for Russia's most famous prelate. He is forced to move house temporarily to escape the opprobrium. Into the breach steps his young friend, the thirty-six-year-old Grigory Rasputin. On 31 October, the tsar and his wife pay a visit to the Montenegrin princesses, Stana and Milica. There, they are acquainted with Milica's new protégé—"the man of God, Grigory."

Their new acquaintance makes a strong impression on the imperial family. The emperor and empress are still in shock over the 17 October manifesto, which goes against their belief that the tsar's power is God-given. Rasputin thinks so, too (or so he says). Nicholas and Alexandra perceive him as the true conveyor of the thoughts and feelings of the common people; he tells them what they want to hear and offers to help knock down the "wall" of officials and courtiers (as well as liberals and intellectuals) that separates the tsar from his people. Rasputin appears just when the tsar is flirting with democracy; he will gradually come to replace that democracy with his own vision; he will become for Nicholas the voice of God and the voice of the people. In modern parlance, he will act as a focus group and the most reliable opinion poll.

"It is strange that such a clever man could have erred in his attempts to pacify," Nicholas II writes to his mother about Count Witte. Indeed, there is no pacification in sight. Nosar, Trotsky, and the Petersburg Soviet are still urging the workers to go on striking indefinitely. The situation is not as desperate as it was in early October, but is still the opposite of what Witte had promised.

In late October Prime Minister Witte receives a delegation of workers, all former activists of Gapon's organization. The workers request an amnesty for Gapon and the return of the confiscated sum of 30,000 roubles* that was in the organization's accounts. Witte promises to return the money, but refuses to amnesty Gapon. But Gapon comes back all the same, under false papers.

The city has changed immeasurably since January. Without his cassock and beard, no one recognizes Gapon (he writes that without his robes he feels like Samson without his hair). The former priest goes into the building of the Free Economic Society, where, disguised, he and Gorky had addressed the crowd in the evening of 9 January. It is now the home of the Petersburg Soviet, headed by Nosar. There Gapon meets an old friend, Pinhas Rutenberg, who has been granted an amnesty.

Rutenberg advises Gapon to walk into the conference hall and say to Nosar: "I, Georgy Gapon, ask for your protection," in which case no one will dare touch him and he will soon be amnestied. But Gapon disagrees, believing that his life will still be in danger. Moreover, he does not want to be in hock to the Petersburg Soviet and wants to revive his own organization.

But while Gapon ponders his next move, the situation changes very quickly. News arrives from Crimea on 11 November that several warship crews have mutinied. Lieutenant Pyotr Schmidt has appointed himself commander of the Black Sea Fleet.

The newspapers have only scraps of information about the uprising, but it is clearly a fatal blow to Witte's pacification policy. After the adoption of his manifesto, things have only become worse. The influence of the *silovik* Interior Minister Durnovo increases as a result. Even Witte himself starts demanding stricter measures.

The government issues a decree imposing new penalties for striking: up to eighteen months in prison for participants and up to four years for organizers. Troops are dispatched to Sevastopol.

On 13 November, the Petersburg Soviet discusses a new general strike, but decides not to announce one. The next day enterprises and factories begin mass layoffs of more than one hundred thousand workers.

It is at this point that Witte remembers Gapon and comes up with a new role for him. The prime minister has no interest in using Gapon to cajole the Petersburg workers, for his connections abroad are far more

---

*About $395,500 in 2017.

useful. Gapon is approached by Witte's personal assistant, the former police agent Ivan Manasevich-Manuilov, who promises to help revive the workers' organization and even finance it, in return for assistance. Although less popular in Saint Petersburg than before, Gapon is still revered among the Russian opposition abroad. Witte's new government is desperately in need of a huge loan—the economy is spluttering and all negotiations with France's bankers have stalled. Gapon's task is to go to Paris and inform local media that the Russian government under Witte is stable and efficient; there will be no revolution and all loans are risk-free.

Gapon agrees. He is given 500 roubles for the trip,* and the promise of the return of his organization's confiscated funds. The government requests that he keep this payment a secret, to which he consents. He is firmly convinced that it is he who is using Witte, and not the other way round.

November 21st marks a long-awaited grand event: the reopening of Gapon's Assembly of Petersburg Factory Workers, attended by four thousand people. Gapon is happy to have achieved his goal once again. As the leader of a powerful organization, he is a force to be reckoned with.

However, the opening of Gapon's organization on 21 November is overshadowed by another far more significant event: the first meeting of the "Union of the Russian People." The authorities allocate the building of the Mikhailovsky Manege for the occasion. A raised platform is set up in the center of the arena for the speakers. The total number of participants is not clear: the Interior Ministry employee Vladimir Gurko estimates around two thousand, but the Black Hundred newspaper publisher Pavel Krushevan is sure it is twenty thousand.

The participants recall a tense atmosphere: "The air was electric." There are fears that after the meeting there will be smashing and looting.

The intermittent raids and pogroms that the monarchists and their sympathizers carry out are the flip side of the unrest of autumn 1905. On one side of the street Marxists bear red flags calling for strikes, while on the other "right" side of the street there are banners and portraits of the emperor. The monarchists often force passers-by to remove their hats (sometimes violently). In addition, they often beat up anyone they consider to be Jewish or a student—the perpetrators of the unrest in their eyes. Even in Saint Petersburg (and especially in provincial towns) a man in glasses is not safe.

This repels many from the monarchist movement. On the eve of the gathering on 21 November, Dr. Dubrovin and his friends visit Saint

---

*About $6,592 in 2017.

Petersburg Metropolitan Anthony, asking him to bless the flags and banners of the Union. But in these more liberal times Metropolitan Anthony, who four years previously signed the excommunication of Tolstoy, no longer feels the need to oblige the Black Hundreds, even if they enjoy the backing of the Interior Ministry. "I do not support your right-wing parties and consider you to be terrorists," Metropolitan Anthony tells Dubrovin. "The left-wing terrorists throw bombs, while the right-wing parties hurl stones at anyone who disagrees with them." He shows the unionists the door. Dubrovin is very offended and does not forgive Metropolitan Anthony.

The meeting of 21 November, however, passes without incident. The speakers include Dubrovin himself, a few monarchist publicists, and two bishops. All believe that the rally in support of the regime in the midst of revolution is a success. On 27 November the union starts publishing its own newspaper under the title *Russian Banner*. The protagonist of every issue is Prime Minister Witte (a.k.a. "Count Semi-Sakhalin"), whom Dubrovin and his associates despise with a burning intensity. Witte's resignation is called for in almost every publication. The union receives money from the government, but that does not prevent it from waging war on the prime minister.

Dr. Dubrovin goes into overdrive. He meets with all officials who are dissatisfied with Witte, and offers them his services. In early December, Dubrovin is received by Grand Duke Nikolai Nikolaevich, who six weeks earlier had implored the emperor to take on Witte, and now bitterly regrets it. "Witte, egged on by the Jews, is leading Russia to revolution and disintegration," Dubrovin exhorts the grand duke. Nikolai Nikolaevich promises to arrange a meeting between Dubrovin and the tsar's right-hand man, Trepov.*

Witte is caught in the crossfire between the attack from the left led by Trotsky and the one from the right led by Dubrovin. As a result, the prime minister loses most of his support. Almost all of liberal society is under the influence of the revolutionaries, and the officials who yesterday supported Witte are today more attuned to the Union of the Russian People.

THE END OF THE SOVIETS

On 25 November Gapon, as agreed, sets off for Paris. The day after, the chairman of the Petersburg Soviet, Nosar-Khrustalev, is arrested. The new

---

* Attacks on the government, but not on the leader of the nation, are a very typical feature of Russian politics in early twenty-first century. Even loyal journalists and members of the "United Russia," let alone the puppet opposition, often criticize the government (for instance, Dmitry Medvedev), but Vladimir Putin is regarded as sacred and above any criticism.

chairman is his deputy, Leon Trotsky. But Gerasimov does stop there. He demands the arrest of the entire Petersburg Soviet.

The now twenty-six-year-old Trotsky is one of the youngest revolutionaries, and the most energetic. Like Gapon, he takes instant decisions and infects others with his self-assurance. More experienced leaders pale in comparison. Even Martov and Lenin are sidelined. The latter writes for *New Life*, but has no role in the Petersburg Soviet.

The executive committee of the Petersburg Soviet discusses how to respond to "the government's kidnapping of Comrade Nosar," and adopts a so-called "financial manifesto." It urges people to take out their savings from the banks and demand that all settlements, including salaries, be paid in gold. This will be a huge drain on the State Bank's gold reserves and will accelerate the government's financial crisis. Even without the appeal, savings are being withdrawn: by early December the State Bank's gold reserves have shrunk by 250 million roubles.*

On 2 December eight newspapers publish the "financial manifesto." All copies are immediately withdrawn from circulation, and the papers are closed down, including Lenin and Andreyeva's *New Life*, Martov and Trotsky's *Beginning*, and the new Kadet newspaper edited by Milyukov, *People's Freedom*.

The next day the police surround the building of the Free Economic Society. An officer presents an arrest warrant, but the presiding Trotsky does not give him the floor: "Please do not interrupt the speaker. If you wish to speak, give me your name, and I will ask the assembly if it wishes to hear from you." The bemused officer waits for the end of the speech and then reads out the warrant. Trotsky says that the Petersburg Soviet will take note of it and asks the officer to leave the room. He goes to get reinforcements. Trotsky, however, tells a different story. Before his arrest, having learned that the building is surrounded by troops, he orders that there be no resistance. There is a clanging of metal as deputies throw their revolvers to the floor. Either way, the entire Petersburg Soviet is soon under arrest.

On the eve of the arrest of the Petersburg Soviet, Witte orders the printing of a thousand copies of Gapon's appeal to the workers: "Stop! Proletariat, beware of an ambush. Not a step forward, not a step back. No sudden movements so as not to provoke the dark, embittered reactionary monster. Avoid bloodshed, enough has been spilt already." It is a surprising about-face—in January Trepov used regime-loyal workers to oppose Gapon's march; now Witte wants to use Gapon as a counterweight to the Petersburg Soviet.

---

* About $3,295,833,333 in 2017.

Gapon, meanwhile, gives a scheduled interview to the French press. "Mr. Witte's current policies at least partially satisfy the requirements of the Russian people," says Gapon in an interview with the newspaper *Le Matin*. "Although Mr. Witte refused to grant me an amnesty, I have changed my negative opinion of him. I think that he is the only one who can save us. If the revolutionaries find a common language with him, it could form the basis of the liberation of Russia."

Two weeks later Gapon arranges an informal press conference and invites correspondents from several newspapers, both Russian and French, for breakfast in order to refute accusations that he is working for Witte. "Under Witte, there is freedom to write and speak. It is better that Witte be in power than Durnovo. That's all. Any talk of dealings between me and Witte is nonsense," says Gapon.

As the leader of the opposition in exile, Gapon's popularity soars once more. After the arrest of members of the Petersburg Soviet, he is invited to all sorts of events on the situation in Russia: he is summoned to the French parliament, and meets with the Socialist leader Jean Jaurès and the writer Anatole France.

Gapon's next port of call is the south of France. All the while, he yearns to return to Russia and be officially pardoned. In the meantime, he acts as an intermediary for Witte in negotiations in Monte Carlo. Soon the Russian tabloids are writing that Gapon was seen playing roulette while blood was flowing in Moscow.

Gapon's appeal has no effect in Saint Petersburg or Moscow. Unlike the Petersburg Soviet, the Moscow Soviet of Workers' Deputies is still calling for the general strike to turn into an armed uprising. Leaflets to that effect are scattered around the city. Moscow is becoming a crucial battleground.

MOSCOW CARNAGE

The Moscow protest is full of youthful folly. One member of the Moscow Soviet, the SR Vladimir Zenzinov, recalls that the decision to start a rebellion was taken on the spur of the moment. There is no chance of success. The rebels are students and young workers armed with "lousy revolvers," seemingly ready to sacrifice themselves for the sake of a revolutionary whim. Zenzinov in December 1905 is twenty-five years old, and many protesters are even younger.

There are no social media or mobile devices back then—even the ordinary telephone is not available to everyone. But thousands of twenty-year-old Muscovites are under the spell of newspapers and discussion groups. They are ready and even willing to die. Years later, Zenzinov will say that the December massacre in Moscow was all a childish prank: "It was a peculiarity of those times. Even when blood was spilt, it was all seen as a bit of fun, just childish defiance." Zenzinov recalls that, in the early stages, unarmed boys and girls laughingly disarmed police officers, who were too bemused to resist.

On 7 December, the situation becomes more serious: railways, post offices, telegraphs, trams, and factories in Moscow go on strike, and newspapers are not published. The lack of news creates panic: it is rumored that the Black Hundreds are starting to eradicate the intelligentsia, although most members are, in fact, at home.

On 8 December, a ten-thousand-strong crowd gathers at the Aquarium Garden. Police surround it and arrest those who are armed. However, the protesters do not want to surrender and most of them jump over the fence and take cover. The rally ends without bloodshed, but rumors spread that the gathering was dispersed violently. The young revolutionaries, led by Zenzinov, decide to take revenge. They throw a bomb at the building of the Moscow Police Department. The result is better than expected: the explosion rips off the roof and the building burns to the ground, along with the officers inside. Henceforth, it is no longer a game.

Zenzinov's comrades, the SR leaders, are in Saint Petersburg at the time, preparing an armed uprising in the capital. Azef appoints Boris Savinkov to lead it. Having recently returned to Russia, Savinkov lives on Ligovsky Avenue and is surprised not to have been arrested. He does not try to hide and even writes articles under his real name. At the same time, he sees that city residents do not want an uprising of any sort. They are even growing tired of striking.

Savinkov goes to a meeting of the district combat unit commanded by Rutenberg. Rutenberg, Gapon's SR friend, delivers a fiery speech. But that is tempered by Savinkov, who says that it is important to understand what sort of fight local residents are ready to engage in.

There are three groups, he says. The first consists of volunteers willing to engage in terrorism by attacking Witte's house or blowing up government and other such buildings. The second is a revolutionary army that could attempt to seize the Peter and Paul Fortress. The third is made up of people willing to defend their neighborhoods. The absolute majority belongs to the third group. They are willing to defend themselves, but not participate in any kind of uprising or terrorism.

Late in the evening of 6 December, Interior Minister Pyotr Durnovo learns that the Moscow Soviet is publishing leaflets calling for a general strike and an armed insurrection. He decides not to disturb his immediate superior, Sergei Witte, and places a direct call to Tsarskoye Selo, waking up the tsar. The following morning, they meet at 7 a.m. and decide that drastic action is called for: "Clearly, it is either us or them. The situation cannot continue. I authorize you to take any measures you deem necessary," says Nicholas II.

Durnovo gives Gerasimov the go-ahead to start mass arrests. He is happy to do so. He writes in his memoirs that he actually started preparing for repressive measures almost immediately after the signing of the manifesto on 17 October. On the first day over three hundred and fifty people are arrested in Saint Petersburg, and around four hundred the next. People are detained at random: for example, the twenty-four-year-old lawyer Alexander Kerensky, who does not yet have anything to do with the revolutionaries (he wanted to join the military organization of the SRs, but was not accepted). In twelve years' time Kerensky will issue an arrest warrant for General Gerasimov.

When Prime Minister Witte wakes on 7 December, he cannot believe his eyes. His power has disappeared literally overnight. The tsar, Durnovo, and Gerasimov have decided everything without him.

But the main events take place in Moscow. The city's governor-general, Dubasov, asks Grand Duke Nikolai Nikolaevich for reinforcements. The latter answers that he has no spare forces, so Dubasov takes matters into his own hands.

A civil war breaks out in the heart of the city. Gorky is delighted: "The public mood is amazing! Honest to God, I didn't except anything of the sort. It's businesslike when fighting mounted police and building barricades, but fun and playful in between. An excellent atmosphere!" Gorky is thirty-seven years old, but infected with youthful revolutionary zeal. He is not bothered by people being killed: "We're used to gunshots, wounds and corpses. When a fire fight starts, people happily join in. Sure, the authorities will win the battle, but not the war."

Dubasov continues to insist on reinforcements. Finally, on 15 December fresh troops from the Semenov Regiment are dispatched, having suppressed the recent Kronstadt mutiny in exemplary fashion. Dubasov also enlists more and more volunteers from the Union of the Russian People.

The insurgents employ what today would be described as guerrilla or even terrorist tactics: they hide in homes and fire at the soldiers from the windows and roofs. The latter respond with artillery fire. Most of the victims are civilians. The sympathies of the majority of Muscovites lie with the revolutionaries. "The population is terrorized and embittered, while the revolutionaries are fearless," writes the monarchist publicist Lev Tikhomirov in his diary. "I pity the dying residents, soldiers and revolutionaries themselves. So much blood and for what? To preserve the incurable ulcer that is ravaging Russia?"

Even more outspoken is the Saint Petersburg police chief Gerasimov: "The most dangerous part was that the revolutionary parties had the active support of the entire population, even where you wouldn't expect to find it. We, the custodians of law and order, were isolated. It pains me to say that there were very few people willing to oppose the revolution as a matter of principle, not simply for material gain. The revolutionaries who sought not only to overthrow the tsarist government, but to overturn the very foundations of the existing order had support and sympathy at every step."

The total death toll is unknown. The newspapers report two thousand injured and estimate at least one thousand killed. There is an information blackout, and Muscovites remain in the dark for a week. Fanciful rumors spread that the true aim of the revolutionaries was to lure as many troops as possible from Saint Petersburg so as to overthrow the government in the capital. The idea that, in fact, the young revolutionaries had no objectives at all is difficult to believe, especially for the relatives of victims and residents of neighborhoods destroyed by artillery fire, who want to think that there is some underlying reason. They would not understand this explanation given by the young Zenzinov: "There are times when people go into battle with no hope of victory—it is not a matter of strategic or political calculation, but of honor. So it was with the Decembrists, who faced certain defeat."

Incidentally, Vladimir Zenzinov is neither killed, nor injured, nor arrested—he calmly buys a train ticket and slips away to Saint Petersburg. Opposite him in the carriage is the red-bearded Peter Struve, who resents what is happening and "blames both sides." Zenzinov has "no desire to argue with him."

KRASNOYARSK REPUBLIC

Rebellion in the name of revolution and democracy is not only big-city entertainment. In autumn 1905 the entire empire is infected with the epidemic. The October strike is nationwide, and its effects are visible everywhere. It happens in parallel with the demobilization of troops, who are returning from the Far East to European Russia. Demoralized by the senseless war, the soldiers spread revolutionary sentiments along the way, stirring up the local population. The soldiers put forward demands and refuse to move until the officers comply. Such a strike is instigated in Krasnoyarsk by the 3rd Railway Battalion. The soldiers find a common language with local workers, and together they set up a joint soviet of workers' and soldiers' deputies, which begins championing the rights of Krasnoyarsk residents. The chairman of the soviet is Warrant Officer Andrei Kuzmin.

The main cause of the resentment among the workers is the elections to the Krasnoyarsk Duma. Under the existing electoral law, only the propertied classes are allowed to vote. In Krasnoyarsk, that means only around one hundred people have the right to elect the fifty-member city council. The Krasnoyarsk Soviet intends to right this wrong.

It is all surprisingly simple: the soldiers peacefully disarm the police, take over responsibility for law and order, and announce forthcoming elections on the basis of universal suffrage, including women. The former Krasnoyarsk authorities look on in amazement. They do not interfere because they can't. Even the governor-general loses his administrative functions to the "President of the Republic of Krasnoyarsk" Andrei Kuzmin. Meanwhile, the Soviet sets up an electoral commission, the legitimacy of which is recognized even by the old city council and the local cell of the Kadets, which sends a delegation of representatives. The election commission draws up a list of voters. Meanwhile, life in the city goes on: theatres, shops, and newspapers all continue as normal. Public meetings are held almost every day to discuss current issues.

Krasnoyarsk's democratic utopia begins on 10 December—the same day that civil war breaks out in Moscow. The "utopia" lasts for two weeks. Only on 17 December, after learning about the suppression of the Moscow uprising, does the governor request reinforcements to suppress the "Krasnoyarsk republic" (apparently the thought never occurred to him before). Finally, on 24 December, soldiers arrive from the Omsk Regiment. They occupy the post office and put up posters around the city declaring martial law. The rebellious soldiers and workers barricade themselves inside workshops and are besieged by the loyalist troops until 2 January. Almost all the leaders of the uprising, including the "President" Kuzmin, somehow manage to escape. Kuzmin moves to France. In early January about five hundred rebels are arrested.

The tale of Krasnoyarsk is typical for the autumn of 1905. Democratic governments spontaneously emerge in Chita, Sochi, Kharkov, Poland,

Georgia, and in the suburbs of Moscow. These "republics" exist from one week to two months before the imperial authorities recover from the shock and restore order.

Leo Tolstoy at this time is living at his Yasnaya Polyana estate, where the situation is much calmer. He spends the whole of December writing an "Appeal to the Russian people: the government, the revolutionaries and the common folk." It outlines his political agenda, which is both anti-government and anti-revolutionary. It closely corresponds in spirit to the natural processes occurring in the country. Tolstoy argues that the Russian people do not need a government—they can work out for themselves how to live: "If urban and rural working people ceased to obey and serve the government, its power would vanish, and with it the conditions of slavery in which they live. These conditions are enforced by the regime. You feed this enforcement yourselves." The micro-republics mushrooming around the country, albeit briefly, embody Tolstoy's idea.

Although Tolstoy is equally critical of the intelligentsia ("a parasite on the body of the people") and the revolutionaries ("who want to replace one form of violence with another"), he considers the present government to be doomed: "Whether or not the revolutionaries are right to pursue their goals, they seek a new system of life. They want one thing: to be in the same favorable position as those who wave the banner of autocracy, albeit with constitutional amendments."

THE PARTY OF POWER

Although Tolstoy opposes the revolution, in conservative eyes he is considered its progenitor and root cause. Tolstoy's sworn enemy is John of Kronstadt. The seventy-eight-year-old writer and the seventy-nine-year-old priest represent the two poles of Russian society. They do not lead public opinion (the tone is set by the younger generation), but they are viewed by most as living symbols: Tolstoy represents the struggle against the regime; Father John symbolizes the Black Hundreds.

In 1906, John of Kronstadt applies for membership to the Union of the Russian People. He donates 10,000 roubles* to its coffers and attends the solemn consecration of its gonfalon. Everyone forgets Metropolitan Anthony's rejection of the organization: the "people's priest" is a far more popular figure than the head of the church.

---

*About $131,833 in 2017.

John of Kronstadt speaks about his motives for joining the Union of the Russian People in an interview with the foreign correspondent of the British newspaper *The Guardian*: "Our people are very ignorant; so it is better not to give them a reason to stray from the true path. . . . Our intelligentsia is not fit for purpose and full of godless anarchists like Leo Tolstoy, whom they adore but I strongly condemn. That is why they hate me so much and want to erase me from the face of the Earth. But I'm not afraid of them and pay no heed."

In December 1905 the Union of the Russian People and Dr. Dubrovin hit the peak of their popularity. The crackdown on the revolution leads to an incredible surge in the Black Hundreds movement across the country.

In early December, Dubrovin sends Nicholas II a telegram requesting him not to release the arrested members of the Petersburg Soviet and others suspected of revolutionary activity. "Quite right," replies Nicholas. On 22 December, immediately after the suppression of the Moscow uprising, the tsar officially receives a group of representatives of the Union of the Russian People, headed by Dubrovin, at Tsarskoye Selo.

Dubrovin reads the emperor an appeal on behalf of the union. "We, Sire, shall defend You faithfully and unflinchingly, just as our fathers and grandfathers defended their Tsars, now and forever."

The appeal sets forth three conditions for preserving the "strength and power of the Russian State": the autocratic power of the tsar, the suppression of "the handful of evil mutineers," and a solution to the agrarian issue.

Nicholas II is content. He accepts the ensign of the union, which the unionists interpret as a gesture that he and the tsarevich have joined the organization. Nicholas even mentions the meeting in his diary, albeit skimpily. This means that it made a great impression upon him.

More importantly, Dubrovin makes the acquaintance of Empress Alexandra and totally charms her. She always knew that "real" Russian people love the tsar, and now she has proof. Alexandra becomes the main lobbyist for the Union of the Russian People and the organizer of her husband's meetings with the Black Hundreds—sometimes informally, without the knowledge of the imperial court or the chancellery.

The meeting is a turning point in the history of the Union of the Russian People. The organization effectively turns into a state institute, the "party of power."* Although not a political party as such, the Union of the Russian People receives copious public funding (10 million roubles† in the

---

* As the pro-Putin party United Russia is called.
† About $131,833,333 in 2017.

first year alone) and forms a vast network of branches across the country. It enjoys plentiful administrative resources, and its regional leaders are often local government officials who believe in the cause.

The Union of the Russian People is thriving, and Dubrovin is an excellent fundraiser. According to those close to him, he is "skilled at collecting private donations off the record." One of his major sponsors and female admirers is Poluboyarinova, a rich widow, who makes regular contributions to the union and eventually becomes its accountant.

By a curious coincidence, both the liberal People's Freedom Party and the monarchist Union of the Russian People appear at roughly the same time and both are fronted by a middle-aged, charismatic leader (the fifty-year-old Dubrovin and the forty-six-year-old Milyukov) funded by a besotted female millionaire (the forty-year-old Poluboyarinova and the thirty-two-year-old Morozova). However, the similarity ends there. In everything else, the "allies" and the Kadets are polar opposites. They despise each other passionately and spare no expense in the struggle. Incidentally, Milyukov and Morozova's romance does not last long, while Poluboyarinova remains true to Dubrovin until her death.

However, not all monarchists want to join the Union of the Russian People. State Council member Boris Stürmer believes that it is "pitiable and laughable" to listen to the Union of the Russian People "histrionically advocating autocracy." For Stürmer, the problem is not Dubrovin, but Nicholas II. "He's to blame for these so-called 'knights of sorrowful countenance,' these Don Quixotes. As long we have this tsar, there will be no order in Russia," he says. In ten years' time the tsar will appoint Stürmer to the post of prime minister.

But the imperial favorite at the moment is Dubrovin. He regularly and frequently discourses with senior government officials: on 30 December, he is received by Trepov, and on 15 January by the emperor once again. But in particular proximity to Dubrovin is the new governor of Saint Petersburg, Major General von der Launitz. Despite being an ethnic German, von der Launitz becomes a fierce supporter and lobbyist of the organization of "true Russian people."

On 13 February the Union of the Russian People celebrates Shrovetide with pancakes. The atmosphere, recall witnesses, is highly charged. In his speech Dubrovin alleges, perhaps metaphorically, that Witte has "put the tsar in a cage." The crowd becomes frenzied: "Where does Witte live? Let's go and kill him!" Saint Petersburg only narrowly avoids mayhem.

Since October 1905, pogroms have been taking place throughout Russia. Whereas hearsay once attributed them to the Interior Ministry, it is now believed that they are the work of the Union of the Russian People. Dubrovin's printing press is said to print not only the newspaper *Banner*, but also pamphlets calling for attacks on Jewish socialists. They circulate throughout the Pale of Settlement.

It is Dr. Dubrovin who, during the Moscow uprising of December 1905, begins to promulgate the idea that the revolution can only be defeated by fighting fire with fire. If the revolutionaries are armed and are trying to incite nationwide revolts, waiting until the rebellion breaks out would be a mistake. The unionists must be permanently on guard and ready to quash it at any moment. They are the anointed defenders of the Faith, the Tsar, and the Fatherland.

By December 1905 Dubrovin's ideas are already being put into practice: combat units are created under the aegis of the Union of the Russian People. Union members are issued weapons by the Interior Ministry. The weapons are delivered in batches and stored in the basement of Dubrovin's house, where they are handed out to the combatants against written acknowledgement of receipt. The operation is overseen by Governor von der Launitz.

One member of the Union of the Russian People, Nikolai Markov, who will soon challenge Dubrovin for the leadership, proudly believes that it is the world's first fascist organization: "The people's movement appeared long before the rise of Fascism and National Socialism. It was their prototype. . . . The Union of the Russian People battled for control of the streets, and the mighty Russian fist, braving the bombs and pistols, delivered such a blow to the skull of the Judeo-Masonic revolution that for many years it hid underground, not daring to show its nose."

All of this Markov will write thirty-two years later, in 1937 in Berlin, as an ardent supporter of Adolf Hitler. He goes on to compare the invention of fascism to the invention of the light bulb: "We, Russians, never bring our inventions to completion. The light bulb, for instance, was invented by our compatriot Pavel Yablochkov long before Edison. It worked, everyone was gasping with amazement, but nothing came of it. Then Edison came along and invented exactly the same thing. The Union of Russian People was made up of Yablochkovs, all vaguely aware of the need to resist internationalist evil with a popular-national idea."

The Union of the Russian People is both anti-Marxist and anti-liberal. It professes populist ultra-nationalism, romanticizes violence, and rejects democratic values. In January-February 1905, when preparations begin for the elections to the State Duma, Dubrovin is single-minded: he refuses to recognize the validity of the exercise and declares that the Union of the

Russian People will not participate. He firmly believes that Russia should be governed autocratically, and that the tsar has no need for a State Duma in any shape or form.

GAPON FALTERS

As the Union of the Russian People gains strength, Gapon's "assemblies" start to receive money allocated by Witte. The cashier Matyushensky supposedly receives two large payments from a "merchant in Baku," after which one of Gapon's assistants lets slip that the money is from Witte. A scandal erupts. Gapon hastily convenes a meeting in Finland to explain to other members where the money came from. It later transpires that there is no money after all—Matyushensky has taken the cash and fled.

Gapon's position is desperate. He is in Finland illegally, and his name is being dragged through the mud in the tabloids. He is accused of being an agent of Witte, and his own organization splits in two—one man even kills himself during the meeting.

But worst of all for Gapon is the lack of news: there is no amnesty from the authorities, and the Interior Ministry has not authorized the assemblies or the opening of new branches. It turns out that Witte has abandoned him—or, rather, Interior Minister Durnovo is no longer under Witte's thumb. Having suppressed the Moscow uprising, Durnovo realizes that liberalism is out of fashion and stops listening to the prime minister. So there is no need to allow Gapon's assemblies.

Gapon is back to square one. He has to start again from scratch and try to rebuild relations with the authorities. He is advised to speak to Rachkovsky.

Gapon tells his associate Rutenberg about the meeting with Rachkovsky, which Rutenberg reports to his boss, Azef, who makes a quick decision: "Let's get rid of that rat Gapon." The task is assigned to Rutenberg himself. Savinkov likes the plan, while Chernov sympathizes with Rutenberg, who has to become an unwilling murderer. "Azef and especially Savinkov had Rutenberg pinned to a wall. Savinkov was seething with rage, tearing into the poor, bedraggled Rutenberg. . . . Rutenberg was their whipping boy."

Meanwhile, new accusations are being made against Gapon, not only of collaborating with the government: the tabloids also discuss his relations with women, saying that "Gapon lives high on the hog in Monte Carlo, burning money at the roulette table, dressed to the nines and surrounded by courtesans."

On 21 February Gapon writes a detailed letter to the newspaper *Rus*: "My name is being trashed by hundreds of newspapers, both Russian and foreign. They slander and reproach me. Deprived of civil rights and denied an amnesty, I am being attacked mercilessly from all sides. They call me a thief and a provocateur. They want to see me crucified." Gapon asks to be tried by a "comrades' court": "I will answer all the accusations. My conscience is clear."

Petersburg Gazette publishes a piece entitled "At Gapon's"—a journalistic report describing how modestly he, his wife Uzhdaleva (a former fosterling at the orphanage where he worked), and newborn son live in a small, huddled apartment.

Preparations are made for the court session. Gapon finds a lawyer, and participants in the "comrades' court" are selected, including the history professor and liberal politician Pavel Milyukov and the journalist Alexander Stolypin, who works for Suvorin and is the brother of the governor of Saratov, Pyotr Stolypin, the future prime minister.

Gapon eagerly awaits the trial. He writes letters to the newspapers and to the Saint Petersburg prosecutor's office, proposing that he be either amnestied or tried as a runaway criminal. Gapon does in fact want to be arrested, for it would greatly enhance his reputation. But the prosecutor's office ignores his plea.

On 27 March Gapon goes to the Saint Petersburg District Court asking for a case to be brought against him as a runaway criminal. He is unexpectedly given a certificate of amnesty backdated to 27 October the previous year. In other words, Witte simply lied to him that he had not been amnestied together with the other workers.

It is a weight off Gapon's shoulders. He can now restore his reputation and revive the "assemblies." The next day he goes to meet Rutenberg at Ozerki Station, north of Saint Petersburg.

Having met on the platform, they head for Rutenberg's rented house. Along the way the newly inspired Gapon outlines his plans to his supposed friend: "I'm going to help the workers. We'll create workshops and bakeries. That's what we need. In time we'll have a factory. You'll be the director." Politics is in the past—it is now all about the "theory of small deeds.'"

They enter the house. Four men appear from a side room. Gapon tries to resist as they put a rope around his neck. Rutenberg leaves so as not to witness what comes next.

---

* See chapter three.

TIME TO LEAVE THE COUNTRY

In Saint Petersburg almost no one is looking for Gapon. Last year's hero is forgotten, and his corpse hangs at an abandoned dacha outside Saint Petersburg.

The winter of 1905-1906 is probably the most frustrating time, and the worst hangover, in Russian history. Everything that Russian society has been so passionate about over the past two years has all been a letdown. There is the closure of newspapers, more and more arrests, nationwide strife, the omnipotent Black Hundreds. . . . "It's time to leave the country" is the mood of the middle classes in Saint Petersburg and even more so in Moscow. After the suppression of the December uprising, Muscovites want a new regime or emigration.

Even some revolutionaries—who returned under Witte's amnesty and now face new criminal charges—want to leave. Apolitical types are also packing their bags. They initially took interest in the "democratic spring," but now have no desire to participate in the dirty, brutal struggle that has ensued.

Dima Filosofov moves to Paris, followed by Gippius and Merezh-kovsky. They are "doing a Herzen,"* says Diaghilev disparagingly, but soon he too leaves—he wants to organize an exhibition of Russian art, again in Paris.

For Maxim Gorky and his civil wife Andreyeva, departure is the only way out, so to speak. They spend January 1906 performing in Finland, sending all the money from their readings to help victims of the December clashes (i.e., to the Social Democrats). However, Finland is part of the Russian Empire, so to avoid arrest Gorky and Andreyeva move to Berlin.

There Gorky writes an appeal entitled "Do Not Give Money to the Russian Government."† The article is one of the most amazing texts ever written by a Russian oppositionist. Today it would be described as Russophobic: "Is Europe really so unconcerned about having as its neighbor a country of 140 million people whom the authorities are trying to turn into animals, instilling in them hostility and hatred for anything that is not Russian, inculcating not just cruelty and violence, but a passion for violence? Do

---

* The writer and thinker Alexander Herzen was a fervent supporter of revolution in Russia, but preferred to live in self-imposed exile abroad.
† Gorky's appeal can be compared only to the views of the most radical members of the Russian opposition in early twenty-first century—for instance, Garry Kasparov, ex-world champion in chess. In the 2010s Russian civil society is mostly moderate. Many people leaning towards opposition even advocate lifting sanctions against Russia.

Jewish bankers in Europe understand that they are giving money to Russia to fund Jewish pogroms?"

For this article, a new criminal case is filed against Gorky in Russia. But he does not plan to return to his homeland, and sets off to America.

Gorky's trip with his wife is arranged by Lenin, who is grateful for the money they sent from Finland. Lenin asks Gorky to promote the Bolsheviks abroad and to continue agitating against the tsarist government. Lenin plans everything in minute detail, right down to hiring a PR man and security guard.

In New York, the writer is received enthusiastically. At the port, he is met not only by journalists, but also by crowds of Russian émigrés. Gorky's photo appears on the front pages of newspapers. Everywhere he is recognized and welcomed. He and Andreyeva ride on the underground. Fellow passengers look at the photos in the papers they are reading and say: "Hey there, Mr. Gorky." On day two, a dinner is held in his honor, attended by the seventy-year-old Mark Twain. Gorky is only thirty-seven and worships the master of American prose, who also admires his young Russian colleague. Together, they announce the creation of a fund to collect money for the Russian revolution. The press describes Gorky as the "Russian Jefferson." Plans are made for a trip to Washington and a meeting with President Theodore Roosevelt.

But everything goes sour on 15 April. An American tabloid uncovers that "Mr. and Mrs. Gorky" are not husband and wife after all. The real Mrs. Gorky (i.e., Ekaterina Peshkova) is in Russia with their two children. She and Gorky are not divorced. Meanwhile, the woman pretending to be the writer's wife is none other than the famous Russian actress Maria Andreyeva.

The *kompromat** has a shuddering effect. The United States in 1905, it turns out, is far more puritanical than the Russian Empire.

The tour is derailed: events in Boston and Chicago are cancelled, and the White House withdraws its invitation. A group of female supporters of the Republican Party demand Gorky's deportation. The writer is forced to leave his hotel and find a room in a hostel, which he also has to vacate. Two complete strangers unexpectedly come to the rescue: Prestonia and John Martin invite Gorky and Andreyeva to live in their house: "We cannot let an entire country descend upon an unprotected young woman, which is why we offer you both our hospitality," they say.

Gorky accepts. They move first to the Martins' luxurious villa near New York City, and then to their estate in the north of New York State, near the

---

* Meaning "compromising evidence," a new word in English thanks to Donald Trump.

Canadian border. There will be no more touring, Gorky decides. Instead, there in the tranquil American outback, he writes the novel *The Mother*, which will become a major work of Soviet literature, the "Bible of the Revolution," and Lenin's favorite book.

HOWLING CATS, SODDEN APPLES

Witte is also disgruntled. The man who in October handed the tsar a philosophical treatise on the pursuit of freedom now speaks with fear and disgust of the State Duma that he himself conceived. During endless government meetings, he says that Russian society is uncultured and that ministerial sessions cannot be made public, otherwise ministers will be showered with "sodden apples and howling cats."*

On 11 December, he publishes a new electoral law—just after Durnovo has arrested all of Saint Petersburg's dissidents and a full-scale war has begun in Moscow. Witte's electoral law makes a mockery of all the principals he preached only a couple of months ago.

It is far from offering the universal, equal suffrage by secret ballot that oppositionists long for. Under the new law, one electoral delegate represents two thousand nobles, or four thousand townspeople, or thirty thousand peasants, or ninety thousand workers. But not everyone has the right to vote, only those who own property or pay sufficient tax. In the cities, for example, students do not have the right to vote: voters must either have their own accommodation or be employees.

Both the Socialist-Revolutionaries and the Social Democrats decide to boycott the Duma elections. In fact, the only real political party in the country is the Kadets, the liberal People's Freedom Party, created by Milyukov on the basis of the Liberation Union.

Peter Struve, having returned from Paris, is also going through a testing period. He wants to resume the publication of *Liberation*, but Milyukov is having none of it. He does not need Struve's hard-hitting publication and wants to set up his own newspaper. With money from a new sponsor, an engineer by the name of Yulian Bak, Milyukov founds the newspaper *Speech*, which he not only manages by himself, but also writes all the editorials. *Liberation* never sees the light of day again.

The election produces a sensation, with the Kadets claiming a stunning victory. With hindsight, it is not so remarkable—it is the only party that

---

* The art of cat-throwing dates back to the Middle Ages, apparently.

conducted an election campaign and the only opposition party that took part, since both the Socialist-Revolutionaries and Social Democrats boycotted the vote.

Nicholas II and his entourage are perturbed. They do not know what to expect from the "seditious" liberals. Witte tells the tsar that Interior Minister Durnovo is to blame for everything—his repressive measures angered society, which then voted for the opposition.

The new Duma has not yet assembled, but everywhere there is talk of its imminent dissolution. Nicholas II criticizes Witte's electoral law, saying that it would be better if there were more representatives of the peasantry in the Duma, since the common man loves the tsar, unlike the intelligentsia. He is told that the peasants would almost certainly demand land. "Tell them to lump it," says Nicholas II. "They will rebel." "Then send in the troops," comes the dismissive response.

WHAT IS TO BE DONE?

The ongoing struggle with the liberals is the main issue of 1906 for Russian Marxists. While Gorky is relaxing in America, Leon Trotsky is at the Peter and Paul Fortress, outraged by the betrayal of the liberals. In February 1906, he writes an article cursing his ideological enemy Peter Struve. According to Trotsky, the liberals in the Duma should: 1) demand the resignation of the government, 2) form a new government themselves, 3) hold elections to a constituent assembly, 4) dismiss and replace regional officials, and 5) put the former authorities on trial. But, of course, Trotsky sneers, the Duma liberals will do nothing of the sort—they will simply tiptoe around and negotiate with the tsarist officials, achieving nothing.

At the same time, similar conversations are being held by conservatives in the opposite camp. They fear that the Duma will soon announce the convocation of a constituent assembly.

Despite the success of the Kadets, the party leaders remain outside the Duma. The central election commission bars both Milyukov and Struve from the elections. The former does not qualify under the property rules, while the latter is under investigation for extremist publications. But other prominent liberals become members of Duma, including Ivan Petrunkevich, Prince Dolgorukov, Prince Shakhovskoy, and Fyodor Rodichev. Aware of their role as the first parliamentarians in the history of Russia, they worry about how strident their tone should be. Meanwhile, Milyukov complains that the liberals are trapped between Scylla and Charybdis: the conservatives consider them enemies and revolutionaries, while for the Marxists they are traitors and government agents.

"RUSSIA IS A MADHOUSE"

In mid-April, Gorky and Andreyeva, still living at the Martins' Adirondack estate, receive a telegram from Russia. The lawsuit between Krasin and Morozov's widow over the health insurance left to Andreyeva has ended in a payout of 100,000 roubles* to the latter. They happily spend the whole evening dancing; even their cordial hosts the Martins join in.

At the same time, another telegram is received by Witte—from Paris on the negotiations about a loan to Russia. The French banks have finally given the nod. As the talks come to an end, French Prime Minister Clemenceau suddenly asks the Russian emissary: "Tell me, why doesn't your sovereign invite Mr. Milyukov to head the new government?" The imperial envoy Kokovtsov replies that the tsar will appoint whomever he chooses.

On learning that the loan has been approved, Nicholas II summons the trusty Trepov and asks him to select a new prime minister, because he cannot tolerate Witte any more: "I have finally parted company with Count Witte, and we shall not meet any more," he states categorically.

The tsar's main criteria are that the new prime minister should be the complete opposite of Witte, lack personal ambition, and not bury the tsar with reform projects. In a word, he must be loyal. The ideal candidate is Ivan Goremykin, the former interior minister. Goremykin's reputation precedes him. He is said to be a politician who is "totally uninterested in politics" and "indifferent to everything."

Witte's departure means the dissolution of the government. Witte learns of his "resignation" a week before the opening of the new State Duma. "Before you there stands the happiest of mortals. The Sovereign could not have done me a greater favor than to relieve me of the hard labor in which I was languishing," he says to Kokovtsov, recently arrived from Paris. "I am going abroad for treatment. I want nothing more to do with matters here. Russia is a complete madhouse, the intelligentsia above all." However, he is striking a wounded pose. Witte is sure that everything will collapse and he will be needed once more.

---

* About $1,318,333 in 2017.

Kokovtsov, the tsar's choice of finance minister, declines the position, asserting that the government that prepared the draft laws should be the one to push them through the Duma. But the new Prime Minister Goremykin reassures him that the previous government did not draft a single bill.

The Union of the Russian People rejoices—its main enemy, Count Witte, has fallen. Dr. Dubrovin writes an article about his vanquished foe. However, the struggle is not over. As the convocation of the State Duma draws nearer, he and his associates become increasingly convinced of the need to employ the same methods as their revolutionary opponents, namely terrorism. The enemies of autocracy must be destroyed, says the doctor.

|| Chapter 8 ||

in which Pyotr Stolypin and
Dmitriy Trepov suggest two different
ways of reforming Russia

GETTING TO KNOW THE PEOPLE

April 26, 1906, is a day of celebration in Saint Petersburg—it is the first meeting of the State Duma of the Russian Empire. The newly appointed parliamentarians board small steamers and sail up the river from the Tauride Palace to the Winter Palace, where they are to be received by the tsar. The Duma members are in a combative mood. Many feel betrayed that the main laws have been adopted without their involvement, in violation of the manifesto of 17 October. They are determined to fight back.

A prayer service is held at the Winter Palace, after which Nicholas II greets the members of Duma. To the right of the emperor stand members of the imperial family, courtiers, and ministers in their gold-embroidered uniforms; to the left are the State Duma members. The two halves of the hall examine each other with curiosity.

The first visual contact is a shock for both sides. Most of the parliamentarians are peasants. For them, the opening of the Duma is their first public event in the capital. There is no dress code. No one prepared the parliamentarians for the meeting, and no one informed them of the proper protocol or court etiquette. All are dressed as if celebrating a holiday. "Very few were in tails and frock-coats. The overwhelming majority of those standing closest to the throne, as if purposely, were attired in workers' clothes, while behind them were some peasants in national costumes. There were also many Duma members from the clergy," recalls Finance Minister Kokovtsov.

It is a meeting of two worlds: the Duma members gaze upon Nicholas II in the flesh, not the "tsar-father" that they have been told about and imagined since childhood; he and the courtiers look back at the people, whom they have never bothered to imagine at all.

Metropolitan high society discusses the meeting at the Winter Palace as if it were some kind of monstrous scandal, although nothing unseemly happens. The mere appearance of the members of Duma seems so disrespectful that the Petersburg elite concludes that nothing good will come of the Duma, since, in their view, it is full of die-hard revolutionaries. After the ceremony Kokovtsov tells the Empress Dowager Maria Feodorovna that the Duma should be dissolved and the electoral law amended so as to prevent the election of such riff-raff in the future.

During the ceremony, one member of the government eyes the parliamentarians even more suspiciously than most. He is on the lookout for potential terrorists among them: "I cannot help thinking that one of them may be concealing a bomb," he says out loud. "However, perhaps there is nothing to fear. The response to such an incident would be too unfavorable for these gentlemen."

The man is Pyotr Stolypin, who a week ago was the governor of Saratov. Now he is the newly appointed interior minister.

"WITHOUT THE TSAR, YOU WOULD ALL BE BEGGARS"

Stolypin is a new face in Saint Petersburg, and his appointment took many by surprise. In dismissing Witte's government, Nicholas II's intention was to replace it with its antithesis. Boris Stürmer, the archconservative, was earmarked for the post of interior minister, but Prime Minister Ivan Goremykin preferred to go for an outsider, so the choice was made in favor of Saratov Governor Pyotr Stolypin.

Saratov province is problematic: peasant unrest has been ongoing since 1905, and landowners' estates are burning. Stolypin copes as best he can (not very well), but things get even worse when help arrives in the form of General Sakharov, who is murdered by terrorists at Stolypin's own home just one week after arriving in Saratov. Strangely enough, the tragedy bolsters Stolypin's reputation, if only because he has been in charge of such an explosive region for three years and has managed to remain alive.

Stolypin is far from being a liberal. In all his speeches, he repeats: "Without the tsar, you would all be beggars, and we would all have no rights!" Unsurprisingly, the new interior minister and the new prime minister see eye to eye.

Goremykin is not thrilled by the prospect of running the country at such a turbulent time. However, he does not actually believe that he needs to. In his view, the tsar, as the anointed one, should rule the country. Besides, he knows that Nicholas II gets very jumpy when any of his top officials try to usurp his power. Moreover, Goremykin is the type of official that we now describe as a technocrat: he has no long-term program of any sort, but understands clearly what is—and what is not—required of him. He knows how to react to external stimuli, believing that in most cases no reaction is preferable. Things will sort themselves out.*

---

* Goremykin's method will be very popular among Russian state officials a hundred years later as well. Many high-ranking government and Presidential Administration employees will be making a huge effort not to make any enemies—and the best way to achieve that is through doing nothing. During Mikhail Fradkov's term as prime minister (2004-2007) this principle was phrased "People don't get fired for bad work performance, they get fired for not being loyal." The same logic applied when Dmitry Medvedev became prime minister.

That is precisely his view of the newly elected Duma. He has no intention of engaging with it in any way: "Let them stew in their own juice. The Duma will discredit itself in the public eye," he reckons.

But if anyone is stewing in his or her own juice, it is Prime Minister Goremykin. Russian newspapers print daily reports from the State Duma, which are themselves something of a revolution, so to speak. Henceforth, no topic is off limits for discussion, even ones that previously incurred stiff penalties, up to and including exile. The State Duma cannot change anything yet, but is already becoming a "forum for discussion."*

After all the ceremonies and prayers, the first meeting of the State Duma commences at 5 p.m. on 26 April. The first elected chairman is the fifty-six-year-old Sergei Muromtsev, a member of the Kadet Party and a professor of Moscow University. He immediately gives the floor to the oldest liberal in the hall, Ivan Petrunkevich, who makes a short speech demanding a political amnesty. Then Muromtsev follows with the words: "While maintaining due respect for the prerogatives of the constitutional monarch, we are called upon to use the full force and scope of the rights of the people who elected us," he says.

The government has prepared only two bills for consideration by the Duma: on setting up a public launderette and repairing the orangery at Tartu University. The bills cause a storm of indignation among the parliamentarians. They want to discuss serious matters. During the first week of meetings, they draft their first appeal to the tsar, which is adopted by majority vote. It consists of two parts. Part one outlines the Duma's intentions and wishes, while part two proposes that the government be dismissed and replaced with one that is answerable to the Duma. Moreover, it calls to abolish the State Council, carry out land reforms, alter the system of zemstvos and city institutions, transform the tax system, introduce free and universal primary education, change the electoral law, introduce universal suffrage, and declare an amnesty for political prisoners.

These are the very slogans that the Kadets had been preaching before they entered the Duma. Moreover, many of the points were included in the manifesto of 17 October, but have not been put in practice since then. The parliamentarians intend to submit their long list of demands to the emperor.

On 8 May Nicholas II informs Duma Chairman Muromtsev that he will not receive the delegation of Duma members, and that they can

---

*In the early twenty-first century Boris Gryzlov, chairman of the fourth and fifth Duma, is rumored to have said "Duma is no place for discussions." However, according to the official verbatim, he put it a bit differently in 2003: "The State Duma is not an arena for political battles."

convey their message to Prime Minister Goremykin (whose resignation the Duma also demands in the appeal). Goremykin appears in the Duma and reads out a long, tedious, barely audible official response from the government. The general import is that some demands have been rejected; other will be considered.

Hardly has Goremykin finished when Vladimir Nabokov runs up to the rostrum and shouts: "Executive power, you must submit to the legislature!" The Duma gives him a standing ovation.

Even before the meetings of the First Duma, things are moving in a vicious circle. From the start, the parliamentarians are offended that their powers, as outlined in the manifesto, have been curtailed. They have nothing but contempt for the authorities, and the antipathy is mutual. The government seeks to make sure that nothing will come of the Duma (although Pyotr Stolypin still hopes to use it for his own purposes). Each side is convinced of its own rectitude and appalled by the unacceptable behavior of its opponents.

EVERY REVOLUTIONARY'S NIGHTMARE

Throughout spring, Russia's professional revolutionaries continue to hide. Very few leave the Russian Empire, but they do move to Finland. The local authorities there usually turn a blind eye to the suspects on the run from the Russian government—many Finns even help the fighters in their struggle against the tsarist regime. Finland is home to the leading Marxists Vladimir Lenin, Julius Martov, Boris Savinkov, Yevgeny Azef, and Viktor Chernov.

The SRs, having decided to boycott legal politics and the elections to the State Duma, are expecting a forceful peasant uprising to shake the country at any moment, for which preparations must be made. Plans are drawn up to detonate railways and bridges and interfere with telegraph communications. They decide to return to terror tactics in anticipation of the uprising, but fail to carry out a single successful assassination. The police are on their trail (tipped off by the double agent Azef), and periodic arrests are made of members of the militant organization. Only Savinkov escapes harassment. His accomplice Dora Brilliant ends up in the Peter and Paul Fortress, goes mad, and dies a year later.

The remaining SRs are demoralized. Pinhas Rutenberg tells Savinkov that he has nightmares about Gapon: "He appears in my dreams. I saved him on Bloody Sunday and now he's hanging there." Even Azef is feeling the psychological strain of being the head of the militant organization of the Socialist-Revolutionaries and a police informer at the same time. He declares to Savinkov that he is tired and wants a break. But Savinkov replies that it is totally out of the question.

Azef takes over the leadership of the main operation—an attempt on the life of Interior Minister Stolypin, while Savinkov is sent to Crimea to assassinate the admiral who suppressed the October uprising in Sevastopol.

Savinkov has barely arrived in Crimea when an unrelated incident occurs. A sixteen-year-old boy throws a bomb at the commandant of Sevastopol Fortress. It does not explode, but another bomb being carried by his accomplice is accidentally detonated, killing the terrorist himself and six innocent passers-by. The police begin to arrest all suspicious types, including Savinkov this time.

They await trial. A "sympathetic" prison guard says that they will all be executed.

A DEMOCRATIC GENERAL

On 6 May 1906 Nicholas II celebrates his thirty-eighth birthday. All the ministers are invited to the palace. Trepov openly discusses which Duma members could make up a government of national confidence. Finance Minister Kokovtsov is uncomfortable about discussing such a delicate topic in front of everyone. But Trepov continues: Does Kokovtsov think that a government answerable to the Duma is the "equivalent of a coup against the monarch, reducing him to a decorative role?" It might be even worse, replies Kokovtsov.

Not all state officials believe that the Duma should be dissolved. General Trepov still considers it his duty to prevent a new insurrection, and is therefore nervous about disbanding the Duma. But the issue cannot be swept under the carpet. On 13 May, the Duma almost unanimously passes a vote of no confidence in the government—only seven parliamentarians abstain.

On 16 May Goremykin summons his ministers to discuss their response. Only Foreign Minister Izvolsky opposes the dissolution of the Duma, saying that it would complicate relations with Europe. All the rest, most vociferously Interior Minister Stolypin, say that the Duma should be broken up.

The newly democratic Dmitry Trepov visits the tsar with a proposed list of cabinet members in the event that the Duma's demand for a new government is satisfied. *Inter alia*, he proposes Duma Chairman Muromtsev as prime minister, Milyukov as interior or foreign minister, and Mikhail Herzenstein, a Moscow representative and the architect of the agrarian reforms, as finance minister. Trepov assures Nicholas II that this is the only way out of the impasse.

Moreover, Trepov says that he has already done the groundwork: he has held secret talks with the two potential ministers Muromtsev and Milyukov to learn about their agendas.

Nicholas is interested, but does not fail to consult with the ardent supporters of the dissolution of the Duma. He summons Finance Minister Kokovtsov, who, horrified by Trepov's proposal, explains that the appointment of a government of people's representatives would deprive the tsar of all influence over state policy—he would not even be able to dismiss the government. "We are not grown-up enough for a constitutional monarchy," warns Kokovtsov.

Trepov, the court commandant, gives an interview to the news agency Reuters. In it, he openly declares that it is necessary to form a new government "made up of Kadet parliamentarians because they are the strongest party in the Duma," adding that a government formed without Duma representation "will not bring peace to the country." He admits that it is a great risk, but necessary: "If it does not work, we shall have to resort to more extreme remedies."

Trepov's opponents decide that "extreme remedies" means Trepov's own personal dictatorship. They say that it is a ruse to form a Kadet government, which will put forward unacceptable conditions, allowing Trepov to dissolve it and seize power for himself.

The interview is an all-or-nothing gamble, and it fails. The idea of a government responsible to the Duma is opposed by Empress Alexandra, and the emperor himself has always believed in the inalienability of his power. "My mind is made up," he assures his finance minister at the end of June. "There was never any real doubt, for I have no right to forgo what was bequeathed to Me by my ancestors and what must be passed on to My son."

Nicholas II is ready to dissolve the Duma, but wants the initiative to come from the government. But Goremykin is afraid to take the initiative. He is waiting for the tsar to order him to dissolve the Duma.

The resolute Stolypin comes to the aid of the indecisive tsar and prime minister. According to Stolypin's plan, everything will go smoothly if the Duma is dissolved at the same time as the government is dismissed, with the appointment of a popular compromise figure as the new prime minister instead of Goremykin. This idea appeals to the tsar, who orders Stolypin to look for candidates.

He summons Milyukov for talks and asks the leader of the Kadets how much he and his fellow party members are prepared to compromise, which members of the current cabinet they are happy to cooperate with, and whether the liberal Kadets realize that they will have to get their hands dirty—for instance, they will be in charge of the gendarmes.

According to colleagues, Milyukov is sure that the prime minister's office is his. He believes that the meeting with Stolypin is a mere formality.

But Stolypin has another scheme. He summons Dmitry Shipov, a former zemstvo and opposition leader who suffered at the hands of Plehve, and offers him the post of prime minister in the new government. More than that, he tries to present him with a *fait accompli*. The dissolution of the Duma is a done deal; Shipov's candidacy has already been approved by the tsar, and tomorrow, 28 June, Nicholas II expects to receive him at the palace.

Shipov is a rare breed. As a sincere Tolstoyan, political intrigues are alien to him. He is honest and scrupulous in all matters. A year earlier, he refused to join the Witte government, citing the fact that he was a minority among Moscow liberals. Now he brusquely rejects Stolypin's proposal, saying that he considers the dissolution of the Duma to be not only unconstitutional but also criminal.

Stolypin tries to persuade Shipov to accept. Will Shipov agree to head a coalition government if the Duma is not dissolved, he asks. Shipov replies that the Duma majority belongs to the Kadets, which means that Stolypin should offer the post of prime minister to Milyukov. The interior minister acknowledges that he has spoken to Milyukov, but does not fancy the prospect of having him as prime minister. In the end, the only thing that Stolypin achieves is a promise that Shipov will meet the tsar the next day for talks.

Immediately afterwards, Shipov goes to see Duma Chairman Muromtsev and tells him everything. He says that he will refuse the post of prime minister, but will suggest Muromtsev instead. Muromtsev also refuses: for one thing, he is not certain that the new government will last long (the position of Duma chairman seems to him to be more stable), and for another, he cannot circumvent Milyukov, because the latter "already feels like the prime minister."

After talking with Muromtsev, Shipov, as promised, pays a visit to Nicholas. Shipov tries to persuade the tsar to form a government from the

Duma majority (i.e., the Kadets). They will soften their tactics on assuming power, he promises. The tsar wants to talk about specific individuals: Who should he appoint as prime minister? Despite the earlier conversation, Shipov recommends Muromtsev, adding that Milyukov could be the new interior minister. He leaves the palace in high spirits, thinking that the tsar has agreed to everything.

"They say Shipov's a smart man, but he revealed his hand to me and I didn't reveal mine," Nicholas says to his wife after the meeting.

Muromtsev is livid when he learns that Shipov has recommended him as prime minister, and Milyukov as interior minister: "What right have you to meddle in an internal party issue?" Shipov starts to talk about the good of the country, but Muromtsev says that he will not be able to work with Milyukov: "Two bears cannot live in one den."

However, Muromtsev is starting to think that he cannot avoid becoming a minister. The next day, during the Duma session, he summons Milyukov (who is not a parliamentarian, but goes to the Duma every day to observe the proceedings from the press gallery). "Which of us will be the next prime minister?" Muromtsev asks by way of greeting. Milyukov replies: "In my opinion, neither of us." But seeing Muromtsev's persistence, he continues: "As for me, I am happy to offer the premiership to you."

The party starts preparing to form a government. On 3 July Milyukov gathers together the various factions and informs his comrades about his negotiations with Trepov and Stolypin. Many are shocked by the admission, believing that the secret meetings with Trepov and Stolypin are a disgrace and that the Kadets should not agree to the tsar's proposal. However, most still agree that their primary duty is to their country, so they set about discussing the government's future program.

The Duma, meanwhile, continues to function. The situation is slightly schizophrenic: the government is demanding the resignation of the Duma members, yet the latter continue to draft unadoptable laws. The key issue is land reform, championed by the Moscow representative and economics professor Mikhail Herzenstein. He is developing a bill on the alienation of landowners' land for the purpose of transferring it to the peasants. Although it does not recognize the Duma's right to make such laws, the government is involved in the debate. The discussion is very lively. Herzenstein says that if land reform is postponed, the peasants will rise up and start burning the aristocrats' estates.

A baptized Jew, Herzenstein is fast becoming a hero among the peasant members of Duma. During speeches by right-wing opponents of the reforms, the peasants usually chant, "Herzenstein! Herzenstein!" The right-wingers hate him. He becomes a prime target for the Black Hundred press attacks and begins to receive threatening letters. He claims not to take the anonymous letters seriously, but insures his life for 50,000 roubles*.

The Union of the Russian People is also full of zealots. They bombard the government with telegrams demanding the dissolution of the Duma, writing that they can "barely contain the righteous indignation of the tsar's loyal subjects who want mob law applied to the enemies of the Orthodox Church, the Tsar and the Russian people."

In late June, the government issues an address to the public, stating that land reforms will not be imminent. In response, the Duma parliamentarians draft their own address to the people, outlining the reforms that they have prepared. On 8 July Goremykin and Stolypin pay a joint visit to the tsar at Peterhof. Stolypin persuades Nicholas that there is no time to lose: the Duma is calling on the peasants to revolt, so it should be pre-empted and dissolved immediately. Both Nicholas and Goremykin are pleased that someone else is taking the responsibility for this momentous decision. Moreover, Goremykin resigns as premier. The tsar appoints Stolypin as his successor.

Stolypin tries to refuse, citing inexperience, but Nicholas insists and blesses him with an icon. As if expecting such a turn of events, Stolypin pulls out a ready-made plan to suppress the unrest, which can be put into practice after the dissolution of the Duma.

On leaving the tsar's office, Goremykin and Stolypin bump into Trepov: "It's terrible! The whole of Saint Petersburg will be up in arms," says Trepov, and hurries off to try to change the emperor's mind.

Prime Minister Goremykin holds one last government meeting. He says that he feels that he has broken free and wants only one thing—peace.

A TRIP TO VYBORG

On Sunday morning, 9 July, Milyukov receives a call from the printing house that is typesetting the manifesto to dissolve the Duma. He jumps on his bicycle and rides around to the homes of all members of the Central Committee, summoning them to the house of Petrunkevich. The party lawyer, Fyodor Kokoshkin, convinces the Kadets that the manifesto is unconstitutional because it does not provide for new elections. The alarmed liberals ask Milyukov to write an appeal to the people to boycott the

---

* About $659,167 in 2017.

government (i.e., through non-payment of taxes and draft avoidance). They decide to convene a Duma meeting, but preferably outside the city to avoid being arrested.

Struve is sent to round up all fellow party members. He runs to the "Kadet club," where everyone usually gathers, stands on a chair in the middle of the hall, and makes a speech. He says that all the parliamentarians have to go to Vyborg, a small town in Finland, an hour's train ride from the Russian capital, where they will be able to discuss what to do next. The Duma members are opposed, saying that running from the capital is tantamount to desertion and acceptance of the dissolution order. "If the Duma remains in Saint Petersburg, there will be blood and disarray," Struve tries to outshout everyone.

A few hours later a crowd of people gathers at Finland Station to begin the exodus to Vyborg—the travelers include not only members of Duma, but also journalists, friends, relatives, and sympathizers.

During the short trip they talk about what will happen. Some believe that another revolution is inevitable; others are sure that the old order will be restored—politics will stop and autocracy will return as before. Many do not understand why they are fleeing to Vyborg. Stolypin, for one, is taken by surprise. He has instructed the police to arrest the Duma members if they try to assemble unlawfully and to expel them from Saint Petersburg. Yet instead, they seem to be expelling themselves.

When they arrive in Vyborg, many find that they have nowhere to stay. All the hotels are full. They have to spend the night on the station floor. The next morning a meeting is held at the Belvedere Hotel. Petrunkevich presides at the first session; Muromtsev arrives later.

For two days the parliamentarians argue over the text of their appeal to the Russian people, blaming each other for being too soft or too revolutionary. In the end, they reach a compromise text, which becomes known as the Vyborg Manifesto. When the members of Duma leave Vyborg, a crowd gathers at the station to see them off. At every station they are welcomed and waved at. The parliamentarians throw leaflets with the text of the appeal out of the train windows. Arriving in Saint Petersburg, the Duma members are surprised to find that no one is there to arrest them. The capital is a picture of calm.

Following the dissolution of the Duma, many Kadets rent out summer villas on the coast of the Gulf of Finland. There, the former parliamentarians continue their meetings to discuss further the party's plan of action. The forty-six-year-old Mikhail Herzenstein is incensed by the gathering in Vyborg: "What foolishness. You made this bed, now you'll have to lie in it. In any case, you're incapable of doing anything intelligent," he grumbles.

He and his family spend the summer nearby at Terioki (now Zelenogorsk in Russia, not Finland). Herzenstein plans to run for the post of head of the Moscow Duma, since he is still very popular in the city. On 18 July, he is strolling along the beach with his wife and seventeen-year-old daughter. They are accosted by a man with a gun. He shoots twice, climbs over a fence, and runs away. The gunman's name is Alexander Kazantsev.

The former Duma member is killed, and his daughter is wounded. The authorities forbid a funeral in Moscow, fearing unrest, and insist that he should be buried in Finland. Suspiciously, a whole hour before the shooting the reactionary newspaper *Lighthouse* had carried the front-page headline: "Herzenstein is assassinated!"

Since the killing took place in Finland (a grand duchy of the Russian Empire) it is investigated by the Finnish police. Had it taken place in the Russian heartland, there would have been no investigation at all, for the head of the Saint Petersburg Police Department knows full well that the assassination was committed by the militant wing of the Union of the Russian People, created by Dubrovin under the aegis of head of city police von der Launitz.

The murder provokes a major scandal inside the union itself. The fact is that von der Launitz paid 25,000 roubles* to the head of the militant wing for Herzenstein's head, but only 300 roubles[†] apiece to the foot soldiers. They are displeased.

The chief of the Petersburg secret police, Gerasimov, hears about it and reports what has happened to now Prime Minister Stolypin. The latter frowns in disgust: "I will tell Launitz to wash his hands of this affair," he says.

The investigation continues for nearly three years, but Dubrovin is never tried or even questioned as a witness. All the accused are pardoned by the tsar at the request of Stolypin. Herzenstein's assassination is the first of many operations carried out by the military wing of the Union of the Russian People.[‡]

---

* About $329,583 in 2017.

† About $3,955 in 2017.

‡ The actions of military wings of the Union of the Russian people are strikingly similar to the affair of the military wing of Russian Nationalists in the early twenty-first century. Activists of this organisation have killed a judge Eduard Chuvashov in 2010, a lawyer Stanislav Markelov, and a journalist Anastasia Baburova in 2009, and several leaders of anti-fascist movements. During the trial the accused stated that the military wing of Russian Nationalists is supervised and funded directly by the Presidential Administration.

AN EXPLOSION ON APTEKARSKY ISLAND

On Saturday, 12 August 1906, Prime Minister Stolypin is at his residence on Aptekarsky Island in the Neva River in Saint Petersburg, receiving visitors. On the upper balcony, directly above the entrance to the house, sits his three-year-old son, Arkady, known in the family as Adya, with his nanny. The boy scrutinizes the arriving visitors. A carriage pulls up with two gendarmes inside, holding briefcases. They stride into the house, pushing the porter out of the way, but are stopped by General Zamyatin, the prime minister's assistant. He is suspicious. Something about their uniforms is not right. Faced with the general, they throw their briefcases onto the floor. An explosion rings out.

Stolypin's daughter Maria says that she was just about to open the door to her bedroom when there was a sudden roar. In a split second, her door turned into a gaping hole in the wall, offering a view of the river.

The terrorists, the porter, and General Zamyatin are "ripped to pieces," says Maria Stolypina. Another thirty people are also killed by the blast. The explosion is so powerful that the windows of a factory on the other side of the river are shattered.

The only room in the house that is not damaged is the prime minister's office, the farthest from the entrance. At the time of the explosion, Stolypin is at his desk. The shock wave causes a bronze inkwell to empty its contents over the prime minister. But otherwise he is unharmed.

He runs out into the street to look for his wife. "Olga, where are you?" yells Stolypin. She runs out onto the balcony. "Are the kids with you?" "I can't find Natasha and Adya."

Stolypin has six children: five elder girls and one youngest son. The fourteen-year-old Natasha and the three-year-old Adya are eventually found alive under the rubble: he has a broken leg, while both her legs are splintered in several places. Adya's seventeen-year-old nanny, who was with the boy on the balcony, has had her legs blown off.

The explosion is heard from afar. At the neighboring dacha, Deputy Interior Minister Kryzhanovsky is receiving Dr. Dubrovin, the head of the Union of the Russian People. According to hearsay, he rushes to the scene and starts administering first aid. He is said to be the first person to talk to the ink-stained, plaster-covered prime minister in the immediate aftermath. "Go and have a wash," he says to the victim, and only then does he recognize Stolypin. When the latter realizes that it is Dubrovin, he allegedly says to him: "Do what you like, the reforms will not be stopped!" The story is improbable, but very popular among the reactionaries.

After the assassination attempt, Stolypin continues as if nothing has happened. "We were amazed by his serenity and composure," says Finance Minister Kokovtsov. Stolypin seemed to come of age and take charge. He was not afraid to speak his mind to anyone."

The next day the tsar offers Stolypin compensation, which he turns down: "Your Majesty, I do not sell the blood of my children." Soon, the Stolypin family relocates to the Winter Palace, since the tsar still prefers to reside at Tsarskoye Selo.

The terrorist group led by Azef spent several months preparing for the attempt on Stolypin's life. Azef informs his supervisor Gerasimov about the operation in June, before the dissolution of the Duma. The two-faced head of the militant organization says that it would be a mistake to arrest all his subordinates and threatens to quit if they are. Gerasimov promises not to arrest all the terrorists.

But Gerasimov wants to know about all the movements of the militants, so that the police can carry out surveillance and, in some cases, let them know that they are being watched. Typically, on noticing a tail, the terrorists abandon their safe houses and lie low for a few weeks from Saint Petersburg. That way, the militant organization is paralyzed. In any case, arresting only the foot soldiers inside a safe house would be a short-term solution.

But Gerasimov forgets about a group of young radicals who split from the SRs when the party declared the terror was over—the so-called "maximalists." They have lost contact with the SRs and are not subordinate to Azef. The leader of the maximalists is Sokolov, nicknamed "Bear"—it is he who coordinated the operation against Stolypin on Aptekarsky Island.

Savinkov, meanwhile, who has been arrested in Sevastopol, avoids the death penalty and escapes with the help of a sympathetic guard. He makes his way to Heidelberg, where the seriously ill Mikhail Gotz lives. The latter is not happy about the explosion on Aptekarsky Island.

Gotz believes that the preparations were shoddy. Stolypin is usually hosting a cabinet meeting at his dacha on the island, but the terrorists chose a time when not a single minister was there. Moreover, the large number of civilian casualties was deplorable. However, he does agree with the idea to assassinate Stolypin as the right response to the dissolution of the Duma, so the maximalists deserve some credit, especially since the SRs' militant organization is making no progress whatsoever. "Don't you see that the militant organization is paralyzed?" says the equally paralyzed Mikhail Gotz.

He suggests that Savinkov should refrain from terrorism until a new approach is devised. Savinkov moves to France, and Gotz dies a few weeks later after an unsuccessful operation on his spinal cord.

Despite Gotz and Savinkov's despondency, their cause is more popular than ever. The SRs' militant organization no longer enjoys a monopoly on terror. A couple of years earlier, all the high-profile attacks in the Russian Empire were the work of Azef and associates, but now there is no centralized organization for political assassinations—rather it is a popular ideology, spreading like a virus. Terrorist attacks against state officials are carried out across the country by young people who have never seen Gotz or Azef. The explosion on Aptekarsky Island is followed by several copycat attacks.

In Peterhof, a terrorist shoots Major-General Kozlov in full public view. During his interrogation, it becomes clear that he thought his target was Trepov. A day after the assassination attempt on Stolypin, Colonel Min, the commander of the Semenov Regiment, who distinguished himself during the suppression of the December uprising in Moscow, is assassinated at Peterhof train station. On the same day, again in Peterhof, General Staal survives an attack, again having been mistaken for Trepov. By June 1906, thirty-seven attacks have been made on major government officials, and the number continues to climb. Later in the year, even the curator of the Union of the Russian People, Petersburg Governor Vladimir von der Launitz, is shot and killed. The assassin commits suicide on the spot—and his head is gruesomely preserved in alcohol and put on public display. It does not help to identify the anonymous terrorist.

Trepov is shaken by the crime spree. In early 1905, he survived a fairly inept attempt on his life, but the assassinations of officials mistaken for him are a cause for alarm. He also fears for the life of the emperor. Moreover, he seems to have lost the ear of Nicholas II, who now listens more to Stolypin. The latter has not only replaced him at the Winter Palace, but is also outperforming him as an "effective manager"* of a hopeless situation.

The general public calm following the dissolution of the Duma is proof for Nicholas II that Stolypin was right and that Trepov was being alarmist. But the latter considers the growing number of terrorist attacks to be evidence of rising discontent that will soon erupt. Trepov believes that by not forming a government from the parliamentary majority and by returning to autocracy, Nicholas II is exposing himself to a fatal peril.

---

* A term applied later to Stalin and Putin among others, and considered a great compliment in Russia.

In September the tsar and his family go on a yacht trip to the Finnish fjords, leaving the fifty-year-old court commandant Trepov behind. It is an open snub. During the cruise, Nicholas II is informed of his sudden death. The tsar instructs his chancellor Mosolov, Trepov's brother-in-law, whom the latter recommended to Count Fredericks six months ago, to find out what has happened.

Petersburg society believes that Trepov has committed suicide, but Mosolov states that the autopsy showed signs of a heart attack. The question on everyone's lips is whether or not the tsar will interrupt his cruise to attend the funeral. He does not. Mosolov goes through Trepov's papers and documents and takes all the most important to Nicholas II. "I am greatly saddened by this sudden death," says Nicholas in a businesslike tone. "The Emperor certainly appreciated Trepov, but did not feel any personal liking for him," Mosolov writes in his memoirs.

Others close to Nicholas II remember Trepov as a brave man devoted to the tsar, but one who showed weakness by trying to persuade the emperor to become a constitutional monarch. However, it soon becomes apparent that Trepov, not Stolypin, was right. The dissolution of the Duma and the subsequent crackdown do not create lasting stability, and the sword of Damocles continues to hang over the tsar. Stolypin survives Trepov by just five years, Nicholas II by twelve.

STOLYPIN'S NECKTIE

A week after the assassination attempt on Stolypin, the Council of Ministers declares a "war on terror" and introduces military courts. For the Russian Empire, which has operated a trial-by-jury system for over half a century, it is a game changer. According to the new system, if a crime is so clear-cut that "there is no need for an investigation," the criminal should be tried by martial law. Such courts are set up by regional governors-general. Court verdicts are to be delivered within twenty-four hours of the crime; the usual sentence is, of course, the death penalty.

Russia at this time has a very special relationship with the death penalty. In 1741, Elizabeth, the daughter of Peter the Great, when preparing to mount a palace coup, vowed before an icon to repeal the death penalty if she became empress. Thereafter, the death penalty in Russia is more the exception than the rule—after Empress Elizabeth any death sentence must be approved personally by the monarch, which happens only in extreme cases. Catherine II, for instance, authorizes the execution of the ringleaders of the Pugachev uprising. In 1825, thirty-one Decembrists are sentenced to death, but only five are hanged in the end; the others have their sentences commuted to hard labor.

The death penalty is applied more frequently in wartime by military courts. Execution by firing squad is the usual penalty for military crimes, while serious political offenses are punishable by hanging. On average, the death penalty is handed down only a dozen times a year. It is not applied to persons under the age of twenty-one or older than seventy. Women can be sentenced to death only for an assassination attempt on the tsar, his family, or his government.

But with the onset of the twentieth century, the situation changes for the worse. Military courts spring up during the suppression of the December 1905 uprising—that month alone 376 people are executed. In the second half of 1906, 574 are sentenced to death, and the numbers climb even further: 1,139 people are hanged in 1907, 1,340 in 1908, and 717 in 1909. The gallows—the government's preferred tool to crush the revolution—will be nicknamed "Stolypin's necktie."

The purges have no obvious effect. Even the head of the secret police, Gerasimov, says that the military courts do more harm than good: they often deliver arbitrary verdicts and swell the ranks of enemies of the regime. Not only terrorists are tried by them, and often the judges are ordinary officers who are not legal experts, so the sentences end up being based on gut feelings and personal enmities. "By introducing military courts, the government seemed to be taking revenge, which was undignified," says Gerasimov.

The ordinariness of the death penalty is a sign of the times; it even becomes a common motif in Russian literature. The main opponent of the death penalty is still the ageing Tolstoy. Two years later, in May 1908, he writes an article entitled, "I Cannot Remain Silent." In it, he asserts that the authorities are worse than the revolutionaries: "You, government people, describe revolutionary deeds as villainous, but there is nothing that they have done that you yourselves have not done to a far greater extent."

AGRARIAN REFORM

Prime Minister Stolypin uses the dissolution of the Duma to launch his most ambitious reform—agricultural. His proposal is completely unlike Herzenstein's and does not foresee alienating land from the landowners and handing it over to the peasant cooperatives or communes.

In early twentieth-century Russia there is no individual land ownership for farmers—every peasant is inseparable from the commune. The land is tilled jointly according to strict rules within the commune. Stolypin's revolutionary idea is to encourage the breakup of the communes by selling land to individual peasants, making them private owners. Peasants can leave the commune and receive a slice of land; also, they get an opportunity to buy plots of land on credit through the new Peasant Bank. Land sold to the peasants is to be redeemed from the landowners by the bank at market prices. Under the scheme, the bank also receives land belonging to the tsar and his family.

Stolypin's project is very unpopular with imperial family members. It takes Stolypin a long time to bring him round to the idea.

Nevertheless, Stolypin manages to adopt a land reform law on 9 November, less than six months after he took charge of the government. He is following the advice of his predecessor, Sergei Witte, who once said that any reform in Russia needs to be done quickly or not at all.

The reform, which is adopted without the approval of the dissolved Duma, provokes a hostile reaction from both opponents and supporters of the regime. The socialists believe that the landowners' land should be confiscated, not redeemed, and distributed, not sold, to the peasants. The Union of the Russian People is equally critical, but from a different angle. Dubrovin considers the peasant commune to be a pillar of the autocratic regime. Stolypin's project, writes the right-wing press, only benefits the Jewish Freemasons, who seek to undermine the autocratic system. But Stolypin's influence over the tsar is firm, and the law is signed into force.

A BARREL OF CABBAGE

Most appalled of all by Stolypin's reforms are the SRs, the heirs of the populist Narodniks. Like the Black Hundreds, they too idealize the peasant commune, but believe that the communes should receive all land—both state-owned and belonging to the landowning class.

However, when Stolypin is busy persuading the grand dukes to accept his reforms, the attention of the SRs is focused elsewhere. They are trying to arrange the escape of their leader, Gregory Gershuni, from prison. It is now three years since Gershuni created the SRs' militant organization, in which time Russia has undergone radical change. It was after Gershuni's arrest that the SRs went on to commit their most high-profile terrorist attacks. Gershuni was not included in the amnesty of October 1905, and by autumn 1906 he is at Akatuysky prison in eastern Siberia.*

The inmates' work involves packing sauerkraut and pickles in barrels and delivering them to the neighboring villages. One morning, Gregory Gershuni climbs into a barrel—he is small in stature, so manages to squeeze in, albeit with difficulty. He immerses himself fully in the mushy contents, using a tube sticking out as an inconspicuous breathing apparatus. The barrel with Gershuni inside is carried out of the prison. He starts to choke and the sour liquid is stinging his eyes, but he manages to remain quiet. Finally, several hours later in the evening, some accomplices in the village help him out of the barrel, give him a horse, and show him to the railway station. A couple of days later, he boards a ship in Vladivostok bound for San Francisco.

In the United States, Gershuni is greeted by those in the know as a superhero returned from the dead. Russian émigrés welcome him with open arms, and the SRs beg him to do what Gorky could not—travel around America raising funds for the revolution. He holds a number of events for the Jewish community, at which the donations flow in. Still, he is eager to return to Europe. Before departing, Gershuni narrowly avoids a scandal when the Russian embassy sparks a rumor that the fugitive terrorist has spoken disrespectfully of President Theodore Roosevelt. The latter writes a letter to the *New York Times* (which the newspaper prints) to say that Gershuni has nothing but respect for the American president.

In February 1907 Gershuni gets back to Russia—or rather the part of the empire where he is relatively safe, Finland. It is expected that he will breathe new life into the weakened militant organization, but Gershuni shocks his fellow party members by appealing for a more peaceable solution. He argues against attacks on other oppositionists (even the Kadets), calls for the creation of a unified socialist party, and condemns the new generation of terrorists for killing too many passers-by.

Leon Trotsky, meanwhile, is inside the Peter and Paul Fortress, reading French novels. "Lying on my prison bunk, reading these books, I became intoxicated with the same sense of physical pleasure that connoisseurs get from sipping a fine wine or puffing on a fragrant cigar," he recalls. He even

---

* The Akatuy prison (nowadays non-existent), where Gregory Gershuni served his time in 1905-1906, is located about 100 kilometres away from the Krasnokamensk prison, where Mikhail Khodorkovsky served his first time (2005-2006).

expresses some regret when his solitary confinement comes to an end in order to face trial.

The trial of the Petersburg Soviet begins on 19 September. In the words of Trotsky, the authorities want to discredit Witte's liberalism and his "soft spot" for the revolution. The trial turns into a major show with more than two hundred witnesses testifying in court. Trotsky transforms it into a piece of theatre. His frail parents are there in the courtroom, and his mother likes her son's speeches so much that she thinks he should be rewarded, not punished.

But the main (absent) protagonist is neither a defendant, nor a lawyer. It is Alexei Lopukhin, the former director of the police department, appointed by Plehve and fired by Trepov in February 1905 after the assassination of Grand Duke Sergei. During the trial, Lopukhin decides to go public with all the facts known to him: for instance, the provincial gendarmerie is printing leaflets calling for pogroms, and the police themselves are responsible for organizing the Black Hundred gangs. According to Lopukhin, the capital escaped mass unrest and pogroms only thanks to the Petersburg Soviet.

All this is read out in a letter on 13 October by a lawyer for the defense. Lopukhin states that he was ready to appear in court as a witness, but was turned down by the judge. On hearing this, the defendants protest and refuse to take any further part in the court proceedings. The trial ends without the defendants in the courtroom. They are sentenced to perpetual exile in Obdorsk (now Salekhard, in northern Siberia). Despite the severity, it is a let-off, for everyone was expecting hard labor. Lopukhin's letter apparently softened the verdict.

Trotsky and the other convicted members of the Petersburg Soviet are transported to northern Siberia in February 1907. The weather is ferocious. Along the way, in the settlement of Berezovo, Trotsky simulates an attack of sciatica and is allowed to remain there. The other exiles go on. Some local residents help Trotsky find a guide to take him seven hundred kilometers west to the Urals on board a reindeer sled. The sled driver is blind drunk for most of the journey and on several occasions nearly kills both himself and his passenger. Having made it to the Urals, Trotsky covers the distance back to Saint Petersburg in record time—just eleven days. His comrades take him for a ghost, believing him to be in northern Siberia—news of his escape has not yet had time to reach the capital.

Taking his wife with him, Trotsky heads for Finland to see his closest comrades, Lenin and Martov. In Finland he writes a book about his escape and uses the fee from the publisher to move to Stockholm.

BOMB IN THE CHIMNEY

One reason Trotsky's escape goes unremarked for a while is that Saint Petersburg is not short of other news. In late January 1907 Dr. Dubrovin asks his private secretary, Prusakov, to provide him with a plan of Witte's residence on Kamennoostrovsky Avenue in Saint Petersburg. He says that the tsar suspects Witte of being a secret revolutionary and wants the police to look for incriminating documents inside the house. Dubrovin promises Prusakov a thousand roubles* and the title of honorary citizen.

A few days later, rummaging through some papers on his boss's desk, Prusakov discovers a draft article written in Dubrovin's own hand, blaming the "assassination of Count Witte" on the socialists. Prusakov is surprised. He has not heard about any assassination attempt on Witte, successful or otherwise.

That same day, two peasants called Stepanov and Fedorov approach Witte's house via the backyard, climb onto the roof, and lower two time bombs (known in Russia back then as "infernal machines") down the twin chimneys. They think that they are carrying out an assignment on behalf of the "party of anarchists" (i.e., the socialists). Having descended from the roof, they approach Alexander Kazantsev, a member of the militant wing of the Union of the Russian People. This is the same Kazantsev who six months ago murdered Herzenstein. Posing as an anarchist, he hired the peasants and gave them the bombs. The three of them head for a tavern, where Kazantsev gives them two roubles† apiece for their work.

Come evening, Kazantsev is in a bad mood. No explosions have occurred. The bombs were discovered by a stoker while cleaning the chimneys. Noticing a rope hanging down from one of the chimneys, he pulls it. The "infernal machine" tumbles to the floor, but, fortunately for him, does not go off, since the device is amateurish. During a search of the house, the former Prime Minister Count Witte asks the head of the secret police Gerasimov who could have planned the assassination. "I don't know, but they were not revolutionaries," he answers.

Gerasimov delivers a report to Stolypin, pointing the finger at the Union of the Russian People. "It's a disgrace," says Stolypin, horrified. "These people do not understand what difficulties they are creating for me and the whole government. Drastic measures are called for."

Meanwhile, the peasants Fedorov and Stepanov are again approached by Kazantsev. Both are in need of work and accept the offer to go to

---

* About $13,183 in 2017.
† About $26.40 in 2017.

Moscow. There, Kazantsev puts them up at his own apartment and explains that the new target is a "dangerous man, a member of the Black Hundreds." Fedorov is the more able shooter, so he is the one to track down and kill the "enemy."

The next day, Stepanov and Fedorov learn from the newspapers that they have killed the former State Duma member Gregory Yollos. He was a Jew, a Kadet, and a close friend of the late Herzenstein. Only then do they realize that they are working for the Black Hundreds. They decide to kill Kazantsev. At their next meeting, Fedorov severs his carotid artery. Dubrovin, meanwhile, is drawing up a list of enemies of the Russian people. The next targets are Vladimir Nabokov and Pavel Milyukov.

Stolypin cannot take any drastic measures against the Union of the Russian People, for it has too many influential patrons. Von der Launitz is dead, but the new court commandant, Dedyulin is also an admirer of the Black Hundreds; he holds receptions between union members and the tsar. But the union's real power lies in the fact that Nicholas and Alexandra are adherents. They love the flattery heaped upon them by Dubrovin and his associates.

In December Stolypin presents the tsar with a decree to abolish a number of restrictions on the Jews. Nicholas promises to sign, but soon returns the document without his signature: "Despite the very strong arguments in favor, My inner voice tells me not to sign. My conscience has never lied to Me. Therefore, I intend to obey it," explains Nicholas II. "The heart of the Tsar lies in God's hands."

Shortly before that, in 1906, the so-called All-Russian Congress of the Russian People takes place in Kiev, involving members of the Union of the Russian People and other organizations. "Each of us suffers for himself, but there is one who suffers for all of us, for the whole of Russia," says Dubrovin in his eulogy to the tsar. The audience agrees. Nicholas II, Alexandra, and Father John of Kronstadt send congratulatory telegrams. It is the largest ever official gathering of the Black Hundreds, with more than five hundred people from across the country.

The monarchists have long discussed the question of unifying all the right-wing organizations, but the Union of the Russian People has no desire to integrate with other groups. But the right-wingers do have a common rallying point: the upcoming elections to the proposed Second Duma. Although Dubrovin himself still does not recognize the Russian parliament, many of his fellows run as candidates. Stolypin, though ostensibly unhappy with the Union of the Russian People, allocates money for its election campaign. At the prime minister's request, the right-wing activist and former police officer Vladimir Purishkevich is invited from Chisinau to enter the Duma.

The campaign starts in December and turns into a real election race. Whereas the First Duma elections were ignored by most parties, both right and left, now everyone is taking them seriously. Moreover, the government this time decides not to leave things to chance. In the elections to the First Duma, Witte interfered in neither the campaign nor the vote-counting process, and ended up with a disloyal Duma as a result. Stolypin does not intend to repeat his predecessor's mistakes.

This time around, only legally registered parties are allowed to campaign. The legal parties include, for instance, the Union of 17 October and the Union of the Russian People, but not the Kadets. Members of the latter can stand as independents, but are not allowed to even mention their party in pre-election events.

The Kadets' main election tactics are to scare voters with the threat of the Black Hundreds and to position themselves as the only real opposition. A vote for the radical left, they say, is a vote wasted, for they will not enter the Duma, leaving the way clear for the monarchists.

The winners of the previous Duma election, the Kadets, face huge obstacles. Not only are all the former Duma members who signed the Vyborg Manifesto forbidden from running, but others are, too, including the party leader Milyukov, who once again does not qualify under the property rules—he has owned an apartment for less than a year, which means he cannot be elected to the Duma.

At the same time, the other oppositionists accuse the Kadets of being in league with the authorities. Milyukov is constantly reminded of his secret talks with Stolypin, and there are rumors that they have met during the current election campaign—Milyukov is supposedly trying to get his party legalized in return for promising not to enter into an alliance with the left.

For the first time in recorded Russian history, the authorities use "administrative resources."* Rural leaders are encouraged to support the right-wing parties. Meanwhile, the Holy Synod enjoins all priests to vote (albeit without specifying for whom).

The left is also in full campaign mode, although with different objectives. The Bolsheviks believe that the Duma can be used as a platform from which to agitate for another revolution, while the Mensheviks see the Duma potentially as an independent decision-making body capable of

---

* A common term in modern Russia to describe state tools to influence elections.

266 | MIKHAIL ZYGAR

turning Russia into a normal parliamentary democracy. Lenin, of course, considers this view a betrayal, and so contrives to derail the Mensheviks at every opportunity, even when the two faces of Marxism are campaigning jointly as part of the so-called "left bloc."

The results are staggering for the government. As Finance Minister Kokovtsov recalls, Stolypin's own staff assured the prime minister that the right-wingers would secure the largest faction. Instead, it goes once again to the independent-running Kadets (again without Milyukov, but this time Peter Struve is elected to the Duma). Another, even worse surprise is the success of the left parties: they get a third of the seats in the new Duma, far more than the right.

The Second Duma opens on 20 February at the Tauride Palace—this time without the tsar. During the opening ceremony, confusion reigns when all the right-wing Duma members insist on standing up whenever the tsar's name is mentioned, while their left-wing adversaries remain firmly seated—with one exception. A tall, red-bearded man rises alone from among the leftist faction. His comrades chide him: "Sit down, will you!" He obeys at first, but then gets to his feet again. It is Peter Struve.

A YOUNG MAN FROM KUTAISI

On 6 March members of the government visit the Duma. Their families sit in the visitors' gallery. From the podium, Stolypin reads out the government's program. The members of Duma sit quietly, which surprises the ministers. Whenever Goremykin addressed the previous Duma, he was greeted with loud cries of "Resign!" Now the government dares to believe that the Duma wants to engage constructively.

In fact, the members of Duma have a different motivation. They regard the government members as enemies. The dissolution of the First Duma, the military courts, the executions, the exile of political prisoners, and the omnipotence of the Black Hundreds are all symbols of authoritarianism. To most members of the Duma, Stolypin and his ministers seem like bloodthirsty tyrants. The Kadets decide to greet them with "proud silence." But the Social Democrats believe that silence might be interpreted as capitulation.

Stolypin's speech is very different to Goremykin's the previous year. The former prime minister was convinced that the Duma was unruly and not interested in cooperation. Stolypin, on the other hand, proposes a detailed list of draft laws. They include the government's nascent land reforms, laws to guarantee individual inviolability, amendments to the Criminal Code, school reforms, and others. It is a striking contrast to last year's launderette and orangery.

Curiously, in describing the situation in the country, Stolypin uses the word *perestroika*, meaning "restructuring": "The country is going through a period of *perestroika* and unrest," says the prime minister. For him, every detail of every new law is important for the country's future.

When Stolypin finishes speaking, the twenty-five-year-old Menshevik Irakli Tsereteli, a Duma member from the Georgian city of Kutaisi, takes the floor. He is the leader of the Social Democratic faction and is responsible for delivering the Duma's response to the forty-five-year-old Stolypin's opening address.

Tsereteli belongs to one of the oldest noble families in Georgia. In 1900 he entered the law faculty of Moscow University—in the midst of the student unrest. When the seventy-two-year-old Leo Tolstoy was excommunicated, the eighteen-year-old fresher Tsereteli was convicted for taking part in the resultant protests and exiled to Siberia, where he spent almost three years. In 1903 Tsereteli returned to Georgia, before moving to Berlin, where he enrolled at Humboldt University. In short, the young Tsereteli has already amassed a great deal of political experience.

He is not at all impressed by Stolypin's conciliatory speech, saying that the prime minister is untrustworthy because his government has already "trampled over the existing laws, filled Russia's prisons with freedom fighters, and introduced 'medieval' torture." Tsereteli says that during the election campaign the authorities made every effort to hinder the Duma opposition, but the people's "hatred for the government overcame the thousands of obstacles." Stolypin cannot be trusted, Tsereteli sums up.

The right-wing parliamentarians, in particular the representatives from Chisinau Purishkevich and Krushevan, shout out "Lies!" and "Away!" The Duma chairman calls for quiet. In his opinion, Tsereteli's words are not a breach of etiquette.

Tsereteli recalls that a year earlier, after the speech of the former Prime Minister Goremykin, Vladimir Nabokov approached the podium, demanding that the executive branch submit to the legislature. It is now clear, Tsereteli says, that the executive branch has no intention of submitting to the Duma. Moreover, it is highly likely that the new Duma, like its predecessor, will be dissolved "within perhaps a week." But the people, argues Tsereteli, will get their way with or without the Duma—the government should obey the will of the people before it is too late.

The right-wing Duma members protest, and the chairman asks Tsereteli to refrain from calling for an armed uprising. He replies that he is not calling for an armed uprising: on the contrary, it is the government's repressive measures that are provoking a surge in violence.

The left applauds, the right hisses. Stolypin mounts the podium again for an impromptu response. The forty-five-year-old prime minister wants to put the twenty-five-year-old parliamentarian in his place. He declares that, at the behest of the tsar, the State Duma is not permitted to express disapproval or censure of the government. However, as the head of the government, he will be glad to cooperate with all members of the Duma who are prepared to work constructively. He is happy to listen to constructive criticism and would welcome the exposure of official abuse of power in Russia. But, warns Stolypin, he will not tolerate Duma members seeking to "paralyze the will" of the government by causing it to surrender. The government will not be bullied, he says, before departing from the Tauride Palace.

Stolypin and Tsereteli are talking at cross-purposes. Neither wants a revolution, yet each considers the other to be provoking one. For Tsereteli, the real revolutionary is Stolypin, since his repressive measures are radicalizing the population; for Stolypin, it is the non-systemic oppositionist Tsereteli who is rocking the boat.

"Both of us shall answer to history," says Stolypin. History, for its part, seems to justify Tsereteli. Despite his efforts, Stolypin failed to prevent another revolution. And it played out exactly as described by the twenty-five-year-old member of Duma from Kutaisi.

THE TRIAL OF LENIN

"The government has again declared war on the people," writes the Bolshevik leader after the opening of the State Duma, signing his article "Nikolai Lenin." He lives in Kuokkala in Finland, an hour's ride from Saint Petersburg. Every day he writes long articles about the political situation in the capital, never missing an opportunity to pick a fight or humiliate his opponents. He rails deliriously at the Kadets, the Socialist-Revolutionaries, and the Duma faction which consists of Socialist Revolutionaries. But his favorite targets are his "comrade" Mensheviks and the Social Democratic faction inside the Duma headed by Tsereteli.

Lenin accuses Tsereteli and the Mensheviks of betrayal. In his opinion, the only reason for partaking in the Duma is to "explain to the masses the illusory nature of hoping for a peaceful outcome to the power struggle"—the Duma members should not swerve from the original revolutionary creed of the Russian Social Democratic Labor Party (RSDLP). There can be no peaceful outcome—only war, revolution, and the dictatorship of the proletariat. In his view, any activity that is not aimed at bringing about a bloody denouement is betrayal and sabotage. The Menshevik parliamentarians are "raising hopes for a peaceful outcome among the masses," which Lenin finds outrageous. "They are disrupting the 'revolutionary forces' inside the Duma," he opines.

Lenin's insults and claims that the Mensheviks are toadying up to the Kadets test the patience of fellow party members. They decide to hold a "party trial" of Lenin to punish him for his mocking comments.

Lenin is "tried" internally by nine judges: three from the Mensheviks, three of Lenin's own choice, and one each from the Latvian and Polish Social Democrats and the Bund. The "defendant" Lenin immediately goes on the attack, arguing that it was not he, but Tsereteli and other Mensheviks from the Duma, who split the party. If the party is indeed split, then it is dead and no longer exists. He believes himself to be free from any moral obligation in respect of party members, whom he considers traitors. Since the Social Democrats are trying to negotiate with the liberals ("political enemies"), he will continue to preach hatred among the masses and lead the fight to destroy them.

This blunt statement marks the end of the trial. The judges have nothing to say in response. It is almost a carbon copy of Lenin's "trial by comrades" in exile in Siberia, at which he said that he did not give a damn about the opinion of his fellows.

ARMY FOR FIGHTING OPPOSITIONISTS

Emperor Nicholas II closely follows the sessions of the Second Duma. He is fed regular transcripts of the liveliest exchanges. At the same time, right-wing parliamentarians deliver excerpts from the Duma speeches to Empress Alexandra.

In early April the right-wingers put forward a resolution condemning the spate of political killings. The SR Duma members cannot bring themselves to vote for it, and even the Kadets feel that the left-wing press will label them stooges of the regime if they back the resolution. As a result, the Duma majority votes against the condemnation of political terror.

Another crucial day is 17 April. The Duma is paid a visit by War Minister Rediger to submit a bill introducing regular army conscription. The bill is opposed by the Menshevik member of Duma Arshak Zurabov from

Tbilisi. In his speech, he accuses the army of being only capable of fighting oppositionists, but not of waging a real war.

The right is in uproar, and the Duma chairman tries to calm them down to no effect: they demand that Zurabov issue an apology. The chairman says that he has heard nothing to warrant an apology. War Minister Rediger goes up to the podium and states that he considers it beneath his dignity to respond to such a remark, and leaves. The chairman announces a recess. During the break, he rereads a transcript of Zurabov's speech and changes his mind. He asks for an apology, but it is not enough.*

Zurabov's remark is reported to Stolypin, who demands that Zurabov be expelled from the Duma. If not, no minister shall ever again cross the threshold of the Russian parliament. When extracts from Zurabov's speech are shown to the emperor, he reacts even more firmly, asking why the Duma cannot be dissolved forthwith. Stolypin replies that the Second Duma cannot be dissolved before the drafting of a new electoral law—if the next Duma is elected under the current rules, things will only get worse. Stolypin believes that the Duma cannot be dissolved without a proper reason and without taking precautions—every effort must be made to blame the dissolution of the Duma on the left. Nicholas reluctantly agrees.

Members of the Union of the Russian People and his wife Alexandra persistently ask the tsar when the Duma will be dissolved. He is becoming increasingly irritated by Stolypin's perceived tardiness.

A SOCIALIST CONSPIRACY

On 29 April 1907, a student hostel at the Polytechnic Institute in Saint Petersburg hosts a meeting of local socialists. It is attended by soldiers and students, among them the young activist Ekaterina Shornikova. She brings with her a petition in the name of the capital city's soldiers addressed to members of the State Duma. The petition calls for an armed uprising and the overthrow of the existing order.

The petition was not, however, written by Saint Petersburg's soldiers, but by the secret police on the orders of Colonel Gerasimov. Shornikova, a police agent, has rewritten the text in her own hand to make it look authentic.

---

*In the early twenty-first century public officials will also often feel offended and use such cases against their political opponents. Moreover, in most cases officials would feel offended not for themselves personally, but for the religious or for the veterans of World War II. Article 282 of the criminal code carries punishment for "dishonoring a social group" (for instance, the group of "public officials").

Gerasimov, instructed by Stolypin to find incriminating evidence against Tsereteli and his fellow Social Democrats, shows the petition to the prime minister. The latter believes that the document can be considered proof of a conspiracy and authorizes arrests to be made as soon as the soldiers hand the petition to the Duma members.

At 7:30 p.m. on 5 May, police officers arrive at the head office of the Social Democratic faction on Nevsky Prospekt. They conduct a search of the room—a violation of parliamentary immunity—but find no trace of any petition. However, the case still goes ahead, based solely on the testimony of Shornikova, who states that she was there when the document was handed over.

According to the official version, there exists an underground military organization led by Tsereteli and the Social Democrats. On 5 May a group of soldiers came to the Social Democrats' office with a petition asking for assistance to start an armed uprising, but it, along with other evidence, was destroyed by the Duma members before the police had time to carry out a search.

The next session of the Duma on 7 May is a tempestuous affair. The right-wing parliamentarians demand to know if the attackers planned to assassinate the tsar. Stolypin arrives at the Duma to deliver a report. He begins by saying that the government is not obliged to disclose such confidential information, but, given the exceptional circumstances, he feels able to reveal some details: yes, there was indeed a conspiracy—a hitherto unknown terrorist group, now neutralized, planned to murder Emperor Nicholas II and Grand Duke Nikolai Nikolaevich. The general import of Stolypin's words is that the "war on terror" is going well.

After that, the Social Democrats inquire as to the lawfulness of the search of their premises, to which Stolypin replies that the uncovering of a major conspiracy involving members of the State Duma is sufficient justification and constitutes grounds to dissolve the Duma.

The threat of dissolution (once again) is a nightmare for many parliamentarians. The Duma's main advocate, Peter Struve, wants parliament to become a proper institution able to fight for the gradual reform of the Russian political system and to work constructively with the government. The slogan of the Kadets and Struve is: "Save the Duma." He argues incessantly with the right, which insists that the Duma is behaving unacceptably and trying to "take power by storm." "Gentlemen, we have assembled here to lay siege to the old order for the benefit of Russian statehood," asserts Struve.

The influence of the one-time leader of public opinion is on the wane, and not only because he is a constant target of Trotsky, Lenin, and the leftist press. The publicist Struve, who has fought so hard for Russia to have an open forum for debate, is totally inept at speaking from the parliamentary rostrum, says Ariadna Tyrkova, the press secretary of the Kadets in the Second Duma. In March the Kadet faction asks him to make a speech on economic issues. He runs to the podium with an armful of papers, and arranges them in front of him on the stand. He starts to speak, at times too loudly, at times too softly, all the while adjusting his pince-nez and rummaging through his notes.

His papers get mixed up. Frantically trying to sort them, he ends up strewing them all over the floor. His fellow Duma members help to pick them up. The chairman is trying not to laugh, but the journalists and opposition parliamentarians are roaring out loud.

Despite his eccentric professor image, Struve begins secret talks with Stolypin in order to rescue the Duma. He visits the prime minister at night, together with his Duma colleague Mikhail Chelnokov. They describe their visits as "scientific expeditions." The talks are held without the knowledge of other members of the Kadet party. Stolypin, meanwhile, is also in negotiations with the liberals, which he hides from the right for fear of being attacked. They have been ongoing for several months and address the question of how to form a stable majority in the Duma and what laws it should be allowed to pass.

In late May, after the start of an investigation into the "conspiracy," the Duma starts to discuss the agrarian law—not Stolypin's version, but its own. The Kadets intend to propose that land belonging to the landowners, the church, and the tsar should be distributed to the peasants for long-term use.

The parliamentary discussion of the Kadets' draft land reform effectively means the end of Struve's attempt to find common ground with the government. It is at this meeting that Stolypin delivers a famous speech culminating with the phrase: "You desire great upheaval. But we desire a great Russia."

On 1 June Stolypin again visits the Duma and demands that fifty-five members of the Social Democratic faction be stripped of their parliamentary immunity and taken into custody. He accuses them of having created a criminal organization bent on the violent overthrow of the state by means of a popular uprising and the establishment of a democratic republic. The Duma offers to set up a twenty-two-man commission that will deliver a response to Stolypin's demand.

That same night Struve and three other Kadet members of Duma go to see Stolypin in one final attempt to persuade him not to dissolve the

Duma, asking why he seeks to aggravate the improving relations between the government and the Duma. Stolypin replies that he sees no such improvement, but suggests a compromise: "Rid the Duma from them [the Social Democrats], and you really will see an improvement." The four Kadets answer that the Duma will not dismiss its own members. "In that case, the Duma will be dissolved and the responsibility shall be yours," says Stolypin.

The parliamentarians leave the prime minister's residence at 12:30 a.m. and head for the nearby park on Yelagin Island to drink champagne and devise a solution.

The next day a new session of the Duma opens, and Tsereteli proposes an immediate discussion of the agrarian law. The chairman objects, saying that it is not on the agenda. "When we are on the verge of a coup d'état, formalities should be discarded," objects Tsereteli. "The government has bayoneted the agenda."

But his proposal is rejected, and the session continues as planned. In the evening the Second Duma disbands, never to meet again. That night, the city is plastered with posters announcing the decree to dissolve the Duma. The round-up of its members commences, starting with Tsereteli.

Information about the secret talks between Stolypin and the Kadets leaks to the press. Soon Saint Petersburg's newspapers are printing cartoons of Struve bowing obsequiously in front of Stolypin with the caption: "Taking power by storm." Struve's party members are incensed, and his political career is effectively over.

A "SHAMELESS" LAW

By the time the Duma is dissolved, a new electoral law has not only been written, but also adopted by the government and the State Council. The text of the new law is penned by the civil servant Kryzhanovsky. To avoid any leaks to the press, Stolypin bans even ministers from having a hard copy. It is simply read out orally at a government meeting. There are no objections.

Two versions of the law are initially drafted. The more radical of them is nicknamed the "shameless law," which Nicholas II prefers.

"The State Duma must be Russian in spirit," states the text, which is published on 3 June. This means that other peoples and nationalities "should not be the arbiters of questions that are purely Russian." This primarily concerns the Caucasus and Poland, whose representatives in the

Duma are sharply reduced. Other regions "where the population is not sufficiently developed in terms of civil society" have no representatives in Duma at all (for example, Central Asia and Yakutia).

Most important of all are the changes to the proportions of representation. Henceforth, one Duma member is elected from two million peasants or sixteen thousand landowners. This means that, by default, two-thirds of the Duma is elected by the nobility and the wealthiest subjects.

For some sections of society, the date 3 June remains a symbol of state repression and disregard for the law for a long time to come. The opposition-minded part of society is one of them. The conservatives also are unhappy, but for a different reason. Whereas Stolypin wants to replace the disobedient Second Duma with a more servile one, the Union of the Russian People believes that the Duma should be abolished and the old order (before the manifesto of 17 October) restored. Dubrovin boasts that if the Union of the Russian People were to take part in the Duma elections, it would win every seat. However, it does not do so because it considers the Duma to be an unlawful institution: "I have no right to justify with my presence the existence of this assemblage that encroaches on the unlimited power of the Sovereign," he explains.

To prove to Nicholas II that the Duma is unnecessary, Dubrovin arranges regular "pilgrimages" by ordinary Russian folk to see the tsar. One of these delegations, from Tsaritsyn (today's Volgograd), is headed by the monk Iliodor, who is recommended by both the Union of the Russian People and Grigory Rasputin. Iliodor is invited to the Interior Ministry for an interview, where he preaches that the State Duma is dangerous and must be destroyed (in the case of the socialist Duma members, he means physically) and that the old dogma about the divine origin of imperial power must be adhered to. Even the tsar, says Iliodor, has no right to change this fundamental law. To Interior Ministry staff, Iliodor seems like an overzealous ragamuffin, and it is decided not to grant him an audience with Nicholas II. Stolypin orders him and his associates to leave the capital. However, Iliodor does not go away. He is given lodging by Rasputin's mentor, Archimandrite Theofan.

This episode is one of many manifestations of the conflict between Dubrovin and Stolypin. The Union of the Russian People starts campaigning vigorously against the election of a new State Duma, which gradually turns into a campaign against the prime minister, despite the fact that the government is the main source of funding for the union.

Stolypin orders that the funds be distributed not to Dubrovin, but to his deputy Vladimir Purishkevich, a former State Duma member from

Chisinau. This produces a schism inside the Union of the Russian People: Dubrovin and Purishkevich accuse each other of embezzling party funds. As a result, the latter withdraws from the organization, taking most of the government funding with him, and sets up his own right-wing party called the Union of Archangel Michael.

BEST FRIEND

On 30 April 1907 Empress Alexandra's twenty-two-year-old maid of honor, Anna Taneyeva, gets married. Her fiancé is the naval officer Aleksander Vyrubov. Although no beauty, she is a good catch, for her father is in charge of the Imperial Chancellery and she herself is very close to the empress. Marriage means that Anna will have to quit her palace employment, which upsets her. She loves the empress and the emperor, but does not like her husband at all.

A week before the wedding, Empress Alexandra asks her closest friend at that time, the Montenegrin Grand Duchess Milica, to introduce Anna to Grigory Rasputin. The Siberian mystic makes a powerful impression on the young woman.

The wedding, held at Tsarskoye Selo, is attended by the entire imperial family: Nicholas and Alexandra, their daughters, and even the tsar's sixteen-year-old cousin, Grand Duke Dmitry, who will take part in Rasputin's murder a decade later.

The Vyrubovs' matrimonial bliss does not get off to a good start. Rumors spread that on their wedding night the groom gets blind drunk and becomes abusive. His wife is so frightened that she does everything possible to avoid the bedroom. After their unsuccessful wedding night, the newlyweds effectively stop talking to each other. According to Anna, her husband is psychologically damaged and still going through a nervous breakdown after the debacle at Tsushima. He spends whole days lying in bed, refusing to see anyone. Sometimes he beats her, Anna tells her friends.

During one of her husband's fits, she calls the empress and asks for help. Alexandra immediately drapes a coat over her diamond-encrusted dress and walks out of the palace to the Vyrubovs' house (they live nearby at Tsarskoye Selo). Anna's husband is sent to Switzerland for treatment, and a year later she asks for a divorce.

This unhappy family saga will have a huge impact on Russian history. The twenty-three-year-old Anna becomes the closest friend of the thirty-six-year-old empress, and her most trusted adviser. Anna really does love

Alexandra and cannot tolerate any criticism of her. Over the next ten years she will carefully and accurately recount to the empress all the rumors and gossip going around the city, and inform her of any potential adversaries, sometimes based on the look in their eyes. For the unsociable and cloistered Alexandra, Anna Vyrubova becomes the main source of information about the outside world.

Even after her divorce, Anna continues to live at the small house in Tsarskoye Selo that she and her husband rented. This innocent-looking building turns into the nerve center of government decision-making. Vyrubova, incidentally, never regains her official position as maid of honor—she is simply a friend of the empress, an unemployed friend.

"THANK GOD, NO PARLIAMENT SO FAR"

Elections to the Third Duma get underway in September. Whereas the authorities did not intervene at all in the first election, and employed "administrative resources" in the second, now they do whatever they can to ensure a compliant Duma. "The new law handed the government a powerful and flexible tool with which to influence the elections," says the author of the "shameless" electoral law, the civil servant Kryzhanovsky.

Sergei Kryzhanovsky, previously mainly a copywriter, now becomes a full-fledged political consultant and Stolypin's right-hand man. Inside the imperial administration, he is responsible for the smooth conduct of the elections.* He summons the regional governors, instructs them to pick the "right" candidates to the State Duma, and gives them money for the election campaign. Moscow Governor Dzhunkovsky, for instance, recalls that Kryzhanovsky "opened his iron cabinet," took out some tightly packed bundles of money, and invited him to take 15,000 roubles,† saying "I hope that is sufficient." The Moscow governor replied that he did not need such a large sum ("It never occurred to me that it was a bribe," says Dzhunkovsky). In the end, Kryzhanovsky gives him 5,000 roubles‡ with the

---

*Kryzhanovsky can be considered a pioneer in organizing Russian elections—in the early twenty-first century Russia it will be done almost the same way. The Presidential Administration knows the desired outcome in advance and is strictly regulating the process. There is nothing that can stop public officials from achieving their target result. Compared to the results of Vladislav Surkov and Vyacheslav Volodin the achievements of Kryzhanovsky, who combined moderate bribes and slight rigging, seem to be quite small.
† About $197,750 in 2017.
‡ About $65,917 in 2017.

parting words: "More is available if required." Other regional governors walk away with far larger sums in their pockets.

As a result, the overwhelming majority of the parties are loyal to Stolypin, including the Union of 17 October, led by Alexander Guchkov, and various right-wing parties. There are no supporters of Dubrovin in the new Duma, but Vladimir Purishkevich wins a seat. And, for the first time, Pavel Milyukov, the leader of the Kadet faction, crosses the threshold.

The new Duma assembles on 20 November and immediately demonstrates that it is unlike its predecessors. In his opening speech, Stolypin accuses the left of "open robbery" and of "corrupting the younger generation," saying that it will be countered by force. The members applaud.

A priority issue for the Third Duma is the unprofitability of Russia's railways. Milyukov, donning the mantle of the Duma's main, albeit cautious, opponent of the government, tells Finance Minister Kokovtsov that he should set up a parliamentary commission to look into the matter. The minister dismisses the suggestion out of hand: "We don't have a parliament so far, thank God." The left boos and whistles, while the right, recalls Kokovtsov, greets his words with "thunderous applause."

But it is not the finance minister but Duma Chairman Khomyakov who provokes Stolypin's ire. Calling for order, Khomyakov says: "I had no way of preventing the finance minister from uttering such an unfortunate expression." Stolypin believes that Duma members have no right to denigrate ministerial remarks. The chairman is forced to apologize for his "incorrect" tone in respect of the minister.

At the same time, the trial of the fifty-five arrested socialist members of the previous Duma begins. It is held behind closed doors to "maintain public order." As a sign of protest, the defendants walk out of the courtroom. They are found guilty *in absentia* and sent to prison. One of the prosecution's main arguments is the RSDLP's calls for revolution in Russia made at their congresses abroad.

The signatories of the Vyborg Manifesto, all of them members of the First Duma, are also tried. They are sentenced to three months in prison. When the former Duma Chairman Muromtsev leaves the courtroom, he is showered with flowers by well-wishers.

|| Chapter 9 ||

SERGEI DIAGHILEV

in which art fan Sergei Diaghilev and
religious fanatic Sergei Trufanov (Iliodor)
try to stay independent from the state
and even use it to their advantage

RUSSIAN CHIC IN PARIS

In October 1906, an exhibition of Russian art opens at the Grand Palais in Paris. The main guest of the *vernissage* is the fifty-nine-year-old Grand Duke Vladimir, the president of the Imperial Academy of Arts and Emperor Nicholas II's uncle, one of the most senior and respected members of the House of Romanov. Until recently, he commanded the Petersburg Military District, in which capacity he opened fire on the Bloody Sunday procession in 1905. However, in Paris he is known as a patron of Russian art, not a military despot.

A year ago, Vladimir took great offense at Nicholas and Alexandra for not approving the marriage of his son Kirill and then expelling him from Russia. As a result, Vladimir and his entire family now spend most of their time in Europe.

The French have never seen an exhibition quite like it: the exposition begins with a collection of religious icons (unprecedented), followed by eighteenth-century art and contemporary works by Vrubel, Serov, Benois, and Bakst. The whole thing is the brainchild of the thirty-four-year-old Sergei Diaghilev.

The public reaction is immense. The critics are raving, and even the French president and other luminaries attend. The grand duke is highly satisfied, so much so that Diaghilev convinces him to consolidate the success by treating the French to some Russian opera. The grand duke agrees.

Not all of Diaghilev's friends are ecstatic about his venture: Benois, for instance, says that it is risky to take money from the grand dukes. The former imperial darling Serov, who since Bloody Sunday has not worked for the Romanovs, considers it unseemly to have dealings with an "executioner." Diaghilev replies that it is impossible to put on exhibitions abroad without big money, and no one except the imperial family is prepared to splash out.*

Meanwhile, Diaghilev takes the exhibition to Berlin, where he arranges a private viewing for Kaiser Wilhelm II. Spotting a portrait by Bakst of Diaghilev himself, the German emperor inquires about the identity of the elderly lady propped up in the background. Diaghilev replies that it is his old nanny Dunya. Wilhelm takes a great interest in how Dunya is getting on.

---

*In the early twenty-first century Russian cultural society will once again be wondering if it is ethically fine for cultural workers to receive state funding. Most people say yes: just like Diaghilev, they believe it to be impossible to find any other sources of funding, while funding cultural development of the country is one of the governmental duties.

Diaghilev enjoys the life of a European celebrity.

The grand duke likes splendor, and Diaghilev is happy to indulge his sponsor's tastes. Vladimir continues to provide funding (increasingly from the state budget, not his own pocket). When in 1908 Diaghilev stages a production of *Boris Godunov* at the Grand Opera in Paris, with Chaliapin in the title role, the luxury of the scenery and costumes surpasses anything that has gone before. "Let the grandeur drive the French out of their minds," Nikolai Rimsky-Korsakov describes his plan for staging Mussorgsky's unfinished opera, which he has undertaken to complete. The performance turns into a grotesque, exotic carnival revolving around an idealized view of Russian antiquity. Grand Duke Vladimir likes the costumes so much that he decides to put them on display at the Hermitage.

The grand duke's favor rescues Diaghilev. The cost of staging *Boris Godunov* at the Grand Opera is so vast that it cannot possibly be recouped. Russian cultural officials demand that Diaghilev be prosecuted for embezzlement. But the grand duke intercedes and thwarts any legal action: the sum of 100,000 francs* owed by Diaghilev to his contractors is ultimately paid out of the Russian treasury.

HOLY TERROR

The left bank of the Seine at this time is home to Diaghilev's cousin, Dima Filosofov, and his associates Zinaida Gippius and Dmitry Merezhkovsky. Having moved to Paris, they continue to invent their own version of Christianity. Back in 1905, Merezhkovsky propounded the notion that "autocracy comes from the Antichrist" and later that "the Russian revolution is not only political, but religious." In Paris they make the acquaintance of Boris Savinkov and other émigré revolutionaries.

For the self-styled *Troyebratstvo* ("brotherhood of three"), the revolution is a new religion. Merezhkovsky pens an article entitled "Devil or God?"—essentially a response to the late Dostoevsky's novel *Demons*, the title of which was a reference to its revolutionary protagonists. Merezhkovsky highlights what he describes as the torment of the Socialist-Revolutionaries, comparing them with the early Christians in the Roman Empire: "They endured torture and death in order to bring the Good News."

The terrorist Boris Savinkov is as far removed from Christianity as can be, yet Zinaida is fascinated by him. For hours on end, she questions him

---

* About $487,783 in 2017.

about how it feels to kill someone. In between assassinations, Savinkov is fond of composing verse. He shows some of his poems to Gippius, who assures him that he has talent. She bestows him with the pseudonym "Ropshin" and persuades him to pursue his literary endeavors.

The justification of violence in the name of revolution is the main theme of Gippius, Merezhkovsky, and Filosofov's symposia. Together, they write a philosophical treatise under the title "Tsar and Revolution," which begins with a political analysis of the situation in Russia by Filosofov, before developing into an unprecedented justification of terrorism by Gippius.

In his article "Tsar-Pope," Filosofov concludes that Russia is a theocratic state, wherein the emperor is the head of the Orthodox Church, just like the Roman pope leads the Catholic Church. Hence, any struggle against the regime must aim to destroy Orthodoxy. Nicholas II cannot grant a constitution, writes Filosofov, because for him it would be a betrayal of his faith. Orthodoxy is the soft underbelly of Russian autocracy.

But the most seminal article in the collection, which is called *Revolution and Violence*, is penned solely by Gippius. In it, she postulates that murders committed in the name of revolution can—and should—be justified. After all, she remarks cold-bloodedly, there are situations, such as duels or wars, where killing is natural. What is more, killings "committed for the sake of the future and inspired by reason and moral feeling" are acts of holy self-sacrifice. In her opinion, terror that strikes a blow to autocracy is godly and pious. "Tsar and Revolution" goes down a storm in Paris. Merezhkovsky's lecture "On Violence" at the Sorbonne attracts so many people that a larger hall has to be found.

Meanwhile, Boris Savinkov is obsessed with a new idea. Disillusioned with the previous tactic of terror, which involved small, secret cells that spent years tracking down victims, he wants to raise terror to a new level. The situation in Russia demands a struggle on a grander scale with an army of terrorists and a "secret order" of assassins led by Gershuni, assisted by Savinkov and Azef. However, neither Gershuni nor Azef likes the plan. Azef (himself a double agent) says that any more than fifty people in the organization will lead inevitably to police penetration. The central committee of the Socialist-Revolutionary Party declines to support Savinkov.

Instead, Gershuni proposes that all efforts be focused on one target: the tsar. The successful terrorist attacks against Sipyagin, Plehve, and Grand Duke Sergei forced the government to adopt reforms, but were followed by a clampdown. Now the time is ripe to set up a militant organization with the aim of assassinating Nicholas II.

Gershuni's plan takes shape in October 1907. At the same time, he receives a disturbing letter from fellow party members in Saratov alleging that Azef is a police agent. Gershuni, the party leader, trusts Azef like a second self, and cannot believe that his chosen successor, the man who has organized all the most high-profile terrorist attacks so far, is a traitor. Yet neither can he dismiss the allegation out of hand. So he asks his colleagues to investigate further.

Meanwhile, the Petersburg police are busy rounding up a large terrorist cell for plotting to commit the most audacious attack in Russian history. Members of the Socialist-Revolutionary Party were planning to blow up the State Council, the upper house of the Russian parliament. They are sure that they were betrayed by one of their own.

Gershuni's health after his Siberian exile is failing. He goes to Switzerland, where he is diagnosed with advanced lung sarcoma. The news demoralizes the Parisian SRs. In March 1908 they receive a visit from the "Sherlock Holmes of the revolution" Vladimir Burtsev, a journalist who specializes in exposing illegal policing methods. Burtsev tells the party's central committee that he is in possession of evidence that unmasks Azef as an agent. Burtsev even hypothesizes that the SRs' entire military organization is a police operation, and that almost all the party's acts of terrorism were secretly sanctioned by the authorities.

For the SR leaders, Burtsev's words seem hysterical. Chernov and his comrades lay into him, finding hundreds of contradictions in his investigation and describing the main source as a misinformer. Nevertheless, Burtsev's theory is reported to the sickly Gershuni. To disprove the charges, Gershuni wants to go to Russia with Azef and assassinate the tsar together. Most likely they will both die, but at least it will clear the militant organization of the false accusations. But just days later Gershuni passes away.

Thus, within a brief interval, Russia's most powerful opposition party is deprived of its two most charismatic leaders—Gregory Gershuni and Mikhail Gotz. It is Viktor Chernov who becomes the most significant of the party leaders. The Saratov investigation ordered by Gershuni is discontinued.

WALKING ON THIN ICE

In the winter of 1907 Nicholas II summons the head of the Moscow secret police, Colonel Gerasimov, to find out why he has not dealt with the terrorists. The tsar is concerned about the ongoing assassinations of officials.

According to rank and protocol, Gerasimov does not have the right to sit in the presence of the tsar, so both men spend the nearly two-hour-long conversation standing by the window, looking out over the park.

Nicholas asks why Gerasimov has not managed to destroy all the terrorists. Gerasimov's answer is simple: Finland. The Finnish border is only two hours away from Saint Petersburg; the revolutionaries are able to commit crimes in the Russian capital and hop across the border where the Finnish police are hostile to the Russian authorities and are themselves revolutionary. Russian police officials investigating in Finland are routinely detained themselves and sent back to Saint Petersburg, complains Gerasimov.

Nicholas is astonished. What should be done, he asks. Gerasimov advises him to annul the constitution granted to Finland: "I am ready to do everything to put an end to this intolerable situation. I shall talk to Stolypin," replies the tsar.

Surprisingly, despite having been part of the Russian Empire for a century, Finland in 1907 is the freest "country" in Europe. Back in 1807, Emperor Alexander I had concluded an alliance with France (against Britain) and joined the "continental blockade" of the British Isles. Since Sweden was an ally of Britain, Russia launched an attack on the former, and by 1809 the Swedish territory of Finland was in Russian hands. It was Russia's "fee" for not interfering in Napoleon's conquest of Europe. By 1812, with Europe duly conquered, Napoleon took the fateful decision to invade Russia. When the dust and cannon balls settled, Napoleon's empire was no more, and there was nothing to prevent Finland from remaining an autonomous principality within Russia. The reformer Alexander II allowed the Finnish Sejm (parliament) to convene, although he did not sign a Finnish constitution.

Problems arose at the turn of the century, when Plehve became the state secretary of Finland. He, along with Governor-General Bobrikov, launched a Russification program in Finland that poisoned Finnish minds against Russia. In 1904 both Plehve and Bobrikov were assassinated before the end of their reforms. Come 1905, Finland was a revolutionary breeding ground.

The "Finnish revolution" is a considerable success. By 1906 all of Bobrikov and Plehve's repressive laws have been abolished, and Nicholas II has signed the newly drafted Finnish constitution: Finland is the first country in Europe to implement universal adult suffrage, including votes for women. It is effectively a separate country, a kind of "domestic offshore territory."

But in 1907 the pendulum swings back. Nicholas II asks Stolypin to "put an end to the intolerable situation," and in October that same year the Russian government dissolves the Sejm and starts to "cleanse" Finland of Russian revolutionaries, who all relocate to Western Europe.

In December 1907 Lenin leaves Helsinki. On board the train he suspects that he is under police surveillance and jumps off. The next part of the journey involves traversing the Gulf of Finland. The ice is thin, yet Lenin decides to make the crossing on foot—a Jesus Christ moment later immortalized by Soviet historians. The ice is cracking underfoot, and Lenin is sure that he will go under. There is only one thought running through his head: what a stupid way to die! A month later he arrives in the tranquil Geneva. Things look hopeless: there is political stability in Russia, and the revolution has been suppressed. Lenin starts to think that this gloomy backwater will be his final resting place.

In May 1908 Stolypin submits his plan for solving the Finnish question to the State Duma. For generations, Finns have considered their country a special legal state. However, says Stolypin, Russia also has rights: not for nothing did Peter the Great "shed streams of Russian blood" on the shores of the Gulf of Finland in constructing his mighty capital. Losing Finland "would inflict incalculable damage on the Russian state," since "Russian moral and spiritual power has been invested in the cliffs and waters of Finland," he asserts. The Duma members applaud and vote to grant the government sweeping powers with respect to Finland. Within two years Finnish autonomy is almost a distant memory.

Like his predecessors Plehve and Bobrikov, Stolypin will not live to reap what he has sown. Lenin, for his part, is destined to return to Finland in 1917, whereupon the Finns will do everything they can to help him seize power.

The open political debates of 1905-6 were seriously limited by 1907. The Third Duma, under the thumb of the authorities, is "not a place for discussion." All conversations are now conducted secretly behind closed doors, often inside private clubs.

The disillusionment with politics revives an old pastime—Masonic lodges. Freemasonry first appeared in Russia in the 1700s, and by the early nineteenth century it is an important cultural trend, as described by Tolstoy in *War and Peace*. However, in 1822 Alexander I forbids all secret societies and the tradition is curtailed. But eighty-five years on, after the dissolution of the First Duma, the Russian liberal intelligentsia once again imports

Freemasonry from France. Following the dissolution of the Second Duma, clandestine Masonic life strikes deeper roots.

On 8 May 1908, the Freemasons Bertrand Seneschal and Georges Boule arrive in Saint Petersburg to officially open the "Polar Star" Masonic lodge in Russia. Freemasons in the capital hold meetings inside a rented apartment directly above the office of the Duma faction of the Kadets. The French duo also opens the "Revival" Masonic lodge in Moscow.

Rumors about the Freemasons spread faster than the lodges themselves. The right-wing press comes up with the term "Judeo-Masonic" to describe almost anyone who is not a monarchist. The Black Hundreds cannot stand the Jews or Western intellectuals. The Duma, too, often blames Russia's woes on the Masons, although there are probably fewer than a hundred of them in the whole empire.

Nicholas II reads the right-wing press and believes it. He asks Gerasimov about the link between the revolution and Freemasonry. Gerasimov replies that the Masons have nothing to do with it, but the emperor does not believe it. He orders an investigation into Russian and foreign Masons, and instructs the police to set up a special commission to counter the movement.

There is a real stir among the Masons when one of their "brothers," Prince Sergei Urusov, makes it known that Yevgeny Azef is a police agent. Urusov learns about it from his brother-in-law and best friend, the ex-police chief Alexei Lopukhin, Azef's former boss. The news horrifies the Masons. They are not so much worried about the SRs as fearful for themselves, because their ranks could also be dotted with agents, but they do warn the SRs of the impending danger.

MASONS AGAINST CONSPIRACY

Nikolai Morozov of the Moscow lodge, a former member of People's Will, is entrusted with the task of warning the SRs of Azef's treachery. In May 1908, he travels to Paris and meets with his People's Will boyhood friend Mark Natanson, now a member of the central committee of the Socialist-Revolutionary Party. The latter refuses to listen and advises Morozov to remain silent about Azef; otherwise, despite his past accomplishments, he will become an enemy of the Socialist-Revolutionaries.

Nevertheless, Natanson sets up a commission that carries out a six-month investigation that fails to unmask a traitor. "Sherlock" Burtsev continues to voice his suspicions and in August, at their next congress in

London, the SR leaders decide to hold an internal party trial of the journalist (an "honor trial") for having slandered the militant organization by describing it as the brainchild of the Interior Ministry. Three of the most respected party veterans are selected as the "judges": Prince Peter Kropotkin (sixty-one years old, thirty-two in exile abroad), German Lopatin (sixty-three years old, over thirty in prison and exile abroad), and Vera Figner (fifty-six years old, sentenced to death, then spent twenty years in prison). The opinion of these living legends is law.

The decision to hold an "honor trial" in Paris is not to everyone's liking. Savinkov, for instance, is against giving Burtsev's insinuations the oxygen of publicity.

But Chernov and Azef insist on the trial. Savinkov suggests that he and Azef go together to Russia: if they are arrested or even executed, it will restore the honor of the militant organization, says Savinkov. But Azef declines. He believes that only by trying Burtsev in front of the party "will the absurdity of all these suspicions be revealed."

Meanwhile, news of the forthcoming trial leaks to the Parisian public. The Freemasons, in particular, are outraged. They try to frame a plan to smoke out Azef and help Burtsev, who needs a witness whose testimony could turn the tide—for instance, his source, Alexei Lopukhin, the former police chief and Azef's former handler.

In early September, the Masons send Burtsev a letter informing him of Lopukhin's whereabouts in Germany. The so-called Russian Sherlock Holmes tracks him down and eventually catches him on board a train from Cologne to Berlin. They have a chat.

The train is already approaching Berlin when Burtsev opens up that he has unmasked a mole inside the Socialist-Revolutionary Party. Burtsev only wants to hear yes or no, and cannot believe his luck when Lopukhin mouths the real name of the police agent—Yevno Azef. No one but Lopukhin refers to Azef, his former protégé, by the name in his passport.

REVELING IN REVEL

On 27 May 1908 King Edward VII of the United Kingdom, who goes by the nickname of "Europe's uncle," pays an official visit to Russia. He is the son of Queen Victoria and the uncle of both Empress Alexandra of Russia and Kaiser Wilhelm II of Germany, while his spouse, Queen Consort Alexandra, is the aunt of Emperor Nicholas II of Russia and the sister of his mother, Maria Feodorovna. The two monarchs intend to discuss the new military alliance between Russia, Britain, and France: the Triple Entente.

The visit causes considerable consternation. Edward VII wants to go to Saint Petersburg, but Nicholas II is against the idea: "In England he's used to strolling around wherever he wants, and will do the same here. I know him. He'll walk to the theatre and the ballet, and probably go and inspect some factories and shipyards." The tsar is worried because the Russian capital is full of terrorists. In the end, the meeting is transferred to the quiet city of Revel (today's Tallinn in Estonia).

But the terrorists are on the ball. Long before Edward VII's visit, Azef informs Gerasimov of a plot to assassinate Nicholas II—and Revel happens to be one of their favored locations. There are two options: either attack the imperial train or assassinate the tsar during a visit to the country estate of one of his courtiers. Azef manages to thwart both attempts, but informs Gerasimov afterwards that he is tired of working for the police and wants to "live in peace." Gerasimov does not try to talk him out of it and even offers to keep paying him a thousand roubles a month.*

THE TRAGEDY OF THE YUSUPOVS

On 22 June 1908 the richest family in Russia (the Yusupovs, not the Romanovs) suffers a tragedy. The twenty-five-year-old Nikolai Yusupov, the elder son of Princess Zinaida Yusupova, the sole heiress to the family fortune, and Count Felix Sumarokov-Elston (who took his wife's name to become Prince Yusupov), is killed in a duel.

The reason for the duel is heartbreak. Nikolai's parents forbade him from marrying his beloved Marina, so she married another. The lovelorn Nikolai turns to an occultist by the name of Shinsky for help. The mystic says that Nikolai's guardian angel is calling upon him to challenge his rival to a duel.

After the death of her elder son, Zinaida Yusupova is close to insanity. Nikolai was the pride and joy of the family. Now the Yusupovs' only son is the twenty-one-year-old Felix. His parents make every effort to "correct" his behavior, which is uncommon, even for a spoilt heir.

On one occasion as teenagers, Felix and his elder brother were thinking of ways to amuse themselves (since they were too young to visit the local amusements). Nikolai's friend, a girl of humble origin called Polenka, had

---

* About $13,183 in 2017.

the idea of dressing Felix up as a woman, which the latter greatly enjoyed: "I realized I could go anywhere dressed as a woman," he recalls. "From that moment on, I led a double life. By day I was a schoolboy, by night an elegant dame."

Some friends of their parents learn about Felix's predilection, but Nikolai persuades them to keep silent. Felix's transvestite ways continue. Eventually, Prince Yusupov learns about his son's behavior. Mortified by the shame, he says that hard labor in Siberia would be the only fitting punishment. "I have always resented the injustice shown to those who behave differently," says Felix Yusupov. "You can reproach homosexual love, but not the lovers themselves, because for them normal relations are repugnant. Is it their fault that they are created like that?"

After the death of his brother, Felix is sent for "re-education" at the home of Zinaida's closest friend, Grand Duchess Elizabeth, the sister of Empress Alexandra and the founder of the Marfo-Mariinsky Convent. Felix loves Aunt Ella and helps with her charity work. At the same time, he forms a close bond with Grand Duke Dmitry, Ella's nephew, whom she is also bringing up. Dmitry is four years younger than Felix and effectively replaces Nikolai as his brother.

They spend their summers in Crimea and winters at Tsarskoye Selo. On several occasions, Felix is summoned by Empress Alexandra to discuss his future. He says that he wants to study in Oxford. "Every self-respecting man," says Alexandra, "must serve either the military or the court." Felix says that he will inherit a huge fortune, including land and factories, and that managing it properly will be of service to Russia. Alexandra replies that Russia is not as important as the tsar, because "the tsar and the fatherland are synonymous." Right on cue, Nicholas II enters the room. "Felix is an incorrigible revolutionary," she informs her husband.

KILLING THE EMPEROR

It is 23 September 1908 in Kronstadt. Aleksei Lopukhin has just admitted to Vladimir Burtsev that Azef is a police agent, but no one yet knows about it. There is a month to go before the SRs' "honor trial" of Burtsev in Paris. Meanwhile, at the Russian navy's main base at Kronstadt, Emperor Nicholas II is inspecting the new cruiser *Rurik*, which was built in Glasgow. Neither the emperor nor his attendants are aware that two crewmembers are recruits of the SR militant organization. Their task is to shoot the tsar at point-blank range.

The preparations for the operation have lasted all summer. First of all, Savinkov visits Glasgow. He and another experienced terrorist, Pyotr Karpovich, who in 1900 assassinated Russian Education Minister Bogolepov, interview potential regicides. They find two volunteers willing to assist. The initial plan is for the sailors to find a secluded place on the ship for either Savinkov or Karpovich to live while the vessel sails to Russia, after which the stowaway will assassinate the tsar during the handover ceremony.

Soon the double agent Azef joins the planning phase of the operation. Having discussed everything, the SR leaders conclude that the chances of remaining unseen and then successfully killing the tsar are minimal. It is then that the sailor volunteers announce that they themselves are willing to assassinate Nicholas. As crewmembers, there will be no need for them to hide.

Savinkov is afraid that they "will bottle it" at the critical moment, but in the end sanctions the mission. The men are issued weapons. Savinkov returns to his fellow SRs and his friends the Merezhkovskys in Paris, while Azef goes to see his family in the south of France. Both await the day for Nicholas II to climb aboard the *Rurik* and come face to face with his killers.

Azef says nothing about the plan to Gerasimov; otherwise the inspection of the cruiser would simply be cancelled. Azef seems to be preparing for the "honor trial" in Paris, in which respect a successful regicide in Kronstadt would be a decisive argument against Burtsev's claims.

According to the plan, the first sailor is due to offer Nicholas a glass of lemonade and shoot. But he freezes, as Savinkov feared. The second sailor takes the tsar on a tour of the holds. He, too, fails to pull the trigger. Savinkov says later that he is not surprised: "I knew they'd bottle it."

On 10 October, the "honor trial" of Burtsev begins in Paris—it is important because if he loses, the SRs will be permitted to kill him (according to their own laws). Azef is not present, but his "lawyers" Chernov, Savinkov, and Natanson are in fighting spirit. They exalt Azef as a glorious freedom fighter *nonpareil*.

"That may be true," replies Burtsev, "but only if he is an honest revolutionary. I contend that he is a provocateur, a liar and an utter scoundrel!"

The "judges" are gradually inclining to side with Burtsev. Shortly after the start of the trial, on 11 November, Lopukhin, back in Saint Petersburg, receives a secret visit from Azef himself, who demands that Lopukhin retract his statement. Lopukhin, fearing that Azef has come to kill him, denies ever having spoken to Burtsev. The even-more terrified Azef starts to think that someone else has betrayed him. Leaving Lopukhin's apartment, Azef goes to see his friend Gerasimov, who describes him as "haggard and pale, with the look of a hunted beast."

"It's over," wails Azef. "I'm done for. All my life I've lived in perpetual danger. . . . And now, just when I've decided to put a stop to this wretched game, they're going to kill me." He remembers what he himself did to Gapon, who was only suspected of collaborating with the police.

Gerasimov says goodbye to Azef, gives him 3000 roubles,* and a few fake passports. But Azef does not run—he returns to the SRs in Paris. Meanwhile, a member of the central committee of the Socialist-Revolutionary Party, by the name of Argunov, travels to Saint Petersburg at the request of the "judges" to interview the "key witness." On 18 November Lopukhin tells him about Azef's recent visit.

Lopukhin is afraid that Gerasimov and Azef, both professional killers, will try to silence him. In search of protection, he writes to friends and Stolypin that the head of the secret police is on his tail and, on 23 November, departs for London.

On 23 December 1908, the SRs are due to decide Azef's fate. Lopukhin repeats his testimony and most of the leadership, including Savinkov, votes to kill Azef. But first, it is decided to interrogate him one last time: Chernov, Savinkov, and others go to Azef's home. He is waiting for them.

His comrades have already voted to murder him, but now they give him a reprieve. They tell him that he has been exposed and demand a confession. Azef denies everything. They give him twelve hours to rethink, and then leave. It is all a rather absurd, psychological game. Savinkov, who three years ago together with Azef forced Pinhas Rutenberg to kill his closest friend, Georgy Gapon, now hesitates to kill his own friend Azef, against whom far more serious allegations have been made.

Only now does Azef collect his belongings and bid his wife farewell. He lies, telling her that he is going to Berlin to work as an engineer. In fact, he goes to see his mistress, with whom he has been cohabiting for several years. Azef who has two wives at the same time obviously loves them both and means to be sincere with both of them.

The SRs are demoralized. Some party members, desperate to kill Azef, hire a villa in Italy and try to lure him there, as Gapon was once enticed and murdered at a dacha in Ozerki. They need someone he trusts as bait, like Savinkov. But the latter wants to forget all about the incident. Azef eventually settles in Berlin and continues to travel around Europe. No one pursues him.

---

* About $39,550 in 2017.

The unmasking of Azef makes the headlines in Russia and across Europe. The trial of Burtsev ends with an apology and the resignation of the entire central committee of the Socialist-Revolutionary Party. As if that were not enough, both Savinkov and Chernov are now accused of treachery.

Horrified, many prominent members leave the party. Barely a week later Stolypin reports what has happened to the tsar. Nicholas II is struck by Lopukhin's betrayal—through the Azef connection, it seems that the police are complicit in the assassinations of Plehve and others. Lopukhin is arrested on charges of divulging state secrets, and his trial is held in April 1909. "I hope the sentence is hard labor," writes the tsar on the case file brought to him. The former police chief is indeed sentenced to five years' hard labor. The verdict outrages many, including some officials.

During the preceding two months, Azef is the subject of much debate in the Duma—perhaps the most candid discussions in the history of Russian parliamentarianism. What is the purpose of the special services, asks one member. It seems that they spend vast sums of public money on solving crimes that they themselves have helped to commit!

There at the meeting is Stolypin, who argues long and hard that the Interior Ministry does not have blood on its hands, that Azef did not organize any terrorist attacks and that the government does not engage in the tactics of provocation. However, he does admit that some occasional ugliness is required in order to maintain stability. The government will renounce such tactics when the time permits, and not before, says Stolypin. It is perhaps the best speech of his career: "We, the government, build scaffolding to facilitate the construction process. Our adversaries describe this scaffolding as an eyesore and try to shake it to the ground. The scaffolding will collapse and perhaps crush us all, but if that be so, let it happen when the edifice of the renovated, liberated Russia is already standing. That time is coming, gentlemen, for not only strength is on our side, but truth."

This metaphor will echo throughout the speeches of Russian leaders for decades to come.* In them, the "ugly scaffolding" of government is cited as a temporary but necessary phenomenon required to guarantee future prosperity, while "strength and truth" are always quoted as the bedrock of state power. Stolypin's promise is never fulfilled: "ugliness" does not give

---

*Pyotr Stolypin will be one of the most respected pre-revolutionary politicians in Russia in the early twenty-first century. In 2011 Vladimir Putin orders a monument to Stolypin erected in front of the Russian Government building and even donates his month's salary for it.

way to "freedom from injustice," but is aggravated, spawning ever-greater lawlessness. The scaffolding is never removed.

AS PURE AS CRYSTAL

Having lost their eyes and ears inside the terrorist underground, the secret police are forced to rely on other senses, namely touch. The authorities believe that the SRs' militant organization has been defanged, but know that fanatical individuals and groupings not subordinate to the central committee still exist. Only now there is no way to find out about them. The tsar's security detail is particularly anxious. The new court commandant asks Gerasimov to investigate a group that sometimes gathers in the small house belonging to the former lady-in-waiting Anna Vyrubova in Tsarskoye Selo. Nicholas and Alexandra themselves are often seen there, in the company of a suspicious character, a peasant by the name of Grigory Rasputin. The court commandant puts a watch over him, for he might be a terrorist.

Gerasimov compiles two dossiers: the first about Rasputin's youth spent in Siberia, the second about his life in Saint Petersburg. The Siberian dossier tells that Rasputin led an "immoral lifestyle" in his hometown, while the surveillance in Saint Petersburg indicates that he keeps the company of prostitutes, going with them to the bathhouse. The police question the women, who, according to Gerasimov, describe him as a "dirty, coarse libertine." However, there are no serious charges against Rasputin. He does not even seem to drink (or at least get drunk). However, on the basis of this patchy information Gerasimov concludes that "such a man cannot be allowed within a 'cannon shot' of the tsar's palace," and duly reports to Stolypin. The prime minister agrees: "The life of the imperial family must be as pure as crystal. If a shadow is cast over the tsar in the national consciousness, the moral authority of the autocrat will perish and misfortune will ensue," says Stolypin, and decides to have a word in the imperial ear.

Nicholas II assures Stolypin that he will no longer meet with Rasputin, whereupon the prime minister orders that the preacher be exiled from Saint Petersburg. The police continue to follow Rasputin and decide to arrest him on his return from Tsarskoye Selo, right at the train station. As if sensing the danger, he leaps out of the carriage, hurls himself into a cab, and dashes to the grand palace of his patroness, Grand Duchess Milica of Montenegro. The police keep watch over the palace for several weeks, but he does not step foot outside. The decision to exile Rasputin is eventually forgotten.

DIRTY DANCES

Grand Duke Vladimir continues to offer Diaghilev his patronage. Both he and his wife, Grand Duchess Maria Pavlovna (known as Miechen inside the family), revel in the role of European patrons. Miechen, a princess from a small German principality, is a highly ambitious and influential society lady.

After his first Parisian success, Diaghilev announces that he wants to bring the Russian ballet and opera to the city. His friend Benois writes a libretto for a short ballet entitled *Le Pavillon d'Armide*. The main role in *Le Pavillon d'Armide* is intended for Matilda Kschessinskaya, the thirty-five-year-old prima ballerina of the Imperial Theatres. In her youth, Matilda was the mistress of Nicholas II (before he became emperor), and now she simultaneously cohabits with two grand dukes: the thirty-five-year-old Sergei and the twenty-five-year-old Andrei. Grand Duke Andrei is the youngest son of the arts patron Grand Duke Vladimir and his wife Miechen, and is his rival Sergei's nephew-once-removed. In 1902 Kschessinskaya gives birth to a baby boy, Vova (Vladimir), who is considered the son of Grand Duke Sergei (although Andrei thinks otherwise). Kschessinskaya's remarkable fusion with the imperial family makes her the most powerful *artiste* in Russia.

At the last minute, the capricious prima donna pulls out of the production: she considers *Le Pavillon d'Armide* to be beneath her. Urgently searching for a replacement, Diaghilev stumbles upon the rebellious twenty-six-year-old Anna Pavlova, a friend of the choreographer Mikhail Fokine and an active participant in the theatre strike of 1905. Seeing her on stage, Diaghilev enthuses to Benois: "That's what we'll take to Paris."

The 1909 tour program features several ballets. Diaghilev wants to bring the influential Kschessinskaya back on board, but Fokine is opposed—Kschessinskaya let him down, so he prefers Pavlova. But Diaghilev gets his way. Kschessinskaya, now seemingly not averse to the production, is offered the main role in *Le Pavillon d'Armide*, while Pavlova is given the title role in *Giselle*, which, however, Kschessinskaya takes as an insult.

On 4 February 1909, Grand Duke Vladimir dies at the age of sixty-two. Diaghilev long mourns his patron's death. At the funeral he meets Nicholas

II, who, crossing himself, says: "He was very fond of you." On 11 March, with Diaghilev having won over the tsar, his troupe begins rehearsing at the Winter Palace, right inside the Hermitage Theatre. The conditions are luxurious—royal footmen bring the ballet dancers tea and chocolate during breaks. However, the rehearsals last only one week: Grand Duke Andrei, the son of the late patron and the lover of Kschessinskaya, writes to Nicholas that Diaghilev is a wily operator "who is smearing the good name of my late father." On 17 March the tsar decides to ban the rehearsals in the Hermitage Theatre and to stop paying for the sets and costumes. Kschessinskaya immediately refuses to take part in the enterprise, again.

Diaghilev runs to his patroness Miechen. It is a strange family conflict: the late Vladimir's wife Miechen supports Diaghilev, while his son Andrei is trying to ruin him.

Nicholas takes the side of Andrei and Kschessinskaya. Diaghilev is suddenly deprived of everything. He is forced to find a new rehearsal room, and his artists take their belongings there on foot. The paparazzi have a field day. Their main target is the twenty-five-year-old dancer Ida Rubinstein, the heiress of a wealthy family of Jewish bankers.

Not a classically trained ballerina, Ida is known for arranging and funding her own private performances. In late 1908, she performs a ballet version of Oscar Wilde's biblically themed *Salome*. It is banned immediately.

Rubinstein manages to give only one performance, on 20 December 1908. During the "Dance of the Seven Veils,"[*] she strips practically naked, wearing only a dress made from beads. The public is shocked. It is a blatant attempt to offend the public's religious feelings. The police burst into the hall and seize the papier-mâché head of John the Baptist (who is remarkably unmoved by it all). Soon Diaghilev invites Rubinstein to join his troupe to add a bit of scandal to the upcoming tour. The papers write about indecent rehearsals, describing the whole project as sordid and anti-government.

TWO BELIEVERS AND THEIR RELIGIOUS FEELINGS

The violation of religious feelings is, in fact, part of the wider struggle between Orthodox conservatives and liberal intellectuals,[†] which is the

---

[*] The dance performed by Salome for King Herod.
[†] Which continues to this day: in 2015 Russia's culture minister sacked a Siberian theatre director after the Russian Orthodox Church criticized his modern staging of Wagner's *Tannhäuser*.

main political motif of 1909. The former are becoming so influential that they are beginning to take on the secular authorities, whom they accuse of displaying a criminal lack of spirituality.

It spills over on 20 December 1908, when the Jewish Ida Rubinstein blasphemously prances around naked with the head of John the Baptist on the very same day that John of Kronstadt, a member of the Holy Synod and still the most popular priest in Russia, passes away.

John of Kronstadt is not only the most commercially successful priest-cum-healer, raising hundreds of thousands of roubles,* but also an important political figure. He is the spiritual symbol of the Union of the Russian People and the Black Hundreds, and is the main enemy of the "godless intellectuals." In the last few months of his life, John prays that Leo Tolstoy will die before he does. God is unimpressed; Tolstoy outlives Kronstadt by nearly two years.

During his life, John acquires more than a few acolytes. One is Rasputin, who is flashy but uninterested in politics. Another is the monk Iliodor who, on the contrary, traveled to Saint Petersburg in 1906 to demand the

---

*Equivalent to millions of dollars in 2017.

dissolution (and execution) of the Duma. Gerasimov, the hardboiled police chief, considers him to be a dangerous fanatic.

Iliodor is an active member of the Union of the Russian people, a preacher, and a writer, who curses all Jews and intellectuals. The monk's position is so radical that the Holy Synod forbids him from engaging in literary activity (Iliodor does not obey). His fiery sermons draw vast crowds of listeners. In between his rantings, he casts out devils and "performs miracles."

In the monastery courtyard where he preaches, Iliodor constructs a huge cardboard dragon that he dubs the "hydra of the revolution." At the end of each sermon, he ceremoniously pierces it with a spear in the manner of Saint George and cuts off its head (which miraculously grows back for the following day's performance).*

None of this would matter if Iliodor limited his attacks to Tolstoy, "yids," and intellectuals. But he also denounces the governor of Saratov, the Holy Synod, and even Prime Minister Stolypin. In March 1909, the church authorities decide to punish Iliodor by transferring him to Minsk, now capital of Belarus. The monk goes to Saint Petersburg in search of potential intercessors and finds one in the sympathetic shape of Grigory Rasputin.

In March 1909 Iliodor is twenty-nine; Rasputin is forty. They are completely dissimilar. Iliodor is well educated and accepted in society. He is an articulate orator able to debate with the capital's leading monarchist intellectuals. Rasputin, on the contrary, is a semi-literate peasant who repels more people than he attracts. His fan club includes Empress Alexandra and her associates, but they are ashamed of their friendship with the preacher. The vainglorious Rasputin seeks fame and notoriety. He hires journalists to write about him, but to little avail. So he begins to brag more and more about his proximity to the imperial family.

Iliodor's plea for help greatly flatters Rasputin. He likes the smart and popular Iliodor and wants to assist—not least to demonstrate his own importance. Through his mediation, the Holy Synod revokes its decision to relocate Iliodor.

---

*In the early twenty-first century religious hard-liners have also suddenly gained political strength. In 2012 the State Duma has passed a law against "offending religious feelings" (the phrasing is an exact match to that of the early twentieth century). Moreover, some public initiatives involving limitation of the rights of sexual minorities, state intervention into private life, and checking whether pieces of art correspond with moral norms used to be disregarded, but now they gain massive public attention.

A SECT IN CAPRI

Maxim Gorky, having moved to Capri near Naples, sets about creating his own kind of sect. He rents a huge villa that becomes home to numerous friends, guests, and adherents. The longer he lives abroad, the more he begins to idealize the Russian folk.

Gorky devotes a great deal of time to reading literary works sent to him by workers and peasants. He enjoys it very much, remarking that it is very "biblical" in content. Gorky adopts a more religious mindset, and he is jokingly referred to as the "bishop of Capri." He has his photograph taken with guests in biblical poses: for example, with Gorky as Abraham, his stepson Zinovy as Isaac, and their family friend, the head of the Bolshevik militant organization, Leonid Krasin, as an angel (rather inappropriately).

On the island of Capri, the forty-year-old Gorky gets on particularly well with the thirty-three-year-old art historian Anatoly Lunacharsky. Together, they begin to invent a new religion—a religion without God based upon the principles of Marxism. Both are passionate about "god-building," as they call it. Gorky says that the religious approach to Marxism has far more promise than the traditional version, because the common man will struggle to come to grips with socialist dogma. Lunacharsky aspires to create some rituals to go along with their new religion.

The party comrades leave no stone unturned in their joint venture. Plekhanov comes up with the nickname "Blessed Anatoly" for Lunacharsky. Lenin twice visits Gorky on Capri, where he rests, bathes, and fishes, but on returning to Switzerland he continues the attacks on his comrades.

The "god-builders" soon move from theory to practice. Party money (partly from smash-and-grab raids) is used to take workers from Russia on trips to Capri, where Gorky lectures them on literature and Lunacharsky and other Marxists teach them about socialism.

RAIDERS OF THE RUSSIAN PEOPLE

The Union of the Russian People continues to grow. It is the largest mass political party in Russia, numbering around four hundred thousand members, and various scandals, such as the murder of the Duma member Herzenstein, have not dented its popularity. The investigation of the latter incident is still ongoing. The killing took place on Finnish soil, and the Finnish justice system intends to get to the bottom of it.

The main surprise of the trial is the unexpected appearance in court of Prusakov, the former personal secretary of Dubrovin, as a witness for the prosecution. He says that the union's combat squads are used to fight political opponents, settle personal scores, and commit robbery and extortion. Inside the Pale of Settlement, they are in the business of racketeering and threatening pogroms. Some of the money goes to the state treasury, but mostly it remains in the pocket of the "scum," as the witness describes members of the combat squads. Dubrovin guarantees them total immunity: crimes are either hushed up or, in more serious cases involving court proceedings, convicted persons are immediately pardoned.

The status afforded to members of the combat squads allows them to escape punishment for all offenses, even ones unrelated to the union. Some, for instance, illicitly sell documents to Jews permitting them to work outside the Pale, including in Saint Petersburg.

Nevertheless, the commander of the combat squads, Nikolai Yuskevich-Kraskovsky, appears before the Finnish court. The court also summons Dubrovin, but he goes to Crimea to visit the local governor-cum-dictator, Colonel Dumbadze, also a member of the union. Dumbadze interferes in everything personally from censoring the press to exiling dissenters and even regulating swimwear on the beach.

In 1907, an attempt is made on Dumbadze's life when a bomb is thrown at him from the balcony of a dacha. He escapes practically unharmed, but, to make a statement, he razes the dacha to the ground without allowing the owners (presumably not the terrorists) to remove a single belonging. The owners sue and even enlist the support of Stolypin, who orders damages of 60,000 roubles* to be paid.

Yet Nicholas II takes a liking to Dumbadze: "If I'd had more people like Colonel Dumbadze a few years ago, everything would have been different," he says to Stolypin. The Black Hundred press, which the tsar devours, extols the Yalta governor and reviles the prime minister, which causes the latter's relationship with Nicholas to deteriorate ever more noticeably.

Stolypin, for his part, does not spare his enemies. While Dubrovin is hiding from the Finnish justice system in Crimea, the prime minister sanctions a forcible takeover of the Union of the Russian People. In July 1909, the organization's headquarters are moved from Dubrovin's apartment to a separate room in Baskov Lane† in Saint Petersburg. In December a new chairman is elected—the Stolypin-loyal right-wing Duma member

---

* About $791,000 in 2017.
† Where Vladimir Putin once lived.

Nikolai Markov. Funding increases immediately: from 1910, the government allocates the union 3 million roubles a year.*

All accessories to the Herzenstein murder are convicted, but are personally pardoned by Nicholas II soon after the trial. However, the combat squads of the Union of the Russian People curtail their official activity as a result of the trial.

NON-RUSSIAN RUSSIAN BALLET

Despite all the efforts of Kschessinskaya and Grand Duke Andrei, on 19 May 1909 Diaghilev's troupe goes on tour to Paris. The first performance is none other than *Le Pavillon d'Armide*. The main role is due to be filled by Anna Pavlova, but her relationship with Diaghilev breaks down, and she ends up organizing her own private tour. That clears the way for Pavlova's understudy, Tamara Karsavina, while the male role is performed by the twenty-year-old Vaslav Nijinsky, arguably the greatest male ballet dancer in history.

It is not just a success, the papers write, but an "invasion," an "explosion," an "eruption." The writer Marcel Proust compares the Russian ballet to the Dreyfus affair—for several weeks the Parisian public can speak of nothing else. The Petersburg press, meanwhile, writes not of the triumph, but of the scandal, the "perversion of classical Russian opera," the "defilement of Russian art." At the same time, both Paris and Petersburg are talking about a rumored love affair between Diaghilev and Nijinsky.

Despite the resounding success, the tour makes a huge loss: 86,000 francs,† which Diaghilev must reimburse to the Théâtre du Châtelet. The producer does not want to pay and tries to negotiate a secret deal with the rival Grand Opera. When the double-dealing is uncovered, Diaghilev's Parisian friends grow cold overnight. The director of the Théâtre du Châtelet informs the press that Diaghilev is a crook and sends a detailed report to the Russian authorities. It is alleged that Diaghilev has been posing as a government official in order to raise funds.

Miechen tries to intercede on Diaghilev's behalf, but her son Andrei, Kschessinskaya, and officials from the Directorate of the Imperial Theatres overrule her. The Ministry of the Court blacklists Diaghilev and vetoes all his projects. The road back to Russia is closed off, so he launches a new venture with a different business model, shorn of government funding or patronage.

* About $39,550,000 in 2017.
† About $419,494 in 2017.

Diaghilev pays off his debts with the help of old Parisian friends from the days of his very first exhibitions, plus new ones in the shape of composers Claude Debussy and Maurice Ravel, as well as a young pupil of Rimsky-Korsakov by the name of Igor Stravinsky. He commissions the latter to write a ballet in the exotically costumed style of *Boris Godunov*, whereupon Stravinsky comes up with *The Firebird*. But the dancers rebel, opining that the ballet has no melody and does not even sound like music. Stravinsky himself plays at every rehearsal, which "the piano finds distressing," joke members of the troupe.

The tour is preceded by a powerful PR campaign, with Stravinsky heralded as the new genius of Russian music. But the main hit is the now-deceased Rimsky-Korsakov's *Scheherazade* with Nijinsky and Ida Rubinstein in the lead roles. Leon Bakst is also lauded for his costumes and scenery. He instantly becomes the world's most sought-after fashion designer: magazines publish interviews with him, and galleries host his exhibitions. Parisian ladies clamber over each other to order dresses "à la Scheherazade."

After this success, Diaghilev faces another problem with Russian cultural officials. They forbid his dancers from taking part in anything Diaghilev-related. The director of the Imperial Theatres, Vladimir Telyakovsky, declares that Russian art should be promoted in Russia, not Europe. So Diaghilev creates his own permanent theatre company, which becomes known as the Ballets Russes. It is a struggle to convince his stars to abandon the reliable state theatres of Russia in favor of his risky venture, but the Russian authorities themselves unwittingly lend a hand.

On 23 January 1911 Nijinsky performs the male role in *Giselle* at the Mariinsky Theatre in Saint Petersburg. There in the hall sits Empress Dowager Maria Feodorovna, plus a sprinkling of grand dukes and duchesses. Maria Feodorovna finds Nijinsky's tight-fitting garments obscene (normal by today's standards). During the intermission, he is requested to change his outfit, which he refuses to do. The next day he is fired. The management hints that if Nijinsky apologizes, all will be forgiven. But he decides to go over to Diaghilev. In April 1911, the Ballets Russes ceases to be Russian when the troupe moves to a permanent rehearsal studio in Monte Carlo.

BISHOPS AND SOCIETY LADIES

In late December 1909, the twenty-two-year-old Felix Yusupov, now a student in Oxford (despite Alexandra's admonition), returns home for

Christmas. His childhood friend Munya Golovina excitedly tells him about an illustrious old man "who has been sent to purify and heal our souls and guide our thoughts and actions." Intrigued, the young Yusupov asks Golovina to introduce him to the "saint." Rasputin's face is "sly and lusty, like a satyr" and "filth exudes through the guise of purity" is how the young prince describes his first impressions, admitting at the same time that this "strange subject" has a mysterious hold on him.

Not only on him. During the winter of 1909-1910 Rasputin is almost a daily visitor at Tsarskoye Selo, where Empress Alexandra and her daughters spend hours in conversation with him. When he does not come, they write him touching letters: Alexandra calls him "my beloved and never-to-be-forgotten teacher, savior and mentor." At the same time, she asks the children never to talk about Rasputin, even to relatives.

But Rasputin is already the talk of Petersburg high society. The rumors are spread mostly by members of the clergy and the ladies-in-waiting. Rasputin once held the elders of the church in great esteem, especially the rector of the Theological Academy, Bishop Theophan, who introduced him to the Montenegrin princesses and other imperial personages. But when Alexandra starts to cold-shoulder the bishops in favor of "folk preachers," Rasputin's respect for his former benefactors evaporates.

Rasputin also falls out with his Montenegrin patronesses, Stana and Milica. They continue to have faith in their spiritual confessor Theophan, while the empress prefers Rasputin. As a result, the Montenegrins lose access to Alexandra, supplanted by the peasant from Siberia. It is a tiff of historical significance, for it causes a rift between Nicholas II and Stana's husband, Grand Duke Nikolai Nikolaevich, which directly affects the outcome of the First World War.

The most common rumor about Rasputin is that he is a member of the banned mystical sect known as the *Khlysts* (a corruption of the word "Christ"), whose acts of worship, according to popular myth, involve trances and orgies. Rasputin was accused of being a *Khlyst* by a local priest back in his native village of Pokrovskoe. The charge was withdrawn after an official investigation, but the stain on Rasputin's (not entirely squeaky-clean) reputation remains.

By March 1910 rumors about Rasputin are everywhere in the press. The monarchist newspaper *Moscow News* accuses him of meeting female admirers in the bathhouse. "This man's victims are convinced that touching Grigory gives them a feeling of angelic purity and heavenly bliss," writes the journalist Novoselov.

The higher clergy continue to feed rumors to the Black Hundred press. The editor of *Moscow News*, Lev Tikhomirov, cites one of his direct sources as Bishop Theophan, who has now "sensed what Grigory is all about, but too late." On 30 April 1910, the paper's front page demands that the Holy Synod investigate Rasputin's *Khlyst* connections.

Rasputin is supported by the monk Iliodor in the latter's own inimitable way: "You, editorial whores, should be nailed to a pillory in full view of all Russia and whipped for having insulted the blessed elder Grigory."

The Black Hundred press revelations are soon picked up on by the liberal newspapers, including the Kadet publication *Speech*, edited by Pavel Milyukov. It prompts another conversation between Nicholas II and Stolypin. On the previous occasion, Nicholas promised never to meet with Rasputin again—this time he is more honest: "I agree with you, Pyotr Arkadievich [Stolypin], but ten Rasputins would be preferable to one hysterical empress," he says to the prime minister, explaining that his wife is seriously ill and believes that only Rasputin can help ease their son's hemophilia (genetic disorder carried by the females in the House of Hesse). Nicholas demands an end to the persecution of Rasputin and the interference in his personal affairs. The government's press committee promptly bans the newspapers from writing about the preacher.

Nicholas asks Rasputin to return home until the hullabaloo dies down. First, he travels to see his friend Iliodor in Tsaritsyn (today's Volgograd), where he is given a magnificent reception. The two monks then travel together to Rasputin's hometown of Pokrovskoe. Exiled and humiliated, Rasputin wants to prove that he is not a spent force. He shows Iliodor some letters he has received in Siberia from Empress Alexandra and her daughters. Iliodor reads them with interest and asks to keep some as a memento. Rasputin unwisely agrees.

TOLSTOY'S TESTAMENT

In January 1910, at his Yasnaya Polyana estate, Leo Tolstoy starts composing a story entitled "Iliodor the Monk." It is not intentionally about the fanatic from Tsaritsyn, but simply that the names coincide. The work begins with the monk suddenly losing faith and the rite of the sacrament becoming a mockery to him. Tolstoy never finishes the story.

Tolstoy does not mention the real-life Iliodor anywhere in his writings. It is a trait of his to ignore those who curse him. Yet, he keeps a close eye on the press and wonders if he should respond publicly. For instance, he reads *Vekhi** and thinks about writing a review of Sergei Bulgakov's article (which says that the intelligentsia's struggle for progress ignores individual rights), but changes his mind.

Tolstoy corresponds with Stolypin for several years. He tries to persuade the prime minister to abolish private ownership of land and condemns the military courts. In August 1909 Tolstoy pens a very personal letter in which he says that Stolypin's "dreadful actions" threaten both the latter's life and posthumous reputation: "Your name will be used as a byword for rudeness, cruelty and deceit." However, he decides not to send the letter to Stolypin. Tolstoy at this time is more consumed by a personal battle against not Stolypin or the church, but his wife. The eternal subject of the dispute is his will.

In the summer of 1909, despite his wife's opposition, Tolstoy leaves Yasnaya Polyana to visit his close friend and disciple Vladimir Chertkov, who is renting a house nearby. Chertkov's wife tries not to let him in, but in vain. During the visit Tolstoy draws up a will, which deprives his wife of her inheritance.

It is a kind of love (or perhaps death) triangle. The sixty-six-year-old Sofia Andreyevna, Tolstoy's wife, and the fifty-six-year-old Chertkov are fighting not for the eighty-year-old Tolstoy's life, but effectively his afterlife. Tolstoy believes that Chertkov understands him far better than his wife does. When he dies, Tolstoy wants all his works to be taken out of copyright so that they belong to everyone, not the family. Sofia is categorically against the proposal, while Chertkov is determined to fulfill his mentor's wish.

On Chertkov's side (and against her mother) is Tolstoy's youngest, favorite daughter, Alexandra. According to Chertkov's scheme, Sasha (Alexandra) will be entitled to all her father's literary works when she turns thirty-five, while Tolstoy's sons and other daughters will get nothing, because only Sasha can be trusted to ensure that Tolstoy's works remain freely accessible to all of mankind and exploited by no one.

It turns into a major scandal. Sofia Andreyevna effectively goes mad with jealousy. She constantly threatens her husband with suicide and promises to write a note blaming him for her death and to send it to all the newspapers. The doctors believe that she is suffering from hysterical paranoia, while the writer himself thinks that his wife is feigning insanity. She, meanwhile, blames Chertkov for everything and discusses with her sons how to declare Tolstoy insane if he really does deprive the family of its

---

* A collection of articles published in 1909 criticizing the Russian intelligentsia.

inheritance. In the autumn of 1910 she announces that she forbids Tolstoy from ever seeing Chertkov again. For Tolstoy, it is the last straw.

On the night of 27-28 October, hearing his wife rummaging around in his possessions in search of his will, Tolstoy leaves home in the company of his personal physician. He wants to visit the Shamordino Convent, where his sister is a nun, and then, together with Sasha and Chertkov, go south to Rostov, Odessa, Constantinople, and Bulgaria. He leaves his wife a farewell note, in which he asks her not to look for him.

But the press makes that unlikely. A day later, the papers report Tolstoy's departure as a major event. Journalists race after him and publish detailed commentaries on where Tolstoy has been and what he ate for breakfast that morning.

Tolstoy and his doctor travel in a third-class compartment with simple folk. To get some fresh air after being cooped up inside the smoke-filled train, the count disembarks at a station and stands on the chilly platform for about an hour. According to his doctor, that is when he catches a cold.

Excommunicated from the church, Tolstoy calls in at the Optina Pustyn Monastery and on to the Shamordino Convent, but the journey is interrupted at Astapovo rail station, for the writer is now ill with pneumonia—his temperature is forty degrees Celsius. He is taken to the stationmaster's quarters, where Chertkov and his daughter Sasha keep vigil by his bedside. It is not long before the rest of the family discovers his whereabouts. They arrive, but the dying Tolstoy does not wish to see Sofia Andreyevna.

He passes away on 7 November 1910: "I love many things. I love everyone," are reportedly his last words, according to his son Sergei. Residents from surrounding villages ask for a funeral service to be held in the station church, but it is forbidden by the Holy Synod.

Tolstoy is buried without church rites or even a cross under a simple mound of earth with no tombstone. Sofia Andreyevna challenges the will in court, but without success. Sasha and Chertkov buy up Yasnaya Polyana from her and, as Tolstoy bequeathed, give it to the peasants.

The news of Tolstoy's death prompts a surge of student demonstrations in Russia's two capitals under the slogan "Down with the death penalty!" In response, the Ministry of Education issues new rules prohibiting student rallies and annulling the autonomy of universities. This sparks another protest. The rector of Moscow University, Manuilov, resigns, followed by several dozen professors in solidarity with him, including the natural scientist Vernadsky and the physiologist Timiryazev—one hundred and thirty people in total. The student unrest worsens, and thousands of students are expelled from Moscow University as a result.

RED TRIANGLE

Vladimir Lenin, together with his wife, mother-in-law, and friend Grigory Zinoviev, move to Paris from Geneva in December 1908. Having made up with his old friend Martov, he launches a new newspaper called *Social-Democrat*, whose editorial board includes Zinoviev and Kamenev. Lenin, as usual, throws tantrums, curses the heresy of his Marxist comrades, and spends a lot of time playing cards with his mother-in-law in the local library.

In 1909, under the pseudonym Ilyin, Lenin publishes the philosophical work *Materialism and Empiriocriticism*. The publicist Semyon Frank, reviewing the work, is surprised that such a meaningless mix of philosophical words and invective can possibly hope to find a publisher and a readership. It is a failure.

Another blow is when Lenin's Social Democratic Party comrades strip him of control over the party finances. Prior to 1910, his duties included managing a large fortune left to the Marxists by a deceased wealthy supporter in Moscow. Now the money is taken from the quarrelsome Lenin and placed at the disposal of a disinterested party, namely the German Social Democrats. The funds are transferred to Germany.

It is a difficult time. Nadezhda Krupskaya, Lenin's wife, recalls that many Russian émigrés live in poverty and suicide among them is a common phenomenon. But the hotheaded Lenin seeks salvation from depression. In 1910 he meets an émigré from Russia, Inessa Armand, the wife of a major Moscow industrialist, who, intoxicated by Marxism, abandoned her husband and went abroad. She is thirty-six years old; Lenin is forty. They have an affair, which Lenin does not hide from Krupskaya. On the contrary, Inessa is a regular guest at their house. Krupskaya even takes a liking to her and spends time playing with her children. Convinced that the relationship between her husband and Inessa is serious, Nadezhda offers her husband a divorce. But Lenin is categorically against the idea. He has grown used to his wife and wants everything to remain the same.

EPIDEMIC OF SUICIDES

The hottest topic in the Russian press is not the epidemic of suicides among Russian émigrés, but the one inside the country, especially among grammar school[*] students. The cheapest and most popular method is

---

[*] Known as *gymnasia* in Imperial Russia.

poisoning by vinegar. The number of suicides sharply rises as political freedoms are curtailed and feelings of despair increase. Young people have been riding a wave of politics and revolution, but now they face the prospect of having all their hopes crushed by the revival of the old order. Many newspapers have a dedicated "Suicides" section.

The popular *Stock Exchange Gazette* publishes a survey in which public figures express their attitude towards suicide. The general feeling is one of sympathy. The writer Fyodor Sologub describes suicide as a "valve" and a "release mechanism for weakness," while the poet Mikhail Kuzmin asks why the Motherland has the right to demand that a man lay down his life for her sake, but forbids him from laying down his life for his own sake.

The publication provokes a storm of indignation. Many publicists, including Maxim Gorky and Leon Trotsky, angrily denounce their colleagues for encouraging people to take their own lives.

In any case, the public mood has changed. Five years ago, people lapped up lectures on political economy, but now politics is out of fashion—mysticism, decadence, and *noir* are in vogue. Private clubs host lectures with titles such as "The Negation of Life," while a stage adaptation of Robert Louis Stevenson's *The Suicide Club* is a hit in all provincial theatres.

CHALIAPIN ON HIS KNEES

In the spring of 1911, Russia's top opera singer, Feodor Chaliapin, wants to shoot himself—or in any case never again set foot in Russia. Chaliapin is being hounded by the press.

It all begins on 6 January. The Mariinsky Theatre is hosting a performance of *Boris Godunov*, and Nicholas II and family are seated in the royal box. During the intermission, Chaliapin speaks with the tsar, who requests him to sing more in Russia and do less touring abroad. Chaliapin is unaware of the ongoing conflict between the Mariinsky Theatre choir and the director of the Imperial Theatres, Telyakovsky, who refuses to raise their salaries. So the choristers appeal to Nicholas himself. When the performance ends, Chaliapin is about to leave the stage when the audience starts shouting, "Anthem, anthem!" The choristers break into a rendition of "God Save the Tsar" and fall to their knees. Chaliapin reluctantly lowers himself on one knee. The choir's trick works, and the tsar raises their wages. Chaliapin duly sets off on tour. Two days later, now in Monte Carlo, he learns that the Russian papers are writing that it was his idea for the choir to kneel down. They publish fictional interviews with him, saying that he has succumbed to patriotic feelings and decided at the same time to ask the tsar to forgive his friend Maxim Gorky.

Even close friends condemn Chaliapin for toadying to the authorities. Gorky himself is upset that Chaliapin is using him to "cover up his underhandedness." The highly principled Valentin Serov sends several newspaper cuttings with the words "Shame on you" scribbled on them, and Plekhanov returns Chaliapin's signed portrait with a short note reading "No longer required."

Chaliapin is horrified. He writes that he does not want to return to Russia: "Life among the Russian intelligentsia has become intolerable. Anyone in a waistcoat and tie considers himself an intellectual and passes judgment as he pleases." He starts to imagine that he is considered to be "a double agent like Azef" and could be killed "by some revolutionary fanatics." Only six months later does Chaliapin venture to write to Gorky to try to justify himself, whereupon he journeys to Capri for an emotional encounter, during which they embrace and make up.

STOLYPIN VICTORIOUS BUT HUMBLED

Throughout 1910 Iliodor the monk feels quite at ease in Tsaritsyn. The governor of Saratov, Tatishchev, is so unnerved by his presence that in the summer of 1910 he packs everything in and moves with his wife to nearby Samara. It is at this point that Stolypin decides to extend his law and order regime to Tsaritsyn.

In January 1911, at the prime minister's insistence, the Holy Synod transfers Iliodor to the Tula diocese as the rector of Novosilsky Monastery, just one hundred and fifty kilometers from Yasnaya Polyana, the estate of the late Leo Tolstoy. But Iliodor refuses to go: "I will not submit to Stolypin. I refuse to let him turn the Church into a police station." He is taken there by force. The new Saratov governor, Stremoukhov, appointed in December, is worried that Iliodor will flee. He does indeed. A month later Iliodor reappears in Tsaritsyn, where he holes himself up inside his former monastery.

Now he starts preaching that the emperor has been captured by the "Judeo-Masonic ministers," of whom the most dangerous is Stolypin himself, who should have "the Masonic spirit beaten out of him." Iliodor's fanatical supporters, many of whom are women, are ready to fight the police for the sake of their leader.

Iliodor spends the month of February waiting for the intervention of friends from the Russian capital. Rasputin cannot assist, for he is currently on a pilgrimage to Jerusalem. But having learnt about his friend's misfortune, he sends Alexandra telegrams in defense of Iliodor. Nicholas II faces a choice: his wife and Rasputin want him to revoke the decision of the Holy Synod. According to the letter of the law, the tsar cannot do this by himself, but Stolypin inadvertently comes to Iliodor's aid.

In early March the prime minister intends to reform the zemstvo system and introduce it to the territory of modern-day Ukraine and Belarus— but with a difference. Since much of the population is non-Russian, including many Poles, Stolypin wants to introduce quotas for ethnic minorities in the new zemstvos.

The Union of the Russian People and other right-wingers oppose the reform. For them, the introduction of elective zemstvos means a greater role for ethnic minorities in government. On 4 March 1910, the Law on the Western Zemstvo, as it is called, is rejected by the State Council.

Stolypin is so angered that he immediately resigns. Nicholas hesitates to accept. On 10 March, he tells Stolypin that he is not ready to part with him and agrees to his conditions, of which there is one: the law must be passed forthwith without the consent of the State Council or the Duma. This is illegal, but there is a loophole: it is possible to announce a temporary recess of the Duma and the State Council, and sign the law during that window. That was how the agrarian reform was adopted.

Nicholas II agrees to Stolypin's sleight of hand: a recess of the Duma and the State Council is scheduled for 12-15 March, and on 14 March the tsar signs a decree on the creation of the Western Zemstvo. There is nothing for the lawmakers to discuss when they convene after their forced break: the law has been adopted and cannot be repealed.

Even Stolypin's supporters are outraged. "You have damaged our young Russian constitution, and yourself even more," says Alexander Guchkov, a representative of the Moscow merchant class, the current chairman of the State Duma and Stolypin's former right-hand man. "You were once a political heavyweight, now you've committed political *hara-kiri*." In protest, Guchkov resigns from his post as chairman of the Duma.

Stolypin does not realize the extent to which Guchkov is right. The episode ruins his relationship with Nicholas II once and for all. The tsar hates being pressured. He has never forgiven Witte for forcing him to sign the 17 October manifesto, and now he accuses Stolypin of blackmail and coercion.

Moreover, Stolypin has lost the moral right to insist that Nicholas observe the laws of the land. When Rasputin asks him to annul the Holy Synod's decree and allow Iliodor to live in Tsaritsyn lawfully, he readily agrees. On 1 April Emperor Nicholas II personally grants Iliodor the right to return to Tsaritsyn, and the next day the Holy Synod repeals its own decree. The church leaders are humiliated. Metropolitan Anthony, who excommunicated Tolstoy a decade previously, suffers a stroke.

But that is not all. In early May Iliodor travels to Saint Petersburg. On the eve of his arrival, the tsar, on the advice of Rasputin, dismisses Lukyanov, the ober-procurator of the Holy Synod (the "minister of the church"), despite Stolypin's protests. The imperial family invites Iliodor to perform a vigil service at the palace church and listens carefully to his sermon. In his memoirs Iliodor claims that during this encounter Nicholas II asked him to obey Rasputin and to attack only his enemies ("Jews and revolutionaries"), not his ministers.

Iliodor returns to Tsaritsyn victorious and sends a letter to the governor, saying that the latter is "cursed." The frightened governor writes to Saint Petersburg, asking for an explanation. He is told that the "curse," which was not approved by a general vote of the members of the Holy Synod, has no legal force.

It is hard to imagine a greater humiliation for Stolypin. At the end of the summer, he meets with Guchkov, his former right-hand man, and complains to him that Iliodor is a threat to the state because he is undermining both local and supreme power. Guchkov describes Stolypin's tone of voice as "forlorn."

While Stolypin is trying to create a zemstvo in Kiev province and fighting Iliodor, an emergency occurs in Kiev: on 20 March the corpse of a twelve-year-old boy named Andrei Yushchinsky is found in a small cave in the forest. He was killed the week before. The body is covered with forty-seven stab wounds and has been exsanguinated.

Rumors of ritual murder immediately abound. At the boy's funeral, leaflets are distributed stating that he was killed by the Jews to use his blood to make *matzo* for Passover. The member of the Union of the Russian People who handed them out is detained, but soon released. The unionists start planning a pogrom. The complicit police persuade them to wait until autumn, since the tsar is due to visit Kiev to mark the fiftieth anniversary of the abolition of serfdom. The Black Hundreds acquiesce.

The police consider various scenarios, one of which involves arresting the boy's mother and stepfather. But Kiev is a city where the Union of the Russian People enjoys great influence, which naturally results in the strong reactionary press insisting that the boy was killed by the Jews. Dubrovin's *Russian Banner* is leading the campaign. The right-wing members in the State Duma, headed by Purishkevich, ask if the government is aware that the Kiev boy was tortured and murdered by a criminal Jewish sect that practices blood libel. The Duma declines to respond, but in any case it is of little consequence.

Anti-Semitism is rife: the public attitude towards Jews is comparable to how modern folk feel about illegal immigrants. Everyone knows that the tsar reads the Black Hundred press and supports the radical anti-Semite Iliodor, against whom even Stolypin is powerless. The government funds right-wing organizations, which are multiplying and competing for public money. The struggle against the "Jewish threat" is considered a noble cause. Therefore, the police need no special instructions to pursue the ritual killing theory. This version of events suggests itself.

On 22 June, the police arrest the Jewish Mendel Beilis, a salesman from a brick factory located not far from the scene of the crime. Thus begins the most high-profile case in the history of the Russian legal system.

SHOTS IN THE STALLS

The celebrations in Kiev on the occasion of the fiftieth anniversary of the abolition of serfdom begin in late August. Stolypin arrives in Kiev on 25 August and discovers that he is *persona non grata*: he is cold-shouldered by the imperial court and denied a place aboard the tsarist steamer on a trip to Chernigov. He does not even have a carriage, and has to hitch a ride from Finance Minister Kokovtsov.

The numerous scandals of recent times, including the Iliodor and Rasputin sagas, have taken their toll. If Iliodor's memoirs are to be believed, in the summer of 1910 Rasputin tells the latter that he will soon force Stolypin out of office (as he did with the ober-procurator of the Holy Synod) and replace him with Kokovtsov. It is not even a matter of personal enmity, but circumstance: the tsar no longer favors Stolypin, and the government is whispering that he could soon be exiled to the post of governor of the Caucasus.

On 1 September Stolypin meets with Russian nationalists in Kiev. "You have my sympathy and support. I think you are the salt of the earth," he says. That same evening the prime minister goes to the opera.

Deputy Interior Minister Kurlov warns Stolypin of a suspected plot to assassinate him. He is given an enclosed vehicle, which he uses, despite the summer heat. The source of information about the assassination plot is a police agent by the name of Bogrov. He warns that the attempt on Stolypin's life will take place at the theatre. Bogrov is given a theatre pass for him personally to point out suspicious types in the audience.

During the interval Bogrov approaches Stolypin's seat in the stalls and fires twice at point-blank range. He is a double agent, like Azef, whom Stolypin recently defended in the Duma. Bogrov is seized. The wounded Stolypin looks around in the direction of the royal box, makes the sign of the cross to Nicholas II, and collapses. He is carried out of the hall, and the orchestra is ordered to start playing the national anthem to restore calm.

The program for the end-of-serfdom anniversary celebrations is curtailed, but Nicholas still makes the trip to Chernigov. Empress Alexandra remains in Kiev and urgently summons Rasputin for consultations (it is rumored) on whom to appoint as the new prime minister.

Stolypin dies in hospital on 5 September. Nicholas II does not visit the bedside of his dying prime minister. Only after the trip to Chernigov, on 6 September, does he go to pay his last respects. He kneels by the coffin and prays. The new prime minister is indeed Kokovtsov. "Do not follow the example of Pyotr Arkadievich [Stolypin], who overshadowed me so much that I was invisible," the tsar exhorts the new head of government.

Stolypin is buried at the Kiev-Pechersk Lavra. His death prompts a wave of laudatory articles in which he is compared to the late emperor-reformer Alexander II.

Stolypin's predecessor, Sergei Witte, however, believes that his death is for the best. Now on an honorary pension as a member of the State Council, Witte hated Stolypin, believing him to have "corrupted the Russian administration, destroyed the independence of the courts and the press, and trampled over the dignity of the State Duma, turning it into his personal department." It is mainly envy, but Witte is right about one thing: Stolypin did indeed take manual control of the courts and the elections. In the post-Stolypin era, this system continues to operate under different management. Meanwhile, the double agent Bogrov is sentenced by a district military court to death and hanged on 12 September.

A LOCAL APOCALYPSE

After the death of his enemy Stolypin, Iliodor becomes even more aggressive, seemingly suffering from progressive mental illness. This time he provokes a scandal with the Moscow City Duma. On learning that the city authorities intend to buy up the estate of Leo Tolstoy at Khamovniki and build a museum, he writes an obscene telegram to the local head Nikolai Guchkov (the brother of Alexander), demanding that the purchase be cancelled or the estate turned into a prison or a brothel. Iliodor hangs up a portrait of Tolstoy inside his monastery, so that visitors can "spit at his despicable mug." Written on Tolstoy's forehead are the words "Satan's servant."

On 26 September, preaching to his flock, Iliodor announces the impending end of the world and the coming of the Antichrist, calling on his followers to dig catacombs under the monastery as a place to hide. In order to keep the enemy out, he orders any curious onlooker to be beaten over the head with a shovel. A total of 991 families volunteer, and the work is done mostly by women and children.

The police files mention a rift between Iliodor and Rasputin, caused by the former allegedly asking the latter to use his government connections to secure funding. Rasputin refuses, whereupon all hell breaks loose.

On 16 December 1911 Rasputin meets Iliodor and Germogen. The fifty-three-year-old Germogen, the last member of the church hierarchy to support Rasputin, begins to accuse him of immorality, demanding that he no longer cross the threshold of the imperial palace. Rasputin verbally insults Germogen and physically pushes him. Iliodor and several others come running and a fight breaks out. Iliodor and Rasputin roll head over heels down a flight of stairs, while the roughed-up Germogen screams blue murder at Rasputin. Rasputin breaks free, swears revenge, and runs away.

Psychiatrists would be fascinated by the case study of Iliodor. He not only predicts the coming of the Antichrist, but also arranges his own local political apocalypse. A couple of weeks after the scuffle, leaflets are distributed in Saint Petersburg bearing the text of letters sent by Empress Alexandra and her daughters to Rasputin—the ones that Rasputin showed boastfully to Iliodor: "How painful it is without you," writes Alexandra in one such letter. "My soul is only at rest when you, teacher, are sitting next to me. I kiss your hands, lean my head on your shoulder and desire only to fall asleep there forever." The letter is signed: "Yours eternally and lovingly." Rumors spread that the empress is Rasputin's mistress.

It is hard to imagine what happens to the introverted empress when she learns that the whole of Saint Petersburg is reading her personal correspondence.

In January 1912, the Holy Synod decides to banish Iliodor (again) to a remote monastery in Vladimir province. Germogen is dismissed from the Holy Synod by imperial decree and sent to Saratov. He refuses to comply and gives interviews to the press, whereupon his diocese is subjected to an "audit." After various infringements are found, he is removed from office and sent to a monastery in Grodno province.

The newspapers try to cover the events, but papers that publish articles in defense of Germogen and against Rasputin are confiscated by the Interior Ministry. The scandal continues all month. On January 24, the leader of the Union of 17 of October Party (the so-called Octobrists), Alexander Guchkov, queries the Interior Ministry about the reason for confiscating the papers. Nicholas II is furious. The ministers in the new cabinet, headed by Kokovtsov, are afraid to approach the tsar, and so they dispatch Count Fredericks to advise him to send Rasputin out of the capital for a while. Finally, on 15 February, Rasputin visits Prime Minister Kokovtsov for a long talk. The next day Rasputin leaves for his home village, most likely having been offered money by Kokovtsov.

There is hope that the situation is improving. On 26 February, the new chairman of the Duma, the Octobrist Mikhail Rodzianko, who was elected after Guchkov's resignation, goes to see the tsar. He brings with him a suitcase full of documents. For two hours he reads out testimonies that Rasputin is a member of the *Khlyst* sect and goes with women to the bathhouse, and shows the tsar letters from repentant women seduced by Rasputin and clippings from foreign newspapers alleging that Rasputin is a revolutionary tool to discredit the Russian monarchy. Nicholas II is struck by the evidence. He asks Rodzianko to compile a detailed report (that he can show to his wife). And as a sign of goodwill, he introduces Rodzianko to his son Alexei, who describes the former as the "biggest and fattest man in Russia."

Rodzianko leaves with the feeling that he has moved a mountain, and starts boasting that the tsar commissioned him to prepare a report to expose Rasputin. On 8 March he informs Nicholas that the text is ready, but the very next day Guchkov, the leader of Rodzianko's own faction, delivers a fiery speech against Rasputin in the Duma: "Let it be known that the Church and the State are in peril. . . . You all know what a painful drama Russia is experiencing. . . . At the center of this drama stands a mysterious, tragicomic figure, like a native from the Other World or a relic of the Dark Ages."

The Duma's discussion of Rasputin is perceived by Nicholas II as a deep personal insult. He no longer receives Rodzianko and does not read his report. Three days later the entire imperial family leaves for Crimea. They are seen off by all the members of the government. Empress Alexandra walks past in silence, not greeting or looking at anyone. "This atmosphere of fibs, gossip and spitefulness is suffocating," Nicholas tells Kokovtsov. "I am leaving now and shall return as late as possible."

BACK TO RUSSIA

The year 1911 is a testing one for Diaghilev. His Italian tour almost falls through, and he has trouble with Stravinsky's ballet *Petrushka*—Bakst is behind schedule with the set designs and Stravinsky himself hurriedly writes the score during rehearsals. Meanwhile, Diaghilev and Fokine are at daggers drawn. There is no theatre available, so the troupe rehearses in a restaurant.

Diaghilev also quarrels with Ida Rubinstein. She is now settled in Paris and loves to shock people: at her apartment she greets guests naked and keeps a living panther, which on one occasion tries to pounce on Diaghilev. Terrified, he clambers onto a table, while Ida laughs. That is effectively the end of their already complex relationship. Lastly, a scandal erupts between Benois and Bakst. Envious of his comrade's success, Benois calls Bakst "a Jewish mug" and refuses to work on Diaghilev's team. "Fifteen years of shameless exploitation have utterly demoralized me," says Benois. Yet despite all the problems, the troubled season ends on a high note: the performance at London's Covent Garden is a triumph, which also makes the company profitable for the first time in its history.

Diaghilev returns to his dream of achieving recognition back home, and for that purpose tries to reach an agreement with his most formidable foe in Saint Petersburg—Matilda Kschessinskaya. Without her favor, it is impossible to perform. The fact is that the twenty-two-year-old Vaslav Nijinsky faces being called up for military service. If he were employed by the Imperial Theatres, he would be exempt, but as things stand, he must remain abroad. Without him, a tour of Saint Petersburg is impossible.

Diaghilev asks Kschessinskaya to help Nijinsky to avoid the army draft in exchange for giving her a chance to perform on the London stage. Kschessinskaya is already forty and dominates Russia, but she has never conquered Europe and time is running out. Diaghilev promises to stage two classical ballets by Tchaikovsky for her in London: *Swan Lake* and *Sleeping Beauty* (neither of which is part of Diaghilev's usual repertoire). "It's a shame," says Valentin Serov. "Despite her merits, she is not an *artiste*. . . . Nor do I see any need for a production of *Swan Lake*." For Serov, the former imperial portraitist, who parted company with the Romanovs after Bloody Sunday, any brown-nosing of the grand dukes is intolerable.

In late September 1911, a Saint Petersburg court unexpectedly declares Nijinsky to be a draft dodger. Moreover, Kschessinskaya is unable to persuade the Imperial Theatres to let Diaghilev use the Mikhailovsky Theatre, so he finds a less prestigious venue: the People's House of Nicholas II—a former pavilion from the All-Russia Exhibition of 1896 that was transported to the capital from Nizhny Novgorod. Nevertheless, some Nijinsky-less performances in the Russian capital are scheduled for February 1912.

Meanwhile, Kschessinskaya and Diaghilev's joint production in Covent Garden goes according to plan. In October 1911 Kschessinskaya arrives in London, accompanied by the grand dukes, and shocks the public with her abundance of jewelry. In addition to Kschessinskaya, the troupe is joined by Anna Pavlova, who dances in *Giselle*. All the performances are attended by the star of London high society—the young Oxford student Prince Felix Yusupov. He is friends with Pavlova, whom he describes as "heaven-sent." Her response is: "You have God in one eye and hell in the other."

On 5 December 1911, far from the triumph of London, Serov, the most principled of Diaghilev's friends, dies in Saint Petersburg. Diaghilev does not have time to attend the funeral, arriving only on 15 December. The next tragedy occurs in late January, when a fire breaks out at the People's House, rendering it unfit for staging a ballet. The frantic Diaghilev approaches Alexei Suvorin, the publisher of *New Time*, an ultraconservative who is totally unpalatable to the metropolitan intelligentsia.

Suvorin has his own private theatre, which Diaghilev begs to be allowed to rent. But Suvorin's price is mockingly unaffordable. "That's how the homeland greets us! It's clear how much we are needed," writes the insulted Stravinsky. "The vile petty hucksters and miscreants serve at the altar of filth, vulgarity and baseness. The presence of so many Suvorins and other riff-raff in Russia is insufferable." In the end, the most famous ballet troupe in the world fails to find a stage in Russia. Diaghilev moves the show to Dresden.

|| Chapter 10 ||

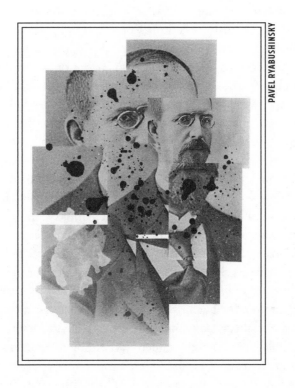

PAVEL RYABUSHINSKY

in which millionaires Alexander Guchkov
and Pavel Ryabushinsky try to engage big
business in managing the country

On 15 April 1912 the steamer *Titanic*, owned by the British company White Star Line, crashes into an iceberg off Greenland. A total of 2,224 people are on board, of which 1,514 perish. The first reports of the wreck of the *Titanic* appear in the world's media on 17 April—except in Russia, which, like its Old Style calendar, lags several days behind. Russians first learn of the incident on 4 May.

The main event in Russia at that moment is the visit of the recently appointed Prime Minister Vladimir Kokovtsov (still also the finance minister) to Moscow, Russia's economic capital. Kokovtsov replaced Stolypin as prime minister more than six months ago, but only now does he decide to talk with big business. He visits the stock exchange, and in the evening Grigory Krestovnikov, the head of the Stock Exchange Council (a union of industrialists), hosts a ceremonial dinner in honor of the prime minister. The merchant class does its best to make a good impression on the head of government,* who expresses polite regret that industrialists cannot serve in the Duma "in sufficient numbers" because of Stolypin's electoral law.

Big business as a whole is loyal to the authorities, but there are a few troublemakers. Their leader is Pavel Ryabushinsky, the eldest of eight brothers, a banker and an industrialist, and the publisher of the newspaper *Morning of Russia*. During the dinner, Ryabushinsky rises to his feet to talk about the numerous grievances of big business against the government (not least the persecution of the Old Believers, since they form the entire Russian business elite). Ryabushinsky's speech is effectively a challenge to the government, but Kokovtsov fails to hear the message, describing it as "incoherent babble." The "loose-tongued" (according to Kokovtsov) Ryabushinsky ends his tirade with a toast: "Here's not to the government, but to the patient, long-suffering Russian people still awaiting true liberation."

The host Grigory Krestovnikov is livid with Ryabushinsky for such tactlessness. The head of the Moscow Duma, Nikolai Guchkov, a descendant of a merchant family and the brother of the former chairman of the State Duma, Alexander Guchkov, is also indignant: "Pavel Ryabushinsky is the vilest scoundrel ever to have seen the light of day. In this private home, in such an intimate circle, he allows himself to lecture the chairman of the Council of Ministers?!"

---

*In the early twenty-first century large business representatives will still be very careful when dealing with the authorities. The Yukos affair was triggered by Mikhail Khodorkovsky holding a report on corruption at the Russian Union of Industrialists and Entrepreneurs' convention in the presence of Vladimir Putin. After that no more so-called "oligarchs" took a chance with publicly criticizing the authorities. On the contrary, representatives of large business have publicly stated that they are ready to hand over all their property to the state if need be.

But for many entrepreneurs, Ryabushinsky is a hero. "You alone spoke from a nationwide perspective, not as a wheeler-dealer," writes Yuly Guzhon, the owner of a Moscow steelworks. "I am sure that many will follow your example—it's high time." According to the police, who have an eye on the public mood, the speech "causes people to chatter and raises Ryabushinsky's popularity."

Ryabushinsky fronts the "young entrepreneurs"—a group of millionaire Old Believers who actively demand reforms and greater involvement of the merchant class in politics. The most active members of the group are Ryabushinsky's friends, Alexander Konovalov and Sergey Tretyakov (the grandson of one of the founders of the Tretyakov Gallery), who are co-financers of the newspaper *Morning of Russia*. Back in early 1911 they, together with Ryabushinsky, spearheaded the famous "Letter of the 66"—the first protest action by business on a matter that did not directly concern it. That was when the business world spoke out in support of Moscow University professors dismissed after the student unrest in memory of Leo Tolstoy. The press reported at the time that the signees of the "Letter of the 66" were collectively worth more than half a billion roubles.* But writing a letter to a newspaper is one thing, while publicly voicing dissatisfaction with the prime minister in his presence is quite another. Such behavior is for left-wing Duma members, not Moscow tycoons.

On the eve of the upcoming elections, Ryabushinsky and the "young entrepreneurs" create their own party called the Progressive Party, intended to represent the interests of business, fight for reforms, and squeeze out both the Kadets and the Octobrists.

DYING FOR GOLD

On the day when Ryabushinsky publicly slams Kokovtsov at a dinner party in Moscow, six thousand kilometers away a tragedy occurs. In the village of Bodaibo, in the Irkutsk region (in eastern Siberia, near the Lena River, about 4,500 kilometers from Saint Petersburg), the capital of the Russian gold mining industry, striking workers hold a rally for better pay, improved housing conditions, and the release of arrested comrades. The troops open fire on the demonstrators, killing around one hundred and fifty to two hundred people, according to various sources, with as many wounded. The gold deposit belongs to the British company Lena Goldfields, and its

---

*About $6,591,666,667 in 2017.

shares are traded on the London Stock Exchange, although it is managed by Russian shareholders—the Ginzburg family.

The Lena massacre makes the headlines. Journalists cite Kokovtsov's speech the previous day to Moscow's bankers, in particular his words that "state power should set an example of respect for the individual. It must value human life." The shooting of the workers provokes a new conflict among big business. The conservatives, led by Krestovnikov, believe that another wave of strikes throughout the country must be avoided at all costs by imposing fines on all strikers and dismissing the instigators. Ryabushinsky and his supporters oppose the suggestion. They believe that what happened in Bodaibo was a crime, and big business should support the protestors by protesting themselves.

Police reports say that Ryabushinsky's popularity is growing, which worries the Octobrists loyal to Guchkov. What is more, the term of the current Duma is about to expire, with only four months remaining before the next elections.

On 9 April, after the Easter recess, the State Duma holds a meeting. Its chairman, Mikhail Rodzianko, begins by expressing his condolences to the "friendly English nation" in connection with the recent sinking of the *Titanic*. He makes no mention of the Lena massacre. Only after lunch do three Duma factions raise the matter with the government, comparing the tragedy at Bodaibo with Bloody Sunday in 1905. Even Guchkov, a recent ally of Stolypin, sides with those calling for an investigation of the incident.

Two days later Interior Minister Makarov attends a Duma session to explain what happened: "When a crowd is spurred on by malicious agitators to attack the army, the only option for the soldiers is to open fire. That is how it was and how it will be!" This last phrase provokes an unlikely reaction. Two investigations are launched simultaneously: the government sends former Justice Minister Manukhin to Bodaibo, while the Duma opposition conducts its own fact-finding mission, headed by the renowned lawyer Alexander Kerensky. The Siberian execution puts an end to the political hibernation of recent times. The Duma, loyal to the government for the past five years, starts to loosen the shackles.

MAN-AT-ARMS

On 22 April 1912, the recent chairman of the State Duma, Alexander Guchkov, arrives in the Saint Petersburg suburb of Staraya Derevnya, not

ALEXANDER GUCHKOV

far from the palace where his close friend Pyotr Stolypin resided before his assassination. Guchkov has come to fight a duel with Colonel Sergei Myasoyedov, the head of military counterintelligence and an aide to the war minister. The colonel misses with his shot, while the Duma member shoots into the air. Both are unscathed. The reason for the duel was an interview with Guchkov for the paper *New Time*, in which he accused Myasoyedov of spying for Austria. Guchkov had no evidence—some officer friends from the General Staff had simply mentioned that Myasoyedov seemed a suspicious type. In the end, the colonel challenged Guchkov to a duel.

Alexander Guchkov is a hotheaded politician for whom dueling is commonplace. He once very nearly fought with Pavel Milyukov (their seconds dissuaded them). Later, on becoming chairman of the Duma, he drew pistols with another parliamentarian and wounded him. After this latest, bloodless duel, Myasoyedov resigns, while the newspapers print cartoons and satirical articles with headings such as "Cyrano de Guchkov."

The Guchkovs, a family of Moscow Old Believer merchants, who made their fortune in textile production, have always dabbled in politics: Alexander

Guchkov's grandfather served as the head of the Moscow City Duma, while his father and uncle were its members. Alexander is the same age as Savva Morozov and Konstantin Stanislavsky, and ten years older than Pavel Ryabushinsky. Unlike them, he has never been infatuated with the theatre or art. Back at school, he wanted to fight for Russia in the war against Turkey, but ended up following in his father's footsteps, becoming a member of the Moscow City Duma by the age of thirty. At thirty-seven, he suddenly left for South Africa—to fight in the Anglo-Boer War on the side of the Boers. He was wounded and taken prisoner. Four years later, in 1903, he took part in the Macedonian uprising against the Ottoman Empire. During the Russo-Japanese War he worked in the Red Cross and was again captured, having refused to retreat from Mukden and been abandoned by the Russian army. By the age of fifty, Guchkov has earned the reputation of an honest lunatic, someone who is ready to die for his beliefs.

In 1905 Guchkov headed the Union of 17 October, Sergei Witte's party of reformists, after which he fell in with Stolypin. Despite his merchant roots, inside the Duma he represents the interests not of business, but of the military. He witnessed for himself the horror of defeat in the Far East and understands its causes, for which reason he dreams of reforming the army and turning it into a modern and combat-ready force. Something akin to an officers' circle forms around Guchkov, in which the question of reforming the armed forces is paramount.

At the same time, the irascible Guchkov does not excel in the field of military discipline. He delivers a blazing speech in the Duma, blaming all the woes of the army on the tsar's relatives in command, calling on the grand dukes to resign. After this speech, Milyukov runs up to him: "Alexander Ivanovich [Guchkov], what have you done? They'll disband the State Duma!"

From that moment on, Guchkov and his officers' circle are looked upon with suspicion and likened disparagingly to the Young Turks (a political reform movement in the Ottoman Empire). Guchkov's references to the Turkish experience only strengthen these suspicions. His officer allies are gradually dismissed from the General Staff, including some very senior figures. The new war minister, Sukhomlinov, tries to hide important matters from the Duma defense commission, of which Guchkov is a part. Guchkov believes that Sukhomlinov rose to prominence by telling jokes to the tsar, instead of feeding him with reports. Sukhomlinov is clearly not interested in army reforms, believes Guchkov.

Guchkov's duel with Sukhomlinov's friend and aide Myasoyedov is only the start of the cold war between them. Sukhomlinov reports to

Nicholas II that Guchkov's "Young Turks" hate him for his loyalty to the sovereign. After a recent speech about Rasputin, Nicholas II considers Guchkov, himself a monarchist, an enemy of the regime.

7,200 GRAMOPHONES

The third "Stolypin" Duma, having served its term, is dissolved. September 1912 sees the start of the pre-election race. The government has developed a taste for power and makes use of "administrative resources" to secure the right outcome. The 1912 elections are unprecedented on that score.

A full two years before the election, Stolypin ordered 4 million roubles* to be allocated to support the government's chosen candidates. The philosopher Sergei Bulgakov, one of the authors of *Vekhi*, who recently castigated the Russian intelligentsia, cannot believe his eyes: there is widespread intimidation of voters; candidates are excluded at the last moment; and there is direct interference on the part of officials. To the horror of the deeply religious Bulgakov, the driving force behind the electoral manipulation is the clergy—for it is they who ensure the desired result at the polling stations. "The voting public has been replaced by 7,200 priests," says the Kadet candidate Fyodor Rodichev during a campaign rally. "It's the same as cranking up 7,200 gramophones and saying that it is the voice of the people."

Oppositionists begin to unite against the bureaucratic onslaught in the summer of 1912. New life is breathed into the Freemasonry movement. The liberal parliamentarians need a non-partisan organization to act in unison and nominate single candidates to stand against the government's intended placeholders. The Kadets suggest using the Freemasons as a vehicle.

With that in mind, the Freemasons overhaul their organization: one of the main reformers is the thirty-two-year-old Kadet Duma member Nikolai Nekrasov. He and his comrades propose simplifying the admission procedure, abolishing the system of Masonic degrees, rejecting past rituals, and basically creating their own Masonic brotherhood, independent of the French, to be called the "Great East of the Peoples of Russia." Parliamentarians from various factions are invited to join the new lodge—even the head of the Social Democrats, the Duma member from Tbilisi, Nikolai Chkheidze. Up-and-coming politicians who intend to run for the Duma are welcomed, too. One is the lawyer Alexander Kerensky, who is winning

---

* About $52,733,333 in 2017.

hearts and minds with his investigation of the Lena massacre. Ryabushinsky and Konovalov also join the Moscow lodge.

Nekrasov is duly elected chairman of the Masonic convention. The new organization is far more active than all previous versions. It is not a pre-election campaign office, but a platform for discussing joint plans.

As a result, despite the immense pressure from the authorities, the Duma ends up being fairly heterogeneous. Ryabushinsky's Progressive Party is the most impressive debutant, gaining forty-eight seats (about 10 percent of the Duma). Ryabushinsky himself did not run, but his friend Konovalov was elected.

The thirty-one-year-old Alexander Kerensky is elected for the first time, having run a very active campaign both in the press and through the Masonic lodge. A candidate from the Socialist-Revolutionaries, during his recent trip to Lena to investigate the massacre he met and befriended the legendary SR exile Babushka Breshko-Breshkovskaya. Now in the Duma, he becomes the leader of the Socialist-Revolutionary faction.

The Social Democrat faction is very small, just eight Mensheviks and six Bolsheviks. The most curious figure among them is the Bolshevik Roman Malinovsky, the new star of the party. Having met Lenin just two years ago, he is already an insider. It is through Malinovsky's efforts that the now-legal Bolshevik newspaper *Pravda* is published for the first time. At the same time, Malinovsky is a secret police agent—and the Interior Ministry's greatest infiltration since Azef.

THE TSAREVICH IS DYING

The imperial family spends most of 1912 away from the capital: spring is whiled away in Crimea, summer is spent swimming off the coast of Finland, and September sees a trip to Belovezhskaya Pushcha.[*]

Emperor Nicholas II is bogged down in family problems. His mother dislikes his wife, and his younger brother Mikhail is having an affair with his adjutant's wife. They have an illegitimate child and want to marry, but Nicholas is firmly opposed to the idea.

Meanwhile, Nicholas's second cousin, King Constantine I of Greece, has started a war against Turkey, in alliance with Bulgaria, Serbia, and Montenegro. The idea of helping their "Slavonic brothers" is very popular

---

[*] Territory on the border of modern Belarus and Poland where the Belavezha Accords were signed in 1991 declaring the dissolution of the Soviet Union.

in Russian society. The newspapers immediately send correspondents to the Balkans, including Leon Trotsky for *Kiev Life*.

Grand Duke Nikolai Nikolaevich, the tsar's uncle and commander of the imperial guard, is especially keen to fight. His wife Stana and her sister Milica, the daughters of the Montenegrin king, beg Nicholas II to help their father. The late Stolypin had always strongly opposed any military action, saying that Russia cannot afford a war until the internal enemy is defeated. Now the role of "pacifist-in-chief" is taken by Rasputin. According to Vyrubova, practically on his knees, he implores the tsar that "Russia's enemies are waiting for her to get caught up in this war," and that "Russia will suffer inevitable misfortune."

In early October, the imperial family goes hunting in Poland for a month. There, the eight-year-old heir to the throne is playing by a pond. As he tries to jump into a boat, he bangs his leg and suffers an internal hemorrhage. Unable to move his foot, he screams in pain day and night, while Empress Alexandra sits by his bedside. On 19 October, the heir develops a fever. The doctors, duly summoned from Saint Petersburg, say that his condition is hopeless. "When I die, put up a small monument to me in the park," Alexei says to his mother. Nicholas, on leaving his son's room, sobs violently in front of his retinue.

The minister of the court, Baron Fredericks, insists on issuing an official press release regarding the health of the tsarevich, but Nicholas and Alexandra consider his illness to be a state secret. The empress asks Vyrubova to send a telegram to Rasputin. "The illness is not as dangerous as it seems," he replies. "Just make sure that the doctors do not torture him." The boy does indeed begin to recover.

On 17 October Grand Duke Mikhail, despite promising not to, secretly marries his civil-law wife, Natalia Wulfert, in Austria. Nicholas II punishes him by dismissing him from all his posts and barring him from entering Russia.

THE ROMANOVS 300 YEARS LATER

The year 1913 marks the three hundredth anniversary of the House of Romanov. Lavish celebrations are due to begin on 21 February—the day when the first Romanov, Mikhail I, became tsar in 1613.

That month the imperial family moves from Tsarskoye Selo to the Winter Palace. Alexandra is in very low spirits. She remembers life at the Winter Palace a decade ago, when seventeenth-century balls and costumes were in vogue at court. Since then, her health has deteriorated sharply, and she hates public appearances: "I'm a wreck," she says to Vyrubova.

The celebrations continue into spring with a royal trip to Kostroma, Yaroslavl, and Nizhny Novgorod. The peasants, seeing the tsar's steamer, wade waist-deep into the water, singing the national anthem. Such scenes of popular adoration convince the empress that the common folk really do love her husband, and that all of Russia's woes stem from the evil intelligentsia. The Moscow leg of the festivities is a triumph. With the sun smiling, Nicholas II enters the Kremlin on foot at the head of a procession of censer-swinging clergymen, while Alexandra and Alexei ride in an open carriage behind. The bells ring, the people rejoice.

The trip introduces the imperial couple's children to the other Russia. The girls are very patriotic. They speak Russian at home and are horrified that one day they may have to marry and live abroad. Prior to this trip, they have seen almost nothing of their own country, having spent their entire lives shuttling between Tsarskoye Selo and Livadia Palace in Crimea.

The Romanovs almost never travel in Russia, and many family members sojourn at length in Europe. The tsar's mother spends most of her time in Copenhagen, where she was born, or visiting her sister, the queen of England, or vacationing in Biarritz. The tsar's brother Mikhail, meanwhile, is forced to live abroad. Traveling in Europe, the grand dukes and their families stay in the most expensive hotels, reserving not just rooms, but entire floors.

The lifestyle of Kirill, Boris, and Andrei, the children of Grand Duke Vladimir, Diaghilev's former patron, is more extravagant than most: Boris is forever to be found in Nice surrounded by prostitutes. Nicholas regularly complains about such "disgraceful" behavior. Andrei, along with his mistress Kschessinskaya, spends a lot of time in Monaco, since he is a gambler, as indeed is his mother, Grand Duchess Miechen.

The luxury of the Russian court is renowned across Europe. Rumors about the enormous accounts held by the tsar and his relatives in European banks are not groundless: after 1905, when Nicholas II was thinking about fleeing Russia for Germany, secret accounts were opened for him at the Berlin bank Mendelssohn & Co (up to 20 million roubles*), plus smaller amounts with Crédit Lyonnais and the Bank of England.

Their good knowledge of Europe is combined with a poor knowledge of Russia. Years later, Grand Duchess Maria, a cousin of the tsar, writes that neither she nor her relatives had any idea of the extent to which the Russian and European provinces differed in terms of standard of living.

---

* About $263,666,667 in 2017.

"COME TO YOUR SENSES!"

In 1913, Russian society gradually comes out of hibernation, and the debates and polemics resume. The investigations of the Lena massacre and the murder of Andrei Yushchinsky in Kiev are the two hottest topics. Both cases are highly politicized: the left-wing parties use the Lena incident as revolutionary propaganda, while the Beilis case is exploited by the right-wing parties to promote anti-Semitism.

Senator Manukhin finishes his report in the autumn of 1912. It remains classified for quite a while, meaning that the Duma discusses it only in the spring of 1913. The conclusions of the senator coincide completely with those of Kerensky: the living conditions at the mine are horrendous; the demands of the strikers were purely economic; and the shooting was totally unprovoked. The government, however, does seek to punish the guilty—a few managers are fired, and the officer who ordered the shooting is demoted, but nothing more. The inquiry into the sinking of the *Titanic*, which occurred almost on the same day as the Lena massacre, resulting in the deaths of around fifteen hundred people, is also a whitewash.

Kiev, on the other hand, sees the start of a high-profile court case. Mendel Beilis is arrested, which splits society, just like during the Dreyfus case in France fifteen years earlier.

Back in November 1911 the "conscience of the nation," the fifty-eight-year-old writer Vladimir Korolenko, wrote an open letter stating that "blood libel"—the charge that Jews drink the blood of infants—was originally a pagan slur against the early Christians.

Korolenko's open letter is signed by nearly all the leading Russian intellectuals of the day: Maxim Gorky, Dmitry Merezhkovsky, Zinaida Gippius, Dmitry Filosofov, Leonid Andreyev, Alexander Blok, Alexander Benois, almost the entire liberal bloc inside the Duma, and hundreds of professors and journalists. A campaign is also launched in Europe in support of Beilis. Supportive letters are written by some of the continent's most famous writers, including Thomas Mann, H.G. Wells, and Anatole France. The "blood libel" charge is rejected by many nationalists, too, including, for instance, the publisher of the newspaper *The Kievite*, Dmitry Pikhno, and his son-in-law, Vasily Shulgin, the one who tried to prevent the Kiev pogrom of 1905. Pikhno writes an article against his own Black Hundred acolytes: "You yourselves make human sacrifices!" *The Kievite* publishes an in-depth and convincing account of the murder of Yushchinsky, effectively proving that Beilis is innocent and pointing the finger at the black marketeer Vera Cheberyak and her accomplices.

WHO KILLED ANDREI YUSHCHINSKY

The Beilis trial becomes a matter of national—and international—significance. The prosecution is led by the conservative Justice Minister Ivan Shcheglovitov. Despite the flimsy evidence, he decides to press ahead with court proceedings so that he and the government are not accused of "selling out to the yids." In an effort to please the authorities, officials go after anyone who criticizes the investigation or the prosecution: newspapers containing articles in support of Beilis are confiscated.

The trial begins on 23 September. "It feels like the sixteenth century," writes Korolenko inside the courtroom, although "outside lies modern Kiev, with beautiful houses, signboards, newspapers and electricity." The makeup of the jury (comprising seven peasants, three members of the bourgeoisie, and two minor officials) is unusual—not a single intellectual, which is rare for a university city. The paper that publishes Korolenko's article, which goes on to accuse the authorities of manipulation, is confiscated, and he himself faces criminal charges.

The loudest protest comes from big-city lawyers: they write an appeal describing the trial of Beilis as violating the foundations of communal existence and abasing Russia in the eyes of the world. The text is published by four newspapers in Saint Petersburg and Kiev. After the trial, the instigators of the appeal—Alexander Kerensky and Nikolai Sokolov—are sentenced to eight months in prison for insulting the authorities.

On the final day of the trial, 28 October 1913, everyone is expecting a guilty verdict and a mass pogrom in Kiev. Pogromist forces have already assembled in advance.

The jury vote comes as a surprise: six return a verdict of guilty, and six of not guilty. According to the legal rules, if there is no majority guilty verdict, the defendant is acquitted. Beilis is released right there in the courtroom. "The nightmare is fading," writes Korolenko about the pogrom so narrowly avoided, for now the authorities will prevent it. It is a victory for the liberal section of society. Beilis and his family leave Russia for Palestine, and the investigation is closed. The fateful question of who killed Andrei Yushchinsky is not raised in public again.

THE SCANDAL OF SPRING

On 29 May 1913, a theatre on the Champs Élysées hosts the premiere of Diaghilev's new ballet *The Rite of Spring*. Even before the premiere,

Diaghilev talks of a musical revolution. Right from the start, it is clear that this is no ordinary performance, full of imitation pagan dances to the accompaniment of Stravinsky's atonal composition. For the twenty-four-year-old Nijinsky, it is a special moment—his debut as a choreographer. Recently the papers have been writing that he is "a young terrorist who has throttled the ballet."

The audience starts whispering, and soon the murmurs turn into chortling, whistling, and outright swearing. Stravinsky's nerves fail, and he leaves the theatre. Fans of Diaghilev's troupe shout back at the dissenters: the poet Gabriele D'Annunzio and the composer Claude Debussy leave their private box and charge at the audience with fists practically flying. With the performance still in progress, a major scuffle breaks out, reminiscent of a football match, not a night at the theatre. Diaghilev orders the lights in the hall to be turned on and off to try to placate the public, but eventually the police have to be called. In the midst of the catcalling and brawling, some audience members cheer and applaud: Nijinsky and Diaghilev even come on stage for a bow.

Diaghilev is delighted by the scandal: "Just what I wanted!" he cries. The whole company goes out to dinner, before strolling through the Bois de Boulogne until sunrise. Jean Cocteau recalls that during the taxi ride back Diaghilev starts muttering something in Russian. Stravinsky and Nijinsky listen to him attentively. When Diaghilev starts weeping, Cocteau asks what the matter is. They say that Diaghilev is reciting his favorite poem by Pushkin.

But the scandal backfires. Covent Garden, the Grand Opera, and other theatres refuse to stage ballets choreographed by Nijinsky for fear of the audience reaction. Orchestras revolt against Stravinsky's music. Diaghilev himself considers *The Rite of Spring* to be overlong and wants it cut, but Stravinsky is possessive. On top of everything, Bakst refuses to design costumes and scenery for Nijinsky's ballets, while the lovers Diaghilev and Nijinsky quarrel endlessly. Diaghilev is jealous of Nijinsky's relationships with women, and they often have bitter arguments in public.

Nijinsky's diary, which he starts to keep much later when suffering from mental illness, describes their separation in detail. He depicts with disgust Diaghilev's dyed-gray hair and false front teeth, comparing him to an old woman. They sleep in different rooms, and Nijinsky keeps his door locked at all times. When he goes to visit prostitutes, Diaghilev orders a servant to follow him.

In August 1913 the troupe goes on tour to Latin America—without Diaghilev, who is afraid of steamboats. On board, Nijinsky makes the acquaintance of Romola de Pulszky, the daughter of a Hungarian aristocrat. Almost immediately on arrival in Buenos Aires, he proposes to her, and on 10 September 1913 they are married. The dancer's sister and mother are at that time in Saint Petersburg and learn about the wedding from the newspapers. Diaghilev is on vacation in Venice. When he receives a telegram with the news, he becomes hysterical. He immediately fires Nijinsky, who then tries to form his own troupe. His efforts to entice Stravinsky are not successful, and a tour to London ends in failure: he gives two performances, announces that he is ill, and rips up the contract.

Diaghilev is lucky: in the autumn of 1913 he meets the seventeen-year-old dancer Leonid Myasin, who is the complete opposite of Nijinsky. Neither tall nor handsome, Myasin is more cerebral and intellectual. Diaghilev also finds new set designers in the shape of Natalia Goncharova and Mikhail Larionov. The twenty-three-year-old composer Sergei Prokofiev is also eager to come on board.

Diaghilev no longer seeks recognition in Petersburg high society, which is alien to new concepts and "persistently defends outdated traditions." Instead, he focuses on the intelligentsia and the merchant class—"the middle class that made the Moscow Art Theatre a success." Turning his back on Saint Petersburg, he plans a series of performances at Mamontov's former opera house in Moscow. The tour is scheduled for January-February 1914.

THE NEW AMERICA

The year 1913 is the peak of Russia's economic development, the apogee of the "stable, well-fed years." Russian GDP is the fourth largest in the world, behind only the United States and Germany, but ahead of Britain.

Capitalism has transformed the face of Russia. The tsar's brother-in-law, Grand Duke Sandro, notes with irritation that in Saint Petersburg everyone seems to be "doing business": officers discuss the rise in steel prices; society ladies invite "financial geniuses" to their salons; even priests dabble in the stock market.

The main driver of the Russian economy is the merchant class. "It is time for the Russian merchants," says Pavel Ryabushinsky, "to become the preeminent social class and proudly wear the label of 'Russian merchant' without chasing after the degenerate nobility." Debates are raging about whether Russia will become the new America, a new breed of economic giant.

The government even develops a new policy to that effect. It is the brainchild of Agriculture Minister Alexander Krivoshein, one of the co-authors of the late Stolypin's agrarian reforms and the latter's former right-hand man. Now Krivoshein comes up with a program to stimulate economic growth: he wants to invest in the creation of major state enterprises, build new railways, and carry out large-scale land improvement. It smacks of Franklin Roosevelt's "New Deal," which will appear in the depression-hit United States only sixteen years later. Though, as agricultural minister, Krivoshein is primarily focused on agribusiness.

Krivoshein's plan runs counter to the policy of the incumbent prime minister, Vladimir Kokovtsov. A thrifty financier, Kokovtsov wants a deficit-free budget and a curb on government spending. Industry should be developed on the back of private investment, he believes.[*]

While Nicholas II is away on vacation, the government intrigues become more Machiavellian. In his struggle against the prime minister-cum-accountant Kokovtsov, the reform-minded Krivoshein decides to enlist the help of the new interior minister, Nikolai Maklakov, who is popular with the imperial family for his ability to tell anecdotes and perform entertaining mime routines. His party trick is the "jump of the amorous panther," which greatly amuses the royal daughters. Maklakov is not a reformer at all, having recently drafted a new censorship law. But like Krivoshein, he despises Kokovtsov and wants to ruin him.

A campaign is launched against the prime minister. Krivoshein convinces the tsar that the Russian Empire needs financial reform, which Kokovtsov is hampering (this much is true). Krivoshein believes that it is high time to abolish the state monopoly on the alcohol trade and to introduce income tax. The campaign against Prime Minister Kokovtsov is joined by the sixty-four-year-old former prime minister, Sergei Witte. He wants to head the government once more and starts to openly criticize the Finance Ministry's law to combat drunkenness, saying that Kokovtsov (who is also the finance minister) is pushing the country into alcoholism, which was certainly not the case when he, Witte, was in charge. Witte finds an unusual ally in the shape of Grigory Rasputin. The "elder" increasingly complains to "mother" and "father" (Alexandra and Nicholas) that the

---

[*]Differences between Kokovtsov and Krivoshein are very similar to the dilemma that Russia will face exactly 100 years later, in the "fat noughties." Finance Minister Alexei Kudrin, just like his predecessor, will be advocating for a stabilization fund while many of his opponents will insist that excess profit from oil trade should be invested in infrastructure development and modernization of the Russian economy. This conflict will end almost the same way as the one of the early twentieth century: the "fat noughties" will come to an end and no reforms will have taken place.

Russian people are taking to the bottle—and the alcohol monopoly is to blame.

The tsar dismisses his prime minister, but even Rasputin's influence is not enough to resurrect Witte's career in government: "Mother and father hate Witte's guts," he says. Nicholas offers the post of prime minister to Krivoshein. But Krivoshein knows from the experience of Stolypin and Kokovtsov how difficult the job of prime minister is—a balancing act between taking action and not provoking the tsar's irritation. Moreover, he is suffering from a heart condition. Krivoshein decides to remain in the shadows and promote the candidacy of a "puppet" prime minister. The role is perfectly suited to the seventy-four-year-old Ivan Goremykin, the same aged placeholder who gleefully handed power over to Stolypin in 1906. Seven years later he is offered the prime minister's chair again—and submissively accepts the appointment.

Goremykin's appointment comes as a real shock to society. Particularly outraged are Ryabushinsky and other young Moscow-based progressive entrepreneurs hoping for political reform. "The government has taken insolence to a new level, ignoring all opposition in the belief that the country is sound asleep," says the businessman Konovalov.

Ryabushinsky invites that selfsame opposition to attend a meeting at his home, including members of not only the Progressivists, the Kadets, and the Octobrists, but also the Socialist-Revolutionaries, Mensheviks, and even the Bolsheviks. The Bolsheviks, of course, have no intention of agreeing to anything. Lenin instructs his comrades to use the opportunity to get some money from the industrialists: "No less than 10,000 roubles."* The other oppositionists take the meeting with Ryabushinsky more seriously.

SECTARIANS AND PROVOCATEURS

The end of 1913 sees a general amnesty for all sorts of enemies of the regime, of which the monk Iliodor is one. He sits inside a monastery prison and writes letter after letter, cursing Rasputin, Vyrubova, and the "minister of the church" Sabler. In May Iliodor petitions the Holy Synod to defrock him. Saint Petersburg acquaintances write to him that there is no need to hurry: there will soon be an amnesty, so just calm down and wait. "Let my tongue fall out before I calm down!" is Iliodor's response. "My whole being is consumed by a tormenting thirst for holy vengeance. . . . I will never

---

*About $131,833 in 2017.

accept a pardon. Only criminals are pardoned. I am not a criminal. I have accomplished a great feat."

In December 1913, realizing that the Holy Synod is planning to hush the matter up, Iliodor writes another repudiation of the church—this time he cuts a vein and signs it in blood. Again he curses the church leaders for being in league with Rasputin, ending his missive with the words: "Henceforth, I do not know your God. I do not recognize you as hierarchs." Only now is Iliodor defrocked and let out of the monastery prison. He returns to his parents' village on the Don River. There he creates a sect called "New Galilee," and invites his former parishioners from Tsaritsyn to join.

While this is going on, Maxim Gorky is busy abandoning his "sect" on the island of Capri and heading back to Russia. The long-anticipated amnesty in honor of the tercentenary of the House of Romanov allows political émigrés to return to their homeland. Gorky goes to Finland, although other Social Democrats do not dare to follow suit, since, despite the amnesty, they are still being hunted in Saint Petersburg—so far in 1913 the secret police have arrested all the prominent Bolsheviks they can find.

The Mensheviks believe that there is a traitor inside the party and point the finger at Roman Malinovsky. Lenin is sure that this is revenge for Malinovsky's anti-Menshevik activity. However, one of Malinovsky's next victims (for he is indeed a double agent) is the Bolshevik Josef Dzhugashvili, who returns to Saint Petersburg under false documents and becomes the editor of the newspaper *Pravda*, taking the pseudonym Stalin. Malinovsky invites his "comrade" to a masquerade ball, where the police are waiting. Stalin tries to escape, even changing into women's clothing, but he is caught, arrested, tried, and exiled to Turukhansk, a village in western Siberia. Stalin's attempt to flee dressed as a woman is never mentioned in later Soviet history books. In fact, it is the Bolsheviks' enemy Alexander Kerensky who is accused of such an unmanly action.

NOTHING DEPENDS ON US

Many contemporaries will later assert in their memoirs that they saw the coming of the First World War. However, there is nothing in their behavior to suggest such foresight. In early 1914, it is (lack of) business as usual. Intellectual oppositionists and monarchist courtiers alike are sure that nothing will change and that nothing depends on them.

But the supreme authorities are also treading water. Tired of bad news, complaints, ultimatums, and intrigues, the tsar is very rarely seen in the capital and lives with his family elsewhere on near-permanent vacation. In Crimea he receives ministers, but during his summer yachting trips around the Gulf of Finland he isolates himself from officialdom. Rumors circulate in Petersburg salons that Rasputin is in charge of the country, but in reality no one is. Rasputin lives in his Siberian village and corresponds with Empress Alexandra. Prime Minister Goremykin tries very hard to do nothing at all—after all, his brief is "not to overshadow the tsar."

In the spring of 1914 Alexandra begins to harbor terrible suspicions. She is jealous of her husband over Anna Vyrubova. Alexandra suffers from migraines, heart trouble, and nervous seizures. During that summer's yachting in the Gulf of Finland, she keeps repeating that this is their last trip. Many years later Vyrubova will interpret these words as a premonition of war.

Most members of the imperial family move to London. The tsar's mother, Empress Dowager Maria Feodorovna, spends June with her beloved sister, Queen Alexandra, the wife of the late Edward VII. The youngest son of Maria Feodorovna, Mikhail, expelled from Russia for his *mésalliance*, is also in London, as are Maria's husband, Prince Shervashidze, daughters Olga and Xenia, son-in-law Sandro, and granddaughter Irina and her husband—the young Felix Yusupov. Felix knows London very well, the star of the local *beau monde*. The family has a great time. Almost every day is spent going to the theatre and strolling in Hyde Park. On the morning of 15 June (according to the Old Style Russian calendar) they are having breakfast at Buckingham Palace when they are informed that Archduke Franz Ferdinand of Austria and his wife have been assassinated in Sarajevo, the capital of Bosnia and Herzegovina. "What savagery! Thank God that when they died they were together," Maria Feodorovna writes in her diary. In the evening, they go to Castle Combe, where Chaliapin is performing.

FOUR MURDERERS

What a century later looks like a carefully conceived plan was, in fact, nothing more than a string of random occurrences. On the day when the Austrian emperor's nephew and heir, Franz Ferdinand, arrives in Sarajevo, a group of nine terrorists is plotting to assassinate him. In 1908 the Ottoman territory of Bosnia and Herzegovina was annexed by Austria-Hungary and now, just six years later, the anti-Habsburg movement is flourishing.

The Young Bosnia movement that wants to kill Franz Ferdinand consists more of fanatics than professional killers. Many of them are sick with tuberculosis, for which reason they are perfectly willing to die for the cause. On the day of the assassination, the leader of the group, the nineteen-year-old Nedelko Chabrinovich, stands in the crowd and greets the archduke's motorcade with everyone else. As the archduke's car approaches, Chabrinovich throws a grenade into the road. The driver sees it coming and puts his foot to the floor. The explosion occurs under the car behind, injuring some of its occupants, but the heir to the Austrian throne is unharmed. Chabrinovich takes a capsule of cyanide and jumps into the nearby Miljacka River. But the poison is ineffective, and the river is too shallow. The terrorist is caught alive.

The archduke asks to go with the wounded to the local hospital, but the driver takes a wrong turn. The accompanying general stops the car and orders it to be turned around. This hiccup occurs a just few meters from where Gavrilo Princip, a nineteen-year-old Young Bosnia activist and tuberculosis sufferer, is standing. Unable to believe his eyes, he runs up to the car and shoots at the couple. Franz Ferdinand and his wife Sofia die a few minutes later. Like Chabrinovich, Princip tries and fails to commit suicide.

The next day, 16 June (Old Style), a woman named Khionia Guseva arrives in the village of Pokrovskoe in Siberia, home to Rasputin. She is thirty-three years old and has lost her nose to syphilis. Khionia is a fan of Iliodor. When she lived in Tsaritsyn, he called her his spiritual daughter, and now she is a member of New Galilee.

The defrocked monk preaches to his followers not to consider themselves Orthodox, for the Russian Church has been hijacked by the false prophet "Grishka" Rasputin. "My dear father, Grishka is indeed a devil. I'll kill him! I'll slaughter him like the prophet Elijah, on God's command, slaughtered the 450 false prophets of Baal! Father, give me your blessing," she asks. She sets off for Rasputin's hometown and duly finds him. Dressed as a beggar, Guseva approaches and stabs him in the stomach. Rasputin runs off, but she goes after him. Rasputin grabs a metal bar lying on the ground and hits her over the head. Khionia falls to the ground. The next day the newspapers publish reports of Rasputin's death, but a day later they are refuted. Rasputin is alive, but in the hospital, where he remains for some time.

On 31 July a man with a notebook is walking around Montmartre. He is twenty-nine-year-old Raoul Villain, a member of the League of Young Friends of Alsace-Lorraine, and a fanatic like Princip and Guseva. The notebook is used to chart the movements of Jean Jaurès, France's preeminent leftist politician, the leader and unifier of the French socialists.

Jaurès is a pacifist and opposes the retaking of Alsace-Lorraine (annexed by Germany during the Franco-Prussian War). For the nationalist Villain, this is treason. He enters the cafe *Croissant* and sees Jaurès dining at a table by the window. He shoots Jaurès twice in the head, killing his victim instantly.

Chabrinovich and Princip are both sentenced to twenty years in prison, where they die from tuberculosis. Khionia Guseva is sent to a psychiatric clinic, where she regales inmates with her story of how she "killed Grishka." "I'm a national hero," she says. In 1917 she is released, whereupon she immediately tries to assassinate Patriarch Tikhon.[*] Raoul Villain will spend five years behind bars before being acquitted in 1919 to the delight of French nationalists, who believe that by killing the pacifist he helped secure victory in the First World War. The legal costs are charged to the widow of the murdered Jaurès.

CHRONICLE OF A GROWING PATRIOTISM

The murder of the heir to the Austrian throne in Sarajevo fails to stir the Russian press, which writes that his death is a positive development, since Franz Ferdinand was anti-Russian.

On 10 July Austria-Hungary presents Serbia with an ultimatum. Leon Trotsky, working as a journalist in Vienna, is struck by the patriotic excitement of the Austrians—the slogan "Death to the Serbs" is ubiquitous.

On 15 July Austria-Hungary declares war on Serbia, whereupon Saint Petersburg starts to discuss its response: Should Russia mobilize in support of its Orthodox ally? The empress telegraphs Rasputin: "We are horrified. Do you also think war is a reality? Pray for us, advise us." Still in hospital, Rasputin replies: "Do not go to war. It will be the end of Russia."

The next day Nicholas II sends a telegram to his wife's cousin, Kaiser Wilhelm II of Germany, with a proposal to discuss the Austria-Serbia question at an international conference in The Hague. It is a delaying tactic. Russian officers are sure that war is inevitable, but believe that it will last no longer than six months.

On 18 July Nicholas II publishes a national mobilization order. Anna Vyrubova runs to Empress Alexandra, who tells her that it must all be some mistake—only the provinces bordering Austria need to be mobilized.

---

[*]Patriarch of Moscow and All Russia in 1917-1925 elected for the reinstated Moscow Patriarchate.

Alexandra hurries to her husband and leaves him in tears, crying: "It's over. We are at war and I didn't even know anything about it."

On 19 July Nicholas receives a telegram from Wilhelm, who urges him to stop the mobilization of the Russian army and to meet for talks. "What will I say to my people?" the tsar asks his wife. Later that evening, the German ambassador to Russia hands Sazonov a piece of paper with a declaration of war. The empress sobs, but Nicholas perks up: "Now at least we know where we stand." On the same day, the former monk Iliodor, now Sergei Trufanov, secretly crosses the Russian-Swedish border. He has gone into hiding after Guseva's failed attempt on Rasputin's life.

On 20 July Russia publishes an imperial manifesto declaring war. The mood everywhere is upbeat: people are patriotic and enthusiastic. A huge banner-waving rally is held on Saint Petersburg's Palace Square. Nicholas goes onto the balcony and the entire crowd falls to its knees and sings "God Save the Tsar!" "They're all sober," remarks the tsar's cousin, Grand Duke Andrei, referring to the fact that during the mobilization period all liquor stores across the country have been closed. The measure is subsequently extended throughout the war, effectively introducing a dry law.

On 21 July Germany declares war on France. It is just three days since the murder of Jaurès. Although he was a pacifist, his party supports the war. Likewise, that same day, the German Social Democratic Party unanimously votes for the war. Lenin, having received the latest issue of the party's newspaper *Vorwärts*, believes that it is a hoax: his Second International comrades could not do such a thing.

ATROCITIES AND DEFEATISTS

On 22 July Saint Petersburg is gripped by a powerful patriotic surge: a mob storms the German embassy on Saint Isaac's Square, smashing it for more than an hour under the tolerant gaze of the police. The wine cellar is looted, and crystalware, antique paintings, and a collection of Renaissance-era bronze artifacts are destroyed. Only the portraits of Nicholas and Alexandra in the reception hall are left intact, although they are removed and carried through the city by the crowd to the tune of the national anthem.

People climb onto the embassy roof, where there stands a huge bronze statue of the Greek mythological twins Castor and Pollux, holding their horses' bridles. The statue is somehow toppled off the building to cheers from below. The embassy is set on fire, and it burns to the ground. The next day the Russian Foreign Ministry expresses deep regret over the incident.

However, it is only the beginning of the campaign. On 31 July Saint Petersburg's anti-German Czech community calls for the city to be renamed. Without hesitation, Nicholas II adopts the name "Petrograd." No one cares to remember that the name "Petersburg" is in fact of Dutch origin (Peter the Great spent several months working incognito in the Netherlands), for it sounds the same in German—and anti-German sentiment is snowballing. Theatres remove Schiller and Goethe from their repertoires, and the Imperial Theatres prohibit the staging of Wagner's operas. Newspapers suggest replacing the German "Butterbrod" with the English "sandwich."

According to the census of 1897, almost two million ethnic Germans live in Russia, speaking German at home. And the number of Russified Germans with German surnames is even greater. Threatened with anti-German pogroms, many start to change their names. German bakeries and sausage shops close down. Describing the "German atrocities" in Europe, Russian newspapers write that Germany is no ordinary foe, but the "enemy of civilization itself." The portrayal of Germans as cruel and barbaric is a common motif in the Russian press.

Russian subjects vacationing in Europe hurry home. Everyone faces difficulties, and their stories are published in the "German Atrocities" section that graces every newspaper.

Empress Dowager Maria Feodorovna returns from London by train. In Berlin she is informed that she cannot proceed overland and must travel to Denmark and onwards by sea. The husband of her granddaughter Irina, Felix Yusupov, is arrested by the Germans—albeit just for a day. When war breaks out, Grand Duke Konstantin is receiving treatment in Germany. He and his family are allowed to leave, but the train does not take them all the way to the border, and the journey must be completed on foot, which the infirm fifty-six-year-old grand duke cannot do. A Cossack detachment discovers him and his family sitting on the roadside.

Members of the imperial family start withdrawing money from European banks, and soon Nicholas orders all foreign-held funds to be returned to Russia.* Around seven million roubles† cannot be withdrawn from banks in Berlin.

Leon Trotsky manages to take his family from Vienna to Zurich. Lenin, meanwhile, is in Galicia, the western-most territory of modern

---

* Similar to Vladimir Putin's 2013 bill banning Russian officials from holding foreign bank accounts.
† About $92,283,333 in 2017.

Ukraine (then part of Austria-Hungary). He is arrested and jailed for two weeks. Yevgeny Azef, who lives in Berlin under a false passport, is confident that his Russian origins will not be uncovered, but he is mistaken—a year later, in 1915, he is sent to prison for being a Russian anarchist.

The war is welcomed by most denizens of the Russian Empire, and even some long-term émigrés, including Prince Kropotkin, Georgy Plekhanov, and Boris Savinkov. Seized by patriotic fervor, "Sherlock" Vladimir Burtsev returns to Russia, whereupon he is immediately put on trial and exiled to Turukhansk in Siberia, where Stalin is serving time. Meanwhile, Savinkov, the former leader of the militant organization of the Socialist-Revolutionaries, quarrels with party comrades over the war. Savinkov's slogan is "Victory before revolution." He even writes an open letter saying that in wartime any démarche against the tsar is a démarche against Russia. His relations with former party members are severed, and Savinkov goes to Paris to work as a war correspondent for various Russian newspapers.

Russia experiences unprecedented political unity: "Even Purishkevich now acknowledges the Jews and shakes Milyukov's hand. Sheep and wolves are lining up together—they've found a common enemy they can both eat," quips Gippius. Ivan Bunin, a future Nobel laureate, writes an anti-German appeal. It is signed by several thousand people, including Chaliapin, Struve, Stanislavsky, and his friend Gorky. The latter is surprised that "yesterday's anarchists are now patriotic statists."

Amongst all the flag-waving rhetoric, the few doubting voices are ear-jarring. They belong to the so-called "defeatists." Gippius is one of them. Never one to follow the crowd, she has no desire to partake in the "patriotic pacing through the streets" or be a "chip of wood in the stream of events." Any war that ends with the victory of one state over another is the germ of a new one, believe Gippius and Merezhkovsky. On the side of the "defeatists" is the Merezhkovsky family's new friend, Duma member Alexander Kerensky. However, the most inveterate pacifists are the socialists. Throughout the entire autumn and winter of 1914, Lenin and Trotsky use the press to pour scorn over the patriots, especially Plekhanov. Lenin writes an article entitled "Studenthood on Its Knees," in which he accuses Russian university students of betraying the revolution and caving in to jingoism.

Later, in 1915, Lenin, Martov, Trotsky, Zinoviev, and the SRs Chernov and Natanson (plus representatives from other belligerent nations, but far fewer) will gather in the Swiss town of Zimmerwald to adopt a declaration, penned by Trotsky, calling for "peace without annexations and indemnities." Come 1917, this phrase, advocating the rejection of all military gains, will be the most popular slogan in Russia.

On 26 July 1914, an emergency meeting of the Duma and the State Council is convened. The parliamentarians are heartened by the outpouring of patriotism on both sides of the political divide. However, it soon transpires that the government has no plans to make use of this unprecedented unity. In connection with the war, Interior Minister Maklakov proposes that the Duma be suspended for a year—until autumn 1915. Rodzianko manages to persuade Prime Minister Goremykin that the members of Duma could be of use, as a result of which the recess is shortened. The next meeting of the Duma is scheduled for February 1915.

The political struggle inside the country seems to be ending. Most former oppositionists sincerely believe that all efforts should be focused on helping the army and securing victory, and only then should the political infighting resume. Pavel Ryabushinsky begins to raise funds from the stock exchange and merchant societies for mobile hospitals, and personally oversees their dispatch to the front. His newspaper, *Morning of Russia*, becomes a popular patriotic publication. Alexander Guchkov goes to the front to work with the Red Cross, as he did during the Russo-Japanese War.

THE POLISH QUESTION

The fighting on the Eastern Front erupts in two places: Russian troops advance on East Prussia (today's Kaliningrad region) and on Galicia (today's western Ukraine). In other words, the war breaks out in lands inhabited by Poles and Ukrainians, who face the prospect of having to fight their own people who, divided by history, happen to live on the other side of the border in Germany and Austria-Hungary.

The question of what to do with Poland and how to motivate the Poles to fight for Russia is crucial. Poland at this time is split between three empires: the central and eastern parts, including Warsaw, belong to the Russian Empire; the northern part, including Danzig (today's Gdansk) belongs to Germany, while the southern region, including Krakow, is part of Austria-Hungary. In none of these empires do the Poles have autonomy.

Throughout the nineteenth century Poland was the main hot spot of the Russian Empire. The great-grandfather of Emperor Nicholas II, Nicholas I, brutally suppressed the Polish Uprising of 1830-1831, vowing to obliterate Warsaw should it reoccur. But now, with the outbreak of global war, the Russian authorities have an entirely different goal—to win Polish hearts and minds.

The first step, on 16 August, is when the new supreme commander of the Russian armed forces, Grand Duke Nikolai Nikolaevich (the tsar's uncle), publishes a manifesto promising to reverse the unjust partition of Poland and grant the Kingdom of Poland autonomy, should all Polish territories be conquered by Russia: "Let the borders that divide the Polish people be erased. And let them be reunited under the scepter of the Russian Tsar."

Despite the grandiloquent words, the war in Poland is not going well. The Germans are advancing on Warsaw with worrying speed. One option discussed is to consolidate Poland's status within the empire by holding another coronation of Nicholas II in Warsaw, in order to demonstrate Russia's special respect for the Poles—just as Emperor Franz Joseph I of Austria was re-crowned in 1868 in Budapest to appease the Hungarians, renaming his empire Austria-Hungary in the process.

Russian Foreign Minister Sazonov, the brother-in-law and friend of the late Stolypin, believes that the Poles should be granted self-administration and the right for schools to teach in the Polish language without delay.

THE UKRAINIAN QUESTION

The offensive on the Southwestern Front, in Galicia, is far more successful. Russian troops take Halych and Lvov (today, cities in western Ukraine), and begin a siege of Przemysl in modern Poland. In the occupied territories, Russia creates two new provinces—Lvov and Ternopil, followed by two more around Chernovtsy and Przemysl. Most of the pro-Russian local intelligentsia was arrested and sent to Thalerhof internment camp before the offensive of the Russian army, so the new authorities had nobody to work with.

Local officials are mostly appointees brought in from other regions of Russia. Meanwhile, some members of the Lvov elite suspected of harboring sympathy and spying for Austria are exiled to remote regions of Russia. Russian laws are enacted prohibiting Jews from owning land; land belonging to local Jews is expropriated, and several thousand of them are deported to the other side of the front line to Austria-Hungary.

As Russia captures the Ukrainian-speaking territories from Austria, the Ukrainian media raise the "Ukrainian question." It all begins when Konstantin Levitsky, who represents Lvov in the Austro-Hungarian parliament, publishes an article in the German newspaper *Berliner Tageblatt* on

1 October, proposing the creation of a unified Ukrainian state under the rule of the Austrian emperor that would include Galicia and Bukovina (today's western Ukraine, at that time part of Austria-Hungary) and the Ukrainian-speaking provinces of the Russian Empire. "Muscovite Russia should be pushed back from the Black Sea, and the Ukrainian lands should become a wedge between Russia and the Balkans," writes the Duma member Levitsky. In response, Peter Struve, now a patriotic publicist, calls Levitsky impudent and ignorant for asserting that Odessa, Nikolaev, and Kherson are Ukrainian cities, when they were built on land taken from the Ottomans: "If Ukrainian nationality is to be recognized at all, then Ukraine's historical right to these Russian cities is even weaker than Turkey's," writes Struve.

Even before Levitsky, the concept of a "single Ukrainian state" has been discussed in Lvov and Vienna for many decades. A major contributor to the debate is Mykhailo Hrushevsky, a professor of history at Lvov University. His multivolume work *The History of Ukraine-Rus'* posits Ukraine's existence as a separate entity from Russia. In December 1914 Hrushevsky is sent into exile—first to Simbirsk, then Kazan. When eminent academics and writers intercede on his behalf, his place of exile is changed to Moscow.

THE ARMENIAN QUESTION

On the day when Nicholas II stands on the balcony of the Winter Palace with the crowd kneeling in front of him, singing the national anthem, Turkey signs a secret treaty with Germany. Under the treaty, the Turkish army passes under German command. The officer Enver Pasha yearns to avenge the Ottoman Empire's defeat in the recent Balkan Wars and the loss of its European territories. In October 1914, the Turkish fleet raids Sevastopol, Odessa, Novorossiysk, and Theodosia; the Young Turks declare a *jihad* on the countries of the Triple Entente, whereupon Russia opens another front—the Turkish Front.

The role of the Poles on the German Front, and the Ukrainians on the Austrian Front, is, on the Turkish Front, played by the Armenians. Both empires, Russian and Ottoman, try to win over the Armenian population, which lives on either side of the border. The Russian governor in the Caucasus poses the idea of Armenian autonomy (although no such plans exist), while the Turkish authorities try to persuade the Armenian Revolutionary Federation (a political party also known as "Dashnaktsutyun") to organize a pro-Turkish uprising in the Russian Transcaucasus. The party's leaders declare that the Armenians of Russia and Turkey will fight to a man for an independent Armenia.

The military conflict between the Ottomans and the Russians begins in December. In January Russian troops take the city of Sarakamish (in today's eastern Turkey). A consequence of the Ottoman defeat is a brutal repression of the empire's Armenian population. War Minister Enver Pasha claims that his men were betrayed by the Armenians. The Armenian soldiers in the Ottoman army are disarmed and executed.

In February 1915, at the request of the Russian command, Britain and France, Russia's allies, open up a second front in Turkey. A landing force is dispatched to the shore of the Sea of Marmara, launching the Gallipoli Campaign. Soon afterwards, the Turkish authorities take the decision to deport 1.8 million Turkish nationals of Armenian origin. "Deportation" is a misnomer: in the period 1915-1918 anywhere from 600,000 to 1.5 million people, according to various estimates, will perish in the Armenian Genocide.

NEW HEROES

Nicholas II initially plans to lead the Russian army himself, but he is persuaded not to, since the mobilization of troops will be a drawn-out process and there could be early setbacks. Nicholas is advised not to harm his image during the initial phases, but to lead the army a little later when victory is assured.

In August 1914, supreme command of the Russian army is handed to Grand Duke Nikolai Nikolaevich, "Uncle Nikolasha" as the tsar calls him. He is fifty-seven years old and considered the most experienced military leader of all the Romanovs. Churches across the empire are ordered daily to pray for the health of the supreme commander, and his portrait hangs in every home. Uncle Nikolasha's popularity irritates Nicholas, who does not like to be overshadowed, and Alexandra, who is jealous.

The initial front-line skirmishes produce heroes and anti-heroes. One of the first battles ends in disaster when the First Army under General Samsonov, advancing into East Prussia, is surrounded. The general commits suicide.

Many officers and reporters are convinced that Samsonov's death is the fault of the Second Army under General Rennenkampf, who suppressed the unrest in Siberia in autumn 1905 and rooted out the self-proclaimed Krasnoyarsk Republic. Everyone discusses Rennenkampf's German roots, and many in the army are sure that he is a traitor who deliberately delayed sending in his army to relieve Samsonov. Grand Duke Andrei recounts that Rennenkampf ordered his units not to shell areas in Germany that belonged to his relatives and issued them "protection letters" to safeguard their estates from looting. The tsar refuses to believe the stories at first, but his cousin Grand Duke Dmitry persuades him otherwise. Rennenkampf is summarily dismissed and investigated.

However, according to the French ambassador Maurice Paléologue, Rennenkampf is not to blame for the rout of the Samsonov's army: the decision to sacrifice it was taken intentionally by the High Command. On the Western Front the German army was threatening to take Paris, so the French command asked the allies to distract the Germans by all means available. Hence, Samsonov contributed to the Anglo-French victory on the Marne and helped save Paris.

The main heroes in the eyes of the Russian press are the victorious commanders in Galicia—General Nikolai Ivanov and General Mikhail Alekseyev. Lvov is occupied by the Third Army under General Nikolai Ruzsky, assisted by the Eighth Army under General Alexei Brusilov. These four commanders are extolled in the press throughout the autumn of 1914. They are the main protagonists of Russia's war, upon whom the country's military and political fate hinges.

Though, not everyone considers Ivanov, Alekseyev, Ruzsky, Brusilov, and Supreme Commander Nikolai Nikolaevich to be brilliant strategists. Another grand duke, Nicholas Mikhailovich, a friend of the late Tolstoy and a well-known historian, the most educated member of the imperial family, is sure that the early victory in autumn 1914 paved the way to eventual defeat. The commanders do nothing to protect their soldiers, and the losses of the victorious Russians (killed, wounded, or captured) are comparable to those of the vanquished Austrians. The country's finest forces have already perished, Nicholas Mikhailovich believes, so the war will now have to be waged with poorly trained recruits, meaning almost certain defeat in spring 1915.

THE OMNIPOTENT VYRUBOVA

As soon as the war breaks out, many women in the imperial family become nurses, known as "sisters of mercy." Olga, the tsar's own sister, goes to the front. Empress Alexandra sets up an infirmary at Tsarskoye Selo, where she, her daughters, and Vyrubova help wounded soldiers.

Anna Vyrubova goes everywhere with Alexandra and feeds her with reports about every stare and incautious word. There are enemies in the woodwork, it seems. The officers at the infirmary become accustomed to Alexandra's visits and cease to accord her due respect. Vyrubova advises her to go less frequently to the infirmary as their punishment.

On 2 January 1915 Vyrubova takes a train from Tsarskoye Selo to Petrograd. About six miles into the journey, it comes off the rails. Vyrubova, who was traveling in the first carriage, is found beneath the rubble. She is placed on a makeshift stretcher and taken to a lodge for the wounded and dying. Her memoirs recount her emotions in detail. She lies on the floor for four hours without assistance. The doctor finally arrives and says: "She's dying, don't touch her." It is then that Rasputin arrives, having recovered from his own ordeal in Siberia, and declares that Vyrubova "will live, but remain a cripple."

As a result, the thirty-year-old Vyrubova becomes like another dependent daughter to the empress, and starts to behave like a capricious child. The empress visits her every day and practically abandons the infirmary. Vyrubova starts to feel important and even allows herself to reproach Rasputin for not praying enough for her health. Other members of Alexandra's entourage start to despise her.

Rasputin is right. Vyrubova does indeed survive, but spends the rest of her life in a wheelchair or on crutches.

GRAND DUKE ANDREI

Come winter, the fighting on all fronts subsides to be replaced by intrigues inside the High Command and the imperial court. They are meticulously documented by a young officer, the supreme commander's nephew and another of the tsar's cousins, the son of the late Vladimir and his wife Miechen, and the lover of Matilda Kschessinskaya, Grand Duke Andrei. He is the only member of the imperial family to have been present at the trial of Gershuni, and was the one to persuade the tsar to deprive Diaghilev of government patronage.

In the army Grand Duke Andrei is a minor figure. An avid gambler, even during the war he spends more time in the restaurants and casinos of Warsaw than at the front. When he is commended for an award, he confesses that he has never been in the zone of military operations and does not deserve it.

According to Grand Duke Andrei's diary, it is easy to see how the attitude of the officer corps changes over the winter of 1915. After the destruction of the army's most combat-ready units, more and more soldiers surrender to captivity, often entire divisions. "Everyone is now afraid for their own skin," writes Grand Duke Andrei. The officers discuss what to do: deprive the capitulators of Russian citizenship or shoot them (assuming they survive captivity)?

Yesterday's triumphant military leaders are losing their resolve. General Ruzsky, victor of Lvov, is appointed commander-in-chief of the Northern Front. He quarrels incessantly with his former head, the commander-in-chief of the Southern Front, General Ivanov. Each commander argues that, given the circumstances, retreat is the best option for them, while asserting that the other commanders should go on the offensive.

In the winter of 1915 Nicholas II asks Grand Duke Andrei if it is true that General Ruzsky is addicted to morphine. Andrei is shocked by the question. The tsar is known for his delicacy and desire to avoid bluntness. Andrei himself has issues with Rutzsky. The general does not communicate with his soldiers and barely leaves his quarters for fear of catching cold. He is very religious and carries a huge icon everywhere he goes. At the front there are rumors that Ruzsky is about to be dismissed and replaced by Kuropatkin, the former war minister and anti-hero of the Russo-Japanese War.

On 18 March Ruzsky is indeed dismissed for health reasons and replaced with Alekseyev. Grand Duke Andrei reproaches the new commander for having no empathy with the troops and for sugar-coating reality by reporting only successes. Andrei's irritation is perhaps explained by the fact that he dreams of victories, but the cautious Alekseyev issues an order to retreat.

SPIES AND SHELLS

The main reason for the setbacks is that the Russian army has run out of artillery shells and cartridges. The War Ministry did not plan for a long-term war, expecting to finish it in six months. Unsurprisingly, the army blames War Minister Sukhomlinov. Supreme Commander Nikolai Nikolaevich goes so far as to accuse Sukhomlinov of espionage and treason, refusing to countenance the view that inadequate training, incompetence, and corruption are the main factors. The supreme commander is on the lookout for saboteurs—the army's failings are all down to traitors, he believes. He is not alone. The High Command and Petrograd are also in the grip of spy mania.

On the night of 19-20 February, Colonel Myasoyedov (who fought a duel with Guchkov) and fifteen others, including his wife (a close friend of Ekaterina Sukhomlinova, the wife of the war minister), are arrested on suspicion of espionage. It is a serious blow to Sukhomlinov's reputation.

For the grand duke, Nikolai Nikolaevich, it is a clear-cut case: "We need to put an end to this affair as soon as possible." He demands that a guilty verdict be delivered before Holy Week, when, according to tradition, death sentences are not carried out. Myasoyedov is executed on 20 March, despite the lack of evidence—the supreme commander does not need any.

Myasoyedov's execution is a high-profile event. Everyone believes in his guilt, which prompts a witch-hunt for other spies and traitors. Alexander Guchkov becomes known as the man who unmasked "Myasoyedov the spy" long before the war even began.

In the midst of the Myasoyedov affair, on 9 March, Russian troops gain another victory when they take Przemysl Fortress. The public rejoices and glorifies the military genius of Grand Duke Nikolai Nikolaevich. No one suspects that this will be the Russian army's last success of 1915.

By early April, the German troops are advancing to the north, where they seize the territories of modern Latvia and Lithuania. Simultaneously, an Austro-German offensive breaks through the Russian line at Galicia. In late May they retake Przemysl from the Russians, followed by Lvov in June. The "great retreat of the Russian army" begins.

GET THEE TO A NUNNERY

On 13 May the leaders of the Young Turks movement issue a law on the deportation of most of the Armenian population of the Ottoman Empire. That same day, the newspaper *Voice of Moscow* publishes an article demanding the deportation of all subjects of Germany and Austria-Hungary living in Russia's second capital—two thousand people in all. The paper was founded by Guchkov, a Russian admirer of the Young Turks, and is the official mouthpiece of his Octobrist Party. May 17th sees the appointment of Felix Yusupov Sr. as the new commander of the Moscow Military District, and by 23 May he has ordered the deportation from Moscow of all subjects of states that are at war with Russia.

The defeats at the front cause a wave of anti-German publications in the press: "Battling the secret influence of the Germans," "German espionage in Russia," "The German stranglehold on music," and "Moscow merchants in the fight against German dominance" are all headings in Guchkov's *Voice of Moscow*. The anti-German mood is naturally shared by the supreme commander. The High Command decides to deport all Germans living in the front-line areas, including the indigenous inhabitants of the Baltic regions. They are forcibly evicted at their own expense.

The anti-German propaganda even affects Empress Alexandra. An ethnic German by birth, she was born and lived in Germany until the age of eight. Her brother, Grand Duke Ernst-Ludwig of Hesse, serves in the German army. The accusations soon extend to Alexandra's sister Ella, despite the latter's impeccable reputation and enormous popularity in Moscow. Rather outlandishly, she is said to be a German spy and rumored to be hiding her brother inside the Marfo-Mariinsky Convent.

It all leads to an anti-German pogrom in Moscow, which begins on 26 May when several women try to find employment with the charity organization of Grand Duchess Ella, but are turned away. They start complaining, and soon an anti-German throng assembles by the home of the governor-general. Several thousand people gather in no time at all. The governor-general does not disperse them. Neither does the head of city police, Andrianov, who says that "the crowd is good, cheerful and patriotic." There begin three days of violence and looting. Mobs force their ways into shops, private houses, and apartments, demanding to see the owners' documents. If the surname sounds German, everything is smashed. Five people are killed, and hundreds of shops destroyed. On the third day, the crowd gathers on Red Square and hurls insults at the empress and her sister, demanding that they be exiled to a convent. They also call for Rasputin to be hanged and for the tsar to abdicate in favor of Grand Duke Nikolai Nikolaevich.

The Moscow City Duma convenes on 28 May. One of its members announces in horror that people are saying that the government has sanctioned four days of pogroms. A modern Saint Bartholomew's Day massacre is again expected. Only on the fourth day are the troops brought in to quell the unrest. Twelve people lie dead as a result. Nicholas and Alexandra are briefed in detail about what has happened. The empress is irritated and angered by the anti-German hysteria—but even more so by the popularity of the supreme commander.

EVERYTHING FOR VICTORY

The setbacks in the war stir society. As early as March the chairman of the Duma, Rodzianko, proposes that the country's rich industrialists should start supplying the army. The supreme commander instructs War Minister Sukhomlinov to arrange a meeting between big business and the heads of the Main Artillery Directorate.

Pavel Ryabushinsky spends the entire winter and spring at the front, where he oversees the setting up of mobile hospitals and infirmaries. On 15 May he receives a message that Moscow's industrialists have nominated him for the position of head of the stock exchange committee. Ryabushinsky returns to Moscow. His newspaper, *Morning of Russia*, for the first time raises the topic of big business becoming involved in the war effort. It could not do so before, because the existing censorship forbade writing about problems in the army.

It marks the start of a new phase in Russian politics and the war: big business proposes to save the army, but wants political power in return.

On 27 May Petrograd hosts the Industrial and Commercial Congress, where Ryabushinsky proposes that private industry should start producing shells and rifles at its own expense. For this purpose, military-industrial committees should be set up consisting of officers and business representatives to coordinate the production and supply of weapons to the army. Ryabushinsky's speech makes a deep impression on both participants and journalists: "Never before has the challenge of the 'third estate' to the obsolete forces of Russian statehood been so boldly expressed," writes *Stock Exchange News*.

Rodzianko attends the congress, but is afraid that the entrepreneurs' appeals will seem too revolutionary to the authorities, and that Interior Minister Maklakov will disperse the gathering and arrest the leaders.

After Ryabushinsky's speech, the creation of a central military-industrial committee and a regional network is discussed. Guchkov is nominated as the chairman of the central body, with Konovalov as his deputy, while Ryabushinsky heads the Moscow committee. Finally, the congress participants demand the convocation of the State Duma. The proposal is strongly supported by Grand Duke Nikolai Nikolaevich.

Not only industrialists but also the whole of society takes up the cause. Since the state has failed to defend the country, volunteers must do the job. "The whole of Russia should become a vast military organization, a gigantic arsenal for the army," says Prince Lvov, chairman of the Union of Zemstvos and the Union of Towns.

But the proposals do not please the empress. "It is proposed that you should order factories to manufacture shells," the empress writes to her husband. "Just demand to see a list of factories and then select a few. It's better to do it yourself than through commissions that spend weeks chattering without solving anything."

However, the government's decisive meeting on this matter is held not in Petrograd, but at the High Command. Under pressure from society and the supreme commander, the tsar dismisses Sukhomlinov and appoints General Polivanov, a friend of Guchkov and a member of his circle, as the new war minister. Sukhomilov's removal is followed by that of other ministers *non grata*: the interior minister, the justice minister, and the "minister of the church."

A new government is formed and factories start producing munitions, but the catastrophe at the front continues. "The Germans' overwhelming artillery and inexhaustible supplies of shells are forcing us to retreat," the newly appointed War Minister Polivanov reports at a government meeting on 16 July. "Our artillery is forced to remain silent even during major clashes. The enemy bears almost no losses, whereas our people are being killed by the thousands."

Goremykin did not plan to convene the State Duma until August, but parliament meets in early July. A week later German troops take Warsaw. The Duma demands an investigation to ascertain whether Sukhomlinov is a traitor (like his sidekick Myasoyedov) or simply a corrupt official. Also on the agenda is the resignation of Grand Duke Sergei, the head of the Artillery Department, who is also suspected of corruption: his mistress, Matilda Kschessinskaya, is said to have interfered in the placement of defense contracts and received large bribes from factories in return for preferential treatment.

Russian troops withdraw from Kaunas (a city in modern Lithuania, then named Kovno) on 9 August and from Grodno (a city in modern Belarus) on 19 August; the Germans are advancing towards Riga (today, the capital of Latvia). The great retreat continues as the situation becomes increasingly desperate. There is even talk of moving the tsar and the government from Petrograd to Moscow.

A MOSCOW ORGY

On 1 June Deputy Interior Minister Vladimir Dzhunkovsky, a former Moscow governor, brings Nicholas II a report—having waited patiently for all the details in it to be confirmed. It tells that on the night of 26 March Rasputin and some cohorts visited Yar, a fashionable restaurant for the Moscow Bohemia. Everyone was drinking, singing, and dancing. The inebriated Rasputin began to boast in front of strangers (mostly a female choir) that his shirt had been sewn by the empress herself (whom he called "Mama" and "old lady"). Then, according to the police report, Rasputin exposed his genitals while talking with the singers, before dancing around in a trance, oblivious to his surroundings. Rumors of the "Yar orgy" spread throughout Moscow, and witnesses confirm them during the subsequent investigation.

The investigation is the catalyst for the year's main political intrigue. Rasputin defends himself, describing the Yar story as slander concocted by enemies of the tsar. He easily persuades the empress of his version of events, for "Our Friend" (as she calls Rasputin in her letters) can do no wrong. Alexandra is convinced that she is surrounded by ill-wishers. Rasputin listens to her attentively, praises those whom she likes, and curses those whom she does not. It is most likely during these conversations that the idea of evil forces conniving against Nicholas II is born.

Above all, Alexandra and Rasputin dislike Nikolai Nikolaevich. It is said in Petrograd that relations between the preacher and the supreme commander deteriorated when the former wanted to visit the High Command and duly sent the latter a telegram: "I will come and console you," to which the grand duke allegedly replied: "Come and I will hang you." In fact, matters are far more complicated. Grand Dukes "Nikolasha" and "Petyusha" (Peter Nikolaevich), and their Montenegrin wives, have long known Rasputin. They believe all the stories emanating from the high clergy. Rasputin and Vyrubova, in turn, feed gossip to the empress about the supreme commander: that the Montenegrins want to make him king of Galicia or Poland, that the people call him Nicholas III. It hits home. The empress is vexed by his rising political influence as well as by the creation of the military-industrial committees and the government meetings he holds at the High Command.

Besides Nikolasha, the empress and Rasputin collectively view the enemy as the "Moscow clique," which includes Alexandra's sister, Grand Duchess Ella, who hates Rasputin and tries to voice her concerns about him. The clique also features Deputy Interior Minister Dzhunkovsky and the new minister of the church, Samarin, plus a fair few anti-Rasputin Muscovites.

By July, the jigsaw puzzle of suspicion is nearly complete: the supreme commander and his brother, together with the Montenegrin princesses, are hatching a plot. They allegedly want to exile the empress to Moscow and relocate to Petrograd. Two months later the empress openly tells her relatives, including Aunt Miechen, that she fears a conspiracy.

But there is no evidence of a plot, other than Alexandra's inner conviction. In early August she and Rasputin persuade Nicholas II to dismiss his uncle, the supreme commander, and exile him to the position of viceroy of the Caucasus, and to assume command of the army himself.

On 5 August, after supper, the tsar asks his family to pray for him as he enters the next room to announce his decision to the assembled ministers. Vyrubova gives him an icon. The meeting lasts for several hours. Unable to bear it, Alexandra takes the children for a walk in the park outside and peeks through the window into the meeting room.

Nicholas II returns in good cheer: "I was resolute. Look how I'm sweating! After listening to all the long boring ministerial speeches, I said: 'Gentlemen! My will is made of iron. I am leaving for the High Command in two days.' Some of the ministers looked crestfallen."

Almost all the assembled ministers vainly try to dissuade the emperor. Nicholas' mother is pole-axed by the news: "Grigory's evil spirit has returned. A[lexandra] wants Nicky to take over as supreme commander in place of Grand Duke Nikolai Nikolaevich. One has to be insane to want such a thing." On 12 August, she visits her son to try to change his mind, for everyone will say that he is obeying Rasputin's orders. They speak for two hours, but Nicholas does not back down. "It is not Nicky, it is not him. He is sweet, honest and kind. It is all *her* doing," the empress dowager complains to her nephew, Grand Duke Andrei, after talking with her son. Andrei, for his part, does not consider it to be so bad—the arrival of the tsar could inspire the troops.

Nicholas appoints General Mikhail Alekseyev as his chief of staff. Henceforth, it is Alekseyev who will de facto lead the entire Russian army, since Nicholas II knows nothing of military affairs and has no interest in them.

THE SOCIETY HATES YOU

In August the investigation into the orgy at the Yar restaurant is coming to an end. An imperial aide-de-camp journeys to Moscow to interrogate the witnesses once again. Whether the new investigator formulates the questions differently, or makes it clear that Rasputin should not be slandered, is unknown. In any case, the witnesses change their testimony. They now say that everything was perfectly innocuous and that Rasputin did not mention the imperial family or take off his trousers. Dzhunkovsky is dismissed from the Interior Ministry and sent to the front. Also fired are the tsar's old friend and adjutant Vladi Orlov and Felix Yusupov Sr., who hates Rasputin, gets on well with Nikolai Nikolaevich, and sees the underhanded plotting of the "German party" everywhere.

At the same time, a new scandal erupts: on the way to his native village aboard the steamship *Tovarpar,* Rasputin gets drunk and starts flinging money around. He takes some soldiers to the onboard restaurant, forces them to sing, and threatens the other passengers. No one dares report his behavior to the authorities or the tsar.

"Madness is to isolate oneself and discard one's truly loyal friends," the tsar's mother writes in her diary. In conversation with Grand Duchess Miechen and her son, Grand Duke Andrei, she says that she is afraid for her son, who, she believes, has not a single devoted person left—as in the time of Pavel I, who in the last year of his life began to distance himself from loyal supporters and was eventually assassinated by members of his inner circle. "The grievous end of our great-grandfather looms before her in all its horror," writes Miechen.

The whole family blames the situation on Alexandra. But whereas the empress dowager hates her, Miechen feels sympathy. According to the prevailing gossip, in a private conversation she tells Alexandra (apparently with the best of intentions) that society hates her. Alexandra, in no need of tough love, ends their relationship.

THE CABINET OF DEFENSE

At that very moment, Pavel Ryabushinsky is promoting his idea of creating a "defense cabinet." On 4 August he proposes to his colleagues that they collectively solicit the tsar to appoint a government consisting of representatives of the public. According to the police report (the police have an agent among the participants), Ryabushinsky says that the "incompetence and inactivity of the ruling classes" and "the government's inability to secure victory" can no longer be tolerated, calling for steps to be taken to seize executive and legislative power. The author of the police report believes that the Moscow City Duma and the Moscow stock exchange committee will soon demand a change of government.

Ryabushinsky does not hide in the shadows: as early as 13 August *Morning of Russia* publishes a proposed list of future government members, the "Cabinet of Defense." The current chairman of the Duma, Rodzianko, is to be prime minister, with Guchkov as interior minister, Milyukov as foreign minister, Konovalov as trade and industry minister, and the Kadet and head of the Masonic supreme council Nekrasov as transport minister. The other key positions are to be left for members of the current government: for instance, Polivanov could remain in the post of war minister and Krivoshein as agriculture minister.

That same day the leaders of the Progressive Party begin talks about unifying with representatives of other factions and mounting a joint struggle for a new "Duma" government. Krivoshein, the current agriculture minister, supports the idea of a government of national confidence and offers the tsar a compromise: appoint Polivanov as prime minister and instruct him to form a cabinet. Nicholas II refuses.

On 19 August, on behalf of the Moscow stock exchange committee, Ryabushinsky sends a telegram to the tsar with a request for the government to include "persons enjoying broad public trust" and for them to be granted full authority. The next day he even travels to Petrograd with a delegation of representatives of society, expecting to be received by the tsar. The royal reply is that the merchants should stick to taking care of the wounded and not meddle in politics.

Finally, on 25 August, the Duma signs an agreement on the creation of the Progressive Bloc, which includes the Kadets, the Octobrists, the Progressive Party, and even some nationalists. The declaration on the creation of the bloc calls for "new persons entrusted with the confidence of the country to join the Council of Ministers forthwith." On the same day, Ryabushinsky gathers the merchants together for an emergency sitting of the Moscow military-industrial committee: "We will not send any more telegrams," he says. "We have nothing to fear; they will meet us halfway out of necessity, for our [Russia's] armies are scattering before the enemy." The meeting backs the Progressive Bloc's demand, and a resolution to that effect is adopted at the next Old Believer congress.

Moscow's merchants have already raised 4.5 million roubles* for the military-industrial committee, bought two plants, equipped them with machinery from the United States and Sweden, and laid railway lines to supply them. In the autumn of 1915 the factories begin to produce shells. Over the remainder of the year, rifle production almost doubles, shell production nearly triples, and machine-gun production quadruples.

In September Guchkov and Ryabushinsky are elected to the State Council as representatives of industry. But the negotiations on the creation

* About $59,325,000 in 2017.

of a new government do not resume. The main supporter of the "Cabinet of Defense" among the acting ministers is Alexander Krivoshein, who resigns, having mistakenly believed that he could be the "de facto prime minister" under Goremykin. Nestled in the prime ministerial chair, Goremykin is not a feeble old man at all, but an immovable bureaucratic monster. Having failed to form a government of national confidence, Krivoshein leaves to work for the Red Cross at the front.

On 3 September the tsar issues a decree to suspend the State Duma indefinitely. On the eve of the dissolution, Duma member Alexander Kerensky phones his friend Zinaida Gippius. "What will happen now?" she asks. "There will be . . . something beginning with 'a,'" he replies, reluctant to say the word in full, for the phone is tapped. He means anarchy.

|| Chapter 11 ||

GRIGORY RASPUTIN

in which Grigory Rasputin becomes the most powerful kleptocrat and the most hated pacifist in Russia

AN ICON WITH A BELL

Once Nicholas has departed for the front, the mode of governance completely changes. Alexandra convinces her husband that she and Rasputin are his only reliable advisors. The fact that she has lost touch with her husband's relatives is not a misfortune in her view, but an asset. She has in her possession a miraculous icon with a bell (presented by Dr. Philippe), which she believes will ward off evil-doers. That is why, Alexandra is sure, the tsar's relatives are shying away from her—they are frightened by the icon. "It is not my will—it is God who wants your poor wife to be your helper," she writes to her husband.

Alexandra does not travel to the capital, so government ministers make the trip to Tsarskoye Selo. She receives them regularly and takes pride in it. Rasputin calls her the "new Catherine the Great"—a comparison that greatly flatters the empress: "Not since the time of Catherine has the Russian empress had such power," she writes. In letters to her husband, she complains that she is burdened by the responsibility, but Nicholas understands that his wife enjoys being in charge. He thanks her for taking control of the country while he is at the front.

In almost everything Alexandra is guided by Rasputin. Never for a moment does she doubt the advice of "God's man." He, in turn, openly flaunts his influence. The staff turnover rises rapidly as Rasputin advises her to replace this or that minister. The empress, for her part, conveys the advice to her husband since "a country whose sovereign is guided by 'God's man' cannot perish."

Almost all of Rasputin's requests are fulfilled—albeit with some delay, since the tsar does not like sudden changes. As a rule, his wife has to write to him three or four times for any particular piece of advice to be implemented.

At the same time, the rumors swirling around Rasputin monstrously exaggerate his role. To the metropolitan intelligentsia, he is the devil incarnate—a fiend who holds drunken orgies at Tsarskoye Selo while the naive tsar is at the High Command. "Grisha [Grigory] rules and drinks and fucks the lady-in-waiting and Feodorovna," writes Zinaida Gippius in her diary on 24 November 1915. It is not true, of course. Since both the empress and her friend Vyrubova genuinely consider Rasputin to be a saint, there can be no sexual subtext to their relationship.

NEW YEAR SURPRISE

Despite Rasputin's influence, almost all the ministers in the tsarist government write in their memoirs that they hardly notice his interference, apart from a handful of isolated cases, such as the appointment in 1915 of a new interior minister, church minister, and metropolitan archbishop of Petrograd. It is not long, however, before Rasputin starts casting around for a new prime minister.

The empress has a soft spot for the incumbent prime minister, Ivan Goremykin, but he is seventy-six years old and, it is said, decrepit. That does not bother Alexandra, for she values his loyalty, yet at the same time she wants to find someone with more backbone who will take the fight to the opposition and the State Duma and restore order. Alexandra believes that the elderly prime minister is to blame for the activation of civil society, because he lacks the strength to tighten the screws.

On being dismissed (not for the first time), the apathetic head of the government is delighted that the torment is over. On the previous occasion, he happily gave way to Stolypin; this time he is replaced by the sixty-eight-year-old Boris Stürmer, Stolypin's former opponent, whom Rasputin recommends as a disciplinarian: "Grigory rates him highly, which is very important," the empress writes to her husband.

Stürmer (whose German surname means "storm-trooper") comes from a family of Russified Germans, for which reason he is overly keen to demonstrate his Orthodox credentials.

Rasputin expects Stürmer to be obedient. The preacher has in fact built his own system of power: about once a week he visits the Peter and Paul Fortress, where he holds secret meetings with Prime Minister Stürmer and the newly appointed Metropolitan Pitirim. However, according to Stürmer's assistant, the former secret police agent Manasevich-Manuilov, Rasputin soon suspects that the prime minister is becoming too independent. During a meeting at the fortress, he gives him a dressing-down: "How dare you oppose the will of our mother [Alexandra]!" he cries, and proceeds to explain to those present that "the little old man should be put on a lead; otherwise he might break his neck."

TO KILL RASPUTIN

Stürmer does not take offense at Rasputin, unlike the latter's other protégé, the new interior minister, Alexei Khvostov (nicknamed "Fatty" by Rasputin and the empress). Khvostov is just forty-three years old and very ambitious. He himself wants to head the government, but Rasputin mocks his prime ministerial pretensions: "Fatty wants too much," he says. Khvostov is incensed by the way Rasputin manages state affairs and belittles members of the government in public. The interior minister summons his deputy, the police chief Stepan Beletsky, responsible for Rasputin's security, and orders him to kill the preacher.

The head of the imperial guard, General Spiridovich, has his own theory: the ambitious Khvostov intends to get rid of all rivals, including Rasputin and Beletsky. Khvostov's plan is supposedly to get his deputy to do the dirty work (or blame him if it goes wrong), take the glory as the country's deliverer from Rasputin, and become the next prime minister, and a popular one at that.

Beletsky, realizing the danger of the errand, procrastinates: he promises Khvostov to arrange an assassination attempt, but in fact does nothing. A few weeks later, on discovering that Beletsky has been idle, Khvostov comes up with another plan that involves Rasputin's now bitter foe, the former monk Iliodor.

Sergei Trufanov (the real name of the defrocked Iliodor) now lives in Norway. Before fleeing Russia, he met with Maxim Gorky and shared his plan to write a revelatory book about Rasputin. Gorky is delighted: "Iliodor's book about Rasputin will be very timely and greatly informative for the public. I will arrange its publication abroad," he writes to a friend. In 1915 Trufanov does indeed write a book called *The Holy Devil*.

The former Iliodor is known as Rasputin's number one enemy, so he is the man to kill the preacher, believes Interior Minister Khvostov. He sends an assistant to Oslo (then called Christiania), where Iliodor lives, to put the proposal to him. On his way back, however, Khvostov's envoy is detained at the Russian border on the orders of Deputy Interior Minister Beletsky. After a short interrogation in Petrograd, he confesses everything and hands Beletsky a letter from Iliodor addressed to Khvostov.

The Interior Ministry deprives Rasputin of his security. Sensing that he is being targeted, he takes his grievances to Vyrubova. She tearfully complains about it to Empress Alexandra, who does the same to her husband: "He [Rasputin] is fraught. He is afraid to go anywhere for fear that he will be killed."

A SPY IS BORN

"Nothing can stop me. It's my call whether Grishka [Grigory] gets to go to a brothel or is thrown under a train," boasts the interior minister in conversation with the head of the tsar's personal guard, Spiridovich. "Didn't you know, general? Grishka's a German spy!" he adds, throwing a pile of police agent reports on the table in front of him. "I could not believe my ears or eyes. This chubby, rosy-faced man with foolish, cheery eyes did not seem like a minister, but a highwayman," recalls Spiridovich. He decides not to mention this conversation to the tsar.

Nicholas, for his part, decides not to fire Interior Minister Khvostov. On 27 February 1916, he visits Tsarskoye Selo for a Sunday service at Saint Fyodor's Cathedral. To mark the first week of Lent, the entire imperial family receives Holy Communion whereas Rasputin stays in the altar. After the service, Rasputin is taken to the palace, where he congratulates the royals, drinks tea with them, and talks about how Khvostov wanted him killed. Rasputin knows this from the aide who was sent to meet with Iliodor.

Nicholas II calms Rasputin, saying that Khvostov is as good as dismissed, before departing for the front without even speaking to Khvostov. "I despair that through Gr[igory] we recommended Khv[ostov] to you," the empress writes to her husband. "The devil himself took possession of him, there's no other way to describe it."

Two days later Khvostov delivers a report to the tsar, who pretends that nothing has happened. Khvostov returns to Petrograd in a sanguine mood, but soon learns of his resignation from the papers. He rushes back to Nicholas, but the tsar does not receive him.

The whole sordid affair ends unexpectedly. Former Deputy Interior Minister Beletsky tells what has happened to a journalist acquaintance, who immediately publishes an "interview with Senator Beletsky" without even asking the latter's permission. Russian society has never before seen such revelations. Beletsky resigns. Stürmer sets up an investigative commission, which sits on its hands, for it would be unseemly to admit that the interior minister dabbled in contract killings.

Khvostov remains a State Duma member. He insists to his Duma colleagues that Rasputin is a German spy, asserting that he just wanted to expose him but was thwarted in the attempt.

The label of German spy sticks surprisingly readily to Rasputin. Only yesterday he was a *Khlyst*, but today he is an agent of Berlin. General Spiridovich investigates Khvostov's claims and finds them to be pure bluff, backed up by no evidence whatsoever.

Nevertheless, the rumors multiply, and Rasputin does little to dampen them. For one thing, Rasputin is an anti-war pacifist. He has always described the war as evil, saying that the people dying on both sides of the conflict are essentially the same. He frequently implores the empress to ask her husband to avoid senseless casualties and look after the soldiers.

The war is the dividing line in Russian civil society, an issue that breaks up families. Anyone who is not jingoistic is branded a traitor and a defeatist.

Rasputin also preaches compassion for minorities. He pleads on behalf of German prisoners of war (which pleases the German-born Alexandra). He offers patronage to sectarians and schismatics (like Tolstoy once did). Lastly, Rasputin has extensive connections among the Jewish bankers of Petrograd—the role of Rasputin's secretary is performed by the merchant Aron Simanovich, while a frequent drinking companion of the preacher is the banker Dmitry Rubinshtein. Jewish bankers in Petrograd are widely suspected of being in league with the Germans.

No one considers Rasputin to be a genuine preacher of humanism. His religious tolerance is put down to the fact that he is a *Khlyst*, and his concern for the Jews by the fact that he is in their pockets (which is partly true, Jewish bankers thank Rasputin for his support with gifts, such as a new sable fur coat). Meanwhile, his charity towards German prisoners of war is a clear sign of espionage, it is said.

FAREWELL, ISTANBUL

At the beginning of January 1916, the Gallipoli Campaign, a joint Anglo-French operation to seize Istanbul, comes to an end.

Germany and Turkey, the main opponents of the Triple Entente, have blocked both the Baltic and Black Seas, meaning that the only port city through which Russia can link up with its allied countries is the distant Arkhangelsk on the White Sea.

The Allies try to break through the blockade. Britain's First Lord of the Admiralty, Winston Churchill, plans an operation in the Dardanelles to take control of the straits and carve a passage to Russia. The battle lasts almost a year, during which Britain loses around thirty-four thousand men, France ten thousand, Australia nine thousand, and New Zealand three thousand. For the latter two countries, these are the most serious military losses in their entire history. In December 1915 Britain decides to evacuate from Turkey, and the Allies admit collective defeat. The British are unable to take control of the Mediterranean straits, open up the shortest sea route to Russia, and knock the Ottomans out of the war. Churchill resigns as Britain's navy minister.

One of the leaders of the defense of the Dardanelles is Mustafa Kemal (the future Ataturk). The triumph makes him a national hero and paves his way to becoming the first president of the Turkish Republic.

The failure of the Dardanelles operation is a blow for Russian society. For many inhabitants of the Russian Empire, the whole point of fighting in the First World War is to seize Istanbul and the Bosporus. After the defeat at Gallipoli, people start to question the war effort: "Everywhere I hear the same thing: 'What's the point of fighting if Constantinople is lost?'" writes the French ambassador Maurice Paléologue in his diary in January 1916, after the evacuation of Allied forces from Turkey.

In Petrograd, parallels between the two obsolete empires of Russia and Turkey are drawn. Turkey looks in better shape: its young military nationalists have taken power, introduced a constitution, and have now won a decisive battle.

Similar comparisons are made by Empress Alexandra. For her, the leader of the Russian "Young Turks" Guchkov is enemy number one. During the British evacuation, Guchkov falls ill with serious post-flu complications. "Let him depart for the next world. My wish is not sinful, for it is for your sake and for the whole of Russia," she writes to her husband on 4 January.

Guchkov is not the only ailing politician. In 1916, many suddenly develop serious health problems that prevent them from operating at full capacity. One is Pavel Ryabushinsky. In early 1916, his tuberculosis worsens. According to the police, who keep watch over the businessman and liberal politician, "his weakness and constant bleeding from the throat prevent him from leaving Moscow." As a result, Ryabushinsky is forced to cease all political and public activity. Only in March is he able to leave for Crimea, where he stays almost until the end of the year.

Duma member Alexander Kerensky suffers from a similar problem— renal tuberculosis. His condition takes a long time to be diagnosed, whereupon his tubercular kidney is removed. Recuperating in Finland, he does not take part in the Duma for seven months.

The imperial couple, meanwhile, are addicted to tranquilizers (which were quite rudimentary at the time). The tsar is more apathetic than ever. Rumors circulate that his wife sends him powders made by a Buryat healer called Dr. Badmaev, prepared using hashish. Alexandra confesses to a friend that she is "literally soaked in veronal" —a psychotropic drug, the first barbiturate, which in the early twentieth century is used as a sleeping pill. It becomes addictive after two weeks of use and has many side effects, including weakness and headaches. The symptoms are even known as "veronalism." The drug often leads to depression and nightmares, while withdrawal results in irritability, panic attacks, and convulsions.

Over the course of 1916, ill health becomes a major factor in Russian politics, resulting in a mass insanity at the end of summer.

ON THE OFFENSIVE

Guchkov survives, but the empress does what she can to get rid of his ally, War Minister Alexei Polivanov. She impresses upon her husband that he is a conspirator, a traitor, and a "Young Turk."

In early March Nicholas II acts on his wife's advice and dismisses Polivanov. As a result of cleansing the top brass of "Young Turks," the new commander of the Southwestern Front is General Alexei Brusilov, who replaces Ivanov. He tells the tsar that the army is in excellent shape and will be ready for a new offensive by 1 May.

At a war council meeting, Brusilov's initiative is approved, despite the fact that the commanders-in-chief of the Northern and Central Fronts, Generals Evert and Kuropatkin, say that they cannot vouch for its success.

The Brusilov Offensive commences on 22 May. General Evert's Western Front is due to advance immediately afterwards, but Evert asks to postpone his offensive until June 5 because of bad weather.

"My dearest darling! Our Friend [Rasputin] sends a blessing to all the Orthodox soldiery," the empress writes to her husband on 4 June. "He entreats us not to advance too far north . . . for we will suffer great harm. He says it as a caution."

The next day the tsar replies: "My dear! I thank you tenderly for your dear letter. . . . A few days ago, Alekseyev and I decided not to advance to the north, but to focus all our forces further south. But, please, do not tell anyone about this, not even our Friend."

Come 5 June, Evert does not advance, and instead regroups. Brusilov is mad at Chief-of-Staff Alekseyev: "I was afraid of being abandoned, and that is what has happened. The enemy will direct troops against me from all sides, and I will be forced to halt."

Alekseyev reports that Evert's decision has been approved by Nicholas II and "cannot be reversed because the emperor's decision is final." Brusilov believes that Nicholas has nothing to do with it, "since in military matters he is an infant."

The Brusilov Offensive begins successfully. On 7 June, his armies take Lutsk (city in modern Ukraine). The breakthrough is greeted enthusiastically by Russian society. The commander-in-chief is inundated with telegrams from peasants, workers, aristocrats, clergymen, and even intellectuals. He is very touched by a personal note from Grand Duke Nikolai Nikolaevich, but the tsar's congratulations, on the contrary, seem very dry and formal.

Brusilov is even less enamored of Alexandra. She receives him during a visit to the High Command shortly before the offensive. She greets him coldly, giving him an icon of Saint Nicholas the Miracle Worker. It is not long before the enamel image of the saint's face is erased, leaving only a silver plate. "Amazed, some superstitious people suspected that the saint was embarrassed by such an insincere blessing," recalls Brusilov.

POLITICAL TOURISM

The soldiers suspect Empress Alexandra of being a German spy, but they hate former War Minister Sukhomlinov even more. The sixty-six-year-old general is already accused of fraud and embezzlement, and the Duma adds high treason to the list of charges. Not everyone believes that Sukhomlinov is a traitor, but almost all rejoice at such an unprecedented achievement of civil society. A criminal case is brought against him and he will answer to the law—something that has never happened before in the history of Russia.[*]

The State Duma seems to be riding a wave. For the first time, the "progressive bloc" feels like a real political force. Pavel Milyukov recalls that during this period he is called the "leader of the Duma," the "leader of the opposition," and the "leader of the progressive bloc."

On 16 April, a Duma delegation embarks on a two-month trip abroad. The parliamentarians want to introduce themselves to future negotiating partners. The delegation is headed by the deputy chairman of the Duma, the Octobrist Alexander Protopopov, and the group includes the Kadets Milyukov and Shingarev, and a dozen other parliamentarians. In Britain, they meet with King George V, members of parliament, and the writers

---

[*] It is a striking coincidence that 100 years later there will be a huge corruption scandal in the Russian government that will also involve the Russian Minister of Defense—Anatoly Serdyukov. His story is partially similar to that of Sukhomlinov who was accused of corruption because of the prodigality of his common-law wife, Ekaterina (among other things). Evgeniya Vasilieva, identified as Anatoly Serdyukov's lover in the press, will symbolize corruption in the Russian Ministry of Defense in the early twenty-first century. However, unlike Sukhomlinov, Serduykov will never be arrested or accused of corruption: he will be a witness in the case while Evgeniya Vasilieva will spend three months behind bars.

H.G. Wells and Arthur Conan Doyle. After that, they travel to France, Italy, Norway, and Sweden. Milyukov and Protopopov are warmly received everywhere thanks to their excellent knowledge of languages, liberal ideas, and promise not to permit the signing of a separate peace.

In late May news breaks that the British cruiser HMS *Hampshire* has been blown up by a German mine in the Baltic Sea, killing the secretary of state for war, Horatio Kitchener, who was sailing to Russia. The general's visit had not been announced in advance, and Petrograd is whispering that the Germans were tipped off by a top official, allowing them to target Kitchener's vessel.

On the way back to Russia, in Stockholm, Protopopov decides to amuse himself. "Are there any interesting Germans in this city?" he asks, wishing to prolong his political tour. A German businessman by the name of Warburg is found. They drink and talk about global politics, Germany and Russia, war and peace. The next day Protopopov recalls the conversation and notes down a summary of it. Returning to Petrograd, he goes to see Milyukov and reads out Warburg's ideas from his notebook, which include the annexation of Lithuania and Courland (today's Latvia) to Germany, a revision of the borders of Lorraine, the return of all colonies, the redivision of Poland into two parts: Russian and Austrian, and the restoration of Belgium's independence—all as part of a separate peace. Milyukov advises Protopopov not to tell anyone about his conversation with the German, but the latter does the exact opposite. A month later, as a result of this random conversation in Stockholm, Protopopov is accused by some, including Milyukov, of having held secret negotiations with a German agent.

On 20 June, the day when the Duma delegation returns from its sojourn abroad, Prime Minister Stürmer announces a postponement of the next sitting of the Duma—the session is rescheduled for 1 November.

THE AMERICAN MIRACLE

Back in January 1916 Sergei Diaghilev and his troupe board a steamer in Bordeaux on tour to America. Everyone is incredibly nervous, especially Diaghilev, who is afraid of water. Ever since a fortune-teller predicted that he would "die on the water," he has been afraid of drowning. But needs must. Europe is being torn apart by war, and the tour to America is a life-saving opportunity for the Ballets Russes, which has been inactive for six months.

The negotiations with the Americans are not easy: they want to see Nijinsky, but Diaghilev has not been in touch with his former star for two and a half years. Nijinsky is presently under house arrest in Budapest (as an enemy of Austria-Hungary). But for the sake of the American tour, Diaghilev starts to arrange Nijinsky's release—after all, the Metropolitan Opera in New York has paid him a 45,000-dollar advance.* This rescues Diaghilev from bankruptcy and finances his company's rehearsals and upkeep for the whole of 1915. By the end of the year, the money is running out, and Diaghilev, terrified, sets off across the Atlantic. On the ship, he locks himself in his cabin, and sends his servant Vasily to say prayers on the deck to ward off trouble. Diaghilev's fears are not entirely unfounded: the war is being fought at sea as well, and passenger steamers are often the accidental targets of German U-boats and underwater mines. Sinkings are regularly reported in the newspapers, horrifying Diaghilev.

However, the crossing is uneventful. Diaghilev takes a liking to New York, saying in one of his first interviews that he has long admired Broadway and its art. After his troupe's first performances in New York, they head for the American outback: Chicago, Milwaukee, Atlantic City, Kansas City, and elsewhere.

The tour is never far from scandal (often initiated by Diaghilev himself). He dismisses his leading ballerina, Ksenia Makletsova, replacing her with the US resident Lydia Lopokova (who would later become the wife of economist John Keynes). Makletsova tries to sue and demands that Diaghilev be arrested. On top of that, the conservative American public is outraged by the openly erotic scenes in *Scheherazade* and *The Afternoon of a Faun*. The most shocking part is not the sexual overtones of the dances, but the fact that the male dancers, made up to look black, are embracing white women. Under public pressure, the controversial scenes are cut from both ballets.

Throughout the tour, Diaghilev continues to seek the release of Nijinsky—at the very least in time for the tour finale at the Metropolitan Opera. The US State Department and the US Embassy in Vienna intercede on behalf of the dancer, who is finally allowed out in March.

Nijinsky arrives in New York on 4 April and sees Diaghilev for the first time in three years. The meeting is acrimonious. Nijinsky does not want to go on stage until Diaghilev pays him what he is owed for past performances. The dispute is eventually settled when Diaghilev agrees to hand over 24,000 dollars. On 12 April, Nijinsky dances his trademark role in *Petrushka* on the stage of the Metropolitan Opera.

---

*About $1,153,871 in 2017.

The New York leg runs for over three weeks and is very successful. An invitation is extended to return in the autumn. Diaghilev accepts, but proposes that Nijinsky should manage the new tour. Diaghilev himself returns to Europe with his troupe for performances in Spain. The way back is just as nerve-wracking. Diaghilev panics, while Vasily prays.

A SECRET SLAUGHTER

Brusilov's offensive is a national triumph. After the endless setbacks of 1915, there is a renewed surge in optimism and patriotism. The admiration for Brusilov is matched only by the contempt for General Kuropatkin, whose name is already a byword for the humiliating defeat in the Russo-Japanese War, but who is now accused of indecisiveness in not having come to Brusilov's aid. All other news recedes into the background, including an uprising in Central Asia—today's Kazakhstan, Kyrgyzstan, Uzbekistan, Turkmenistan, and Tajikistan.

In June, Prime Minister Stürmer drafts a conscription order for the entire male population of Turkestan (Central Asia) aged nineteen to forty-three to perform front-line duties—the plan is for around two hundred thousand locals to dig trenches. According to Russian law, non-Russian inhabitants of the empire (as the entire Muslim population of Central Asia is categorized) are not subject to compulsory military service. But the new order changes everything.

It causes a wave of protests: the transfer of all the region's adult men to the front effectively dooms the remaining women, children, and elderly to starvation. The problem is aggravated by the fact that the publication of the decree coincides with the start of the cotton-picking season. Moreover, Russia's Muslims do not want to fight against the caliph—the sultan of the Ottoman Empire. The tipping point is the abuse of office by petty officials: since local residents have no documents, their age is determined by a quick inspection, meaning that people can be given whatever age they want by paying a bribe.

The first unrest begins in the Tajik city of Khujand—it is a "women's revolt." Local women throw themselves at the feet of the Cossack soldiers, begging them not to take their men. The insurrection gains traction in the Samarkand region, and then spreads to the so-called Semirechye (Seven Rivers) region—now in the southeast of Kazakhstan and the north of Kyrgyzstan, the territory around Almaty and Bishkek, former capital of Kazakhstan and capital of Kyrgyzstan, respectively. There are many Russians living there, and what ensues is effectively a civil war: the Kirghiz butcher the Russians, and the Russians try to exterminate the Kirghiz.

On 17 July 1916, martial law is declared across the whole of Central Asia, and Kuropatkin is sent in to quell the uprising—just six months after his appointment as commander-in-chief of the Northwestern Front. Despite being opposed to the call-up of local residents, he is the one tasked with crushing the insurgency.

At any other time the uprising in Central Asia would have provoked a major international reaction, far greater than the Lena Massacre or the Chisinau Pogrom. But it is eclipsed by the First World War. During the crackdown, up to sixty thousand people are killed; the exact number is unknown.

The region is soon paid a visit by Alexander Kerensky on a fact-finding mission on behalf of the State Duma. Kerensky has only just returned to active politics following his illness. Eager to resume his Duma role, he willingly travels to Central Asia.

Initially, Kerensky sees no signs of a pre-planned uprising: no weapons have been brought in. Clearly, it was a spontaneous, elemental outbreak of anger by a local population driven to despair. In Kerensky's view, the talk of a "pan-Islamic revolt" or "German agents" is nonsense. "It will be very difficult for us now to speak about 'the Turkish atrocities in Armenia' or 'the German atrocities in Belgium' when the world has never seen anything like what has just happened in the mountains of Semirechie," Kerensky reports to the Duma on 13 December. Cries of "Shame!" are heard from the left and "Lies!" from the right.

POLAND AND THE MARK OF THE DEVIL

In late June 1916, Foreign Minister Sergei Sazonov visits Nicholas II at the High Command, bearing a ready draft of the new Polish constitution. He is adamant that the document must be signed forthwith, since the Kingdom of Poland is now occupied by Germany. The only way for Russia to curry favor with the restless Poles is to grant them their own constitution with a view to presenting Russia as the guarantor of a freer and more prosperous Poland. The fact that Poland could ultimately become an independent country does not worry Sazonov. On the contrary, he considers the inclusion of Poland into the Russian Empire to have been a historic mistake—Poland is a cancerous growth inside the Russian state, and Russia will only benefit from having it surgically removed.

To increase the pressure on the tsar, Sazonov shows the draft constitution to Chief-of-Staff Alekseyev, who supports the idea and offers himself to present it to the tsar. Nicholas II complacently approves the document and asks that it be submitted to the government for further discussion. In fulfillment of the tsar's request, Sazonov hands the document to Stürmer and, in anticipation of the Duma discussion, goes on a short vacation to Finland.

While he is showing the draft constitution to the tsar, Sazanov has no idea that he is already doomed. Grigory Rasputin believes that the foreign minister is "marked by the devil," while Empress Alexandra says that his "cowardice before Europe will be the death of Russia."

While on vacation, Sazonov learns that the Council of Ministers has rejected the draft constitution of Poland, that he himself has been fired and that Prime Minister Stürmer is now, additionally, the foreign minister.

TWO CONSPIRACY THEORIES

After the initial success, the Brusilov Offensive peters out. The commander-in-chief continues to commit Russia's best units to the operation, but the front line fails to advance any further. He expects the two fronts to the north of him to join the offensive, but they hardly budge. It is not just indecision on the part of the respective commanders-in-chief: the Western and Northwestern Fronts face powerful German resistance with a well-entrenched defensive line. Brusilov knows that breaching it will be a far harder task than breaking through the Austrian defense. The High Command believes that the Austrian line is the weak link, and so redeploys additional units from the north to help Brusilov.

But Brusilov's successes come to end. The armies of the Southwestern Front advancing on Kovel (in the northwest of modern Ukraine) suffer huge losses. The German and Austrian troops put up fierce resistance. The Russian army loses about half a million men killed, wounded, or captured. The army elite—the Imperial Guard—perishes in the "Kovel meat grinder." Rasputin blames Brusilov personally. He advises the empress to tell her husband that General Brusilov should preserve his soldiers and not continue the offensive to the Carpathians: "The losses will be too great."

There is no more good news from the front. In July, on the crest of optimism prompted by the Brusilov Offensive, Romania enters the war on the side of the Entente. But the Romanian army proves to be a weak fighting force and is completely decimated by August.

Russian society is in the throes of disappointment. Brusilov is still considered a hero, but Evert is accused of cowardice and even treason. The only explanation considered by the chattering classes is that the operation was subverted by the "German party": Empress Alexandra, Stürmer, and Rasputin thwarted Brusilov's victory by not allowing the rest of the army to assist him.

However, this conspiracy theory is soon counterbalanced by another. In the summer, Vyrubova goes on vacation to Crimea, where she makes the acquaintance of the *gakhan*, the spiritual leader of one of the local ethnic groups, the Karaites. He makes a strong impression on Vyrubova, primarily because he shares her opinion that a conspiracy is being hatched against the empress. According to the *gakhan*, the instigator is the British ambassador to Russia. Vyrubova is so astonished that she invites him to visit Tsarskoye Selo to share his theory with the empress. As a result, the idea of a British-led conspiracy takes root among Alexandra's entourage, and by autumn 1916 the Russian elite is split into two unequal parts: one (Duma members and sympathizers) suspects the other (the empress's entourage and the government) of involvement in a German conspiracy; while the latter suspect the former of complicity in a British conspiracy. Alexandra, naturally believing her entourage, demands that her husband write to his cousin George V and take up the matter with the British ambassador, George Buchanan.

THE NEW LORD OF THE BLACK SEA

In July, the new commander-in-chief of the Black Sea Fleet, Admiral Alexander Kolchak, arrives in Sevastopol. His first move is to send warships to mine the Bosphorus so as to prevent the Turkish-German fleet from entering the Black Sea. His predecessor considered this venture a near impossible task, but Kolchak copes admirably. As a result, Turkish and German ships are "jammed" in the Bosporus. Thereafter, Kolchak lays the groundwork for an even more ambitious objective—the seizure of the Black Sea straits and Istanbul, which was only recently considered a lost cause.

The slogan "Raise a cross over Hagia Sophia"—an obsession among some sections of Russian society for many decades—is not considered a fantasy, but a reality. According to Kolchak's calculations, the Turkish army has been bled dry by the Battle of Gallipoli and the constant setbacks in Palestine, Egypt, and Armenia, not to mention the fact that Turkish troops were sent to Galicia to aid the Austrian army. In the area of the straits, only three Ottoman divisions remain. Kolchak insists that the operation to seize Istanbul must be carried out before the weather deteriorates (i.e., no later than September). He asks Alekseyev to supply him with landing troops.

According to Kolchak, only five divisions will be needed to capture Istanbul—half the number suggested by Alekseyev. In 1916, the city is home to more than 1.5 million people. The question of what to do with them is not discussed.

Emperor Nicholas II approves the plan. However, it turns out that the preparations and military training will require three to four months. The operation cannot be carried out in the autumn or winter due to the stormy weather, so Kolchak has to postpone the maritime offensive until the spring of 1917.

The cancellation of the operation plunges Kolchak into a state of depression, aggravated by a tragedy that occurs in October. Aboard the battleship *Empress Maria*, a keg of gunpowder self-ignites, causing a massive explosion inside a shell room. A fire breaks out. Kolchak sails to the battleship and personally oversees the fire-fighting operation, but despite all the efforts, the battleship sinks. Admiral Kolchak is the last man to leave the ship. The loss of the *Empress Maria* is a body blow to Kolchak. He becomes withdrawn, stops eating, and receives no one. His entourage fears for his sanity.

MAD AS A HATTER

"My dearest darling wife! Yesterday I met a great man—Protopopov," Nicholas writes to Alexandra on 20 July. "He traveled abroad with other members of the Duma and told me lots of interesting things."

It is the start of a beautiful friendship. Returning from his foreign tour, Protopopov feels triumphant. His ambition is said to be running wild. He dreams of becoming a minister, and the chances look good. Protopopov knows that back in spring Rodzianko recommended him to the tsar as the new trade minister. But Rodzianko does not know that Protopopov has even more influential patrons. The fact is that the deputy chairman of the Duma was recently treated for a venereal disease by Dr. Badmaev, who specializes in Buryat and Tibetan medicine. The healer introduces him to Rasputin, and now Rasputin recommends him to the empress.

Soon after returning from Europe, Protopopov attends a reception at Tsarskoye Selo. Alexandra also takes a liking to the Duma deputy chairman. She urges her husband to appoint Protopopov to the post of interior minister: "He has known and loved our Friend for at least four years, which redounds greatly to his credit."

On 16 September the deputy chairman of the State Duma is duly appointed acting interior minister. To his colleagues in the Duma, it comes as a complete surprise. He did not forewarn anyone about the appointment. They are outraged.

The fuss surrounding Protopopov's appointment intensifies when he orders the transfer of former War Minister Sukhomlinov from prison to house arrest. Protopopov is acting at the behest of the empress and Rasputin, who pity the old man locked up in the Peter and Paul Fortress.

On his way back from Central Asia, Duma member Kerensky stops over in Saratov (which happens to be his electoral constituency), where he holds several meetings. There he learns about Protopopov's elevation and is initially heartened by the news: Protopopov is a fellow native of Simbirsk (as is Lenin), and they have good relations. But back in Petrograd, Kerensky discovers a telegram reporting the arrest of everyone he recently met in Saratov. He immediately goes to see Protopopov.

Interior Minister Protopopov promises to sort everything out. They start to chat informally. Kerensky notices a reproduction of the painting *Christ with Crown of Thorns* by Guido Reni on Protopopov's desk. Intercepting his gaze, the interior minister explains that he always seeks advice from the picture: "When a decision has to be taken, He points the way." Protopopov proceeds to outline his messianic plan for saving Russia. Kerensky cannot understand what has happened—he knew Protopopov as a person of sane mind: "Is he a madman? Or a charlatan who has adroitly tailored his views to the musty atmosphere of the tsaritsa's apartments and Anna Vyrubova's 'little house'?" wonders Kerensky.

Rumors of Protopopov's insanity quickly spread around the capital. "He symbolizes the fact that all ministers are *non compos mentis*," writes Zinaida Gippius in her diary. "There are quiet idiots who, with a smirk on their sagging lips, enjoy starting fires. Protopopov is one. No one can prevent his arsonist activity, because his power comes from above."

AMERICAN PSYCHO

In the autumn of 1916 Diaghilev divides his troupe in two: he and his dancer Myasin remain in Spain, while the other part, as arranged, returns to America under the direction of Nijinsky. Diaghilev used to mock his former prima ballerina Anna Pavlova for having performed in circuses and hippodromes, laughing at her for devaluing high art by dancing in arenas for dogs and horses. Now Nijinsky performs at similar venues, but Diaghilev does not protest. On the contrary, he pockets the money from it.

The program of the American tour is intense: fifty-three cities. In New York Nijinsky stages his new ballet *Till Eulenspiegel*, but it bombs. The American tour turns into a horror story, and the troupe is exhausted by the constant traveling.

By the end of December the company is running out of money. On the way to Los Angeles and San Francisco, the dancers practically starve. Nijinsky sends telegram after telegram to Diaghilev, begging for help and imploring him to come over. But Diaghilev cannot stomach the thought of another Atlantic crossing. He does, however, dispatch Vasily.

With Vasily of no assistance whatsoever, Nijinsky has a nervous breakdown and is unable to perform. No one yet realizes it, but this is the onset of madness. The upcoming 1917 will be the last year of his ballet career. After that, he will spend the rest of his life in psychiatric clinics.

The tour is interrupted, and the Metropolitan Opera suffers huge losses, which are passed onto Diaghilev's enterprise. He tries to economize on everything—even on the services of his friend Stravinsky, with whom he now quarrels over every centime. Their ping-pong telegrams to each other are full of mutual reproaches.

Despite the mess, Diaghilev still dreams of performing in Russia as soon as the war is over—which he thinks will happen very soon.

GO TO SLEEP

Pavel Milyukov leaves for Europe at the end of the summer. He and Struve are invited to Cambridge, where they are to be awarded with honorary professorships. There is nothing for them to do in Petrograd at the present time, for the Duma is in recess until November. Throughout the trip Milyukov is continually asked whether Russia intends to conclude a separate peace and about the influence of Rasputin. He gets so carried away on this latter topic that he decides to conduct his own journalistic investigation. Milyukov is no professional, and his inquiries are limited to reading newspapers and a handful of interviews. He is, however, an excellent orator and delivers talks about his work as if he has discovered a new continent.

During his trip, he stocks up on rumors. In London he meets with the elderly Russian ambassador, Count Benckendorff, who says that British diplomats dislike Stürmer; in Lausanne he converses with Russian diplomats and immigrants (who feed him with gossip about clubs for Russian Germanophiles, which Milyukov takes with a pinch of salt). Trips to Paris, Oslo, and Stockholm also furnish him with hearsay, whereafter he returns to Petrograd in September.

He is just in time for the first meeting between Duma members and their former colleague Protopopov, now the interior minister. On 19 October Duma Chairman Rodzianko invites the leaders of the Duma factions and the freshly baked minister to his home. Protopopov amazes his old comrades by turning up dressed as a gendarme. No minister since Plehve has worn a police uniform. Protopopov insists that their conversation remain confidential, but Milyukov replies that the time for secrets is over, and that he will duly report to his faction.

"What's happened? Why don't you want to talk like comrades?" Protopopov is surprised. Milyukov shouts back that Protopopov is serving the interests of Stürmer, whom the whole country considers a traitor. Moreover, he is hounding the press and his appointment was made largely thanks to Rasputin. "I am the personal choice of the Sovereign, whom I have grown to love," replies Protopopov. He goes on to say that he has in no way defected to the monarchist camp, for he has always been a monarchist and never considered himself a member of the "progressive bloc." What is more, he asserts, he will never allow the government to become answerable to the Duma. "I began my career as a humble student, giving lessons for 50 kopecks,'" he exclaims. "All I have is my personal support for the Sovereign, which I will retain to my dying day, regardless of what you think of me!" The parliamentarians respond to the chest-thumping minister's histrionic speech with the words: "Go to sleep."

The next day a transcript of the meeting spreads around Petrograd. Milyukov claims that he recalled the details of the conversation from memory, while Protopopov is sure that Rodzianko planted a stenographer behind the wall. No newspaper risks publishing the text. But the smile-inducing transcript is printed unofficially and transmitted from hand to hand and lauded as a fine example of humorous prose.

However, there are more strings to Pavel Milyukov's literary bow than political satire. For the new session of the Duma, he prepares a revelatory address using all the materials collected during his recent travels. The

---

* About $6.60 in 2017.

Duma opens on 1 November, whereupon Milyukov gives perhaps the most famous speech in the history of the Russian parliament.

He says nothing not already discussed in the average Petrograd living room, but he says it openly and candidly. He states that Russia is rife with rumors of betrayal and treason, of dark forces fighting for Germany, asserting that if the Germans wanted to ferment disorder in Russia, they would do no better than to follow the example of the Russian government, and goes on to cite numerous cases of corruption, fraud, and errors of judgment by the authorities. Recalling the phrase of War Minister Shuvaev, "I may be a fool, but I'm not a traitor," Milyukov poses a rhetorical question: Is the Russian government stupid or treacherous?

The "raw nerve" moment of the speech pertains to Rasputin and Empress Alexandra's entourage, who effectively decide government appointments. Despite it being a forbidden topic, Milyukov cannot keep silent. He knows that he will be cut short if he says anything construed as an "insult to the supreme authority," so Milyukov craftily quotes an extract from a Swiss newspaper in German about the role of the empress and her "party of courtiers." Rodzianko has prudently left the hall, so the acting chairman at that moment is his deputy, Varun-Sekret, who does not know German and so does not interrupt the speaker.

The refrain of Milyukov's speech is highly symbolic. He feels obliged to answer his own rhetorical "stupid or treacherous" question. He thinks that traitors exist, that there is a "pro-German party" and that the government cannot be full of idiots—there must be some wicked intent somewhere. A century on, we know the answer to his question: it is stupidity. None of the bureaucrats he exposed were spies. They were just feckless pen-pushers.

The speech is a sensation, for it marks the first time that the whispers have sounded in public. The censor forbids its publication, so newspapers simply print empty columns where it would have been. However, the text of Milyukov's speech (sometimes considerably embellished) spreads throughout the country: it is read by soldiers and workers. According to Colonel Denikin, many officers, including the top commanders, agree with Milyukov. Moreover, the points he touched upon are no longer taboo, but openly discussed during officer meetings.

A week after the speech Rasputin and Protopopov are so worried that they advise Alexandra that the elderly Stürmer should be sidelined for a while—because his German surname is a "red flag for the lunatics" who believe in espionage theories. The empress passes on the request to her husband.

INVISIBLE TROUSERS

Nicholas II lives at the High Command in Mogilev (a city in modern Belarus, then in the west of Russian Empire) with his ailing son. He corresponds constantly with his relatives, who all live apart: his wife and daughters at Tsarskoye Selo, his mother, sister Olga, and brother-in-law Sandro in Kiev, and the rest either at the front, in Petrograd, or in Tiflis.

The correspondence between the imperial couple in the autumn of 1916 is a monument to their insane love and devotion. They do everything they can to help each other. Alexandra sincerely believes that by consulting with Rasputin on any matter and conveying his recommendations, she is helping her husband.

In his letters, Nicholas ironically refers to himself as a "weak-willed hubby," while Alexandra displays resoluteness. She writes that she has a strong will and wears "invisible trousers," making her the only real man among the feeble ministers. She demands that her husband be merciless towards their enemies (i.e., the Duma). She wants to see Guchkov hanged and Polivanov, Lvov, and Milyukov sent to Siberia.

On 1 November, the day of Milyukov's speech in the Duma, Grand Duke Nicholas Mikhailovich, a liberal and a friend of the late Tolstoy, visits the High Command. Without consulting the leader of the Kadets, he delivers a speech to the tsar, which also touches upon the "dark forces" surrounding Alexandra. He says that the whole country is gossiping about Rasputin: "Russia cannot be ruled like this anymore." Moreover, he warns the tsar that his life is under threat: "You are on the threshold of a new era of unrest and assassinations."

Nicholas is silent. Nicholas Mikhailovich hands him a letter in which he further develops his thoughts. "You have faith in Empress Alexandra. That is understandable," writes the grand duke. "But what comes from her lips is smoke and mirrors, not the truth," he writes. Nicholas, even without breaking the seal on the letter, sends it to his wife. She replies that Siberia is the only fitting punishment for such a letter, "since it borders on high treason. . . . He and Nikolasha [Nikolai Nikolaivich] are my greatest enemies inside the family, not counting the black [Montenegrin] women."

A week later, on 6 November, "Nikolasha" and his brother "Petyusha" pay a visit to the High Command—for the first time since his dismissal as supreme commander. Alexandra is fraught: "You must be cold-blooded with this wretched gang," she writes to her husband. The tsar's uncle picks a fight with his nephew: "You ought to be ashamed of yourself for thinking that I wanted to dethrone you. You've known me all my life; you know how I've always been devoted to you. Shame on you, Nicky." The tsar shrugs his shoulders in silence. "It would be better if you cursed or struck me than keeping silent. Don't you see that you are losing the crown?" says his uncle, urging the tsar to appoint a government of national confidence that is answerable to the Duma. "You are delaying everything. There's still time, but soon it will be too late."

Nicholas II maintains his stubborn silence. In the end, he decides to dismiss Stürmer. Empress Alexandra is very upset. She bombards her husband with hysterical letters, demanding that Nicholas Mikhailovich be exiled and complaining that the new prime minister, Trepov, dislikes her and "great difficulties will arise" with him. Finally, she urges her husband not to fire Protopopov and essentially not to do anything until she herself comes to see him at the High Command.

DREAMS OF A CONSPIRACY

On 7 November, Emperor Franz Josef I of Austria dies after a sixty-eight-year rule: that is to say, he was on the throne long before Nicholas II and Alexandra, and most of their relatives, were even born. The death of the "eternal emperor" makes a great impression on the Russian imperial family: on the one hand, they say that it will bring about the defeat of Austria-Hungary and end the war; on the other, there is talk of the need for changes at the top in Russia, too.

The discussions about "saving Russia" by replacing Nicholas and Alexandra are not new, of course. But in November 1916 the emperor's abdication and the empress's exile to a monastery are the most fashionable debates in almost every Petrograd living room. Opinion is split on one point in particular: If Nicholas II renounces the throne in favor of his son, who will become the regent? His brother Mikhail, his uncle Nikolasha, or perhaps Grand Duke Dmitry?

The most influential woman in Petrograd is Grand Duchess Miechen, around whom the entire imperial court rotates, since the two empresses do not live in the capital (Alexandra hardly ever leaves Tsarskoye Selo, and Maria Feodorovna has moved to Kiev). The grand duchess has a deep-seated grudge against Alexandra. First, she has not forgotten how her eldest son Kirill was expelled from Russia for marrying a princess who had rejected Alexandra's brother. Second, Miechen wanted to marry off her son Boris to the imperial couple's eldest daughter, Olga. Alexandra refused without hesitation. What is more, Miechen is eyeing the throne for one of her own sons: Kirill, Boris, or Andrei.

In November Miechen visits the chairman of the Duma, Mikhail Rodzianko. She says that Alexandra is ruining the country and putting the tsar and the whole dynasty at risk. She needs to be sidelined, asserts Miechen. Many share this view. No one wants to get their hands dirty, but everyone prods each other and openly speaks about the need for concerted action.

Even Protopopov talks about a plot. Shortly after his appointment, he told the head of the Zemstvo Union, Prince Lvov, that he would prohibit the union from meeting because its members allegedly want to arrest the tsar and force him to adopt a constitution.

Lvov was not planning anything of the sort back then, but the idea got him thinking. In October, he visits the High Command to discuss the political situation with Chief of Staff Alekseyev. Various scenarios are considered: for instance, the empress could be arrested during one of her visits to the High Command. In this case, Nicholas would willingly agree to anything and would certainly appoint Lvov as prime minister.

After this conversation, both fall ill from exhaustion. Alekseyev is so stressed that on 3 November he cannot get out of bed. On 8 November, he goes to Crimea for treatment. Meanwhile, on 14 November Empress Alexandra arrives at the High Command.

In early December the Zemstvo Union holds a congress in Moscow. It is officially banned, so the delegates meet at the home of Prince Lvov. One of them is the Armenian politician Alexander Khatisov, the head of Tiflis (i.e., the head of the City Duma of present-day Tbilisi). Lvov tells Khatisov how much better it would be if Grand Duke Nikolai Nikolaevich were the sovereign instead of Nicholas II. As a former supreme commander with an iron will, he is convinced of the need for dialogue with society. He was one of those who insisted on the dismissal of Sukhomlinov and other odious ministers, and urged the tsar to sign the manifesto on 17 October 1905. Prince Lvov has no desire to orchestrate a coup d'état himself—he wants the coup to be carried out by the grand duke. Nikolai Nikolaevich is so popular that everything will go swimmingly, he is sure.

Khatisov travels to Tbilisi to see the grand duke. According to protocol, the duke should, in fact, summon an adjutant and order the arrest of the conspirator—but instead he listens attentively before asking Khatisov to come back the following day. When Khatisov returns the next day, he is met by the grand duke with his wife, the Montenegrin Stana, and his chief-of-staff, General Yanushkevich. Khatisov repeats everything and sees that the idea of a coup greatly appeals to the grand duchess. Yanushkevich doubts whether the army will follow the grand duke, fearing that there could be a mutiny at the front. Nikolai Nikolaevich thanks Khatisov and bids him farewell. The conversation is over. The next time they see each other will be in February 1917.

PLOTS

During his trip around Europe, Milyukov was repeatedly tormented by the questions of "Who if not Nicholas II?" and "What will happen if there is another revolution?" Returning home, Milyukov decides to discuss this topic with his comrades: Who indeed? Many of his colleagues regularly discuss this issue at their Masonic lodge meetings, but Milyukov is not a Freemason and is not party to these conversations. He summons Rodzianko and the leading Kadets, including Nekrasov, the chairman of the Masonic supreme council, and some non-Duma members, including Guchkov and the young tycoon Mikhail Tereshchenko, heir to a sugar-refining dynasty (he is also a Freemason, and Nekrasov brings him along).

They discuss the likelihood of a street uprising, which the current government will not be able to handle. In this case, one of two things will happen: either the authorities will form a government of national confidence, or the protesters themselves will come to power. Guchkov listens in silence to these arguments and then replies that the new government will be formed from the forces that make the revolution, not outsiders. On this thought, the discussion ends. Almost everyone concludes that Guchkov knows about a brewing conspiracy, but is not letting on.

After the meeting Guchkov again falls ill and goes for treatment to Kislovodsk (the spa city in the south of the Russian Empire). When he returns, he is immediately approached by Nekrasov, with whom he is not very familiar; Nekrasov wants to know about the rumored conspiracy.

As the doyen of Russian Freemasonry, Nekrasov loves secrecy and mystery. He tells his friends that his dream is to become an *éminence grise*, whom "no one knows" but who "does everything." He disseminates rumors of a possible conspiracy inside the Masonic lodges themselves. The leader of the Social Democratic faction in the Duma, Nikolai Chkheidze, recalls that some of his colleagues regularly voice the need to finance and stage a coup, which would include holding lectures in the regions to prepare public opinion. But since the Russian Freemasons are a network of discussion clubs, and not a secret organization (everyone knows about it), Nekrasov needs Guchkov's assistance.

Guchkov says that there is no conspiracy just yet, but the time has come to start thinking about one. The plan that Guchkov comes up with is almost a carbon copy of the Young Turk Revolution. He wants to force the tsar to abdicate in favor of another. He himself has no intention of entering government, for at heart he is a monarchist and simply wants a different emperor.

The details of the plan are as follows: it is difficult to detain the tsar at the High Command (it would require the involvement of senior officers), and an attempt at Tsarskoye Selo could result in bloodshed, so the most opportune moment would be to intercept the tsar's train en route from Mogilev to the capital. No violence would be necessary, just a bit of psychological pressure to persuade Nicholas to abdicate in favor of his son, with his brother Mikhail as regent. Since everyone loves little Alexei, it would boost support for the monarchy across society. After that, everything will be done by the book: Mikhail will expel Rasputin and Protopopov and refill the government with decent types, such as the reformer Krivoshein and former Foreign Minister Sazonov.

According to Guchkov's memoirs, there is no plan B: if the tsar refuses, the conspirators will not insist, but surrender, which means arrest and possible hanging.

The thirty-seven-year-old Nekrasov involves his Masonic "brother," the thirty-year-old Tereshchenko, in the conspiracy. Together they begin searching for military units able to intercept the imperial train on the journey from Mogilev to Tsarskoye Selo. But they are hard to come by.

Elsewhere, another couple of plotters are hatching a plan: the twenty-nine-year-old Felix Yusupov and his friend, the twenty-five-year-old Grand Duke Dmitry, a potential pretender to the throne. They have been thinking about assassinating Rasputin for several months now, even consulting with friends and family. For instance, on 20 November Felix writes to his wife Irina, the tsar's niece: "My dear darling, I'm terribly busy with plans to eliminate R. It is now absolutely necessary, or else everything will be finished." It is believed that Rasputin intends to lobby for a separate peace with Germany before the end of 1916.

As a result, many people learn about their intentions, including Irina's father and the tsar's childhood friend, Grand Duke Sandro, and Alexandra's sister, Grand Duchess Ella. Initially, Yusupov plans to use his wife Irina as bait. Rasputin wants to make the acquaintance of the tsar's niece, which means he will willingly accept the invitation to their home. But Felix then decides not to involve Irina, which offends her greatly.

Felix and Dmitry have entirely different motivations. Both are under the influence of what they have heard from their families. Grand Duchess

Ella hates Rasputin and has made a mortal enemy of her sister the empress because of him. Felix's father, meanwhile, the former Moscow governor-general Felix senior, is consumed by other prejudices and conspiracy theories. Yusupov senior is sure that there is a secret German lobby inside Russia in control of Rasputin and the government. He believes that it was the Germans who secured his dismissal the year before. Felix shares all his father's convictions. Their circle believes that Rasputin is a spy and that it was his doing that enabled the Germans to sink Lord Kitchener's ship as it sailed to Russia.

But that is not all. Felix is used to being the center of everyone's attention, and is forever plotting increasingly extravagant ways to achieve this. Aged thirteen, strolling around the World Exhibition in Paris with his parents, Felix grabbed a fire hose and began spraying passers-by. He was detained by the police and his parents paid a fine. The case was hushed up and they did not punish their son. Later, at a more mature age, while studying in Oxford, he was the star of London's balls—his suits were always the most colorful and expensive. Now grown up, he is a student of an elite military school—the Pazhesky Corps—and craves glory. He wants to be a superhero, the savior of the Fatherland. Dmitry, on the other hand, judging by his letters, harbors more modest ambitions and is ready to follow his idol, Felix.

In early December the two friends find themselves an unexpected accomplice: State Duma member Vladimir Purishkevich, a former leader of the Union of the Russian People, who, with government funding, split the movement in two and founded his own Black Hundred organization. On 20 November Purishkevich amazes everyone by leaving the right-wing faction, joining the opposition, and making a provocative speech in the Duma against corruption inside the imperial court.

Purishkevich's speech is no less explosive than Milyukov's. That same day Felix Yusupov calls him to arrange a meeting at which Felix opens up about the plan to kill Rasputin. A few more assistants are found, among them Lieutenant Sukhotin, the stepson of Leo Tolstoy's daughter Tatiana.

The operation is scheduled for 16 December. Yusupov calls the preacher beforehand to invite him to his parents' home on the Moika River in Petrograd, saying that Irina wants to meet him. Rasputin agrees and arrives in secret, without the knowledge of his own bodyguards. "It's strange and frightening to think how easily he agreed to everything, as if he himself was helping us in our difficult task," recalls Yusupov.

At 11 p.m. Grand Duke Dmitry and the other conspirators arrive. According to Yusupov, one of the accomplices, Dr. Lazovert, laces a plate of chocolate cakes with poison—the dose is many times stronger than necessary for a fatal outcome. After the murder, the plan is for one of the conspirators, Lieutenant Sukhotin, to put on Rasputin's hat and coat and walk back in the direction of the preacher's house on Gorokhovaya Street, where he lives with his daughters, to create an alibi. Purishkevich is to burn Rasputin's clothes, while Grand Duke Dmitry will take the corpse to Petrovsky Island in his car.

FOUR SHOTS AND AN ICE-HOLE

At about midnight on 16–17 December 1916, Rasputin opens the door to Yusupov, who has come to pick him up. The preacher is well attired—Yusupov has never seen him looking so dapper. Rasputin says that he has promised Interior Minister Protopopov to stay at home: "'They want to kill you,' he says. 'Evil people are plotting bad things. . . .' Well, let them try. They won't succeed. They're not up to it."

For some reason, the preacher trusts Yusupov, which, for a moment, makes the latter feel "ashamed and loathsome." Later, Grand Duke Nicholas Mikhailovich suggests that Rasputin had a "carnal passion for Felix."

They go to the Moika Palace. Seated at the table, Rasputin refuses a drink for a long time, waiting for Irina Yusupova to appear (although she won't, for she is no longer part of the plan). Felix says that she and his mother-in-law are entertaining guests, and that his wife will come down as soon as they leave. Finally, Rasputin begins to eat and drink. At 3:30 a.m. Felix runs upstairs and complains to his accomplices that the cyanide in the cakes and wine is not working. He takes Dmitry's revolver and goes back.

Rasputin is sitting at the table as before, head down, breathing heavily. He complains that his "head is heavy and his stomach is burning." He asks for another glass and suggests going to see some local gypsies. Yusupov, according to his own account, points to the wall and says: "Grigory Yefimovich [Rasputin], why don't you take a look at that crucifix and pray in front of it." He takes the revolver from behind his back and shoots. Rasputin "roars like a wild animal and falls heavily onto the bearskin rug."

Grand Duke Dmitry and the other conspirators leave the house, according to Yusupov's version. Only he and Purishkevich remain. Felix takes a closer look at the "corpse" when suddenly it moves. Yusupov runs to Purishkevich, shouting: "Where's your revolver, he's still alive!" He grabs a truncheon and runs back. The resurrected Rasputin crawls away, "moaning and growling like a wounded beast."

He stumbles into the street and screams: "Felix, Felix, I'm going to tell the tsaritsa everything!" Purishkevich runs after him and shoots four times, twice missing, twice hitting the target. He catches up with his victim and kicks him in the temple.

Hearing shots, a policeman by the name of Vlasyuk runs to the palace. The inebriated Purishkevich confesses in the heat of the moment that they have killed "Grishka Rasputin, who destroyed our Motherland and our tsar, and sold us to the Germans," and if he [Vlasyuk] loves Russia, he must remain silent. The policeman agrees, yet informs his superiors after leaving the palace.

Yusupov again inspects Rasputin: he is "irresistibly drawn to the bloody corpse." He starts beating the body with his truncheon. Purishkevich cannot stop him. Grand Duke Dmitry arrives with his car, and the corpse is stuffed inside and taken to Petrovsky Island, where they throw it from the bridge into a pre-prepared ice-hole. But they forget to tie a weight to the legs. Rasputin's galoshes slip off. They throw them after him into the hole, but in the darkness no one notices that they miss.

Yusupov orders a servant to kill one of his dogs and throw it into the snowdrift where Rasputin fell—in case the police notice that the fresh snow has been disturbed.

THE LAW-BREAKING EMPRESS

On the morning of 17 December, Anna Vyrubova receives a phone call from Rasputin's daughter Maria. She says that her father left late at night with Yusupov and did not return. That is followed by a call from Interior Minister Protopopov to report the on-duty policeman's version of the previous night's events. Another policeman saw a car without headlights drive off from the palace.

Empress Alexandra and Vyrubova are beside themselves with worry. They pray and cry, telling each other that they do not believe that Rasputin is dead. Alexandra fears that the death of Rasputin means the death of her son—without his healing powers, the tsarevich cannot live.

At 10 a.m., when Felix Yusupov wakes up, a police officer is already waiting outside his palace. He has come to ascertain whether Rasputin was with him the night before. Yusupov denies it. The officer says that the policeman who spoke to Purishkevich during the night has reported everything to his superiors. Yusupov feigns surprise and says that the previous night he had simply received guests. One of them got so drunk that he killed a dog. The inebriated Purishkevich had simply been comparing Rasputin to this dog when he spoke to the policeman, alleges Yusupov.

Alexandra asks Protopopov to continue the investigation and conduct a search of the Yusupovs' palace on the Moika River. She also begs her husband to return as soon as possible. Nicholas II receives her telegram during a war council meeting with the commanders-in-chief from all the fronts. Despite its importance, he interrupts the meeting and leaves for Tsarskoye Selo.

In the evening Purishkevich is due to go to the front line aboard a medical aid train (he is in charge of medical aid), Felix heads for Crimea, while Dmitry goes to the High Command. Felix writes to the empress, claiming that he had invited Rasputin to visit, but the meeting was cancelled. Then, according to his version, he calls on his aunt's husband, the chairman of the Duma, Mikhail Rodzianko. In the evening he, together with his wife's brothers, who are the tsar's nephews, goes to the station and finds it cordoned off by police. Alexandra has ordered that Felix be forbidden from leaving Petrograd.

Grand Duke Dmitry goes to the Mikhailovsky Theatre. There, as a renowned Rasputin-hater, he is greeted with applause. Embarrassed, he quickly leaves. In the evening, he phones the empress at Tsarskoye Selo, but she refuses to talk to him.

On the morning of the 18th, a policeman goes to Rasputin's house and shows his daughters one of the bloodstained galoshes found near Bolshoi Petrovsky Bridge.

Felix Yusupov collects his things and moves to the home of Grand Duke Dmitry. The house of the grand duke is inviolable, and so he will not be arrested there, he believes. Dmitry is very surprised—he thought that Felix was already on his way to Crimea. At that moment the phone rings from Tsarskoye Selo, reporting that Grand Duke Dmitry is under house arrest on the orders of the empress. The two friends are indignant: according to the law, only her husband the emperor can arrest the grand duke. Dmitry immediately writes telegrams to his relatives. All are outraged: the empress has clearly exceeded her authority.

Grand Duke Nicholas Mikhailovich pays several visits to supply the arrested duo with fresh rumors that Alexandra is demanding a military trial that will sentence them to death by firing squad, but Protopopov is urging her to wait for her husband's return. A telegram is received from Dmitry's beloved Aunt Ella in Moscow: "May God grant Felix strength after his patriotic act," writes the founder of the Marfo-Mariinsky Convent.

A copy of the intercepted telegram is immediately brought to Empress Alexandra, who a few months earlier had quarreled with her sister over Rasputin and banished her from Tsarskoye Selo. Now the sobbing Alexandra is convinced that Ella was part of the conspiracy.

LONESOME AT NEW YEAR

On the morning of 19 December Rasputin's fur coat is found in the icehole, followed by his corpse frozen to the ice. He is taken to the Chesmensky Almshouse for an autopsy. When the corpse thaws, the medics establish that the cause of death was a gunshot—no traces of poison are found. A search of the Yusupovs' Moika Palace reveals a trail of blood. Forensic analysis establishes it to be human, not canine.

The next morning Protopopov arrives at Tsarskoye Selo and reports that the murder of Rasputin marks the start of a new wave of terrorist attacks; hence, the security of the empress is paramount. Under suspicion are the grand dukes, the Yusupovs, Rodzianko (who is related to them), the prime minister, and the justice minister, who is hampering the investigation. Nicholas, having recently returned, dismisses his justice minister, sanctions the house arrest of Dmitry, and asks for Rasputin's body to be brought to Tsarskoye Selo.

Yusupov and Grand Duke Dmitry feel both fear and pride. They deny that they killed Rasputin, yet their relatives congratulate them and talk about the tremendous public reaction: people are said to be kissing in the streets, like at Easter, rejoicing at the death of Rasputin. But it is an exaggeration. On the third day, the newspapers are banned from writing about Rasputin, and the detainees become depressed. Yusupov clearly expected the assassination to change the world: "Yusupov was intoxicated by the importance of his role. He had a great political future mapped out for himself," recalls Dmitry's sister, Grand Duchess Maria.

On 22 December Sandro, Yusupov's father-in-law, goes to Tsarskoye Selo. The grand duke says that Felix and Dmitry are not common murderers, but patriots misguided by an overwhelming desire to save the Motherland. "You speak very well," the tsar replies with a smile, "but you will agree that no one, whether a grand duke or a simple peasant, has the right to kill."

Dmitry, meanwhile, writes to Nicholas to say that he will shoot himself rather than face a military tribunal. The next morning, he is summoned to Tsarskoye Selo and told that he is being exiled to Persia; Felix is banished to his Rakitnoye Estate near Kursk. They are not allowed to phone or correspond with relatives. Purishkevich and the other conspirators are not mentioned, seemingly forgotten.

"They are neuropathic aesthetes, everything they did was a half-measure," writes the fifty-six-year-old Grand Duke Nicholas Mikhailovich in his diary. "We must definitely put an end to both Alexandra Feodorovna and Protopopov." He dreams of killing the empress ("rendering her harmless," in his words), but does not know who to involve after Purishkevich's departure.

On New Year's Eve, Miechen's palace hosts a gathering of family members, who sign a collective letter to the tsar with a request to mitigate Dmitry's punishment. In their opinion, exile to Persia is a death sentence. "No one has the right to kill. I know that there are other guilty minds out there, for Dmitry Pavlovich did not act alone. I am surprised by your appeal to me," Nicholas replies. The three grand dukes who signed the letter, Nicholas Mikhailovich and Miechen's sons Kirill and Andrei, are subsequently expelled from the capital.

Nicholas and Alexandra cease all communication with their relatives. Protopopov continues to supply them with new letters whose authors regret that Rasputin's killers did not finish the job by getting rid of "Her." New Year 1917 is a lonely time for the Romanovs. They see in the New Year with only Anna Vyrubova for company, whom the empress no longer allows out of Tsarskoye Selo for fear of her life. Protopopov is now their main source of information from the outside world. He tries his best to make up for the absent Rasputin—he summons the psychic medium Charles Peren from abroad and asks him to invoke the spirit of Rasputin. It is said that a double of the late preacher has been seen inside Protopopov's office. The interior minister tells the empress that he has seen Rasputin in his sleep, standing there with arms open wide, blessing Russia. It calms her down.

THE CURTAIN CALL

On New Year's Eve, the tsar dismisses his prime minister, replacing him with a wholly unexpected face. It belongs to the sixty-six-year-old Prince Nikolai Golitsyn, who is almost unknown to the public and lacks experience. His only selling point is that the empress trusts him, for he runs her personal charity committee. Golitsyn implores Nicholas not to appoint him, but the tsar insists and hands the new prime minister a dateless decree for the dissolution of the Duma, allowing Golitsyn to disband parliament at any moment, even when Nicholas is away at the High Command.

Golitsyn is horrified. He asks the tsar at least to fire Protopopov, because it will be impossible to work with him. But Nicholas refuses. Protopopov is the most influential member of the government, who believes that the Duma should be dissolved because it is teeming with revolutionaries. In the meantime, the next session of the Duma is postponed until 14 February. Alexandra expects further decisive action from Protopopov—and he duly orders the arrest of members of the so-called Working Group under the Central Military-Industrial Committee, headed by its Menshevik chairman Kuzma Gvozdev. It is the most high-profile political arrest for several years. The interior minister boasts at Tsarskoye Selo that he has beheaded the revolution.

When the Duma finally sits, the meeting kicks off with a scandal. Kerensky delivers a speech unrivalled for its acerbity: "Do you understand that the historical task facing the Russian people is to destroy the medieval regime whatever it takes?" he asks his colleagues. Having read a transcript of the speech, Alexandra writes that "Kedrinsky" (misspelling his name) should be hanged.

The main word on people's lips this winter in Petrograd is "tails," referring to the snake-like queues in front of every store. There are fuel shortages in the capital, and goods cannot be delivered. It is a nationwide problem: everywhere from Petrograd to Moscow to the provinces ration cards are issued for bread, sugar, and meat. The "tails" are not only a source of food, but also of information. While standing endlessly in line, people exchange rumors. Some talk about an impending famine, which does little to calm the already hungry queuers.

However, it is not only a question of bread. Many, even the most loyal monarchists, sense that the regime is doomed: "Soon all of us will be hanging from the lamp-posts," Admiral Nilov, an imperial adjutant, often says in public, while the elderly lady-in-waiting Naryshkina is eager to leave Tsarskoye Selo for the month of Lent, since she is unable to help the empress, whom she asserts is "under the influence of Satan."

There is a similar feeling in Moscow. "I often puzzle over the question of how to save the monarchy. I see no available means," writes the publicist and monarchist Lev Tikhomirov in late January.

It is the same all over the country. The gendarme officer Zavarzin spends several months on a round trip to the Far East: from Petrograd to Vladivostok and then back to Arkhangelsk by train. He marvels at how calm and assured people are. On board the train and in the streets the talk everywhere is of imminent revolution and the abdication of the tsar. The death of Rasputin is universally approved ("Let a dog die like a dog"), and the imperial couple is hated ("Why waste words on them, they'll soon be gone"). Everyone is waiting for the government to become answerable to the Duma. The gendarme is shocked and angered at first, but soon realizes that a nationwide clampdown would be futile: "State power is atrophied, and we are on the verge of the abyss."

On 22 February Nicholas suddenly departs for the High Command, although there is nothing for him to do there. He has not been back since interrupting the war council meeting in late December, and has no interest in frontline affairs or the new offensive scheduled for spring. It is simply that he cannot stand the atmosphere at Tsarskoye Selo and needs to get away. He even leaves the sick Alexei. A few days later he writes to his wife from Mogilev that he is "resting his head."

The day after his departure the children suffer a bout of measles, as does Vyrubova. The empress changes into her nurse's uniform and takes care of her children. The palace at Tsarskoye Selo turns into a sick ward.

On 23 February riots break out in Petrograd due to bread shortages. The police open fire, killing some protesters. Public transport and factories come to a halt when up to seventy thousand workers go on strike. "Boys and girls are running around, shouting that they have no bread just to create a commotion," the empress writes to her husband. The commander of the Petrograd Military District, Khabalov, bans mass rallies in the streets, but that causes even greater crowds to gather, with a corresponding rise in the number of victims.

Previously, whenever the tsar left for the High Command, Alexandra took over state business, receiving ministers and reading reports. Now she has her hands full with the sick children, so she devolves the running of the state to her friend Lili Dehn. On 26 February Dehn receives an Interior Ministry official on behalf of Protopopov, who reports that the situation is under control. The ministers are taking proactive measures and tomorrow everything will be calm, he says.

Alexandra goes to the grave of Rasputin to pray, after which she sends her husband a piece of wood she found near the burial site. "I think everything will be fine," she writes to him. "The sun was shining so brightly and I felt such peace and tranquility at his dear graveside. He died to save us."

By 25 February the trams are no longer running, and many members of the capital's bohemia have to walk to the centrally located Mikhailovsky Theatre, where Mikhail Lermontov's tragedy *Masquerade* is being performed. The director Vsevolod Meyerhold has just spent five years rehearsing the play—a monstrous show with grandiose scenery that comes sliding off the stage into the auditorium. All the tickets are sold out several months in advance. Lines of black cars hug the entrance to the theatre. "It is a gathering of all the nobility, plutocracy and bureaucracy of Petrograd," writes the newspaper *Theatrical Life*.

There is shooting in the city, and a stray bullet kills one theatre-goer right on the threshold of the building. As the capital's elite sit there watching the performance, a revolution breaks out in the street. What unfolds outside the theatre is even more dramatic than what is happening inside.

The press leaves no stone unturned in trashing the play. *Theatrical Life* writes the following: "a Babylon of preposterous luxury. The audience gasps, 'Oh, how splendid, how lush!', while outside the hungry crowds shout for bread and Protopopov's police drench them with bullets."

At the finale, a church choir comes on stage and sings a dirge. The curtain, when it falls, resembles a funeral shroud. It feels like a requiem for the audience.

|| Chapter 12 ||

ALEXANDER KERENSKY

in which there is a second leader of
popular protest in Russia: his name
is Alexander Kerensky

BRAND-NEW DAY

At 8 a.m. on 27 February 1917, member of State Duma Alexander Kerensky wakes up his wife. One of his deputy comrades has called to report an insurrection at the Volynsky Regiment. Moreover, the Duma is being dissolved, and Kerensky is needed urgently at the Tauride Palace, in the center of Saint Petersburg, where the Duma usually sits. He rushes to the phone to find out the latest news, and then to the palace, which is only five minutes from his apartment.

Soldiers at the barracks of the Volynsky Regiment are up much earlier than Kerensky. Line-up is scheduled for 7 a.m., but they assemble an hour earlier. Petty Officer Kirpichnikov suggests that they disobey the officer corps' orders to shoot the demonstrators in the city. When the officers come, the plan is to shout "Hurray!" and then disarm them. All the soldiers readily agree.

Two officers enter the barracks at 7 a.m., the appointed time. In response to the greeting, "Hello, brothers!" the soldiers cry, "Hurray!" and start banging their rifle butts on the ground. Regiment Commander Lashkevich tries to shout "Attention" in order to read out an order from Commander Khabalov of the Petrograd Military District and a telegram from Emperor Nicholas II. But nobody is listening. He runs out—and gets a bullet in the back.

Members of the Volynsky Regiment, now under the command of Kirpichnikov, go to the barracks of the Preobrazhensky and Litovsky regiments, which join the insurgents. Alongside them are workers from the Imperial Arsenal. Together, they head off to seize and set fire to administrative buildings. This is the moment at which Alexander Kerensky wakes up.

While he is en route to the Duma, the insurgents seize the Arsenal and set fire to the district court. The commanders of the neighboring regiments are quick to hear the news. The Moskovsky Regiment, still loyal to the government, is deployed on Liteyny Bridge to stop the rebels. A firefight begins—and ends quickly when the Moskovsky Regiment shoots its own officers and joins the uprising.

A huge crowd gathers on Nevsky Prospekt, and scuffles break out between police and protesters. French Ambassador Maurice Paléologue looks from his window and cannot believe his eyes: "The bridge, usually so lively, was empty. But on one side there appeared a disorderly crowd with red banners, while on the other side was a regiment of soldiers. It seemed there would be a clash, but they went towards each other and began to fraternize. The soldiers received the rebels as brothers."

THE END OF DUMA

When Kerensky enters the meeting room, his colleagues surround him. They believe that he, the most left-wing member of the Duma, is likely to be better informed about what is happening. Kerensky says that the revolution has begun and that the duty of the Duma members, as representatives of the people, is "to welcome the insurgents and work together to resolve common issues."

The members of Duma are initially in a state of panic, but "the excitement was so great that soon all anxiety disappeared," Kerensky recalls. Everyone wonders how the government will respond. Rumors are flying that Interior Minister Protopopov plans to provoke unrest and use it as a pretext to crush the uprising, and then conclude a separate peace with Germany. It is far-fetched, yet the people really do view Protopopov as the embodiment of evil.

At 11 a.m. Duma Chairman Mikhail Rodzianko reads out a decree issued by Nicholas II to dissolve the Duma until April. What to do next? The left-wing parliamentarians, headed by Kerensky and Chkheidze, propose not to obey the imperial decree, continue the session, and assume supreme authority—after all the capital is in the throes of revolution.

But no one is sure that the revolution will last. Everyone is expecting to hear the sound of machine-gun fire. All are sure that Protopopov is about to crack down on the insurrection. Rodzianko and Milyukov suggest that, rather than disperse, the Duma members should move from the large hall to a small semicircular room behind the presidium, where the informal sitting continues for another two hours.

The parliamentarians dare not disobey the order of the tsar and so come up with a compromise called the "Provisional Committee of the State Duma." What it is and what its functions and powers are, no one knows. Yet it includes all the most prominent Duma members: Rodzianko, Milyukov, Kerensky, Chkheidze, Shulgin, Nekrasov, and representatives of all parties, except the right. The right-wingers did not come to the Tauride Palace that day—no one informed them of the session.

A stone's throw from the Duma, Zinaida Gippius observes what is happening from her balcony: "All the adjacent streets are packed with soldiers who seem to have joined the movement," she notes in her diary.

CALMNESS IN HIGH COMMAND

Before relocating to the semicircular hall, the chairman of the Duma, Rodzianko, who himself is no revolutionary, sends another panic-stricken telegram to the tsar, in which he accurately sums up the situation: by disbanding the Duma, the tsar has destroyed the last bulwark of law and order; the regiments have rebelled and, together with crowds of people, are moving towards the buildings of the Interior Ministry and the Duma. Civil war is about to break out, he writes.

Rodzianko's aim is to persuade the tsar to revoke the decree to dissolve the Duma and appoint a new government: "Sire, do not delay. If the movement reaches the army, the Germans will triumph, and Russia and her dynasty will collapse. . . . The decisive hour has struck for you and the Motherland."

Rodzianko's telegram is kept secret from his colleagues. Many members of Duma—for instance, Kerensky—believe that it is already too late. Nicholas reads it and, with his usual disdain, says to Alekseyev: "That fatso Rodzianko has written another pile of nonsense, which I will not even reply to."

The emperor is unmoved. At 1 p.m. War Minister Belyaev reports to him that the disturbances have been "vigorously" suppressed, and order shall once more reign in the capital.

But by this time the rebellious soldiers have moved to the Vyborg Side and seized the infamous Kresty prison; other regiments are joining them.

SOLDIERS AT THE GATE

At 1 p.m., when the informal meeting of the Duma is still in progress, the Tauride Palace is surrounded by troops. Kerensky rushes to the window. "From the window I saw soldiers," he recalls. "Surrounded by citizens, they lined up along the opposite side of the street. They looked bewildered without the officer corps." Kerensky and Chkheidze run out to greet the soldiers and ask them to protect the Duma should Protopopov's government-loyal troops arrive. Together, they enter the sentry house to disarm the guards. But there is no one there. The guards have already fled for their lives.

Returning to the Duma building, Kerensky discovers a crowd of onlookers who are convinced that the revolution is over. Seeing the parliamentarian, they shower him with questions: What will happen to the old tsarist officials? How will they be punished? Kerensky replies that the main thing is to avert bloodshed; the most egregious offenders under the old regime shall be arrested and punished, but the people "must not take the law into their own hands."

The crowd continues to swell. By 3 p.m. the excitement inside the Duma is bordering on hysteria: no one understands what is happening, and rumors are rife. The phones are not working, and there are stories of massacres in the streets. At 4 p.m. Kerensky is requested to find a room inside the Tauride Palace for the newly created Soviet of Workers' Deputies to assemble.

Such a body existed in Saint Petersburg in 1905 and was the symbol of that year's revolution. Hence, the creation of a new soviet (council) with the same name is a symbolic gesture. Rodzianko allocates room No. 13. The most popular socialist members in the State Duma are chosen as its leaders: Chkheidze becomes chairman, and Kerensky deputy chairman.

Now there are two bodies inside the Tauride Palace—the Soviet and the Provisional Committee—battling against the old regime, not noticing that the latter is disintegrating all by itself.

UNDER SIEGE

At the same time as the soldiers are taking over the Duma, members of the government are gathering at the home of Prime Minister Prince Golitsyn. The evening before they unanimously voted for the dissolution of the Duma and the severest measures against the demonstrators, proposing a de facto dictatorship without delay. But since yesterday, their mood has radically altered: they have all seen with their own eyes what is going on in the city. Now the ministerial talk is of dismissing Interior Minister Protopopov. The prime minister says that they do not have the formal right to do so, but the interior minister could conveniently "fall sick and resign." Protopopov, who is there in person, gets up and leaves, saying (according to Golitsyn): "I guess all that remains is for me to shoot myself." The other ministers do not even say farewell.

They are all afraid for their own security, so Prime Minister Golitsyn suggests moving from his apartment to the Mariinsky Palace, where the security is better and there is less likelihood of an enraged crowd breaking in. They are inside by 3 p.m., but the palace does not seem safe either: the ministers peek out of the windows, paralyzed with fear. They themselves telegram the tsar asking to be dismissed and for a new government of national confidence to be appointed, headed by a man of the people. Nobody wants to risk his life for the sake of a ministerial portfolio.

The French ambassador visits Foreign Minister Pokrovsky and tells him that the city is blazing. "Let me remind you that in 1789, 1830 and 1848 three French dynasties were overthrown because they underestimated the force of the movement directed against them," says the ambassador. "Is there really no one who can open the emperor's eyes?" "The emperor is blind," replies the foreign minister.

GOVERNMENT PAVILION

At 4 p.m. Ivan Shcheglovitov, the former justice minister, now the chairman of the State Council (the upper house of parliament), arrives at the Tauride Palace to discuss the situation with Rodzianko. The chairman of the Duma shakes his hand, bows, and invites his guest into his office. Suddenly Kerensky bursts in, shouting: "No, Shcheglovitov is not a guest." With the other members staring in amazement, Kerensky runs up to the chairman of the State Council, stands between him and Rodzianko, and asks: "Are you Ivan Grigoryevich Shcheglovitov?" Shcheglovitov nods. "I kindly ask that you follow me. You are under arrest. Your safety is assured," states Kerensky.

Rodzianko and the members are dumbfounded, but they dare not argue with Kerensky, who has the backing of the insurgent soldiers. He takes Shcheglovitov to the "government pavilion"—a reception room inside the Tauride Palace where traditionally ministers wait before addressing the Duma. The area is now an improvised prison.

At 7 p.m. the perplexed ministers receive a visit from the two people on whom their last hopes are pinned: the tsar's brother, Grand Duke Mikhail, and the chairman of the Duma, Mikhail Rodzianko. They meet with Prime Minister Golitsyn in private. It is proposed that Grand Duke Mikhail "assume a dictatorship over Petrograd" (i.e., take responsibility and do something to stop the mayhem). He is asked to dismiss the government and demand that the tsar appoint a new government of national confidence. Mikhail refuses to take power, but agrees to talk to his brother, although he is unsure what good will come of it. The grand duke goes to the residence of War Minister Belyaev, where there is a special communication link with Mogilev, in Belarus, where the tsar is located as commander-in-chief of the Imperial Army.

As they are leaving, the Mariinsky Palace is surrounded by insurgent soldiers there to arrest the ministers. Terrified, the officials run through the back door as the palace is stormed. The government effectively dissolves itself.

Almost simultaneously, the tsar responds to the prime minister's telegram requesting his resignation: "I personally bestow upon you all rights necessary for civil administration. In the circumstances, I consider personnel changes to be unacceptable." The words do not reach their audience: the telegraph is no longer working, the ministers have fled, and soldiers are ransacking the Mariinsky Palace, looting valuables and even icons.

"THE REBELS HAVE NO PLAN"

By evening, almost the entire Russian capital has been smashed. Police stations and courts have been set on fire, and many administrative buildings seized. The epicenter is the Tauride Palace, where waves of insurgents gather periodically before moving on to their next target.

The Kresty prison is taken in the morning, followed in the afternoon by another jail, Litovsky Fortress, which becomes the Russian "Bastille"— it is burnt to the ground. The house of Count Fredericks, the minister of the court, and the Hotel Astoria are also vandalized.

Throughout the city, shops are looted and vehicles are stolen. Communication lines are severed and telegrams are not delivered. "It seems that the rebels have no plan," the naval staff officer Kapnist reports to his commander, somewhat understatedly.

In the afternoon a crowd breaks into the Mariinsky Theatre and is about to start smashing it to pieces when a noise from the ventilation pipes on the roof is mistaken for machine-gun fire. The mob backs off. The city is swirling with rumors of shootings and random killings. There is talk of a mysterious black car driving around Petrograd, shooting at the police. Yet the reality is even worse: at the corner of Znamenskaya and Basseinaya streets, a crowd bursts into a policeman's apartment. Not finding him at home, they brutally murder his wife and two young children. Another crowd, storming the building of the gendarmerie, savagely beats and then shoots the sixty-three-year-old commander, Lieutenant-General Ivan Volkov (having sent his colleagues home, he alone is on duty).

NEW ATTEMPT

The High Command is still calm, mainly because of the lack of accurate information. Only at 7 p.m. does a message arrive from War Minister Belyaev to report that the mutiny cannot be suppressed; more and more units are joining the uprising, and the city is engulfed in flames. The head of the capital's Military District, Khabalov, cannot cope and demands new troops loyal to the regime. An hour later Khabalov himself telegraphs to say that most units have rebelled and are refusing to fight against the insurgents.

Khabalov's failure means he must be replaced by someone more dependable, the emperor decides. He sends a new commander to Petrograd, General Ivanov, along with two infantry regiments, two cavalry regiments, and a machine-gun crew to quell the unrest. The sixty-six-year-old Ivanov is a favorite of Empress Alexandra, who calls him a "devoted old man." Nicholas II is sure that he will quickly suppress the uprising. Ivanov is ordered to travel to Petrograd the very next day, 28 February.

At Tsarskoye Selo, Alexandra is less sanguine. At 10 p.m. Belyaev orders that she and the children depart the royal residence immediately; morning may be too late, for an angry crowd could arrive from Petrograd at any moment. Alexandra is nervous and wants to go to her husband. But when she telegraphs the High Command, Nicholas tells her to remain where she is, because he will come to see them tomorrow.

At half past ten the telephone rings at the High Command. It is Grand Duke Mikhail, calling from the home of the war minister and insisting that Chief of Staff Alekseyev take urgent action to dismiss the Council of Ministers and appoint a new government headed by the popular Prince Lvov. The grand duke also advises his brother, the tsar, to postpone his visit for several days.

The chief of staff promises the grand duke that he will talk to the emperor. Mikhail can do nothing except wait for Alekseyev to ring back. It is remarkable how Adjutant-General Mikhail Alekseyev, the son of a rank-and-file soldier, has become the tsar's right-hand man and the main intermediary between Nicholas and his family. Yet at the time Alekseyev is suffering from a severe cold and spends most his time on the couch, rising only to speak with Nicholas or Petrograd.

Grand Duke Mikhail waits several hours. Finally, the chief of staff calls back. The answer to everything is "no." Nicholas refuses to delay his trip to Tsarskoye Selo (he intends to leave immediately), and there will be no changes in the government until he returns (i.e., he needs time to consult with his wife). General Ivanov is preparing to set off for Petrograd, so there is nothing to worry about, the tsar is sure.

The conversation finishes at 3 a.m., whereupon Grand Duke Mikhail leaves the house of the war minister to travel to his imperial residence at Gatchina. But the station there is already in the hands of the rebels, so he turns around and heads for the Winter Palace.

WHO'S IN CHARGE HERE?

At night, when most of the uninvited guests abandon the Tauride Palace, members of the State Duma's Provisional Committee discuss their next move. Almost the entire Petrograd garrison has revolted, and without officers the insurgents cannot be controlled. The military is in a chaotic mess, which frightens the committee members.

But even more frightening is the prospect that the old regime could survive. They fear that Interior Minister Protopopov's police could still materialize with their near-mythical machine guns, or that the tsar might redeploy troops from the front line to suppress the revolution. If that were to happen, the rebellious, commander-less soldiers would simply turn and flee.

According to Kerensky, Rodzianko is the most hesitant of all, for he does not want to take responsibility and declare disobedience to the emperor. So, the Provisional Committee members frighten him into action. If Rodzianko does not assume supreme authority, then the rival Petrograd Soviet, assembled in the next room, will fill the breach. Rodzianko reluctantly agrees to arrogate power to the Provisional Committee until an interim government is formed.

What to do with the rest of the country? Who is now in charge? There is mayhem in the capital; the government has fled, and the emperor is uninformed about what is happening. Members of the Provisional Committee argue until they are hoarse: "Whatever happens, one thing is certain: we have absolutely nothing in common with that bastard," Milyukov voices his opinion of Nicholas II.

To prevent frontline veterans from returning to Petrograd, the train stations need to be seized. With all the guards gone, the task is readily accomplished by the Duma commissars.

The Provisional Committee knows nothing about what is happening outside the capital. And vice versa: the country knows almost nothing about the events in Petrograd. The Provisional Committee sends its member Alexander Bublikov to the central railway telegraph. The forty-two-year-old Bublikov, a former railway worker, helps to spread the revolution throughout Russia. On the morning of 28 February, he sends a message on behalf of Rodzianko to all railway stations across the country: the regime has collapsed. "I address you [railway workers] on behalf of the Motherland. She expects more than fulfillment of duty; she expects heroic exploits."

Bublikov's telegram notifying the whole of Russia of the revolution means there is no turning back for the Provisional Committee members.

LOST CONTROL

On the night of 28 February, Emperor Nicholas II hastily departs the High Command at Mogilev on board the imperial train. Not wishing to hinder the movement of troops to the capital to suppress the insurrection, he takes a detour via Smolensk, Likhoslavl, and Bologoye, assuming that General Ivanov and his men will travel the shorter route through Vitebsk.

However, the meticulous General Ivanov is in no hurry. On the morning of 28 February, he telephones General Khabalov: "Which units are causing a nuisance?" he asks, completely unaware of the situation in the capital. Khabalov answers that he has lost control of all of them: the stations are in the hands of the revolutionaries, there is no telephone link to the city, ministers have been arrested, and all artillery is controlled by the rebels.

At 8 a.m. Khabalov informs Alekseyev that no more than six hundred infantry and five hundred cavalry troops remain loyal to the government, with fifteen machine guns and eighty cartridges between them. The last bastion of the regime in the capital is the Admiralty, from where Khabalov intends to fight to the bitter end.

Meanwhile, the imperial train leaves Mogilev in the direction of Tver, halfway between Petrograd and Moscow.

THE MORNING AFTER

The next day, almost everyone in Petrograd is hungover, either literally or metaphorically. The euphoric bravado of the day before now turns to fear. Mikhail Rodzianko has declared himself the head of the self-proclaimed government; Alexander Kerensky has begun to arrest former officials; Alexander Bublikov has sent a nationwide telegram about the transfer of power to the Duma. Yet they were all acting on the spur of the adrenaline-filled moment, and are now having second thoughts. The question on everyone's lips is when will the regime strike back; when will the tsarist troops begin the long-awaited assault on Petrograd?

In the morning of the second day of the revolution, almost nothing happens. The violence raging through the night comes to a temporary halt. The soldiers who disobeyed and shot their officers, the students who thronged around the Tauride Palace, and the workers who smashed and looted stores seem shocked by their own recalcitrance. Almost everyone spends the day at home, waiting for the tsarist troops' savage crackdown. But it does not materialize.

By midday Petrograd is alive again, and the violence begins anew. Now police stations and police archives are on fire: former stool pigeons terrified of being unmasked are trying to save themselves. In the afternoon, a crowd bursts into the Central Police Department and begins smashing it up.

The new authorities do nothing to stop the disorder. By evening almost all the imperial ministers have been arrested. Finance Minister Pyotr Bark even suffers the ignominy of being detained by his former footman. The justice minister is found and arrested at the Italian Embassy, and, despite his resistance, Commander of the Petrograd Military District Khabalov is detained at the Admiralty. The French and English ambassadors go to see Foreign Minister Pokrovsky. "You've just passed through the city," says the foreign minister. "Do you think the emperor will retain his crown?" Paléologue replies that anything is possible, but the emperor must "acknowledge the *fait accompli*," appoint members of the Provisional Committee as ministers, and amnesty the insurgents. "If he personally appears before the army and the people, if he states from the parvis of Kazan Cathedral that a new era has begun for Russia, it would be welcomed. . . . But tomorrow will be too late."

At 11 p.m. a man in a fur coat arrives at the Duma and addresses the duty officer: "Please take me to the executive committee of the State Duma. I am the former interior minister, Alexander Protopopov. I wish only the best for the country, and so have come on my own volition. Take me wherever I must go." Protopopov is assigned to the government pavilion, which saves his life from the marauders.

NOT THE TSAR'S ESTATE ANYMORE

Throughout the whole of 28 February Tsarskoye Selo is in a state of fear, although not much happens. In the morning, the condition of Tsarevich Alexei worsens—he has a high temperature. Empress Alexandra asks the servants to prepare everything for the move to Gatchina (imperial residence, more distant from Petrograd than Tsarskoye Selo). Half an hour later she is informed that everything is ready, but now she changes her mind. Her entourage unanimously advises her to flee, if not to Gatchina, then perhaps to Novgorod, where a couple of months ago she was received enthusiastically by the local population.

At 3 p.m. soldiers from the Tsarskoye Selo garrison leave the barracks. They intend to release prisoners from local jails and smash some wine shops. The imperial guards do not leave the palace, since they do not know what is happening in the city. Alexandra says that all the children are sick and, in her capacity as a "sister of mercy,"* turns the palace into a makeshift hospital.

In the evening the empress calls Grand Duke Pavel, the father of Rasputin's killer, Grand Duke Dmitry, who has just been exiled to Persia. She has no one else to turn to, since all her relatives have left Tsarskoye Selo. When he arrives, she starts blaming the family for everything that is happening, to which Pavel answers that she "has no right to doubt his loyalty, and now is not the time to drag up old quarrels." The main thing, he says, is for the tsar to return as soon as possible. Alexandra informs him that her husband is due to arrive at 8 a.m. the next morning, and Pavel promises to meet him at the station.

The grand duke's wife, Olga Paley, tells her husband that workers from the city of Kolpino are said to have rebelled and to be on their way to loot Tsarskoye Selo. The terrified family leaves the estate and spends the night elsewhere with friends. The rumors do not end there: Protopopov is said to have fled and to be in hiding with Anna Vyrubova; workers everywhere are supposedly on the rampage.

In the evening a crowd of insurgent soldiers comes to the Alexander Palace at Tsarskoye Selo. The guards, loyal to the empress, remain on duty around the perimeter. The soldiers and the guards hold talks, after which both sides agree to dispatch representatives to the Petrograd Duma. The tension subsides.

At 10 p.m. a telegram arrives from Nicholas II: "I hope to be home by tomorrow morning." Alexandra is relieved and decides to go outside, along with her seventeen-year-old daughter, Grand Duchess Maria, to see the troops guarding the palace. The other children are too unwell. They walk among the ranks, nodding silently at the men in uniform.

The whole retinue decides to spend the night at the palace. Late that night Count Apraksin, a courtier, asks the empress to send Vyrubova away from the palace, for he believes that she is cursed and will bring the wrath of the people upon the imperial family. "I do not betray my friends," replies the empress tearfully.

STOP THE EMPEROR

At 1 p.m. on 28 February, General Ivanov, the new "military dictator" (i.e., head of the capital's Military District), leaves Mogilev for Petrograd to put

---

* The term used to describe Russian nurses in World War I.

down the rebellion and restore order in Petrograd. Station managers have already received the telegram from the new Railway Transport Minister Bublikov requesting that all trains moving to Petrograd be reported and, if found to be carrying troops or ammunition, halted.

In Petrograd confusion reigns. Bublikov's assistant, Yuri Lomonosov, recalls how the new railway bosses tried to get instructions from the Duma about whether to allow the imperial train through to Tsarskoye Selo or direct it elsewhere. The Provisional Committee members cannot decide and do not give any orders.

In the meantime, the decision to turn the train around is taken by the emperor himself. In the town of Malaya Vishera, a railway guard stops the train, since the next station, Luban, is in the hands of rebellious soldiers. The head of the imperial train wakes the tsar to inform him that the route is blocked, so Nicholas II orders the train to go to Pskov.

Only at 9 a.m. on 1 March does the Petrograd Duma take the decision to detain the train. Bublikov sends a telegram to block the route between the stations of Dno and Bologoe. He sends another to the wireless telegraph aboard the imperial train, instructing it to remain at Bologoe and wait for the arrival of Duma Chairman Rodzianko, who hopes to persuade Nicholas II to recognize the authority of the Provisional Committee.

Petrograd is awash with rumors that the emperor's real intention is to head for the bastion of Moscow, from where he will lead a campaign on Petrograd together with regiments still loyal to him. This version is recounted in the diary of the French ambassador, Paléologue, adding some typically blasé words allegedly spoken by Nicholas: "If the revolution triumphs, I will renounce the throne. I shall go to Livadia (imperial summer palace in Crimea); I adore flowers."

Bublikov's order is ignored, and at 7 a.m. the imperial train passes unhindered through Bologoe towards Dno. Already there, having come by a different route, is General Ivanov. In anticipation of the emperor's arrival, he and his troops have restored order at the station, just as the Kronstadt mutiny was suppressed twelve years previously: he approaches the "nuisance" soldiers and yells: "On your knees!"

The revolutionaries immediately obey. They are disarmed, and the unruliest among them are put on Ivanov's train. One of them bites the general on the hand. Pausing for a moment, he decides to spare the man's life. A total of seventy armed soldiers (some drunk) are arrested, and the weapons they stole from their officers are confiscated. Having subdued the soldiers, Ivanov moves on towards Tsarskoye Selo.

VICTORY DAY

At 8 a.m. on 1 March, the tsar's uncle, Grand Duke Pavel, having promised the empress to meet Nicholas II, goes to Tsarskoye Selo station. Neither he nor anyone else knows that the train was turned around at Malaya Vishera and is now on its way to Pskov. Having waited some time for his nephew, the grand duke leaves the station.

Psychologically, 1 March is make-or-break day. Petrograd sees the publication of the newspaper published by the so-called *Committee of Petrograd Journalists,* which reports that "soldiers have entered the Tsarskoye Selo Palace" and the imperial family is in the hands of rebel forces. It is not true, but has the effect of making the revolution seem irreversible. If the imperial troops have not arrived by now, they never will, the people of Petrograd think to themselves. There begins a wave of oaths of allegiance to the new government.

On that day, according to Kerensky's memoirs, military units file into the Duma one by one, filling the Catherine Hall. Rodzianko's address, calling for them to put their trust in the new authorities and maintain discipline, is drowned in a squall of overenthusiastic cries and applause. The jubilant soldiers demand speech after speech. "Finally having the opportunity to talk freely with the newly liberated people, I felt a sense of giddy delight," recalls Justice Minister Kerensky.

The main symbol of the revolution is the red ribbon: on clothes, cars, horses. On apartment blocks and houses, red flags are flown.

One of the first divisions to swear allegiance to the Duma is the Cossack detachment of the imperial guard. This is highly symbolic, because Nicholas II has not yet abdicated; yet his personal security is already loyal to the new government. The apogee of the parade of loyalty is the appearance of Grand Duke Kirill, the tsar's cousin and the fourth in line to the Russian throne. He enters the hall at the head of his own detachment with a red ribbon pinned on his chest, and submits to the authority of the State Duma.

The capital is daring to hope that the tsarist regime is gone for good. Matilda Kschessinskaya's mansion has been looted. Ambassador Paléologue recalls that, close to the Summer Garden imperial residence, he saw one of the Ethiopians* who used to stand guard at the emperor's door. The "dear negro" is now dressed in civilian clothes, and there are tears in his

---

*Dating back to Peter the Great, the Abyssinian Guards were a regiment of Ethiopian troops hired to guard the Russian tsar.

eyes. Paléologue tries to comfort him and shakes his hand in farewell. "Surrounded by the collapse of the entire political and social system, he stands for the monarchical splendors of yesteryear, the charm of the now meaningless words, 'Russian Court,'" recalls the ambassador. Clearly the French ambassador considers the imperial doorkeeper to be far more civilized than most Russian folk.

NEW GOVERNMENT

State Duma member Vasily Shulgin says that Rodzianko and the entire committee are paralyzed by distractions: "Instead of working, every minute the head of the Provisional Committee has to run into the street and shout 'Hurrah!', and members of the government are overwhelmed by the number of supplicants they have to deal with."

Nestled inside two small rooms at the Tauride Palace, the committee is supplied with nuggets of information by Kerensky: for instance, a document that has been obtained from the Foreign Ministry pertaining to secret negotiations between Russia and foreign powers during the war. Nobody knows what to do with the priceless text. There is not even a filing cabinet in the room, so the papers are "hidden" under a tablecloth. Next, Kerensky brings a suitcase full of money: "Two million roubles* from some ministry or other," he says. "Right, we need to appoint commissioners. Where's Mikhail [Rodzianko]? Outside shouting 'Hurrah'? No time for that. Gentlemen, to business!"

Shulgin persuades Milyukov "not to run the country from under the table," but to form a government. Literally on a napkin, Milyukov begins drawing up a list of commissioners. "Milyukov's mind gave birth to this list on the edge of a table in a whirlwind of madness. He clutched his head in both hands as if squeezing out the thoughts. Future historians and Milyukov himself will say that it was the fruit of profound insight, but I'm telling it how it was in reality," recalls Shulgin.

In the morning of 1 March, a long-expected guest arrives in Petrograd. Very few can recognize him, but almost everyone has heard his name. It is Prince Georgy Lvov from Moscow, head of the Zemstvo Union and the leading candidate to head the new government. He arrives just as the new cabinet is taking shape and Milyukov's list is being discussed. The hardest part is the negotiations with the executive committee of the Petrograd

---

*About $26,366,667 in 2017.

Soviet, which also sits at the Tauride Palace and enjoys greater influence over the masses than does the Provisional Committee.

Milyukov offers two seats in the new government to the socialists Kerensky and Chkheidze. The latter, although part of the Provisional Committee, does not take an active role in its business. He chairs the executive committee of the Petrograd Soviet, and so decides to decline the post of labor minister. Instead, he puts forward some demands: the Petrograd Soviet will support the soon-to-be Provisional Government if it declares a general amnesty, guarantees freedom of expression, holds elections to a Constituent Assembly, and promises not to withdraw and disarm the rebel troops of the Petrograd garrison. All the points are accepted.

The post of war minister goes to the politician with the most extensive military connections, Alexander Guchkov, while Milyukov himself becomes Russia's new foreign minister. But there are some surprises: the new finance minister is the thirty-two-year-old sugar empire heir, art collector, socialite, and Freemason Mikhail Tereshchenko.

However, the carving up of the ministerial posts is not the most important event taking place at the Tauride Palace. What is happening in the next room is of greater interest.

SOLDIERS VERSUS OFFICERS

Most military units are delighted by the transfer of power to the State Duma, but some consider it insufficient. Many soldiers want more authority for themselves and do not want to remain subordinate to the officer corps. The shine is beginning to wear off the Provisional Committee as a result of its reconciliatory efforts to restore order. In the afternoon of 1 March, the military commission of the Provisional Committee issues an order forbidding soldiers to seize weapons from officers. A couple of hours later, the Preobrazhensky Regiment, the one that initially started the uprising, again rebels. While rehearsing their oath of allegiance, the soldiers take away the officers' sabers.

The attitude of the Petrograd Soviet of Workers' Deputies towards the State Duma begins to mirror that of the soldiers towards their officers. The Petrograd Soviet is becoming an alternative center of power and a rival to the Provisional Committee. Its members decide to bring in more soldiers' representatives, renaming the body the Petrograd Soviet of Workers' and Soldiers' Deputies in the process. Whereas in the early days it was a place for letting off political steam with little to show for it, the Petrograd Soviet now has a distinct purpose: to support the soldiers in their struggle against the officer corps.

The soldiers' representatives sit apart from the others, who still assemble in room No. 13 at the Tauride Palace. The lawyer Nikolai Sokolov, a former ally of Kerensky and Chkheidze, presides over the soldiers' meetings. The soldiers, each more radical than the one before, take turns to speak from the podium to great applause. The speeches are so rapid-fire that the stenographer can barely keep up.

The soldiers' deputies believe that General Ivanov's troops are advancing on Petrograd, and that the officers should be disarmed in case they switch sides again. The Provisional Committee is trying to re-establish the old order, they think, which must be stopped. The soldiers demand that authority be transferred from the officers to elected soldiers' committees, which are to have custody of all weapons, and that equal rights be granted to the "lower ranks."

Sokolov takes the hastily written text to the editor of *Izvestia* (a newly founded newspaper, mouthpiece of the Petrograd Soviet of Workers' Deputies)* and refers to the proclamation as an "Order." The next morning "Order No. 1," addressed to the soldiers of the Petrograd garrison, appears in the newspaper and is replicated on leaflets. The Petrograd Soviet distributes the text to prevent General Ivanov and his tsarist troops from suppressing the uprising. Nobody pays attention to the fact that the "Order" is addressed solely to the Petrograd garrison, for all soldiers in the Russian Empire will get the message to disobey their officers. The "Order" has a powerful impact. The officers will later say that it destroyed the army, but members of the Petrograd Soviet recall that the decision was made deliberately to avert a counter-revolution and the restoration of the old regime.

The Provisional Committee is horrified. "Those bastards are in league with the Germans. . . . They're traitors. . . . What will happen now?" cries Rodzianko. There is nothing they can do. The text is already plastered all over the city.

REFORMS OF GENERAL ALEKSEYEV

The chief of staff of the supreme commander, General Mikhail Alekseyev, who only a day before was in control of the tsar, now cannot contact him.

---

*The newspaper will become one of the most important daily news publications of the Soviet period, and in 2007 will be bought by Yury Kovalchuk, president Putin's close friend and Russia's most influential media tycoon.

Ill with fever, he receives information at his sickbed in Mogilev in dribs and drabs. "There is total revolution in Moscow," reports the head of the Moscow Military District. News arrives from Kronstadt that the port commander has been killed by the anarchists. The Baltic Fleet has recognized the authority of the Provisional Committee of the State Duma.

"If I am offered a choice between the Sovereign and Russia, I will choose Russia," said General Brusilov in late 1916, furious at the ignominious failure of his frontline offensive and hypothetically ready to choose between country and emperor. Come the end of February 1917, almost all officers are thinking along the same lines. The main priority for them is victory over the Central Powers. For that, they are ready to do anything, including insubordination. General Alekseyev already knows that the army is threatened by anarchy, which is undermining the war effort against Germany and Austria-Hungary. These words he repeats again and again in his telegrams to Nicholas II.

In the afternoon of 1 March, Nicholas finally arrives in Dno, where he is due to meet with Rodzianko. But the latter is late, so Nicholas goes on to Pskov, where the headquarters of the northern front are located. Alekseyev telegraphs Pskov, detailing the horrors that inaction will incur and asking the emperor to appoint a "person whom Russia will believe in" as the head of the government. When Nicholas arrives in Pskov in the evening, a staff officer informs him of Alekseyev and Grand Duke Sergei's request for him to appoint Rodzianko as the head of the new government.

The commander of the northern front, General Nikolai Ruzsky, spends the whole evening discussing Alekseyev's telegrams with Nicholas, urging him to assent to the "government of national confidence." Ruzsky tries to persuade the tsar to surrender unconditionally to the Provisional Committee, but Nicholas is having none of it.

The general loses his temper and openly blames Nicholas for bringing the situation upon himself, above all through his blind faith in Rasputin. The emperor and his entourage are shocked by such impudence. Admiral Nilov, deeply affected by the conversation, believes that Ruzsky should be demoted, arrested, and executed. With someone more loyal in charge, things will sort themselves out, he thinks.

At 10:30 p.m. on 1 March, Alekseyev sends the tsar a draft imperial royal decree on the appointment of Rodzianko as prime minister. Nicholas II informs Ruzsky that he has agreed to sign it. A phone call to the Tauride Palace immediately follows, requesting that the new chairman of the State Duma report at once to the emperor in Pskov. The response from Petrograd is that Rodzianko will not go anywhere.

Far more disturbing for the emperor, however, is that he cannot get to Tsarskoye Selo to see his family. "It's shameful and disgraceful that I cannot get to Tsarskoye. All my thoughts and feelings are there! It's terrible for poor Alix to have to bear all these event alone. Lord, help us!" he writes in his diary.

The evening of 1 March is pivotal not only for Petrograd, but for the emperor and his entourage, too. Hitherto, they have been sure that, if all else fails, they will be able to drown the revolution in blood. The thought that the soldiers might refuse to fire on the insurgents never crosses anyone's mind.

LIBERALS VERSUS SOCIALISTS

Rodzianko is really unable to go anywhere. For years he has been nervously expecting the tsar to dissolve parliament, and now that the moment has arrived his confidence totally deserts him. Ever since 27 February when, in front of his very eyes, Kerensky arrested the chairman of the State Council, Ivan Shcheglovitov, Rodzianko has understood the precariousness of his own position. For Kerensky, the former Justice Minister Shcheglovitov is a personal enemy, but for the refined nobleman and court chamberlain Rodzianko, he is a kindred spirit. The recent events in Petrograd are a living hell for Rodzianko and many other members of the State Duma. They are terrified of the crowds, which today are smashing up someone or other's mansion. Tomorrow it could be theirs.

The threat hanging over the revolutionary capital is symbolized by the Petrograd Soviet. This wholly unelected body assembled in the Tauride Palace is a magnet for revolutionaries, but a dangerous gang of impostors in the eyes of the Duma. Its members do not yet know about "Order No. 1," which will be published on 2 March and plunge them into a state of catatonic fear.

The dislike is mutual. Barred from all previous elections, the "non-systemic opposition"* inside the Petrograd Soviet has never tasted power before now. To the Petrograd Soviet, the tsarist Duma is a mockery of democracy, a puppet parliament elected exclusively by the propertied classes, meaning that most residents in the insurgent Petrograd can rightfully say: "You do not represent us."

Shulgin recalls how one of Rodzianko's speeches to a crowd at the Tauride Palace was suddenly interrupted: "The chairman of the State

---

* The term used in today's Russia to describe real, non-fake opponents of the Kremlin.

Duma [Rodzianko] asks you, comrades, to save the Russian land. . . . Mr. Rodzianko does indeed have something to save, for he owns a nice chunk of this very land of which he speaks. . . . Rodzianko and other landowners in the State Duma—princes, counts, barons—describe their domains as 'Russian land'. . . . In that case, comrades, you should indeed save it."

Rodzianko's nerves are playing up: "Bastards! We sacrifice our sons for this country, and they think we begrudge a bit of soil. Damn the wretched soil. What good is it to me if there is no Russia? Filthy scum, the lot of them. I'd give the shirt off my back to save Russia."

On another occasion a group of revolutionary sailors tells Rodzianko to his face that he, as a "bourgeois," should be shot. Whereas yesterday the capital was gripped by fear of a tsarist crackdown, now the overriding feeling is mutual loathing between the haves and the have-nots. Zinaida Gippius writes that during the revolution her home turned into a "command center for acquaintances and semi-acquaintances (sometimes non-acquaintances) trudging towards the Duma." They—the Merezhkovskys and Filosofov—supplied food and tea, and a chance to get warm. In the morning of 1 March, Gippius is optimistic about the revolution, but by evening that feeling is gone. She is paid a visit (again to warm up) by the writer Ivanov-Razumnik, who says "with horror and disgust" that the Petrograd Soviet is a bunch of rebels.

Many hate Rodzianko with equal passion. "I'd like to strangle that son of a bitch with my own hands. Noble spawn! He's a royal footman who wants to sit on his master's throne," writes the peasant poet Nikolai Klyuev. "He will oppress the peasants as his master was oppressing him. . . . Heavy it is to wear the cap of Monomakh,* but to let go is heavier still."

Sensing the threat and rivalry from the socialist Petrograd Soviet, the liberal Provisional Committee meets in secret late on 1 March to agree on the future form of government. All present are unanimous that the monarchy must be preserved, only without Nicholas II. "The tsar must not be overthrown by force," says Alexander Guchkov. "Only through his voluntary abdication in favor of his son or brother can a new order be established without major upheavals." It is decided at the secret meeting that Guchkov and Shulgin—the two staunchest monarchists—shall visit the emperor to persuade him to abdicate in favor of his son.

---

* A quote from Pushkin's historical play *Boris Godunov*, written under the influence of Shakespeare; the line is said to have been inspired by: "Uneasy lies the head that wears the crown" (*Henry IV, Part 2*).

THE MOST IMPORTANT PHONE CALL
IN RUSSIAN HISTORY

At 3 a.m. on 2 March, General Ruzsky telephones Rodzianko to say that he is disheartened by the latter's failure to travel to Pskov. It was not possible, explains Rodzianko: General Ivanov's regiments had disembarked at Luga Station and blocked all the approaches to the capital.

Ruzsky says that Nicholas II has decided to appoint him the head of the new government and has already drafted a manifesto to that effect. Rodzianko asks to receive it forthwith, adding: "His Majesty and your good self are clearly unaware of what is happening here." He says that the emperor's inaction has led to anarchy, which can no longer be stopped: the demoralized soldiers are killing their officers, hatred for Empress Alexandra knows no bounds, and almost every minister has had to be locked up in the Peter and Paul Fortress for his own safety. "I greatly fear that a similar fate shall befall me," says Rodzianko. "What you offer is too little, too late. The very future of the dynasty is now at stake."

What this means is that the people are demanding the abdication of Nicholas II in favor of his young son under the regency of Grand Duke Mikhail Alexandrovich. Rodzianko explains that hatred for the imperial family runs deep, and the people want the war against the Central Powers brought to a victorious end. He proceeds to list all the errors of judgment committed by Nicholas II and Alexandra, including unwise appointments to key posts, the role of Rasputin, the purges and crackdowns that caused the revolution in the first place—in short, everything that "alienated His Majesty from the people."

Ruzsky says that the emperor has already sent a telegram to General Ivanov not to use force, and reads out the draft manifesto: "Striving to unite the forces of the people to achieve swift victory, the Emperor deems it necessary to form a government responsible to the people, headed by Mikhail Rodzianko, made up of persons having the confidence of the whole of Russia."

Ruzsky says that he has followed his heart and done everything he can to restore order for the sake of the army. Spring is approaching, which means it will soon be time to launch another frontline offensive.

"My heart is torn, Nikolai Vladimirovich [Ruzsky]," says Rodzianko. "You can imagine the enormity of the task in front of me. I am hanging by a thread, and power is slipping out of my hands; the anarchy is such that I must now appoint an interim government in the dead of night. Unfortunately, the manifesto was late, it should have been released immediately after my first telegram; the moment is lost, there is no going back. . . . I pray that God grant the strength to at least stay within the borders of the present disorder of minds, thoughts and feelings, though I fear worse is to come."

Rodzianko's heart really is torn. Deep down he longed to be appointed the head of government under Nicholas II. But he has only just attended a meeting at which the decision was taken to demand the tsar's abdication, and that cannot be undone.

THE MARCH OF IVANOV

Ruzsky learns from Rodzianko that General Ivanov was unable to get to Tsarskoye Selo: his troops apparently left the train at Luga and went over to the rebels. But this is not true.

Approaching Tsarskoye Selo aboard the train, General Ivanov is shocked to receive the news that the Tsarskoye Selo garrison has mutinied. At 1:30 a.m. he receives a telegram from Nicholas II: "Do not take any action until my arrival." He shows the telegram to Empress Alexandra, when they meet later that night. The highly-strung Alexandra Feodorovna asks him to leave the town to avoid bloodshed and not to endanger her and the children.

General Ivanov orders his units out of the train at Vyritsa Station and sends telegrams to the frontline commanders asking for reinforcements. He does not know that they will not arrive, for on the morning of 2 March Nicholas II recalls all troops brought in to suppress the rebellion back to the front line.

KERENSKY ON THE EDGE OF A NERVOUS BREAKDOWN

On the night of 2 March, when Ruzsky is talking with Rodzianko, and General Ivanov with Empress Alexandra, Alexander Kerensky is close to a nervous breakdown because of the overwhelming stress of the past few days.

The reason is because Kerensky is desperate to please both the liberals of the Provisional Committee and the socialists of the Petrograd Soviet. He goes here and there, mixing with all, reveling in the exceptional role that has befallen him. Yet there is one insurmountable problem: his comrades from the State Duma are increasingly at odds with his comrades from the Petrograd Soviet. That night, 2 March, he realizes that he is falling between two stools. He has to make a choice.

He does not want to be left out of the Provisional Government, especially since he has been offered the post of justice minister. But the Petrograd Soviet is adamant that he, like his State Duma comrade Nikolai Chkheidze, should refuse the offer of a ministerial post without hesitation. Kerensky feels obliged to do so as not to lose credibility in the eyes of the workers and soldiers, the SRs and the Mensheviks. The dilemma is driving him crazy. Having decided nothing, he sets off home.

"It was strange walking down familiar streets without the usual escort of secret police agents," recalls Kerensky, "walking past the sentry posts and seeing smoke and tongues of flame still gushing from the building of the gendarmerie, where I was interrogated in 1905."

After lying in bed for two to three half-conscious hours, he comes up with a potential solution: he will accept the government post and then defend the decision before the Petrograd Soviet, explaining the benefits of having someone inside the government. He calls Milyukov, his Provisional Committee fellow member, in the middle of the night to tell him about his decision.

In the morning, Kerensky goes to the Duma. There, he meets members of the executive committee of the Petrograd Soviet, who greet him "with sour faces." Kerensky announces that he has decided to become a minister. They try to dissuade him, but he has already figured out how to overcome their veto. He goes into the next room, where a meeting of the Petrograd Soviet is in full swing, like a never-ending political rally. He asks for permission to address the meeting and climbs onto the table (otherwise no one will see or hear him). He delivers a fiery speech, saying that he has decided to represent the workers and soldiers in the new government, and asks for approval. The ordinary workers give their hero Kerensky an ovation, but the hardened revolutionaries of the executive committee are outraged: Kerensky has deceived them—he agreed to boycott the liberal Provisional Government and has now spat that promise back in their faces. But there is nothing they can do about it.

"NO TIME FOR PLEASANTRIES"

When Ruzsky and Rodzianko are having their nocturnal telephone conversation, the tsar is asleep. The first to receive a shorthand transcript of the conversation is Alekseyev in Mogilev. He demands that the emperor be woken immediately ("This is no time for pleasantries," he says) and be informed of Rodzianko's words: "The only option left is abdication."

Alekseyev believes the myth propagated by *Izvestia* that Tsarskoye Selo is in the hands of the rebels, and that, if the emperor does not agree to abdicate, they will kill his children and spark a civil war, whereupon the German juggernaut will crush Russia.

However, Alekseyev is informed that Nicholas II has just fallen asleep and will not be disturbed for at least half an hour. So he takes the initiative into his own hands, and by 3 a.m. has received telegrams from Evert, Brusilov, and even Grand Duke Nikolai Nikolaevich—the three frontline commanders in the war. All of them, including the tsar's uncle, beg the emperor to abdicate. The generals have one objective: to continue the war at all costs. For them, the prospect of the army refusing to fight is too terrible to contemplate. They believe that the abdication of the toxic tsar will help secure victory. The very next day some of them will realize how wrong they were.

THE CHOICE OF KERENSKY

On the morning of 2 March, Pavel Milyukov addresses an audience of workers, soldiers, and bystanders in the Catherine Hall of the Tauride Palace. He announces that the Provisional Committee has taken the decision to form an interim government.

The softly spoken fifty-eight-year-old professor with old-fashioned diction is not the most electrifying orator, certainly not in comparison with the young Kerensky. Milyukov does not feel the crowd and does not know how to say what it wants to hear. He reads out a list of members of the new Provisional Government, adding that Nicholas II is abdicating in favor of his son under the regency of Grand Duke Mikhail and that a constitutional monarchy will be established in Russia. This is not at all what the audience wants to hear, and Milyukov's speech is drowned in cries of indignation.

"Who elected you?" asks a caustic voice from the crowd. "The Russian revolution elected us," responds Milyukov pompously. At a hastily convened meeting of the executive committee of the Petrograd Soviet, Kerensky is quizzed as to why he concealed from them the Duma's desire to preserve the monarchy and make Grand Duke Mikhail regent. For the socialists, it means a complete rollback to the old ways. They want to establish a republic and fear that the Duma is in collusion with the old elite.

Kerensky tries to convince his comrades that he knows nothing and that there is no cause for alarm. He is lying, of course. He knows everything that goes on inside the Provisional Committee, and is aware that the

Duma emissaries Guchkov and Shulgin are planning to go to Pskov to request the tsar's abdication. His now not-so-comradely fellow socialists realize that Kerensky is two-faced, and announce that they will send their own delegation to Pskov, or at least hamper the efforts of the Duma.

When Kerensky departs, he is now sure which side he is on. He feels like a member of the new government and senses that the insurgents of the Petrograd Soviet are a threat. He needs to ensure that Guchkov and Shulgin get to the tsar before the Soviets do.

THE FIRST ABDICATION

The next morning, in Pskov, Nicholas II reads the transcript of the night-time talk between Ruzsky and Rodzianko, proposing for the first time that he should abdicate. The prospect does not seem totally unacceptable to the tsar.

The day before, he has taken the far more painful decision to appoint a government of national confidence: the idea to curb his own power always seemed like a crime to Nicholas. Since childhood, he has been inculcated by his father and Pobedonostsev with the belief that the monarch bears responsibility for Russia before God. To adopt a constitution would be to violate his coronation oath. Despite being unable to influence the situation in the country, he—not the government—is responsible before God. For Nicholas, his oath to God precludes even the idea of a constitutional monarchy. His wife adheres to autocracy no less dogmatically than he does. For her, the adoption of a constitution would be a crime against her son and a violation of his birthright. Paradoxically, abdication seems less daunting a prospect. Vacating the throne will relieve him of his divine responsibility, and, hence, whatever he does thereafter will not be a crime in the eyes of God.

At 1 p.m., walking along the platform of Pskov station, the tsar says to Ruzsky that he is seriously considering abdication. An hour later, Ruzsky receives the telegrams from the frontline commanders (the ones already sent to Alekseyev), and takes them to the tsar. The message is clear. Nicholas II orders the drafting of a manifesto by which he shall pass the throne to his son and appoint his brother Mikhail as regent. The manifesto is to be sent immediately to Duma Chairman Mikhail Rodzianko in Petrograd and Chief of Staff Mikhail Alekseyev in Mogilev.

At 3 p.m. Ruzsky leaves the tsar with the signed text in his hand, but is stopped by members of the royal entourage. Court Commandant Voeikov,

Court Minister Fredericks, and others are completely unprepared for such a step. They are shocked by the ease with which the tsar has abdicated ("How is it possible to give up the throne as if handing over command of a squadron?" says one of the generals). "What was I supposed to do when I've been betrayed by everyone," the tsar explains his action to Voeikov.

Voeikov requests that the telegram not be sent immediately. He knows that the Duma emissaries Guchkov and Shulgin are on their way from Petrograd, and the court commandant believes that there is a chance to undo the decision—the Duma representatives are bound to be more compliant than Ruzsky and will surely not insist on abdication.

Meanwhile, Nicholas is pondering what to do next. He dreams of sitting out the war somewhere abroad, coming back to Russia, and settling in Crimea to raise his fragile son in the temperate climate. But he is informed that that is out of the question; he will not be able to live with his son for he will be forced into exile. Troubled by the thought of separation, he inquires about the chances of Alexei ever recovering from his illness. The family doctor, Fedorov, replies that modern science has yet to find a cure for hemophilia. Belatedly, he starts to think that abdicating in favor of his son is a mistake.

THE SECOND ABDICATION

Meanwhile, Guchkov and Shulgin are traveling to Pskov. It takes a long time, for they have to keep stopping at stations along the way to speak to the assembled crowds. At one stopping point, they receive a phone call from General Ivanov. To their surprise, he complains that he was ordered to suppress the revolt and wait for two divisions recalled from the front, but they never arrived. Moreover, the two battalions in his command are now refusing to obey orders. Ivanov wants to meet with the deputies, which they decline.

Guchkov and Shulgin get to Pskov by 10 p.m. in a state of severe nervous exhaustion: after several sleepless nights Shulgin has severe headaches. Nevertheless, they are immediately taken to the tsar. In a highly respectful tone, Guchkov informs Nicholas of the situation in the capital. He says that no one planned the uprising; it simply flared up spontaneously and turned into anarchy. Sending troops from the front is bound to fail. The only feasible option is abdication in favor of Tsarevich Alexei under the regency of Grand Duke Mikhail.

Shulgin describes what is happening at the Tauride Palace and the Duma's attempts to restore order and save arrested members of the old regime from mob law, adding that it needs assistance in the fight against "leftist elements." When Guchkov says that the tsar has twenty-four hours to think it over, the latter replies that he has already decided to abdicate in favor of his son. But now, realizing that he does not want to be parted from his son, he changes his mind and renounces the throne on behalf of both himself and his son in favor of his brother.

There is a somber silence, after which Ruzsky asks Guchkov if the Duma can guarantee that Nicholas will not be separated from his son. He replies in the negative. A short while later, Guchkov addresses a crowd of curious onlookers in Pskov: "Do not worry, ladies and gentlemen. The emperor has agreed to do more than we expected." They had expected more resistance to the idea of abdication.

Later, legal experts will state unanimously that abdication on behalf of an infant heir is contrary to the laws of the Russian Empire and the manifesto of succession signed by Emperor Pavel I. However, Guchkov and Shulgin do not think about that.

Finally, around 11 p.m., Nicholas signs the last set of manifestos. When it comes to appointing a new prime minister, he has reached the point of indifference: "Who do you think?" he asks. "Prince Lvov," replies Shulgin. "Ah, let it be Lvov," Nicholas says, signing the paper. Another document appoints Grand Duke Nikolai Nikolaevich as the new supreme commander of the armed forces.

Meanwhile, the new authorities in Petrograd are developing a new policy. Justice Minister Alexander Kerensky sends telegrams to prosecutors throughout the country freeing all political prisoners and offering the new government's congratulations. A priority is the immediate release of "Babushka" Yekaterina Breshko-Breshkovskaya and five members of the Social Democrat Party, who were exiled to Siberia in 1915.

The very next day, Babushka, who lives in Achinsk in Siberia, receives an official notification of her release. "When news arrived of the overthrow of the old regime, all local officials evaporated," recalls Breshko-Breshkovskaya.

There was no one shouting at us. There was no one to salute to. There was no one to be afraid of. At one station I met a tall man who bowed to me and said in a low voice:

'Is it true?'

'Looks like it. And who are you?' I asked.

'I am the gendarme who brought you here.'

'And what are you going to do now?'

'I'm going to war. We, the gendarmes, have long wanted to serve at the front, but we were always refused.'

He was the last representative of the tsarist bureaucracy I ever met. They all crawled away like miserable, beaten dogs to hide until the storm blew over.

The old-regime prisoners are quickly replaced by new arrestees. "The victims of the anointed sovereign were released from Siberia. The plan was to replace them with new, more 'contemporary' [exhibits]," the modern artist Kazimir Malevich notes ironically in his diary.

Throughout the day the most odious members of the tsarist government are taken into custody, including former War Minister Sukhomlinov, former Prime Ministers Stürmer and Goremykin, former Interior Minister Maklakov, and Dubrovin, the head of the Union of Russian People (the world's first fascist organization).

By 2 March there are so many detainees that Kerensky decides to transfer them all to the Peter and Paul Fortress to stop them from being lynched. For many ministers, being arrested is salvation from death. War Minister Belyaev asks the Provisional Government for protection after an armed mob breaks into his apartment and smashes it up. He is told that the safest place to be is at the fortress. The next day Bublikov receives a call from former Prime Minister Trepov, asking to be arrested. He laughs in response, but sends a detachment to take Trepov to the fortress.

"RUSSIA NEEDS A TSAR"

Late in the evening the Tauride Palace is hosting a session of the new government when news arrives from Guchkov and Shulgin. Kerensky recalls that the first to break the silence was Rodzianko, saying that Grand Duke Mikhail cannot ascend to the throne for he has never shown any interest in public affairs and is married to a woman of lower social rank, for which, officially, he is even forced to an exile. This is pure court rationale, and many members of the imperial family think likewise. Kerensky is about to interrupt him to say that at this stage of the revolution there can be no tsar in any shape or form, but instead Milyukov takes the floor. He starts to argue that "Russia needs a tsar. The Duma never aspired to found

a republic, but simply to see a new figure on the throne. In close cooperation with the new tsar, the Duma can calm the raging storm."

It is already morning when the session breaks up. Kerensky wants to use
the pause to prevent the publication of the tsar's abdication manifesto in
favor of his brother. Rodzianko travels to the home of the war minister,
from where he can contact Alekseyev. The latter reports that the manifesto
is being distributed among the frontline soldiers and many have already
sworn allegiance to Emperor Mikhail II. Rodzianko asks him to stop the
process immediately.

Alekseyev inquires as to why the tsar's order is not to be divulged. Rodzianko explains evasively that Petrograd society would accept the accession
of Tsarevich Alexei, but never that of Grand Duke Mikhail.

Alekseyev cannot believe what he is hearing. He is horrified that he
trusted Rodzianko and persuaded the tsar to abdicate: "I will never forgive
myself for having faith in the sincerity of certain people and for sending a
telegram about the tsar's abdication to the commanders," he says.

Rodzianko contacts Ruzsky with the same request not to distribute the
abdication manifesto. "A soldiers' mutiny has flared up, the like of which
we've never seen," exaggerates Rodzianko to substantiate his request. "The
crowd is shouting 'Down with the dynasty,' 'Down with the Romanovs.'"
It is not true.

MIKHAIL II

At 6 a.m. Rodzianko returns to the Duma building. The Provisional Government is pondering how to get in touch with Grand Duke Mikhail, who
does not know that during the night he became emperor. He is still a
resident in Petrograd, but not at the Winter Palace. He now stays for a
night in the mansion of Princess Putyatina on Millionnaya Street.

When the government delegation goes there to meet him, the grand
duke greets them with the words: "I'm like the king of England, eh?" "Yes,
Your Highness, it's easy to rule when there's a constitution to abide by,"
says Milyukov, smiling.

Rodzianko and Lvov spell out the majority view: the grand duke, in
their opinion, must abdicate. Then, to everyone's surprise, Milyukov
launches himself into a long and flowery speech urging the grand duke, on
the contrary, to accept the throne. He talks and talks without end, which
greatly irritates Mikhail.

In fact, Milyukov is holding out for the arrival from Pskov of Guchkov and Shulgin, who will back him up and maybe convey to the grand duke a personal message from his brother, after which he will dare not renounce the throne. But they are nowhere to be seen.

The fact is that the Provisional Government emissaries have been detained by the crowd at the station. Upon learning that the emissaries have in their possession an abdication manifesto in favor of the tsar's brother, the angry workers detain Guchkov and Shulgin, and want to destroy the document: they do not want the tsar replaced; they want the monarchy abolished. The original document survives the ordeal by being crumpled in the pocket of Bublikov's assistant, Lomonosov. Guchkov and Shulgin are not detained for long, however. Some workers are on their side: "We ourselves invited them. . . . They trusted us and came here. . . . And what do you do? Try to lock them up? I tell you, comrades, you are worse than the old regime," recalls Lomonosov.

Shulgin and Guchkov arrive at the house on Millionnaya Street just as Milyukov's long speech is coming to an end. They express their support for Milyukov's position, but Kerensky immediately interjects: "I beg you in the name of Russia to make this sacrifice. . . . Otherwise, I cannot vouch for the personal safety of Your Highness. . . . Your life will be in danger should you accept the throne."

Mikhail retires to a separate room with Lvov and Rodzianko. On returning, he announces that he is ready to accept the throne only at the request of the Constituent Assembly when it is convened by the Provisional Government. From this point on, Russia de facto becomes a republic.

Sitting in the antechamber is the specially summoned law professor Vladimir Nabokov, father of the future world-famous writer; Prince Lvov has asked him to draw up an act of renunciation. Mikhail ponders for a long time how to sign the document: Grand Duke Mikhail Alexandrovich or Emperor Mikhail. In the end, he chooses the former. Half an hour later, placards are posted around the city: "Nicholas abdicates in favor of Mikhail. Mikhail abdicates in favor of the people." "God knows who put him up to signing such a vile thing," Nicholas writes about his brother's decision.

RUSSIA WITHOUT A TSAR

The news that the tsar is no more is greeted by yesterday's subjects with delight. The red flag is raised above the Winter Palace, and along Nevsky

Prospekt all heraldic eagles and signs reading "Supplier of the Imperial Court" are removed from shops and pharmacies.

In addition to the red ribbons pinned to the chests of Russia's former subjects (now citizens), a second symbol of change appears: sunflower seeds. Soldiers and workers freely roam the streets constantly snacking on seeds. There are no police to maintain order, so the streets are not cleaned. As a result, a thick layer of husks is deposited on the pavement and trampled underfoot.

Zinaida Gippius, who only yesterday was afraid of the Petrograd Soviet, now rejoices: she waves a red rag and throws red ribbons and flowers at demonstrators under her balcony. She and Filosofov pin all their hopes on Kerensky, who for them is "the living incarnation of the revolutionary pathos. He is guided by intuition, and every time it is the intuition of genius."

The artist Alexander Benois is amazed at the swiftness of the succession: "It's as if the tsar never reigned. Everyone has taken the news in their stride."

According to Paléologue, the imperial family was abandoned: "All the courtiers, senior officers and dignitaries, who once acted as the heaven-born defenders of the throne, simply fled." Others assert that it is not the court that betrayed the emperor, but the emperor who betrayed the court, his family, and the entire Russian people.

However, every rule of thumb has the odd exception. Sergei Zubatov, the disgraced founder of the first trade unions and security policing in Russia, on hearing the news from his wife of the tsar's abdication, gets up, leaves the room, and shoots himself.

"THEY'RE INFECTED BY SOME KIND OF MICROBE"

On the morning of 3 March, the tsar's uncle, Grand Duke Pavel, visits Alexandra, who is still dressed as a sister of mercy and caring for her children. The seventeen-year-old Grand Duchess Maria, who was the only healthy child, now, too, is seriously ill with a fever. The former empress has not yet been informed of her husband's abdication.

Pavel has good reason to dislike Alexandra. Fifteen years previously, in the wake of his secret wedding, it was she who insisted on his exile from Russia and opposed his second wife ever being admitted to the Russian court. It was she who ordered the arrest of his son Dmitry after the murder of Rasputin, and insisted on the latter's exile to Persia, then considered the equivalent of the death penalty. However, despite having suffered from

Alexandra's ill disposition towards him, the grand duke is the only relative to visit her in the days after the revolution.

"The grand duke quietly approached her and pressed a lingering kiss on her hand, unable to utter single a word. His heart was ready to burst," recalls his wife, Olga Paley, whom Alexandra so despised. "Dear [Alix]," says the grand duke at last. "I wanted to be by your side at this difficult time for you."

Alexandra does not believe the news at first. After speaking to the grand duke, she runs to her room. Her friend Lili Dehn has to catch hold of her to stop her from falling. Leaning on her desk for support, she repeats in French, "Abdiqué!" "My poor dear is suffering all alone. . . . God, how he must be suffering!" she sobs.

The situation becomes more complicated with each passing day. There is no news from Nicholas. Alexandra's own telegrams are returned with the inscription in blue pencil: "Addressee whereabouts unknown."

Lili Dehn advises Alexandra to burn her diaries and letters, so they do not fall into the hands of the revolutionaries. And during the next three days, together they burn everything that the former tsarina has carefully compiled over the years. Not knowing where her husband is, Alexandra writes countless letters to different addresses and dispatches servants on missions to find him.

"The Duma and the revolutionaries are two snakes that, I hope, will bite each other's heads off—that would rescue the situation," she writes in one of her letters. "I feel that God will do something. What a lovely sunny day it is today, if only you were here! Even the *equipage* left us today—they don't understand anything; they're infected by some kind of microbe." To Alexandra, the revolution is unnatural, even supernatural.

THE EMPEROR'S FAREWELL

Having signed the abdication, Nicholas returns to the High Command. This prompts a nervous reaction in Petrograd, where it is feared that he is gathering loyalist troops to launch a counter-revolution. However, Nicholas is far from such thoughts. Instead, he sends a telegram to his mother, Maria Feodorovna, who lives in Kiev, asking her to come to him in Mogilev.

Tormented by what has happened, a couple of days later he summons Alekseyev and tells him that he has changed his mind and wants to abdicate in favor of his son, handing his chief of staff a corresponding telegram addressed to the Provisional Government. Alekseyev politely but firmly declines to send it, explaining that they will both look ridiculous. After hesitating for a while, Nicholas again asks Alekseyev to send it and walks off.

Instead, Alekseyev sends his own telegram to Petrograd asking for Nicholas to be allowed to return to Tsarskoye Selo and be reunited with his wife and sick children, before traveling to Murmansk and sailing to England. The Provisional Government acknowledges the request.

British Ambassador Buchanan informs Milyukov that King George V has agreed to provide his cousin and family shelter in England, provided their upkeep is paid for by Russia's Provisional Government.

Justice Minister Kerensky arrives in Moscow and addresses a crowd, during which he is asked about what will happen to "Nikolai Romanov": "The revolution has been bloodless so far, and I shall not be the one to stain it. Soon, under my personal supervision, the former tsar shall be taken to a harbor and from there by boat to England."

But inside the Petrograd Soviet, other conversations are taking place. Its resident Bolsheviks (primarily Molotov, Stalin's future foreign minister) demand the immediate arrest of the imperial family. The Provisional Government reconsiders and, on 7 March, authorizes the arrest to go ahead. This is the first order drawn up by the chief administrator of the Provisional Government, Vladimir Nabokov.

In Mogilev, meanwhile, Nicholas is communicating not with the officer corps, but with his mother and childhood friend Sandro, who have arrived from Kiev to offer their support. In the evening of 7 March, a group of commissioners headed by Bublikov arrives from Petrograd to arrest the former tsar. Nicholas addresses the troops one last time: "Anyone who thinks now of peace is a traitor. Perform your duty well, defend our great Motherland, serve the Provisional Government, obey your superiors, and remember that any weakening of the chain of command only benefits the enemy." Chief of Staff Alekseyev and many others are in tears; some fall to the ground.

That same evening, the new commander of the Petrograd garrison, General Lavr Kornilov, arrives at Tsarskoye Selo to inform Alexandra that she, too, is under arrest.

The tsar's abdication is welcomed by all classes of Russian society, including the nobility and clergy. "It is God's will," reads an official statement of the church. "The Holy Synod prays devoutly that the Almighty bless the initiatives of the Russian Provisional Government."

Only among the officer corps is there discontent, but not much. General Denikin recalls that he was aware of only two senior officers who placed themselves and their forces at the former emperor's disposal. Count

Fyodor Keller and Huseyn Khan Nakhichevansky send a telegram to Nicholas requesting permission to dispatch their units to Petrograd to suppress the revolution. Nicholas does not accept the offer. In any case, it is unlikely that the rank-and-file soldiers under their command would show the same loyalty to the old regime.

Count Keller refuses to swear allegiance to the Provisional Government. Gustaf Mannerheim, the future first president of independent Finland, who at that moment is a general in the Russian imperial army, tries to convince him to see reason. Keller does not, and resigns from his post.

Nakhichevansky is the only one who tries to mount a resistance against the Provisional Government. Together with Prince Yusupov Sr., the father of Rasputin's murderer, he travels to Kharkov, where Grand Duke Nikolai Nikolaevich, the newly appointed supreme commander, receives them. The latter is journeying from Tiflis (modern-day Tbilisi) to the High Command in Mogilev, via Kharkov. Yusupov and Nakhichevansky meet him at the station and ask him to remain in Kharkov to lead the fight against the Provisional Government. The grand duke consults with his brother Petyusha, General Yanushkevich, and other members of his entourage before eventually deciding to continue onwards to the High Command.

He arrives in Mogilev on 10 March and even has time to take the oath of supreme commander, but in vain. He soon receives a telegram from Prime Minister Lvov requesting his immediate resignation for the sake of public order. Petrograd society, especially the Petrograd Soviet, is outraged that the new supreme commander is another Romanov. And although the grand duke still enjoys enormous prestige at the front, common sense prompts him to hand over his post to General Alekseyev. His next destination is Crimea.

THE POWER OF TOLSTOY

At one of the first meetings of the Provisional Government, Justice Minister Kerensky delivers a short speech proposing to abolish the death penalty. Vasily Shulgin, who is not a member of the government but in attendance as a guest, asks: "Alexander Fedorovich [Kerensky], in proposing to abolish the death penalty, do you mean for *all*? Do you understand what I am getting at?"

Shulgin is, of course, referring to the Romanov family. "I understand, and my answer is yes, for all," replies Kerensky. The death penalty is abolished unanimously.

At a time of war and revolution, when human life is practically worthless, it is a landmark decision. Not far from the capital, at Kronstadt, Helsinki, and Tallinn, the Baltic Fleet is revolting against the new authorities. Dozens of officers have been killed, including the commander-in-chief, Admiral Nepenin, the first of the tsarist military leaders to recognize the Provisional Government. He is knifed in the back on his way to a meeting with a group of commissioners from Petrograd.

Non-violent resistance to evil is a core principle of the new government headed by the Tolstoyan Prince Lvov. "The government has displaced the old governors and shall not appoint replacements," the prime minister telegraphs to the regions. "Such matters should be decided locally by the people, not by the center."

"Listening to Lvov, I realized for the first time that his great strength comes from faith in the common man—reminiscent of Kutuzov's faith in the common soldier," recalls Kerensky. "We really had nothing else other than faith in the people, patience and a decidedly unheroic realization that there was no turning back."

On 17 March the Provisional Government announces a program of unprecedented reforms that only yesterday were unimaginable: guaranteed freedom of the press and freedom of assembly; a general amnesty; the immediate convocation of a constituent assembly based on universal, equal, and direct suffrage by secret ballot; and the formation of people's militia units to replace the police (recently disbanded by the Provisional Government).

Russia is the first country in the world to outlaw the death penalty and one of the first to give women the vote.* Neither Britain, nor France, nor the United States has anything like it at the time. Almost overnight, the legally and politically backward Russian Empire turns into the most humane and democratic country in the world.

---

* In 1917 only citizens of Australia, New Zealand, Denmark, and Norway had electoral rights; in one part of the Russian Empire (Finland), women's suffrage had existed since 1906.

|| Chapter 13 ||

VLADIMIR LENIN

in which Irakli Tsereteli tries to turn
Russia into a parliamentary democracy and
Vladimir Lenin stands in his way

HOLED UP IN SWITZERLAND

"We old-timers might not live to see the decisive battles of the coming proletarian revolution. But I have great confidence that the young people of the socialist movement will have the good fortune not only to fight it, but to win it," a Russian émigré tells a group of young Swiss Marxists. It is late February 1917, a couple of weeks before Russia is hit by revolution.

The man has been living in Switzlerland for almost eleven years and signs his name as "Nikolai" Lenin. The leader of the Bolshevik Party, over the past seventeen years he has changed his name so many names it is hard to keep track: Ilyin, Petrov, Frey. He is still fanatically devoted to the revolutionary cause and is sure that it will happen one day. Yet the forty-seven-year-old Vladimir Ulyanov (his real name) is psychologically prepared for the fact that that he may not live to see the day.

Russian émigrés in Switzerland are cut off from what is happening back home. Most of them left Russia more than fifteen years earlier and have no idea what the Russian people are saying or thinking. The émigré community has turned into a sect, and even a number of warring sub-sects. They have come to despise their compatriots who remained in Russia, whom they view as traitors or compromisers. Almost all émigrés believe that they are the only true bearers of the ideas of the Russian revolution—only they are real; everyone else is a fraud. This messianic approach, however, is a psychological defense mechanism. They want to believe that their dull, shabby existence in a European backwater is a noble sacrifice. Lenin's self-hypnosis is the most complete of all.

For a decade-and-a-half he has not felt like a Russian politician—his debating opponents are all Swiss or German Marxists. What very little he hears from Russia does not interest him. His "pen pals" (his closest friend, Grigory Zinoviev, and mistress, Inessa Armand) also live in Switzerland.

By 2 March, the revolutionary events in Russia seem to be ending. The tsar has abdicated and the Provisional Government is in place. Yet Ulyanov still knows nothing about it. He and his wife, Nadezhda Krupskaya, are having dinner when a Polish neighbor comes running, asking breathlessly if they have heard the news from Russia. Lenin throws on his coat and dashes to a newspaper stand. That same day he writes to Zinoviev in Bern, asking him to travel to Zurich immediately.

The revolution wakes Ulyanov out of his stupor. He feverishly analyzes the political situation, but cannot get a hold on it. For one thing, he is sure that the tsar has escaped and is preparing a counter-revolution. Then he assumes that the revolution could not possibly have gone so smoothly had it not been the result of a conspiracy by the English and French in order to continue their imperialist war and prevent the tsar from concluding a peace treaty.

Despite his hazy view of the situation, he instructs his friend Alexandra Kollontai, who is able to travel to Petrograd from her position in Norway, not to offer Bolshevik support for the Provisional Government.

The main problem for all Russian émigrés in Switzerland is that they cannot get out. Switzerland is surrounded on all sides by belligerent countries. This common problem temporarily unites the warring socialist factions. A discussion is held, the tone of which is set by Julius Martov. This is logical, for his party comrades, the Mensheviks, are the ones in charge of the Petrograd Soviet. Ulyanov does not attend the meeting, but sends Zinoviev as his representative. Martov suggests two options for returning home: via Germany or via England.

Martov looks at both and concludes that England is too difficult. He, like Lenin and all other Russian émigrés, is a pacifist (i.e., antiwar, not anti-murdering Russian officials). Under martial law, antiwar propaganda is a crime. A couple of months previously Leon Trotsky was arrested in France and deported to Spain, and then to the United States, for such an offense. Traveling through France to England (and then by steamship to Sweden and onwards to Russia by train) is an option only for revolutionaries who publicly support the war: for example, the old leader of the Marxists, Plekhanov, who in one of his last interviews urged Russian women not to marry their soldier fiancés until they have returned victorious from the front. Martov and his comrades make fun of the sixty-year-old Plekhanov's newfound jingoism. Yet they are envious, because they cannot go to Russia.

The second option suggested by Martov is also highly dubious. Safe passage through Germany, which is at war with Russia, seems impractical. But Martov can call upon an influential comrade in Russia: Nikolai Chkheidze, the Menshevik chairman of the executive committee of the Petrograd Soviet. He wants the new Russian government to exchange German prisoners of war in Russia for revolutionaries holed up in neutral Switzerland. Martov fears that, in the turmoil of the revolution, his fellow party members now in power will forget about their émigré comrades. He writes letter upon letter, including ones to Gorky, Korolenko, and other illustrious acquaintances requesting assistance to get back to Russia.

Unlike Martov, Ulyanov does not have high-placed friends at home in Russia. The few Bolsheviks in the Petrograd Soviet have absolutely no influence whatsoever and cannot help their stranded leader.

Nadezhda Krupskaya recalls that her husband is losing sleep as he obsesses about how to escape from Switzerland. Flying by plane is impossible without the right documents. Another of Ulyanov's ideas is to obtain Swedish passports for himself and Zinoviev. But he and Zinoviev do not know a word of Swedish, so they would need the passports of deaf-mute Swedes. It is no joke. Ulyanov even sends a photograph to his comrade Yakub Ganetsky, who lives in Stockholm, asking him to find a Lenin-lookalike, deaf-mute Swede whose passport (indicating deaf-mute status) could be stolen. Krupskaya pokes fun at her husband: "Who are you kidding? You might start talking in your sleep. You'll dream about the Kadets* and start swearing."

A third option involves a fellow party member (and potential lookalike) Vyacheslav Karpinsky. Ulyanov proposes that Karpinsky give him his passport to travel to Russia and lie low for a couple of weeks in a sanatorium in the Swiss Alps. He even promises to pay all accommodation expenses. Karpinsky refuses.

In desperation, a fourth option is mooted, reviving Martov's idea of traveling through Germany. But the plan this time is to contact the Germans directly, without relying on the Mensheviks in Petrograd. For this, Lenin dispatches another comrade, Karl Radek, to meet with the German ambassador in Switzerland. Radek conveys Lenin's terms to the ambassador: "The German government shall let [the revolutionaries] through without asking their names, and the transit passengers shall have the privilege of extraterritoriality." The ambassador is taken aback: "Sorry, but I believe that Mr. Ulyanov and his associates are asking for permission to travel through Germany. If that is the case, the terms and conditions of passage shall be set by us." Nevertheless, he conveys the Bolsheviks' demands to Berlin.

BACK FROM SIBERIA

Most of the convicts exiled by the tsarist authorities to Siberia learn about the revolution no earlier than the Swiss emigrants. On that same day, 2 March, when Lenin and Krupskaya are avidly reading the newspapers at a kiosk near Lake Geneva, news of the revolution arrives in Irkutsk, the capital of Eastern Siberia. Crowds of people waving red flags pour onto the streets: rallies are held, and speeches are made. The atmosphere "vividly

---

* Members of the Constitutional Democratic Party.

IRAKLI TSERETELI

evokes the spirit of 18 October 1905 in St. Petersburg," recalls one of the exiles. "It was the same intoxication, the same uncertainty, the same vague anxiety. But there was also one significant difference: this time the troops were with the people."

Having learned about the revolution, the thirty-six-year-old former State Duma deputy Gerasim Makharadze runs to the nearest rail station. He is in a hurry to get to the village of Usolye to tell his friend Irakli Tsereteli, Russia's most famous political prisoner, about what has happened. The two of them, Tsereteli and Makharadze, were once members of the Second Duma from the Georgian city of Kutaisi. In 1907, both were accused by Stolypin of attempting a coup, and both were exiled to Eastern Siberia, six thousand kilometers from Georgia. Makharadze quickly finds Tsereteli, and the following day they enter the city as conquerors. Irkutsk is Russia's "premier" political prison. It is here, in the early nineteenth century, that a group of leading aristocratic officers, known as the Decembrists, were exiled for their dreams of turning Russia into a constitutional monarchy. At the beginning of the twentieth century, the resident Social Democrats, among them Tsereteli, dream of making Russia a democratic republic. Hitherto, they have gathered here illegally to discuss the latest news. But on 3 March they meet in order to set up the Irkutsk Soviet of Workers' Deputies—the new authority in town. Irakli Tsereteli and another exile, the Socialist-Revolutionary Abram Gotz, the brother of the party's late ideologist Mikhail Gotz, speak to the soldiers, who greet them with cries of "Long live the free Russia!" and "Long live the free soldiers!"

The very next day Tsereteli has to intervene in a conflict between Irkutsk soldiers and officers. "We are the predominant force," say the soldiers, stating that they will no longer obey the officers. "Yes, you are," agrees the exiled deputy Tsereteli, "because you are carrying out the will of the people. But the moment you place your own desires above the will of the people, you will become an insignificant bunch of rebels." His resoluteness makes a deep impression on the soldiers, and the conflict is settled.

Tsereteli stays a week in Irkutsk until the situation finally stabilizes. On 10 March he, along with other exiles, boards a train bound for Petrograd. Decorated with flags and posters, "the train of the Second Duma" stops at every station along the way, where the passengers alight to speak to the locals.

Tsereteli himself does not leave the train, for he is ill. He remains inside his compartment, perusing the papers and pondering his plans. The main task ahead is to unite all the former oppositionists, leave all disputes behind, and build a new Russian democracy together. To this end, Tsereteli tells his fellow passengers that he must meet with Lenin face to face in order to explain to him the folly of "maximalist experiments"* and convince him of the need for joint action.

At the same time, another living legend is departing from Krasnoyarsk. She is "Babushka" Breshko-Breshkovskaya. The most striking thing for her is that officialdom everywhere seems to have evaporated, yet law and order prevail: "The mood was respectful. People were confident that justice had finally arrived." Unlike the former deputies, however, she is not in a hurry to get to Petrograd. The legendary convict spends an entire month travelling around all the major towns and cities from Krasnoyarsk to Petrograd, where thousands of people come out to pay homage to their "queen."

MINISTRY OF ARTS

Meanwhile, many in Petrograd sense that the time is nigh. Swift action is needed to make the most of the unprecedented and long-awaited opportunities opened up by the revolution.

---

* In the words of Tsereteli's friend Vladimir Voitinsky.

On the morning of 4 March, the telephone rings at the house of the artist Alexander Benois. It is his colleague Kuzma Petrov-Vodkin, urging Benois to go to Gorky's place immediately, for a gathering of the creative intelligentsia is set to take place to elect a new minister of the arts. According to Petrov-Vodkin, the obvious candidate is Sergei Diaghilev. Benois rings around other friends, and all are infected with the same enthusiasm. The artist Konstantin Somov says that in view of the effective abolition of the Ministry of the Court, which oversaw the Imperial Academy of the Arts, action must be taken.

After dinner everyone gathers at the home of Gorky. His small living room is packed to the rafters. Benois recalls that the meeting was something of a muddle. Gorky repeats several times that artists themselves must assume responsibility for protecting museums, while his wife, Maria Andreyeva, appeals to Chaliapin to save the Russian theatre. All the while the "great oaf" Vladimir Mayakovsky (future greatest poet of Communist revolution, now wearing a simple soldier's uniform) is swearing his head off. In the end, Benois, Gorky, Chaliapin, Roerich, and other artists are chosen as delegates to attend the Duma the following day.

On the way back from Gorky's home, Benois is struck by the calm in the city: "A few patrols sat around campfires. No screaming or swearing. No drunks at all. It's all a bit surreal. You have to pinch yourself and ask: are Russians really so mature?"

The next day the stellar delegation goes to the Duma, where it finds a huge crowd through which they miraculously make their way thanks to Gorky's "magic" pass. After spending half a day in crowded reception rooms, they are informed that the chairman of the Council of Ministers has issued a decree to set up a special police unit to protect monuments and museums, which "only remains to be signed." At the same time, it turns out that the Provisional Government has relocated to the building of the Interior Ministry, where the delegation now goes. This time Chaliapin is the "pass," since everyone either knows or wants to know him. The young finance minister, Mikhail Tereshchenko, approaches the group ("with the demeanor not of a democratic minister, but of a gracious prince," writes Benois, "speaking in a husky voice"). It turns out that Tereshchenko's dream is to create a separate Ministry of the Arts headed by Diaghilev: "We must put it in writing right away, Alexander Nikolayevich!" he says to Benois.

Finally, the delegation makes the acquaintance of the star of the Provisional Government—Alexander Kerensky, whom Benois initially considered to be an "overzealous clerk." Kerensky takes the delegates to the next room and says that, as the justice minister, he has already visited the

Winter Palace and Tsarskoye Selo and posted guards there. Moreover, he is sure that the Winter Palace is wholly inappropriate as a venue for the constituent assembly.

"The man had clearly not slept for many nights," recalls Benois. "Having encountered so much mediocrity and inborn Russian apathy, Kerensky made a fine impression. He exudes talent, willpower and watchfulness. A born dictator!"

It transpires that Kerensky is a step ahead and has already secured Prime Minister Lvov's signature on the decree to set up a police unit to protect the palaces. He thanks the delegation, saying that he relies on the support of such artistic luminaries. Then, without saying goodbye, he dashes from the room on urgent business.

The next day the newspapers publish a report on the creation of a new arts commission, which includes Gorky, Benois, Petrov-Vodkin, Roerich, Chaliapin, and other celebrities. Young artists and poets are against this "dictatorship of stars." They demand a congress of artists, which convenes at the Mikhailovsky Theatre on 12 March, presided by Professor Vladimir Nabokov Sr. The theatre director Vsevolod Meyerhold and the young poet Vladimir Mayakovsky are in a tempestuous mood, the latter demanding a "constituent council of artists," not some "ministry of arts."

Perplexed, Benois and Nabokov leave the meeting. Benois calls Elena Diaghileva, Sergei's stepmother, to find out his current address and urge him "to return to Russia for the sake of the common task" (and lead it, most likely). Elena is sure that Sergei will agree because great opportunities beckon. Benois admits that he is somewhat concerned for Diaghilev, should he return: "Let him be spared from partaking of the bitter cup of our machinations."

HEAVE-HO

In March 1917 a new season of Diaghilev's Ballets Russes begins in Rome. When Igor Stravinsky arrives from Switzerland, the whole team is already assembled: the choreographer Leonid Myasin leads the rehearsals, while Léon Bakst and Pablo Picasso are putting the finishing touches to the stage set. The Rome program includes Stravinsky's *Firebird* and *Fireworks*. All performances traditionally begin with the orchestra performing the Russian national anthem, but Diaghilev considers "God Save the Tsar" to be no longer appropriate. Instead, he instructs Stravinsky to arrange—and the orchestra to play—a stirring rendition of the traditional ballad "*Ey, ukhnyem*" (literally "Heave-ho," more commonly known as "The Song of the Volga Boatmen")—the song of the "barge haulers" (laboring men dragging barges on rivers), probably the most deprived members of society.

Having received Benois's telegram, Diaghilev does not take long to refuse. He is finishing work on a new grandiose staging of Erik Satie's ballet *Parade*, with scenery once more by Picasso. Diaghilev's previous seasons have not been very successful, and this time he is hoping for a breakthrough.

"I've been working abroad for too long," Vaslav Nijinsky's wife, Romola, recalls the words of Diaghilev, whom, incidentally, she detests. "I wouldn't survive in the new Russia and prefer to remain in Europe." Benois eventually accepts his point of view: "Let Sergei remain abroad. We'll all have to emigrate too when everything turns sour."

Back in Russia, the lack of a national anthem is a problem. As the "official" anthem of the revolution, the French *Marseillaise* is normally chosen for formal occasions. Yet Russian composers are eager to write a new tune. Alexander Grechaninov, Alexander Glazunov, and Sergei Prokofiev all compose versions of their own. Grechaninov asks the poet Konstantin Balmont to write some words. He pens the following:

> Long live Russia—land of the free!
> Free and elemental, great is your story.
> O mighty power, o shoreless sea!
> The mist is dispelled by your fighters of glory.

Zinaida Gippius and Valery Bryusov are also rumored to try their hand at composing a verse or two.

The new country still has no symbols or traditions. The first ritual needed is for the funerals of victims of the revolution, so-called "festivals of freedom." The Petrograd Soviet seriously considers the idea of burying its fallen comrades in Palace Square, with the fraternal grave crowned by a grandiose monument.

But members of the "commission for the arts" are horrified. Benois is worried that hundreds of thousands of people will attend the ceremony and make a dash for the Winter Palace and the treasures of the Hermitage. He asks Gorky to go to the Petrograd Soviet of Workers' Deputies and use his influence to suggest that the burial take place, for instance, in front of Kazan Cathedral—the site of numerous clashes with police under the former regime. But the Petrograd Soviet insists on Palace Square, and work begins to dig it up.

However, it proves impractical due to the frozen ground and crisscrossing pipes. In the end, the decision is taken to hold the mass funeral for victims of the revolution at the Field of Mars, a spacious park named after the Roman god of war. On 23 March an immense procession of almost a million people takes place ("Two million," says Gippius, "and no Khodynka tragedy"). The fact that such a vast memorial service passes without incident is praised even by skeptics, such as the French ambassador to Russia, Maurice Paléologue: "Innumerable crowds escorted the slow-moving red coffins—an extraordinarily magnificent spectacle. The tragic effect was intensified by once-a-minute cannon fire. Russians have an innate sense of the dramatic."

WITHOUT PRIESTS

Non-religious funerals come as a great shock for many residents of the capital. "No priest, no icons, no prayers, no cross. Only one song: the *Marseillaise*," the French ambassador continues. "Only yesterday peasants, soldiers and workers could not walk past an icon without doffing their caps. What a contrast to today!"

The lack of priests at funeral ceremonies is the talk of the town, not least at the home of the Merezhkovskys. Zinaida Gippius, the founder of her own "domestic church,"* is indignant. "How can they just bury people without even singing the Memory Eternal?" she asks guests seated around her kitchen table.†

"Why not?" responds one of her soldier guests. "There was a choir from every regiment. They sang in a comradely manner. Why bother with priests? If the other side had won, the victims would now be swinging on the gallows." Gippius concurs, recalling that the Russian Orthodox Church forbade prayers for the saintly Tolstoy, while the devil-incarnate Rasputin's burial service was performed by the metropolitan himself.

The church itself tries to show loyalty to the new government. "It is God's will. Russia has embarked on a new path," announces the Holy Synod three days after the abdication of Nicholas II. "The Holy Synod prays that the Almighty bless the deeds of the Provisional Government."

The Provisional Government is busy developing its own secular rituals. Kerensky, for his part, believes that Russia "needs more fine gestures."

---

* The so-called "Brotherhood of Three" composed of herself, her husband, and Dmitry Filosofov.
† A eulogy sung at the end of Orthodox funerals.

Benois does not really know what he means, but agrees all the same. The next "fine gesture" of the new government is a gala concert at the Mariinsky Theatre in honor of the revolution.

At the theatre, members of the Provisional Government and the executive committee of the Petrograd Soviet sit in the stalls. All eyes are trained on the royal box, which is now full of thirty people: old men and a few old women with gaunt yet strangely expressive faces glancing around in surprise at the audience. They are terrorist heroes and heroines, who only returned from Siberia a few weeks ago, including the legendary Vera Zasulich and Vera Figner of People's Will.

"I was horrified to think of all the physical and mental suffering they had endured in silence. What an epilogue to Dostoevsky's *House of the Dead*," says the French ambassador, moved by the scene.

To the delight of the audience, Justice Minister Kerensky appears on stage. He is followed by the aforementioned sixty-five-year-old Vera Figner. In 1881, she was the only member of People's Will who managed to avoid arrest after the assassination of Alexander II. But not for long. Two years later she was captured and sentenced to death, later commuted to lifelong hard labor. But in 1906 she was humanely released for medical treatment abroad, where she founded the committee for political prisoners, the first human rights organization in Russian history (based in Paris). Now she is on stage at the Mariinsky Theatre, speaking on behalf of "the innumerable army of all those who sacrificed their lives for the Revolution, who died anonymously in prison and in Siberia." "A whisper of sympathy and reverence, a kind of silent ovation, swept through the hall," recalls Paléologue. Her speech is followed by a funeral march, and the room starts to weep.

"IT'S NOT EVERY DAY THAT TSERETELI ARRIVES"

On 18 March the Petrograd Soviet is in a flutter: tomorrow the "train of the Second Duma" is set to arrive, bringing with it the legendary revolutionaries and leaders of the Socialist-Revolutionaries and Social Democrats from Siberian exile. The most famous of them is Tsereteli. The Petrograd Soviet arranges a guard of honor made up of soldiers and sailors, an orchestra, and an official delegation for his arrival. Some want to tone down the occasion for fear of provoking a stampede. "It's not every day that Tsereteli arrives, you know," replies Moisei Uritsky, a member of the executive committee. In less than a year's time, now on the side of the

Bolsheviks, it is Uritsky who will be responsible for dispersing the Constituent Assembly and persecuting Tsereteli in his role as head of the Petrograd Cheka, the security agency set up to fight enemies of the new regime.

The red carpet is indeed rolled out (along with red flags), setting a precedent for greeting other newly arrived "great revolutionaries." The heroes are borne aloft by the crowd and taken to the Tauride Palace, where more triumphant speeches are delivered.

For Tsereteli, returning to the Tauride Palace is a symbolic moment. It was here, a decade before, that he listened to his sentence being read out, with the approval of the then-deputies Guchkov, Milyukov, and Rodzianko, who now sit in the new government. Tsereteli makes a speech in which he forgives his erstwhile enemies and states his willingness to work with them for the sake of Russian democracy.

"We, more than anyone else, know the price of the bourgeoisie. On our bones, on the crypt of the Social Democrats of the Second State Duma, the Fourth Duma was raised," he says, presenting himself as a martyr. Tsereteli argues that power should lie in the hands of the Provisional Government and that strict discipline should be enforced in the ranks of the proletariat, effectively announcing that his goal is to curb the Petrograd Soviet and put an end to the revolutionary chaos. He explains this task from a Marxist viewpoint: "The time has not yet come to implement the end objectives of the proletariat," these "bright ideals will be implemented through the joint efforts of the world proletariat," but for now the Russian working class "hand in hand with the progressive bourgeoisie" must build a new democratic state and "defend freedom from the forces of darkness."

Lastly, Tsereteli boldly declares that the "great schism" in the ranks of the Russian Social Democrats is over: "For years we have rebelled against each other in fratricidal warfare. Not any more. Today we stand as representatives of the Social-Democratic faction, which has united the Bolsheviks and Mensheviks as a single whole."

Meanwhile, the Bolshevik and Menshevik ideologists themselves, Lenin and Martov, are also trying to unite to return to Russia, unaware that many of their comrades no longer need them all that much.

The Bolshevik Party is experiencing an internal transformation: among the returning exiles are the famous revolutionaries Lev Rosenfeld and Joseph Dzhugashvili. They are received into the executive committee of the Petrograd Soviet and immediately seize editorial control of the party newspaper *Pravda* in a coordinated "raid." Rosenfeld and Dzhugashvili are better known by their pseudonym surnames Kamenev and Stalin. Brutalsounding pseudonyms are in vogue among the Bolsheviks: Stalin (from the Russian word for "steel"), Kamenev ("stone"), Molotov ("hammer"), Lomov ("crowbar").

Dzhugashvili, according to one of his so-called colleagues, is like a "gray, indistinct spot." The new party line is set by Kamenev, who renounces Lenin's intransigence in the spirit of Tsereteli, who believes that the stability of the new democracy must be ensured. Kamenev and Tsereteli see eye to eye. Moreover, they know each other from their school days back in Tbilisi (then Tiflis).

Many top positions inside the Petrograd Soviet are occupied by Georgians. In 1917 no one is bothered by it, since they all claim to be patriots of Russia and uninterested in the issue of Georgian autonomy.

In the spirit of universal reconciliation, the legendary Babushka makes a triumphant tour of the country. Arriving at long last in Moscow, she is taken in the once imperial carriage to the Moscow Duma. Then, on moving to Petrograd, she is met at the train station by Kerensky himself and taken to the buildings of the Petrograd Duma and the Petrograd Soviet. She gives speeches at both. Kerensky lodges the seventy-three-year-old Babushka in his own apartment.

Benois, however, believes that the hero-worship of convicts is excessive: "They've overegged it. Babushka is spoilt forever." Benois thinks that the humble Breshko-Breshkovskaya, who once roamed the villages, is now a living museum exhibit. Yet the Provisional Government does not turn her into a propaganda tool. She simply lives at Kerensky's apartment, seemingly more fascinated by him than he is by her. Speaking in public, she never fails to extol his virtues.

KERENSKY THE SAVIOR

Babushka is not the only one enamored of the young justice minister, Alexander Kerensky. Every woman in Russia, it seems, is in love with him, while men speak of him in reverential terms as the savior of the Fatherland. Less than a month after the tsar's abdication, in a country without television and radio, talk of the superhero minister is spreading like wildfire.

Kerensky is walking on air and his energy knows no bounds. He is literally everywhere and said to be the only member of the new government who never sleeps. Foreign journalists are amazed that Kerensky gives interviews at 7 a.m. Despite looking tired, he still manages to infect others with his enthusiasm.

"I really want to be in close contact with him. I could be useful to him," Alexander Benois writes in his diary after his first meeting with Kerensky. "What unbridled rapture his appearance aroused," Ekaterina Peshkova remembers a speech by Kerensky. "It was such a joy to listen to him and realize that such a person exists." "Who's our savior? Kerensky!" Benois's daughters and maids chant in unison in the family kitchen.

Kerensky's appeal reaches far beyond the capital. "I worship Kerensky, the leader of our revolution. . . . My darling, wonderful Kerensky!" writes the Odessa music teacher Elena Larier in her diary. "There is only one person who can save the country," states the British military attaché Alfred Knox, who expects nothing good to come of the revolution.

On 12 March Kerensky pays a visit to his old friend Zinaida Gippius, and asks her husband Merezhkovsky to write a pamphlet about the Decembrists to be published with a circulation of one million copies. Kerensky explains that the work is needed to quell the soldiers' hatred of their officers and show that the Russian revolution began with an uprising among the nobility and aristocracy back in 1825.

The ever-cynical Gippius listens to Kerensky and recalls how two years previously, at a meeting of the Religious-Philosophical Society, she saw Kerensky next to a portrait of Nicholas II and was struck by the likeness: "I'll never forget it. Who'd have thought that today the mutineer would be a minister and the tsar under arrest?"

Kerensky leaves the Merezhkovskys as hastily as he came, asking for the visit to be kept secret. "Kerensky is now the only one," writes Gippius in her diary. "It's scary. He may be brilliant, but not all-powerful. The task could swallow him."

Two months later Merezhkovsky puts the finishing touches on his book, *The Firstborns of Freedom*, and devotes it to "the successor of the Decembrist cause: A.F. Kerensky."

THE DUUMVIRATE

Kerensky is indeed the most active and most popular politician in the new Russia, but Gippius is right that he is far from being all-powerful. The most popular word in Russia in the spring of 1917 is *dvoyevlastiye*, meaning duumvirate or dual power. It appears endlessly in newspapers, diaries, and memoirs. The fact is that since the beginning of the February Revolution, both the Provisional Government and the Soviets (in Petrograd, Moscow, and hundreds of cities all over the country) have been functioning simultaneously. They are not opposed to each other, but their very coexistence is confusing for society.

The new system that emerged after the abdication of the tsar is well understood in the twenty-first century, when the division of power into legislative and executive branches is commonplace. But in the early twentieth century, for Russian society accustomed to rigid, top-down, one-man rule, the mere existence of two centers of power seems unnatural and dangerous. The ordinary citizen has no concept of checks and balances or how such a system should work. Throughout its twelve-year existence of opposition, the State Duma has never had an opportunity to influence political decisions, let alone form a government.

Yet the Petrograd Soviet does not claim to be an organ of supreme state power (the slogan "All power to the Soviets" will sound much later from the archenemy of the existing system, Lenin). Nikolai Chkheidze, the chairman of the executive committee of the Petrograd Soviet, admits in one of his speeches that only once did the Petrograd Soviet permit itself to intrude into the realm of executive responsibility: in the first days of the revolution, fearing that the tsar would raise an army and lead a counter-revolution, members of the Soviet wanted to send soldiers to have him arrested. However, they later ceded the executive function to the Provisional Government.

According to Chkheidze, the Soviet exercises civilian, or parliamentary, control over the activities of the government. The majority inside this quasi-parliament belongs to the left-wing socialist opposition, with the liberal government being more to the right.

The democratic nature of such a system is a moot topic: the Soviets are elected by labor collectives of enterprises and military units, not by the entire population. However, the previously elected bodies—the Duma and the zemstvos—were also far from being truly democratic, because the requirement to own property largely ruled out peasants, workers, and soldiers. Now it is the workers and soldiers who have assumed the role of choosing the new representative bodies. The fact that the Petrograd Soviet sits at the Tauride Palace, the building of the State Duma dissolved by the tsar, is symbolic.

The system of checks and balances between the Petrograd Soviet and the Provisional Government swings into action when Tsereteli arrives in Petrograd. He does not occupy public office yet, but he is the ideologist and "spiritual leader" of the Petrograd Soviet.

An unofficial body of power is taking shape around Tsereteli, which his detractors call the "star chamber"—a group of likeminded individuals,

Socialist-Revolutionaries, and Mensheviks, who dominate the executive committee of the Petrograd Soviet. Every morning they gather for breakfast at the flat of Duma deputy Skobelev, also home to Tsereteli, who does not have his own apartment. Also present are Chkheidze, Abram Gotz, Fyodor Dan (one of the Menshevik leaders), and several others. Tsereteli uses these morning briefings to instruct his comrades.

The reason for Tsereteli's potent influence is that he alone has a clear plan; all other politicians are lost. According to his colleague Voitinsky, the more complex the political situation and the more hesitant those around him, the more Tsereteli is sure of himself. In terms of self-belief, Tsereteli has only one rival—Lenin.

AN INEFFECTIVE MANAGER

The fact that the Provisional Government feels squeezed by the Petrograd Soviet is not surprising. The former has no leader and no effective management: the super-popular Kerensky is more a lone wolf than a team player, and the formal leader, Prince Lvov, does not want to hog the limelight. He is in no hurry to establish relations with the regions. As the new interior minister, Lvov dismisses all former governors, replacing them with the heads of provincial zemstvos (i.e., elected officials are vested with power, not appointees). However, they tend to be local noblemen respected in their own circles, but removed from the common folk and slightly afraid of them.

At the same time, the government does not regulate or hinder the emergence of local self-government bodies—an endless number of committees and soviets (councils). In the opinion of Prince Lvov, there is no need for a special program to set up local authorities, since they are self-generating and already exist in embryonic form, preparing the people for future reforms.

At first this is not a problem. As recalled by the leader of the Socialist-Revolutionaries, Viktor Chernov, "the popular enthusiasm about the fall of the old regime was so great that its heirs literally choked on the stream of telegrams expressing sympathy, support and unlimited hope."

But within a month, there is discontent among the people, which the Provisional Government fails to notice because it does not have its ear to the ground. Its members are surprised to learn that working people consider them *bourgeoisie*.

Neither does the "Tolstoyan" Provisional Government of Prince Lvov know how to deal with the police. With the old tsarist police disbanded, most of its leaders are behind bars. No one is responsible for law enforcement, and throughout the country there is a sharp increase in crime. Local soviets respond by creating their own volunteer worker and student militias. Only a month later does the Provisional Government issue a decree to legitimize them.

A BUTTERFLY ON THE WHEEL

The former tsar and his family have been living under arrest now for two weeks. Nicholas spends his time clearing snow from around the palace and keeping the ponds free of ice. The guards mock him, saying, "Hey, colonel, you're not allowed over there," and shove him around with their rifle butts. But overall, the two weeks have been calm. Nicholas and Alexandra's attention is mainly on their children, who are only just beginning to recover from their illness—all except Maria, who now has pneumonia.

On 21 March, the calm inside the palace is disturbed by the arrival of Justice Minister Kerensky. His first port of call is Anna Vyrubova:

"Are you Ms. Anna Vyrubova?"

"Yes," she answers, barely audibly.

"Get dressed and follow me."

Vyrubova is silent.

"What the devil are you doing in bed?" inquires Kerensky.

"I'm sick," she whimpers.

Kerensky turns to the accompanying officer. "Put a guard on the door. I'll go and speak to the doctors. No one is to enter or leave this room without my permission." He then swiftly proceeds to the quarters of Nicholas and Alexandra. "I'm Kerensky, you probably know my name," he says. They are silent. "You must have heard of me? I don't know why we are standing up. Let's sit down, that will be more comfortable." The former empress pointedly ignores all the minister's questions, so he asks her to leave him alone with Nicholas. Alexandra runs out of the room. "Mum, what's going on?" ask her worried elder daughters Olga and Tatiana.

"Kerensky insisted that I leave him alone with the Sovereign," replies Alexandra. "They'll probably arrest me."

However, Kerensky takes into custody only Alexandra's two friends—Anna Vyrubova and Lili Dehn—on suspicion of political conspiracy. He is acting largely under the influence of the press, which every day publishes new lurid details about the lives of the imperial family. Such publications are no secret to Vyrubova. On the morning of the day of her arrest, for instance, she reads in the papers that she and Dr. Badmaev allegedly tried to "poison the Sovereign and the heir."

Vyrubova sobs all the way to Petrograd. But once in the capital, curiosity takes over. For the first time, she sees the revolutionary city, the crowds of soldiers, the long queues, and the "dirty red rags" on all the buildings.

"You see, Lili. After the revolution, things are no better," she says to her friend.

"Not a single policeman," writes Dehn. "Law and order ceased to exist, but groups of strange people were gathered on the street corners. No doubt the loiterers were Jews. . . . It's no wonder that Petrograd acquired a small-town mentality."

In the pre-trial detention cell, Dehn takes the remaining letters from Vyrubova. There was no stove in the house, so she tore the ones she could find into small pieces and flushed them down the lavatory, so that the jailers would not find anything "compromising."

The soldiers and officers who arrested Alexandra's ladies-in-waiting are surprised to discover that the renowned Vyrubova is not a wanton high-society *belle*, but an invalid on crutches who looks much older than her thirty-two years.

"We must give them their due. The soldiers were very gentle with this butterfly that had fallen under the wheels of a car," notes Dehn ironically.

After one night in prison together, they part company: Vyrubova is taken to the Trubetskoy Bastion of the Peter and Paul Fortress—one of Russia's worst jails, where political prisoners were detained in the days before the revolution. As for Dehn, a few days later Kerensky demands her release. For a start, she has never engaged in politics, and besides, she has a seven-year-old child at home. She is set free.

THE PRISON POET

On 26 March Alexander Blok arrives in Petrograd from the front line. He is thirty-six years old, the same age as Kerensky, and for several years has been one of the most famous poets in Russia. The last few months he has spent in the swamplands of Belarus, serving as an army clerk.

As it happens, his arrival in the capital coincides with the burial of victims of the revolution at the Field of Mars. Blok wanders the streets and looks at the "joyous, mellowed people" in the unswept, police-free streets. To him, it seems like the first of many miracles: "There is nothing to be afraid of here. The city is like a dream world."

He goes to see the Merezhkovskys, who receive him kindly and bring him up to speed on the revolution. Their story further convinces him that something supernatural has occurred.

On his first day back in the capital, an old acquaintance offers Blok a job as a secretary at the newly created investigative commission, which is tasked with interrogating all arrestees of the old regime and unpicking their crimes. The chance to be close to history in the making appeals to Blok: "I'll be in the Winter Palace at the heart of government business," he explains to his mother. He accepts the post.

Meanwhile, the Peter and Paul Fortress is filling up with persons whom the new government suspects of crimes: in addition to Vyrubova, there is the head of the Union of Russian People Dubrovin, the corrupt former palace commandant Voeikov, the former war minister Sukhomlinov and his wife, the former prime ministers Stürmer and Goremykin, and the former interior minister Protopopov. Just a few days after the revolution, almost all former ministers, high-ranking police officers, and other undesirables of the former regime find themselves under arrest.

They are kept in terrible conditions. When Vyrubova is brought to her cell, the soldiers remove the mattress from the bed and an extra pillow, tear off the gold crucifix from around her neck, and confiscate her icons and gold rings. "The crucifix and icons fell into my lap. I cried out. One of the soldiers punched me and spat in my face. They left, slamming the iron door behind them," Vyrubova describes her first few moments in the cell.

The head warden comes to see her. He is Andrei Kuzmin, a former ensign who, after the Russian-Japanese War, spent two weeks as the "president of the Krasnoyarsk republic."* Vyrubova knows nothing of his past, except that he did fifteen years' hard labor in Siberia. "I tried to forgive him, knowing that he was just taking out his grievances of the past years on me; but how hard it was to endure such cruelty on the very first evening!" recalls Vyrubova.

It only gets worse. Vyrubova says that she soon fell ill with pleurisy from the dampness.

Suffering from a severe fever, she cannot rise for weeks. On the floor in the middle of her cell is a huge puddle, and sometimes she falls off her bunk in a slumber right into it and wakes up dripping wet. The prison doctor, she says, is a sadist, who enjoys mocking the prisoners.

"I literally starved. Twice a day they brought half a bowl of slop, which the soldiers often spat and put pieces of glass in. It often stank of rotten

---

* He led an armed uprising in the region against the imperial regime.

fish. I held my nose and swallowed a little, so as not to die of hunger. The rest I poured down the toilet. . . . It was a slow death penalty."

The cells are occasionally visited by investigators, including the new secretary of the investigative commission, Alexander Blok. Despite being a refined romantic (the "lunar poet" in the words of his friend Zinaida Gippius), Blok feels no compassion for the prisoners. "This feeble-minded harlot lies with her crutches all day long in bed," Blok writes to his mother about Vyrubova. "She is thirty-two years old and might even be beautiful, but there is something terrible in her. . . ."

Almost all the prisoners provoke Blok's disgust: "An insignificant creature" (about Voeikov); "a hideosity with a greasy mug, a plump tummy and a new jacket" (about Prince Andronnikov); "a pathetic, sick monkey" (about the gendarme Sobieschansky); "what foul eyes" (about Dubrovin). Put simply, Blok is a real revolutionary investigator: "I would hang Madame Sukhomlinov, although the death penalty has been abolished. This gold-digging, bribe-taking spouse [of former War Minister Sukhomlinov] has forever ruined his reputation," the poet writes to his mother.

The dampness in the cells soon makes all the prisoners ill. Voeikov writes that his belly is swollen from hunger. So it continues until Ivan Manukhin, a renowned doctor who treated Gorky's tuberculosis, as well as a neighbor and close friend of the Merezhkovskys, joins the medical staff of the investigative commission. Manukhin insists that the prisoners be fed normally and forbids the use of the freezing-cold punishment cell: "Prisoners were never treated as harshly under the old regime or during the first few months after the October revolution," Manukhin recalls. In her memoirs, Vyrubova describes the doctor as her savior.

A TERRIBLE SOCIALIST

Meanwhile, on the other side of the world in New York, a former prisoner of the Peter and Paul Fortress is about to return home. On learning about the revolution in Russia, Leon Trotsky hurries to the Russian consulate, where they have already taken down the portrait of Nicholas II. He is issued documents, and soon he and his family are on board a Norwegian steamer bound for Europe. However, at the port of Halifax in eastern Canada, British security officials interrogate the "terrible socialist." On 3 April he and his family are taken off the steamer for further questioning and subjected to a search far more humiliating that anything he ever experienced at the Peter and Paul Fortress.

Trotsky is unaware, of course, that the British ambassador in Petrograd, Buchanan, is at that very moment asking Russian Foreign Minister Milyukov about what to do with the exile in Canada. Milyukov, the former leader of the Kadets, is well aware that Trotsky is a socialist and a pacifist. For him, all pacifists are enemies and traitors, so he asks Buchanan to keep Trotsky in custody. Only two weeks later, under pressure from Kerensky and his colleagues, does he ask the British to release the detainee.

While Trotsky is at the Amherst internment camp in Nova Scotia (which he describes as a "concentration camp"), a crucial event happens: the United States enters the war on the side of the Entente powers. It seems to many that this will decide the outcome.

A "RED LINE" IN CHALK

Germany agrees to give passage to the revolutionaries "willingly, even too willingly," worries the Marxist Anatoly Lunacharsky. The German Foreign Ministry and General Staff come to the conclusion that it is in their interests to hand over the pacifist revolutionaries to Russia. The political decision has been made, yet it remains to be implemented on the ground.

Lenin wants to set off immediately. Krupskaya tries to dissuade her husband: in Germany they risk arrest, while in Russia they face accusations of treason. He tries to secure the signatures of Swiss and French socialists in support of his passage through Germany to prove that he is not a German spy.

At noon on 9 April, Lenin and Zinoviev draw up a list of those requesting passage to be presented to the authorities. According to the agreement, they are not required to show passports. Lenin tries to fill the list with as many non-Bolsheviks as possible, so that not only his party is accused of having ties with Germany. He does not succeed all that well: only four of the thirty names do not belong to Lenin's Bolsheviks. At 3:30 p.m. they all go to the station, where they are awaited by a crowd of enraged compatriots, all shouting "German spies!" Yet many of the people shouting would like to be on the train to Russia.

The train starts rolling. Lenin with Krupskaya and his mistress Inessa Armand, Zinoviev with his ex-wife and his current wife, and another twenty-four people set off for their homeland.

The border crossing is a nerve-wracking affair. All the passengers are taken out of the carriage and into the customs hall—the men and women are separated. They are sure that they will now be arrested, and Lenin is to be the first. To protect their leader, they surround him on all sides, shielding him from the German border guards. But after half an hour of waiting, the emigrants are unexpectedly allowed to continue their journey.

Under the terms and conditions laid down by Germany, the passengers are not to communicate with anyone and avoid the slightest contact with German people, so as not to fuel accusations of spying for Germany.

The "sealed carriage" has since become the stuff of legend. In fact, it is not entirely sealed: there is a door leading to the other carriages, but Fritz Platten, the main organizer of the trip, draws a line on the floor in chalk that no one, Russian or German, is allowed cross except him. This chalk line serves as a boundary between the Bolsheviks and Germany.

From the start, Lenin turns the carriage into a microcosm of the Russian state that he wants to build. After the nervy border crossing, the passengers relax and smoke cigarettes, but Lenin bans smoking inside the carriage. A queue forms outside the single toilet (where smoking is allowed), and Lenin introduces "toilet passes," which he issues personally.

ARMORED CAR IN THE SPOTLIGHT

After resting in Stockholm, the Bolsheviks leave aboard a train to Petrograd. But even now Lenin is very afraid that they will be arrested—in Russia. At Beloostrov Station on the Russian border, he is greeted by some comradely faces: his sister Maria, his friend Alexandra Kollontai, and Kamenev (whom he chastises for the overly moderate tone of the party newspaper, *Pravda*, which he oversees).

But the first question Lenin asks is: Will he be arrested? They smile back. The workers who have met Lenin at the border station give him an ovation and carry him aloft into the waiting room. Lenin does not understand what is going on and thinks that he is about to be torn to pieces. He does not give a speech and instead limits himself to a couple of slogans.

Soviet textbooks will describe Lenin's triumphant arrival at Finland Station in Petrograd itself on 16 April as something unique. In fact, it is just one of many "revolutionary homecomings": Tsereteli, Babushka, Plekhanov, Vera Zasulich, Vera Figner, the Socialist-Revolutionary (SR) leaders Chernov and Savinkov, the anarchist Kropotkin, and the leader of the Mensheviks Martov are all greeted by enthusiastic crowds.

A guard of honor welcomes Lenin with a rendition of the *Marseillaise*. He is handed a huge bouquet of flowers and taken to the royal pavilion to meet a delegation from the Petrograd Soviet. The head of the Petrograd

Soviet, the Menshevik Chkheidze, delivers a welcoming speech, which sounds more like a warning. He urges Lenin to collaborate with his comrades from other parties and to help rally all political forces in support of the nascent democracy. But Lenin, the head of the most radical Marxist party and the *enfant terrible* of the revolution, seems not to hear. "Comrades, soldiers, sailors, workers!" he shouts. "The predatory imperialist war marks the start of civil war across Europe. . . . The sun of the global socialist revolution has risen. In Germany the soil is ripening. We will observe the gradual collapse of European imperialism. . . . Long live the global socialist revolution!"

Lenin is carried to a crowded square, illuminated by spotlights. A day earlier this journalist and political theoretician from Zurich was barely known; now he is greeted as a revolutionary hero.

Lenin is raised aloft and placed in an armored car. His slogans are drowned in the noise of the crowd. But what happens to Lenin himself at this moment? A month ago he described himself as an old man who would not live to see his dream. Three days ago he was mortally afraid that he would be shot by German soldiers. An hour ago he was sure that he would be arrested on the station platform. He, the authoritarian leader of a small sect, suddenly turns into a superstar. He stands in the spotlight and is applauded by everyone in the giant square. It is unlikely that Lenin ever expected such a triumph (so far completely undeserved), but the greeting at the station gives him confidence. Lenin is taken from the armored car to the mansion of Matilda Kschessinskaya, which now serves as the Bolsheviks' headquarters.

LIVES OF THE FORMER ONES

The euphoria of the February revolution continues in Petrograd for several months. However, many are horrified by what is happening—not only members of the old government who have ended up in prison, but also all the former elite, the former *beau monde* of Petrograd. Their symbol is Matilda Kschessinskaya, Russia's most famous ballerina.

Forced to flee from her house with her son Vova, Kschessinskaya is now in hiding at the apartment of the actor Yuryev, who is currently playing the lead role in a monumental production of Meyerhold's *Masquerade*. The apartment is inspected by soldiers and sailors, but they do not know Kschessinskaya in person and so leave her alone. There are rumors in the city that she has been killed. When the revolution comes to an end, she meets with Kerensky and asks to be allowed to return to her house. She also writes to the Petrograd Soviet, but to no avail.

The life of the imperial family also changes forever. In addition to Nicholas and Alexandra, Miechen is also under house arrest, as well as her two sons and Grand Dukes Andrei and Boris, in the town of Kislovodsk. They are not charged with any crimes. Miechen's eldest son, Kirill, the first member of the imperial family to swear allegiance to the Provisional Government, remains in Petrograd. He gives an interview to the *Petrograd Gazette* in which he disassociates himself from the former regime.

None of the Romanovs is able to preserve their former way of life. The emperor-not-to-be Mikhail still lives at Gatchina. On one occasion, in response to a request for a private train from Petrograd to his residence, the Ministry of Railways replies that Citizen Romanov can buy a ticket at the booking office like everyone else. Even the little Princess Maria, the former tsar's cousin, who worked as a nurse in a military hospital in Pskov, is forced to quit and move to Tsarskoye Selo—the authorities say that Pskov is no longer safe for her.

Grand Duke Dmitry, exiled to Persia for the murder of Rasputin, decides not to return to his homeland. "Am I supposed to go back and calmly observe the unfolding chaos and be subjected to insults for bearing the name of Romanov? This I cannot do," he writes to his father and relocates instead to the Persian capital, Tehran.

However, another of Rasputin's assassins, Felix Yusupov, returns from exile to Petrograd immediately after the tsar's abdication.

EXECUTION IN KIEV

Empress Dowager Maria Feodorovna, having said goodbye to her son in Mogilev, returns to Kiev, where she moved a year ago. She is in a state of shock. Her son-in-law, Grand Duke Sandro, tries to persuade the sixty-nine-year-old former empress to leave Kiev for his Crimean estate, but she refuses, saying that she would prefer to be "arrested and imprisoned."

Yet the revolution in Kiev is bloodless. The most notable incident is a symbolic execution on Dumskaya Square (now Maidan Nezalezhnosti, or Independence Square). There stands a monument to former Prime Minister Pyotr Stolypin, who was killed six years earlier at the Kiev Opera House. On 16 March a ceremonial trial of Stolypin (as a symbol of the old regime) is held, during which he is sentenced to death by hanging. A gallows-like structure is set up and used to drag the statue from its pedestal.

Petrograd looks kindly upon Ukrainian self-determination: in March the Provisional Government authorizes Kiev to offer teaching in the Ukrainian language, with the proviso that Russian-language tuition would still be available.

Regular rallies are held in Kiev, which members of the imperial family who live in the city find disturbing. Grand Duke Sandro recalls a demonstration under the slogans: "Bring our sons and husbands back from the front!" "Down with the capitalist government!" "We want peace and an independent Ukraine!"

In late March the Provisional Government finally decides to send Maria Feodorovna, along with her daughters Xenia and Olga, and her son-in-law Sandro, from Kiev to Crimea. The decision saves all their lives.

In April, in Crimea, their dwellings are searched by a group of commissioners, who turn up at 5:30 a.m. when everyone is asleep. The search lasts five hours, during which Maria Feodorovna's papers are all confiscated. Above all, she bemoans the loss of her deceased husband's letters and a Danish copy of the Bible, a present from her mother.

Maria Feoderovna and her daughters live at the Ai-Todor estate, owned by Sandro. Nearby, at the Dulber estate, lives the retired supreme commander-in-chief, Grand Duke Nikolai Nikolaevich, with his brother Peter and their Montenegrin wives.

PRISONERS OF TSARSKOYE SELO

The imperial family members cooped up at Tsarskoye Selo have no idea of the behind-the-scenes wrangling in Petrograd and elsewhere over their future. The papers continue to publish revelations, as if making up for years of censorship. Before the revolution, the only permissible object of political satire was Germany's Kaiser Wilhelm II. Now Nicholas, Alexandra, Rasputin, and any member of the imperial family and the court are fair game.

On 1 April the press publishes Alexandra's final telegrams to her husband, in which she urges him to be tough. "The empress seems scared. The public agitation against her is rising," recalls her lady-in-waiting Elizaveta Naryshkina.

The imperial family's relocation to England seemed a done deal a month ago. However, King George V now has cold feet. Despite being Nicholas's maternal—and Alexandra's paternal—cousin, the British monarch is more concerned with the domestic political situation in England than any sense of moral or familial duty. The British press is closely following the events in

Russia and publishes reports from Russian newspapers. George V fears that the appearance of the Romanovs will provoke unrest, ruin his reputation, and destabilize the shaky (in his view) British monarchy.

On 5 April the king's private secretary, Lord Stamfordham, writes to Foreign Minister Arthur Balfour with a request to withdraw the invitation to Nicholas and Alexandra. He argues that the arrival of the disgraced Russian monarch and his family is opposed not only by the aristocrats inside their private clubs, but also by the Labour Party in the House of Commons and the man in the street. "The King believes that the presence of the Russian imperial family (especially Empress Alexandra) in this country will cause numerous complications," he writes. "I am sure that you understand how difficult this situation will be for our royal family."

The government does not demur. "Perhaps we should suggest Spain or the south of France as more suitable destinations for the tsar?" says Lord Balfour.

The imperial family at Tsarskoye Selo knows nothing of this. Their only link with the outside world is via Justice Minister Kerensky, who visits them from time to time. Soon enough, even the imperial family falls under Kerensky's spell. Naryshkina regrets that Nicholas did not surround himself with people like Kerensky when he was on the throne: "If the Sovereign had rid himself of the cult of autocracy, both mystical and political, and encircled himself with sensible minds, instead of a bunch of scoundrels, everything would have been different." Nicholas himself takes a liking to Kerensky.

The former emperor's diary in the spring of 1917, after his abdication, reads like that of a bored gardener. Nicholas does not yet know that his cousin George V has abandoned him. In fact, he knows nothing about his future at all. He has no idea how long his family will remain at Tsarskoye Selo, or whether they will be allowed to join their relatives in Crimea.

THE END OF LENIN'S CAREER

Having arrived from Finland Station to Kschessinskaya's mansion, Lenin greets the crowd from the balcony, after which he returns inside the mansion and delivers a keynote address to a group of his most ardent supporters. His speech is like that of an alien who has just fallen to Earth. Charismatic as always, Lenin cajoles his listeners, but what he says is beyond the realm of fantasy. For the crowd, the collapse of the monarchy and the revolution are a blessing. But Lenin maintains the opposite: there is nothing good about the revolution or the new democratic government. The new regime is already growing weak and should be replaced, he says. The defense of the Motherland, in his view, is only about protecting one gang of capitalists from another. The imperialist war (against Germany) must turn into a civil war (against Russia's own capitalists). The defensive war must be stopped, the land and banks nationalized, and the property of the landowners and aristocrats confiscated, whereupon the peoples of other countries will immediately join the Russian revolution. It is during this speech that he proposes renaming his political organization the "Communist Party."

"I felt like I was being hit over the head with a chain," recalls Nikolai Sukhanov, a member of the executive committee of the Petrograd Soviet. "One thing was clear: I, a free man, did not see eye to eye with Lenin."

The next day the Tauride Palace hosts a meeting of the All-Russian Conference of Soviets of Workers' and Soldiers' Deputies—the new quasi-parliament now includes delegates from all over the country. Lenin goes there, having barely slept. His speech, which becomes known as the "April Theses"—shocks the entire assembly. He proposes to stop the war, even in self-defense, to destroy the state, including the army (replacing it with "armed people's units"), the bureaucracy, the police, and the banks, to overthrow the Provisional Government and to transfer power to the Soviets. It sounds like the end of the world. The last point about the Soviets should, in theory, be well received, but after all that has gone before the audience looks at Lenin as if he is deranged and dangerous. Lenin is desperate to prevent the unification of the Bolsheviks and the Mensheviks, because in this case he will become an ordinary party figure inside a huge party led by Tsereteli.

There is pandemonium. Tsereteli mounts the podium and adopts a rather affable and conciliatory tone. Citing Marx, he says that lone figures can make mistakes, but not the people. He is willing to forgive Lenin's errors of judgment and to offer him his hand. After Lenin's hysterical speech, Tsereteli's assured manner wins the day. Lenin leaves the building angrily, accompanied by many, but by no means all, fellow party members. Some Bolsheviks prefer the more constructive Tsereteli to their own leader.

"Deny the revolution if you want to, but the rest of us here will continue along this path," says the presiding Nikolai Chkheidze in Lenin's wake.

"Yesterday Lenin completely failed in front of the Soviet," Milyukov gleefully reports to Ambassador Paléologue. There follows what Krupskaya describes as "baiting." All the papers quote his "defeatism" and, recalling that he and his comrades returned to Russia with the consent of the German emperor, call him a German spy. The commander of the sailors' detachment tells reporters that he is ashamed that he greeted "Lenin the traitor" at Finland Station. Anti-Lenin crowds gather beneath the windows of the Bolsheviks' headquarters. He goes out on the balcony to speak to them, but ends up having to hide inside the building. It seems that his political star has begun to wane after just one day.

NO ANNEXATIONS OR INDEMNITIES

The war remains an acute problem and the most polarizing factor in society. Nobody argues against the need to continue it (except Lenin), but there is no consensus inside the Provisional Government as to how it should end. Foreign Minister Pavel Milyukov and War Minister Alexander Guchkov are piously sure that the centuries-old dream of starry-eyed Russian imperialism is to be fulfilled, and that Russia is destined to seize Constantinople. However, the idea is not shared by all. Kerensky, for instance, is convinced that the war should be purely defensive—Russian territory should be freed from German occupation, but nothing more than that. He is against new conquests and "annexations and indemnities." The words "annexations and indemnities" are on everyone's lips—in trams, theatres, and soldiers' barracks.

Tsereteli and, hence, almost all the socialist deputies share Kerensky's opinion. They believe that the war should be conducted only in self-defense to liberate Russian soil from German troops with no further offensives or assistance to France to regain Alsace-Lorraine or to Britain to win even more colonies. In other words, the new democratic government must reject any secret agreements made between the tsarist regime and the Entente powers, say the socialists.

In mid-March the Petrograd Soviet adopts its "Appeal to the peoples of the world"—the foreign policy doctrine of the new Russian state. It states that the revolution will not allow Russia to be crushed by hostile military forces, and that there will be "no annexations or indemnities," only the "free self-determination of peoples." Since the Russian democratic state genuinely considers itself to be the most progressive in the world, it wants to set an example to all. Such values will enter the global mainstream only after the Second World War. The "Appeal to the peoples of the world" is ahead of its time; its principles are exactly the same as those outlined in the Helsinki Accords, signed in 1975.

A split appears in the Provisional Government: seven of the twelve ministers are on the side of Kerensky and the Petrograd Soviet, including Prime Minister Lvov, Finance Minister Tereshchenko, and Industry Minister Konovalov. Against are Guchkov and the Kadets, led by Foreign Minister Milyukov. Milyukov tells French Ambassador Paléologue that he will stand his ground—if the government rejects its commitments to its allies and abandons its claim to Constantinople, he will immediately resign.

"EAT, DRINK, RUN"

Alexandra, the favorite daughter of Leo Tolstoy, works as a frontline nurse during the spring of 1917. She describes some of the arguments among the soldiers: "Why the hell do we need this revolution?! Instead of the tsar, we've got these Lvovs and Kerenskys. All the same, we're still sat in the trenches, covered in dirt and lice," complain shell-shocked soldiers in the hospital, smearing muddy tears across their faces.

"Enough of fighting the Germans. It's time to fight the *bourgeoisie* and take the land from the landowners and the factories from the factory owners," says a paramedic.

"You're all cowardly bastards. You want to sell your homeland to the Germans. A soldier's duty is to fight for Russia until the bitter end," responds a platoon commander.

The paramedic is a Bolshevik agitator, and his argument seems convincing to many soldiers.

Petrograd is plagued by the same doubts. Whereas today peace and human life are universal values (at least on paper), their equivalents a century ago are war and debt. Refusing to fight is considered shameful not only by the officer corps, but by most members of the intelligentsia as well. Gippius is outraged by the "stupid, ignorant" and "cynical, naive" deserters: "They have no glimmer of conscience. They are guided by three instincts: eat, drink, run," she writes. Gippius wants the war to end, of course, but with dignity, for that is the "only way to redeem the past, preserve the future and recover one's senses."

The poetess hopes that her friend Kerensky will be sufficiently firm and resolute. She fears that he is not up to the task.

People from various political camps believe that victory is the main objective of the war, including another friend of Gippius, the former terrorist Boris Savinkov. Savinkov arrives by boat from France, along with his fellow SR party member Viktor Chernov. Their paths immediately diverge.

Chernov joins the executive committee of the Petrograd Soviet (and Tsereteli's "star chamber"), becoming one of its leaders. Savinkov, to the surprise of many, departs for the front line as a commissioner of the Provisional Government to campaign for "war to the bitter end."

"WE ARE NO LONGER ABLE TO"

Gippius's archenemy, someone she has long despised as a symbol of all things vile and cowardly, is Maxim Gorky. "Weak, pitiful and dull-witted" are among the epithets she attaches to him.

The Merezhkovskys' apartment on Shpalernaya Street and Gorky's home on Kronverksky Avenue can be regarded as the two oppositely charged poles of Petrograd. Gippius, Merezhkovsky, and Filosofov live near the Tauride Palace, and their abode is the headquarters of the liberal movement, a place often frequented by ministers. Gorky and Andreyeva live in the middle class district, next to the house of Kschessinskaya and the Peter and Paul Fortress. Their guests and associates are socialists and members of the executive committee of the Petrograd Soviet.

Yet both Gorky and Gippius have doubts about the war: "Tens of millions of the healthiest, most able-bodied people have been severed from their productive existence to go and kill each other," writes Gorky. He is horrified by the outbreak of violence in the country after the revolution and hopes that the "outpouring of spiritual filth" and the "festering storm" are, in fact, signs of healing. Gorky preaches in an almost Tolstoyan spirit, calling for non-violence—the only difference being that he does not believe in God, but in education: "Politics and religion divide people; nothing rectifies the human soul as swiftly as the influence of science and art."

On 13 March Alexander Benois, Gorky's friend, pays a visit to Paléologue. "The war cannot go on," says Benois, who, as his name suggests, is of French origin. "I know that Russia's honor is linked to its alliances. But necessity is the law of history. No one is obliged to perform the impossible."

In response, the French ambassador lectures the artist on modern geopolitics. France and Britain are rich enough to wage war until victory is secured, especially now that America has entered the war. For them, "domination of the seas and control over Mesopotamia, Thessaloniki and Germany's colonies" are at stake. If Russia pulls out of the war, it stands to lose Kurland, Lithuania, Poland, Galicia, and Bessarabia at the very least, not to mention its prestige in the East and the prospects of winning Constantinople. According to Paléologue, it is not just a question of Russia's honor and well-being, but also its "national existence."

Perplexed, Benois tearfully says that he does not disagree, but Russia cannot continue the war: "Really, we are no longer able to."

He is not exaggerating. In early April German troops suddenly break through the Russian lines at the Stokhod River in western Ukraine. It is a particularly painful blow, for this is the site of the Brusilov Offensive of 1916, a great victory for Russia. Now, a year later, the Russian army has been defeated at exactly the same spot, with another twenty-five thousand men killed or captured. Moreover, it is the first battle since the revolution took place, and it demonstrates that the army has lost the will to fight.

ARMY IS SICK

Guchkov, the new war minister, tries to boost morale and discipline in the army by setting up a commission that includes members of the Petrograd Soviet as well as officers. Guchkov appoints his old friend Alexei Polivanov, the former war minister, as its head. To Guchkov's dismay, the commission soon drafts a "Declaration of soldiers' rights," granting them the civil rights to join a political party, send correspondence confidentially, and wear civilian clothes when off duty. The generals believe that the declaration spells the end of all discipline. Polivanov throws up his hands, saying that he could do nothing to prevent it.

In mid-April the conflict between Kerensky and Milyukov over their opposing war aims reaches a climax. Kerensky (without consulting Milyukov) tells the press that the government plans to clarify its war objectives in respect of Russia's wartime alliances. The very next day Milyukov denies it, saying that nothing of the sort is planned. Rumor has it that Foreign Minister Milyukov is about to be sacked and replaced by the "thinker" Plekhanov.

Under pressure from the Petrograd Soviet and his ministerial colleagues, Milyukov publishes a formal appeal to Russia's allies, which formulates the country's rejection of the idea of capturing Constantinople and its readiness for peace without annexations or indemnities. But, at the last minute, he cannot help adding a short preface of his own, saying that the "popular desire" in Russia is to see the war through to the bitter end, to secure "sanctions and guarantees" that will make future wars impossible, and to "fulfill Russia's obligations to its allies."

The note is signed on 18 April, the day when the rest of the world is celebrating Workers' Day (1 May, according to the Gregorian calendar). By decision of the Petrograd Soviet, the Russian capital hosts its own "May Day" demonstration.

Prince Lvov sends the note to the Petrograd Soviet. Tsereteli recalls that the content stunned everyone who read it. "Milyukov is the evil spirit of the revolution," whispers Chkheidze.

The very next day Milyukov's note is published. There is uproar. "The revolutionary Russian democracy plans to shed blood not only for the restoration of Belgium and Serbia, but to give England more colonies in Africa, as well as Palestine and Baghdad, give France the left bank of the Rhine, and give Italy Dalmatia and Albania, because everyone knows that these are Russia's 'obligations to its allies,'" storms the left-wing publicist Razumnik Ivanov. The Petrograd Soviet flies into a rage. Milyukov has hoodwinked everyone. Kerensky is accused of knowing about and approving what becomes known as the "Milyukov note." Kerensky considers resigning.

On the morning of 20 April, Prince Lvov meets Tsereteli for urgent talks. News has arrived that soldiers from several regiments are on their way to the Mariinsky Palace to arrest the Provisional Government. It comes as a surprise, even to the executive committee of the Petrograd Soviet—everyone is angry with Milyukov, but no one is planning an armed uprising.

It turns out to be the handiwork of Lenin. Milyukov's note has restored yesterday's political corpse to life. He and his Bolshevik agitators have always said that the Provisional Government is "bourgeois," "imperialist," and waging war in the interests of foreign capitalists, not their own people. Milyukov's note has merely confirmed what they knew all along.

Coincidentally, the Provisional Government is saved from arrest by Guchkov. Because of his illness, the ministers adjourn to his apartment on the Moika River. The insurgent soldiers and sailors, having reached the Mariinsky Palace, discover it to be empty. Members of the executive committee of the Petrograd Soviet go to meet them to clarify the situation, and to make sure that Milyukov's note is not a pretext to overthrow the government. The regiments disperse, and the first Bolshevik coup ends in failure.

That same evening, the executive committee of the Petrograd Soviet and the Provisional Government meet to discuss their future plans. Prince Lvov says that he has no desire to cling to power and is ready to hand it to the Petrograd Soviet if its leaders are confident that they will cope better with the situation. But the socialists do not want to form a new government, knowing that it will be much more difficult for them to consolidate society, for example, to find a common language with the officer corps and big business. They do not demand the resignation of the entire government, only Milyukov.

Guchkov delivers an impassioned speech in which he says that he, a devout monarchist, was forced to choose between his sovereign and his country, for he was sure that the weak emperor was the main obstacle to victory in the war. He and many officers forswore their oaths and joined the revolution to save Russia. But a month later it seems to have been in vain, for victory is now an even more remote prospect.

The meeting ends with no decision taken. The next day, a new demonstration takes place at the Mariinsky Palace, this time in support of Milyukov and Guchkov, and in favor of continuing the war. Milyukov delivers a balcony speech in which he says that the shouts of "Down with Milyukov" really mean "Down with Russia." The crowd cheers and applauds.

On 21 April the government holds a meeting at the Mariinsky Palace until late into the night. Milyukov, Rodzianko, and the head of the Petrograd Military District, General Kornilov, speak from the balcony, trying to calm the crowd. Rumors are circulating that a massacre is about to begin; Kornilov is alleged to have summoned government-loyal troops from Tsarskoye Selo to Petrograd.

The main item on the government's agenda is how to pacify the crowd. Guchkov says that he has at his disposal several thousand very reliable soldiers. He admits that they should not be used to suppress the unrest, but if an armed attack were to be launched on the government, there would have to be some kind of resistance. "Alexander Ivanovich [Guchkov], I warn you that I shall resign if one drop of blood is spilt," he is told by Alexander Konovalov, Russia's industry minister and a childhood friend. Konovalov has the backing of almost all the other ministers: any use of weapons would deprive the Provisional Government of its moral authority and set it on the path of tsarist repression.

That same evening the executive committee of the Petrograd Soviet, for a period of three days, bans all demonstrations and forbids the military from leaving its barracks without the consent of the Soviets. This also applies to Kornilov's units and the ones the Bolsheviks tried to use to "arrest the Provisional Government." The disorder immediately comes to an end.

DICTATOR, COALITION, AND HOUND OF
THE BASKERVILLES

Thus, the Petrograd Soviet demonstrates its ability to control the situation and calm the unrest provoked by the Bolsheviks, making the executive authorities look feeble by comparison. General Kornilov resigns. Prince Lvov, a true democrat, says that if the Petrograd Soviet enjoys such authority, it should be invited into the government.

The same idea is suggested by Kerensky. He is thoroughly fed up with the incessant reproaches and complaints coming from members of the Petrograd Soviet. But things are not so simple. Tsereteli does not want to enter the government, for he believes that his place is in the Petrograd Soviet. The executive committee rejects the proposal.

The government crisis deepens with every passing day. Milyukov departs for the front line, and the next government session turns into a demonstration against him. Guchkov listens in silence to the insults addressed to his absent colleague. In years gone by, he would have challenged the offenders to a duel, but now he just leaves the room and writes a resignation letter to Lvov. To make it final, he sends a copy to a newspaper. After resigning, Guchkov immediately leaves Petrograd to serve at the front as a simple warrant officer.

The Provisional Government is only two months old, but its authority is already undermined. On the day of Guchkov's resignation, the former emperor Nicholas, isolated in his palace at Tsarskoye Selo, mentions politics in his diary for the first time since his abdication. "Yesterday I learnt about Gen. Kornilov's departure from the post of commander of the Petrograd Military District, and tonight about the resignation of Guchkov," writes Nicholas, who blames the Soviets for both. "What is Providence preparing for poor Russia? May God's will reign over us." After this brief digression, he returns to domestic issues. That day, for instance, he notes that he has been reading *The Hound of the Baskervilles* to his children.

Kerensky, meanwhile, is continuing talks on cooperation with the Petrograd Soviet, which Guchkov's resignation should facilitate. Prince Lvov holds parallel talks with Tsereteli, which bear fruit: the executive committee votes to enter the government by forty-four votes to nineteen.

Milyukov promptly resigns, and exhausting negotiations begin with the Petrograd Soviet on who will take which position. The socialists and liberals manage to come to an agreement. Tsereteli, according to Milyukov, "sacrifices himself" to avert a civil war by accepting the minor post as head of the Ministry of the Post Office and Telegraph, which will allow him to continue his work in the Petrograd Soviet. The leader of the SR Party, Viktor Chernov, becomes the new agriculture minister, responsible for agrarian reform. The question of filling the post vacated by Guchkov is assigned by Prince Lvov to Commander-in-Chief Alekseyev, who, having consulted the generals, nominates Kerensky. As a result, Kerensky is appointed the new war minister. The socialists (the Mensheviks and the SRs, including Kerensky, now a member of the latter) get six seats. Hence, the new government can claim legitimacy by representing all political forces, except for the Bolsheviks. The political crisis is resolved peacefully.

THERE IS NO SUCH PARTY

On 4 June the first Congress of Soviets—the parliament of the Russian revolution—is convened in Petrograd, including representatives of hundreds of soviets from all across Russia. Tsereteli addresses the congress, saying that hitherto the supreme representative body of revolutionary power in the country was *de facto* the Petrograd Soviet, but now it should hand over its authority to the congress. The congress should then elect its own executive committee and hold a vote of confidence on its predecessors, who are now part of the Provisional Government.

Sitting there in the hall is Lenin, who is effectively the target of Tsereteli's speech when he accuses the Bolsheviks of "agitation" to applause from the audience.

In response to Lenin's demand to stop the war, Tsereteli says that a separate peace is impossible, because the war cannot be ended unilaterally. As for the accusation of being unable to solve the country's pressing problems, he says that in two months no one could. A key point in Tsereteli's speech concerns the "unification of all living forces" (i.e., the government should allow its opponents to operate freely, not just its supporters).

At the same time, the government should be strong enough to "resist the reckless experiments that threaten the future of the revolution, challenge the authorities and risk sowing the seeds of civil war."

"At the moment, there is no political party in Russia which is prepared to take full power on itself," says Tsereteli. "Yes, there is!" shouts Lenin from his seat. "There is not a single party able to lay claim to power," continues Tsereteli, "but there have been statements to that effect from irresponsible groups on both the right and the left."

In his view, Lenin is a fringe counter-revolutionary. The audience applauds. The next day it will be Lenin's turn to speak from the podium, and

462 | MIKHAIL ZYGAR

the audience will laugh when he says that the Bolsheviks are in fact ready to seize power at any moment.

Tsereteli's proposals receive the most votes, and Lenin's are rejected. The Congress of Soviets issues a vote of confidence in the Provisional Government, the Petrograd Soviet, and Tsereteli's strategy. It seems that democracy has passed its first test.

A PARADE IN PARIS

In April, Diaghilev's troupe moves from Rome to Paris. They have heard bits and pieces about what is happening in Russia, and are infected with the revolutionary spirit. They instigate a revolution of their own—in the world of art and ballet.

Having suffered greatly under the imperial regime, Diaghilev has reason to rejoice at its downfall. However, his main opponents in recent years have been show-business magnates who have stolen his artists, wrecked his plans, and ruined the public's artistic tastes with low-quality entertainment. Diaghilev wants to lead his own revolution against the lowest common denominator, against mass culture. The forty-five-year-old Diaghilev enlists the help of some younger associates: his new set designer is the thirty-six-year-old Pablo Picasso, his script writer is the twenty-eight-year-old Jean Cocteau, and his choreographer (and male lover) is the twenty-year-old Leonid Myasin.

Cocteau wants to add circus-like elements to the ballet, while Picasso is keen to design the sets and costumes in the new Cubist style. Most of all, Diaghilev likes Picasso's idea of depicting French and American capitalists in the form of animated, rectangular billboards representing the vulgarity of the magnates and show business itself. In creating the American skyline, Picasso paints a collage with a skyscraper, a mosaic of faces, and a flashy billboard with the word "Parade"—which becomes the title of the production they are creating.

Before the premiere of *Parade* in Paris, Diaghilev's troupe stages their trademark *Firebird* by Stravinsky. The ballet finale usually sees the appearance on stage of the Russian folk hero Ivan Tsarevich wearing a crown. But in view of the new political realities, this time Diaghilev decides that he should don a red cap and hold a red flag. Diaghilev is sure that in republican France such a salute to the Russian revolution will be received enthusiastically. He would be advised to follow the news more closely.

The Russian revolution was indeed popular in Paris, but not for long. The French public had hoped that it would not interfere with Russia's war effort. But the debacle at the Stokhod River—the Russian army's only battle in the spring of 1917—showed that it was ill prepared. The emboldened Germans, fighting on two fronts, feel able to deploy massive forces to the West and put up unexpectedly strong resistance to the Franco-British Nivelle Offensive: in one month the French lose one hundred and eighty thousand men, the British one hundred and sixty thousand, and the Germans another one hundred and sixty thousand.

The Russian "betrayal" and the terrible losses are the main topics of the French papers. In this context, the red flag in the hands of Ivan Tsarevich incenses the patriotic Parisian public. Afterwards, Diaghilev tries to explain in an interview that the red flag is just a symbol of the struggle for freedom. But he is slated by the press and theatre critics, and his business partners threaten to tear up his contract and torpedo *Parade*. For the next performance of *Firebird*, Diaghilev makes sure that Ivan Tsarevich wears a crown.

However, the real scandal lies ahead. The premiere of *Parade* on 18 May comes at the most inopportune moment: the Nivelle Offensive has failed and patriotic Parisians are ready to be offended by anything. They believe that they are being mocked by Picasso's Cubist scenery and Cubist costumes. The last straw for the audience is the onstage appearance of a Cubist horse with a Cubist muzzle. The audience hurls insults at Picasso and Diaghilev, calling them Germans. That is followed by the chant "Death to the Russians!" People in the stalls go up to the stage and bang their fists on it, demanding the curtain to come down.

However, for Parisian bohemians, *Parade* is a resounding success. Claude Debussy tries to contact Diaghilev to congratulate him on his artistic, if not political, triumph, but "it is easier to get in touch with the Lord our God," says the composer.

PERSUADER-IN-CHIEF

Kerensky, the new war minister, does what Guchkov refused to do: he signs the "Declaration of soldiers' rights." He does not believe that the war should end, however. On the contrary, he wants to show that under his command Russia can achieve victory and save France and the Western Front from the German onslaught. According to Kerensky, the German command plans to "paralyze the Russian Front through peaceful propaganda and fraternization, so as to concentrate the full might of the German army on the Western Front and deliver a crushing blow before the arrival of American troops." To thwart this plan, someone in Russia needs to take the initiative and resume hostilities.

On 14 May Kerensky publishes an order to attack along with a pathos-filled proclamation addressed to the soldiers: "In the name of saving the free Russia, go where your leaders and government take you. . . ." Kerensky then sets off on a nationwide tour in his new role as war minister. He visits army units, confident that his charisma will work wonders. It does not let him down: even his detractors admit that Kerensky is an accomplished propagandist.

Kerensky is compared to both Napoleon and Joan of Arc. He travels around by any means of transport there is: plane, car, foot. He greets war heroes and bandages wounds himself. Skeptical officers call him the "persuader-in-chief," but he is not offended.

The plan to go on the offensive was approved before the revolution by Nicholas II. The main strike is to be aimed at the Southwestern Front under the command of General Brusilov—just like the year before.

The offensive begins on 18 June, and Kerensky is there at the frontline command. Following the first successful attack, the Petrograd press praises Kerensky and the military to the skies. In the space of three weeks, Kalush and Galich (then part of Austria-Hungary, today in Ukraine) are occupied, thousands of Austrians are captured, and the front line advances thirty kilometers to the west. The Russian military loses around forty thousand men. On the one hand, it is not much compared to the French losses on the Western Front or during the Brusilov Offensive (which killed ten times as many). But the fallen soldiers belong to elite units, which are the only ones still committed to the cause. Almost immediately the advance starts to stall.

"NEITHER REBELLION NOR SUBMISSION"

In early July, Kerensky, who now spends almost all his time at the front, goes instead to the rear—to Kiev to hold talks with the Ukrainian Central Rada.* A serious problem is brewing between Kiev and Petrograd. For several months, the Central Rada has been developing plans for Ukrainian autonomy. On 16 May a Ukrainian delegation headed by Volodymyr Vynny-

---

* The Ukrainian parliament.

chenko had travelled to Petrograd, but was not received by any ministers. The Ukrainian question was postponed until the convocation of the Constituent Assembly.

In Petrograd there is no consensus about how Russia should be structured. The Kadets believe that the country should be indivisible, while the SR leader Chernov suggests creating a "United States of Eastern Europe, Siberia and Turkestan." Either way, the Provisional Government prefers to hide behind the promise of the Constituent Assembly, without deciding anything.

So Kiev opts for more decisive action. In early June, at the height of mobilization, and contrary to a ban imposed by Kerensky, the First All-Ukrainian Military Congress is held in Kiev, at which the creation of a separate Ukrainian army is put forward as a key demand. At the same time, the Central Rada publishes the First Universal—the main policy document and manifesto of the new Ukraine. It is a constitution in everything but name, drafted according to the principle of "neither rebellion nor submission" propounded by Vynnychenko.

On 28 June a top-level delegation from the Provisional Government arrives in Kiev: Tsereteli, Foreign Minister Mikhail Tereshchenko (who was born in Kiev), and War Minister Kerensky. The negotiations are successful. The Provisional Government agrees that Ukraine should be granted autonomy, but only when the issue of the Russian Constituent Assembly has been decided. The Central Rada promises not to proclaim autonomy unilaterally.

The negotiators depart from Kiev with a sense of accomplishment. On 1 July, Kerensky, Tereshchenko, and Tsereteli return to Petrograd. But even before their arrival back in the Russian capital, it becomes apparent that the agreement with Ukraine could bury the Provisional Government. The Kadet ministers put forward an ultimatum: they will leave the government if the agreement with Ukraine is approved.

THE END OF THE LIBERAL DREAM

The Russian liberals (i.e., the Kadets) are reeling. Four months ago they were the Russian opposition and the main force behind the "progressive bloc" in the Duma. They were the ones who made the February Revolution—or at least picked up the pieces of power that had fallen from the hands of Nicholas II. The Kadet leader, Pavel Milyukov, drew up the first list of names of the Provisional Government virtually on a napkin and read it out for the first time to soldiers gathered in the foyer of the Tauride Palace.

However, four months later the situation has changed so much that the liberal Kadets now seem like conservatives: many of them would prefer a constitutional monarchy to a republic, but if a republic is inevitable, they would at least like it to be based on established practices.

In the post-revolution period, yesterday's main opposition is too moderate to be popular. In late June, elections are held in Moscow to the Duma, which are seen as "primaries" ahead of the elections to the Constituent Assembly. Moscow has always been a bastion of liberals, in particular the Kadets, in contrast to Petrograd, where the political mood in the street is set by the one-hundred-thousand-strong garrison.

Throughout June, a pre-election campaign runs in Moscow under the slogan "Like in Europe." The seven parties involved plaster campaign posters over fences and drop leaflets from airplanes. The Kadets' campaign is sluggish, and their wealthy voters are more passive than those of the left-wing parties. They seem to think that they will win because the party is listed first on the ballot paper.

In the end, the SRs score a convincing victory in Moscow, winning 116 seats out of 200 (57.98 percent of the vote). The liberal Kadets come second with 34 seats (16.85 percent of the vote). The remaining seats are divided between the Mensheviks and the Bolsheviks, with 11 percent each.

The Kadets are the only party without leftist convictions. However, it is not their economic beliefs, but their international policy that marks them out. The liberals of the early twentieth century are imperialists. They want Russia to be free and democratic, yet remain an empire. They oppose regional self-determination, condemn Finland for its "betrayal," and are outraged by the behavior of Ukraine.

The next day the Provisional Government votes by a majority to ratify the agreement with the Central Rada. Four Kadet ministers announce their resignation, and a fifth, Nekrasov, withdraws from the party. Kerensky returns to the front in a calm state of mind, not realizing that the departure of the liberals from the government marks the start of a new revolution.

|| Chapter 14 ||

LEON TROTSKY

in which Leon Trotsky and Lev Kamenev don't wish for a Bolshevik revolt anymore, since they believe it to be completely unnecessary

A CIRCUS STAR

When Leon Trotsky finally gets back to Petrograd after being released from the Canadian "concentration camp," the revolution is already two months old. Trotsky goes to a meeting of the Petrograd Soviet, the organization he headed twelve years previously during the 1905 uprising. Back then, he was twenty-six years old. Now thirty-eight, he is surplus to requirements inside the Petrograd Soviet. As a "veteran," he is found a place on the executive committee in an "advisory capacity," but he has no influence on policy. All the roles have been assigned: Tsereteli is in charge; Trotsky is late.

Looking for something to do, he goes to the Modern Circus, located not far from Kschessinskaya's former mansion. It is a favorite haunt for Petrograd locals who are addicted to mass demonstrations. It is here that Trotsky, having lived abroad for so long in isolation, hones his oratorical skills. The daily rallies at the circus are attended by armchair politicians. They satisfy their thirst for entertainment by listening to mostly third-rate speakers who find themselves outside of the political machine but still eager to be heard. Trotsky makes this audience his own.

He criticizes Kerensky and the war against the Central Powers, saying that the government thinks that Russia's soldiers are made of clay and utterly dispensable. He accuses Kerensky of clowning around instead of addressing the soldiers' grievances. Trotsky himself gives very simple answers: to achieve freedom, the war should be stopped and the land should be taken from the landowners. He soon becomes the star turn at the circus—none of his political opponents dare cross the threshold of Trotsky's bastion. But whenever he shows his face at the Petrograd Soviet, he is met with the words: "This isn't a circus, you know."

The first clash between Trotsky and Tsereteli takes place in May. The Petrograd Soviet is trying to stop the ongoing rebellion at Kronstadt. The officers were imprisoned by the sailors during the February revolution and are still locked up. Tsereteli tries to negotiate with the sailors. Having spent eight years in prison, he is horrified by what he has seen and asks the sailors how they can hold people in such conditions. Tsereteli describes Kronstadt as a hotbed of rebellion that could derail the revolution. Some defend the sailors, saying that Kronstadt represents a "deeper" phase of the revolution. One of them is Trotsky.

The popularity of the Bolsheviks and their allies (including the so-called "Interdistrictites," a faction of the RSDLP to which Trotsky belongs) is growing among the soldiers and sailors. Despite being called "pacifists," the Bolsheviks do not speak for peace, but for turning the "imperialist war" into a civil conflict "against the bourgeoisie." Their leaflets state that the revolution has not brought about economic improvements, because the government is controlled by "bankers" and "speculators." It cannot be tolerated any longer—everyone must leave the barracks and overthrow the capitalist ministers, handing over all power to the Soviets, say the leaflets.

Tsereteli's patience runs out on 10 June. He has personally built a fragile coalition of all political forces and now asks his colleagues to disarm the Bolsheviks. Trotsky "trolls" Tsereteli in response: Why pay so much attention to such a small group as the Bolsheviks? Tsereteli responds that the Bolsheviks are indeed a small group, almost unrepresented in the Petrograd Soviet, but they are the weak link that could ruin the revolution: "What the Bolsheviks are doing is not ideological propaganda, it's conspiratorial. Revolutionaries who do not know how to handle a weapon should have it taken from them."

The situation becomes stormy: "Sir, if you are a man of your word, then arrest me!" cries the Bolshevik Lev Kamenev. Most of the Socialist-Revolutionaries and Mensheviks in the Petrograd Soviet disagree with Tsereteli, and his proposal is rejected; the Soviet limits itself to a verbal condemnation of the Bolsheviks' behavior. "Tsereteli was in the minority, yet he was right," his main opponent that day, Leon Trotsky, will write many years later.

WEAK LINK

On 2 July Trotsky, along with fellow art historian Lunacharsky, speaks at a rally at the barracks of the First Machine-Gun Regiment. Trotsky turns the event into a powerful anti-government demonstration: "The mood was upbeat. Everyone cursed Kerensky and swore allegiance to the revolution."

Incited by Trotsky, the machine-gunners head off that same evening to overthrow the Provisional Government under the slogan "The first bullet is for Kerensky." The war minister himself is at that moment just about to depart on a visit to the front for an update on his offensive against the Germans.

The First Machine-Gun Regiment is a strange formation: at the beginning of the year it had around twenty thousand soldiers, almost the same number as a division. Prior to the revolution, its soldiers were sent to the front. Afterwards, they were deployed in the capital to "guard the revolution." A third of them have deserted, while the rest remain at their barracks, actively engaged in the political upheaval. With the start of the June offensive, Kerensky tries to return the regiment to frontline duty, but the soldiers disobey.

On the morning of 3 July, the agitated soldiers of the First Machine-Gun Regiment hold another rally. News breaks that "five capitalist ministers" have resigned (in fact, four Kadets have departed over the situation in Ukraine). The soldiers' favorite slogan (which happens to be "Down with the ten capitalist ministers") has been half fulfilled, which ignites them even more.

The First Machine-Gun Regiment dispatches couriers to the other barracks in Petrograd to inform them that they intend to overthrow the government. One column of soldiers goes to the Mariinsky Palace, where the Provisional Government sits, and another to the Tauride Palace, home of the Petrograd Soviet, to seize power from the former and hand it to the latter. "All power to the Soviet of Workers', Soldiers' and Peasants' Deputies!" and "Down with Kerensky and his offensive!" are written on their banners. It is War Minister Kerensky, the country's most popular politician, who is in the crosshairs of the Bolsheviks. They describe him as a "little Napoleon" who has sacrificed half a million lives in the war.

The crowd arrives at the Mariinsky Palace, but it is empty once again. This time the ministers are meeting at the apartment of Prime Minister Lvov. Some of the marchers start looting shops out of frustration.

The soldiers stop cars in the street and "confiscate" them in the name of the revolution. They even steal Tsereteli's car. There is a feeling of déjà vu: law and order has broken down again, and this time the soldiers are seizing power for themselves. The weather is summery, and this adds to the feverish atmosphere. The soldiers drive around the city in the open cars they have commandeered. Some machine-gunners ride on the fenders for effect. "When will this outrage come to an end?" mutters Grand Duke Nicholas Mikhailovich, walking through the Summer Garden, now "Citizen Romanov," a cousin of the former tsar and once the most liberal of his relatives.

The soldiers approach the former mansion of Kschessinskaya. A perplexed Lev Kamenev comes out onto the balcony—he missed the previous evening's rally, so the militancy of the regiment takes him by surprise. He tries to persuade the machine-gunners to return to their barracks, but they do not listen to him. So Kamenev returns to confer with his comrades—all are in a state of confusion. Lenin is not in the capital. Feeling unwell, he has decided to recuperate at a sanatorium in Finland, departing with his sister on 29 June. The remaining Bolshevik leaders vote against an armed uprising. Trotsky also says that it is premature to overthrow the government. Kamenev and Zinoviev write an article in the next issue of *Pravda*, urging restraint.

LEV KAMENEV

The Tauride Palace hosts another exhausting meeting of the executive committee. Tsereteli, who is simultaneously the leader of the Petrograd Soviet and minister for post and telegraph communications inside the Provisional Government, is in the middle of a speech when news arrives that regiments are approaching to seize power from the government. The Bolshevik Stalin jumps up and tells Tsereteli and Chkheidze that the Bolsheviks have nothing to do with it and that they oppose the uprising. They do not believe him.

Tsereteli's position is unique: Petrograd is essentially undergoing another revolution, which requires him to consolidate power in his own hands, but he resolutely refuses to do so, because the very idea of dictatorship is anathema to him: he wants democracy and is ready to fight against the insurrection. Being a Marxist, he is convinced that the government should consist of representatives of the bourgeoisie. That was the decision of the Congress of Soviets, and the Petrograd Soviet does not have the right to violate it.

The Petrograd Soviet issues another order forbidding the soldiers to leave their barracks, but this time no one obeys: at 8 p.m. on 2 July soldiers from across the city gather near the Tauride Palace. A disorganized mob without orders or objectives, it simply hangs around outside.

The panicky discussions at Kschessinskaya's mansion continue. Various speakers go out onto the balcony to try to calm the soldiers. They are implacable—hence the only option is to join them and lead them, believes Trotsky. Zinoviev and Kamenev's article calling for calm is scrapped. The next morning's issue of the Bolshevik mouthpiece *Pravda* is published with a blank front page.

Instead of the article, a leaflet is printed with the words: "The Provisional Government has collapsed... a new supreme power is needed.... This power can only be the Soviet of Workers', Soldiers' and Peasants' Deputies." The text is written by the editor of *Pravda*, Joseph Stalin.

By midnight all the streets around the Tauride Palace are occupied by armed soldiers. At 2 a.m. they are joined by thirty thousand workers from the Putilovsky plant. Surrounded by the crowd, the executive committee of the Petrograd Soviet realizes, perhaps for the first time, that it is powerless in the face of such an elemental force.

In the morning military vessels sail from Kronstadt to Petrograd, and Lenin boards a train to return to the capital. It is a short distance from Finland Station to Kschessinskaya's mansion. By noon he is there on the balcony. Still swarming below is the feverish crowd. But Lenin is out of sorts. For one thing, he is still sick, and for another, he, like his comrades, is not convinced that the uprising will succeed. "You must show steadfastness, endurance and vigilance," he tells the crowd rather aimlessly. The soldiers are disappointed.

Lenin is clearly nervous: he believes that it is not the right time for an insurrection. A frontline offensive has just begun, Kerensky is popular with the majority of the army, and the Provisional Government can deploy regiments from the front to suppress the uprising at any moment. Zinoviev recalls a talk he had that day with Lenin and Trotsky over lunch at the Tauride Palace: "No, we cannot seize power now because the frontline soldiers are not yet ours," says Lenin. "The frontline soldiers have been brainwashed by the liberals and will cut the Petrograd workers' throats."

INTO THE JAWS OF THE CROWD

On 4 July the city center is still crawling with Kronstadt sailors; local residents are in hiding. There are skirmishes here and there as the sailors randomly shoot at the windows of houses along Nevsky Prospekt, leaving dozens dead.

The sailors arrive at the Tauride Palace and ask to speak to Justice Minister Pereverzev, demanding that he immediately release the Kronstadt sailor. The justice minister is not there, provoking more rage. The sailors start smashing down the gates of the Tauride Palace. "There's one of the traitors!" a sailor shouts out, catching sight of the leader of the Socialist-Revolutionary Party, Agriculture Minister Viktor Chernov, who is dragged into the street. He tries to jump onto a nearby barrel to explain to the crowd that he is trying to reform the land laws, but no one is listening. The crowd yells that the land should be distributed immediately. Chernov, the leader of the oldest and largest political party in Russia, the Socialist-Revolutionaries (SRs), is just moments away from being torn to pieces, like tsarist generals and policemen during the February Revolution. But Chernov is lucky. Instead of being lynched, he is arrested and stuffed into a car. A worker shakes his fist in Chernov's face, shouting: "You should take power, you son of a bitch, when it's being offered to you." The minister's clothes are torn, and he himself is badly shaken.

The executive committee of the Petrograd Soviet, which is meeting inside the palace, learns about what has happened a few minutes later. Chkheidze yells at Kamenev and Martov, who supposedly have influence over the crowd, demanding that they immediately release the agriculture minister. While they procrastinate, the crowd becomes more and more aggressive. Trotsky goes out to speak to them. An experienced tamer of the crazed masses, he picks out the ringleader, goes up to him, and embraces him.

"You have all proved your devotion to the revolution. Every one of you is ready to lay down his life for it. I know it," he cries. "Give me your hand, comrade! Give me your hand, my brother!" he says, trying to shake hands with everyone. Some avoid Trotsky's handshake. The sailors know Trotsky well from his speeches at Kronstadt, during which he urged them to be merciless towards their enemies. Now he is trying to pacify them, and they do not like it.

He jumps onto the hood of the car with Chernov still inside, shouting: "Who here is for violence? Raise your hands!" With the crowd somewhat dumbfounded, he takes the opportunity to grab the deathly pale Chernov from the car and take him back to the Tauride Palace.

THE ANATOMY OF PROTEST*

The sailors are still looking for Justice Minister Pavel Pereverzev. As a lawyer before the revolution, he defended members of the Bolsheviks who

---

* The title of a Russian documentary maligning the anti-Putin protests of 2011-12.

were being tried at Stolypin's request. Now he himself is preparing to accuse them of treason: he claims to have documents proving that Lenin and company are German spies.

The charges are based on the testimony of a warrant officer by the name of Yermolenko, who in late April surrendered to Russian counterintelligence and admitted that he worked for Germany, listing other German spies operating in Russia in the process. Among the first names he cites is Lenin. According to the documents presented by Yermolenko, Lenin is in the pay of German intelligence.

There is one drawback: the evidence is fake. It is a stitch-up, and not a very subtle one at that: a humble warrant officer could not possibly be in possession of documents exposing the entire German spy network. Pereverzev is well aware of this (and maybe even ordered the forged documents himself). His motive is to get rid of all enemies threatening the stability of the government. On 3 July the justice minister decides to make the documents public: his people invite representatives from different regiments of the Petrograd garrison to the general staff to show the soldiers the putative evidence of the Bolsheviks' betrayal.

At the same time, Pereverzev sends the "Yermolenko papers" to the press. Unexpectedly, the first scandal erupts when the justice minister discusses the operation at a government meeting. Prime Minister Prince Lvov is outraged. The accusations against the Bolsheviks are obviously bogus, he cries. Lies are inadmissible even in the struggle against one's opponents, as this will undermine the authority of the government.

Lvov demands that all newspapers refrain from publishing the documents; he personally rings round the editorial offices. Heeding the prime minister's authoritative tone, the newspapers comply—all except one; the tabloid *Living Word* refuses to pass up such a sensational story. An article entitled "Lenin, Ganetsky* & Co Are German Spies" has already been written and is due to be published the next morning.[†]

---

* An "Old Bolshevik" and a close associate of Lenin.

† The way authorities spread accusations against Bolsheviks in the press is very similar to the persecution of the Russian opposition in the early twenty-first century. In 2011 the TV channel NTV will broadcast two features: "Anatomy of Protest" and "Anatomy of Protest 2" based on candid videos, possibly shot by the Russian secret service. These videos will allegedly prove that Russian opposition is being funded by the Georgian secret service. Later criminal charges will be brought against three activists of the "Left front" based on "Anatomy of Protest 2"—all of them will be sentenced to prison.

TO SEIZE OR NOT TO SEIZE

In the evening of 4 July, the Tauride Palace is still besieged by armed sailors and soldiers. There is shooting in the streets, and demonstrators occasionally break into the assembly hall, shouting out their demands. The nerves of those assembled are stretched to the limit.

Tsereteli explains that the Petrograd Soviet cannot accept the demands of the soldiers. The Congress of Soviets met less than a month ago and agreed to support the coalition Provisional Government. If the executive committee now yields to the insurgents and opposes the government, the whole country will view it as succumbing to the will of the violent minority. While the executive committee ponders the matter, a strong summer downpour drives almost all the protesters away. Some run to the barracks, others to the mansion of Kschessinskaya or the Peter and Paul Fortress. In the deserted street outside the Tauride Palace, a few armored cars stand abandoned in the pouring rain.

The executive committee is still in session late that night when members hear the trampling of soldiers' boots in the corridor. There is panic in the hall, but it turns out to be regiments loyal to the Provisional Government that have just returned from the front. The executive committee duly votes for a resolution in support of the Provisional Government, and that same day the Provisional Government decides to hold elections to the new Constituent Assembly on 17 September and to draft a land reform bill in advance of them.

Tsereteli approaches Stalin, whom the Bolsheviks have sent to negotiate with the Petrograd Soviet, hoping that the two Georgians will see eye to eye. The Bolsheviks know, Stalin says, that the government intends to dispatch troops to the mansion of Kschessinskaya. However, the building is armed with Bolshevik detachments, so any attempt to seize the house and arrest the Bolsheviks will inevitably result in bloodshed.

"There will be no blood split in Kschessinskaya's mansion," Tsereteli says. "So the government will not send troops there?" asks Stalin. "The government will send troops, but there will be no bloodshed, for the Bolsheviks will see that resistance is useless." Stalin walks away. In all his subsequent speeches and books, he will always describe Tsereteli as the chief victimizer of the Bolsheviks.[*]

---

[*] In the period between February and October 1917 not a single Bolshevik is killed; it is Stalin who will repress almost all the party members after 1927.

END OF THE BOLSHEVIKS

Early in the morning of 5 July the Bolsheviks learn from the newspaper *Living Word* that they are to face espionage charges. They describe the charges as "another Dreyfus affair" by analogy with the trial of a French officer falsely accused of spying for Germany in the 1890s.

"They will shoot us one by one. Now is their time," Lenin says to Trotsky, who agrees. The Bolshevik leaders hastily leave the *Pravda* printing house, narrowly avoiding the arrival of government troops, who then head for the mansion of Kschessinskaya.

"Comrades, a most heinous act of villainy has been committed," shouts Zinoviev, running into the meeting room. "A monstrous piece of populist slander has appeared in the press, which is intended to mobilize the most benighted section of the population." Ironically, the Bolsheviks do not consider as "populist" their calls for the soldiers to desert the front and seize the land from the landlords and the factories from the bourgeois.

The Bolsheviks' supporters from the machine-gun regiment are still holding on to the Peter and Paul Fortress, but on the morning of 5 July they are disarmed. There are no mass executions of the Bolsheviks, which Trotsky in his memoirs many years later will describe as a mistake by the Provisional Government: "Fortunately, our enemies lacked determination," he writes. Tsereteli, even in exile, will maintain that he and his comrades did the right thing, because they wanted to implant democracy, not terror.

PRINCE MYSHKIN

War Minister Kerensky is at the front during the entire uprising. Only on the evening of 4 July does he receive a telegram from Prince Lvov with an urgent request to return to the capital. He immediately goes back and sends irate telegrams demanding the arrest of all the Bolsheviks. Along the way, a catastrophe happens: a locomotive slams into Kerensky's train at full speed. The minister is not injured, but he is severely shaken and convinced that it is an assassination attempt, although there no evidence to prove it.

At the last station before Petrograd, he is met by Foreign Minister Tereshchenko, who has made the journey specifically to meet him and discuss the situation in the capital. The uprising is a big blow for Prime Minister Lvov. The latter intends to resign in favor of Kerensky.

Kerensky is deeply irritated by what is happening in Petrograd. On arriving in the capital, his first act is to dismiss the commander of the

Petrograd Military District, General Polovtsev, despite the latter having pacified the Bolshevik insurrection.

A telegram is received from the Southwestern Front with news that the Germans have broken through the Russian defenses. With this telegram in hand, Kerensky strides into the hall where the Provisional Government and representatives of the Petrograd Soviet are meeting. "Are you still opposed to arrests?" he says, waving the telegram. He is sure that the German offensive and the Bolshevik insurrection are connected.

Kerensky finds Prime Minister Georgy Lvov in a state of severe depression. As a Tolstoyan, he has always defended the interests of the people. The slogans damning the "capitalist ministers" are weighing heavily on the prime minister. Who does he represent if the people themselves are against him?

"There is nothing left for me to do," says Lvov. "To rescue the situation, we have to disperse the Soviets and open fire on the people. This I cannot do. But Kerensky can."

In his resignation letter Prime Minister Lvov cites the main reason for his departure as his conflict with the leader of the SRs, Agriculture Minister Viktor Chernov, who wants to distribute the land without waiting for approval from the Constituent Assembly. Lvov believes that this is illegal and simply wrong. Moreover, he accuses Chernov of justifying the peasants' unlawful land grabs (Chernov does indeed believe that this is the lesser evil, when the alternative is to keep the peasants hanging in limbo).

Prince Georgy Lvov is a unique figure in Russian history. The first head of the Russian republic, essentially the Russian George Washington, he was—and still is—generally unknown. The first American president, according to the recollections of colleagues, was clearly aware that he was shaping history with his own hands. Prince Lvov, too, is historically unprecedented. Unlike Russia's previous leaders, he shuns the idea of becoming an emperor. A friend of Leo Tolstoy, Prince Lvov turns into the Prince Myshkin* of Russian politics. This highly principled (and hence transient) leader of Russia could not tolerate violence and did not aspire or cling to power.

On leaving his post, Lvov departs for Optina Pustyn—a monastery that Tolstoy visited on several occasions, the last time just before his death.

ESCAPE FROM THE BATTLEFIELD

The German counteroffensive inflicts a crushing psychological blow on the Russian army and the country. The newspapers write that the 607th

---

* The pacifist protagonist of Dostoevsky's *The Idiot*.

Regiment has deserted. Later, Kerensky will assert that such reports were deliberate lies to demoralize the army, leading to its collapse.

Boris Savinkov telegraphs from the Southwestern Front that most of the units are falling apart; there is no discipline, and the lines of deserters stretch for hundreds of miles. Rumors spread that the fleeing infantrymen are shooting anyone who tries to stop them, killing officers, and robbing local residents. In what is known as the "Tarnopol disgrace," the Russian army loses all the territories it gained during the previous year's Brusilov Offensive, and much more besides.

Kerensky blames the press for the failure of his offensive, and orders the restoration of military censorship. General Kornilov, the new commander-in-chief of the Southwestern Front, telegraphs Petrograd to say that the reintroduction of the death penalty for "traitors and cowards" will save "many innocent lives." His telegram is reprinted by all the newspapers. Without waiting for approval from the Provisional Government, Kornilov orders that deserters should be seized and hanged from lampposts, with plaques listing their crimes attached to the corpses.

TO RAZLIV

The frontline defeat causes shock and hysteria in Petrograd. Lenin and the Bolsheviks are blamed for being "German spies." The papers write that they are complicit in the failure of the Kerensky Offensive and the Russian army's retreat: "Thanks to them—Lenin, Zinoviev, Trotsky, et al.—Wilhelm II has achieved everything he dreamt of," writes Vladimir Burtsev, Russia's real-life Sherlock Holmes, who unmasks double agents and provocateurs. For him there is no doubt: Lenin is a traitor.

The first to be arrested is Kamenev, followed by the commander of the Kronstadt sailors, Midshipman Raskolnikov. Lenin and Zinoviev go into hiding, which the press reports as proof of their guilt.

Even many Bolsheviks do not understand why the party leaders are hiding instead of facing trial and proving their innocence, like in the Dreyfus affair. But as usual, Lenin does not care about what his comrades think. Wearing a wig and clean-shaven, he travels to Lake Razliv in Finland under a false passport. There, he and Zinoviev live in a hut by the waterside. Lenin builds a wooden "office," which even Zinoviev is not allowed to enter. He devours all newspapers he can get hold of and plots a new armed uprising against the Provisional Government, taking into account the previous unsuccessful attempt.

Trotsky is at liberty, but members of the executive committee treat him like a leper. He still goes to the buffet inside the Tauride Palace, where he sups on black bread with cheese and red caviar. Trotsky notices that at the height of the Bolshevik persecution his tea and sandwiches suddenly taste nicer: staff members sympathize with the Bolsheviks and give Trotsky the best food and drink that they can find.

Trotsky writes an open letter in support of the Bolsheviks and declares that he intends to defend them in court. However, on 10 July he himself is arrested and sent to the Kresty prison.

THIRTEEN SPEECHES A DAY

After the July uprising many in Petrograd believe that the Bolsheviks are finished. But the accusations of spying for Germany spread further: the next victim of the patriotic press is the leader of the SRs, Viktor Chernov.

The SRs, the oldest and largest party in the country, who enjoy tremendous influence over the peasantry, now have a leadership problem: the legendary Mikhail Gotz and Gregory Gershuni did not live to see the revolution. In his memoirs, Chernov (writing about himself in the third person) complains that he lacks their charisma and experience. He has neither the determination, nor the vision of the party's deceased leaders, yet he is still the party's only option. Chernov is loved by the peasants, who gladly listen to his speeches—up to thirteen a day, it is reported.

The SRs triumph in all local elections, but inside the government coalition Tsereteli is clearly in charge. The former head of the party's militant organization, Boris Savinkov, and the former head of its faction in the Duma, Alexander Kerensky, are now trying to distance themselves from the SRs and from Chernov. Both consider themselves to be sufficiently popular in their own right.

Chernov wants to fulfill the dream of the Russian peasantry by giving them "land and freedom." A faithful disciple of Babushka, the agriculture minister believes that the growing tension among the peasants can only be relieved through the rapid redistribution of the land. Therefore, he vests the regional land committees with the authority to take land from the landlords and transfer it to the peasants. At the same time, the Provisional Government is adamant that a land law should be drafted by the forthcoming Constituent Assembly; if the peasants are given land, it warns, all the frontline soldiers will desert in order to get their share. Chernov counters this by saying that, on the contrary, the reform will spur the soldiers to fight for what is now their land.

Chernov's land policy is the reason for the espionage campaign against him—at least that's what he thinks. He is labeled a defeatist and a spy in the pay of the Germans. The leader of the SRs even resigns temporarily to devote all his time to proving his innocence. The party stands by him and puts forward a condition to Kerensky: they will support the new government only if Agriculture Minister Chernov remains a part of it.

A FIRM HAND

When the Kerensky Offensive was going well, it seemed that the whole army adored the new war minister. But when the retreat begins, the antagonism between the generals and Kerensky comes to the surface at a meeting of all the commanders on 16 July in Mogilev.

Kerensky arrives from Petrograd with Boris Savinkov, the government's frontline commissioner. When Kerensky's train pulls up, he refuses to disembark because only Brusilov's adjutant is there to meet him, not the supreme commander himself. Kerensky waits in the carriage until Brusilov arrives. It is not a requirement of protocol, just a personal whim.

Kerensky's late arrival delays the meeting by an hour and a half. General Denikin, long irritated by Kerensky, blames him for the collapse of the army and for undermining the authority of the officers. Kerensky is amazed. He listens to the accusations, holding his head in his hands, before thanking Denikin for his "bold and sincere words."

Brusilov reports that to save the army, the soldiers must be deprived of the right of assembly and barred from politics, including the abolition of all soldiers' committees. Kerensky listens carefully, but on returning to Petrograd, his first act is to dismiss Brusilov, who takes his grievances to the press.

Kerensky's new supreme commander is Lavr Kornilov, the only member of the top brass to be absent from the controversial meeting in Mogilev. Having recently commanded the Petrograd Military District, Kornilov is remembered for clashing with the Petrograd Soviet. Now he is gaining a reputation for his de facto reintroduction of the death penalty by hanging deserters.

The idea to appoint Kornilov belongs to Savinkov, a former terrorist who has grown to admire the former tsarist general. Savinkov likes Kornilov's "attitude to the death penalty, his understanding of the causes of the rout at Tarnopol, and his resoluteness in the fight against Bolshevism."

However, in response to the telegram informing him of his appointment, Kornilov lists his conditions for accepting the post, which include the freedom to act as he sees fit and to be "responsible only to his own conscience and the people." Kerensky has second thoughts, but it is too late—the press is already trumpeting the appointment.

THE KERENSKY GOVERNMENT

Kerensky, too, tries to strike a more resolute tone: "The main task now is to unite power," he says in an interview after returning from the front. "The government will save Russia. It is ready to forge national unity with blood and iron if rationality, honor and conscience do not suffice."

His behavior becomes increasingly erratic, yet few notice the signs of emotional burnout. He is still considered the country's most effective leader and its most popular politician. With the departure of Prince Lvov, it is not clear who should form the next government. The former prime minister "bequeathed" the chair to Kerensky, but the position is not hereditary and there are no laws or institutions governing the transfer of power. There begin endless negotiations between the Petrograd Soviet and government members. Kerensky does not take part, demonstrating that he is above such squabbling and too busy saving the motherland.

Lvov also served as Russia's interior minister, and that position is taken by Tsereteli. He becomes the de facto leader of the government while Kerensky is at the front. He is in fact opposed to Kerensky becoming prime minister, because he lacks faith in the latter's organizational skills. Yet Tsereteli does not fight for power himself. The press is waiting for a conflict to break out between Kerensky and Tsereteli over the post of prime minister, but instead they issue a joint statement saying that they are ready to work together.

Faced with never-ending talks between the government and the Petrograd Soviet, War Minister Kerensky pointedly refuses to accept power and departs on vacation for Finland, leaving Savinkov in the role of acting war minister. He also writes a resignation letter to Deputy Prime Minister Nekrasov.

Petrograd is in a flurry. Nekrasov holds a government meeting in the Malachite Hall of the Winter Palace with the participation of the Petrograd Soviet, the Provisional Committee of the State Duma, and the leaders of all political parties except the Bolsheviks. All decline to take power. Milyukov suggests to Tsereteli that the Soviets should form a government (which happens to be one of Lenin's slogans). Tsereteli, for his part, believes that the bourgeoisie should be represented, meaning that the Kadets should be part of any Soviet-led cabinet.

In the end, a compromise is found: the absent Kerensky is given the right to appoint a new cabinet at his own discretion. Tsereteli is opposed and declines to join the new government.

With the new ministers accountable only to Kerensky, the result is a strange semi-monarchical system. Almost all the old faces remain in their positions. In addition to his new prime ministerial functions, Kerensky retains the post of war minister, even though the War Ministry is now de facto managed by Savinkov.

The new government finally takes up residence in the Winter Palace, relocating from the Mariinsky Palace, and Kerensky, having returned from Finland and now not averse to power, settles there with his "mascot"—Babushka Breshko-Breshkovskaya. He is increasingly suspected of harboring dictatorial and even imperial tendencies. It is rumored that his signature looks like "Alexander IV." Moreover, every time Kerensky leaves the Winter Palace, the red flag above it is lowered, just like the Imperial standard in the old days.

FINNISH GRIEVANCES

While Kerensky was resting in the Finnish wilderness, a dramatic event occurred: the Grand Duchy of Finland, part of the Russian Empire, decided to opt for autonomy—even more determinedly than Ukraine. The spark was the July uprising in Petrograd. At the peak of the anarchy, the Finnish Social Democrats in Petrograd (supporters of the Bolsheviks) proposed that the Finnish Sejm (parliament) should declare itself the supreme authority in Finland and implement the slogan "All power to the Soviets" at the local level.

The Sejm adopts this decision, making the situation for the Russian government even more precarious. There is no stable governance in Russia, the front line in western Ukraine is turning into a catastrophe, the supreme commander has been dismissed, and War Minister Kerensky is threatening and pretending to resign: Finnish autonomy is the last thing that anyone needs. But the Provisional Government decides to play even tougher with the Sejm than it did with Ukraine's parliament, the Central Rada. The Sejm is dissolved and its building occupied by Russian troops. New elections are held, and all previous decisions on autonomy are annulled.

The Finns are incensed by the crackdown. Henceforth, as in tsarist times, Finland becomes the unruliest of all Russia's unruly regions. Lenin does not spend long in his log cabin by Lake Razliv. He soon moves to Helsinki, where he receives the personal protection of the head of the Finnish militia. It is in the latter's apartment that Lenin continues to develop plans for a new uprising. The Finnish authorities are happy to assist as revenge for their thwarted autonomy.

TO TOBOLSK

On 11 July Kerensky pays a visit to Tsarskoye Selo. The former emperor, Nicholas, is pleased to see him. He is appalled by the July uprising, yet happy about the restoration of order and the reintroduction of the death penalty at the front.

For the imperial family, Kerensky's visit eclipses all the alarming news of the previous days. He reports that the prisoners of the Alexander Palace (i.e., the imperial family) are to be allowed to travel to the south "in view of the proximity of Tsarskoye Selo to the turbulent capital." The whole family is in a state of nervous excitement. "It is strange that we are being moved after four months of seclusion here," writes Nicholas in his diary (we also learn that on that day the former tsar reads Conan Doyle's "The Poison Belt" to his daughters). Two weeks later the imperial family is told that Crimea is not an option. It is not yet clear where they are going, but they are advised to pack some warm clothes. There is talk of a three or four-day journey to Siberia. That evening Nicholas reads the children *A Study in Scarlet*, again by his beloved Conan Doyle.

The departure is scheduled for late that same evening. The whole family dresses and goes out into the street at midnight, but the car due to take them to the station arrives only in the morning. All are terribly nervous, but calm down once they board the train. Nicholas has time to admire the sunrise over Petrograd, where they change trains. At the station in Petrograd they finally learn that their destination is Tobolsk, the historical capital of Siberia.

Alexandra is terribly agitated the whole way. The journey will take them close to the home of Rasputin, which she regards as a mystical sign. In Tyumen they are transferred to a steamship and, on 5 August, they sail past the village of Pokrovskoe, the birthplace of the preacher. The whole family stands on the deck in prayer. The next day the ship steams into Tobolsk, where they discover that their accommodation is not ready. The

Romanovs joke about the Russian people's "astonishing inability even to arrange lodging"—and spend another week living on the boat.

At precisely the same time, the Provisional Government publishes a decree on elections to the Constituent Assembly to be held on the basis of universal, equal, and direct suffrage by secret ballot. Electoral rights are denied only to persons that are insane, deaf-and-dumb, or incarcerated—as well as all members of the House of Romanov.

The imperial family itself is not investigated, but members of the inner circle are. In early summer the prison doctor, Ivan Manukhin, notes that the soldiers guarding the Peter and Paul Fortress have stopped taking orders from the investigators and are starting to administer their own justice. He decides to rescue the prisoners, or at least take them to other prisons that are "less Bolshevik." According to Manukhin, the soldiers hate Anna Vyrubova most of all, and she is likely to be the first victim.

The doctor states that Vyrubova is a virgin, so the rumors about her and Rasputin are fiction. And while the charges against her relate to her role in state policy, not her personal life, the investigative commission takes note of her chastity: on 12 June she is transferred to a "detention house" with a more lenient regime, and on 24 July released for lack of evidence.

Another patient of Manukhin is the sixty-nine-year-old former Prime Minister Boris Stürmer. He is seriously ill with uremia. The doctor insists on his release, but Kerensky decides to transfer him to the "softer" Kresty prison, where he dies from complications on 5 September.

"HANG FROM THE LAMPPOSTS"

Kerensky does not approve of the Kornilov-Savinkov plan to reintroduce the death penalty—and not only because he does not trust them (the feeling is mutual: at a meeting with the prime minister at the Winter Palace, Kornilov came surrounded by armed Turkmen guards). The main reason is because it runs contrary to his convictions. It calls for the execution not only of rebels, but of agitators, too—something that didn't happen even under Stolypin and his "neckties." Kerensky is a lawyer who has spent his life defending opponents of the regime. However, he does not voice his opposition to Kornilov's face, and instead promises to think about it.

The altercation takes place on the eve of a major public conference in Moscow, which Kerensky needs to give the government legitimacy and convince himself of the need for more stringent measures. On the eve of the Moscow conference, he postpones the Constituent Assembly elections from September to November. However, Kerensky's public propaganda show is hijacked by Kornilov, who becomes the new hero of Moscow.

Kornilov at that moment is quite popular, especially in Moscow. The city is home to big business and merchants, who have long eyed Kornilov as the one person capable of restoring order. But the old generals do not rate him very highly: Mikhail Alekseyev once said that he had "the heart of a lion and the head of a sheep," while Brusilov described him as the head of a guerrilla group. Yet on the eve of the Moscow conference, all the talk is about Kornilov.

The day before, Moscow's conservative circles hold a meeting of their own, including the entrepreneur Pavel Ryabushinsky, the two recent supreme commanders Alekseyev and Brusilov, as well as Mikhail Rodzianko and the Kadets, led by Milyukov. The main outcome of the meeting is that they will support Kornilov as the man to bring order to the country and disperse the Soviets.

As soon as Kornilov arrives at the train station in Moscow, he is met like the lord of the realm and pelted with flowers by women. He goes to the Iberian Gate near the Kremlin to pray to the Iveron Theotokos icon (as the tsars used to do when visiting Moscow). Russia's supreme commander then meets with advisers, who report on the country's finances and the international situation.

On the second day, Kornilov speaks at the Bolshoi Theatre—after Kerensky, who has just delivered a one-and-a-half hour speech full of promises to restore order with "blood and iron." When the supreme commander appears on stage, half the hall gives him a standing ovation, but the soldiers (who prefer Kerensky) refuse to rise.

Kornilov's speech is a direct challenge to Kerensky and the members of the Petrograd Soviet there in the hall. He says that the liberated Russia has inherited a combat-ready and "self-sacrificial" army, but that the new laws have turned it into a "mad rabble of people who value only their own lives." Peace, he says, is impossible, and even if one were concluded, the "rabble" would then proceed to crush its own country. Lastly, he tells the audience that he and Savinkov have suggested a reform plan to Kerensky, and that he has no doubt that it will be adopted shortly.

Having said his piece, Kornilov departs from the theatre and heads for the High Command at Mogilev. His speech makes a huge impression on the audience.

The last day of the Moscow conference sees the opening of the Local Council of the Russian Orthodox Church—the first time since the seventeenth century. It is a symbolic act, representing the restoration of the Patriarchate after it was abolished by Peter the Great and replaced by the Holy Synod in 1721 as part of his reforms of the church. The ceremony is attended by Kerensky and the last Minister of Religion of the Synod, Anton Kartashov.

But the main talking point for the press that day, 15 August, is not the end of the political conference or the opening of the Local Council, but the largest manmade disaster in the history of Russia (at that time). An arms factory watchman in Kazan throws a cigarette butt to the parched ground, which sparks a fire that spreads to a warehouse containing ammunition and oil cisterns. Panic sets in when the explosion bellows across the city. The fire kills twenty-one people and destroys almost the entire arsenal sorely needed by the army. The papers claim that it is the work of German agents. The tragedy is compounded by a surge in looting, especially among the rampant soldiers (according to the press).

TIME FOR HANGING

The fire in Kazan is still raging when the Germans take Riga, stopping five hundred kilometers short of the Russian capital. Kornilov decides to create a separate Petrograd Front, directly subordinate to the High Command, while the city itself remains under the control of the Provisional Government, which duly appoints Savinkov as governor-general.

On the eve of the Moscow conference, Kornilov sends troops to the capital: a cavalry corps under the command of General Krymov and the so-called "Wild Division," consisting of troops from the North Caucasus. The High Command understands that the intent is to take control of Petrograd. "It's time to hang Lenin's German stooges and spies, and disperse the Soviet of Workers' and Soldiers' Deputies," Kornilov tells his chief of staff, Alexander Lukomsky, adding that he is not opposed to the Provisional Government, and hopes to reach an agreement with it.

Kerensky is still hesitant about declaring martial law and adopting the repressive measures proposed by Kornilov. He tells Savinkov that the government's authority is spent and that the High Command is full of counter-revolutionary sentiment. Moreover, he says that Savinkov must go to Mogilev to straighten things out. In response, the latter says that he is still offended by their last conversation: "Have you forgotten it?" he asks. "Yes,

I have. I seem to have forgotten everything," says the prime minister, smiling oddly. "I'm sick. I'm a corpse. That conference killed me."

Savinkov meets with Kornilov on 24 August at the High Command to discuss the plan: Kerensky signs all the repressive laws, while Kornilov leads his troops into the capital to suppress the protests. Supreme Commander Kornilov tells Savinkov of his dislike for Prime Minister Kerensky, whom he considers a lame duck. The government, believes Kornilov, will function better without him. He is sending troops to Petrograd to defend the city not only from the Germans and the Bolsheviks, but also from Kerensky. Savinkov tries to win Kornilov over: "I know and admire Kerensky," he says. "Kerensky is a man of integrity, but you're right about one thing. He's weak." Savinkov eventually persuades Kornilov to work with Kerensky.

Savinkov asks Kornilov not to appoint General Krymov as the commander of the Petrograd operation and not to send in the Wild Division, because "the mountain dwellers don't care who they kill." Kornilov appears to agree, but goes ahead anyway and appoints Krymov. Both the cavalry corps and the Wild Division continue to advance on Petrograd.

"Krymov is known for his bloody-mindedness. Savinkov is just afraid that he might hang more people than necessary," the supreme commander tells his chief of staff. He is sure that Savinkov will thank him later for ignoring his requests.

THE HIGHS OF OFFICE

On the day when Savinkov leaves for the High Command, his friends Gippius, Merezhkovsky, and Filosofov pen a letter to Kerensky. They call on him to take drastic measures and to "wield power"—if he is unable to do so, he should hand over to someone "more capable" like Savinkov, and he himself should become a "symbol."

That same day, Kerensky is visited at the Winter Palace by a former member of the Provisional Government, Vladimir Lvov, who just a month previously was dismissed from his post as minister for religion. He once described Kerensky as a mortal enemy, but has now come to warn him of the impending danger. Lvov says that Kerensky's popularity is declining, while hinting vaguely at the existence of "certain circles" that could support him. Kerensky agrees to enter into negotiations with these "certain circles."

After receiving the Merezhkovskys' letter, Kerensky goes to see them for an explanation. Only Filosofov is at home when he calls by. "Take decisive action, smash them to pieces!" Filosofov advises him. "Remember that you are the 'president' of the republic. You are the chosen one of the new democracy. You are, and not the socialists." After this short conversation, Kerensky runs off as quickly as he arrived. "He seemed like a morphine addict who only comes alive after a fix," recalls Filosofov. "I'm not sure he even heard what I said, never mind remembered it."

Meanwhile, Vladimir Lvov begins his shuttle diplomacy. On 25 August he approaches Kornilov, allegedly on Kerensky's instructions, and says that the latter is ready to retire, but will continue as prime minister if he has Kornilov's support. He asks Kornilov to put forward his demands. The latter replies that after the capture of Riga, the Kazan fire, and the nationwide unrest, only a dictator can rescue the country, be it himself, Kerensky, General Alekseyev, or anyone. Kornilov says that a dictatorship is required because the Bolsheviks are planning a coup in Petrograd for late August. Lvov replies that Kornilov could be the one to lead this dictatorship.

After spending the whole day discussing the makeup of the government, Kornilov proposes to set up a "Council of National Defense," headed by him with the participation of Kerensky, Savinkov, Alekseyev, Kolchak, and High Command Government Commissar Filonenko. The talks with Vladimir Lvov come to an end. Kornilov does not even suspect that he is dealing with an impostor: Lvov is only pretending to be acting on behalf of Kerensky.

Kornilov writes to Savinkov that the troops will arrive in Petrograd on 28 August, on which day martial law and his package of repressive measures can be implemented, including the death penalty. This will lead to immediate protests, whereupon General Krymov's cavalry corps will suppress the rioters and "hang the Soviet of Workers' Deputies from the lamp-posts."

Lastly, Kornilov asks Lvov to tell Kerensky and Savinkov that they should go to the High Command to ensure their safety during the fighting in Petrograd. With that, Lvov takes his leave. He has the feeling that Kornilov is trying to lure Kerensky there in order to assassinate him. Moreover, Lvov recalls that an officer of Kornilov's staff spoke openly to him about a plan to kill Kerensky.

THE PENCIL IS MIGHTIER THAN THE SWORD

Lvov heads back to Petrograd in a daze. He did not expect that his unsolicited mediation would lead to the discovery of an assassination plot. He can barely contain the importance of what he has to convey to Kerensky.

Meanwhile, Savinkov gives Kerensky the text of the repressive measures to be approved by the government. Seeing that Kerensky is again having doubts, Savinkov snaps that his indecision is criminal and his weakness is ruining Russia. Kerensky promises to adopt the "Kornilov package" during that evening's cabinet meeting. Kerensky is horrified: the repressive laws are contrary to his beliefs. He is far from being a professional killer like Savinkov or a swashbuckler like Kornilov.

While Kerensky is still racked with doubt, he is paid a visit by an agitated Vladimir Lvov, who reports that he has come from Kornilov with a request that he, Kerensky, should resign, transfer all military and civil authority to the supreme commander and, together with Savinkov, go to the High Command for their own safety.

Kerensky is shocked. He believed that his mediator in dealing with Kornilov was Savinkov, who never mentioned Kerensky's resignation or leaving for the High Command. On the contrary, it was Kerensky who was to introduce the emergency measures in Petrograd, not Kornilov. Kerensky perceives the words of the trembling Lvov as an ultimatum from Kornilov.

"It seemed like either he was insane or something major had happened," Kerensky recalls this conversation. Seeing Lvov's anxious state, he asks him to formulate the ultimatum on paper so as to convey it accurately to the government. Armed with pencil and paper, Lvov writes:

1) Martial law is to be declared in Petrograd.
2) All military and civil power is to be transferred to the Supreme Commander.
3) All ministers, including the Minister-Chairman,* are to resign, and temporary control of the ministries shall pass to their deputies until the formation of a cabinet under the Supreme Commander.
Petrograd. 26 August 1917
V. Lvov

As soon as Lvov begins to write, Kerensky's remaining doubts vanish. He had been warned of a conspiracy among the generals and of Kornilov's excessive popularity. Now a picture of betrayal emerges in his mind, and he sees clearly that everyone is against him.

"Will you go to the High Command?" asks Lvov. "Of course not. Do you really think I can serve under Kornilov?" snarls Kerensky.

---

* The prime minister.

Lvov, whom Kerensky believes to be Kornilov's envoy, confesses that Kerensky is right not to go, because he believes that there is a plot to assassinate him. Kerensky is surprised: "And what if they were just pulling your leg, Vladimir?" he says.

FATEFUL CHAT

When Lvov departs, Kerensky goes to the War Ministry to talk with Kornilov over a direct telegraphic link. They do not know each other very well, having spoken only a few times. Now the main showdown between them occurs via "telegraph chat." This exchange of telegrams will change the world.

Kerensky asks Kornilov to confirm that Lvov is indeed acting on his behalf. Kornilov confirms the request for Kerensky and Savinkov to come to the High Command at Mogilev. Kerensky says that it is impossible at the moment, and asks if Savinkov is required. Kornilov replies that both men should appear by 27 August at the latest.

Kerensky tries to clarify: "We are to come only if the rumors of an offensive on Petrograd come true?" Kornilov says that they should visit the High Command in any event. "See you soon," Kerensky signs off informally.

Kerensky takes this vague conversation as proof of a conspiracy. He runs to the Winter Palace and bumps into Lvov on the steps. He takes the latter inside and asks him to recount the whole story from the very beginning. An Interior Ministry official stands guard behind a screen. When the conversation ends, Kerensky draws back the screen and announces that Lvov is under arrest. He is taken into the next room.

Kerensky arrives late for a government meeting at which the repressive Kornilov measures are due to be discussed. His lateness is compounded by sending Kornilov a telegram informing the supreme commander of his dismissal.

At the meeting Kerensky demands that the ministers grant him dictatorial powers. Almost everyone agrees—except for the Kadets, who state that they would rather resign. The meeting breaks up at dawn, but assembles again at 11 a.m. at the request of Kerensky, although he himself fails to appear. The ministers continue the discussion till evening: Is it possible to salvage the situation? Can an agreement be reached between Kerensky and Kornilov?

Kornilov receives Kerensky's telegram that same morning and immediately responds that he will not obey. Savinkov persuades Kerensky not to leak the news of Kornilov's supposed resignation to the press, whereafter he convinces Kornilov to come to Petrograd for talks with Kerensky.

Kornilov refuses to come, explaining to Savinkov that Lvov cannot be trusted. At the same time, he orders the troops loyal to him—General Krymov's corps and the Wild Division—to continue their advance on Petrograd. Kerensky's circle is aware of the developments: "While you were talking on the wire, the people from the Caucasus were on their way to Petrograd," Kerensky's horrified deputy Nekrasov tells Savinkov.

The talks between Savinkov and Kornilov are cut short when the deputy war minister, Savinkov, learns that Kerensky has ordered the publication of an official government statement branding General Kornilov a traitor. Kerensky's telegram is forwarded to all military units.

The Petrograd Soviet learns of the unfolding crisis from this official statement, and its members rush to the Smolny Institute, where the Soviet is headquartered. Lunacharsky, a Bolshevik, is pleased. For him, it is "a storm that will clear the unbearably stifling atmosphere" and "revenge" for the July repression of his party. The leader of the Petrograd Soviet, Tsereteli, is depressed: "It's celebration time on Bolshevik street," he says to Lunacharsky. "It's your time again."

Throughout the night of 27-28 August, Savinkov, Alekseyev, and Tereshchenko try to figure out what to do in the morning when the newspapers publish Kerensky's statement about Kornilov's resignation. Savinkov asks Kerensky if he is aware that it will ruin army morale. Kerensky replies that, on the contrary, "inspired by the victory over the counter-revolution, the soldiers will charge into battle and defeat the enemy."

THE AUGUST *PUTSCH*

On the morning of 28 August, the entire country learns from the papers of a coup by the supreme commander against the government. At 7 a.m. Kornilov issues an appeal not to obey Kerensky: "A great provocation is threatening the Fatherland. Russia is dying. The hour of death is drawing near!" Kornilov accuses the Provisional Government of assisting the Germans, arguing that, under pressure from the Bolshevik-led Soviets, the government is "killing the army and shaking the country to its foundations."

The army is on the side of Kornilov. The High Command at Mogilev believes that the insurgents have the upper hand in terms of military force: the entire command staff and the overwhelming majority of the officers, the Cossacks, the military schools, and the top combat units all support

Kornilov. Moreover, General Krymov's corps and the Wild Division are almost in Petrograd. The Provisional Government is close to panic: a full-scale civil war is about to erupt on the streets of the capital.

The Petrograd Soviet becomes the new headquarters of the resistance against the advancing troops. Since the July revolt, the Soviet has been fairly inactive. On learning of the coup, it comes alive, as do the Bolsheviks. They understand that if Kornilov enters the city, his troops will immediately hang the Bolsheviks who were arrested by Kerensky back in July.

At the suggestions of Lev Kamenev, one of the most prominent Bolsheviks, a counter-coup military revolutionary committee is set up, consisting of three representatives each from the Bolsheviks, the Mensheviks, and the SRs. They draw up plans to oppose Kornilov. The Petrograd Soviet and the Bolsheviks are sure that they will be "hanged from the lamp-posts."

The committee does everything to prevent General Krymov's troops from entering Petrograd. Telegrams are dispatched nationwide, and the railways along which Krymov's echelons are moving are blocked with logs. Meanwhile, some experienced heads, including members of the Congress of Muslim Nations, led by the grandson of Imam Shamil,* are sent to parley with the Wild Division to halt its advance on Petrograd. At the same time, the new Military Revolutionary Committee starts to arm the workers.

NEW PETROGRAD SOVIET

While the Petrograd Soviet is making efforts to protect the capital, the government ministers at the Winter Palace are discussing what to do next. They propose that Kerensky resign in favor of a new government headed by General Alekseyev, the former tsar's chief of staff. Kerensky summons Alekseyev, but he declines both the post of prime minister and the post of supreme commander in place of Kornilov. Alekseyev has never been a leader and prefers to be second in command. He urges Kerensky to take over as supreme commander himself, and he, Alekseyev, will serve as his chief of staff.

In the evening it is reported that Kornilov's troops have halted. The mood inside the once-loyal units has changed radically. They were ready to march on the capital with the intention of rescuing it from the Bolshevik uprising, but on hearing that Kornilov has been declared a traitor, their enthusiasm wanes. General Krymov's corps disperses at Luga on

---

* The leader of the anti-Russian resistance during the Caucasian War of 1817–64.

the approach to Petrograd. Interestingly, precisely six months earlier, General Ivanov's offensive against Petrograd had crumbled at exactly the same place.

General Krymov travels to Petrograd alone to find out what is happening there. He meets with Alekseyev and then Kerensky. Taking leave of Kerensky, he writes a farewell note to Kornilov—and shoots himself. That same day, the commander of the Southwestern Front, General Denikin, is arrested by his own soldiers—the Provisional Government has to work hard to save him from mob law.

On 1 September, the new chief of staff, Alekseyev, goes to the High Command at Mogilev, where he arrests Kornilov and his closest officers, and imprisons them inside a monastery in the town of Bykhov with double perimeter protection. Kornilov and his loyal Turkmen fighters are guarded by soldiers from the Provisional Government. But only a few days later, on 7 September, Alekseyev resigns under pressure from the Petrograd Soviet, which considers him a "reactionary general" and a supporter of the old regime. After the failed coup* Kerensky dismisses many members of his inner circle. He appoints Savinkov as governor-general of Petrograd, but dismisses him three days later on learning of his dealings with Kornilov. Even his loyal deputy Nekrasov is suspected of treason; Kerensky removes him from the government and exiles him to Finland as the region's governor-general.

The Kornilov revolt is a milestone in the history of the 1917 revolution. It is hard to imagine a more absurd train of events. It causes a spike in the Bolsheviks' popularity and leads to the October uprising. Typically, none of the protagonists ever admit that they made serious blunders; both sides will remain convinced to their dying day that they were the victims of a vile conspiracy.

---

* The parallels between the Kornilov revolt of 1917 and the *putsch* of August 1991 are striking. Both had the same objectives: enact revenge and restore the old order. In both cases, the coups were instigated by fanatics of an empire in the throes of agony and led by members of the military and the old elite. State power (Kerensky, Gorbachev) played a passive, ambiguous role: it has been suggested that both times the head of state and the putschists were in collusion. A portion of the cultural intelligentsia sided with the coups, but most people in the capital cities opposed them. It was civil society, rather than the government, that defeated the coups. As a result, the failed coups led to the exact opposite of what the conspirators intended, accelerating the collapse of their beloved regimes. Moderate, transitional forms of government were ruled out as radical opponents of the former empires gained the upper hand. In both cases, the state—which the putschists had vainly tried to save—split into pieces. Were it not for the coups, the territorial integrity of the Russian Empire and the Soviet Union might have been preserved.

"THE SAD PIERROT OF THE REVOLUTION"

"Hope in the once-demigod Kerensky is fading fast," writes Alexander Benois, who back in March was so desperate to be of use to him. Kerensky's credibility has been fatally undermined, and those who idolized him are disillusioned.

"Kerensky is a pitiful sight," describes Kartashov, the minister of religion, in conversation with Gippius. "Yes, he doesn't physically hear what is said to him," adds Gippius. She, like many others, considers Kerensky to be the aggressor and Kornilov the victim. Kerensky is soon labeled "the sad Pierrot* of the revolution."

Kerensky is likely suffering from bipolar disorder combined with exhaustion: it is said that he has not slept properly for months. Back in March, Gippius suspected that he would burn out, and, come August, he has. His public behavior increasingly resembles that of a drug addict (he is now said to be sniffing cocaine). His bouts of euphoria vie with periods of prolonged depression, during which time he loses all interest in government business. All the while he brags to his colleagues that he is still constantly being asked for his autograph.

Alexander Benois retells a common piece of gossip that the prime minister allegedly spent his days at the Winter Palace in the former quarters of Alexander III, where he would "sing opera arias and take all kinds of junk." Arias and drugs in the imperial chamber is probably an exaggeration—akin to Rasputin's supposed orgies with Anna Vyrubova and Empress Alexandra. But the public laps it up.

Vladimir Lvov, the self-styled mediator in the negotiations between Kerensky and Kornilov, having spent a short spell at the Peter and Paul Fortress, is eager to confirm all the rumors about Kerensky. He tells that on 26 August, after being arrested at the Winter Palace, he was locked up in the former bedroom of Maria Feodorovna and could not sleep all night because in the late Alexander III's chamber next door Kerensky was pacing up and down, belting out operatic arias. The craziest rumor of all alleges that after the revolution Kerensky divorced his wife (true) in order to marry one of the former tsar's daughters (not so true).

The Kornilov revolt completely changes the balance of power in Petrograd. The Bolsheviks played a crucial role in defending the capital and dispersing Kornilov's troops. The Petrograd Soviet demands that Kerensky release the hundreds of Bolsheviks arrested during the July uprising. The

---

* A character from French mime.

Bolsheviks scream that it is the Kadets' turn to be rounded up for having supported Kornilov. But this does not happen, save for an isolated incident in Crimea, where the Simferopol Council of Workers' Deputies arrests the tycoon Ryabushinsky on suspicion of sympathy for Kornilov. He is released only after Kerensky's intervention.

After the defeat of Kornilov the Bolsheviks see their popularity soar. On 1 September a plenary session of the Petrograd Soviet is held at the Smolny Institute—it is so crowded and tumultuous that virtually no decisions are taken. The Bolsheviks put forward a resolution consisting of their traditional populist slogans: offer universal democratic peace to all belligerent nations; abolish the death penalty at the front; abolish the private ownership of landed estates; and transfer power to the proletariat and the revolutionary peasantry. The Petrograd Soviet adopts the resolution by a majority vote.

But this event is eclipsed by the same-day announcement of Kerensky's new government (a directory of five persons). He also dissolves the State Duma and, without waiting for approval from the Constituent Assembly, declares Russia to be a republic.

The next day, 2 September, Trotsky is released from the Kresty prison on a bail of 3,000 roubles*—the Provisional Government does not consider him to be a threat. On 4 September Kerensky orders the dissolution of the Military Revolutionary Committee, which was set up to defend the capital from Kornilov. An announcement to that effect is published in *Izvestia*, the official mouthpiece of the Petrograd Soviet. The very next day *Izvestia* publishes the dates of the committee's next sittings. The still-intact committee has no intention of obeying Kerensky.

By 9 September the executive committee—a narrow circle of leaders of the Petrograd Soviet—has come to realize that it no longer controls what goes on inside. Many of them, including Chkheidze, Tsereteli, and Chernov (most of the former ministers in the Provisional Government) decide to snub the Petrograd Soviet using a favorite tactic of Kerensky: they announce their resignation. They disapprove of the Bolshevik resolution adopted on 1 September. Tsereteli and company do not want to resign; on the contrary, they wish to fight against the Bolsheviks for influence and win back their supporters who have been seduced by the Bolsheviks.

Meanwhile, Trotsky actively campaigns against the old presidium: "The ghost of Kerensky now sits between Fyodor Dan[†] and Chkheizde," he declaims. "Remember that by approving the policy of the presidium, you are

* About $39,550 in 2017
† A Menshevik leader.

approving the policy of Kerensky!" The result of the vote on the Bolshevik resolution is a shock to the leaders of the SRs and the Mensheviks: they secured four hundred votes in the Petrograd Soviet against five hundred for the Bolsheviks.

This is a far greater political earthquake than the endless updates of the Provisional Government. The composition of the Petrograd Soviet has not changed since the revolution began. It has been the de facto parliament and the guarantor of stability throughout all the turmoil: from the Milyukov note in April to the July uprising and the August muddle between Kerensky and Kornilov. Now the executive committee has resigned.

"We are stepping down," says Tsereteli, "in the knowledge that over the past six months we have honorably held the banner of revolution. Now the banner is in your hands. We can only hope that you will be able to hold it aloft for at least half that period."

A week later the Petrograd Soviet elects a new executive committee and a new chairman in the shape of Leon Trotsky. The new Bolshevik-led Petrograd Soviet behaves quite differently from its predecessor. A "workers' militia" is set up to continue arming the workers, even though Kornilov's troops are no longer a threat. In spring 1917, after the February revolution, Tsereteli and the previous executive committee had made every effort to disarm the workers, who were called the "Red Guards." Now Trotsky reverses this policy.

A week later the triumph of the Bolsheviks spreads to Moscow: the Moscow Soviet adopts the same Bolshevik resolution as in Petrograd and its moderate members resign.

After the July uprising the Bolsheviks seemed a spent force, banished forever to the political margins. But the Kornilov coup has seen them democratically elected in Moscow and Petrograd. Kornilov and the generals, who were convinced that they could change things for the better by stringing a few people up, are no more.

DARK AND SLIMY

Autumn sets in, and the fleeting euphoria is supplanted by depression. Everywhere—from the front line to civvy street—the word is that Russia is lost. In Petrograd the weather is terrible. "It's so dark and slimy, even in daytime," writes Gippius.

The newspapers talk about the horrors of Riga. Before the city was captured by the Germans, it was apparently ransacked by "comrade soldiers" (now a euphemism for armed troublemakers). The press claims that the rapes and murders were perpetrated not by the Germans, but by the departing Russians. There is nationwide chaos, with soldier and peasant uprisings in Astrakhan, Irkutsk, Saratov (now cities in the Russian Federation), Gomel (in modern Belarus), Tashkent (capital of modern Uzbekistan), Kiev, Kharkov, Chernigov, and Odessa (cities in modern Ukraine). According to the new war minister, Verkhovsky, there are two million deserters.

After the tragedy in Kazan, an arson epidemic breaks out: some say it is revenge against the propertied classes; others are sure that the owners themselves are burning down their properties for insurance payouts. The newspapers, meanwhile, blame everything on German agents provocateurs.

The Provisional Government has no economic policy or even a finance ministry. In September the decision is taken to print new twenty- and forty-rouble notes. They do not replace the old tsarist money, but are supposed to complement it. The printing of these worthless pieces of paper, known as "kerenkas" (after Kerensky), spirals out of control—within a few months the money supply increases severalfold.

At the same time, labor productivity is plummeting: workers spend more time rallying than toiling. Living conditions after the revolution deteriorate, largely due to inflation. Throughout 1917 the government tries to reform the labor law, but is afraid of adopting drastic measures without the approval of the Constituent Assembly (which still hasn't been convened) and cannot reach a compromise with the oligarchs, who claim that in wartime the socialists' demands (for example, widespread wage increases) will bring industry to a standstill.

Pavel Ryabushinsky, who represented Moscow business at the congress of industrialists in August 1917, says that life punishes those who violate the laws of economics: "Unfortunately, we need the bony hand of hunger and poverty to grab the throat of the faux friends of the people—members of all the countless committees and soviets—so that they come to their senses." This sentence becomes a catchphrase for the left-wing newspapers, which cite it as proof of corporate callousness.

In autumn many enterprises experience not strikes, but "takeovers": workers start arresting their bosses. The most uncontrollable situation is in the Donbas (the Donets Basin in modern Ukraine).* "The miners have gone utterly mad," the mine owners telegraph Petrograd.

---

*Eastern part of modern Ukraine occupied by two self-proclaimed states—Donetsk People's Republic and Luhansk People's Republic—which are waging war against Ukraine supported by Russia.

On 25 September the three ambassadors to Russia for the European Allies—Britain, France, and now Italy—inform Kerensky that they intend to stop all shipments to Russia until the fighting capacity of its army is restored. When the railways go on strike, the economic collapse is complete. The forthcoming winter promises famine and even worse unrest than during the "bread riots" of 1917.

BACK TO GEORGIA

Everyone is tired of the endless political debates, yet the chin-wagging continues. Kerensky arranges a "democratic conference" at the Alexandrinsky Theatre that sits for two weeks and finally elects from its ranks a "pre-parliament."

The Bolsheviks announce that their nominated delegates are Lenin and Zinoviev. It is a test to see whether the Bolsheviks have been forgiven, for both leaders are still on Kerensky's wanted list. Kerensky duly announces that Lenin should be arrested as soon as he sets foot in the theatre.

Tsereteli believes that the pre-parliament can save Russia from the Bolsheviks. Together with the Kadet Vladimir Nabokov, he begins to draft a Russian constitution. Nabokov recalls that Tsereteli spoke endlessly about the threat of the Bolsheviks coming to power. "Of course," says Tsereteli, "they won't last more than two or three weeks, but just think of the damage they could still do. That must be avoided at all costs."

However, in early October Tsereteli unexpectedly drops everything and returns to the Georgian capital on family business. It is his first trip home for ten years.

A PROVINCIAL STRATEGIST

"Vladimir Ilyin" (a.k.a., "Nikolai Lenin") is still living in Finland under the protection of the local authorities. But he is restless. The "good" news about the Bolsheviks' ascendancy does not please him: he thinks they should be more proactive and seize power.

It is a repeat of the situation in early March, when all the seminal events took place in the capital while Lenin was away in some secluded backwater. Only this time he is hindered not by borders, but political expediency. He is still a wanted man. The party's central committee is anxious that he should be protected and that to return him to Petrograd would be dangerous. Lenin is furious and curses his comrades, especially Trotsky, but stays put.

The Bolshevik Party is led by Lev Kamenev and Leon Trotsky (whose first names, incidentally, both mean "lion"). Both are "effective managers": Kamenev led the Bolsheviks in the workers' struggle against the Kornilov coup, while Trotsky's eloquence has secured Bolshevik control over the Petrograd Soviet. Now a second Congress of Soviets is convened that is set to consolidate Bolshevik influence even more. Unlike Lenin, they believe that another armed uprising will ruin everything.

Lenin is afraid that the moment will be squandered. In one newspaper he reads that the British could soon conclude a separate peace with the Germans, and in another that Kerensky is planning to surrender Petrograd to Berlin, so that the Germans will deal with the revolutionaries. The bottom line is that action is required.

By late September Lenin can stand it no longer and ups sticks from Helsinki to Vyborg, half the distance to Petrograd, but still in Finland (in those days). There, he is visited by an old friend, Alexander Shotman, who informs him of the severe economic crisis. No one knows how to fix it, least of all the Bolsheviks, who lack expertise, Shotman says.

"Nonsense!" screams Lenin. "Any worker can become a minister. No special skills are needed." He continues: "There is nothing simpler than solving the problem of inflation. We'll print new notes to replace the old ones. It will be done by experts. They will have no choice but to work for us."

According to Lenin, the priority is to seize power and issue decrees to endear the people to the Bolsheviks, namely: declare peace to win over the army; take the land from the landowners to win over the peasants; and give the factories to the workers. "Who will oppose us after that?" says Lenin, smiling. Shotman goes to Petrograd, leaving Lenin in the quiet, provincial Vyborg to draw up a plan.

TO SURRENDER PETROGRAD TO THE GERMANS

Petrograd is buzzing with speculation that German troops are at the gates. The alleged plan to surrender the city to the Germans is seized upon by Trotsky, who turns it into a rhetorical device. In all his speeches he brands Kerensky as "the head of the government of national betrayal," who is plotting a counter-revolutionary coup with the Germans. He knows that no such plans exist, but skillfully exploits the public anxiety.

Interestingly, in September and October 1917 the Bolsheviks accuse the Provisional Government of everything that they themselves will do just a few months later, including disrupting the Constituent Assembly, restoring the death penalty, and moving the capital from Petrograd to Moscow. Moreover, they say that Kerensky's economic policies are leading to starvation and ruin.

The impending coup is on everyone's lips. The Bolsheviks have not started planning for it, yet Petrograd is discussing when it will happen. Gippius ponders the idea of writing a short, sharp manifesto against the Bolsheviks on behalf of the "silent intelligentsia": "In view of the government's criminal feeble-mindedness," she writes and then changes her mind: "It's only words, damn it. It won't have any effect." Public opinion craves a strong hand, a dictator capable of imposing order. "Everyone is dreaming of bayonets," admits Gippius.

THE NEW RASPUTIN

Even before the Kornilov affair, the papers were writing about a counter-revolutionary coup and the restoration of the monarchy. In early August, in response to such rumors, the Provisional Government placed the former grand dukes Mikhail (the tsar's brother) and Pavel (his uncle) under house arrest.

A month later they are freed. In September Pavel is visited by a young officer, who says that he is an envoy of Colonel Igor Sikorsky, the legendary aeronautical engineer. He offers the family an escape plan: one of Sikorsky's aircraft will make a nighttime landing in the park outside the grand duke's home, and he and his family will be whisked away to Stockholm.

"Dear friend, I am deeply touched by the proposal, but it sounds like something from the pages of Jules Verne," replies the grand duke. They will be spotted, he says, and refuses to even try.

Anna Vyrubova, the former lady-in-waiting of Empress Alexandra, lives quietly in Petrograd. That is until 25 August, when she suddenly learns from a newspaper report that she and her associates are to be exiled from Russia as "particularly dangerous counter-revolutionaries." But on their way to Helsinki the car with the "counter-revolutionaries" is unhooked and all the passengers are dispatched to prison. It is only by some miracle that the sailors don't kill them. By some miracle, the sailors who found them spare their lives.

Vyrubova and the others are taken to the Sveaborg Fortress on board the *Polar Star*, a yacht that belonged to the imperial family. Vyrubova has sailed on it many times before. "In that filthy, spit-covered, smoke-filled cabin, it was impossible to recognize the wonderful dining room of Their Majesties. At their table, there sat a hundred 'rulers'—all dirty, brutal sailors," she recalls.

Vyrubova spends a month in prison, until her mother somehow manages to get hold of Trotsky in the hallway of the Petrograd Soviet. He orders the release of "Kerensky's prisoner." On 3 October Vyrubova is taken to the Smolny Institute in Petrograd, where she meets Kamenev and his wife Olga, Trotsky's sister. They give her dinner, after which Kamenev says that he will personally vouchsafe her freedom. Thereafter, the press begins to write that Vyrubova is now associated with Trotsky and Kamenev and has allegedly turned into a Bolshevik. "It's just like before," she exclaims in her diary, "only this time the papers have replaced Rasputin with Trotsky."

THE DIE IS CAST

Meanwhile, Lenin is putting the finishing touches to his article "Can the Bolsheviks keep hold of state power?" Finally, on 6 October, he journeys to Petrograd. The fact that the Bolsheviks are planning an armed uprising is hardly a secret: even children know about it. The Military Revolutionary Committee orders the Petrograd garrison not to carry out any orders without Bolshevik approval. Trotsky tables a resolution with the Petrograd Soviet calling for the seizure of power by the workers and soldiers. He is getting carried away by the moment, just like Gapon on the eve of Bloody Sunday a dozen years before.

Local residents prepare for the uprising as if expecting some kind of Saint Bartholomew's Day massacre: they are sure that armed soldiers and sailors will break into their homes and slaughter them in their beds. Local residents set up the so-called "house committees" for keeping watch and reporting signs of imminent danger.

On 10 October, the Bolsheviks gather at the home of the Menshevik Sukhanov, who, incidentally, is absent from his own apartment. Twelve of the twenty-four central committee members are present, including Trotsky, Kamenev, Zinoviev, Stalin, and a clean-shaven gentleman wearing a wig and thick horn-rimmed glasses. It is "Comrade Ivanov," known occasionally as Lenin.

The meeting reveals a split among the Bolsheviks. The head of the Bolshevik faction in the Petrograd Soviet, Kamenev, is categorically opposed to the planned uprising; he is supported by Zinoviev, supposedly

Lenin's right-hand man. Lenin calls them traitors, saying that Kerensky is preparing to surrender Petrograd to the Germans and launch another Kornilov offensive. Urgent action is needed, says the party leader Lenin. The remaining Bolsheviks understand the power of newspaper gossip, yet do not argue: they believe in Lenin's sixth sense and do not think he has been duped by the press. Trotsky is intoxicated by the feeling of power flowing into his hands. In the end, only two vote against the uprising, with ten in favor.

Trotsky earmarks 25 October as the date of the uprising, when the Second Congress of Soviets is due to commence in Petrograd. The plan is simple and even "democratic": the Congress will deliver a vote of no confidence in the Provisional Government and form a new one. Whereas the first congress in June was led by Tsereteli and recognized the authority of the Provisional Government, the second will be headed by the new leaders of the Petrograd Soviet—Trotsky and Kamenev. Back in June, Lenin had interrupted Tsereteli when the latter stated that there was no party in Russia capable of seizing power. This time around there will be no need for interruptions.

Trotsky believes that the congress will legitimize the coup, but Lenin is impatient and cannot understand the need to justify the uprising. "Everything is set for 25 October," says Trotsky. Lenin labels him a "25 October fetishist," but cannot overrule the leader of the Petrograd Soviet.

LENIN AND HIS TOOTHACHE

Lenin fears that Kerensky will recover his wits and disarm the Bolsheviks, as was the case in July. He is desperate to strike while the Provisional Government is weak. Lenin's fears are grounded. At a meeting of the Provisional Government on the night of 23-24 October, Kerensky does indeed say that all members of the Military Revolutionary Committee should be arrested immediately. The prime minister is aware of the Bolshevik plan and understands the threat posed by the Congress of Soviets. But ministers have doubts and propose a softer measure: ban the Bolshevik press.

That night, government troops are sent to the Bolsheviks' printing house and confiscate all copies of the latest issues of its newspapers. This pre-emptive strike plays into the hands of Lenin's supporters, who now agree that urgent action is required, otherwise they will be arrested ahead of the congress. Lenin, now hiding in a safe house, does not receive his morning edition of *Working Path* and fears that Kerensky has started a crackdown. However, at 10 a.m. Bolshevik-friendly soldiers arrive at the printing press and drive away the young government troops, who are only student cadets.

At the Smolny Institute, the headquarters of the Petrograd Soviet, the Bolsheviks are continuously in session. Observing them is the American journalist John Reed,* who remarks that the Bolsheviks barely eat or sleep: Trotsky and Kamenev address the workers and soldiers, sometimes speaking for six, eight, or even twelve hours a day. It is decided that all members of the Bolshevik central committee should reside permanently at Smolny. The guards at the entrance are supplied with machine guns, and extra regiments loyal to the Bolsheviks are called in. The Baltic Fleet sails warships into the capital along the Neva. Fearing that the government will try to sever the communication lines, the Bolsheviks send troops to guard the post office and the telegraph.

The soldiers and workers are getting itchy feet: When will the Bolsheviks arrest the Provisional Government? Trotsky replies that if Kerensky acquiesces to the resolutions of the Congress of Soviets, there will be no need for any arrests. Meanwhile, the increasingly restless Lenin joins the workers and soldiers in demanding the immediate arrest of the government. He writes to the Petrograd Soviet, urging his comrades to disarm the government cadets and seize power. In the evening, without waiting for a reply, he goes to the Petrograd Soviet in person. He is unrecognizable: not only has he shaved off his beard and moustache, but he now also has a handkerchief wrapped around his face, as if suffering from a toothache.

THE BLIND LEADING THE BLIND

On the morning of 24 October, Kerensky arrives for a meeting of the pre-parliament. Speaking clearly and convincingly, he states that waiting is not an option and calls on his ministers to sanction the arrest of the Bolsheviks. As usual, the call for immediate action prompts a lengthy discussion. The debate continues well into the night.

Throughout the next day preparations are made to defend against the Bolshevik offensive. Troops supposedly loyal to the Provisional Government are brought in, including cadets and women soldiers. Adult men—in particular, soldiers of the Petrograd garrison—cannot be relied upon. The bicycle infantry that used to guard the Winter Palace declare that they no

---

* The author of *Ten Days That Shook the World*.

longer wish to serve the government and leave their barracks to hold a spontaneous rally.

However, the cadets and women soldiers are not as pliable as expected. When the First Petrograd Women's Battalion arrives at the Winter Palace and is ordered to guard the building, many ask to return to the barracks, saying that they were expecting to take part in a parade. But by evening around two hundred women soldiers and two thousand cadets have surrounded the Winter Palace, in the company of slightly more than one hundred officers.

The commander of the Petrograd Military District orders all bridges in the capital to be raised, but the order is not carried out. The Women's Battalion is afraid to approach the Troitsky Bridge because it is in range of the cannons of the Peter and Paul Fortress, where the garrison supports the Bolsheviks.

A unit of cadets goes to the central telegraph building to relieve the guard, but the on-duty troops refuse to leave. They have gone over to the Bolsheviks and force the cadets to back off. That night the soldiers seize the post office building, not far from the telegraph.

The uprising is only just beginning, but it is already clear that the authority of the Provisional Government is crumbling—everything is much calmer and less bloody than it was at the start of the February revolution.

RUNNING OUT OF ENERGY

Lenin, meanwhile, is making his way to the Smolny Institute. Only on trying to enter the building does he encounter a problem: he has no pass. But he manages to slip inside with a bustling crowd of workers. It is Lenin's first time inside the Smolny Institute. He wanders from room to room, looking for familiar faces, and inadvertently stumbles upon a meeting of the Mensheviks, who, mistaking him for a hungry worker, offer the disguised Bolshevik leader a sausage sandwich.

Even more in need of a sausage sandwich at that moment is Trotsky. He recalls how, after another interminable meeting, he collapsed onto a nearby couch, asked Kamenev for a cigarette, and promptly passed out. Regaining consciousness, he sees Kamenev's alarmed face: "Do you need some medicine?" he asks. "How about some food," replies Trotsky. "I can't remember the last time I ate. It certainly wasn't yesterday."

The Provisional Government sits until 2 a.m. and leaves the Winter Palace, leaving Kerensky there alone. He is still trying to summon a Cossack regiment to protect the palace, but without success.

That same night the Smolny Institute hosts a meeting of the Bolshevik central committee. Heartened by how the revolt is progressing, Lenin suggests forming a government made up solely of Bolsheviks. However, the only affirmative decision he takes is to go to sleep—right on the floor of Trotsky's office.

A STAR-SPANGLED DEPARTURE

On the morning of 25 October, pro-Bolshevik soldiers continue seizing the main facilities in Petrograd without resistance. Around seventy of them approach the telephone exchange, which is guarded by a few dozen cadets. Seeing their numerical inferiority, the cadets surrender the building without a fight. On entering the telephone exchange, the soldiers sever all lines to the Winter Palace.

That same morning Lenin writes an appeal, "To the Citizens of Russia," in which he states that the Provisional Government has been overthrown and power has passed into the hands of the Military Revolutionary Committee. This is a great exaggeration, since the Petrograd garrison soldiers are simply moving around the city, placing guards at key institutions. They calmly take control of the state bank and release all Bolsheviks from the Kresty prison.

Kerensky is afraid that the Bolsheviks will come for him before his promised reinforcements arrive. At 9 a.m. he goes to his office at the Winter Palace and starts burning documents. The commander of the Petrograd Military District, Colonel Polkovnikov, reports that the situation is hopeless: the Provisional Government has no more soldiers at its disposal. Kerensky instructs Deputy Prime Minister Konovalov to call a ministerial meeting. He himself runs to the General Staff building, where he learns that there are indeed no new troops. The commanders of the cadets and the Women's Battalion say that their forces are insufficient to defend the Winter Palace, but are still hopeful of receiving Cossack reinforcements and battle-hardened troops from the front.

Kerensky tells Polkovnikov that he intends to leave the city to meet the troops supposedly heading to Petrograd from the Northern Front. Polkovnikov tries to find Kerensky a car, but it is not so straightforward. There are no vehicles in the palace garage, so inquiries are made at the local foreign embassies. The Italians refuse, but the Americans agree. The secretary of the US embassy, the appropriately named Sheldon Whitehouse, delivers two vehicles to the Winter Palace, replete with star-spangled banners.

Kerensky asks him to inform the other ambassadors not to recognize the Bolshevik government under any circumstances, since he will return in five days at the most with reinforcements.

At 11 a.m. the two vehicles pull off with Kerensky and his adjutants inside. An hour later the Provisional Government assembles at the Winter Palace for what is to be its last meeting and is surprised to discover that Kerensky has disappeared.

THE LAST SUPPER

On 25 October the Winter Palace hosts the last and most remarkable sitting of the Provisional Government. Those in attendance know from the start that they are doomed. The Winter Palace guards do not mince words when reporting that they cannot offer protection against a Bolshevik assault. The ministers believe that their leader Kerensky has fled, and they know that they do not have the support of the masses. Yet they stubbornly continue to sit and wait.

Ten government members are there from the start, later joined by three more. Who are these people? Four millionaire tycoons, two lawyers, two professors, an engineer, an economist, a doctor, a theologian, a naval officer, and a worker. All of them are between thirty-one and fifty-four years old. Three of the entrepreneurs—Konovalov, Tretyakov, and Smirnov—are the "young capitalists" who, together with Pavel Ryabushinsky, sought freedom and reforms on the part of the authorities. Prosecutor-General Malyantovich is a prominent lawyer who defended Trotsky in 1906 and also won Maria Andreyeva's case against Zinaida Morozova, ironically securing 100,000 roubles* from the widow of Savva Morozov for the Bolsheviks. The labor minister is the thirty-five-year-old worker Kuzma Gvozdev, who in January 1917 was arrested on the orders of then Interior Minister Protopopov. It was his arrest that effectively kick-started the February revolution. Now he himself is a member of the latest government to be overthrown.

The session is opened by Deputy Prime Minister Alexander Konovalov, who informs his colleagues of the previous night's events and of Kerensky's whereabouts. Naval Minister Verderevsky says that he does not understand why the meeting has been convened, since the ministers have no real power. He is given short shrift by Dr. Kishkin, an old Kadet, one

---

* About $1,318,333 in 2017.

of the founders of the Liberal Party: "We are not the Petrograd Provisional Government, but the All-Russian Provisional Government. If we have lost power in Petrograd, it does not mean that we have lost power in Russia." Deputy Prime Minister Konovalov suggests that the ministers remain at the Winter Palace, despite the threat of arrest. The proposal is adopted without objection.

The meeting also votes to appoint Dr. Kishkin as the minister responsible for the city's defense. But what can he do? The only hope is the Cossacks, who will never support the Bolsheviks. But neither Konovalov nor Kishkin can persuade them to side with the government.

To the aid comes Pinhas Rutenberg, the famous SR, "friend" and killer of Georgy Gapon; Rutenberg has recently been appointed by Kerensky as vice-governor of Petrograd. He recalls that his comrade Savinkov is in touch with the Cossacks. Savinkov promises to help and goes to meet with the Cossack leaders.

In the afternoon the ministers learn that posters are being plastered around the city announcing the new Bolshevik government, including Prime Minister Lenin and Foreign Minister Trotsky. Soon after, the news arrives that the Bolsheviks have dispersed the pre-parliament.

Vladimir Nabokov, the deputy chairman of the pre-parliament, goes to the Winter Palace. The mood there is one of extreme despondency. He is approached by Sergei Tretyakov, a Moscow tycoon and the grandson of one of the founders of the Tretyakov Gallery. He is very angry with Kerensky, who has betrayed them, he says, adding that the situation is hopeless. Foreign Minister Tereshchenko interjects that troops loyal to the government are on their way—they just need to hold out for forty-eight hours.

Nabokov leaves the Winter Palace as discreetly as he arrived. The other ministers could also depart, but instead they stubbornly sit and wait. At 6:30 p.m. they go to the dining room, where they are served soup, fish, and artichokes. Immediately after dinner, an ultimatum is issued by the Bolsheviks: the ministers have twenty minutes to surrender. If they do not, the cruiser *Aurora*, which has already pulled up alongside the Winter Palace on the Neva, will open fire.

The telephones at the Winter Palace start trilling. In order to talk in peace, the ministers retire to a side room with no annoying modern means of communication. They decide unanimously to reject the ultimatum.

Cups of tea are ordered in anticipation of the onslaught. But the storm does not begin. The clock strikes eight, then nine. All the while, the naval minister is desperately trying to persuade his colleagues to surrender: "Do you know what will happen if the *Aurora* opens fire? The Winter Palace will be turned into a heap of rubble." But the ministers do not listen.

It is odd, for the ministers understand that they no longer hold power. During the analogous February uprising, it did not take long for the imperial government to scatter, even though its members still saw themselves as appointees of the Anointed One. Why now do the ministers risk their lives and the lives of the women soldiers and cadets guarding them?

A COMMON MAN

At 3 p.m. Leon Trotsky ascends the podium at the Smolny Institute and announces that the Provisional Government is no more: "I know of no other example in the history of the revolutionary movement to have involved such a huge mass of people and to have been so bloodless. Kerensky's Provisional Government is dead. The broomstick of history has swept it aside." This phrase is Lenin's cue to enter the hall. Trotsky gives him the floor. Lenin delivers the first of many triumphant speeches, listing the immediate objectives of the new government: create an entirely new state apparatus; end the war; and destroy the propertied classes. "You are pre-empting the will of the Congress of Soviets," shout a few disgruntled voices in the hall.

The Congress of Soviets is due to meet later that night. Lenin demands the storming of the Winter Palace and the arrest of the Provisional Government before the Congress starts. He prowls around the small hall like a caged lion.

Trotsky says that "the common man has been sleeping peacefully and does not yet know that power has been transferred." He is right: most inhabitants of Petrograd suspect nothing. There are posters around the city stating that the old government has been overthrown, but there is no evidence of it, other than the *Aurora* alongside the Winter Palace.

At around 10 p.m. the opera singer Feodor Chaliapin is on stage. He is dressed in a purple robe, holding a scepter, and wearing a crown. He is playing the role of King Philip of Spain. He surveys his subjects and . . . suddenly a cannon shot rings out. Then another. The actors are frightened and slowly edge their way off the stage. The audience is also jumpy. A minute later, an official runs on stage and informs the hall that the shells are not being fired in the direction of the theatre, so there is nothing to fear: "Ladies and gentlemen, the cruiser *Aurora* is shelling the Provisional Government inside the Winter Palace," he announces. Clearly nothing to worry about. . . .

At roughly the same time, Kerensky arrives in Pskov and inquires as to whether his government-loyal troops are heading towards the capital. Kerensky, now the supreme commander as well as the prime minister, issued an order to that effect in the morning. But he learns to his horror that the commander-in-chief of the Northern Front, General Cheremisov, cancelled the order because he considered it pointless: "The soldiers will not fight for Kishkin." There are no troops on the move. Kerensky goes to the Pskov apartment of his brother-in-law, General Baranovsky, where, according to the latter, he "suffers the torments of hell and despair."

When the *Aurora's* first salvo rings out, the defenders of the Winter Palace immediately start to surrender, including three hundred Cossacks (who have decided to join the Provisional Government), followed by the Women's Battalion. A few cadets remain on duty inside the palace.

At 10:40 p.m. the Congress of Soviets gets underway at the Smolny Institute. Of the 670 participants in the congress about three hundred are Bolsheviks. "The mood of those assembled is festive. There is great excitement and not the slightest panic, despite the fact that fighting is still raging around the Winter Palace," rejoices the art historian Lunacharsky. In truth, only the Bolsheviks are celebrating. Their opponents are "panic-stricken, angry, confused and nervous." One of the Mensheviks runs up to the art historian and shouts: "The *Aurora* is bombarding the Winter Palace! Do you hear, Comrade Lunacharsky? Your cannon are destroying Rastrelli's masterpiece!" The Winter Palace is, in fact, under fire from three sides: from the *Aurora*, from the Peter and Paul Fortress, and from guns mounted on the arch of the General Staff building. Some cadets are wounded, and Dr. Kishkin does his best to patch them up. There is a fire in one of the rooms, and the ministers do what they can to put out the flames.

"We are here in the Winter Palace, completely abandoned," says Agriculture Minister Semyon Maslov. "It was democracy that sent us here. But my last word will be to curse that wretched democracy for failing to protect us."

Back at Smolny, the Menshevik leader Julius Martov demands an immediate halt to the shelling of the Winter Palace and for negotiations to begin. "The revolt of the people needs no justification," smiles Trotsky. "What has happened is an uprising, not a conspiracy. The masses have won victory under our banner, and now you want them to make concessions and come to an agreement? With whom? I ask you, with whom do we have to reach an agreement?" "In that case, we shall leave," cries Martov.

They do indeed. Most of the Mensheviks and the SRs get up and walk out. Only the Bolsheviks and their allies remain in the hall. Trotsky yells after them that they are making a feeble and criminal attempt to disrupt the genuine will of the workers and soldiers.

At 1:30 a.m. around three hundred Bolsheviks, led by Vladimir Antonov-Ovseyenko, one of three new war ministers, go to the Winter Palace. The troops take a long time to find the Provisional Government inside the huge building. During the search, they come across the former office of Nicholas II, which has been left intact for the creation of a museum. They smash it to bits.

They eventually find the ministers: "The pressure of the crowd caused it to burst through the door. It came spilling in, flooding all corners of the room like water," recalls Justice Minister Malyantovich.

Antonov-Ovseyenko describes the scene: "[The ministers] were sitting at the table, blurred into a single grey, pallid, quivering blob. 'In the name of the Military Revolutionary Committee, you are under arrest!' I said to them. 'Members of the Provisional Government, I order you to surrender in the interests of avoiding bloodshed,' said Konovalov."

The ministers are taken from the Winter Palace across Troitsky Bridge to the Peter and Paul Fortress. Along the way a crowd gathers, demanding their heads to be cut off and thrown into the water. By 4 a.m. they are all inside prison cells at the fortress.

Before that, at 3 a.m., Kamenev reads out a telegram from the podium of the Smolny hall: the Winter Palace has been taken. The congress rejoices and approves the decision to set up a new revolutionary government headed by Lenin.

"You know," Lenin says to Trotsky, "after all the persecution and underground activity . . ." He tries to find the right phrase in Russian, but gives up. He says, "*es schwindelt*,"* and gestures that his head is spinning. He and Trotsky exchange glances and chuckle.

---

* It's intoxicating.

EPILOGUE

Only in history textbooks does the October Revolution seem like a watershed moment that changed the country forever. Most people in Russia do not notice any major upheavals either on 26 October 1917 or over the days that follow. The Petrograd City Duma does not recognize the Bolshevik government and sets up the Committee for the Salvation of the Motherland and the Revolution—a substitute for the Provisional Government and an alternative to the Bolsheviks' Council of People's Commissars.

No one believes that the Bolsheviks will be able to cling to power, which is why the Mensheviks and the Socialist-Revolutionaries withdraw from the Congress of Soviets—as a form of punishment. They are certain that without them the Bolsheviks are doomed. "The Bolsheviks might be able to seize power, but they will not keep it for more than three days," the American journalist John Reed quotes one of the Mensheviks. "They do not have the people to run the country. The best thing is probably to let them try—they will fall flat on their faces." On 29 October, however, the Bolsheviks disperse the Committee for the Salvation of the Motherland and Revolution and consolidate their grip on Petrograd.

The Bolsheviks won popular support in the first place thanks to three bombastic slogans. Their first promise is peace. To that end, on 26 October the Congress of Soviets adopts the newly drafted Decree on Peace, which appeals to the warring parties to conclude a peace without annexations or indemnities. However, the war does not end. On 9 December Trotsky travels to Brest-Litovsk for talks with Germany, but refuses to accept Berlin's conditions. Germany launches a new offensive and seizes additional territories, as a result of which the Treaty of Brest-Litovsk is signed on 3 March 1918 under far more onerous terms: Germany annexes around one million square kilometers of Russian territory and forces Russia to pay an indemnity of 6 billion marks (2.75 million roubles*). But even that does not put a stop to the killing. The end of one war sees the start of another—this time a civil conflict.

---

*About $36,208,333 in 2017.

The Bolsheviks' second promise is to provide land for the peasants. However, they do the opposite: on 27 October the Congress of Soviets adopts the Decree on Land, abolishing the right of private land ownership entirely. At that time, a fifth of all land in Russia belongs to the peasants, but now the state takes it away from them and implements a redistribution and utilization program. But that is not all: less than six months later, in the spring of 1918, a "food dictatorship" decree is issued under which "committees of the poor" confiscate "surpluses" from the peasants, which amounts in practice to almost everything they produce.

The third and most important promise—to hand over the factories to the workers—is also unfulfilled. All enterprises are nationalized. The workers' dream of controlling the factories and receiving some of the profits is shattered.

More than six months after the February Revolution, people are still waiting for the Constituent Assembly to convene to determine the identity of the new Russian state. But having come to power, the Bolsheviks lose interest, contemptuously referring to it as the *uchredilka*.[*]

Nevertheless, the long-awaited elections to the Constituent Assembly begin five days after the overthrow of the Provisional Government, on 30 October. But a month later, even before the results are announced, the new Bolshevik Government disbands the election committee which oversees the elections to the Constituent Assembly. The Bolshevik Moisei Uritsky is appointed its new chairman.

On 28 October Lenin signs a decree banning the Kadets as "a party of enemies of the people"; all its leaders face arrest and a revolutionary tribunal. The Kadets Andrei Shingarev and Fedor Kokoshkin, former members of the Provisional Government and newly elected to the Constituent Assembly, are arrested that same day. They will die the next day after the opening session, for they are killed by sailors in a prison hospital in early January.

According to the official election results, the Bolsheviks win Petrograd and Moscow, but nationwide the Socialist-Revolutionaries are in front. On 5 January the Constituent Assembly convenes at the Tauride Palace in Petrograd for a single day. On this day, soldiers from the Petrograd garrison open fire on a demonstration of supporters of the Constituent Assembly and kill about fifty people. The next day the deputies return to the Tauride Palace only to find it closed—a carbon copy of how Prime Minister Stolypin dissolved the First and Second Dumas.

---

[*] A pejorative contraction of *Uchreditelnaya sobraniye* (Constituent Assembly).

In the winter of 1918 the Bolshevik government relocates to Moscow, away from the front line and the fickle Petrograd garrison, which poses a threat to any regime.

Throughout the country, including Petrograd, the winter of 1918 sees the onset of famine. Politics gives way to the more basic question of how to put food on the table. What to do? Stay at home and wait? Flee to the Cossacks on the Don River, where opponents of the Bolsheviks are gathering? Try to sneak abroad? During this winter period, about a million people leave Petrograd to escape the hunger and cold.

However, not everyone has a choice. In March 1918 Zinoviev and Uritsky order the remaining members of the Romanov family to be exiled from Petrograd. In June-July 1918 Sverdlov and Lenin make the decision to execute the tsar and his family, who are already in exile in the Urals. The first to be murdered is the tsar's brother, Grand Duke Mikhail. He (together with his personal secretary, an Englishman by the name of Johnson) is kidnapped in Perm, taken to a forest, and shot. A month later, in Yekaterinburg, in the basement of Ipatiev House, Nicholas II, Alexandra, their children, and four servants are shot by firing squad. The next day, one hundred and fifty kilometers from Yekaterinburg, in the city of Alapaevsk, eight people are dumped alive down a coalmine shaft, including Alexandra's sister, Ella, and a number of grand dukes, where they die in agony from their wounds.

On 30 August, in Moscow, Fanny Kaplan, a member of the Socialist-Revolutionary Party, shoots Lenin three times in retaliation for the dispersal of the Constituent Assembly, seriously injuring him. On the same day, Moisei Uritsky, the now former head of the Central Election Commission, who now runs the City Emergency Commission, is assassinated in Petrograd. In response to the attempt on Lenin's life and the murder of Uritsky, the Soviet government launches what becomes known as the "Red Terror": "The death of one of our fighters must be paid for by the lives of thousands of enemies," writes the Petrograd newspaper *Red Newspaper*.

On 5 September Moscow's Petrovsky Park witnesses the new regime's first public execution: former tsarist officials and prominent members of the Union of the Russian People are shot, including the ex-ministers Nikolai Maklakov, Alexei Khvostov, and Ivan Shcheglovitov, and the former deputy minister Stepan Beletsky.

The papers publish a list of "hostages" who are to be shot if a single Soviet worker is killed. The list opens with the names of four grand dukes, including the liberal Nicholas Mikhailovich. Gorky tries to intercede for him, for the grand duke is a renowned historian. "The revolution does not need historians," Lenin reportedly replies. The four grand dukes are executed at the Peter and Paul Fortress in late 1919. Yuly Martov, on learning of their death, pens an article entitled "Shame!"

Those members of the imperial family lucky enough to have made their way to Crimea are able to escape: Britain's King George V dispatches the battleship HMS *Marlborough* to pick up his aunt, Empress Dowager Maria Feodorovna, and other relatives (the late tsar's sisters, Olga and Xenia, his brother-in-law Sandro, the former supreme commander Nikolai Nikolaevich, the Montenegrin princesses, and members of the Yusupov family). The ship takes them to Britain.

By this time, there exist two Russias: one Red, the other White, with its capital in Omsk. This alternative Russian state is led by the remnants of the Provisional Government, headed by the Socialist-Revolutionary Nikolai Avksentiev, and later by Admiral Kolchak, who establishes an anti-communist government in Siberia. It is his government, and not the Bolsheviks, that is de facto recognized by the international community.

The Russian Civil War lasts almost six years and ends in victory for the Bolsheviks. It claims the lives of more than 10 million people—five times more than the number of Russian casualties in the First World War, which the Bolsheviks promised to end. Of that figure, 2.5 million are killed in battle, another 2 million fall victim to the Red (and White) Terror, while around 6 million die from hunger and disease. On top of that, approximately 2 million emigrate. A significant portion of the country is destroyed; the coal industry in the Donetsk region (in modern Ukraine) and the oilfields of Baku (in Azerbaijan) are particularly affected.

In February 1919 the publicist Vasily Rozanov dies of hunger in the town of Sergiev Posad near Moscow. In April 1921 the founder of the Union of the Russian People, Alexander Dubrovin, is shot on the orders of the Cheka, the Soviet secret police. Yuly Martov initially fights to reform Soviet power from within, but admits defeat in 1920 and moves to Berlin, where he dies from tuberculosis.

Members of the creative intelligentsia react differently to the Bolshevik victory. The poet Alexander Blok, for instance, welcomes the October Revolution. Many of his friends break off contact with him. In 1919 Blok bumps into Zinaida Gippius on board a tram. "Will you give me your hand?" he asks. "Personally, yes. Publicly, the bridges between us have been blown up," she replies.

Many dream of leaving Petrograd, but it is soon prohibited. The only way to get out of the city is by joining the Red Army. Merezhkovsky is lucky—he manages to obtain permission to give lectures to Red Army soldiers on the history of Ancient Egypt. But instead of lecturing, he, Gip-pius, and Filosofov make their way to Poland. There, the "Brotherhood of Three" disbands forever: Filosofov remains in Warsaw, with Savinkov, to fight against the Bolsheviks, while the Merezhkovskys depart for Paris.

Blok, too, eventually asks to leave the country. Gorky, Lunacharsky, and even Kamenev petition on his behalf. Lenin refuses several times. In August 1921 Blok dies from heart disease, still waiting for permission.

As for Gorky, he turns into a leading critic of the Bolsheviks, but is allowed to leave for treatment in Berlin for his past merits as an opponent of tsarism. Maria Andreyeva, Gorky's ex-civil wife, and her lover, a secret police agent, follow Gorky to spy on him for the Soviet government. They keep tabs on his expenses, monitor all his publications, and report everything he does to Moscow. Only in 1924 does he manage to shake them off by moving to Italy.

Tsereteli and Chkheidze, together with other Georgian socialists, try to create an independent Georgian republic, but are forced to emigrate after a successful offensive by the Bolsheviks. Chkheidze commits suicide in Paris in 1921. Tsereteli, meanwhile, outlives his fellow countryman Stalin, dying in the United States in 1959.

The former monk Iliodor, now the layman Sergei Trufanov, returns to Tsaritsyn in 1918 and declares himself to be "Patriarch Iliodor." In 1922 he leaves for the United States, becomes a Baptist, and works as a hotel door-man, dying in New York in 1952.

Relations between Russian émigrés are complex, to say the least. The liberal monarchists and the Black Hundreds are literally at each other's throats: the latter blame the former for the revolution. In 1921, in Berlin, Guchkov is attacked by a group of radical monarchists. A year later the Black Hundreds try to gun down Milyukov for having insulted the empress in his infamous "Stupidity or Treason?" speech before the Duma. Milyukov survives, but Vladimir Nabokov, the father of the future writer, is killed on the spot and nine others are injured.

Most members of the Russian imperial family remain in France. In 1924 Miechen's son, Grand Duke Kirill, declares himself "emperor in exile," but he is recognized by neither Empress Dowager Maria Feodorovna, nor the former supreme commander Grand Duke Nikolai Nikolaevich, nor Grand Duke Dmitry.

Nikolai Nikolaevich dies in Antibes in 1929, while Grand Duke Dmi-try passes away in Switzerland in 1942 and Felix Yusupov in Paris in 1964. In the 1940s Felix's daughter, Irina, meets and even befriends Rasputin's daughter, Maria.

The arrested Anna Vyrubova miraculously escapes due to the slovenli-
ness of the Red Army soldiers escorting her. She goes into hiding in Petrograd for a long time, before eventually moving to Finland with her mother.
She lives to be eighty years old and dies in 1964, a few months before
Brezhnev replaces Khrushchev as the head of the Soviet Union.

Many members of the nobility and intelligentsia who stayed in Soviet
Russia and survived the civil war somehow build new lives: they find work
in Soviet institutions and departments. In the 1920s it seems as if the upheavals are over. But their peaceful existence lasts barely a decade, ending
abruptly with the onset of the Stalinist terror of the 1930s.

The former head of the "Masonic Supreme Council" and former deputy
prime minister in the Provisional Government, Nikolai Nekrasov, changes
his surname to Golgofsky, finds employment in various Soviet ministries
and lectures at university, but in the 1930s he is arrested and sent to the
White Sea Canal gulag. There, he works in the design bureau and even
receives the Order of the Red Banner of Labor for delivering the project
ahead of schedule. Despite that, he is shot in 1940.

He is not alone. Another seven former ministers of the Provisional
Government are executed during the Great Terror, and the rest spend a
significant part of their lives in Soviet prisons. Vladimir Lvov, the perpe-
trator of the "Kornilov putsch," dies in jail in Tomsk in 1930.

Boris Savinkov agrees to cooperate with the Bolsheviks and is lured
back to Russia in 1924. But it is a trap set by the OGPU, the Soviet body
for combating counter-revolutionary activity. He is arrested and sentenced
to death. He allegedly commits suicide at Lubyanka, the secret police
headquarters in central Moscow. His friend Filosofov cannot believe Savinkov's betrayal. He dies alone in German-occupied Warsaw in 1940.

When the purges of the "old Bolsheviks"—Stalin's opponents—begin in
the late 1920s, many describe it as an internal squabble among "spiders in a
jar." Following Lenin's death in 1924, Zinoviev, Kamenev, and Stalin initially
unite against Trotsky to prevent him from becoming Lenin's successor. But
then Stalin turns against all his rivals. He manages to sideline Kamenev by
having him appointed as the Soviet ambassador to Italy. In 1927 Zinoviev
and Trotsky join forces and hold anti-Stalin opposition rallies, dedicated to
the tenth anniversary of the revolution, but crowds of Stalin's supporters
disperse the rallies with shouts of "Down with the oppositionist Yids!"

In 1929 Trotsky is expelled from the Soviet Union and murdered by
Stalin's agents in Mexico in 1940. In 1936 Lev Kamenev and Grigory Zinoviev are tried and executed, followed by several hundred others inside

the Soviet leadership. Despite the pervasive fear of the Great Terror, it still comes as a shock to its victims.

The Second World War challenges the belief system of many émigrés. Grand Duke Sandro, a childhood friend of Nicholas II, praises Stalin for having reconstituted the Russian Empire. Stalin's actions also win the approval of Milyukov, now residing in France. He supports the war against Finland: "I pity the Finns, but Vyborg belongs to Russia." Struve, too, opines that Nicholas II was too soft—all the revolutionaries, including himself, should have been physically eliminated, says the former Marxist and liberal. Milyukov dies in 1943, Struve in 1944.

In 1941 the Paris resident Merezhkovsky delivers an anti-Bolshevik speech for German radio (nobody hears it, but it quickly becomes the stuff of legend). Accused of harboring fascist sympathies, he and Gippius are totally isolated from the Russian émigré community. He dies in December 1941, she in September 1945, both at the age of seventy-six.

Alexander Kerensky outlives almost all his ill-wishers and only just fails to see his ninetieth birthday. He lives abroad in Britain, France, Australia, and the United States. In 1968 he tries to visit the Soviet Union. He asks permission from Brezhnev, stating that he has no regrets about what happened and that the October Revolution and all subsequent events were natural developments. But his return is stymied by the Prague Spring; the Soviet leadership has no time for Kerensky. He dies in 1970 in New York and is buried in London.

The beloved daughter of Leo Tolstoy, Sasha, who received the copyright to her father's works, lives to the age of ninety-five. She spends the 1920s in the new Soviet Union working as a human rights activist. Arrested several times by the Cheka, she finally emigrates in 1929. She dies in the United States in 1979.

The Bolshevik empire itself collapses in 1991. From a historical perspective, those who predicted a speedy end to Bolshevik rule were almost right. For history, seventy years is the blink of an eye.

The Russian Revolution was an event on a planetary scale. It was a tectonic shift that plunged a vast, highly developed civilization into the depths of Hades. Moscow, the current capital of Russia, has preserved about as much of its pre-revolutionary heritage as the Italian capital has of Ancient Rome or Mexico has of the Maya Empire.

This disaster was not an act of God, but anthropogenic. I do not consider it much of an exaggeration to describe it as the biggest manmade catastrophe in history.

The colossal difference in wealth and education made the country extremely unstable, as indeed is any system based on segregation. Sooner or later, the prosperous minority becomes unable to withstand the pressure of the dispossessed majority pushing up from below.

The imperial family, the court, members of the government, the Black Hundreds—thousands of people were unable to renounce their belief in the medieval dogma of the divine origin of tsarist power. Their archaic conviction and stubborn resistance to the bitter end prevented reform and the country's political development. Time and again they brushed aside all moderate evolutionary scenarios.

The tragic culmination was in no way the only possible outcome. The idea of preordained karma—that it was the Russian people's destiny—is currently in vogue in Russia. I hope that this book will cast doubt on that theory. Nothing is known in advance, nothing is 100 percent predetermined. History is one long blunder. The protagonists of this book are forever making plans and predictions, acting on the basis of what always seems to them to be careful calculation. But they almost always delude themselves. Time passes, and all these delusions fade from memory. The protagonists themselves, and the historians who study them, begin to believe that the plan was indeed well-founded, that everything that happened was not accidental, but the fruit of their original intention.

During the writing of this book, I was constantly amazed by the recollections of those who took part in the events. Hundreds of eye-witnesses wrote the most detailed memoirs about what happened and why their (often wildly different) opinions were correct. This is not surprising. The cause of my amazement lay elsewhere. Most of the memoirs were written after the two revolutions of 1917. Their authors already know how the story ends, yet almost none revise their attitude or point of view. All are convinced that they are right. Few consider themselves complicit in the tragic dénouement. They all sank their utopian Atlantis together, but they all point the finger at each other. The gendarme believes that he was right to tighten the screws, and only regrets that he didn't turn them all the way. The revolutionary is sure that he was right to throw bombs, and worries only that he did not hurl more of them. All believe that their intentions were good, but, alas, looking back, they recognize the road that their good intentions have paved—and where it leads.

The tragedy of the early twentieth century is imprinted in Russia's cerebral cortex. Even a century later, the middle class unconsciously expects a recurrence. Russia in the early twenty-first century looks nothing like its early twentieth-century counterpart: society today is incomparably more educated and prosperous than a hundred years ago. Nevertheless, the psychological trauma is still felt. The experience of the civil war and the Red Terror forces new generations of Russians to repeatedly ask themselves: Should I leave? Will it soon be too late?

Like a century ago, many people today share the values of the Black Hundreds, while others justify the purges and the Red Terror. For them, the departure of dissenters from the country is like the discharge of ballast water from a ship—something that will benefit Russia and allow it to sail more speedily. To this day, sections of Russian society continue to wage war on each other and on their historical predecessors.

For the country as a whole, this is yet another tragedy. The cleansing of the intellectual and business elite is eroding its future. Russia has never come to terms with its past; the historical traumas are still raw; the psychological hang-ups persist. Russian history is an illness. Our history has made us all sick. I do not want to die from this illness.

REFERENCES

CHAPTER 1

Andreyeva M. F. *Perepiska. Vospominaniia. Stat'i. Dokumenty* [Correspondence. Memoirs. Artiles. Documents]. Moscow, 1963.

Benois A. N. *Moi vospominania* [My Memoirs]. Moscow, 1980.

Chaliapin F. I. Stranitsy iz moei zhizni [Pages of My Life]. Feodor Ivanovich Chaliapin. Vol. 1. *Literaturnoe nasledstvo. Pis'ma* [Literary Heritage. Letters]. Moscow, 1976.

Dnevniki imperatora Nikolaia II [Diaries of Emperor Nicholas II]. Vol. 1. 1894-1904. Moscow, 2011.

Grand Duke Konstantin Konstantinovich Romanov. (K.R.) *Dnevniki. Vospominaniia. Stikhi. Pis'ma* [Diaries. Memoirs. Poems. Letters]. Moscow, 1998.

Gapon G. *Istoriia moei zhizni* [Story of My Life]. Leningrad, 1926.

Gippius Z. *Sobranie sochinenii v 15-ti tomakh* [Collected Works in 15 Volumes]. Moscow, 2016.

Gorky M. *Pis'ma v 24-kh tomakh* [Letters in 24 Volumes]. Moscow, 1998-present.

Milyukov P. N. *Vospominaniia* [Memoirs]. 1859-1917. Moscow, 1990.

Pis'ma Pobedonostseva Aleksandru III. [Letters of Pobedonostsev to Alexander III]. Moscow, 1924-1926.

Pobedonostsev K. P. *Velikaia lozh' nashego vremeni* [Great Lie of Our Time]. Moscow, 1993.

Tolstoy L. N. *Polnoe sobranie sochinenii v 90 tomakh* [Complete Collected Works in 90 Volumes]. Moscow, Leningrad. 1928-1958.

Tolstaya S. A. *Moia zhizn'* [My Life]. Moscow, 2014.

Witte S. U. *Vospominaniia* [Memoirs]. Moscow, 1960.

CHAPTER 2

Bogdanovich A. *Tri poslednikh samoderzhtsa* [Three Last Autocrats]. Moscow, 1990.

Dostoyevsky F. M. *Dnevnik pisatelia v 2-kh tomakh* [Writer's Diary in 2 Volumes]. Moscow, 2011.

Dnevniki imperatora Nikolaia II [Diaries of Emperor Nicholas II]. Vol. 1. 1894-1904. Moscow, 2011.

Grand Duke Alexander Mikhailovich. *Vospominaniia* [Memoirs]. Moscow, 2015.

Gippius Z. *Dnevniki* [Diaries]. 1914-1917. Moscow, 2017.

Kolyshko I. I. *Velikii raspad. Vospominaniia* [Great Collapse. Memoirs]. St. Petersburg, 2009.

Lamsdorf V. N. *Dnevnik* [Diary]. Vol. 1 (1886-1890). Moscow, 1926.

Lamsdorf V. N. *Dnevnik* [Diary]. Vol. 2 (1891-1892)). Moscow, 1934.

Milyukov P. N. *Vospominaniia* [Memoirs]. 1859-1917. Moscow, 1990.

Stanislavski K. S. *Sobranie sochinenii v 8 tomakh* [Collected Works in 8 Volumes]. Vol. 1. Moscow, 1954.

Suvorin A. S. *Dnevnik* [Diary]. Moscow, 2015.

Tolstoy L. N. *Polnoe sobranie sochinenii v 90 tomakh* [Complete Collected Works in 90 Volumes]. Moscow, Leningrad. 1928-1958.

Witte S. U. *Vospominaniia* [Memoirs]. Moscow, 1960.

CHAPTER 3

Breshko-Breshkovskaya E. *Iz moikh vospominanii* [From My Memoirs]. St. Petersburg, 1906.

Chernov V. M. *V partii sotsialistov-revoliutsionerov. Vospominaniia o vos'mi liderakh* [In the Socialist Revolutionary Party. Memoirs about the Eight Leaders]. St. Petersburg, 2007.

Dnevniki imperatora Nikolaia II [Diaries of Emperor Nicholas II]. Vol. 1. 1894-1904. Moscow, 2011.

Gapon G. *Istoriia moei zhizni* [Story of My Life]. Leningrad, 1926.

Gerasimov A. V. *Na lezvii s terroristami* [On the Blade with the Terrorists]. Moscow, 1991.

Gershuni G. *Iz nedavnego proshlogo* [From the Recent Past]. Leningrad, 1928.

Korolenko V. G. *Dom № 13-yi* [The House No.13]. Moscow, 1903.

Milyukov P. N. *Vospominaniia* [Memoirs]. 1859-1917. Moscow, 1990.

Partiia sotsialistov-revoliutsionerov. Dokumenty i materialy [Socialist Revolutionary Party. Documents and Materials]. 1900-1907. Moscow, 1996.

Pis'ma Azefa [Letters of Azef]. 1893-1917. Moscow, 1994.

Savinkov B. V. *Vospominaniya terrorista* [Memoirs of a Terrorist]. Moscow, 1991.

Spiridovich A. I. *Zapiski zhandarma* [Notes of a Gendarme]. Kharkiv, 1928.

Witte S. U. *Vospominaniia* [Memoirs]. Moscow, 1960.

Zapiski generala Kuropatkina o Russko-iaponskoi voine. Itogi voiny [Notes of General Kuropatkin about Russo-Japanese War. Results of the War]. Berlin, 1911.

Zenzinov V. M. *Iz zhizni revoliutsionera* [From the Life of a Revolutionary]. Paris, 1919. in Russian.

CHAPTER 4

Andreyeva M. F. *Perepiska. Vospominaniia. Stat'i. Dokumenty* [Correspondence. Memoirs. Artiles. Documents]. Moscow, 1963.

Belokonskii I. P. *Zemskoe dvizhenie* [Zemstvo Movement]. Moscow, 1914.

Iz arkhiva Y. O. Martova. Perepiska [From the Archive of Y. O. Martov. Correspondence]. Vol. 1. 1896-1904. Moscow, 2015.

Kizevetter A. A. *Na rubezhe dvukh stoletii: Vospominaniia* [At the Turn of Two Centuries: Memoirs 1881-1914] 1881—1914. Prague, 1929.

Kokovtsov V. N. *Iz moego proshlogo* [From My Past] 1903-1919. Minsk, 2004.

Lenin V. I. *Polnoe sobranie sochinenii v 55-ti tomakh* [Complete Collected Works in 55 Volumes]. Moscow, 1985.

Milyukov P. N. *Vospominaniia* [Memoirs]. 1859-1917. Moscow, 1990.

Petrunkevich I. I. *Iz zapisok obshchestvennogo deiatelia* [From the Notes of a Public Figure]. Moscow, 1993.

Plekhanov G. V. *Sochineniia v 24 tomakh* [Works in 24 Volumes]. Vol. 9. Moscow, 1925.

Savinkov B. V. *Vospominaniya terrorista* [Memoirs of a Terrorist]. Moscow, 1991.

Shipov D. N. *Vospominaniia i dumy o perezhitom* [Memoirs and Thoughts about the Past]. Moscow, 1918.

Stanislavski K. S. *Sobranie sochinenii v 8 tomakh* [Collected Works in 8 Volumes]. Vol. 1. Moscow, 1954.

Struve P. B. *Patriotica. Politika. Kul'tura. Religiia. Sotsializm* [Patriotica. Politics. Culture. Religion. Socialism]. Moscow, 1997.

Tyrkova-Williams A. V. *Na putiakh k svobode* [On the Paths to Freedom]. Moscow, 2007.

CHAPTER 5

Bogdanovich A. *Tri poslednikh samoderzhtsa* [Three Last Autocrats]. Moscow, 1990.

Chernov V. M. *V partii sotsialistov-revoliutsionerov. Vospominaniia o vos'mi liderakh* [In the Socialist Revolutionary Party. Memoirs about the Eight Leaders]. St. Petersburg, 2007.

Denikin A. I. *Put' russkogo ofitsera* [Path of a Russian Officer]. Moscow, 1991.

Dnevniki imperatritsy Marii Fedorovny [Diaries of Empress Maria Feodorovna]. Moscow, 2005.

Dnevniki imperatora Nikolaia II [Diaries of Emperor Nicholas II]. Vol. 1. 1894-1904. Moscow, 2011.

Gerasimov A. V. *Na lezvii s terroristami* [On the Blade with the Terrorists]. Moscow, 1991.

Grand Duchess Maria Pavlovna. *Memuary* [Memoirs]. Moscow, 2004.

Grand Duke Alexander Mikhailovich. *Vospominaniia* [Memoirs]. Moscow, 2015.

Gurko V. I. *Tsar' i Tsaritsa* [Tsar and Tsarina]. Paris, 1927.

Gilliard P. *Imperator Nikolai II i ego sem'ia* [Emperor Nicholas II and His Family]. Leningrad, 1990.

Milyukov P. N. *Vospominaniia* [Memoirs]. 1859-1917. Moscow, 1990.

Mosolov A. A. *Pri dvore imperatora* [At the Court of Emperor]. Riga, 1938.

Stanislavski K. S. *Sobranie sochinenii v 8 tomakh* [Collected Works in 8 Volumes]. Vol. 1. Moscow, 1954.

Suvorin A. S. *Dnevnik* [Diary]. Moscow, 2015.

Shipov D. N. *Vospominaniia i dumy o perezhitom* [Memoirs and Thoughts about the Past]. Moscow, 1918.

Witte S. U. *Vospominaniia* [Memoirs]. Moscow, 1960.

CHAPTER 6

Andreyeva M. F. *Perepiska. Vospominaniia. Stat'i. Dokumenty* [Correspondence. Memoirs. Artiles. Documents]. Moscow, 1963.

Arkhiv A. M. Gor'kogo [Archive of M. Gorky]. Vol. 4. Pis'ma k K. P. Piatnitskomu [Letters to K. P. Piatnitskii]. Moscow, 1954.

Dnevniki imperatora Nikolaia II [Diaries of Emperor Nicholas II]. Vol. 1. 1894-1904. Moscow, 2011.

Dzhunkovskii V. F. *Vospominaniia* [Memoirs]. Vol. 1-2. Moscow, 1997.

Gorky M. *Polnoe sobranie sochinenii v 25-ti tomakh* [Complete Collected Works in 25 Volumes]. Moscow, 1968.

Gippius Z. *Sobranie sochinenii v 15-ti tomakh* [Collected Works in 15 Volumes]. Moscow, 2016.

Gerasimov A. V. *Na lezvii s terroristami* [On the Blade with the Terrorists]. Moscow, 1991.

Gershuni G. *Ob ekspropriatsiiakh* [About the Expropriations]. Hoover Institution on War, Revolution and Peace, Stanford University, USA. Boris Nikolaevsky Collection. Box 12. Folder 1. P. 7-8.

Kokovtsov V. N. *Iz moego proshlogo* [From My Past] 1903-1919. Minsk, 2004.

Krasin L. B. *Dela davno minuvshikh dnei: Vospominaniia* [Affairs of the Bygone Days: Memoirs]. Moscow, 1934.

Mosolov A. A. *Pri dvore imperatora* [At the Court of Emperor]. Riga, 1938.

Olsuf'ev D. L. Revoliutsiia: Iz vospominanii o deviatisotykh godakh i ob moem tovarishche Savve Morozove, um. 1905 g. [Revolution: From the Memoirs about the Nineties and about my Comrade Savva Morozov, died in 1905]. *Vozrozhdenie* [Renaissance], Jul 31, 1931, №2250.

Posse V. A. *Vospominaniia* [Memoirs]. 1905-1917. Moscow, 1923.

Rutenberg P. M. *Ubiistvo Gapona* [Assassination of Gapon]. Leningrad, Moscow, 1990.

Savinkov B. V. *Vospominaniya terrorista* [Memoirs of a Terrorist]. Moscow, 1991.

Witte S. U. *Vospominaniia* [Memoirs]. Moscow, 1960.

CHAPTER 7

Bogdanovich A. *Tri poslednikh samoderzhtsa* [Three Last Autocrats]. Moscow, 1990.

Dnevnik L. A. Tikhomirova [Diary of L. A. Tikhomirov]. In *Krasnyi arkhiv*, 1930. Vol. 38-42.

Gerasimov A. V. *Na lezvii s terroristami* [On the Blade with the Terrorists]. Moscow, 1991.

Dzhunkovskii V. F. *Vospominaniia* [Memoirs]. Vol. 1-2. Moscow, 1997.

Kokovtsov V. N. *Iz moego proshlogo* [From My Past] 1903-1919. Minsk, 2004. (in Russian)

Lunacharskii A. *Siluety* [The Silhouettes]. Moscow, 1965.

Milyukov P. N. *Vospominaniia* [Memoirs]. 1859-1917. Moscow, 1990.

Nikol'skii B. V. *Dnevnik* [Diary]. 1896-1918. St. Petersburg, 2015.

Padenie tsarskogo rezhima. Stenograficheskie otchety doprosov i pokazanii, dannykh v 1917 g. v Chrezvychainoi Sledstvennoi Komissii Vremennogo Pravitel'stva [The Fall of the Tsarist Regime. Verbatim Transcripts of the Interrogations and Testimony Given in 1917 in the Extraordinary Investigation Commission of the Provisional Government]. Leningrad, 1924-1927.

Shul'gin V. V. *Dni: zapiski* [Days: Notes]. Belgrade, 1925.

Savinkov B. V. *Vospominaniya terrorista* [Memoirs of a Terrorist]. Moscow, 1991.

Trotsky L. D. *Sobranie sochinenii* [Collected Works]. Moscow, Leningrad, 1924-1927.

Voennyi dnevnik velikogo kniazia Andreia Vladimirovicha Romanova [War Diary of Grand Duke Andrei Vladimirovich Romanov]. 1914-1917. Moscow, 2008.

Witte S. U. *Vospominaniia* [Memoirs]. Moscow, 1960.

Zenzinov V. M. *Perezhitoe* [The Lived Through]. New York, 1953.

CHAPTER 8

Bok M. *Vospominaniia o moem ottse P. A. Stolypine* [Memoirs about my Father P. A. Stolypin]. Moscow, 2007.

Chetverikov S. I. *Nevozvratnoe proshloe* [Irrevocable Past]. Moscow, 2001.

Dnevniki imperatora Nikolaia II [Diaries of Emperor Nicholas II]. Vol. 1. 1894-1904. Moscow, 2011.

Dzhunkovskii V. F. *Vospominaniia* [Memoirs]. Vol. 1-2. Moscow, 1997.

Gerasimov A. V. *Na lezvii s terroristami* [On the Blade with the Terrorists]. Moscow, 1991.

Kokovtsov V. N. *Iz moego proshlogo* [From My Past] 1903-1919. Minsk, 2004.

Kurlov P. G. *Gibel' Imperatorskoi Rossii* [The Death of Imperial Russia]. Moscow, 1992.

Lenin V. I. *Polnoe sobranie sochinenii v 55-ti tomakh* [Complete Collected Works in 55 Volumes]. Moscow, 1985.

Milyukov P. N. *Vospominaniia* [Memoirs]. 1859-1917. Moscow, 1990.

Padenie tsarskogo rezhima. Stenograficheskie otchety doprosov i pokazanii, dannykh v 1917 g. v Chrezvychainoi Sledstvennoi Komissii Vremennogo Pravitel'stva [The Fall of the Tsarist Regime. Verbatim Transcripts of the Interrogations and Testimony Given in 1917 in the Extraordinary Investigation Commission of the Provisional Government]. Leningrad, 1924-1927.

P. A. Stolypin: Perepiska [P. A. Stolypin: Correspondence]. Moscow, 2007.

Riabushinskii V. P. *Staroobriadchestvo i russkoe religioznoe chuvstvo* [Old Belief and the Russian Religious Feeling]. Moscow, 2010.

Savinkov B. V. *Vospominaniya terrorista* [Memoirs of a Terrorist]. Moscow, 1991.

Stolypin P. A. *Nam nuzhna Velikaia Rossiia… Polnoe sobranie rechei v Gosudarstvennoi dume i Gosudarstvennom Sovete* [We Need a Great Russia… Complete Collection of Speeches in the State Duma and the State Council]. Moscow, 1991.

Tolstoy L. N. *Polnoe sobranie sochinenii v 90 tomakh* [Complete Collected Works in 90 Volumes]. Moscow, Leningrad. 1928-1958.

Tsereteli I. G. *Vospominaniia o Fevral'skoi revoliutsii* [Memoirs about the February Revolution]. Paris, 1963.

Tsereteli I. G. Rechi, vystupleniia, doklady, stat'i [Speeches, Statements, Reports, Articles]. 1907-1946. Dan F.I., Tsereteli I.G. *Dva puti. Izbrannoe* [Two Paths. Selected]. Part 2. Moscow, 2010.

Voitinskii V. S. *Gody pobed i porazhenii* [The Years of Victories and Defeats]. Berlin, 1923-1924.

Zavarzin P. P. *Zhandarmy i revoliutsionery. Vospominaniia* [The Gendarmes and the Revolutionaries. Memoirs]. Paris, 1930.

CHAPTER 9

Aleksandr Ivanovich Guchkov rasskazyvaet. Vospominaniia predsedatelia Gosudarstvennoi Dumy i voennogo ministra Vremennogo pravitel'stva [Alexander Ivanovich Guchkov Tells. Memoirs of Chairman of the State Duma and War Minister of the Provisional Government]. Moscow, 1993.

Benois A. N. *Moi vospominania* [My Memoirs]. Moscow, 1980.

Berberova N. N. *Liudi i lozhi* [People and Lodges]. Moscow, 1997.

Burtsev V. L. *V pogone za provokatorami* [In Pursuit of Provocateurs]. Moscow, 1989.

Chetverikov S. I. *Nevozvratnoe proshloe* [Irrevocable Past]. Moscow, 2001.

Delo Mendelia Beilisa. Materialy Chrezvychainoi sledstvennoi komissii Vremennogo pravitel'stva o sudebnom protsesse 1913 g. po obvineniiu v ritual'nom ubiistve [The Case of Mendel Beilis. Materials of the Extraordinary Investigation Commission of the Provisional Government on Trial of 1913 on Charges of Ritual Murder]. St. Petersburg, 1999.

Dnevniki imperatora Nikolaia II [Diaries of Emperor Nicholas II]. Vol. 1. 1894-1904. Moscow, 2011.

Gurko V. I. *Cherty i siluety proshlogo: Pravitel'stvo i obshchestvennost' v tsarstvovanii Nikolaia II v izobrazhenii sovremennika* [Features and Silhouettes of the Past: Government and Society in the Reign of Nicholas II Described by a Contemporary]. Moscow, 2000.

Kokovtsov V. N. *Iz moego proshlogo* [From my Past] 1903-1919. Minsk, 2004.

Kurlov P. G. *Gibel' Imperatorskoi Rossii* [The Death Of Imperial Russia]. Moscow, 1992.

Lenin V. I. *Polnoe sobranie sochinenii v 55-ti tomakh* [Complete Collected Works in 55 Volumes]. Moscow, 1985.

Nikolaevskii B. I. *Russkie masony i revoliutsiia* [Russian Freemasons and the Revolution]. Moscow, 1990.

Nikolai II i velikie kniaz'ia (rodstvennye pis'ma k poslednemu tsariu) [Nicholas II and the Grand Dukes (Related Letters to the Last Tsar)]. Leningrad, Moscow, 1925.

P. A. Stolypin. *Programma reform. Dokumenty i materialy* [The Program of Reforms. Documents and Materials]. Moscow, 2011.

P. A. Stolypin glazami sovremennikov [P. A. Stolypin through the Eyes of Contemporaries]. Moscow, 2008.

Provokator: Vospominaniia i dokumenty o razoblachenii Azefa [Provocateur: Memories and Cocuments on the Exposure of Azef]. Leningrad, 1929.

Rediger A. F. *Istoriia moei zhizni. Vospominaniia voennogo ministra* [Story of My Life. Memoirs of a War Minister]. Moscow, 1999.

Riabushinskii V. P. *Staroobriadchestvo i russkoe religioznoe chuvstvo* [Old Belief and the Russian Religious Feeling]. Moscow, 2010.

Stolypin P. A. *Nam nuzhna Velikaia Rossiia* [We Need a Great Russia]. Moscow, 2013.

CHAPTER 10

Bark P. L. *Vospominaniia poslednego ministra finansov Rossiiskoi imperii* [Memoirs of the Last Finance Minister of the Russian Empire]. Moscow, 2017.

Benois A. N. *Moi dnevnik* [My Diary]. 1916-1918. Moscow, 2003.

Buchanan G. *Memuary diplomata* [Memoirs of a Diplomat]. Moscow, 1991. (in Russian)

Buryshkin P. A. *Moskva kupecheskaia* [The Merchantss Moscow]. Moscow, 1990.

Chetverikov S. I. *Bezvozvratno ushedshaia Rossiia* [Irrevocable Russia]. Berlin, 1922.

Delo Mendelia Beilisa. Materialy Chrezvychainoi sledstvennoi komissii Vremennogo pravitel'stva o sudebnom protsesse 1913 g. po obvineniiu v ritual'nom ubiistve [The Case of Mendel Beilis. Materials of the Extraordinary Investigation Commission of the Provisional Government on Trial of 1913 on Charges of Ritual Murder]. St. Petersburg, 1999.

Denikin A. I. *Put' russkogo ofitsera* [Path of a Russian Officer]. Moscow, 1991.

Dnevniki imperatora Nikolaia II [Diaries of Emperor Nicholas II]. Vol. 1. 1894-1904. Moscow, 2011.

Lenin V. I. *Polnoe sobranie sochinenii v 55-ti tomakh* [Complete Collected Works in 55 Volumes]. Moscow, 1985.

Milyukov P. N. *Vospominaniia* [Memoirs]. 1859-1917. Moscow, 1990.

Naidenov N. A. *Vospominaniia o vidennom, slyshannom i ispytannom* [Memoirs of What I Have Seen, Heard and Experienced]. Moscow, 2007.

Paléologue M. *Tsarskaia Rossiia vo vremia mirovoi voiny* [Tsarist Russia during the World War]. Moscow, 1991.

Spiridovich A. I. *Velikaia Voina i Fevral'skaia Revoliutsiia 1914–1917 gg* [The Great War and the Feburuary Revolution of 1914-1917]. New York, 1960-1962.

Taneeva (Vyrubova) A. A. *Stranitsy iz moei zhizni* [Pages of My Life]. Berlin, 1923.

Voennyi dnevnik velikogo kniazia Andreia Vladimirovicha Romanova [War Diary of Grand Duke Andrei Vladimirovich Romanov]. 1914-1917. Moscow, 2008.

Voeikov V. N. *S tsarem i bez tsaria: Vospominaniia poslednego dvortsovogo komendanta gosudaria imperatora Nikolaia II* [With Tsar and Without Tsar: Memoirs of the Last Palace Commandant of the Emperor Nicholas II]. Moscow, 1995.

CHAPTER 11

Bark P. L. *Vospominaniia poslednego ministra finansov Rossiiskoi imperii* [Memoirs of the Last Finance Minister of the Russian Empire]. Moscow, 2017.

Benois A. N. *Moi dnevnik* [My Diary]. 1916-1918. Moscow, 2003.

Bogdanovich A. *Tri poslednikh samoderzhtsa* [Three Last Autocrats]. Moscow, 1990.

Brusilov A. A. *Vospominaniia* [Memoirs]. Moscow, 1963.

Buchanan G. *Memuary diplomata* [Memoirs of a Diplomat]. Moscow, 1991. (in Russian)

Bubnov A. D. *V tsarskoi stavke* [In the Tsar's High Command]. Mosocw, 2008.

Dehn L. *Podlinnaia Tsaritsa* [The Real Tsarina]. Moscow, 1998.

Denikin A. I. *Put' russkogo ofitsera* [Path of a Russian Officer]. Moscow, 1991.

Dnevniki imperatora Nikolaia II [Diaries of Emperor Nicholas II]. Vol. 2. 1905-1918. Moscow, 2013.

Gessen I. V. *Arkhiv russkoi revoliutsii* [Archive of Russian Revolution]. Vol. 8. Berlin, 1923.

Gerasimov A. V. *Na lezvii s terroristami* [On the Blade with the Terrorists]. Moscow, 1991. Spiridovich A. I. *Zapiski zhandarma* [Notes of a Gendarme]. Kharkiv, 1928.

Gippius Z. *Sobranie sochinenii v 15-ti tomakh* [Collected Works in 15 Volumes]. Moscow, 2016.

Nikolai II i velikie kniaz'ia (rodstvennye pis'ma k poslednemu tsariu) [Nicholas II and the Grand Dukes (Related Letters to the Last Tsar)]. Leningrad, Moscow, 1925.

Padenie tsarskogo rezhima. Stenograficheskie otchety doprosov i pokazanii, dannykh v 1917 g. v Chrezvychainoi Sledstvennoi Komissii Vremennogo Pravitel'stva [The Fall of the Tsarist Regime. Verbatim Transcripts of the Interrogations and Testimony Given in 1917 in the Extraordinary Investigation Commission of the Provisional Government]. Leningrad, 1924-1927.

Paléologue M. *Dnevnik posla* [Diary of an Ambassador]. Moscow, 2003.

Perepiska Nikolaia i Aleksandry [Correspondence of Nicholas and Alexandra]. 1914-1917. Moscow, 2013.

Purishkevich V. M. *Dnevnik "Kak ia ubil Rasputina"* [Diary "How I Killed Rasputin"]. Moscow, 1990.

Purishkevich V. M. *Dnevnik chlena Gosudarstvennoi Dumy Vladimira Mitrofanovicha Purishkevicha* [Diary of a Member of the State Duma Vladimir Mitrofanovich Purishkevich]. Riga, 1924.

Rodzianko M. V. *Krushenie imperii. Zapiski predsedatelia Russkoi Gosudarstvennoi dumy* [Fall of the Empire. The Notes by the Chairman of the Russian State Duma]. Moscow, 1992.

Sazonov S. D. *Vospominaniia* [Memoirs]. Minsk, 2002.

Spiridovich A. I. *Velikaia Voina i Fevral'skaia Revoliutsiia 1914–1917 gg* [The Great War and the Feburuary Revolution of 1914-1917]. New York, 1960-1962.

Taneeva (Vyrubova) A. A. *Stranitsy iz moei zhizni* [Pages of My Life]. Berlin, 1923.

Voennyi dnevnik velikogo kniazia Andreia Vladimirovicha Romanova [War Diary of Grand Duke Andrei Vladimirovich Romanov]. 1914-1917. Moscow, 2008.

Yusupov F. F. *Memuary, v dvukh knigakh* [Memoirs in Two Volumes]. Moscow, 1998.

CHAPTER 12

Bark P. L. *Vospominaniia poslednego ministra finansov Rossiiskoi imperii* [Memoirs of the Last Finance Minister of the Russian Empire]. Moscow, 2017.

Barony Vrangeli. Vospominaniia [The Barons Wrangel. Memoirs]. Moscow, 2006.

Benois A. N. *Moi dnevnik* [My Diary]. 1916-1918. Moscow, 2003.

Bublikov A. A. *Russkaia revoliutsiia (ee nachalo, arest tsaria, perspektivy). Vpechatleniia i mysli ochevidtsa i uchastnika* [The Russian Revolution (Its Beginning, the Arrest of the Tsar, Prospects). Impressions and Thoughts of a Witness and Participant]. New York, 1918.

Buchanan G. *Memuary diplomata* [Memoirs of a Diplomat]. Moscow, 1991. (in Russian)

General Kutepov. Sbornik statei [General Kutepov. Collection of Articles]. Paris, 1934.

Globachev K. I. *Pravda o russkoi revoliutsii: vospominaniia byvshego nachal'nika Petrogradskogo okhrannogo otdeleniia* [Truth about the Russian Revolution: Memoirs of the Former Chief of the Petrograd Secret Police]. Moscow, 2009.

Gippius Z. N. *Siniaia kniga. Peterburgskii dnevnik 1914-1918* [Blue Book. The Petersburg Diary 1914-1918]. Belgrade, 1929.

Kerensky A. F. *Rossiia na istoricheskom povorote. Memuary* [Russia at the History's Turning Point. Memoirs]. Moscow, 1993.

Krasnyi arkhiv. 1927. No. 21.

Krasnyi arkhiv. 1928. No. 2 (21).

Krasnyi arkhiv. 1930. No. 40-42.Paléologue M. *Dnevnik posla* [Diary of an Ambassador]. Moscow, 2003.

Lenin V. I. *Polnoe sobranie sochinenii v 55-ti tomakh* [Complete Collected Works in 55 Volumes]. Moscow, 1985.

Lomonosov, Iu. V. *Vospominaniia o Martovskoi revoliutsii 1917 g* [Memoirs of the March Revolution of 1917]. Stockholm, Berlin, 1921.

L'vov G. E. *Vospominaniia* [Memoirs]. Moscow, 2002.Vrangel' N. E. *Vospominaniia. Ot krepostnogo prava do bol'shevikov* [From Serfdom to the Bolsheviks]. Moscow, 2003.

Milyukov P. N. *Vospominaniia* [Memoirs]. 1859-1917. Moscow, 1990.

Paléologue M. *Tsarskaia Rossiia nakanune revoliutsii* [Tsarist Russia on the Eve of Revolution]. Moscow, 1991.

Petrogradskii Sovet rabochikh i soldatskikh deputatov v 1917 godu: protokoly, stenogrammy i otchety, rezoliutsii i postanovleniia obshchikh sobranii, sobranii sektsii, zasedanii Ispolnitel'nogo komiteta, Biuro Ispolnitel'nogo komiteta i fraktsii, 27 fevralia — 25 oktiabria 1917 g [The Petrograd Soviet of Workers' and Soldiers' Deputies in 1917: Minutes, Verbatim Transcripts and Reports, Decisions and Resolutions of Common Sessions, Sessions of Sections, Session of the Executive Committee, the Bureau of the Executive Committee and Factions, 27 February — 25 October 1917]. St. Petersburg, 1993.

Pokrovsky N. N. *Poslednii v Mariinskom dvortse. Vospominaniia ministra inostrannykh del* [The Last One in the Mariinsky Palace. Memoirs of a Foreign Minister]. Moscow, 2015.

Princess Olga Paley. *Vospominaniia o Rossii* [Memoirs about Russia]. Moscow, 2005.

Shul'gin V. V. *Dni: zapiski* [Days: Notes]. Belgrade, 1925.

Spiridovich A. I. *Velikaia Voina i Fevral'skaia Revoliutsiia 1914–1917 gg* [The Great War and the Feburuary Revolution of 1914-1917]. New York, 1960-1962.

Shliapnikov A. G. *Fevral'skie dni v Peterburge* [February Days in St. Petersburg]. Kharkiv, 1925.

Voeikov V. N. *S tsarem i bez tsaria: Vospominaniia poslednego dvortsovogo komendanta gosudaria imperatora Nikolaia II* [With Tsar and Without Tsar: Memoirs of the Last Palace Commandant of the Emperor Nicholas II]. Moscow, 1995.

Velikie dni rossiiskoi revoliutsii [Great Days of Russian Revolution]. Petrograd, 1917.

CHAPTER 13

Chernov V. M. *Velikaia russkaia revoliutsiia. Vospominaniia predsedatelia Uchreditel'nogo sobraniia* [Great Russian Revolution. Memoirs of the Chairman of the Constituent Assembly]. 1905-1920. Moscow, 2007.

Dehn L. *Podlinnaia Tsaritsa* [The Real Tsarina]. Moscow, 1998.

Gippius Z. *Sobranie sochinenii v 15-ti tomakh* [Collected Works in 15 Volumes]. Moscow, 2016.

Kerensky A. F. *Rossiia na istoricheskom povorote. Memuary* [Russia at the History's Turning Point. Memoirs]. Moscow, 1993.

Kerensky A. F. *Poteriannaia Rossiia* [The Lost Russia]. Moscow, 2014.

Krupskaya N. K. *Vospominaniia o Lenine* [Memoirs about Lenin]. Moscow, 1989.

Kschessinskaya M. F. *Vospominaniia* [Memoirs]. Moscow, 1992.

Lenin V. I. *Polnoe sobranie sochinenii v 55-ti tomakh* [Complete Collected Works in 55 Volumes]. Moscow, 1985.

Naryshkina E. A. *Moi vospominaniia. Pod vlast'iu trekh tsarei* [My Memoirs. Under the Rule of the Three Tsars]. Moscow, 2014.

Paléologue M. *Dnevnik posla* [Diary of an Ambassador]. Moscow, 2003.

Sukhanov N. N. *Zapiski o revoliutsii* [Notes about Revolution]. Moscow, 1991.

Tolstaya A. L. *Doch'* [Daughter]. London, 1979.

Trotsky L. D. *Moia zhizn'. Opyt avtobiografii* [My Life. An Attempt at an Autobiography]. Moscow, 1991.

Tsereteli I. G. *Vospominaniia o Fevral'skoi revoliutsii* [Memoirs about the February Revolution]. Paris, 1963.

Voitinskii V. S. *1917-i. God pobed i porazhenii. Kniga vospominanii* [1917. The Year of Victories and Defeats. Book of Memoirs]. Moscow, 1999.

CHAPTER 14

Benois A. N. Moi dnevnik [My Diary]. 1916-1918. Moscow, 2003.

Chernov V. M. *Velikaia russkaia revoliutsiia. Vospominaniia predsedatelia Uchreditel'nogo sobraniia* [Great Russian Revolution. Memoirs of the Chairman of the Constituent Assembly]. 1905-1920. Moscow, 2007.

Dnevniki imperatora Nikolaia II [Diaries of Emperor Nicholas II]. Vol. 2. 1905-1918. Moscow, 2013.

Gippius Z. *Dnevniki* [Diaries]. 1914-1917. Moscow, 2017.

Gippius Z. *Sobranie sochinenii v 15-ti tomakh* [Collected Works in 15 Volumes]. Moscow, 2016.

Knox A. *Vmeste s russkoi armiei. Dnevnik voennogo attashe* [Together with the Russian Army. Diary of a Military Attache]. 1914-1917. Moscow, 2014.

Savinkov B. V. *Vospominaniya terrorista* [Memoirs of a Terrorist]. Moscow, 1991.

Sukhanov N. N. *Zapiski o revoliutsii* [Notes about Revolution]. Moscow, 1991.

Trotsky L. D. Sobranie sochinenii [Collected Works]. Moscow, Leningrad, 1924-1927.

INDEX

© JAMES HILL

Mikhail Zygar is the former editor in chief of the only independent TV station in Russia, TV Rain (Dozhd). Awarded the 2014 International Press Freedom Award by the Committee to Protect Journalists, Zygar is the author of *All the Kremlin's Men*.

PublicAffairs is a publishing house founded in 1997. It is a tribute to the standards, values, and flair of three persons who have served as mentors to countless reporters, writers, editors, and book people of all kinds, including me.

I. F. STONE, proprietor of *I. F. Stone's Weekly*, combined a commitment to the First Amendment with entrepreneurial zeal and reporting skill and became one of the great independent journalists in American history. At the age of eighty, Izzy published *The Trial of Socrates*, which was a national bestseller. He wrote the book after he taught himself ancient Greek.

BENJAMIN C. BRADLEE was for nearly thirty years the charismatic editorial leader of *The Washington Post*. It was Ben who gave the *Post* the range and courage to pursue such historic issues as Watergate. He supported his reporters with a tenacity that made them fearless and it is no accident that so many became authors of influential, best-selling books.

ROBERT L. BERNSTEIN, the chief executive of Random House for more than a quarter century, guided one of the nation's premier publishing houses. Bob was personally responsible for many books of political dissent and argument that challenged tyranny around the globe. He is also the founder and longtime chair of Human Rights Watch, one of the most respected human rights organizations in the world.

· · ·

For fifty years, the banner of Public Affairs Press was carried by its owner Morris B. Schnapper, who published Gandhi, Nasser, Toynbee, Truman, and about 1,500 other authors. In 1983, Schnapper was described by *The Washington Post* as "a redoubtable gadfly." His legacy will endure in the books to come.

Peter Osnos, *Founder*